MICHAEL E. ROLOFF, Editor
GAYLEN D. PAULSON, Editorial Assistant

Communication Yearbook

21

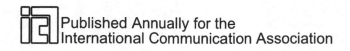 Published Annually for the
International Communication Association

SAGE Publications
International Educational and Professional Publisher
Thousand Oaks   London   New Delhi

P
87
.C5974
V 21

May, 1998

For information address:

 SAGE Publications, Inc.
2455 Teller Road
Thousand Oaks, California 91320
Phone: 805-499-0721
E-mail: order@sagepub.com

SAGE Publications Ltd.
6 Bonhill Street
London EC2A 4PU
United Kingdom

SAGE Publications India Pvt. Ltd.
M-32 Market
Greater Kailash I
New Delhi 110 048 India

Printed in the United States of America

Library of Congress: 76-45943

ISBN 0-7619-1428-5

ISSN 0147-4642

This book is printed on acid-free paper.

98 99 00 01 02 03 10 9 8 7 6 5 4 3 2 1

Acquiring Editor: Margaret Seawell
Editorial Assistant: Renée Piernot
Production Editor: Astrid Virding
Production Assistant: Denise Santoyo
Typesetter: Rebecca Evans
Indexer: Will Ragsdale
Cover Designer: Ravi Balasuriya
Print Buyer: Anna Chin

CONTENTS

THE INTERNATIONAL COMMUNICATION ASSOCIATION

The International Communication Association (ICA) was formed in 1950, bringing together academicians and other professionals whose interests focus on human communication. The Association maintains an active membership of more than 2,800 individuals, of whom some two-thirds are teaching and conducting research in colleges, universities, and schools around the world. Other members are in government, the media, communication technology, business, law, medicine, and other professions. The wide professional and geographic distribution of the membership provides the basic strength of the ICA. The Association is a meeting ground for sharing research and useful dialogue about communication interests.

Through its Divisions and Interest Groups, publications, annual conferences, and relations with other associations around the world, the ICA promotes the systematic study of communication theories, processes, and skills.

In addition to *Communication Yearbook*, the Association publishes the *Journal of Communication, Human Communication Research, Communication Theory, A Guide to Publishing in Scholarly Communication Journals, ICA Newsletter,* and the *ICA Membership Directory.*

For additional information about the ICA and its activities, contact Robert L. Cox, Executive Director, International Communication Association, P.O. Box 9589, Austin, TX 78766; phone (512) 454-8299; fax (512) 454-4221; e-mail icahdq@uts.cc.utexas.edu

Editors of the *Communication Yearbook* series:

Volumes 1 and 2, Brent D. Ruben
Volumes 3 and 4, Dan Nimmo
Volumes 5 and 6, Michael Burgoon
Volumes 7 and 8, Robert N. Bostrom
Volumes 9 and 10, Margaret L. McLaughlin
Volumes 11, 12, 13, and 14, James A. Anderson
Volumes 15, 16, and 17, Stanley A. Deetz
Volumes 18, 19, and 20, Brant R. Burleson
Volumes 21, 22, and 23, Michael E. Roloff

INTERNATIONAL COMMUNICATION ASSOCIATION
EXECUTIVE COMMITTEE

CONSULTING EDITORS

The following individuals helped make possible this volume of the *Communication Yearbook*. The editor gratefully acknowledges these scholars for the gifts of their time and wisdom.

EDITOR'S INTRODUCTION

Welcome to Volume 21 of the *Communication Yearbook*. This collection continues the format, begun with Volume 19, of publishing state-of-the-art reviews of communication research. Under the able editorship of Brant Burleson, *Communication Yearbook* established itself as an essential source for in-depth analyses of communication scholarship representing the broad array of research areas evident within the field. The chapters contained in this volume are of high quality and should add to the reputation of the *Communication Yearbook*.

To help the reader understand this volume, I will describe the process by which the chapters were selected and created, the content of each chapter, and the individuals who played essential roles in putting the volume together.

CHAPTER CREATION

Approximately 18 months prior to the publication of this volume, a call for submissions was circulated. Drafts of chapters and proposals for chapters were solicited that would review important, specific areas of scholarship. An attempt was made to solicit proposals from across research specializations. To that end, copies of the call were sent to the leaders of all divisions and interest groups of the International Communication Association, asking that they identify potential contributors and circulate the call to the membership. I am grateful to those who were contacted for their assistance in identifying potential contributors. The call was also sent to the editors of 20 newsletters published by organizations both within (e.g., the National Communication Association) and outside the field of communication (e.g., the Society for Personality and Social Psychology). Finally, given that dissertations are often a rich source for literature reviews, more than a hundred letters were sent to professors at Ph.D.-granting universities, asking them to identify recently completed dissertations that contained quality literature reviews.

We received 37 new submissions and 5 papers that were begun but not completed during Brant Burleson's editorship. The proposed topics reflected the diversity of our field and included the areas of health communication, intercultural communication, interpersonal communication, mass communication, organizational communication, political communication, racial communication, and rhetoric. All 42 prospective chapters were subjected to blind review by at least two referees. Each referee was asked to make the following assessments: (a) Is the submission a literature review? (b) Is the literature worthy of review? (c) Is the review comprehensive and current? (d) Is there a coherent organizational pattern and procedure for conducting the review? (e) Are the conclusions clear and valid? (f) Is the review sufficiently critical?

and (g) Does the review set forth future issues and directions for research? The authors of those proposals and papers that were judged to conform to all these standards were encouraged to submit chapters for further evaluation. In most cases, the manuscripts went through several revisions.

The 11 chapters contained in this volume are those that survived this rigorous review process. They are truly a select group. Of the total, 8 were drawn from the 37 new submissions and 3 emerged from the 5 projects begun during Brant Burleson's term as editor.

CHAPTER CONTENT

Although proposals were sought from all interest areas in communication, the selection of chapters was based entirely upon judgments of quality. Had the proposals from a single interest area all been judged to be the best, *CY21* would have a singular focus. However, as testimony to the vibrancy of all of our research specializations, the final chapters reflect the diverse interests that compose our field. Therefore, readers will find some chapters that fit into our formal divisional structures and some that blend two or more. Hence readers should find in-depth reviews focused on important topics in their own specializations and well-written syntheses that inform as to scholarship in other domains.

The first chapter, by O'Keefe and Hale, is a meta-analysis of research focused on the door-in-the-face (DITF) persuasion technique. Scholars interested in dyadic influence have long noted that speakers often use messages in a sequential, linked fashion so as to gain compliance from others. The door-in-the-face strategy is based upon the assumption that the rejection of a large initial request increases the likelihood that a target will comply with a second, smaller request relative to the presentation of the second request by itself. The meta-analysis verifies the effectiveness of the DITF technique, but also finds that its effectiveness is moderated by a variety of factors. Even more important, the meta-analysis calls into question some of the current theoretical explanations of DITF. As an alternative, O'Keefe and Hale point to a guilt-based explanation.

Although social influence frequently occurs in dyads, it is not confined to that context. Indeed, the next two chapters highlight the manner in which social influence occurs within organizations. In Chapter 2, Cheney et al. focus on factors that affect workplace democracy. They define *workplace democracy* as "those principles and practices designed to engage and 'represent' (in a multiple sense of the term) as many relevant individuals and groups as possible in the formulation, execution, and modification of work-related activities." In effect, these authors review research that examines how organizations facilitate or inhibit the ability of their members to exert influence over task performance as well as the consequences of allowing these multiple voices to be heard. This chapter represents the first time scholars have brought together the huge volume of interdisciplinary research focused on this important topic.

Allowing individuals to voice their opinions can have an impact on the quality of organizational decision making. However, discovering a good solution to a problem is not the end of the story. One must also find a means to convince individuals to implement the solution. Although a substantial body of research has examined the creation of innovative programs and policies, relatively little attention has been paid to how one might convince individuals to adopt and implement them. In their groundbreaking review, Lewis and Seibold (Chapter 3) pull together the existing research focused on theories that inform as to implementation processes, the implementation strategies that might be employed, and the target characteristics that affect the receptiveness of organizational members to implementing recommended changes in organizational operations. The authors highlight areas in which the advice offered in the popular literature is based upon an inadequate research base.

The ability of organizational members to exert influence and the processes that affect the implementation of innovative ideas are important examples of intraorganizational influence. However, organizational influence often extends beyond the boundaries of the organization. The next three chapters address aspects of extraorganizational influence.

Increasingly, business transactions extend beyond national boundaries. As a result, scholars have turned their attention to intercultural business negotiations. In a first-of-its-kind review, Cai and Drake (Chapter 4) synthesize and critique the interdisciplinary research in this area. One of their surprising conclusions is that much of our knowledge about intercultural business negotiation stems from research that is really intracultural. Most frequently, instead of having negotiators from one culture interact with those from another, the behaviors of dyads of negotiators from one culture are compared with the negotiation behaviors of dyads composed of individuals from a different culture. Furthermore, Cai and Drake note a regrettable lack of theory to guide research.

Organizations also try to present themselves in a desirable fashion to their publics. Increasingly, public relations units of organizations are being required to justify their function within the organization. Unfortunately, the academic literature has not developed a model for conducting such evaluations. In Chapter 5, Ferguson reviews literature that assesses how public relations units might be evaluated for impact and for ethical behavior, and identifies those individuals who might be in the best position to make such assessments.

One of the most difficult tasks facing organizations is determining how to deal with crisis effectively. In Chapter 6, Seeger, Sellnow, and Ulmer view an organizational crisis as "a specific, unexpected, and nonroutine event or series of events that create high levels of uncertainty and threaten or are perceived to threaten an organization's high-priority goals." When a crisis occurs, internal communication mechanisms are activated and challenged as members attempt to understand and manage the crisis. Furthermore, an important component of the response is external, as the organization tries to maintain a positive image with its various publics. Seeger et al. review the extant literature reporting on studies that have employed a variety of methods to investigate the various aspects of crisis management. They also propose several theories that might be useful in guiding research in this area.

The chapters by Cai and Drake, Ferguson, and Seeger et al. demonstrate the importance of studying communication both within and by organizations of all varieties. However, expansive literatures have developed concerning organizations that specialize in the routine production of messages for public consumption. Appropriately, the final five chapters in this volume focus on the communication practices and effects of professionals who are employed by media organizations.

In Chapter 7, Gunaratne examines the current literature surrounding the notion of public journalism. Scholars have conceptualized public journalism in a variety of ways, but Gunaratne defines it as a movement that calls for journalists to redefine news values, question the utility and ethics of objectivity, become more actively involved in their communities, and better reflect the multicultural nature of U.S. society. He identifies similarities between the key tenets of this position and those contained in earlier literatures focused on the social responsibility of the press and developmental journalism. He concludes that public journalism can be seen as the next stage in thinking about the role of journalism in the United States, and that it has evolved with changes in the effect of capitalism on the press.

The impact of the marketplace is also evident in the review by Eastman (Chapter 8). Broadcasters must provide products of interest to their consumers. In light of increasing competition and the greater ability of audiences to avail themselves of alternatives, Eastman reviews literature that demonstrates the substantial changes that have taken place in the ways in which programming is conducted and suggests how programming theory will change with the advent of viewer-controlled, on-line technologies.

Some media professionals combine aspects of news reporting with their own particular slant on the news. In Chapter 9, Mello focuses his review on editorial cartoonists. These pundits express particular interpretations of news events through a relatively simple visual and linguistic form. Their messages are designed for easy consumption by receivers and are often written in a humorous fashion. Mello's literature review highlights the various professional practices of editorial cartoonists and summarizes the effects their messages have on readers.

As Mello notes, the mass media create messages aimed at influencing political opinion. Indeed, some would argue that the mass media have fundamentally altered political processes in the United States. Perhaps the most visible impact has been on the presidency. Accordingly, Stuckey and Antczak (Chapter 10) examine interdisciplinary research focused on the rhetorical presidency. They review scholarship that informs as to how the media have shaped the role of the presidency as well as how presidents have used the media to govern.

Of course, receivers—whether they are listeners, viewers, or readers—are at the heart of media effects. If messages sent by the media are not attended to or not comprehended by their intended targets, then the influence of the media may be more limited than is often assumed. Unfortunately, our understanding of how receivers process messages is limited by ambiguity arising from the manner in which researchers measure attention. Lang and Basil (Chapter 11) review the literature associated with secondary task reaction time measures, which are among the most frequently employed indicators of attention. They note four different interpretations of what these measures assess. Based upon their critique, they propose a model that incorporates the four definitions, and they find that it can account for the majority of findings from prior research.

Although broadly cast, all of the chapters included here address issues that are important for communication researchers and for society as a whole. The reader will find that each chapter provides an excellent summary and critique of the literature. The authors have done a fine job.

ACKNOWLEDGMENTS

Putting together a volume such as the *Communication Yearbook* is labor-intensive, and an editor relies upon the cooperation and goodwill of many people. I would be quite remiss if I did not acknowledge the critical contributions of my support system.

My able editorial assistant, Gaylen Paulson, worked countless hours on this project. He computerized the review process, and his finely honed copyediting skills were invaluable. He kept me on track and was an effective problem solver. He deserves a great deal of credit for the completion of this huge project.

I owe a significant debt of gratitude to my predecessor, Brant Burleson. He set a new direction for the *Yearbook* and passed on to me a series that is in great shape. On a practical level, he provided computer files of forms and contacts that were immensely useful. As noted earlier, three of the chapters in this volume were started and revised during his last year as editor (Chapter 5, by Ferguson; Chapter 9, by Mello; and Chapter 10, by Stuckey and Antczak).

Furthermore, I am especially appreciative of his unbounded willingness to commiserate over the challenges facing *Yearbook* editors!

My colleagues from Northwestern and around the country also contributed to this endeavor. Dean David Zarefsky provided financial support from the School of Speech at Northwestern, as did the Department of Communication Studies. Two Northwestern staff members, Rita Lutz and Martha Kayler, helped me complete the internal paperwork necessary to keep the review process functioning. Professors Peter Miller, Mike Leff, Linda Putnam, and Brant Burleson were extremely helpful in directing me to referees. Two doctoral students at Northwestern, Joy Shih and Lefki Anastasiou, assisted with copyediting tasks. I must also extend my appreciation to the many students who tolerated my delayed responses to their assignments and inquiries when my editorial duties beckoned.

Clearly, a volume such as this could not exist without submitters and reviewers. I am very appreciative of the interest expressed by those who sent in proposals, and I applaud the time and effort they expended on proposals that in some cases did not come to fruition. The referees provided thorough, insightful responses to the proposals, and most were completed in a timely fashion.

I want to acknowledge the assistance and support of the communication editor at Sage Publications, Margaret Seawell, and her assistant, Renée Piernot. They efficiently moved the volume through the production phase.

Finally, I need to express my gratitude to my wife, Karen, and my daughters, Erika, Katrina, and Carlissa, for tolerating my periodic inattention to the travails of family life.

Michael E. Roloff

CHAPTER CONTENTS

1   The Door-in-the-Face Influence Strategy: A Random-Effects Meta-Analytic Review

DANIEL J. O'KEEFE
SCOTT L. HALE
University of Illinois, Urbana-Champaign

A random-effects meta-analysis of research concerning the door-in-the-face (DITF) influence strategy provides evidence supporting more confident generalizations about the role of several moderator variables than that provided by previous reviews. Variations in the identity of the requester, the identity of the beneficiary, the prosocialness of the requests, the medium of communication, and the time interval between requests all appear to influence the size of DITF effects; variations in concession size do not. DITF effects are small in absolute terms (with an overall mean r of .10), but not remarkably small in the context of other effect sizes concerning social influence. However, there is substantial variability in DITF effects, even under optimal conditions. The review's findings are not easily reconciled with most proposed explanations of DITF effects, but appear consistent with a guilt-based account.

THE door-in-the-face (DITF) influence strategy is a much-studied means of social influence. Systematic research concerning the DITF strategy began more than 20 years ago, with Cialdini et al.'s (1975) classic work. Two meta-analytic reviews of the DITF literature appeared about a decade later (Dillard, Hunter, & Burgoon, 1984; Fern, Monroe, & Avila, 1986). A good deal of DITF research has appeared following those reviews, and though there has been some discussion of this research area (e.g., Dillard, 1991), no subsequent systematic review has been undertaken.

This chapter reports a meta-analytic review of the DITF research literature. Our broad purpose is to assess the current state of the literature, taking into account the studies undertaken since the last meta-analytic reviews. In doing so, we also hope to address some uncertainties arising from previous reviews,

Correspondence and requests for reprints: Daniel J. O'Keefe, Department of Speech Communication, 244 Lincoln Hall, University of Illinois, 702 S. Wright Street, Urbana, IL 61801-3631; e-mail dokeefe@uiuc.edu

Communication Yearbook 21, pp. 1-33

to shed light on possible new moderators of DITF effects, and to consider possible explanations for the observed effects.

BACKGROUND

The DITF Strategy

In the DITF strategy, a relatively large initial request is made of a person, which the person declines. Then a subsequent smaller request is made, in the hopes that the person's having declined the initial request (having metaphorically closed the door in the face of the requester) will make the person more likely to comply with the second (target) request. In experimental investigations of the strategy, researchers assess DITF success by comparing target-request compliance rates in a DITF condition with the corresponding compliance rates in a control condition in which participants receive only the target request.

For example, in Cialdini et al.'s (1975, Experiment 1) classic study, people were approached on a campus sidewalk by another student purportedly representing the "County Youth Counseling Program." In the DITF condition, a large initial request was made—that the receiver spend 2 hours a week, for a minimum of 2 years, working as an unpaid volunteer counselor at the County Juvenile Detention Center. No one agreed to this request. The smaller second request was that the receiver serve as an unpaid volunteer chaperone, spending 2 hours one afternoon or evening taking a group of juveniles from the Detention Center to visit the zoo. In the control condition, in which participants heard only the smaller (target) request, 17% consented to serve as a chaperone. In the DITF condition, in which the initial large request had been declined, 50% agreed to chaperone.

Previous Meta-Analytic Findings

The two previous meta-analytic reviews of DITF research reported that the overall observed mean DITF effect (that is, the difference between the target-request compliance in the DITF condition and in a control condition in which only the target request is received) is roughly equivalent to a correlation of .08 (Dillard et al., 1984, p. 471; Fern et al., 1986, p. 150).

These reviews also examined the effects of four specific moderator variables. First, the effects of varying time intervals between the first and second requests were examined by both extant meta-analyses. Each reported that DITF effects were larger when there was no delay between the two requests than when some time elapsed (Dillard et al., 1984, p. 478; Fern et al., 1986, p. 149). Second, the effect of variation in the identity of the requester was studied by Fern et al. (1986, p. 149), who found that DITF effects tended to be larger when the same person made both requests than when different persons made the two requests. Third, the influence of the prosocialness of the requests was reviewed by Dillard et al. (1984, pp. 478-479). They found that DITF effects were larger when the requests came from prosocial organizations (e.g., civic or environmental groups) than when they came from nonprosocial organizations (e.g., marketing firms). Fourth, the role of the size of the concession made—that is, the size of the drop in request size from the first to the second request—was examined by Fern et al. (1986, p. 149). Their review found that variations in the magnitude of concession were not dependably associated with variations in DITF effect size.

Explaining DITF Effects

Cialdini et al. (1975) advanced what is probably the best-known explanation of DITF effects, the reciprocal-concessions explanation. This explanation proposes that the sequence of requests makes the situation appear to be a negotiation or bargaining situation, and hence a situation in which a concession by one side (the requester's making a smaller second request) is expected to be reciprocated by a concession from the other side (the person's accepting the second request). In fact, Cialdini et al. went so far as to label the procedure the "reciprocal concessions technique."

However, as several commentators have suggested, the reciprocal-concessions explanation does not appear to be entirely satisfactory (see, e.g., Dillard, 1991). In particular, the finding that concession size does not influence DITF effects appears inconsistent with the explanation; if the explanation were true, one would expect that larger concessions would yield larger effects. Additionally, this explanation obviously does not provide an explanation for the finding that DITF effects are larger with prosocial than with nonprosocial requests.

Another proposed explanation invokes perceptual-contrast effects (Miller, Seligman, Clark, & Bush, 1976). The suggestion is that the second request is perceived as smaller than it actually is because of a perceptual contrast with the larger first request. That is, the second request appears less demanding when it is seen against the backdrop of the larger initial request (and hence engenders greater compliance).

But the perceptual-contrast explanation appears incapable of accommodating the previously observed effects of moderator variables. Specifically, it does not explain why, from a perceptual-contrast standpoint, DITF effects should vary depending on whether the same person makes the requests. Nor does this explanation appear to offer any clear account of why DITF effects should be larger with prosocial than with nonprosocial requests. Moreover, direct evidence bearing specifically on the perceptual-contrast explanation gives little support to this account (Abrahams & Bell, 1994; Cantrill & Seibold, 1986; Goldman, McVeigh, & Richterkessing, 1984).

Self-presentational concerns have also been suggested as a possible explanation of DITF effects. This account proposes that rejection of the first request makes receivers concerned that they will be negatively evaluated by the requester (Pendleton & Batson, 1979). But the self-presentation explanation is also difficult to square with the research evidence in hand. As Abrahams and Bell (1994, p. 136) have noted, DF effects have repeatedly been obtained in circumstances in which self-presentational considerations should not be especially strong (as, for instance, in interaction between strangers who are unlikely ever to interact again). Moreover, the initial findings suggesting the plausibility of this account (Pendleton & Batson, 1979) have proved difficult to replicate (Reeves, Baker, Boyd, & Cialdini, 1991), and subsequent direct tests (Abrahams & Bell, 1994) have also failed to confirm expectations of the self-presentation explanation.

A final possible explanation is based on guilt (O'Keefe & Figgé, 1997). The suggestion is that DITF success comes about through a guilt-arousal-and-reduction process, in which rejecting the first request induces guilt in the receiver and accepting the second request reduces that guilt. This explanation appears to be capable of encompassing the moderator-variable effects reported in previous meta-analytic reviews. Specifically, the observed effect for prosocialness is explained as a consequence of persons feeling greater guilt when declining prosocial requests than when declining nonprosocial requests. The apparent time-interval effect is taken to occur because with increased delay between the requests, any induced guilt has greater opportunity to dissipate. The observed identical-requester effect is seen to arise because a second request that comes from a different requester does not offer the same guilt-reduction possibilities as a second request from the same person whose request was just declined.

This explanation is also consistent with current research about guilt. (This literature, addressed at some length by O'Keefe & Figgé, 1997, is only briefly summarized here.) For example, this account harmonizes with current theoretical and empirical understandings of the nature of guilt. By way of illustration: Roseman, Wiest, and Swartz (1994) found that among the reactions distinctively associated with guilt were "thinking that you were in the wrong," "thinking that you shouldn't have done what you did," "feeling like undoing what you have done," "wanting to make up for what you've done wrong," and the like (see p. 215). It is easy to imagine how (for instance) refusing to help troubled children might lead to such feelings and how the second request in the DITF sequence might offer the prospect of making up for what one has done. As another example, Baumeister, Stillwell, and Heatherton (1994) have emphasized that guilt arises from interpersonal transactions and is particularly linked to "suffering that oneself has caused" (p. 246); from such a vantage point, the DITF strategy can be seen to involve an interpersonal transaction in which the refusal of the initial request might involve the infliction of suffering on another person.

Additionally, this explanation appears consistent with extant research findings concerning guilt-based social influence. There are two areas of such research. In the first, researchers have explored the relationship between guilt and compliance with altruistic requests by inducing guilt in participants (by having them inflict harm on another) and subsequently making altruistic requests of them. A number of studies have found that guilt induction can enhance request compliance (e.g., Carlsmith & Gross, 1969; Cunningham, Steinberg, & Grev, 1980; Freedman, Wallington, & Bless, 1967; Konoske, Staple, & Graf, 1979), confirming the role that request compliance can play in guilt reduction (for a more detailed discussion of this literature, see Baumeister et al., 1994, pp. 249-251). The second area of research consists of a small body of work concerning the use of guilt appeals in persuasive messages. Such appeals are parallel to the proposed analysis of the DITF strategy: Both involve an initial arousal of guilt followed by the presentation of a course of action that might mitigate that guilt. Research on guilt-based persuasive appeals suggests that it is indeed possible for message variations to induce varying levels of guilt, that the most intense message contents do not necessarily arouse the greatest guilt, and that greater induced guilt can make for greater persuasiveness (Bozinoff & Ghingold, 1983; Coulter & Pinto, 1995; Ghingold & Bozinoff, 1981; Pinto & Priest, 1991; Ruth & Faber, 1988; Yinon, Bizman, Cohen, & Segev, 1976).

The Present Review

The present meta-analysis was motivated by four broad concerns. One was simply a felt need for a new, more thorough review. This need reflects our interest both in reviewing the DITF research that has appeared in the 10 years since the last meta-analytic review appeared and in including unpublished work (which both previous reviews excluded).

Second, the present review was motivated by our interest in addressing some apparent uncertainties surrounding previous reviews. These uncertainties stem primarily from methodological differences between the reviews. One such methodological difference concerns the moderating variables considered in the meta-analyses. No previous review explicitly examined all four of the moderator variables mentioned above. Dillard et al. (1984) considered only the prosocialness of the requests and the time interval between requests; they did not consider variations in requester identity or concession size.[1] Fern et al. (1986) examined the effects of concession size, time delay, and requester variation, but not the prosocialness of the requests. One can have greater confidence in claims about a given moderating variable when independent meta-analyses provide converging evidence about the variable; when those meta-analyses do not examine the same moderators, however, doubt can arise about the conclusions offered. (In a way, thus, there is a meta-analytic parallel to the importance of primary-research replication: Where two or more independent meta-analytic reviews reach similar conclusions, confidence in those conclusions is naturally strengthened.)[2]

A second methodological difference involves the unit of analysis employed. As noted by Dillard and Hale (1992, p. 222), the extant reviews used different analytic units: Dillard et al. (1984) used studies as the unit of analysis, whereas Fern et al. (1986) used more fine-grained units. Apparently, when different DITF implementations were reported in a single investigation, Fern et al. analyzed each separately, whereas Dillard et al. combined them.[3] On the face of the matter, Fern et al.'s procedure seems preferable. It seems unreasonable to treat two different DITF implementations separately if they appear in two different studies but combine them if they happen to appear in one.

This methodological difference has become important because Fern et al.'s findings have been interpreted as casting doubt on Dillard et al.'s claim that prosocialness is an important moderator of DITF effects. Fern et al. did not explicitly consider prosocialness as a possible moderating factor. However, Dillard and Hale (1992, p. 222) have suggested that, because Fern et al. (1986) reported homogeneous DITF effects without partitioning cases on the basis of prosocialness, Fern et al.'s findings imply that prosocialness does not moderate DITF effects.[4] Dillard and Hale (1992, p. 229) have noted the possibility that Dillard et al.'s means of aggregating effect sizes resulted in unrepresentative patterns of DITF effects; under this interpretation, Dillard et al.'s finding of a significant moderating role for prosocialness would be called into question. In this circumstance, it would plainly be informative to have a new meta-analytic review that uses Fern et al.'s fine-grained units of analysis and explicitly considers the possible moderating role of prosocialness. Such a review could clarify whether prosocialness is indeed an important moderator of DITF effects.

The third broad concern motivating the present review was an interest in examining the possible effects of two new moderator variables derived from the guilt-based explanation of DITF effects (O'Keefe & Figgé, 1997). The first is the identity of the beneficiary of the two requests. In a sense, when the initial request is refused, there are potentially two injured parties—the person who made the request and the potential beneficiary of the request. Being able to comply with a second request from the same requester, for the same beneficiary, presumably would provide greater guilt reduction than would (to take the opposite extreme) complying with a smaller request from a different requester, for a different beneficiary. Thus the guilt-based account leads one to expect smaller DITF effects when the beneficiary of the requests differs from the initial to the target request.[5]

The second new potential moderator is the medium of communication. Consideration of this moderator is recommended by the conjunction of two lines of research. The first is work concerning communication media, specifically the idea that "social presence" is greater in face-to-face interaction than in mediated communication. The suggestion is that in face-to-face interaction, the presence of the other (and hence the interpersonal relationship) is more salient, because such interaction provides more communicative modalities than does (for instance) written or telephonic interaction (Short, Williams, & Christie, 1976; for related work, see Sproull & Kiesler, 1991). The second is work emphasizing the fundamentally interpersonal character of the feeling of guilt. Baumeister et al. (1994) have underscored the close connection between guilt arousal and interpersonal transactions (noting, e.g., that a prototypical cause of guilt is the infliction of harm on a relationship partner; see p. 245). Taken together, these two lines of thought suggest that guilt-arousal processes will be stronger in face-to-face interaction than in other communication media, and thus lead to the expectation that DITF effects will be larger in face-to-face implementations than in implementations using other media.[6]

Finally, this review was motivated by our interest in examining DITF effects using a random-effects analysis rather than a fixed-effects analysis. The situation faced by a meta-analyst with multiple message replications is parallel to that faced by a researcher whose primary-research design contains multiple instantiations of message categories. A researcher can analyze such multiple-message designs by treating messages as either a fixed effect or a random effect. There has been considerable discussion of this choice in the context of primary research on messages. The relevant general principle is that replications should be treated as random when the underlying interest is in generalization. This principle reflects the fact that fixed-effects and random-effects analyses test different hypotheses. For instance, when comparing two group means while treating message replications as fixed, the hypothesis that is tested concerns whether the responses to a fixed, concrete group of messages differ from the responses to some other fixed, concrete group of messages. The parallel random-effects analysis tests whether responses to one category of messages differ from responses to another category of messages (see, e.g., Jackson, 1992, p. 110).[7]

Although perhaps not so prominently discussed, the same choice (between fixed-effects and random-effects analysis) faces meta-analysts. A meta-analysis involves a collection of replications, parallel to the message replications in a multiple-message primary-research design. Similar considerations—including whether the analyst is interested in generalization—bear on the choice between the two analyses (for some discussion, see Erez, Bloom, & Wells, 1996; Jackson, 1992, p. 123; Raudenbush, 1994; Shadish & Haddock, 1994). Most meta-analytic work, in communication and in other fields, has commonly employed fixed-effects analyses, despite the analysts' typically being interested in generalizing beyond the cases at hand. Perhaps it is unsurprising that a National Research Council panel should have concluded that meta-analytic work "would be improved by the increased use of random effects models in preference to the current default of fixed effects models" (National Research Council, 1992, p. 185).

In the present review, our interest is naturally not in the fixed sets of messages (request pairs) that happened to be studied by past investigators, but in the classes of messages of which the studied messages are instantiations, and hence a random-effects analysis was the appropriate choice. In a random-effects analysis, the confidence interval around an obtained mean effect size reflects not only the usual (human) sampling variation but also between-studies variance. This has the effect of widening the confidence interval over what it would have been in a fixed-effects analysis (see Shadish & Haddock, 1994, p. 275; for related discussion, see Raudenbush, 1994, p. 306).

Neither previous DITF meta-analysis employed random-effects analysis. Fern et al. (1986) reported mean effect sizes and associated confidence intervals based on a fixed-effects analysis (see p. 147; see also Hedges, 1982). Dillard et al. (1984) focused on the mean effect size in, and the homogeneity displayed by, a given set (or subset) of effect sizes, following procedures described by Hunter, Schmidt, and Jackson (1982) that do not consider between-studies variation in estimating means and confidence intervals.

There is thus room for justifiable concern about the degree to which previous meta-analytic findings represent conclusions about the specific DITF implementations that have been studied, as opposed to broader generalizations. For example, Fern et al.'s (1986) report that the mean DITF effect size is dependably ($p < .05$) positive when the same person makes both requests, strictly speaking, concerns only the particular DITF implementations reviewed.[8] Of course, commonly—including earlier in this report—such meta-analytic findings have been (mis)interpreted as representing dependable generalizations beyond the cases studied. A random-effects analysis, however, provides a better basis for dependable generalization, and hence can address concerns about the evidentiary basis of previous conclusions.

METHODS

Identification of Relevant Investigations

Literature search. Relevant research reports were located in various ways, including personal knowledge of the literature, examination of previous reviews and textbooks, and inspection of reference lists in previously located reports. Additionally, we made searches through databases and document-retrieval services using "door-in-the-face," "DITF," "sequential request," and "request sequence" as search bases; these searches covered material through at least October 1, 1996, in PsycINFO, ERIC (Educational Resources Information Center), CARL/Uncover (Colorado Association of Research Libraries), *Current Contents,* and Medline, and through at least June 1, 1996, in *Dissertation Abstracts Ondisk.*

Inclusion criteria. To be included, an investigation had to meet two criteria. First, the study had to compare a DITF condition (in which, following the rejection of an initial request, a smaller target request was made) with a control condition (in which only the target request was made). Excluded by this criterion were review papers and secondary discussions and studies lacking the appropriate experimental comparisons, including studies in which the second request was not smaller than the first (Cialdini et al., 1975, Experiment 3, equivalent-request control; Miller et al., 1976, gaining-only and yielding-only conditions), those in which no explicit second request was made (Foehl & Goldman, 1983; Grace, Bell, & Sugar, 1988, spontaneous-helping conditions), those in which the target request was preceded by multiple initial requests (e.g., Comer, Kardes, & Sullivan, 1992; Goldman & Creason, 1981, two-face condition), and those lacking a relevant control condition (Goldman et al., 1984, Experiment 2; Yip & Kihoi, 1996).

Second, the investigation had to contain appropriate quantitative data pertinent to the comparison of compliance rates across experimental conditions. Excluded by this criterion were studies of effects on other dependent variables (Cantrill, 1986; Goldman, Gier, & Smith, 1981; Pendleton & Batson, 1979; Stahelski & Patch, 1993; Tybout, Sternthal, & Calder, 1983, Experiment 1) and studies for which appropriate quantitative information could not be obtained (e.g., Brechner, Shippee, & Obitz, 1976).

Dependent Variable and Effect Size Measures

Dependent variable. The dependent variable of interest was the relative success of the target request in the DITF condition and the control condition. Most studies elicited only verbal consent to the target request (as opposed, e.g., to behavioral performance of the requested action), and hence when multiple measures of compliance were available, verbal consent measures were employed to maximize consistency.

Effect size measures. Each comparison between a DITF condition and its corresponding control condition was summarized using r as the effect size measure. Effects were coded so that differences favoring DITF conditions were positive in sign and differences favoring control conditions were negative.

Most effect size estimates were derived from dichotomous indices of compliance, variously reported as frequencies (e.g., 15 of 21 participants complied) or proportions (e.g., 71%). All such reports were cast as frequencies (thus eliminating rounding errors associated with reports of proportions) and converted to r using formulas described by Johnson (1989, pp. 104-105).

In some studies, researchers retained DITF-condition participants who accepted (rather than rejected) the initial request, yielding effects based on an imperfect realization of the DITF strategy. When reports included the appropriate information, frequencies (and hence effect size computations) were adjusted in such cases to include only participants who rejected the initial request.

When multiple control conditions were available, the effect size was based on the comparison that best isolated the effect of the DITF strategy. For example, Wang, Brownstein, and Katzev (1989) had three different "control" conditions, which varied in exactly how the target request was made; the effect size was based on the comparison of the DITF condition to the "standard control" condition, because the second request in the DITF condition best matched the request made in that control condition. Similarly, Tybout's (1978) several "control" conditions differed in various ways from the DITF condition (e.g., with respect to the timing of questionnaires), whereas the "straight persuasion" condition differed only in its lack of a DITF implementation (and hence, because it isolated the effect of the DITF strategy, it provided the appropriate comparison).

Each of us computed effect sizes independently, and we subsequently resolved any discrepancies through discussion.

Independent Variables

Requester variation. Cases were coded for whether the two requests were made by the same person.

Beneficiary variation. Cases were coded for whether the two requests had the same beneficiary, defined as the person or persons who would benefit from the request's being fulfilled.

Prosocialness of requests. Each request was classified as prosocial or nonprosocial. Prosocial requests were those that, if fulfilled, would presumably benefit society at large, directly or indirectly (such as requests for donations to charitable organizations, environmental groups, or civic organizations), or would represent favors to individuals (such as requests for favors from strangers). Nonprosocial requests were requests not meeting these criteria; the exemplary forms of nonprosocial requests were those from commercial (profit-seeking) enterprises. Based on these codings, cases were classified as either using two prosocial requests or not using two prosocial requests (this latter classification thus included cases in which one or both of the requests were nonprosocial).

Medium. The medium of communication used for each request was recorded. All cases involved either face-to-face interaction or telephone communication and were classified correspondingly.

Time interval. The length of time that elapsed between the first and second requests in the DITF condition was recorded, with cases classified as having either no delay (cases in which no more than 5 minutes elapsed between requests) or delay. Delays ranged from 2 to 14 days.

Coding reliabilities. Two coders independently classified 10 randomly selected cases for these five variables, with 96% average intercoder agreement; disagreements were resolved through discussion. The coders subsequently coded all remaining cases independently, with any further disagreements similarly resolved.

Concession size. A separate analysis was undertaken to assess the possible effects of concession size. This moderating variable is distinctive, in that coding cases for concession size is problematic. The most straightforward way of coding each case for concession size would require an assessment (on some universal metric) of the size of each request, which would then provide a basis for classifying cases based on the difference between the values for the first and second requests. But it is not clear that a suitable metric exists or that defensible assessments are obtainable. One cannot now ask the primary-research participants for their assessments of request size, and one might doubt whether request size assessments obtained today would reflect accurately the views of primary-research participants. (For an illustration of the potentially problematic nature of such procedures, see Petty, Cacioppo, Kasmer, & Haugtvedt, 1987, pp. 260-261; Petty, Kasmer, Haugtvedt, & Cacioppo, 1987, pp. 241-242; Stiff, 1986, p. 83; Stiff & Boster, 1987, pp. 252-253. For some general discussion, see Hale & Dillard, 1991, pp. 467-468.) Fern et al. (1986, p. 146) estimated relative request magnitudes in a variety of ways, including dollar ratios (where money was requested), time ratios (where time commitments were involved), and magnitude estimates obtained from marketing research students, though it is not clear whether this last procedure would yield estimates consistent with the other procedures.

An alternative approach is possible, based on studies in which manifestly different-sized initial requests were used with the same target request (or, alternatively, studies in which manifestly different-sized target requests were used with the same initial request). For example, Abrahams and Bell (1994) created two DITF conditions by varying the size of the initial request (labeled "moderate" in one condition and "large" in the other). Because these two conditions used the same target request, they represented different concession sizes: the "moderate" initial request condition involved a relatively small concession, whereas the "large" initial request condition involved a relatively large concession. Thus a comparison of the effect sizes between these two conditions provides information about the effect of concession size variations.

Examining studies that afford such within-study comparisons avoids any problems associated with post hoc assessments of request size. Moreover, this way of proceeding helps to isolate the effect of concession size: Because the evidence is derived from within-study comparisons, each obtained comparison reflects similar procedures and circumstances with respect to other possible variables.

Every study providing such a within-study comparison was identified and used in a separate analysis.[9] The comparison of interest concerns how DITF effects (expressed as *r*s) vary between two conditions (namely, larger and smaller concessions), and thus required a distinctive effect size index. The relevant effect size index is that for a comparison of two correlations; Cohen's q (the difference between the z-transformed rs) provides such an index (Cohen, 1988, p. 110). This index was computed such that positive values reflected larger DITF effects with larger concessions; negative values indicated smaller DITF effects with larger concessions.

Analysis

Unit of analysis. In our consideration of how to analyze the present collection of studies, attention to the particular requests employed was important. Every analyzed study contains a comparison of the success of a target request under two conditions (preceded, or not, by the initial rejected request), and it might be thought that one could simply straightforwardly derive an effect size measure for each study. But some studies have more than one initial/target request pair, and some initial/target request pairs are used in more than one study. If one is interested in generalizing across messages (that is, request pairs), the common meta-analytic procedure of treating each study as providing one effect size estimate is unsatisfactory.

Thus, in the present analysis, the fundamental unit of analysis was the request pair (that is, the pair composed of a target request and its corresponding initial request). A measure of effect size was recorded for each distinguishable request pair found in the body of studies. For example, a study reporting separate comparisons between DITF and control conditions for multiple different initial/target request pairs contributed multiple observations (e.g., Miller, 1974), whereas a study with a single request pair contributed only one. Similarly, a study with a single target request contributed multiple observations if comparisons were available for different initial requests (e.g., Wang et al., 1989).

Where a study employed an experimental manipulation corresponding to an independent variable in the current report, effect sizes were computed separately for the relevant conditions. For example, Patch (1986) ascribed the requests to either a nonprofit (prosocial) organization or a consulting company (nonprosocial); separate effect sizes were recorded for these two conditions. When an experimental manipulation not germane to this review was employed (e.g., formal versus informal clothing; Williams & Williams, 1989), effect sizes were computed collapsed across such variations.

Usually, a given request pair was used only in a single investigation, and hence only one effect size estimate was associated with the pair. But when a request pair was used in more than one study, there would be several estimates of the effect size associated with that request pair. These multiple estimates were cumulated into a single summary estimate before inclusion in the analysis.

Such cumulation occurred in the following cases: data from Experiment 1 (no-delay condition) and Experiment 2 in Cann, Sherman, and Elkes (1975) were combined and reported as "Cann et al. (1975) no-delay"; data from the second pilot experiment and from the main experiment in Cantrill (1985) were combined and reported as "Cantrill (1985)"; data from Experiment 1 and Experiment 3 in Cialdini et al. (1975) were combined and reported as "Cialdini et al. (1975) Experiments 1 and 3"; data from the moderate-request conditions in Experiments 1 and 2 in Even-Chen, Yinon, and Bizman (1978) were combined and reported as "Even-Chen et al. (1978) moderate"; data from Mowen and Cialdini (1980) Study 1, large-request condition, and Study 2, 15-minute-same condition, were combined and reported as "Mowen & Cialdini (1980) large"; data from Patch (1986, consulting-source condition), Patch (1988), and Dillard and Hale (1992, consulting-source condition) were combined and reported as "Patch consulting"; data from Patch (1986, non-profit-source condition) and Dillard and Hale (1992, nonprofit-source condition) were combined and reported as "Patch nonprofit"; data from Experiments 1 and 2 in Reeves et al. (1991) were combined as appropriate and reported as "Reeves et al. (1991) extremely large" or "Reeves et al. (1991) moderately large" (see Table 1.1).

When multiple estimates were cumulated, the preferred means of cumulation was to combine the raw frequencies; for example, if the DITF compliance rates for a given request pair were 20/35 in one investigation (i.e., of 35 participants, 20 complied with the target request) and 15/25 in a second, the effect size was computed based on a DITF compliance rate of 35/60 (compared with similarly combined control group frequencies).[10] We used this same procedure when collapsing across irrelevant experimental manipulations within a single investigation.

In some cases, the same primary data served as the basis for multiple reports. Whenever a given investigation was reported in more than one outlet, it was treated as a single study and analyzed accordingly. The same research was reported (in whole or part) in Bell, Abrahams, Clark, and Schlatter (1995) and Bell, Abrahams, Clark, and Schlatter (1996); in Cantrill (1985), Cantrill (1991), and Cantrill and Seibold (1986), recorded here under Cantrill (1985); in Cialdini (1975) and Cialdini and Ascani (1976), recorded here under the latter; in Hayes (1982) and Hayes, Dwyer, Greenwalt, and Coe (1984), recorded here under the latter; in Nawrat (1989) and Nawrat (1993); in Reingen (1977) and Reingen (1978); and in Schwarzwald, Raz, and Zvibel (1979) and Schwarzwald, Zvibel, and Raz (1980), recorded here under the former.

Random-effects analysis. For the primary analysis, the individual correlations (effect sizes) were initially transformed to Fisher's zs; the zs were analyzed using random-effects procedures described by Shadish and Haddock (1994), with results then transformed back to r. We employed a random-effects analysis in preference to a fixed-effects analysis because of our interest in generalizing across request pairs.

TABLE 1.1
Cases Analyzed

Study	r	n	Codings[a]
Abrahams & Bell, 1994			
moderate	.362	91	1/1/1/1/1
large	.441	91	1/1/1/1/1
Bell et al., 1995, 1996	.000	112	1/1/1/1/1
Brownstein & Katzev, 1985	.093	48	1/1/1/1/1
Burger, 1986, Experiment 7	.091	38	1/1/1/1/1
Cann et al., 1975			
delay	−.218	47	1/1/1/2/2
no-delay	.366	87	1/1/1/2/1
Cantrill, 1985			
donation-effort	.378	121	1/1/1/1/1
donation-novelty	.438	83	1/1/1/1/1
elderly-effort	.399	117	1/1/1/1/1
elderly-novelty	.164	114	1/1/1/1/1
Cialdini & Ascani, 1976	.178	126	1/1/1/1/1
Cialdini et al., 1975			
Experiment 2 rejection-moderation	.236	39	1/2/1/1/1
Experiment 2 two-requester	−.258	38	2/2/1/1/1
Experiments 1 and 3	.278	96	1/1/1/1/1
Collins & Brady, 1994	−.083	240	1/1/2/1/1
Crano & Sivacek, 1982	−.120	61	2/2/1/2/2
Dillard & Hale, 1992, lobbying	.148	160	1/1/2/2/1
Even-Chen et al., 1978			
Experiment 1 large	.143	116	1/1/1/1/1
Experiment 2 large	.253	67	1/1/1/1/1
moderate	−.190	183	1/1/1/1/1
Foss & Dempsey, 1979			
Experiment 2	.127	59	2/1/1/2/2
Experiment 3	.002	62	2/1/1/1/2
Goldman, 1986			
moderate	.172	152	1/1/1/2/1
target	.211	152	1/1/1/2/1
Goldman & Creason, 1981	.315	64	1/1/2/2/1
Goldman et al., 1984, Experiment 1	.207	100	1/1/1/1/1
Grace et al., 1988	.186	30	1/2/1/1/1
Harari et al., 1980	.227	94	1/1/1/2/1
Hayes et al., 1984	−.123	607	1/1/1/2/1
Katzev & Brownstein, 1989			
math test	−.167	60	1/1/1/1/1
survey	.064	57	1/1/2/2/1
Miller, 1974			
time-time	.319	44	1/1/1/2/1
money-time	.047	44	1/1/1/2/1
money-money	.321	44	1/1/1/2/1
time-money	.189	44	1/1/1/2/1
Miller et al., 1976	.478	38	1/1/1/2/1

TABLE 1.1
Continued

Study	r	n	Codings[a]
Mowen & Cialdini, 1980			
Study 1 very large	.127	128	1/1/2/1/1
Study 2 10-minute same	.000	72	1/1/2/1/1
Study 2 10-minute different	−.143	72	1/1/2/1/1
Study 2 15-minute different	−.030	72	1/1/2/1/1
large	.152	200	1/1/2/1/1
Nawrat, 1989, 1993			
sweater	.286	70	1/1/1/1/1
fiancée	.059	76	1/1/1/1/1
Oliver, 1984			
prosocial low-cost	.000	40	1/1/1/2/1
prosocial high-cost	−.109	40	1/1/1/2/1
commercial low-cost	−.152	40	1/1/2/2/1
commercial high-cost	−.066	40	1/1/2/2/1
Patch consulting	.044	324	1/1/2/2/1
Patch nonprofit	.202	231	1/1/1/2/1
Reeves et al., 1991			
extremely large	.285	120	1/1/1/1/1
moderately large	.220	120	1/1/1/1/1
Reingen, 1977, 1978	.065	128	1/1/1/1/1
Reingen & Kernan, 1977	−.147	84	2/2/2/2/2
Reingen & Kernan, 1979	−.139	196	1/1/2/2/1
Rogers, 1976			
Experiment 1 one-requester	−.051	40	1/1/1/2/1
Experiment 1 two-requester	−.168	40	2/2/1/2/1
Experiment 2	.168	120	1/1/2/2/1
Experiment 3 one-requester	−.168	80	1/1/1/2/1
Experiment 3 two-requester	−.132	80	2/2/1/2/1
Schwarzwald et al., 1979			
20-10	.101	40	1/1/1/1/1
30-10	.436	40	1/1/1/1/1
40-10	.436	40	1/1/1/1/1
50-10	.314	40	1/1/1/1/1
60-10	.000	40	1/1/1/1/1
100-10	−.152	40	1/1/1/1/1
20-15	.420	40	1/1/1/1/1
30-15	.420	40	1/1/1/1/1
40-15	.329	40	1/1/1/1/1
50-15	−.253	40	1/1/1/1/1
60-15	−.451	40	1/1/1/1/1
100-15	−.503	40	1/1/1/1/1
30-20	.408	40	1/1/1/1/1
40-20	.302	40	1/1/1/1/1
50-20	.101	40	1/1/1/1/1
60-20	.000	40	1/1/1/1/1
100-20	−.218	40	1/1/1/1/1

TABLE 1.1
Continued

Study	r	n	Codings[a]
Shanab & Isonio, 1980	.000	80	1/1/1/1/2
Shanab & O'Neill, 1979	.249	80	1/1/1/1/1
Shanab & O'Neill, 1982			
large	.053	80	1/1/1/1/1
very large	.425	80	1/1/1/1/1
Snyder & Cunningham, 1975	−.243	54	2/2/1/2/2
Tybout, 1978, Experiment 1	−.158	120	1/2/2/1/1
Tybout et al., 1983, Experiment 4	.000	105	1/1/2/2/1
Wang et al., 1989			
$10	.009	75	1/1/1/1/1
$25	.105	74	1/1/1/1/1
$50	−.098	77	1/1/1/1/1
Williams & Williams, 1989	.000	136	1/1/1/1/1

a. The coding judgments, in order, are requester variation (1 = same requester, 2 = different requesters), beneficiary variation (1 = same beneficiary, 2 = different beneficiaries), prosocialness (1 = prosocial, 2 = nonprosocial), communication medium (1 = face-to-face, 2 = telephone), and time interval (1 = no delay; 2 = delay).

RESULTS

Overall DITF Effects

Effect sizes were available for 88 distinct request pairs. The number of participants was 7,780, with study sample sizes ranging from 30 to 607. Details on each included case are contained in Table 1.1.

Across all 88 cases, the random-effects weighted mean correlation was .097. The 95% confidence interval for this mean was .049, .144, indicating a dependably positive overall DITF effect.

Moderating Factors

Table 1.2 provides a summary of the results concerning the effects of the five main moderating variables, considered individually. For each variable, the results indicate an important moderating role. The mean effects are dependably positive if the same person makes both requests, if the requests have the same beneficiary, if the requests are prosocial, if the requests are made face-to-face, or if there is no delay between the requests. The mean effects are not dependably positive, however, if different persons make the requests, if the requests have different beneficiaries, if the requests are not prosocial, if the requests are made over the telephone, or if there is a delay between the requests. Indeed, effect sizes are significantly ($p < .05$) larger when the same person makes both requests (as opposed to when different persons make the requests), when the requests have the same beneficiary (as

TABLE 1.2
Summary of Results

	k	r	95% CI	Q (df)
All cases	88	.097	.049, .144	311.3 (87)**
Same requester	80	.116	.067, .166	287.2 (79)**
Different requesters	8	−.110	−.202, −.018	6.0 (7)
Same beneficiary	79	.117	.068, .167	279.2 (78)**
Different beneficiaries	9	−.110	−.223, .003	9.2 (8)
Prosocial requests	71	.120	.064, .176	265.0 (70)**
Nonprosocial requests	17	.012	−.052, .077	33.1 (16)*
Face-to-face	57	.120	.057, .182	202.8 (56)**
Telephone	31	.055	−.015, .125	96.3 (30)**
No time interval	81	.112	.062, .161	293.2 (80)**
Time interval	7	−.080	−.179, .018	6.1 (6)
Optimal moderator values	45	.152	.078, .226	164.0 (44)**
Suboptimal moderator values	43	.039	−.016, .094	115.6 (42)**

$*p < .01; **p < .001.$

opposed to having different beneficiaries), and when there is no delay between the two requests (as opposed to some time interval between them).

As a way of summarizing the effects of these five moderating factors, we classified cases into two categories: cases in which the moderating variables had values that would be expected to maximize the effect size (namely, two prosocial requests having the same beneficiary, made face-to-face by the same requester with no delay between the requests) and cases in which one or more of the moderating variables had a less-than-optimal value.

As indicated in Table 1.2, in 45 cases, all five moderating factors had optimal values, with a mean r across these cases of .152; this mean correlation was dependably ($p < .001$) positive. In 43 cases, at least one of the five moderating factors had a less-than-optimal value; the mean r across these cases was .039 and was not significantly different from zero. Thus, although the 95% confidence intervals for these two means overlap, only under optimal conditions is the mean effect dependably positive.

With respect to concession size, 15 distinguishable comparisons were available between DITF effect sizes obtained with relatively smaller and relatively larger initial requests (see Table 1.3). The n-weighted mean q (difference between z-transformed rs) was .005. Because meta-analytic techniques for handling effect size indices such as q appear not well developed, confidence intervals were not constructed. However, the obtained mean q is literally nearly zero and is obviously substantially smaller than the .10 q value conventionally labeled "small" by Cohen (1988). Of the 15 comparisons, 7 were positive (indicating larger DITF effects with larger concessions) and 8 were negative (indicating smaller DITF effects with larger concessions).

Homogeneity of Effects

There is substantial heterogeneity in the observed effects. Even under the very specific circumstance identified by the conjunction of optimal values for the five key moderator variables, there is significant variability in the set of effect sizes. Homogeneous effects do appear to obtain within some categories; for example, the set of effect sizes involving delay between the two requests is apparently homogeneous. However, the categories within which the null hypothesis of homogeneity is not rejected are also categories that contain relatively few cases, and hence may have low power for detecting heterogeneity.

DISCUSSION

What emerges from this review is a somewhat more complex but also better-evidenced picture of DITF effects than that afforded by previous reviews. We discuss, in turn, the findings concerning moderators of DITF effects, the magnitude and robustness of DITF effects, the explanation of DITF effects, directions for future DITF research, and some methodological aspects of the current review.

Moderator Variables

Individual moderator variables. Previous meta-analytic reviews suggested that three particular moderator variables—requester identity variations, prosocialness of requests, and time interval between requests—play significant roles in influencing DITF effects. However, no previous review offered an appropriate (random-effects) analysis that might underwrite generalizations about these moderators. The current findings, however, do provide a more sound evidentiary basis for these previous suggestions. Specifically, when different persons make the two requests, when the requests are not prosocial, or when a time interval intervenes between the two requests, the mean DITF effect is not significantly different from zero; by contrast, when the same person makes both requests, when the requests are prosocial, or when no time interval separates the requests, the mean DITF effect is dependably positive.

The current evidence for the role of prosocialness is especially noteworthy, given the doubts that Dillard and Hale (1992) have raised. In the present

TABLE 1.3
Concession Size Cases

	q	n
Abrahams & Bell, 1994	.094	182
smaller concession ("moderate") $r = .362$		
larger concession ("large") $r = .441$		
Even-Chen et al., 1978, Experiment 1	.311	232
smaller concession ("moderate") $r = -.165$		
larger concession ("large") $r = .143$		
Even-Chen et al., 1978, Experiment 2	.494	134
smaller concession ("moderate") $r = -.231$		
larger concession ("large") $r = .253$		
Goldman, 1986	−.040	304
smaller concession ("target") $r = .211$		
larger concession ("moderate") $r = .172$		
Mowen & Cialdini, 1980, Study 1	.031	256
smaller concession ("large") $r = .096$		
larger concession ("very large") $r = .127$		
Mowen & Cialdini, 1980, Study 2 same	−.256	144
smaller concession ("15 minute") $r = .251$		
larger concession ("10 minute") $r = .000$		
Mowen & Cialdini, 1980, Study 2 different	−.114	144
smaller concession ("15 minute") $r = -.030$		
larger concession ("10 minute") $r = -.143$		
Oliver, 1984, prosocial	.109	80
smaller concession ("high-cost") $r = -.109$		
larger concession ("low-cost") $r = .000$		
Oliver, 1984, commercial	−.087	80
smaller concession ("high-cost") $r = -.066$		
larger concession ("low-cost") $r = -.152$		
Reeves et al., 1991	.069	240
smaller concession ("moderately large") $r = .220$		
larger concession ("extremely large") $r = .285$		
Schwarzwald et al., 1979, 20-10 vs. 100-10	−.255	80
smaller concession ("20-10") $r = .101$		
larger concession ("100-10") $r = -.152$		
Schwarzwald et al., 1979, 20-15 vs. 100-15	-1.001	80
smaller concession ("20-15") $r = .420$		
larger concession ("100-15") $r = -.503$		
Schwarzwald et al., 1979, 30-20 vs. 100-20	−.655	80
smaller concession ("30-20") $r = .408$		
larger concession ("100-20") $r = -.218$		
Shanab & O'Neill, 1982	.401	160
smaller concession ("large") $r = .053$		
larger concession ("very large") $r = .425$		
Wang et al., 1989	−.107	152
smaller concession ("$10") $r = .009$		
larger concession ("$50") $r = -.098$		

review, the unit of analysis was the request pair, quite unlike Dillard et al.'s procedure in which the study was the unit of analysis. Despite this methodological difference, the present results indicate that DITF effects are indeed significantly positive when prosocial requests are made and not dependably positive otherwise.

These results also provide evidence consistent with Fern et al.'s (1986) failure to find any relationship between concession size and DITF effect size. Notably, this confirmation was obtained in a manner quite different from that employed by Fern et al.; such diversity in method provides even greater confidence in this null result.

Additionally, this analysis has identified two new moderating factors: the identity of the beneficiaries of the request and the medium of communication. When the two requests have different beneficiaries or when the requests are made over the telephone rather than face-to-face, the mean DITF effect is not significantly different from zero, whereas DITF effects are dependably positive when the requests have the same beneficiary or when requests are made face-to-face.

However, a complication arises in the consideration of beneficiary-variation and requester-variation effects, namely, that beneficiary variations and requester variations are largely confounded. In 83 of the 88 cases analyzed here, the requester and beneficiary were either both constant across the requests ($k = 77$) or both varied ($k = 6$). In only 5 cases was one varied while the other was constant: In 3 cases the same person made the two requests but the beneficiaries varied, and in 2 cases the beneficiary was identical but different persons made the two requests.

This confounding naturally makes for interpretive uncertainties concerning the distinctive effects of these two moderating factors. It may be that beneficiary variations are solely responsible for the observed effects, and hence that the effects previously attributed to requester variations are in fact due to beneficiary variations; it may be that requester variations are solely responsible for the observed effects; or it may be that both factors play a role.

The possibility that both factors play a role is supported by an examination of the contrast between cases in which both the requester and the beneficiary differ from the first request to the second ($k = 6$) and cases in which one varies but the other does not ($k = 5$). When both the requester and the beneficiary are different in the two requests, the mean r is $-.168$ and is dependably negative (the 95% confidence interval is $-.274$, $-.061$). When one varies but the other does not, the mean r is $.024$ (the 95% confidence interval is $-.106$, $.154$). Despite the very small number of cases, these two means are nearly significantly different ($p < .12$). In short, it appears that both requester variations and beneficiary variations influence DITF effects, such that effects are especially reduced when both the requester and the beneficiary change from the first request to the second.

Joint operation of moderators. It is worthwhile to consider the joint operation of the five centrally relevant moderator variables (requester variation, beneficiary variation, prosocialness of requests, communication medium, and time interval between requests). This package of variables is obviously informative about the conditions under which DITF effects are to be expected. There is a notable difference between the mean DITF effect obtained under optimal conditions (roughly .15) and that obtained under suboptimal conditions (roughly .04). Indeed, the joint operation of the five key moderating factors is such as to make positive DITF effects unlikely to occur under suboptimal circumstances. When any of the five key moderators was not optimal for DITF effects, the obtained mean effect size was not significantly positive.

At the same time, no value of any one of the five key moderator variables is apparently absolutely necessary to produce DITF effects. Positive (though not necessarily dependably positive) DITF effects have been observed when different persons made the two requests (Foss & Dempsey, 1979, Experiment 2), when the two requests were not both prosocial (Mowen & Cialdini, 1980, Study 1, very large condition), when a delay intervened between the requests (Foss & Dempsey, 1979, Experiment 2), when the two requests had different beneficiaries (Grace et al., 1988), and when the requests were not made face-to-face (Cann et al., 1975, no-delay condition). That is to say, it may be possible to produce DITF effects under suboptimal conditions. Indeed, significantly positive DITF effects have been observed with implementations using nonprosocial requests (Mowen & Cialdini, 1980, large) and with implementations using telephoned requests (e.g., Harari, Mohr, & Hosey, 1980).

Similarly, even apparently optimal conditions are no guarantee of positive DITF effects. A number of cases with optimal conditions nevertheless produced negative (though not necessarily dependably negative) effect sizes (Even-Chen et al., 1978, moderate; Katzev & Brownstein, 1989, math test; Schwarzwald et al., 1979, 100-10, 50-15, 60-15, 100-15, and 100-20 conditions; Wang et al., 1989, $50). Thus, although one cannot confidently specify either necessary or sufficient conditions for obtaining DITF effects, it is nevertheless possible to identify a number of important moderating factors that influence the size of DITF effects.

Magnitude and Robustness of DITF Effects

Magnitude. DITF effects are genuine, as evidenced by the dependably positive overall mean effect size and by the observation of individual cases in which dependably positive effects obtain. But these effects may not appear to be especially large. The overall mean correlation is about .10, and even under optimal conditions the mean correlation is only about .15. Under anything less than optimal conditions, the mean drops substantially, to about .04.

But this appearance may be deceiving. For example, a correlation of .15 corresponds to the difference between a control condition in which 42.5% comply with the target request and a DITF condition in which 57.5% comply (which is a 35% increase in compliance). Even a correlation of only .10 represents the difference between a control condition with 45% compliance and a DITF condition with 55% (a 22% increase in compliance). Thus, although the obtained mean correlations may seem minute when judged against the magnitude of correlations expected in (for example) inter-item reliability assessments, in fact the observed effects are not entirely trivial. (For a general discussion of effect sizes, see Rosenthal, 1994; for some specific discussions concerning the understanding of effect size magnitudes, see Abelson, 1985; Cooper, 1981; Haase, Ellis, & Ladany, 1989.)

Moreover, it is not clear that it is realistic to expect dramatically larger mean effects in social influence research. Consider, for example, that the mean difference in persuasive effectiveness (expressed as r) between one-sided and two-sided messages has been reported as .04—increasing to .08 if only refutational two-sided messages are considered (Allen, 1991). The mean correlation between fear-appeal manipulations and behavior has been estimated variously as .10 (Boster & Mongeau, 1984) and .17 (Sutton, 1982), and that between fear-appeal manipulations and attitude as .21 (Boster & Mongeau, 1984) and .18 (Sutton, 1982). The mean persuasive effect (as r) of variations in the timing of communicator identification has been reported as .26 (O'Keefe, 1987). Segrin's (1993) review of the influence of various nonverbal elements on compliance reported mean correlations of .23 (for gaze), .21 (touch), .18 (interpersonal distance), and .16 (apparel).

In short, other meta-analytic estimates of the effects of various factors on the success of social influence efforts should lead one to expect effects not larger than ones equivalent to a correlation of .30. Cohen's (1988) diffidently offered conventional labels would have a correlation of .50 be a "large" effect, .30 a "medium" effect, and .10 a "small" effect. By this yardstick, factors affecting the outcomes of social influence efforts appear (on the basis of meta-analytically derived estimates) to have no better than small to medium-sized mean effects. Understood in this context, the observed magnitude of DITF effects is not remarkably small.

One should also remember that it is possible in individual implementations to obtain rather impressive DITF effects: effect sizes in excess of .40 were obtained by Abrahams and Bell (1994, large), Cantrill (1985, donation-novelty), Miller et al. (1976), Schwarzwald et al. (1979, 30-10, 40-10, 20-15, 30-15, and 30-20 conditions), and Shanab and O'Neill (1982, very large). A correlation of .40 is equivalent to the difference between a control condition that produces 30% compliance and a DITF condition that yields 70% compliance (which is a 133% increase in compliance). Although DITF effects this large are rare (occurring in about 10% of the cases), a number of different investigators have produced them—although, notably, almost always under conditions that were optimal with respect to the five key moderator variables.

Robustness. Even though there is a significantly positive overall DITF effect, there is also substantial heterogeneity among the effect sizes. Indeed, even under optimal conditions, there is significant variability among the observed effect sizes. What this suggests is that, even though there may be a dependably positive DITF effect under these optimal conditions, one should also expect quite a bit of variability in the success of DITF implementations even in optimal circumstances.

One reaction to such heterogeneity might be to suppose that the phenomenon in question must be poorly understood. Such a reaction would be encouraged by a supposition that the point of meta-analytic research is the establishment of sets of homogeneous effect sizes; from this vantage point, heterogeneity in a collection of effect sizes is something to be squeezed out by ever-finer effect size categorization (see, e.g., Dillard et al., 1984, pp. 465-466). But one might alternatively take heterogeneity to be a fact about the phenomenon. We are accustomed to thinking about the mean effect size as a fact about a given phenomenon, but we might consider effect size variability in a similar way. So, for example, two different compliance techniques might vary not only in their mean effects but in the degree of variability to be expected across implementations. That variability, like the mean effect, is simply one aspect of the phenomenon.

Considered in this way, one interesting fact about DITF effects is their heterogeneity. DITF effects do not appear to be the sort of thing easily produced on demand; there is no hard-and-fast set of requirements for obtaining DITF effects. On the contrary, DITF effects look to be relatively fragile rather than robust. After all, even when experimental conditions are optimized with respect to five demonstrably relevant moderating variables, the size of the observed DITF effect can still vary greatly. In fact, even under apparently optimal conditions, dependably *negative* DITF effects have been observed (e.g., Even-Chen et al., 1978, moderate).

Explaining DITF Effects

Any satisfactory explanation of DITF effects will need to be able to account for the roles of observed moderator variables. The present review, by providing stronger evidence than was previously available about the operation of suspected moderators, thus specifies constraints to be met by any proposed explanation.

The best-known DITF explanation, the reciprocal-concessions account, receives little support in these findings. The reciprocal-concessions explanation leads to the expectation that larger concessions will produce larger DITF effects. However, in this review, as in Fern et al.'s (1986) review using different procedures, we did not find larger concessions to be dependably associated with larger DITF effects.

Moreover, these results suggest roles for two other moderators that are not obviously encompassed by a reciprocal-concessions account. The first is the prosocialness of the requests. There is no obvious reason concessions involving prosocial requests should receive greater reciprocation than concessions involving nonprosocial requests. (Prosocial requests might produce greater compliance than nonprosocial requests, but the issue here is different; it concerns not the difference between prosocial and nonprosocial request compliance rates, but the difference between prosocial and nonprosocial request DITF effect sizes.) Indeed, if anything, given a general familiarity with the existence of bargaining in commercial enterprises (e.g., labor-management negotiation), the reciprocal-concessions account might expect that nonprosocial requests would more easily be perceived as fitting a bargaining/negotiation frame (compared with nonprosocial requests), and hence might predict *larger* DITF effects for nonprosocial requests than for prosocial requests.

The other moderator variable that seems troublesome for the reciprocal-concessions explanation is variations in the identity of the beneficiary. The reciprocal-concessions account can easily explain why variations in the identity of the requester will influence DITF effects (because with different requesters, the pressure to reciprocate a concession vanishes), but it does not explain why changes in the beneficiary of the request should have the observed effects.

These results also offer little confirmation for the perceptual-contrast and self-presentation explanations. The perceptual-contrast explanation does not appear to provide any reason why the prosociality of the requests should influence DITF effect sizes. And neither of these explanations appears to offer any obvious account of why beneficiary variations should influence DITF effects.

By contrast, these results do provide some evidence supporting the usefulness of a guilt-based analysis of DITF effects. First, this review has provided better evidence for the operation of previously suggested moderator variables the expected effects of which can be explained by a guilt-based analysis. As discussed previously, the guilt-based account explains the role of requester variations by suggesting that a second request that comes from a different requester does not offer the same guilt-reduction possibilities as a second request from the same person whose request was just declined. The observed effect for prosocialness is explained as a consequence of persons' feeling greater guilt when declining prosocial requests than they feel when declining nonprosocial requests. And the observed time-interval effect is seen to arise because with increased delay between the requests, any induced guilt has a greater opportunity to dissipate.

Second, two new moderating variables suggested by the guilt-based analysis (beneficiary variations and communication medium) are apparently related to the size of DITF effects. However, these findings do not (and cannot) represent decisive evidence for a guilt-based explanation. These same moderating factors might be explained equally well in other ways; for example, the reciprocal-concessions explanation might suggest that face-to-face interactions would engender greater pressure toward reciprocity than would telephone interactions. As several commentators have observed, when meta-analytic research identifies relevant moderating factors, it is not uncommon for multiple plausible models to be consistent with the data in hand (e.g., Cook et al., 1992, pp. 181-184; Hale & Dillard, 1991). Thus these findings concerning new moderator variables do not uniquely support a guilt-based analysis. Nevertheless, a guilt-based analysis did lead to the identification of these new moderating factors, and the present results are entirely consistent with the expectations of a guilt-based account.

   In any event, the identification of these new moderator variables places additional constraints on any satisfactory explanation of DITF phenomena, as any suitable explanation will need to address how and why the various moderator variables produce their observed effects. And the guilt-based explanation does appear well suited to accommodate the observed pattern of effects and particularly the apparent role of beneficiary variations. Moreover, the apparently fragile character of DITF effects seems consistent with the evanescent nature of an emotional state such as guilt.

Future Research

   Future DITF research might usefully examine more closely the possible role of guilt in DITF processes. Two broad lines of work recommend themselves. The first is the examination of the effects of additional possible moderator variables that might be derived from the guilt-based account. For example, O'Keefe and Figgé (1997) have suggested that, because guilt arises from a person's holding him- or herself responsible for some negatively evaluated outcome, anything that reduces a person's sense of responsibility for first-request refusal will reduce the amount of guilt experienced (and correspondingly affect the success of the DITF strategy). As just discussed, however, there is no reason to suppose that any such possible moderating variable would be uniquely associated with guilt-based processes.

   A second, and empirically more compelling, avenue for research would involve the direct assessment of guilt to see whether guilt arousal and reduction patterns obtain in the ways expected by a guilt-based explanation. As several commentators have noted, it is important to have direct assessment of whatever mediating state is posited by a DITF explanation (Abrahams & Bell, 1994; Dillard, 1991). In the specific case of guilt various assessment procedures are possible, but assessing guilt is not entirely unproblematic (see Bozinoff & Ghingold, 1983; Kugler & Jones, 1992; O'Keefe & Figgé, 1997).

No matter the specific direction of future primary research, it might be noticed that the present results underscore the difficulties and delicacy of producing satisfactory primary-research evidence concerning DITF and any proposed mediating state. DITF effects are elusive, there is no recipe to guarantee their production, and they are commonly of sufficiently small magnitude as to make power requirements potentially daunting (particularly for designs seeking comparisons between different DITF conditions).[11] Useful primary research on DITF effects will plainly require a skilled experimental hand.

Some Methodological Considerations

The present meta-analysis is distinctive in some methodological respects, most notably in using a random-effects analysis. The same considerations that underwrite the choice of random-effects analyses in primary-research designs that contain message replications underwrite the choice of random-effects analyses in meta-analytic research covering message replications. Fixed-effects analyses (e.g., of the sort reported by Fern et al., 1986) cannot provide evidence bearing on general claims about classes of messages. Where meta-analytic work in communication is motivated by an interest in generalizing about message categories, random-effects analyses should be preferred (with message as the unit of analysis).

But the present analysis is also distinctive in reporting confidence intervals around means. Faced with a set of effect sizes, many meta-analysts in communication appear concerned with reporting whether the collection of effect sizes is homogeneous and what the mean effect size is. The assumption seems to be that if a set of effect sizes is homogeneous, then the observed mean effect size *is* the population effect size; this assumption is mistaken, however. A set of effect sizes can be homogeneous and have a nonzero mean, but that mean can still not be significantly different from zero.[12] (For an example, see the DITF cases with some time interval between requests, as summarized in Table 1.2.) Routine reporting of confidence intervals would of course make individual meta-analyses more informative, but it also would facilitate comparison across meta-analyses.

Summary

This random-effects meta-analysis of DITF research provides evidence supporting more confident generalizations about the role of several moderator variables than were possible based on previous reviews. Variations in the identity of the requester, the identity of the beneficiary, the prosocialness of the requests, the medium of communication, and the time interval between requests all appear to influence the size of DITF effects; variations in concession size do not. DITF effects are small in absolute terms but not remarkably small in the context of other effect sizes concerning social influence. However, there is substantial variability in DITF effects, even under optimal conditions. These findings are not easily reconciled with most proposed explanations of DITF effects, but they appear consistent with a guilt-based account.

NOTES

1. Dillard et al. (1984, p. 483) noted that requester identity and delay were confounded, hence they analyzed only delay variations.

2. A reader quite properly cautioned that this parallel is imperfect because two meta-analyses of a given research area rely on the same (or at least overlapping) data (unlike the case of two primary-research reports based on entirely independent data). But those familiar with (for example) the difficulties of extracting effect sizes from research reports will also appreciate that when different meta-analysts independently figure effect sizes, code study characteristics, and undertake statistical analyses, convergence of results is by no means guaranteed. Still, the caveat is well-taken, and the parallel to primary research ought not be overinterpreted.

3. One cannot be entirely certain on this point because Fern et al. (1986) were not sufficiently explicit about the procedures followed.

4. This suggestion does not appear to be entirely well-founded. The finding that a set of effect sizes is homogeneous does not mean it is impossible for a significant moderator to be at work within that set. See Cook et al. (1992, pp. 313-314) or Hall and Rosenthal (1991, p. 440).

5. Fern et al.'s (1986) inclusion criteria were such as to exclude DITF cases if the sponsoring organization was different in the two requests (see p. 147). This might well have had the effect of excluding cases in which the beneficiary of the second request was different from that of the first request.

6. This expectation is obviously not unique to a guilt-based account. Any number of interpersonal processes might be expected to be engaged more intensely in face-to-face interaction than in mediated communication. But the distinctly interpersonal character of guilt does recommend examination of the possible effect of the communication medium on DITF effects.

7. For this reason, a fixed-effects analysis is naturally more powerful than its random-effects counterpart—because the fixed-effects analysis tests a less demanding hypothesis (a hypothesis about the particular collections of messages, as opposed to a hypothesis about the larger classes of messages). Greater statistical power is sometimes touted as an advantage of fixed-effects analyses, but obviously this is no boon unless the hypothesis of interest concerns the particular collection of messages—in which case a fixed-effects analysis would be preferred not for reasons of power but for reasons of appropriateness.

8. As Jackson (1992) points out, in a fixed-effects analysis, a result such as this one "does not establish a categorical difference, even for the messages actually included in the sample." She notes that "any differences between the two concrete groups may reflect nothing more than case-to-case differences occurring even within categories," and hence "the observation that the two concrete groups of messages differ [in a fixed-effects analysis] does not justify the conclusion that the categories differ" (p. 95).

9. When multiple within-study concession size comparisons were available, we used the comparison between the largest and smallest concessions. For example, the comparison derived from a study with small, medium, and large initial request conditions (compared with a given target request) was based on the comparison of the small and large conditions.

10. An alternative procedure is to compute separate effect sizes for the two investigations and then to produce an *n*-weighted average; where raw frequencies were unavailable, we followed this procedure. However, we preferred cumulation based on raw frequencies because

such a procedure minimizes data manipulation and provides consistency with the procedure we followed when collapsing across irrelevant experimental manipulations within a given study.

11. Consider an experimental design hoping to compare two DITF conditions in which different-sized effects are expected. The current results can provide estimates of the relevant population effect sizes: The mean observed DITF effect size under optimal conditions is approximately $r = .15$, and under suboptimal conditions is approximately $r = .04$. To have power of at least .50 (.05 alpha, two-tailed test) in detecting differences of this magnitude (i.e., to have a 50% chance of returning a statistically significant difference between conditions), more than 1,300 participants would be required (more than 650 in each of the two conditions). Even with 2,000 participants, the design's power will be only .65. In the cases reviewed here (as summarized in Table 1.1), the median number of participants was 71.

12. Jackson (1991) has addressed this matter in the context of considering meta-analytic methods for the analysis of primary-research designs containing message replications. Specifically, she points out that testing for homogeneity but failing to test the significance of a mean effect size is (expressed in parallel ANOVA terms) the equivalent of testing the significance of a Treatment × Replications interaction but not the significance of the treatment main effect. A nonsignificant Treatment × Replications interaction is no guarantee of a significant treatment main effect.

REFERENCES

Note: Asterisks indicate studies included in the meta-analysis.

Abelson, R. P. (1985). A variance explanation paradox: When a little is a lot. Psychological Bulletin, 97, 129-133.

*Abrahams, M. F., & Bell, R. A. (1994). Encouraging charitable contributions: An examination of three models of door-in-the-face compliance. Communication Research, 21, 131-153.

Allen, M. (1991). Meta-analysis comparing the persuasiveness of one-sided and two-sided messages. Western Journal of Speech Communication, 55, 390-404.

Baumeister, R. F., Stillwell, A. M., & Heatherton, T. F. (1994). Guilt: An interpersonal approach. Psychological Bulletin, 115, 243-267.

*Bell, R. A., Abrahams, M. F., Clark, C. L., & Schlatter, C. (1995, May). Does it matter who answers the door? An individual differences analysis of two models of door-in-the-face compliance within a fundraising context. Paper presented at the annual convention of the International Communication Association, Albuquerque, NM.

*Bell, R. A., Abrahams, M. F., Clark, C. L., & Schlatter, C. (1996). The door-in-the-face compliance strategy: An individual differences analysis of two models in an AIDS fundraising context. Communication Quarterly, 44, 107-124.

Boster, F. J., & Mongeau, P. (1984). Fear-arousing persuasive messages. In R. N. Bostrom (Ed.), Communication yearbook 8 (pp. 330-375). Beverly Hills, CA: Sage.

Bozinoff, L., & Ghingold, M. (1983). Evaluating guilt arousing marketing communications. Journal of Business Research, 11, 243-255.

Brechner, K., Shippee, G., & Obitz, F. W. (1976). Compliance techniques to increase mailed questionnaire return rates from alcoholics. Journal of Studies on Alcohol, 37, 995-996.

*Brownstein, R. J., II, & Katzev, R. D. (1985). The relative effectiveness of three compliance techniques in eliciting donations to a cultural organization. Journal of Applied Social Psychology, 15, 564-574.

*Burger, J. M. (1986). Increasing compliance by improving the deal: The that's-not-all technique. Journal of Personality and Social Psychology, 51, 277-283.

*Cann, A., Sherman, S. J., & Elkes, R. (1975). Effects of initial request size and timing of a second request on compliance: The foot in the door and the door in the face. *Journal of Personality and Social Psychology, 32,* 774-782.

*Cantrill, J. G. (1985). Testing two cognitive explanations for sequential request efficacy (Doctoral dissertation, University of Illinois at Urbana-Champaign, 1985). *Dissertation Abstracts International, 46,* 3191A. (University Microfilms No. AAC86-00139)

Cantrill, J. G. (1986, April). *Sequential requests and the problem of message sampling.* Paper presented at the annual meeting of the Eastern Communication Association, Atlantic City, NJ.

*Cantrill, J. G. (1991). Inducing health care voluntarism through sequential requests: Perceptions of effort and novelty. *Health Communication, 3,* 59-74.

*Cantrill, J. G., & Seibold, D. R. (1986). The perceptual contrast explanation of sequential request strategy effectiveness. *Human Communication Research, 13,* 253-267.

Carlsmith, J. M., & Gross, A. E. (1969). Some effects of guilt on compliance. *Journal of Personality and Social Psychology, 11,* 232-239.

*Cialdini, R. B. (1975). A test of two techniques for inducing verbal, behavioral, and further compliance with a request to give blood. In S. M. Weiss (Ed.), *Proceedings of the National Heart and Lung Institute working conference on health behavior* (pp. 176-186). Bethesda, MD: U.S. Department of Health, Education and Welfare, Public Health Service, National Institutes of Health.

*Cialdini, R. B., & Ascani, K. (1976). Test of a concession procedure for inducing verbal, behavioral, and further compliance with a request to give blood. *Journal of Applied Psychology, 61,* 295-300.

*Cialdini, R. B., Vincent, J. E., Lewis, S. K., Catalan, J., Wheeler, D., & Darby, B. L. (1975). Reciprocal concessions procedure for inducing compliance: The door-in-the-face technique. *Journal of Personality and Social Psychology, 31,* 206-215.

Cohen, J. (1988). *Statistical power analysis for the behavioral sciences* (2nd ed.). Hillsdale, NJ: Lawrence Erlbaum.

*Collins, B., & Brady, R. M. (1994, November). *Anchoring effects in the door-in-the-face technique.* Paper presented at the annual convention of the Speech Communication Association, New Orleans.

Comer, J. M., Kardes, F. R., & Sullivan, A. K. (1992). Multiple deescalating requests, statistical information, and compliance: A field experiment. *Journal of Applied Social Psychology, 22,* 1199-1207.

Cook, T. D., Cooper, H., Cordray, D. S., Hartmann, H., Hedges, L. V., Light, R. J., Louis, T. A., & Mosteller, F. (1992). *Meta-analysis for explanation: A casebook.* New York: Russell Sage Foundation.

Cooper, H. M. (1981). On the significance of effects and the effects of significance. *Journal of Personality and Social Psychology, 41,* 1013-1018.

Coulter, R. H., & Pinto, M. B. (1995). Guilt appeals in advertising: What are their effects? *Journal of Applied Psychology, 80,* 697-705.

*Crano, W. D., & Sivacek, J. (1982). Social reinforcement, self-attribution, and the foot-in-the-door phenomenon. *Social Cognition, 1,* 110-125.

Cunningham, M. R., Steinberg, J., & Grev, R. (1980). Wanting to and having to help: Separate motivations for positive mood and guilt-induced helping. *Journal of Personality and Social Psychology, 38,* 181-192.

Dillard, J. P. (1991). The current status of research on sequential-request compliance techniques. *Personality and Social Psychology Bulletin, 17,* 283-288.

*Dillard, J. P., & Hale, J. L. (1992). Prosocialness and sequential request compliance techniques: Limits to the foot-in-the-door and the door-in-the-face? *Communication Studies, 43,* 220-232.

Dillard, J. P., Hunter, J. E., & Burgoon, M. (1984). Sequential-request strategies: Meta-analysis of foot-in-the-door and door-in-the-face. *Human Communication Research, 10,* 461-488.

Erez, A., Bloom, M. C., & Wells, M. T. (1996). Using random rather than fixed effects models in meta-analysis: Implications for situational specificity and validity generalization. *Personnel Psychology, 49,* 275-306.

*Even-Chen, M., Yinon, Y., & Bizman, A. (1978). The door in the face technique: Effects of the size of the initial request. *European Journal of Social Psychology, 8,* 135-140.

Fern, E. F., Monroe, K. B., & Avila, R. A. (1986). Effectiveness of multiple request strategies: A synthesis of research results. *Journal of Marketing Research, 23,* 144-152.

Foehl, J. C., & Goldman, M. (1983). Increasing altruistic behavior by using compliance techniques. *Journal of Social Psychology, 119,* 21-29.

*Foss, R. D., & Dempsey, C. B. (1979). Blood donation and the foot-in-the-door technique: A limiting case. *Journal of Personality and Social Psychology, 37,* 580-590.

Freedman, J. L., Wallington, S. A., & Bless, E. (1967). Compliance without pressure: The effect of guilt. *Journal of Personality and Social Psychology, 7,* 117-124.

Ghingold, M., & Bozinoff, L. (1981). Construct validation and empirical testing of guilt arousing marketing communications. In A. A. Mitchell (Ed.), *Advances in consumer research* (Vol. 9, pp. 210-214). St. Louis, MO: Association for Consumer Research.

*Goldman, M. (1986). Compliance employing a combined foot-in-the-door and door-in-the-face procedure. *Journal of Social Psychology, 126,* 111-116.

*Goldman, M., & Creason, C. R. (1981). Inducing compliance by a two-door-in-the-face procedure and a self-determination request. *Journal of Social Psychology, 114,* 229-235.

Goldman, M., Gier, J. A., & Smith, D. E. (1981). Compliance as affected by task difficulty and order of tasks. *Journal of Social Psychology, 114,* 75-83.

*Goldman, M., McVeigh, J. F., & Richterkessing, J. L. (1984). Door-in-the-face procedure: Reciprocal concession, perceptual contrast, or worthy person. *Journal of Social Psychology, 123,* 245-251.

*Grace, C. R., Bell, P. A., & Sugar, J. (1988). Effects of compliance techniques on spontaneous and asked-for helping. *Journal of Social Psychology, 128,* 525-532.

Haase, R. F., Ellis, M. V., & Ladany, N. (1989). Multiple criteria for evaluating the magnitude of experimental effects. *Journal of Counseling Psychology, 36,* 511-516.

Hale, J. L., & Dillard, J. P. (1991). The uses of meta-analysis: Making knowledge claims and setting research agendas. *Communication Monographs, 58,* 463-471.

Hall, J. A., & Rosenthal, R. (1991). Testing for moderator variables in meta-analysis: Issues and methods. *Communication Monographs, 58,* 437-448.

*Harari, H., Mohr, D., & Hosey, K. (1980). Faculty helpfulness to students: A comparison of compliance techniques. *Personality and Social Psychology Bulletin, 6,* 373-377.

*Hayes, T. J. (1982). Comparing the foot-in-the-door and the door-in-the-face techniques of behavioral influence: A blood donor recruitment experiment (Doctoral dissertation, University of Cincinnati, 1982). *Dissertation Abstracts International, 43,* 2773A. (University Microfilms No. AAC82-28799)

*Hayes, T. J., Dwyer, F. R., Greenwalt, T. J., & Coe, N. A. (1984). A comparison of two behavioral influence techniques for improving blood donor recruitment. *Transfusion, 24,* 399-403.

Hedges, L. V. (1982). Estimation of effect size from a series of independent experiments. *Psychological Bulletin, 92,* 490-499.

Hunter, J. E., Schmidt, F. L., & Jackson, G. B. (1982). *Meta-analysis: Cumulating research findings across studies.* Beverly Hills, CA: Sage.

Jackson, S. (1991). Meta-analysis for primary and secondary data analysis: The super-experiment metaphor. *Communication Monographs, 58,* 449-462.

Jackson, S. (1992). *Message effects research: Principles of design and analysis.* New York: Guilford.

Johnson, B. T. (1989). *DSTAT: Software for the meta-analytic review of research literatures.* Hillsdale, NJ: Lawrence Erlbaum.

*Katzev, R., & Brownstein, R. (1989). The influence of enlightenment on compliance. *Journal of Social Psychology, 129,* 335-347.

Konoske, P., Staple, S., & Graf, R. G. (1979). Compliant reactions to guilt: Self-esteem or self-punishment. *Journal of Social Psychology, 108,* 207-211.

Kugler, K., & Jones, W. H. (1992). On conceptualizing and assessing guilt. *Journal of Personality and Social Psychology, 62,* 318-327.

*Miller, R. L. (1974). Facilitating compliance by manipulating the nature of the comparison: Relative cost vs. reciprocal concession. *Personality and Social Psychology Bulletin, 1,* 160-162.

*Miller, R. L., Seligman, C., Clark, N. T., & Bush, M. (1976). Perceptual contrast versus reciprocal concession as mediators of induced compliance. *Canadian Journal of Behavioral Science, 8,* 401-409.

*Mowen, J. C., & Cialdini, R. B. (1980). On implementing the door-in-the-face compliance technique in a business context. *Journal of Marketing Research, 27,* 253-258.

National Research Council. (1992). *Combining information: Statistical issues and opportunities for research.* Washington, DC: National Academy Press.

*Nawrat, R. (1989). Czy mozna manipulowac przechodniami na polskiej ulicy? Empiryczne badanie efektywnosci wybranych sekwencyjnych procedur zwiekszania uleglosci [Is it possible to manipulate passers-by in a Polish street? Empirical tests of effectiveness of selected sequential procedures of increasing submission]. *Przeglad Psychologiczny, 32,* 205-218.

*Nawrat, R. (1993). "Konnen sie 20 minuten auf mein fahrrad aufpassen?" Ein vergleich dur "fuss in der tur"-technik und der technik der "zugeschlagenen tur" ["Could you keep an eye on my bicycle for 20 minutes?" A comparison of the foot-in-the-door and the door-in-the-face procedure]. *Zeitschrift für Sozialpsychologie, 24,* 264-272.

O'Keefe, D. J. (1987). The persuasive effects of delaying identification of high- and low-credibility communicators: A meta-analytic review. *Central States Speech Journal, 38,* 63-72.

O'Keefe, D. J., & Figgé, M. (1997). A guilt-based explanation of the door-in-the-face influence strategy. *Human Communication Research, 24,* 64-81.

*Oliver, D. F. (1984). Understanding the "foot in the door" and the "door in the face" compliance techniques: A reinterpretation of the situation (Doctoral dissertation, University of Southern California, 1984). *Dissertation Abstracts International, 45,* 2735B.

*Patch, M. E. (1986). The role of source legitimacy in sequential request strategies of compliance. *Personality and Social Psychology Bulletin, 12,* 199-205.

*Patch, M. E. (1988). Differential perception of source legitimacy in sequential request strategies. *Journal of Social Psychology, 128,* 817-823.

Pendleton, M. G., & Batson, C. D. (1979). Self-presentation and the door-in-the-face technique for inducing compliance. *Personality and Social Psychology Bulletin, 5,* 77-81.

Petty, R. E., Cacioppo, J. T., Kasmer, J. A., & Haugtvedt, C. P. (1987). A reply to Stiff and Boster. *Communication Monographs, 54,* 257-263.

Petty, R. E., Kasmer, J. A., Haugtvedt, C. P., & Cacioppo, J. T. (1987). Source and message factors in persuasion: A reply to Stiff's critique of the elaboration likelihood model. *Communication Monographs, 54,* 233-249.

Pinto, M. B., & Priest, S. (1991). Guilt appeals in advertising: An exploratory study. *Psychological Reports, 69,* 375-385.

Raudenbush, S. W. (1994). Random effects models. In H. Cooper & L. V. Hedges (Eds.), *Handbook of research synthesis* (pp. 301-321). New York: Russell Sage Foundation.

*Reeves, R. A., Baker, G. A., Boyd, J. G., & Cialdini, R. B. (1991). The door-in-the-face technique: Reciprocal concessions vs. self-presentational explanations. *Journal of Social Behavior and Personality, 6,* 545-558.

*Reingen, P. H. (1977). Inducing compliance via door-in-the-face and legitimization of paltry contributions. *Psychological Reports, 41,* 924.

*Reingen, P. H. (1978). On inducing compliance with requests. *Journal of Consumer Research, 5,* 96-102.

*Reingen, P. H., & Kernan, J. B. (1977). Compliance with an interview request: A foot-in-the-door, self-perception interpretation. *Journal of Marketing Research, 14,* 365-369.

*Reingen, P. H., & Kernan, J. B. (1979). More evidence on interpersonal yielding. *Journal of Marketing Research, 16,* 588-593.

*Rogers, C. M. (1976). The door-in-the-face effect: Concessional reciprocity or dissonance reduction? (Doctoral dissertation, Peabody College for Teachers of Vanderbilt University, 1976). *Dissertation Abstracts International, 38,* 2437B. (University Microfilms No. AAC77-25126)

Roseman, I. J., Wiest, C., & Swartz, T. S. (1994). Phenomenology, behaviors, and goals differentiate discrete emotions. *Journal of Personality and Social Psychology, 67,* 206-221.

Rosenthal, R. (1994). Parametric measures of effect size. In H. Cooper & L. V. Hedges (Eds.), *Handbook of research synthesis* (pp. 231-244). New York: Russell Sage Foundation.

Ruth, J. A., & Faber, R. J. (1988). Guilt: An overlooked advertising appeal. In J. D. Leckenby (Ed.), *Proceedings of the 1988 conference of the American Academy of Advertising* (pp. 83-89). Austin, TX: American Academy of Advertising.

*Schwarzwald, J., Raz, M., & Zvibel, M. (1979). The applicability of the door-in-the-face technique when established behavioral customs exist. *Journal of Applied Social Psychology, 9,* 576-586.

*Schwarzwald, J., Zvibel, M., & Raz, M. (1980). The efficacy of the door-in-the face technique when initial requests are situated within the acceptance or rejection latitude. *Megamot, 26,* 169-178.

Segrin, C. (1993). The effects of nonverbal behavior on outcomes of compliance gaining attempts. *Communication Studies, 44,* 169-187.

Shadish, W. R., & Haddock, C. K. (1994). Combining estimates of effect size. In H. Cooper & L. V. Hedges (Eds.), *Handbook of research synthesis* (pp. 261-281). New York: Russell Sage Foundation.

*Shanab, M. E., & Isonio, S. A. (1980). The effects of delay upon compliance with socially undesirable requests in the door-in-the-face paradigm. *Bulletin of the Psychonomic Society, 15,* 76-78.

*Shanab, M. E., & O'Neill, P. J. (1979). The effects of contrast upon compliance with socially undesirable requests in the door-in-the-face paradigm. *Canadian Journal of Behavioral Science, 11,* 236-244.

*Shanab, M. E., & O'Neill, P. J. (1982). The effects of self-perception and perceptual contrast upon compliance with socially undesirable requests. *Bulletin of the Psychonomic Society, 19,* 279-281.

Short, J., Williams, E., & Christie, B. (1976). *The social psychology of telecommunications.* London: John Wiley.

*Snyder, M., & Cunningham, M. R. (1975). To comply or not comply: Testing the self-perception explanation of the "foot-in-the-door" phenomenon. *Journal of Personality and Social Psychology, 31,* 64-67.

Sproull, L., & Kiesler, S. (1991). *Connections: New ways of working in the networked organization.* Cambridge: MIT Press.

Stahelski, A., & Patch, M. E. (1993). The effect of the compliance strategy choice upon perception of power. *Journal of Social Psychology, 133,* 693-698.

Stiff, J. B. (1986). Cognitive processing of persuasive message cues: A meta-analytic review of the effects of supporting information on attitudes. *Communication Monographs, 53,* 75-89.

Stiff, J. B., & Boster, F. J. (1987). Cognitive processing: Additional thoughts and a reply to Petty, Kasmer, Haugtvedt, and Cacioppo. *Communication Monographs, 54,* 250-256.

Sutton, S. R. (1982). Fear-arousing communications: A critical examination of theory and research. In J. R. Eiser (Ed.), *Social psychology and behavioral medicine* (pp. 303-337). New York: John Wiley.

*Tybout, A. M. (1978). Relative effectiveness of three behavioral influence strategies as supplements to persuasion in a marketing context. *Journal of Marketing Research, 15,* 229-242.

*Tybout, A. M., Sternthal, B., & Calder, B. J. (1983). Information availability as a determinant of multiple request effectiveness. *Journal of Marketing Research, 20,* 280-290.

*Wang, T., Brownstein, R., & Katzev, R. (1989). Promoting charitable behaviour with compliance techniques. *Applied Psychology: An International Review, 38,* 165-183.

*Williams, K. D., & Williams, K. B. (1989). Impact of source strength on two compliance techniques. *Basic and Applied Social Psychology, 10,* 149-159.

Yinon, Y., Bizman, A., Cohen, S., & Segev, A. (1976). Effects of guilt-arousal communications on volunteering to the civil guard: A field experiment. *Bulletin of the Psychonomic Society, 7,* 493-494.

Yip, E., & Kihoi, S. C. (1996, May). *Door-in-the-face in cyberspace: A comparison of compliance-gaining success over computer-mediated communication and face-to-face communication.* Paper presented at the annual convention of the International Communication Association, Chicago.

CHAPTER CONTENTS

2 Democracy, Participation, and Communication at Work: A Multidisciplinary Review

GEORGE CHENEY
JOSEPH STRAUB
LAURA SPEIRS-GLEBE
The University of Montana–Missoula

CYNTHIA STOHL
Purdue University

DAN DeGOOYER, JR.
The University of Iowa

SUSAN WHALEN
KATHY GARVIN-DOXAS
DAVID CARLONE
The University of Colorado at Boulder

This review essay examines a broad multidisciplinary literature on democracy and work, highlighting issues of theory and practice of special interest to communication scholars. The essay treats relevant and selective research from the following fields (in addition to communication studies): the sociology of organizations, political science and public administration, comparative and labor economics, management and organizational behavior, cultural anthropology and organizations, industrial and organizational psychology, labor and industrial relations, and feminist studies of organizations. The following communication-related themes are used to organize the essay and to derive conclusions from the relevant literatures: (a) the boundary-

AUTHORS' NOTE: The authors are listed in the order of their overall contributions to this project. We express our gratitude to Christine Courtade Hirsch of the University of Colorado at Boulder, Alfie Galely of Tom James of Los Angeles, Inc., and David Diamant of the University of New Mexico for helpful bibliographic work. We are also grateful to Dana Cloud of the University of Texas at Austin, in addition to the anonymous reviewers, for helpful critical comments on an earlier draft.

Correspondence and requests for reprints: George Cheney, Department of Communication Studies, University of Montana, Missoula, MT 59812; e-mail gcheney@selway.umt.edu

Communication Yearbook 21, pp. 35-91

spanning potential of organizational democracy, (b) multiple rationalities and motivations in employee participation programs, (c) the microprocess features of workplace democratization, (d) the structural aspects of participation and democracy at
work, (e) the issue of "voice" and the expression of interests in organizational
participation, (f) "adversarial" versus "consensus-based" versions of organizational
democracy, and (g) issues of control, power, and influence in "alternative" versus
traditional organizational structures.

BACKGROUND AND RATIONALE

"Democracy at the Crossroads" was the theme for the International Communication Association's 1996 convention in Chicago. "Democracy in Crisis"
might have been an even more suitable heading, both because of the challenges posed today for the maintenance and revival of participatory politics
all over the world and because of the variety of questions that have been raised
in public discourse about the very nature, meaning, and possibility of authentic democracy (Barber, 1984; Lefort, 1988). Likewise, the realities and
potentialities of active citizen participation in industrialized societies are
being intensely debated (Gould, 1988; Mathews, 1989). Democracy seems to
be both spreading, through new organizational structures and new media, and
diminishing, in terms of the limits of the possibilities for genuine dialogue in
a fast-paced world that is utterly cluttered with symbols. At the same time, of
course, that we witness the assertion of common or even global interests in
certain democratic political movements, we see various expressions of a politics
of identity or "difference"—in some cases leading to tremendous conflict,
bloodshed, and authoritarian reactions (Benhabib, 1996; Elshtain, 1995).
Depending on which of the many popular books on the subject one chooses
to highlight, the prospects for democracy may look bleak, bright, or mixed.

Three things become clear very quickly in any such discussion. First,
democracy itself is an essentially contested term, in that one person's idea of
a democratic arrangement may be another's notion of a constraining and
oppressive system of governance (Gustavsen, 1992). Second, democracy and
democratization are dauntingly complex matters even when we do agree more
or less on our use of terms. Third, critical observers are looking for and at
democratic practices far beyond the traditional domains of politics and civil
rights.

Now is therefore the time for communication scholars to take a serious,
broad-ranging, and long look at issues of democracy in today's world. There
are at least four important reasons for the communication discipline's sustained attention to issues of *workplace democracy*. First, the roots of communication studies are in classical and neoclassical notions of public discussion
and, more specifically, in our ways of understanding how it is that we
influence one another and make decisions in the interest of the wider com-

munity (Grimaldi, 1972). There are now numerous examples of contemporary social theorists whose reflections center on genuine dialogue and a type of "deep" democracy that transcends the domain of politics as typically conceived (Habermas, 1989). Second, issues of democracy and democratization cut across the traditional (and, unfortunately, often rather insular) divisions of the discipline: interpersonal communication, small group communication, organizational communication, mass communication, political communication, rhetorical studies, and intercultural communication (Hegstrom & Kassing, 1996). And, as an example, in the emerging arena of health communication (which itself tends to bridge concerns associated with interpersonal, organizational, and mass communication) issues of institutional centralization versus decentralization, client access, individual "voice," and social control have become hotly debated (Ray, 1996). Third, a responsive and expansive field of communication should concern itself with issues of democracy as they are manifest, emergent, and critiqued in various parts of the world (Harrison, 1992). Thus we are asserting our ethical and practical interest in promoting democratic organizations (Sashkin, 1984) while at the same time seeking to present the empirical research on the subject faithfully and to represent democracy's limits fairly (Gamson & Levin, 1984; Kanter, 1982). Fourth, issues of democracy and participation necessarily involve questions about communication in terms of both structure and process (Harrison, 1994; Monge & Miller, 1988; Stohl, 1995a).

Concepts such as "democracy" and "participation" should be assessed in terms of both how they are constituted or demonstrated in practice and how they themselves (as ideas, ideals, and terms) are discussed and debated (Cheney, 1995, 1997a, 1997b). That is, we should consider not only what practices *count* as democratic but also what the *meanings* of democracy are. Indeed, ideas about what democracy *is* can vary substantially over time in a particular society (or even in a specific organization), just as they can and do across cultures and settings at the same moment. This same principle holds for participation (Stohl, 1993) and other such popular "organizing" terms. Moreover, the discipline of communication stands to learn from what other disciplines and areas of research have said about forms of employee participation and should contribute to those discussions (Seibold & Shea, in press). The theoretical and practical benefits of such an engagement of the discipline in basic and crucial issues about democracy can be enormous. As Deetz (1995) argues, issues of democratization and participation at work are important practically and economically as well as theoretically and philosophically.

We begin this review essay with all four of the above observations firmly in mind, as we consider systematically and broadly what democracy means and could mean in the world of work organizations. Thus, while we focus our attention on the organizational context and even more specifically on employing organizations, we necessarily treat a number of issues that do not fit neatly into the "container" model of organizational life (Putnam, Phillips, &

Chapman, 1996; Smith, 1993; Taylor, 1995). That is, we deliberately urge organizational communication scholars to look beyond the boundaries of an organization to understand fully such organizational practices as participation. This "boundary crossing" makes sense, given the array of practical and theoretical reasons for considering in a fluid manner the organizational-environmental interface (Cheney & Christensen, in press). For many organizations today, it is unclear just where their boundaries are.

Broadly speaking, we employ in this essay a "communication perspective" that emphasizes such concepts as symbols, language, meaning, interactions, networks of relationships, and patterns in discourse. However, throughout we attempt to minimize the use of discipline-specific jargon, preferring instead to highlight the following seven important issues:

- The *boundary-spanning* dimension of democratization and work, referring to important connections between intraorganizational and extraorganizational relations and networks
- The question of *multiple rationalities,* or the extent to which democracy and communication are framed in nontechnical or extratechnical ways in the life of the organization, serving not only the needs of greater production or increased efficiency but also distinctively social or people-oriented ends
- The *structural* aspects of workplace democratization, referring to how structures are created, implemented, and maintained so as to serve as the "architecture" for participation and perhaps also for workplace democratization
- The *microprocess* features of workplace democratization, pertaining to the specific ways in which democracy is enacted through interaction (especially in groups) and in patterns of "talk"
- The *issue of voice,* articulating the ways in which multiple interests may be recognized and expressed and how they may contribute to decision making within the organization
- The tension between *adversarial* and *consensus-based* images or models of organizational democracy, considering how that dialectic is addressed and managed (if at all) and including references to the problems encountered in deep probes of each model
- The *control* question, concerning the potential for or actual reordering of relations of influence and power within the organization, in terms of sources, "directions" (e.g., vertical versus horizontal), strategies, processes, and effects

Each of these sets of issues, derived from our examination of the relevant literature, has significance both within and outside our discipline.

The topics of democracy and participation at work could be neither more timely nor more pressing. Transformations in the world of work surround us. *Reengineering, lean production, downsizing,* and *outsourcing* are just a few of the currently popular terms that suggest a reordering of the workplace—often with a stress on speed, quantity of production, cost-cutting measures, and limited staffing (Rifkin, 1995). Self-directed or semiautonomous work teams, total quality management, continuous improvement, and customer-driven firms represent some of the most common approaches to the restructuring of work processes. They can mean more freedom for employees in certain decisions and activities while also entailing greater responsibility, higher workload, and generally increased pressure (Barker, 1993; Berggren, 1992; Wendt, 1994). Further, many of these programs as implemented do not necessarily produce the anticipated positive results—in either enhanced productivity or boosts in morale—especially in the short term (Zorn, 1997). Also, the disarming and exciting technological changes of today's world (such as computer-mediated communication) raise penetrating questions about these approaches' potential patterns of social organization (Mantovani, 1994; Sclove, 1995), especially in terms of the competing trends of centralization versus decentralization. So-called network forms of organization, involving strong but ad hoc relationships and a high degree of coordination, represent one possibility for "flatter" structures (Monge, 1995; Powell, 1990). And finally, critiques have recently appeared questioning the democratic nature of a "globalizing" world in which the multinational corporation has become perhaps the preeminent social institution (Korten, 1995). These are just a few of the economic and social developments that point to the need for further investigation with respect to democracy and work (see also Arterton, 1987, for a broad-ranging discussion of technology and its implications for democracy).

Obviously, there are a great many definitions and conceptions of terms such as *workplace democracy* and *employee participation* (Warner, 1984). The reader should be aware of the powerful ambiguities surrounding these terms (Berggren, 1992) and should recognize also that terminological shifts (say, from *employee participation* to *employee involvement*; Cotton, 1993) can make enormous practical differences in terms of highlighting certain types of social phenomena and excluding others (Eisenberg, 1984). The use of the word *teamwork,* for example, can highlight or suppress individual differences and distinctive member contributions (Plas, 1996). In any context, *democracy* and *participation* are not only essentially contested terms, but also ideals that may well be "reinvented." These qualities suggest the need for a self-reflexive and process-oriented perspective on workplace democracy (Cheney, 1995; Deetz, 1995; Harrison, 1994).

Here, we would like to offer working definitions of *democracy* and *participation* to orient the reader. Generally speaking, we characterize *workplace democracy* as referring to those principles and practices designed to engage and "represent" (in the multiple senses of the term) as many relevant individuals and groups as possible in the formulation, execution, and modification of work-related activities. *Employee participation programs* may then be considered as typically narrower in scope, referring to cases of organizationally sponsored systems that may or may not have democratization as their primary goal or outcome.

We proceed by examining each of the seven communication-related themes listed above (i.e., boundary spanning, multiple rationalities, structure, microprocesses, voice, adversarial and consensus-based models, and control). We consider these themes with respect to seven identifiable bodies of relevant scholarly literature from across the following disciplines and specialties: (a) politics, democracy, and participation; (b) power in organizations; (c) leadership in organizations; (d) organizationally sponsored employee participation programs; (e) organized labor and workplace democracy; (f) "alternative" organizations (e.g., worker co-ops); and (g) feminism and feminist organizations. (Although technological developments, ethnic and other forms of diversity, and social movements are important and relevant topics for discussion, their treatment is beyond the scope of this particular essay.)[1]

We selected and employed the topics listed above because each represents an identifiable and reasonably coherent body of literature and a corresponding network of scholars. Predominant themes are indeed evident in these literatures. For example, the literature on politics and political life tends to focus *outside* the boundaries of the workplace, yet in recent years it has come to extend the political rights of participation in the larger community to the experience of the employee (Dahl, 1961, 1985). As another example, the literature on worker cooperatives has often been preoccupied with *proving* economic success, but lately it has attended just as much to the maintenance of the social system and mission of the cooperative workplace (Greenwood, 1992; Krimerman & Lindenfeld, 1992; Whyte & Whyte, 1991). Still one more case can be offered here as a prefatory illustration. The research on feminist theory and feminist organizations, which began with emphases on both interpersonal relations and politics, now includes "middle-level themes" such as the potential for transcending or transforming rigid and patriarchal bureaucratic structures (Ferguson, 1984).

The lack of "conversation" between and among these various literatures is shown by the fact that, for instance, the literatures on feminist organizations and labor (on the one hand) and feminist theory and alternative organizations (on the other) exhibit little awareness of or allusion to one another. Similarly, the literature on organizationally sponsored participative systems—such as quality circles, self-directed work teams, and "quality of work life" programs—and the research on "alternative" organizations tend to be rather compartmentalized (Berggren, 1992, is an exception). And we observe that seldom has the vast literature on forms and practices of leadership been brought into direct dialogue with research on employee participation and workplace democracy (McLagan & Nel, 1995, is an exception). Even though "democratic leadership" has been a major theme throughout this scholarly tradition, much of the research has been contained and rather self-referential. This is true also of the writings on power in organizations (see the reviews by Alvesson, 1996; Mumby, in press).

The remainder of the essay is structured as a theme-by-theme examination of the relevant literatures in which we highlight areas where research investigations have spoken explicitly or implicitly to questions of democracy, participation, and communication.

THE BOUNDARY-SPANNING DIMENSION OF DEMOCRACY AND ORGANIZATIONS

The issue of boundary spanning expresses in the most direct way the relationship between "what's going on inside" and "what's occurring outside" the organization. Unfortunately, organizational communication has largely been confined to a "container" model of the organization, relegating affairs beyond organizational borders to the attention of scholars in mass communication, marketing, advertising, and public relations. Such a division in concerns is no longer fruitful or justifiable (Cheney & Christensen, in press; Deetz, 1995; Harrison, 1994). As Dahl (1985) and others (e.g., March & Olsen, 1995) have argued recently, issues of *governance* now pervade our society. It is compelling to consider how rights and practices of participation in the larger community are related to rights and practices of participation in organizations (Mathews, 1989). To be sure, issues of time, abilities, and material resources are relevant to how an individual "participates" in a variety of spheres of activity. At the same time, however, the degree to which each of us is embedded in overlapping and, at times, competing activities and relationships suggests the importance of looking simultaneously inside and outside the organization (Stohl, 1995a).

The research on politics obviously has a great deal to say about "crossing boundaries" in attempts at democratization or the revitalization of existing democratic forms. But we must also hear what the other areas of research say about this matter. In an age when organizational boundaries are made problematic for a host of reasons, the implications for democracy and communication require sustained research.

In this section, we address briefly the interrelationships among such questions as: How do the changing structures of work and the workplace relate to those of the larger society? How is the nature of workplace or work participation shaped and constrained by the larger political context (or culture) within which it operates? What is the relationship (potential or actual) between work-based democratization and political activity of a broader scope? What sorts of political vocabularies are employed within or outside the workplace to refer to participation and democracy? And finally, what are the implications of organizational democracy and employee participation within the larger public sphere? These questions will not be treated serially here, but rather as they are interrelated.

From a political perspective, activities both "inside" and "outside" the organization may be seen as relevant to any claim about democracy or democratic practices. In a straightforward way, Dahl (1985) poses the question, Shouldn't the very rights and privileges we institutionalize in the political realm be relevant also to the market in general and to the for-profit business in particular? Dahl asserts that our economic institutions ought to move toward greater democracy, both in the sense of shared ownership and in the aspect of participatory decision making. Thus Dahl insists on the application of democratic principles and practices to work life.

From the standpoint of communication, a key issue that derives from Dahl's (1985) work is the *relationship* between participatory activity "inside" the organization and political or civic life beyond work. This relationship can be posed in terms of rights, persuasion or influence, and communication networks. Working from a rights-oriented perspective, Pateman (1970) initiated a lively, persistent debate over the possibilities for employee participation being linked to a larger domain of participatory politics. Pateman's call for such a connection has been the inspiration for many empirical investigations focusing on the influences between participation in work and nonwork domains. In essence, Pateman theorized that if workers were given a voice in the important structures and practices of their workplaces, they would consequently use their voice to engage in civic domains outside of work.

Greenberg's (1986) extensive research on plywood cooperatives of the U.S. Pacific Northwest is well-known for its disappointing conclusion that employee participation—which was, at the time of his research in the late 1970s and early 1980s, fairly extensive in many of these worker-owned firms—did not translate into a practice of broader political engagement. That is, worker-owners did not "carry outside" the firm an ideal of wider participatory practice by engaging in the larger political sphere. Huspek and Kendall (1991) closely examined the political vocabulary and concepts of worker-owners in some of the same plywood firms, also in the 1980s. Their conclusions basically paralleled Greenberg's: They found the political vocabulary and consciousness of worker-owners to be highly limited and circumscribed—not at all empowering or expansive for the individual as he or she approached the larger society (or, for that matter, even the top management of the firm).

Still, there have been other case analyses that have revealed nascent possibilities for persuasion or influence spreading out from the participatory firm. Elden (1981) reviewed 10 studies to make the point that workers can learn valuable participatory skills at work that they may later transfer to the larger domains of community and politics. In this meta-analysis, Elden defined "participatory organizational members" as those who spoke up at meetings, wrote articles (e.g., for newsletters), generally attempted to influence others, and tried to air complaints or grievances. However, neither Elden's review nor the 10 articles examined in it address directly and empirically the mechanisms by which these presumably useful skills are in fact transferred to nonwork domains.

Finally, there is what we might loosely call a "network" perspective on the interrelations between forms of participation in work and nonwork domains. Certainly, Putnam's (1993, 1995) work fits here, in that he has encouraged us to consider how a variety of relationships, group activities, and interconnections among domains (say, from sports clubs and community involvement) can lead to either a vital or a vapid public sphere. In this regard, his research contrasting northern and southern Italian participative practices is especially illuminating, suggesting that the multiplicity of social institutions and community groups in the north helps to explain economic prosperity as well as political stability.

Bachrach and Botwinick (1992) call for cooperative and democratic activity in business and at work as a necessary element in a revived public sphere. They articulate connections between truly *public* behavior inside the employing organization and public behavior outside or beyond the organization as both working together. These two seemingly distinct domains ought to be, in their view, linked so that the general trend in the late 20th century toward the privatization of interests can be reversed or countered. And the best way to do so is through the development of active alliances between and among local groups, inside and outside the firm. Labor-oriented groups ought to be involved in the educational programs of their communities, for example, just as corporate interests now are (Parker & Slaughter, 1988, 1994).

In the same work, Bachrach and Botwinick (1992) acknowledge that there is often a struggle involved in the relationship of public to private spaces. Individuals, these theorists claim, are often forced to act dualistically: as private persons maximizing their self-interests and as citizens promoting the common good (Bellah, Madsen, Sullivan, Swidler, & Tipton, 1985). But, as Bachrach and Botwinick continue, "if the major assumption of participatory theory is correct—that participatory experience generates a desire for more participation—then progress toward workplace democracy should instigate increasing struggle by women and feminist organizations for sexual equality in all areas of life, including the home" (p. 139).

Indeed, the political perspective on workplace democracy is highly suggestive of communication-related issues. How and when does influence occur across different domains of activity? What sorts of freedom-of-speech rights ought to be protected and asserted for work *and* nonwork domains? How do networks of communication within and beyond the firm serve as the inspiration for a community or political revival? To what extent is meaningful participation possible or realizable in a postmodern communication environment? These are some of the basic questions that deserve further attention from communication scholars and practitioners.

Although we have deliberately focused this section on issues raised about organizational boundary spanning as they arise in the literature of politics, there are other areas of research that address essentially the same set of issues. Labor activism, in its current emphasis on organizing across domains (Whalen, 1997), and new technologies, in their capacity to create "network" and "virtual" forms of organization, are two examples. We do not have the space here to explore these arenas fully, but we would like to close by highlighting one relevant issue that has emerged as significant in the literature on "alternative organizations" such as worker cooperatives.

Although many studies of worker-owned and -managed cooperatives have addressed the question of the organization's relation to the larger "environment," perhaps no other research has explored this question more systematically than that of Rothschild and Whitt (1986). The central issue here is one of balance, especially for the "alternative" organization: an organization that struggles to shape and define itself *against* typical hierarchical and bureaucratic organizations. Too much exchange with mainstream organizations can mean a loss of distinctiveness or a compromise of the organization's basic values. Too little adaptation can undermine success and continuance (Gamson & Levin, 1984). Many worker co-ops and other alternative organizations adopt what sociologists of religion call a "sectarian" posture, involving simultaneous engagement in and distance from the larger society.

Among the "external conditions" facilitating the development of collectivist-democratic organizations, Rothschild and Whitt (1986) feature "oppositional services and values" and "a social-movement orientation." In essence, they highlight the fact that many alternative organizations perform better and cohere more if they define themselves to some extent with a stance counter to, or at least outside, the "mainstream" of organizational life. At the same time, however, these researchers examine five worker cooperatives in California (a food co-op, an alternative high school, a free clinic, a law firm, and a newspaper) to illustrate the tensions between maintaining a relatively closed system and risking failure or irrelevance and allowing too many outside influences (in the forms of funding, advice, and imitation) to undermine the basic purposes of the organization.

The question of the organizational-environmental interface becomes even more acute in an era of market globalization. From the standpoint of communication, this fundamental issue can be reframed in social network terms. Just as in the case of the individual who must cross organizational boundaries, an organization must decide (even if by default) how to "locate" itself in the communication that constitutes the larger society. For example, what is the effect of a customer- or consumer-driven orientation, which orients organizational activities exclusively toward the "outside," on the structure and parameters of employee participation inside the firm? It may well be that deference to the "sovereign consumer" drastically subordinates the employee's role as employee, as the organization gears all or most of its activities toward an external point of reference and requires a form of "participation" that is largely reactive and rather narrowly circumscribed (Cheney, 1997a).

Also, as Abell's (1988) studies in Fiji, Tanzania, and Sri Lanka show, *the nature of the support system* surrounding a cooperative becomes a vital determinant of the organization's success: The co-op cannot flourish in Third World contexts with either too few linkages or too much interference from without. Thus the democratic organization's relationship with its environment is of supreme importance.

In a broader sense, the boundary-spanning question leads us to consider the nature of the public sphere as both a locus of democratic discussion and a set of practices involving deep forms of participation. And this issue takes on urgency in an era of market globalization. Most notable for promoting a revived public sphere in the sense of rational dialogue and relatively unconstrained communication is Habermas (1989). We do not have the space necessary here to detail Habermas's theory or critical responses to it, but we want to highlight the fact that with reference to his model, a number of communication researchers are considering (a) the interrelations of organizational and extraorganizational domains (Pearson, 1989), (b) the corporation as a potential "site" of democratic participation and negotiation (Deetz, 1995), and (c) the interpretation of various ideas of "public" and "private" with respect to organizing (Metzler, 1996). The crucial point here is that issues of democratization and participation today are leading us toward profound reflections on the very organization of our society.

In sum, the larger boundary-spanning question directs our attention to the multiple ways in which the internal and external affairs of an organization are interrelated. These features of organizing are especially relevant to democracy and participation because of the possibilities for effects of one domain of activity on another. Communication researchers should pay significant attention to the boundary-spanning issue in seeking to comprehend more completely social stability as well as social change, co-optation as well as persuasion, and the meanings of democracy and participation in society at large.

MULTIPLE GOALS AND RATIONALITIES
WITH RESPECT TO WORKPLACE DEMOCRACY

It should come as no surprise that most formal attempts at democratizing work have tended to place the goal of productivity well above the social goal of valuing democracy for its own sake or for the benefits it can give to society (Schiller, 1991). In this regard, it is telling that some authors speak not of *employee participation* but of *employee involvement,* considering from the organization's point of view how it is that employees or members might come to be involved in the affairs *of* the organization *for* the organization, through means designed *by* the organization (Cotton, 1993). The issues entailed in a complete assessment of organizational and individual goals are exceedingly complex. For example, there are cases in which the "rationale" or "rationality" of an attempt at workplace democracy is only a thin disguise for enhanced technical control or even the direct undermining of other democratic processes, such as incipient labor organizing (Grenier, 1988). Many programs for democracy or involving participation at work are not what they may first appear to be, and the scope of a particular program—whether labor sponsored, managerially promoted, or of another type—may actually be quite narrow in conception and implementation (Mason, 1982).

By offering the label of *multiple rationalities,* we intend to consider how different areas of research have treated technical and social goals for participation. Essentially, in this section we probe various historical and contemporary reasons for the fostering of workplace democracy (although our historical references are limited by considerations of space).[2]

Employee participation and at least a degree of democratization can be encouraged in even the most bureaucratic organizations through the implementation of organizationally sponsored systems of employee participation, although programs vary widely in motivation, design, practice, and results (Locke & Schweiger, 1979; Monge & Miller, 1988; Seibold & Shea, in press; Strauss, 1982). This is why Rock (1991) takes pains to specify the "depth" of workers' control over a firm's decision-making processes, with levels ranging from "No right to any say; or right to make suggestions only" to "Workers have a majority of votes (or more) in the decision-making (workers decide)" (p. 44).

In general, worker participation may be thought of as "constituted by the discretionary interactions of individuals or groups resulting in cooperative linkage which exceed minimal coordination needs" (Stohl, 1995b, p. 5). The term *worker participation* covers multiple communicative forms and contents, denotations and connotations. In Europe, for example, the terms *workplace democracy* and *industrial democracy* are often used as synonyms for *worker participation,* whereas in the United States limited employee involvement is equated with participation and the term *democracy* is in fact rarely used. Thus rationales and motivations can differ tremendously.

Concerns with workplace democracy and employee participation are not at all new in the European context. Experiments with worker cooperatives were undertaken throughout the 19th century, for example, in Great Britain, France, Italy, and Denmark. When the harmful and alienating aspects of the Industrial Revolution first became apparent in the early part of the 19th century, social activists in Europe looked to some form of worker participation as a means of reintegrating the urban working class into society (Lindenfeld & Rothschild-Whitt, 1982). Even before World War I, workplace democracy was a major political issue in many Western European nations (Strauss, 1982). By the 1960s, the European Union (formerly the European Economic Community and the European Community) began formal initiatives on worker participation. And the former Yugoslavia pursued extensive restructuring of industry in terms of workers' councils during the 1960s and 1970s (Obradovic, 1975). Today, workplace democracy remains a controversial and unresolved issue within the European Union, often conceptualized as a hybrid of the ideologies of socialism, human relations, and capitalism. In some countries a participative organizational structure is implemented through legal mandates (e.g., German workers' councils and codetermination policies), whereas in others (e.g., Denmark) legal regulations are scarce but cooperative agreements between lower-level and high-ranking employees are commonplace and in fact represent *cultural* institutions. In some nations adversarial union-management relations have represented an undercurrent of the participative initiatives (e.g., in England in the 1970s), whereas in other nations (e.g., in Sweden), cooperation between management and labor has been more easily developed (Wilpert & Sorge, 1984).

In the United States, with the exception of certain labor movements in the first three decades of the 20th century, workplace *democracy* has not been prominent in most discussions of work (re)organization (Lichtenstein & Harris, 1993). Rather, *participation* and *involvement* have been the key terms or concepts, and programs have represented either managerial initiatives or management-labor partnerships (Mathews, 1989). Participation on the job was narrowly circumscribed under scientific management, as "rules of thumb" were replaced by systemic controls over production. Despite the fact that scientific management had appropriated some of the rhetorical power of the Progressive Movement, it jettisoned the Progressives' vision of a more participative, more democratic workplace (Cheney & Brancato, 1993).

The human relations tradition, which began in the middle of the 20th century, emphasized the value and potential of participation, cooperation, and collaboration between and among employees (Lewin, 1947). Extensive, open, friendly, trusting, face-to-face encounters between workers and managers were associated with increasing psychological satisfaction, development and growth of individuals, and increased productivity and efficiency of organizations (Roethlisberger & Dickson, 1939). The human relations movement involved a number of leading organizational theorists in the United States and elsewhere, including names such as Argyris, Barnard, Blake and Mouton, Follet, Herzberg, Mayo, McGregor, and Tannenbaum. Likert (1961), for example, heralded a system of management that he called "participatory leadership," in which managers actively solicit employee involvement and collaboration in the work processes in order to facilitate a climate of cooperation.

Even to begin to summarize the extensive and diverse studies associated with this movement is impossible within the confines of this essay. However, we want to emphasize here several important conclusions: (a) The relationships between employee participation and job satisfaction are complex and to some extent dependent upon the larger social context and the reward structures (Locke & Schweiger, 1979). (b) Group-level variables or factors (such as cohesiveness or consensus) are as important as individual-level aspects of motivation and participation (Seashore, 1954). (c) Employees' interpretations both of programs of participation and of their own individual acts of participation vary widely and may in fact change in the course of an organizational activity or a researcher's intervention (Gillespie, 1991). All of these important findings (which have been revisited over the decades as the contributions of the human relations movement have been periodically reassessed) point to the need for a better understanding of how participation "works" at the level of specific, situated interactions (see also Redding's, 1972, "ideal managerial climate").

In the 1970s, job enrichment and job redesigns were undertaken with the aim of making workers happier, more committed, and hence more productive (Hackman & Oldham, 1980). Job designs typically included some form of limited employee participation that allowed workers input into the production aspects of daily work routines and provided more information to workers. At the same time, more U.S. companies (for example, Lockheed and Honeywell), impressed by the success of Japanese manufacturing (particularly Japanese firms' adaptation of Deming's 1950s quality-control principles; see Deming, 1986), began to implement quality circle programs, giving workers the opportunity to participate in production and quality-related problem-solving groups. By the early 1980s, literally thousands of companies throughout the world had developed quality circle programs, including approximately 90% of U.S.-based Fortune 500 firms.

By the late 1980s, however, the limitations of quality circles in non-Japanese contexts became apparent, and organizations began experimenting with more encompassing quality programs, such as statistical process control and total quality management (TQM). These newer programs emphasize increased autonomy and greater employee involvement, but typically only as these pertain to actual work processes (Wendt, 1994). With all employee participation programs, of course, the question of the authenticity of companies' commitment to them has been raised (Grenier, 1988).

This new preoccupation with total quality also made U.S. organizations more cognizant of the work of sociotechnical theorists (Trist, Murray, & Trist, 1993) and their early focus on semiautonomous work groups. Shell Oil, Staley's, Cummins Engines, TRW, General Motors, and Procter & Gamble, for example, have built new plants utilizing sociotechnical systems, minimizing the distance between workers and managers and maximizing workers' participation in the day-to-day decisions that affect their jobs (Lawler, 1986). These designs are expected to make organizations more flexible and more responsive to change and quality issues, and thus more competitive in the global economy. At the same time, such programs are expected to stimulate employee participation at all levels of the organization, foster more fluid employee relations, and enhance job satisfaction (Lawler, Mohrman, & Ledford, 1995).

In all these cases, note that *participation* refers to limited participation in decision making about processes directly related to doing specific tasks. Moving beyond the small and routine decisions required by a particular job, participation in decision making may address involvement in broader issues, such as job assignments within a given production process, the right to stop an assembly line if something is jeopardizing the quality of the product, or having a say in the way performance appraisals are carried out. However, formal employee participation in the United States rarely means sharing the power to make strategic and long-range decisions. These decisions are still typically considered to be management's prerogative within most large capitalist firms.

In their famous synthesis of the research, Dachler and Wilpert (1978) note that there are at least *four* general orientations toward workplace democratization and employee participation: democratic, socialist, human growth and development, and production and efficiency. In the United States, as we have seen, the last two have been dominant rationales, at least in terms of corporations and government agencies. Research on "social-technical" systems has for decades sought ways of integrating the goals of productivity and democracy through the involvement of employees in key decisions about the structures and employment of technologies (Trist, 1963; Trist & Banforth, 1951; Trist, Murray, & Trist, 1993). The specific studies under the rubric of sociotechnical systems have varied in terms of their emphasis on distinctively social ends (such as job satisfaction and worker participation) and on the goals of organizational productivity and efficiency.

Our goal in this section of the review, after all, is to consider a variety of perspectives on the rationale, goals, and techniques of workplace democracy and employee participation, recognizing that such efforts in most cases are likely to involve mixed motives and more than one working "logic." A preeminent question here is, Can sociopolitical concerns about workplace democracy be realistically pursued within the context of the contemporary global market (Mander & Goldsmith, 1996)? For communication researchers, this question leads not only to a consideration of the variety of forms of interaction within and between organizations but also to the social and technical aspects of discourses about the workplace and workplace democratization. If the social end of democracy at work is privileged, for example, this would suggest that people not be discussed as mere instruments to the achievement of specific goals of productivity and efficiency (Cheney & Carroll, in press). In any case, the diverse literatures we consider with respect to this question also offer diverse perspectives on this question.

The literature on organizationally sponsored programs of participation is especially relevant to this section of the review, as are the bodies of work on feminist and alternative organizations. Organizationally sponsored programs of participation are typically "sold" to organizations based on two arguments.

Managers "buy in" because they expect increased employee participation to allow them to do more with less: to increase their productivity without having to hire more employees and/or without having to invest in a lot of new capital-intensive equipment. Employees are sold on greater participation based on the idea that it will improve their day-to-day work: By taking greater responsibility for decisions made by the organization, employees will gain not only greater satisfaction but also more control over the future of the organization.

Formal organizationally sponsored programs are top-down efforts; they have the approval and sponsorship of traditional management. Because of this, managers usually frame what participation will mean in the organization. This often (but not necessarily) leads an organization to place the ideas of increased productivity and "doing more with less" ahead of any purported benefits to employees. Thus programs designed to further democracy in workplaces often characterize greater employee control, involvement, and satisfaction as by-products of the structures that are designed chiefly to improve organizational productivity, competitiveness, and performance. The obvious question is, Do these formal programs really change anything for nonmanagers, or are they simply an unobtrusive way to "get more out of the employee"?

In their examination of quality circle training manuals, Stohl and Coombs (1988) found that programs may supply trainees with information to develop solutions and make decisions, but they also provide them with a *frame of reference* to employ when approaching problems and decisions. Essentially, training provides organizations with an opportunity to create organizational identification: to demonstrate not only "how these sorts of situations/decisions are handled in our company," but also to indoctrinate workers with organizational norms, values, and decisional premises. Specifically, Stohl and Coombs found that the messages in the training manuals served to narrow employee choices and thoughts in favor of a chiefly managerial perspective.

With respect to new and current team-based systems of organization, it is important to stress that the word *team* may carry with it many different senses. Berggren (1992) explains this well by contrasting European and North American notions of teams against Japanese corporate conceptions of "teamwork." In Europe and North America, teams are semiautonomous units within the organization, whereas in Japan teamwork represents strong devotion to the organization. Certainly, Graham's (1993) firsthand study of a Japanese auto manufacturing "transplant" within the United States points up the same issue by showing how "teamwork" in that context did little to promote group or individual autonomy and in fact served to privilege a highly specified form of loyalty to the *company*. Still, it would be a mistake to see all differences in the conceptualization and practice of teamwork as culturally based. Even within Europe or within North America there may be vast differences in understanding and application (Larson & LaFasto, 1989).

In an interesting analysis of the research literature on teams and teamwork, Sinclair (1992) has observed systematic biases that suggest a particular type of rationality coloring most such discussions. Sinclair describes the assumptions underlying the literature on teams as a dominant team ideology that narrowly defines the concept of work and what constitutes group work, focuses on individual rather than group motivation, treats leaders who adopt participatory behaviors as superior to others, and treats power, conflict, and emotion as undesirable elements of group work. This ideology often sets teams up to fail, in part because the prescriptive measures followed by organizations tend to overemphasize task and underestimate the complexity of working in a group, thus allowing for extremely high expectations for coordination that are difficult to fulfill in practice.

Next, we turn specifically to the literatures on feminist and so-called alternative organizations. The literatures on feminism and feminist organizations are often highly critical of what is seen as an excessive emphasis on technical rationality in the modern organization, finding that the result is not only an obstacle to genuine participation and democratization but also a devaluation of the whole person (Mumby & Putnam, 1992).

But here it is important to maintain a distinction between a feminist critique (broadly speaking) of any organization and an organization that calls itself feminist. Feminist ideology and feminist organizations are two different things, and they should be separated analytically. For example, a feminist perspective (i.e., a feminist theoretical lens) may be applied to any traditional, autocratic organization or to an organization that professes to be feminist. Likewise, an organization could be classified as feminist by an observer even if its workers have little or no knowledge of any feminist ideology. *Feminist perspectives,* for our purposes, are those based in any school of thought that recognizes that women are, generally speaking, an oppressed group, and that this oppression is perpetuated by discrimination. From this point on, we use the term *feminist organization* to refer to any organization that meets one or more of the following key criteria: (a) has a feminist ideology, (b) has feminist guiding values, (c) has feminist goals, (d) produces feminist outcomes, or (e) was founded during the women's movement or as part of the women's movement (Martin, 1990).

Rodriguez (1988) offers the example of a battered women's shelter organization as a self-consciously feminist alternative to the typically more hierarchical social service organization. This shelter is democratic in its approach toward social change for women because it cultivates empowerment and self-responsibility for its members. Rather than compelling members to follow rules imposed by the leaders of the social service organization, which can be seen in a way as parallel to the battering relationship, this organization reflects a more appropriate method for empowering the abused to become independent through a participatory structure in which members determine their own rules. Thus this organization's rationale for incorporating democracy into its everyday practices is to ensure that client-members have a measure of control, which has been stripped away from them in private life.

Here we must also mention the literature on "alternative" organizations (e.g., worker cooperatives). Perhaps the most relevant finding concerns how in the explicit internal communication of organizations the ideal of a foundational and defining *mission* is discussed and treated. The notion of "degeneration," which is a central concept in both the lore and the research on worker cooperatives, often is applied to deterioration in economic strength, yet it is just as relevant to the "social side" of the organization (Cornforth, 1995). The key question, then, concerns maintenance of core social values and organizational integrity—the commitment to "constitutional" values such as democracy, equality, and solidarity (Cheney, 1997a). In addition, there is the temptation to bureaucratize, formalize, and centralize the organization to the extent that its essential mission is lost (Newman, 1980). But, for many cooperatives, the very discussion of democracy and related values becomes an important part of what the organization *is*. Although many such organizations slide into goal displacement, some are so devoted to their "cause" that they may decide to go out of business rather than be economically successful but socially bankrupt. As the five case studies in Rothschild and Whitt's (1986) analysis show, the rationality of an alternative organization may be conceived and discussed as being so different from the mainstream technical rationality of organizations that it may produce the unlikely result of organizational suicide. The point is that, although the dominant logic of contemporary organizational life is oriented toward production, profit, growth, customer responsiveness, and technical control, there are some organizations that defy this logic to some degree and opt for distinctively different value orientations.

We would be remiss here if we did not consider, at least briefly, different rationales and motivations for participation from the perspective of the employee. Although these cannot ultimately be divorced from the context in which the employee is working, they deserve attention in their own right. A few studies bear mention here for highlighting different points. First, extensive research on workers' councils (part of a statewide system) in what was then Yugoslavia revealed the perpetuation of small group control by those workers who were most highly educated, were best connected to the ruling party, and had the highest professional aspirations (Obradovic, 1975), despite the perceptions of many activists that the system was more widely democratic. A detailed analysis of who participates in the Mondragón cooperatives in Basque Spain reveals the complex interrelationships among organizational structures, individual preferences, and individual experiences, showing above all that actual participation levels can be best predicted by two factors: prior interest in and current experience with the council or governing organ in question (Klingel, 1993). Finally, from a communication network perspective, Marshall and Stohl (1993) found in a study of a U.S. manufacturing facility that the exact nature of participation—mere involvement or a richer sense of empowerment—was related closely to both job performance and job satisfaction. With all of these findings, we are reminded to consider not only antecedent and consequent factors with respect to employee participation in decision making at work but also the *interpretations* employees have of their current experiences within a presumably participative or democratic work system.

Given the variety of programs and organizations that call themselves "participatory" or "democratic," it becomes especially important to analyze closely the patterns of discourse that characterize various organizational experiences. Communication research can make an important contribution to the literature by pushing it beyond the confines of *event-* or *decision-centered* studies of workplace democracy and participation. Viewing communication and democracy in organizations in broad terms, we must consider how the very culture of an organization comes to be inclusive or exclusionary with respect to diverse interests, conceptions of what count as issues, and ways of being (Deetz, 1992, 1995).

THE STRUCTURAL ASPECTS AND TYPES
OF WORKPLACE DEMOCRATIZATION

Here we consider issues of how certain structures can both promote and inhibit democratic practices, even as they are designed with increased inter-action and participation in mind. Seibold and Shea (in press) emphasize that the specific *form* of an employee participation program has enormous impacts on outcomes such as job satisfaction, group cohesion, and organizational effectiveness. McPhee (1985) offers a useful heuristic device for the treat-ment of organizational structures in this regard: He defines them as "substi-tutes" for communication, in that once one sets up a procedure, it can be relied upon every time the group holds a meeting. It is in this sense that structure serves as the "architecture" for communication process. Still, as social theo-rist Giddens (1984) reminds us, structures are both resources for and products of interaction. The matter of structure is central to any consideration of democracy at work in that we must scrutinize over time the degree to which certain structures continue to serve the interests of democracy.

These sorts of structural issues are especially relevant to organizationally sponsored programs of employee participation, given the array of possible structures for encouraging, mandating, and enacting participation and democ-ratization (Pacanowsky, 1988). For example, many TQM programs have been implemented with attention largely to technical rather than social aspects, such as genuine participation (Fairhurst & Wendt, 1993). Also, in cases of alternative organizations, the very structures that were at one time established to support efforts toward democracy and equality may, with age, become hindrances to the achievement of those goals (Heckscher & Donnellon, 1994; Stryjan, 1989). And even society- or industrywide participation programs can leave workers feeling that very little has changed in terms of the ways work is done or in how influence is exercised (Rus, 1975). Thus a perspective that highlights both structure and process is useful (Kuhn, 1996), taking seriously the idea that democracy is something requiring renegotiation in an organization or society. In the Mondragón cooperatives of the Basque region of Spain, for instance, the general assembly meetings of each cooperative, which make decisions on a one-person, one-vote principle, have become over 40 years "as predictable as Catholic masses." In this case, dynamic and informal deliberation has been displaced to other less formal arenas (Cheney, 1995). From the standpoint of communication, then, a critical practical element is the maintenance of debate over the structures that guide democratic practices, such that they do not become stagnant, calcified, or unduly circumscribed. This issue applies, of course, not only to organizations designed as democratic but also to democratic transformations of all or part of more traditional organizations (Metzler, 1996). Thus the very structures designed to promote and represent democracy can get in the way of its practice, quite paradoxically.

In this section, then, we not only consider what structure means with respect to communication and democracy at work but also explore how structure-in-action must be a central consideration in any attempt at workplace democratization. To address these issues at a concrete level, we consider some of the common forms that workplace democracy and participation have taken. Each specific type of organizationally sponsored program described below gives workers a greater say in organizational decisions, yet the types differ (a) with respect to how they are structured and (b) in how the workings of the programs themselves can come to modify the organization's structure. Here we give special attention to programs most common in the United States, leaving aside, for example, the codetermination model of Germany and other nationally instituted efforts.

Job enrichment refers to management's effort to redesign jobs to provide for greater participation and involvement of workers, so that the job itself produces internal motivation and job satisfaction (Hackman & Oldham, 1980). Based upon Herzberg's (1966) motivator-hygiene model and Hackman and Oldham's (1980) model of job characteristics (skill variety, task identity, task significance, job feedback), job enrichment programs have been adopted by companies throughout the United States, which have redesigned jobs to increase the experienced meaningfulness of work through employee responsibility and knowledge of results. Job enrichment is typically a "top-down" process in which autonomy is very narrowly conceived, even when employees are actually involved in the redesign efforts.

Quality circles comprise 5 to 15 individuals from the same general work area (but often from across different departments) who voluntarily meet on a regular basis to deal with problems of quality and production. Though usually limited in the domain of problems they are allowed to tackle (e.g., task problems related directly to their own work processes), quality circle members are given training in statistical procedures that help them analyze work-related problems and evaluate potential solutions. Members have partial access to the decision process but cannot make autonomous decisions. Solutions proposed by the circle are evaluated by a management committee, which makes the final decision and determines the procedure used to implement the innovation. There is great variation in the types of rewards associated with quality circle programs (c.g., praise, public recognition, awards banquets, and/or financial rewards based upon the savings/cost reductions of implemented innovations). Quality circles are supplemental to the work process and are not an integral part of organizational structure (Stohl, 1986, 1987).

Quality of work life (QWL) programs represent cooperative agreements between management and unions (or, in the public sector, between government agencies and workers) that are designed to improve relations between managers and workers by increasing workers' involvement in various aspects of organizational life. Although many programs can fall under this rubric, QWL usually describes participation programs that focus on management-union cooperation rather than, say, compensation (Cotton, 1993; Lawler, 1986). Under this "spirit of cooperation," management, for example, supports paid education leave, which is designed to allow workers to become better informed about industry economics, global competition, political climate, and so on. QWL programs also grant workers access to management discussion about specific problems in the company.

Semiautonomous/self-managing/self-directed work teams are the foundation of many presumably "transbureaucratic" or "reengineered" organizations. Workers take on the responsibilities formerly assigned to supervisors, including setting their work schedules, deciding upon the best ways to do the job, monitoring their own work performance, hiring additional workers, conducting inventory and ordering materials, and coordinating the team's efforts with other teams across the organization. Work teams are usually made up of five to nine members (although they are sometimes larger), and each team is responsible for a specified task, such as the assembly of an appliance or the coordination of student services in a university (Barry, 1991). Team members perform all required functions to complete the task. When a team member is absent, no replacement workers are provided; rather, the team is expected to continue its high level of performance by adapting procedures. Fred Emery and Eric Trist (see the reviews in Trist & Banforth, 1951; Trist et al., 1993) have coined the term *sociotechnical system* to describe the network of semiautonomous work teams within an organization, emphasizing that workers make decisions about the implementation of new technologies (among other things). Semiautonomous teams are an integral part of the organizational design and, not surprisingly, their success relies heavily upon worker motivation and commitment. In addition, work teams commonly afford opportunities for (a) broader worker input into decisions, (b) better use of human and technical resources, (c) greater individual freedom and higher employee morale, and (d) opportunities for cross-training and job rotation (Seibold, 1995).

Gain-sharing plans are formal, supplemental compensation programs that focus on rewarding workers for improvements in labor productivity and cost reduction. Gain-sharing plans do not address issues related to increases in sales or profits. *Scanlon plans* are the most common type of gain-sharing programs. Developed in the 1940s by Joseph Scanlon, such plans are designed to involve workers in everyday decisions regarding work and to provide workers with financial rewards based on organizational productivity. Workers' suggestions, innovations, and ideas are evaluated and implemented by a companywide committee that is also responsible for evaluating the success of the idea and the bonus that will be given. As in quality circles, participation in a gain-sharing plan is consultative; the workers cannot make and enact decisions without the approval of management. Unlike in quality circle programs, however, workers receive no formal training in statistics or group problem-solving processes. They have a wider decision domain than do members of quality circles and provide a greater focus on the economic condition of the firm.

Employee stock ownership plans (ESOPs) are the most common form of employee ownership. Surveys suggest 80,000 companies in the United States are, to some degree, employee owned, and about 15% of these are majority employee owned (Rosen, Klein, & Young, 1986). In an ESOP, the company sets up a special trust in which it either contributes cash to buy stock for employees from existing owners or contributes stock directly. As long as an employee works for the company, and the company is profitable, the employee receives an agreed-upon amount of stock. The stock stays in the trust until the employee leaves the company or retires. In the longest-standing ESOPs, employees have full voting rights on their stock and regular opportunities at shareholder meetings to have input into decisions that affect their jobs. Some companies with ESOPs do such things as give employees regular stock contributions, have participation opportunities on the job, treat employees as owners, explain through a series of formal and informal communicative practices how their plans work, and frequently remind employees of their ownership stake in their firm. However, ESOPs vary widely in both the degree of formal ownership afforded employees and in the extent of control over decisions that accompanies ownership.

Although the organizationally sponsored programs discussed above encourage more participation from employees than do traditional bureaucratic models, theorists have been quick to criticize their real democratic potential. Thompson (1961), for example, struggles with the notion of there ever being a true form of democracy when any significant amount of bureaucracy is involved. He notes, "Many of the values we associate with democracy—

equality, participation, and individuality—stand sharply opposed to the hierarchy, specialization, and impersonality we ascribe to modern bureaucracy"
(p. 235). In other words, until an organization's hierarchy is flat, Thompson
would hesitate to call any workplace democratic.

Feminist writers also fall on both sides of this issue. Martin (1990) states
that although early feminist movements "claim they created a new organizational type that organized authority collectively and assured democracy
through a flat rather than a hierarchical structure and through consensus
decision making," in actuality most organizations that consider themselves
"feminist" are really "impure mixtures of bureaucracy and democracy"
(p. 195). An organization can therefore be structured hierarchically and still
consider itself (or be considered by others) a feminist organization due to
other defining characteristics.

Working from another perspective, researchers have argued that certain job
types lend themselves to democratization more readily than do others. Gardell
(1977), for example, argues that when workers have higher demands on both
their manual and their social skills, they seem to become more involved and
participative in their jobs. Gardell asserts that "robot jobs," or assembly-line-
type jobs, should be abolished in industrial life to enable the development of
a more democratic workforce whose members are willing to participate in the
decisions affecting their quality of work life. In a related vein, Russell (1996)
argues that many workers or employees intuitively know how to participate
because the nature of their work requires well-developed communication
skills and a high degree of coordination, but that some jobs do not fit well
with expectations for participation. Similarly, Zuboff (1988) suggests that
developments in information and computer technologies should be considered together with more creative, flexible, and democratic organizational
structures. Thus some work settings are more easily transformed into democratic workplaces than are others. The points cited above remind us to pay
close attention to the nature of the work, including the *pace* of the work,
which may in some cases be so rapid as to inhibit or prevent employee
participation.

Deetz (1992) argues that workplace democracy poses a threat to many
existing structures in corporations. "Managerialism"—meaning a stress on
the culture, prerogative, and superiority of management—has moved top
managers to isolate themselves from other constituencies in the workplace
and to make decisions with fairly narrow technical interests in mind. Workers
and owners alike often find themselves removed from managers and managers' day-to-day tasks. Workplace democracy has the capacity to erode managerial elitism and isolation. Edwards (1979, 1981) has recognized the threat
of this eroded credibility and status to managers. He describes a 1960s
Polaroid worker participation program that worked *too well* and was dis-
banded because democracy "got out of hand." According to Polaroid's training director, "[The experiment was too successful]. What were we going to

do with the supervisors—the managers? We didn't need them anymore. Management decided it just didn't want operators *that* qualified" (quoted in Edwards, 1979, p. 156; emphasis added).

This leads us to consider the structures of workplace democracy explicitly within the context of organized labor (Freeman & Medoff, 1984). At their annual meeting in 1995, the presidents of all the major industrial and trade unions in the United States voted unanimously to endorse company-sponsored structures that encourage employee participation and general efforts at democratizing relations between labor and management. These union leaders viewed structures such as quality circles and work teams as generally encouraging of workplace democratization, but remained concerned that contemporary efforts at democratization in the form of workplace democracy programs take place *within the larger structural context of unionization.*

Still, it is important to note that although labor leaders have been encouraging of such organizationally sponsored efforts, substantial numbers of rank-and-file leaders, labor organizers, and labor scholars have argued against these structural arrangements, seeing them as key in the decline of actual democratic practice on the shop floor (Brody, 1992; Fantasia, Clawson, & Graham, 1988; Grenier, 1988; Parker, 1985; Slaughter, 1983). These commentators view democratization efforts as, at best, tangentially concerned with democracy; they believe such efforts are primarily aimed instead at union busting, breaking down informal work cultures, and increasing productivity.

Substantial research indicates that many company-sponsored programs indeed enhance specific practices of workers' control over important aspects of their work (Stuart, 1993; Thompson, 1991), a most critical element of workplace democratization. For example, workers have been shown to have increased control over time management, the learning and deployment of industrial and trade skills, the negotiation and allotment of wages and benefits, and the election of labor representatives.

Precisely because of the tensions associated with efforts at democratizing traditional capitalist firms, "alternative" organizations such as cooperatives have appeared in various places around the world for nearly two centuries. Worker-owned and -managed co-ops, especially, represent attempts to (a) transcend typical bureaucratic constraints, (b) make economic control *and* access to policy formation available to all members, and (c) overcome the usual division between labor and capital (Whyte & Whyte, 1991). However, experiences over time and in a wide range of cultural contexts reveal that the relationships between economic and social aspects of presumably democratic workplaces are enormously complex. Shared economic control is no guarantee of genuine employee participation (Russell, 1985); nor does it necessarily result in diminished social alienation (Greenberg, 1986). Also, economic success and growth of the organization can in fact threaten the organization's basic internal social goals (Cheney, 1997a; Rothschild & Whitt, 1986). On the other hand, the failure of revitalization in either the economic or the social realm can be devastating to the organization (Batstone, 1983; Cornforth, 1995; Rosner, 1984). Finally, the structures of a democratic organization (such as a worker co-op) can outlive their usefulness by becoming rigid, nonadaptive, or simply irrelevant (Clay, 1994). Again, we are reminded of the interdependence of structure and process, the economic and the social.[3]

Returning to a point made at the outset of this section, we want to underscore the idea that just as structure and process are inextricably interrelated, organizational patterns, routines, and policies serve in ways that are both enabling and constraining. This is precisely why organizational structures aimed at fostering or even enacting employee participation and workplace democracy must be seen not as timeless edifices but instead as portable and alterable buildings that will need periodic renovation. Communication research stands to contribute greatly to the discussion of how structure and process interrelate in the context of workplace democracy and to the even broader question of how social (re)production occurs.

THE MICROPROCESS FEATURES OF
WORKPLACE DEMOCRATIZATION

For many years, the literature on power and power relations paid little attention to what we might call the micropractices that constitute the very exercise of power—that is, control. In recent years, however, both within the discipline of communication studies and in cognate fields of the social sciences and the humanities, scholars have come to ask, How is it that power is exercised in a given situation or a given case (Deetz, 1995; Mumby & Stohl, 1991; Tompkins & Cheney, 1985)? In other words, how does democracy manifest itself in everyday organizational interaction? Communication studies can offer a great deal of insight into the microprocesses or concrete behaviors that constitute "workplace democracy" or "employee participation" (Cheney, 1995; Glaser, 1994; Harrison, 1994; Stohl, 1995a). In fact, participation may be usefully described as a special case of communication that meets a number of specified criteria: say, for example, relatively equal involvement, "deep" engagement in the issues at hand, and the possibility for revision or modification of the very system of participation (Stohl & Cheney, 1997). With these concerns in mind, it is crucial that we look carefully at the range of organizationally sponsored systems of participation or interventions, sorting through their substantive differences in terms of communication and democratic practice.

A recent study of the Grameen People's Bank of Bangladesh explored in depth what democracy and autonomy mean for female members of this large and successful grassroots organization (Papa, Auwal, & Singhal, 1995). The researchers note that although the specific interactional practices of the organization are highly democratic and empowering in certain respects, they also serve to constrain and burden members with a powerful and demanding vision and extremely high expectations for performance. This is just one case in which the enhanced democratic "control" brought about by new organizational forms can be double-edged in actual practice.

An examination of the micropractices of avowedly democratic organizations and those associated with democratic interventions within organizations can help to illuminate this issue and enable us to understand more fully what different models of workplace democracy mean in practice. At the same time, however, we must consider in detailed terms what it means for an employee to be engaged deeply in participative processes. We are treating employee participation as a special case of communication. However, we still must ask at what point an employee's contributions to discussions, to decision making, and to the ongoing and significant activities of the organization *constitute* meaningful participation. And we must recognize that even in an organizational environment that is genuinely democratic, there will be important differences in the persuasive abilities and skills of members (Mulder & Wilke, 1970). Finally, a variety of other factors can affect group-level or organizationwide participation; these include compatibility of work schedules, information resources, member motivation, and leadership (Hirokawa & Keyton, 1995). Clearly, we are seeing employee participation and workplace democracy as beyond the normal, expected level of coordination that typifies organizational experience. In the remainder of this section, we characterize some of the issues of communication roles, discussion-related behaviors, and the bounds of discourse.

Making an organization more democratic involves much more than an alteration of its structure. An essential element of organizationally sponsored programs of participation is a change in organizational member roles and corresponding changes in patterns of communication. Although not explicitly discussed in extant research, role changes seem to function as a basis for a wide variety of other changes in microprocesses that are associated with the move from a traditional to a participatory organization (Schonberger, 1994). To varying degrees, programs to enhance participation ask employees who have traditionally functioned in follower roles to adopt participatory roles and ask managers to become, to one degree or another, partners or coaches or facilitators. The results of such a transformation can be the development of more dynamic communication networks and a shared sense of the "big picture" by organizational members (Stohl, 1986).

The literature on leadership is especially pertinent in addressing the question of how the micropractices of democracy affect employees and managers. The well-known writings on "transformational leadership" (Burns, 1978) emphasize a form of leadership that inspires others, engages them, stimulates them intellectually, and responds directly to their needs and wants. Many authors have applied Burns's transformational leadership style to the workplace (Hater & Bass, 1988; Kotter, 1995; Tichy & Ulrich, 1984), and the style has been found to correlate positively with perceptions of leader effectiveness, employee productivity, and employee satisfaction with work.

Coaching is a leadership style that was recently rediscovered by organizations as a means of promoting workplace democracy. Although the term *coaching* originally described a manager-subordinate relationship similar to that of master-apprentice, it later came to mean coordinating the efforts of the whole team and determining what each member must do in order to ensure the best performance of the team. Today, coaching is considered to be a leadership strategy used to encourage maximum performance from each subordinate (Evered & Selman, 1989). Coaches strive to encourage group-based problem solving, the exploration of issues and diverse views, and an open and trusting communication environment. Coaching is a type of interaction between managers and employees that may be described as "a people based art that focuses on creating and maintaining a climate, environment, and context which enable/empower a group of people to generate desired results, achievements, and accomplishments" (Evered & Selman, 1989, p. 17; emphasis deleted). According to this model, managers create this climate, environment, and context through their interactions with others.

Building on the coaching metaphor, research on leadership has also explored the context of team-based organizational structures (such as semi-autonomous work groups, outlined above). Manz and Sims (1980, 1984, 1987) have examined the specific behaviors required and performed within the paradoxical role of the "unleader," the group facilitator who remains a coequal with others. In such team-oriented situations, leaders exchange their roles of motivator, trainer, and decision maker for those of liaison, "connector," and mediator. Barry (1991) suggests a distributed leadership model that views leadership as a series of roles that can be adopted by any group member. Many of the activities that Barry identifies (e.g., getting acquainted, surfacing differences, presenting information to outsiders, summarizing positions, developing goals and vision) require particular communication skills, and each activity serves to enhance group work by facilitating group members' ability to work together and to accomplish tasks.

As the two examples above demonstrate, much of the literature on teams focuses on the alteration of management behavior, rather than on the changes required of employees. One important exception is the work of Barker and his colleagues (Barker, 1993; Barker & Cheney, 1994; Barker & Tompkins, 1994) that examines the implementation of self-directed work teams in a high-tech manufacturing company. In particular, these researchers found that the transformation of the follower role did not take place in a linear progression, but rather followed a two-steps-forward, one-step-back pattern of adaptation. For example, when faced with a crisis, the team members first asked someone *what* they should do, a habit learned in the formerly autocratic organizational structure.

Researchers who have addressed leaders' communication styles stress that leaders must demonstrate their commitment to the organizational vision and goals through both words and actions (Clement, 1994; Richmond, Wagner, & McCroskey, 1983; Senge, 1990). Other writers specifically emphasize the importance of nonverbal communication to the success of implementing and maintaining organizational programs such as job enrichment and gain sharing (Grunig, 1993; Kouzes & Posner, 1987; Remland, 1981, 1984). A leader may talk the party line, speaking in favor of a democratic, participative workplace, but may communicate dislike for such policies through symbols, gestures, and other nonverbal means. Fairhurst and Sarr (1996) suggest that leaders should model desired behaviors for their employees and employ "framing" (or the inspirational management of meaning) to help employees understand their role(s) in the democratic workplace.

Whether leadership is associated with a team or with a separate manager does not seem to be as important as the attitudes, communication behaviors, and roles adopted by members of organizations trying to encourage participation. Organizationally sponsored programs of employee participation are paradoxically structured by managerial objectives; that is, to what extent are employees *required* rather than *allowed* to engage in participative practices? Many researchers have worked in earnest to develop a model of organization in which participation and democracy are principal characteristics of the organization, and some observers offer feminist organizations as cases in point.

Feminist theorizing about organizations offers much insight into the "reinvention" of democracy in organizations, and certain feminist organizations provide excellent examples of leadership within the context of democratic organizations. Such organizations tend to be based on high member participation, have relatively flat hierarchical structures, and frequently emphasize practices of cooperation (Rodriguez, 1988). Feminist organizations generally strive to be democratic or even consensus based, exemplifying cooperative rather than competitive principles, and are supportive of their members (Iannello, 1992; Pardo, 1995). In this sense, these organizations embody shared leadership.

However, explicitly feminist, egalitarian organizations may encounter special difficulties. Mansbridge (1973) notes that participatory groups, including many avowedly feminist organizations, typically face three challenges: First, decisions tend to take more time; second, decisions demand more emotional involvement and vulnerability than they do in mainstream organizations; and third, participation is not equally available to all participants because they come to the organization with different knowledge, skills, and backgrounds. Glaser (1994) has recast these three dimensions in explicitly communicative terms, arguing that emotional expressions can serve multiple functions in democratic, egalitarian groups or organizations. Again, we are reminded of the need to examine the specific behaviors and patterns in the avowedly democratic organization, being aware of both advantages and disadvantages of particular actions.

Along with the strong connection between feminist theory and workplace democracy, there is a direct connection between feminist ideology and democratic micropractices. Generally, feminists treat the personal side of relationships as being extremely valuable, as the aphorism "The personal is political" expresses. Workplace relationships are seen in this same light. Feminist values, applied to the workplace, tend to emphasize working relationships characterized by mutual support, empowering behaviors, caring, cooperation, and fairness of treatment (Martin, 1990).

Feminist researchers also criticize the separation of the "public" work world from the "private" home (Maguire & Mohtar, 1994; Mumby, 1993). Traditionally, an employee is expected to "check her (or his) private life at the door"—that is, to leave non-work-related issues behind. Maguire and Mohtar (1994) argue that by recognizing both the private and public lives of workers, an employer can begin to value employees' entire reality, to promote a type of participation that acknowledges individual differences and yet does not completely "absorb" the individual into the organization. Levering and Moskowitz (1993) report on an example of this type of working relationship at Patagonia, a U.S.-based outdoor products company. An employee of Patagonia described the company as unique and remarked that mothers employed there are encouraged to breast-feed their babies at work: "A woman walked into a meeting and breast-fed her baby. She gave this great presentation. Everyone agreed with her point, and there was a baby sitting right there. It was so normal and healthy and natural that it just fit" (p. 342).

Although the study of leadership roles and types of behaviors reveals much about what both "democracy" and "participation" can and could mean at the level of organizational activity, a fuller examination of the microprocesses demands attention to patterns of organizational discourse. Here we refer especially to the ways certain linguistic devices implicate the "management of meaning" and therefore serve to delimit or expand the range of democratic possibilities.

Mumby (1988) has written extensively on this topic, usually under the rubric of power and control in organizations. He has demonstrated how narratives or stories in organizations can function to solidify individuals' roles, maintain status differentials, and limit forms of expression. Whitten (1993) similarly reveals how office tales can "keep employees in their place." Whitten relates an often-told story in one corporation of how a dedicated employee was fired for even suggesting that his superior shouldn't worry about being a few minutes late for a meeting while the superior was driving over sidewalks and yards to get to an appointment with a CEO of another company. Such seemingly "interesting" stories at work can serve to dampen dissent, discussion, and dialogue, thereby inhibiting any real movement toward a participative or perhaps democratic work organization. Clair's

(1993) research on sexual harassment shows how the less powerful can participate in their own subjugation by using "framing" devices such as "reification" (e.g., "That's the way it is in our society") and "trivialization" (e.g., "It's not that big a deal").

With respect to language, discourse, and the microprocesses of participation, the ambiguities and vagaries of language itself deserve careful attention. Eisenberg (1984) calls attention to how ambiguity can be exploited as a strategic resource for communication and interaction in organizations. Following in this same line of analysis, Markham (1996) considers how ambiguous messages within the context of one organization's program to stimulate employee creativity and participation are strategically employed as a vertical control measure.

Finally, we return to a brief consideration of the nature, dynamics, and "evolution" of key terms such as *democracy* and *participation*. Not only do such terms, which are important in colloquial organizational discourse and not just scholarly discussion, elicit multiple meanings, but their dominant meanings in particular contexts can shift significantly over time. For example, Cheney's (1997a, 1997b) research on the Mondragón cooperatives shows how a prevailing understanding of participation in terms of a *right* to contribute to decision making and even policy shaping is perhaps giving way to a managerially promoted *demand* for participation "at the level of one's job"— in practice meaning "the giving of one's all" to the job, team, organization, and ultimately the customer (as a point of reference). These examples of discourse in practice suggest the critical importance of delving deeply into the *meanings* of "democracy" and "participation" as well as considering more broadly what practices count as participation or democratic governance.

THE ISSUE OF VOICE IN
ORGANIZATIONAL DEMOCRACY

This criterion for assessment of the extant literatures asks, To what degree does a body of research treat the ways in which multiple voices are expressed, suppressed, repressed, co-opted, or ignored in the discussions that presumably constitute workplace democracy? The literature on power is especially well developed in responding to this question, in that it has ready concepts of interests, voice, hegemony, and so forth (Clegg, 1988; Lukes, 1974). However, as Scott (1990) has shown, these issues are by no means resolved definitively, even within the conversation of those who talk explicitly of power relations (in and about organizations): What appears to be "false consciousness" of majority and/or minority groups in some cases may simply be an adept performance of submitting publicly to a form of domination while maintaining an elaborate system of egalitarian relations among the comparatively disempowered as they act behind the scenes. Thus Scott questions the tradition of presuming *hegemony* of dominant ideologies by observing that subordinated groups—from slaves to secretaries—frequently have their own counterdiscourses, their own hidden and emancipatory "texts."

The questions raised by the literature on power must be considered as well with respect to other literatures that would presume to say something important about the prospect for democracy at work. For example, how does each literature deal with questions of outright coercion versus subtle dimensions of shaping a discussion through the sheer *definition* of terms? The research on alternative organizations, we should observe, has not generally been very reflective about how its very ideals—for example, equality or solidarity or participation—can function as tools of domination by those who hold the keys to defining those values.

In this section we will consider the important matter of voice, reflecting not only on the ways in which it has been treated by a variety of research traditions (Hirschman, 1970) but also on the utility and limitations of the metaphor itself (Mumby & Stohl, 1996; Putnam, Phillips, & Chapman, 1996). Along the way, we will address the ways in which the idea of employee voice, in terms of open expression of ideas (Gorden, 1988; Haskins, 1996), can be related to the notion of "interests." And we will consider the communication-related constraints on the expression of voice by both individuals and groups.

Democracy extends simple participation in the workplace by ensuring that the individual has a voice, may express an opinion, that means something and has the potential for "making a difference" in the larger organizational context. In this sense, the Western rationalist-democratic tradition is strongly biased against silence, in contrast to, for example, many Native American cultural traditions.

Considerations of voice and power in organizations may be closely linked to the function of power structures in the workplace. As indicated above, structures enable and constrain certain democratic practices. On the overt or explicit level, democratization can be operationally defined in terms of the extent of genuine opportunities for dissent or discussion. For example, Gorden (1988) specifies different stances and corresponding communication behaviors associated with voice; these stances—ranging from "active constructive" to "passive destructive"—apply to the larger community as well as to work life within the organization. Among other things, Gorden and his colleagues (e.g., Kassing, 1996) have pointed out differences in employees' perceptions of their free-speech rights at work, both across different organizations in the United States and between different countries (Ewing, 1977).

The most dramatic form of dissent, of course, is whistle-blowing, the act of going outside the organization to express objections to organizational policies or practices (Stewart, 1981). In a sense, however, whistle-blowing can be taken as an indication that the system does not allow for dissent in everyday organizational practice. Thus it is important to consider multiple types, avenues for, and expressions of organizational dissent (Kassing, 1996), acknowledging that fear of reprisal or threat of coercive force can jeopardize the democratic tendencies of any organization.

On the level of ideology and socialization, the ways systems of discourse are shaped are central to our understanding of the range of expression. Mumby and Stohl (1991) analyzed an interaction of team members for their absence and presence in team meetings and gatherings. The work team took issue with a member who had recently been absent, and when the employee tried to explain his absences by referring to "stuff" that had come up, another team member responded, "Come on, there isn't other stuff" (p. 322). As Mumby and Stohl observe, the team forced private issues out of the workplace. The team allowed only those issues directly related to the team's work and tasks to be considered. Other "stuff," such as health or family concerns, had no place in this team and in this particular workplace. A democratic workplace, then, must consider and value various voices and the concerns that diverse voices may raise. The structures of such a workplace must be able to account for the needs of employees. In this way, the metaphor of voice is a useful critical tool.

Deetz (1995) has recently proposed a model that attempts to account for the largely suppressed voices of organizational members and constituencies. The model attempts to position the corporation as a forum for the productive airing of various constituencies' voices. Specifically, Deetz advocates a dialogic model of communication in which various groups of corporate stakeholders not only express their perspectives but also have equal opportunities to influence the decisions made in and by the corporation. Many of the changes that Deetz presents relate to efforts to democratize the workplace and the roles of communication in the democratic workplace: Each member should adopt the *perspective of an owner,* information should be readily accessible, structures should be shaped by those at the bottom of the organization, and interactive discussions and negotiations of values and ends should occur on a frequent basis. From this perspective, the very discourse that characterizes much of the organization is expansive and self-reflexive rather than closed and self-satisfied.

Standpoint feminism (Buzzanell, 1994) is relevant to issues of voice within the workplace. Standpoint feminism argues that women, like men, have a variety of experiences and thus have different "standpoints" or perceptions/opinions from which to view the world. Beginning originally with a critique of social institutions from the perspective of middle-class white women of the industrialized world, standpoint feminism has come lately to consider a variety of excluded or marginalized groups and what can be learned about the reform of society from their multiple viewpoints (Bullis & Bach, 1996). Standpoint feminism, in this sense, highlights the special understandings of the social order held by comparatively disempowered individuals and groups. From this ideological stance, a truly participatory, democratic organization should value, or at least recognize, the voice of each employee, whose life experiences may include the roles of manager, mother, wife, volunteer, victim of sexual assault, and so on. All of these roles or life experiences shape the views of this single employee and all contribute to her overall perspective on life and work (Gottfried & Weiss, 1994). As another example, a single man who lives alone may have a different standpoint on a day-care issue from that of a man who is helping to support five children. The organization should recognize both viewpoints in order to promote continued participation by these employees and to foster a supportive working environment. The essential point here is that a particular workplace issue can look different from a variety of points of view—especially when employees' viewpoints are based in lived experience.

The recognition of multiple voices can, however, pose problems within an organization. Feminist ideals of collectivity and respect are often lost in favor of getting things done. As Ferree and Martin (1995) observed in their study of feminist organizations, "Overtly feminizing efforts started with emphasis on collectivity and consensus of various degrees, but over time they moved to more hierarchy or to representative rather than participatory democracy" (p. 138). Making sure that multiple voices are heard can take time, and, unfortunately, corporations typically equate time with money. This pervasive dilemma is not one that will be easily solved, but it is worth investigating further. Feminist theorist Joan Acker has stated: "I believe it will take radical transformations of the entire society, which we cannot yet imagine, to create conditions that will support alternative and humane forms of organizing. In the meantime, the feminist image of the nonoppressive organization can serve as an ideal against which to judge our actions" (quoted in Ferree & Martin, 1995, p. 141).

A more traditional view concerning voice has been aired by Conte (1986) in his examination of the effects of ESOPs on organizations' performance, productivity, and employee attitudes. This examination was conducted in response to the "participationist" argument that the positive effects of ESOPs on employees' productivity are due not solely to the profits gained by workers, but also to the employees' accompanying right to participate in decision making (or to voice their opinions). Conte asserts that although profits are certainly an incentive for workers to get involved in ESOPs, such systems would be ineffective if employees did not feel they had some say over the decisions their companies make.

Along these same lines, Kornbluh (1984) found that problems may arise when firms try to implement quality circles and QWL programs without also *implementing a democratic form of management.* Workers will be disappointed if they are introduced to such programs and their suggestions are not implemented by management. Kornbluh sees the current U.S. workforce as more resilient to authoritarianism than the previous generation of workers.

Therefore, he argues that it would be ridiculous to spend energy implementing quality circles without also instituting a flatter hierarchy and allowing more worker participation and decision making throughout the organization.

Within the context of organized labor, *voice* as a practical construct refers to autonomous practices of speech that are braced by institutional guarantees. The right of free speech guaranteed to U.S. citizens by the First Amendment largely disappears within the context of the workplace; the Bill of Rights does not protect workers from private sector abuses. Laws that govern speech-related rights within the context of organized labor are thus rooted in an amazingly complicated mixture of Supreme Court rulings, National Labor Relations Board rulings, union constitutions, and agreements made during the course of collective bargaining.

Though many constraints exist within factories and offices that stipulate the kinds of talk appropriate or inappropriate in the workplace, mechanisms do exist that allow workers to channel discontents stemming from conditions of work. Historically, the routine guarantor of voice in the workplace has been the grievance procedure. Brody (1992) has characterized the grievance procedure as the most important mechanism for indicating blue-collar workers' resistance to poor working conditions. Until the wide popularization of company-sponsored employee participation programs, the grievance procedure was usually addressed in labor-related scholarly literature as the one structural guarantee of voice (Chamberlain, 1951; Cooke, 1990; Elkouri & Elkouri, 1980; Herman, Kuhn, & Seeber, 1987; Rothenburg & Silverman, 1973).

Since the mid-1980s, labor scholars rooted in traditions of industrial relations research have discussed voice within the context of the increased participation afforded by the seemingly democratic structures and practices of quality circles and work teams. These scholars note that increased participation often lends to workers a sense of increased workplace control (Marks, Hackett, Mirvis, & Grady, 1986) and crafts for them a perceptual structure of equality of power between labor and management personnel (Stuart, 1993). However, these findings are countered by the publication of occasional, but strong, dissenting research. Kelley and Harrison (1991) found that participation programs do not lead to higher productivity and, importantly, that the democratizing benefits of such programs disappear unless they take place in a union setting.

Ultimately, each presumed case of workplace democratization needs careful scrutiny with respect to such dimensions as (a) the *range of issues* about which participants may speak, (b) the *extent of actual influence* by employees through their exercise of voice, and (c) the *levels of the hierarchy* at which meaningful voice is possible (Bernstein, 1976; Cheney, 1995; Miller & Monge, 1986; Monge & Miller, 1988; Strauss, 1982). Still, any "textual" emphasis on what is said in democratic discussion and participation must be complemented by an exploration of the "counterfactual"; that is, what sorts of expression might be possible within an alternative or different system? In considering both empirical realities and model alternatives, communication research can speak specifically to the issue of voice in terms of what speech practices "count" as meaningful democratic expression and how they can best be promoted and protected.

ADVERSARIAL AND CONSENSUS-BASED IMAGES
OR MODELS OF WORKPLACE DEMOCRATIZATION

The issue of adversarial versus consensus-based models is undoubtedly one of the most important in democratic theory (Mansbridge, 1983). It implicates several concerns, such as organizational size, group homogeneity, and value homophily, and the very definition of democracy itself. And, even more broadly speaking, we encounter the question of possibilities for real consensus, rational dialogue, and a democratic order. Within communication studies, perhaps rhetorical theory has been most directly concerned with this issue. Burke (1969) has offered a vision of rhetoric that is explicitly cooperative rather than oppositional. In terms of the literatures we are reviewing for this project, studies of contemporary organized labor, as well as analyses of feminist and other alternative organizations, are especially relevant. Organized labor has traditionally been a promoter of workplace democratization (Freeman & Medoff, 1984). However, in reaction to some current specifications and enactments of that term, segments of organized labor have argued against a few organizationally sponsored systems of participation (Parker & Slaughter, 1988, 1994). Of course, such opposition is understandable in terms of the union-busting motivation of some programs (Grenier, 1988). Braverman (1974) questions seriously whether such programs can be anything but co-optive within the status quo of labor and industrial relations.

Our chief concern here is how democratic systems *ought* to be constructed (Whalen, 1997). Some would say that only an adversarial model such as Alinsky's (1971) can be truly democratic, pointing to the need for an institutionalized force of opposition or resistance within any organizational system. Other observers, stressing what Mansbridge (1983) would call a "unitary" model of democracy, would argue that a genuinely democratic system ought to strive toward consensus (see Sheeran's, 1983, study of the Friends Church). Obviously, these issues also implicate the literature on power in organizations, especially considering the extent to which true consensus is seen as achievable. How the tension between adversarial and consensus-based models of democracy is resolved in communication practice is just as important as how it is conceived within the various bodies of research covered by this essay. As Mansbridge explains, the crux of the question is in how best to represent the interests of a group or groups.

Therefore, in this section we will consider what each of the literatures reviewed has to say about balancing concerns for oppositional arrangements in discussions versus seeking consensus. For example, some current theories of public relations tend to emphasize "symmetry" in relations between and among organizations (Grunig, 1992). Although such an impulse is democratic in seeking to engage as many organized groups as possible in discussions about salient issues of the day, in practice the model tends to be equated with sheer agreement. In the literature on alternative organizations, we find similar treatments of consensus *within* the organization, essentially begging the question of how disagreement is conducted within the context of an organization that is expressly committed to unity of commitment and homogeneity of values (Westenholz, 1993). Three key questions then emerge: When is unitary democracy possible? How can an organization that embodies a unitary vision of democracy prescribe and truly grant a role for oppositional groups? How can an organization built upon an adversarial model of democracy arrive at a sufficient degree of consensus in order to thrive and maintain the coherence of its governing system? The answers to these questions are interrelated and entail important communication-related concerns.

In her anthropolitical investigations of an array of community organizations, Mansbridge (1983) identifies *size* as a crucial factor in, or even determinant of, the possibilities for a thriving consensus-based democratic order. In this way, her investigations echo the pessimism of both Weber (1978) and Michels (1962), who both saw the growth of an organization as a significant impediment to democratic practices and the maintenance of an egalitarian ethos. However, there is an important distinction to be made here between, for example, a lawlike or deterministic perspective (such as that of Michels and perhaps that of Weber) and the recognition of strong tendencies. Do we push for consensus whenever possible, assuming an achievable unity of interests and goals? Or do we structure an organization so as to ensure and protect the expression of different and even opposing voices? In a study of collectively oriented law firms, Hansmann (1990) takes the side of determinism, arguing not only that unitary democracy is achievable solely in groups of small size but also that it requires groups of highly educated and similarly trained professionals.

Certainly, the recent literature on power in and around organizations cautions us against presuming that real consensus is possible, especially over time, in even small organizations. Lukes's (1974) theory, in the tradition of recognizing social "hegemony" (particularly in terms of how potential minority voices are socialized out of the discussion), and Foucault's (1984) insistence on the importance of there being constant opportunities for the expression of minority voices "on the margins" are two prominent examples. As an empirical case, Westenholz's (1991) longitudinal studies of worker and other cooperatives in Denmark reveal ways in which small as well as large organizations can forcibly try to improve and maintain value consensus, thereby engendering paradox.

The literature on feminist-oriented organizations reveals perhaps the most confident school of research in terms of the prospects for democratic, consensus-based organizations. Feminist organizations are often characterized, by design, as cooperative and consensus based. *Cooperation* is defined here as a willingness to help others rather than to act competitively against them. Cooperation is evident both within feminist organizations and in relations between feminist organizations and other organizations.

Rodriguez (1988) describes a battered women's shelter as being cooperative and nonhierarchical. In this organization decision making is by consensus, hiring is based on a commitment to social service and firsthand experience of the problem rather than professional experience, and the workers' salaries are all the same. Iannello (1992) reflects on the limits of consensus through studies of various women's groups with feminist commitments. Importantly, Iannello recognizes that not all decisions in nonhierarchical or minimally hierarchical feminist organizations need to go through the full consensus process for the organization to maintain its value commitments. Specifically, only those decisions that are deemed vitally important to the group need to be based on consensus—a form of "modified consensus." Thus groups or organizations can decide upon the domains of decision making where consensus is most valued and those where it is thought to be indeed *constitutive* of the organization. This is consistent with Kanter's (1982) analysis of the appropriateness of thoroughly democratic decision making for various organizational situations.

Labor research and theory have also addressed this question extensively. As many labor organizers put it, Can *any* nonoppositional, nonpluralistic system of governance avoid the traps of co-optation and the silencing of important minority voices? This is why labor scholars Mandel (1975), Parker and Slaughter (1988, 1994), and others are so critical of organizationally sponsored systems of participation. Not only do such systems (e.g., quality circles or self-managed work teams) typically have limited scope; they also tend to grant more responsibility to employees without also endowing them with increased decision-making discretion. Whereas the Commission on the Future of Worker-Management Relations (1994) has pronounced the current period a new era in labor-management cooperation, Parker (1993) calls the typical enactments of this philosophy "management by stress."

In fact, the issue of whether or not unions should cooperate with management has been characterized as "the key strategic question for the American labor movement as it struggles to survive the 20th Century" (Banks & Metzgar, 1989, p. 5). In the protracted and sometimes bloody history of labor-management relations in the United States, the central operating assumption has been the materialist assertion that labor and management exist in a *necessarily adversarial relationship*. Further, organized labor has assumed that the different interests that drive labor-management negotiations necessitate a democratic system that operates *independent of* management influence.

A large body of contemporary literature characterizes the efforts of workplace democracy programs in terms of "ideologies of cooperationism." The central issue in this literature revolves around the question of who should control shop-floor knowledge (Bluestone & Bluestone, 1992; Parker & Slaughter, 1989; White, 1989). Organized labor holds that shop-floor knowledge should remain the sole property of labor, and that cooperation with management on related issues means the co-optation of labor's chief domain (Parker & Slaughter, 1989). Management often holds that shop-floor knowledge should be the province of *both* labor and management, and that many benefits accrue to workers in settings where such information is publicly discussed (Bahr, 1989; Swinney, 1989). This issue has important practical implications in terms of communication, in that information and control are closely linked in practice (Burawoy, 1979).

There is little doubt that organized labor has entered a new era, one in which assuming a purely adversarial stance holds little payoff. As Bluestone (1989) notes: "While there is some nostalgic appeal to 'old style' adversarial unionism, the lesson of the cards seems compelling. The union, no matter how militant its stance, has little power to tame the global marketplace or for that matter reign in the multinational firm that moves its operations abroad or outsources its production to avoid the union" (p. 68). Put another way, "if it's the only game in town, then it may be necessary to play" (p. 69). The question is not whether adversarial or cooperative stances are preferable for labor, but rather what models of cooperation are more structurally democratizing and thus preferable to others.

In closing this section, we want to emphasize the essential differences between adversarial and consensus-based models of democratic practice while also recognizing their complementarity. Consensus-based images of organizational democracy often presume that authentic harmony is possible and achievable. Adversarial notions of democracy assume that multiple interests will necessarily be in competition with one another. Although it is likely that the size and nature of an organization, along with the preferences of its members, will point to one model as more suitable than the other, it is also true that each model can be seen as a corrective to the excesses of the other. Seen from this perspective, then, communication would take on multiple formal and informal roles within an organization that incorporate some elements of both consensus-based and adversarial models of democracy.

At the same time, however, we must remain mindful of the postmodern critique that calls into question the very meanings of consensus and the open expression of interests.[4] We should not take adversarial or unitary models of democratic participation for granted; rather, we ought to "deconstruct" each type to reveal the ways in which its operation in practice may undermine its own presumed goals. This is important because most of our models of democratic participation, whether consensus-based or adversarial in orientation, presume that training and engagement in rational discussion represent progressive movement toward democratic ideals (Mumby, 1997). However, as a number of theorists (who may be loosely clustered under the heading of "postmodernism") have shown us, there are real practical limits to our neoliberal conceptions of democracy and to the ways democracy is manifest today: Consensus may be false, shallow, or stale (Phillips, 1996); fragmentation may be essential to democratic vitality (Foucault, 1984); more communication itself may be problematic (Baudrillard, 1983); our frequent and rapid-fire methods of measuring public opinion (e.g., of consumers) may actually *discourage* deep forms of participation (Laufer & Paradeise, 1990); and incipient or overt "corporatism" can privilege the voices of the best-organized and most-resourced bodies, even in an apparently open discussion (Cheney & Christensen, in press).

ORGANIZATIONAL CONTROL
AND DEMOCRATIC REORGANIZATION

We place concerns about control here for three specific reasons: (a) because the verb *to control* is more suggestive of action than is the noun *power* (Tompkins & Cheney, 1985), (b) because we observe both that there exists an identifiable literature on power and that issues of control have surfaced in a variety of areas of scholarship, and (c) because the question of control readily suggests the issues of horizontal versus vertical aspects of organization and reorganization (Mulgan, 1991). Self-directed work teams may promise an increase in autonomy for the employee, yet control may be strongly exercised by the group over the individual (Barker, 1993; Barker & Cheney, 1994). Another example is the debate over whether computer-mediated communication (and other related forms of communication technology) will lead to radically democratic structures or to new forms of centralized control (Mantovani, 1994; Sproull & Kiesler, 1991). Part of what is interesting about this debate is that we are observing emergent communication patterns and structures even as critics and analysts are arguing about where they are headed.

In this section we will examine how control is manifest in the ongoing interactions and activities of work. At least three important issues emerge here. First, we must consider the extent to which horizontally organized systems actually grant enhanced control to individual members of the organization. Second, related to Tannenbaum's (1983, 1986) "control graph" theory, we must consider the extent to which the total control in a system is finite or expandable. What do transformations in the structure of an organization toward greater democracy mean for the *total* amount of control, and how would we explore such a question in terms of the interactions that constitute both communication and the organization? And third, how do language and other symbol systems operate in practice so as to constrain or even undermine presumably democratic practices at work?

Edwards (1979) has argued that to the extent that employee participation programs do not reshape the structures of power in the workplace, these programs remain a tool of management. This idea fits well with much of the empirical evidence provided by a variety of organizational scholars (Barker, 1993; Manz & Angle, 1987). Although we believe that only deep member involvement may significantly reshape the workplace, we recognize that even democratic practices can become structural in nature, enabling certain practices while constraining others (Giddens, 1984). Control becomes an important issue on both the "local" level (e.g., the implementation of self-directed work teams) and the broader organizational level. In both domains, what first appears to be enabling may actually be substantially constraining. Moreover, the various levels of organization can interact with one another in some surprising ways, such as when a team-oriented ideology comes to supersede organizational concerns (Sinclair, 1992). The question of control is evocative of surprise, contradiction, and paradox (O'Connor, 1995; Stohl & Cheney, 1997; Walker, 1996; Westenholz, 1991).

Perhaps the most relevant paradox is what Stohl and Cheney (1997) call the paradox of *design*. This refers to efforts to build the "architecture" for participation in a largely top-down manner. This raises the question of the degree to which workplace democracy can or should be a managerial prerogative. Still, it may be useful to consider under what circumstances a participatory work climate (Redding, 1972) can be fostered or facilitated, with a certain acceptance and perhaps creative transcendence of the paradox.

Russell's (1985, 1996) studies of diverse forms of worker co-ops (including Israeli kibbutzim, San Francisco's taxi driver associations, and emergent employee participation in Russian private firms) reveal the importance of looking closely at the economic and social arrangements characterizing any avowedly democratic firm. In his studies of ESOPs, for example, Russell (1984) surprisingly concludes that under certain conditions, economic ownership (e.g., in the form of guaranteed stock options) can actually result in greater political and social powerlessness for employees, because the symbolism of property ownership can divert workers' attention from labor-oriented interests (such as improvement of working conditions and enhanced participation in decision making).

Probably no other type of organizationally sponsored program of employee participation or workplace democracy has been promoted more in recent years than self-directed, semiautonomous, or self-managing work teams. Katzenbach and Smith (1993), among others, celebrate the transformational possibilities of emerging team-based structures: flatter hierarchies, greater coordination, heightened participation, and, of course, increased productivity for the organization. Consistent with this perspective, Snyder and Graves (1994) summarize the philosophy of empowering employees, both as individuals and as team members. Specifically, they argue that leaders cannot force employees to change; doing so produces only short-term change. Leaders must adapt their visions of the future to employee suggestions when appropriate. Empowerment involves much more than just delegating tasks to employees:

> Empowerment means giving employees jobs to do and the freedom they need to be creative while doing them. It means allowing employees to try new ideas, even ones that have never been considered or that have been previously rejected. It means allowing them to experiment and fail on occasion without fear of punishment. . . . [Leaders] should establish an understanding with employees about the risks they are willing to take in the experimentation process. (p. 6)

It is important to observe, however, that even from this comparatively employee-centered perspective, empowerment is seen as an organizational imperative—defined, interpreted, and applied from the top.

At the same time, there are promoters of work teams who caution organizational leaders against surrendering too much control, urging them to communicate clearly to team members the parameters of the teams' autonomy and organizational jurisdiction. In this vein, Simons (1995) argues for the steady maintenance of leaders' roles both outside and within work teams. In fact, Simons details several strategies to help leaders maintain control: *Diagnostic control systems* allow managers and employees to observe progress toward predefined performance goals. *Belief systems* empower employees at all levels by communicating the company's primary goals and encouraging employees to look for new opportunities. *Boundary systems* are the limits that must be placed on employee efforts to try new ideas and take risks, and might include minimum standards of performance, companies or ventures to be avoided, or practices that are not allowed. Finally, *interactive control systems* help leaders to involve themselves regularly and personally in the decisions of their subordinates. More specific to a team's functioning in terms of group interaction is the potential for greater horizontal (Graham, 1993), "endogenous" (Mulgan, 1991), or peer-based control (Barker, 1993). Although team-based structures are designed and implemented largely with a "post-bureaucratic" motivation, they may well take on strikingly bureaucratic features, as demonstrated by Barker's (1993) study of a midsize high-tech firm. Employee team members in this case came to police one another in terms of strict adherence to rules for attendance and performance, effectively substituting group control for certain dimensions of vertical control over work processes and employee behavior. Especially remarkable in this study was the extent to which team members actually *internalized* these rules, norms, and ideas about appropriate individual performance (see also Sewell & Wilkinson, 1992).

Another dramatic example of increased control over individuals' work behavior comes from Manz and Angle (1987), who examined a different work context that consisted of individual insurance representatives who had formerly experienced a high degree of autonomy, making their own schedules and reporting on their own activities. Manz and Angle found that in this case the implementation of work teams not only *reduced* autonomy for employees but also diminished job satisfaction and harmed customer service.

Perhaps the most vivid published analysis of control in a team-based organization is provided by Graham (1993), who offers an "insider's" look at work processes and social relations in a Japanese "transplant"—specifically, a Subaru-Isuzu plant in West Lafayette, Indiana. In general, Graham found that the Japanese managerial system exerted a rather thorough measure of control over worker behavior. In fact, he felt that only truly collective resistance on the part of workers could overcome such complete control. When an individual resisted by leaving his or her team's place on the assembly line momentarily, production was accelerated by other team members upon that person's return, as a form of peer punishment. In order to analyze the various aspects of control, Graham divided the production process into five *social* components: (a) the preemployment selection process; (b) orientation and training for new workers; (c) the team concept; (d) the philosophy of *kaizen,* or continuous improvement; and (e) attempts at shaping a shop-floor culture. The team concept was implemented on three levels, stressing self-discipline, peer pressure, and the intervention of the team leader. The entire system was set up so that the failure or error of an individual led to "punishment" of the team, resulting in even more intense peer pressure and oversight by the leader. *Kaizen* was implemented so that workers' ideas were appropriated by management, and management decided if, where, and when to employ the ideas. The shop-floor culture was shaped and reinforced through a stress on teams and on an overall team culture; in this way, the company hoped to foster both team-based and organizational identification. For example, everyone wore the same uniform and was referred to as an "associate." The team metaphor was promoted at all levels.

Graham's (1993) study, and the others discussed in the preceding paragraphs, raises the issue of total control in an organizational system. That is, we can examine the implementation of work teams (and other organizationally sponsored systems of participation) not only with respect to the group's exercise of control over the individual, but also with regard to the overall amount of control in the organizational system. In fact, Coleman (1974) argues that although the total amount of control for "natural persons" (unorganized or unaffiliated individuals) and for "corporate persons" (or organizations) has greatly expanded in modern times, the *proportion* of individuals' control has declined relative to organizational power.

On the organizational and institutional level, Tannenbaum (1983, 1986) has devoted significant attention to the question of what changes in organizational structure or practice can increase the total amount of control in a system. In his earlier work, Tannenbaum (1983) asserted that the use of employee participation programs would increase the total amount of control in an organization. Control should not be considered as governed by zero-sum logic, but rather as an expandable dimension of the organization. As employees increased their control of, and responsibility for, organizational processes, the control present in the organization grew. In a more recent article, Tannenbaum (1986) draws on existing literature to demonstrate his earlier argument. Studies of participative/nonparticipative organizations in the former Yugoslavia, Germany, Japan, the United States, and Canada tend to show that the amount of control in participative organizations is greater than the amount of control in nonparticipative organizations. However, Tannenbaum's (1986) idea of participation is left somewhat ambiguous and does not necessarily feature the deep level of involvement that we might posit for true workplace democracy. In some of the examples that Tannenbaum cites, participation programs increased the amount of control in the system while at the same time highlighting the differences in control between managers and subordinates.

With respect to organizational control, one of the distinctive contributions of communication-centered studies of workplace democracy and employee participation is the specification of the precise nature of participatory constraints, possibilities, and activities. On a general level, Mehan (1987) reminds researchers to attend closely to the empirical connections between micropractices that may produce power inequities (e.g., socialization and education). Willis's (1977) detailed study of the socialization of working-class youths in Great Britain shows vividly how a variety of institutional experiences can together serve to reproduce the social order and ultimately limit the participation of individuals in professions, organizations, and the larger public sphere. Knights and Willmott (1987), in their studies of service industries, show how "organizational culture" can sometimes be used as a managerial strategy, a tool for control, that limits rather than widens possibilities for understanding and participation by organizational members. Similarly, Kunda (1992) explains how the normative control associated with a strong organizational culture in a high-tech firm can produce severe tensions between organizational pressures and individual aspirations. Tompkins and Cheney (1985) argue that contemporary reliance on "unobtrusive control" strategies in organizations—especially the fostering of employee identification and the internalization of corporate values—can be double-edged in that it may strengthen social bonds that both enable and constrain the individual. In an extensive study of the U.S. Forest Service, Bullis (1991) considers specific communication practices, such as information dissemination, that serve to inculcate organizationally preferred values and thereby make control over individual decisions more likely. And Alvesson (1996) examines a business informational meeting to show how subtle dimensions of power are operative even in apparently value-neutral activities. All of these studies remind us of the importance of analyzing *socialization* (in its various forms) as we consider the potential for and actuality of workplace democracy.

We close our review with a brief discussion of the views of one of the most prolific writers on the subject of communication, power, and democracy, Stanley Deetz. Deetz (1992, 1995) considers the organizational domain for democracy both in terms of ideas of dialogue and the public sphere (Habermas, 1989) and in light of constraining notions of communication and its capacity for marginalization (Foucault, 1984). Although highly skeptical about the potential for real democracy through organizationally sponsored systems of participation, Deetz sees hope in such efforts as (a) enhanced education about participation, (b) broader access to a variety of communication channels, (c) further development of communication skills, (d) widespread involvement in decision making, and (e) the development of genuine dialogue between and among various groups of organizational stakeholders.

Ultimately, then, workplace or organizational democracy should be understood in terms of a wide range of communication practices as well as with respect to economic control. And, given that these very practices may be seen as constituting democracy, they must be open-ended, adaptable, and subject to scrutiny, within any work or organizational context we may consider.

CONCLUSION

Rather than offering a detailed summary of this large review, in this concluding section we would first like to suggest a few areas for further exploration, in terms of theorizing, empirical investigation, discussion, and democratic practice. We return here to the categories that organize our review. First, it is clear that more work is needed concerning the relations between organizational democracy and wider practices in the community. In fact, we are led to consider at the broadest level the relationship between democratic practice and multinational corporate capitalism in an era of "globalization." This issue is of enormous practical as well as theoretical importance, particularly as numerous societies are considering ways to stimulate citizen participation and revitalize democracy. Specifically, the limitations of the market as a substitute for vibrant and expansive democratic practice should be examined closely. Also, the possibilities and the challenges of new computer-mediated technologies should be considered, especially in terms of their capacities for simultaneously encouraging some forms of participation and stifling others.

Second, the rationalities of and motivations for employee participation and workplace democracy need to be considered seriously in an age when the "social contract" between the individual and the employing organization is being questioned, redefined, and reshaped. We take the position that, although the kind and extent of organizational democratization need to be geared to the nature of the work, all types of organizations would benefit ultimately by making genuine commitments to their employees and their goals (even though such commitments may be less than permanent). From a communication standpoint, the discourse surrounding the implementation of programs of workplace democracy and employee participation is revealing in terms of the motives and organizing symbols that come to predominate in any particular case.

Third, the possibilities for the survival of "postbureaucratic," relatively egalitarian organizations remain debatable. Although the evidence weighs heavily against the long-term maintenance of the "integrity" of highly democratic organizations, what remains to be assessed in depth are highly adaptable, process-oriented models of organization. Clearly, communication patterns within and between presumably democratic organizations and their environments are among the deciding factors in this issue.

Fourth, with respect to the "microprocess" or specific behavioral aspects of workplace democracy, it is important that the extensive knowledge gained from a century of leadership study be brought into the examination of contemporary programs of employee participation. The demands and dilemmas of team leadership must be explored more fully; behaviors and persuasive strategies should be examined in varied social contexts. At the same time, the prevailing and marginal discourses of the organization should be examined more closely for how the activities of leadership and participation are understood, framed, and practiced within them.

Fifth, the issue of employee voice should be investigated more thoroughly, both with respect to apparent opportunities for individual expression and in terms of organizational constraint. For example, it has become evident in recent years that a degree of coercion persists in organizations beyond what had been commonly recognized. In analyzing both unobtrusive and overt forms of control, we must consider that the line between them is often blurred, and that there can be covert forms of direction or even coercion (hidden from the observer's view), just as there can be not-so-subtle instances of unobtrusive control (as in deep and vocal allegiance to a corporate mission).

Sixth, the question of adversarial versus consensus-based models of organizational democracy represents an important practical matter for policy makers and decision makers in organizations. Specifically, size/growth, value homogeneity, and means to achieving group cohesion all should be seen as topics for periodic review. Moreover, from a broader practical and philosophical perspective, our very notions of consensus have been challenged by postmodern critiques (just as presumptions about conflict have been challenged by feminist authors). This further intensifies the need for more detailed empirical analysis of the (non)expression of interests in real situations.

Finally, the ironies of power and control in presumably democratic organizations merit attention as well as self-reflection. Control in this sense must be seen simultaneously as interpersonal and systemic and as an immanent but changing dimension of interaction at work. We should therefore be attuned to the surprises, contradictions, and paradoxes entailed in organizational transformations toward presumably greater employee "empowerment," seeing these challenges as part of the ongoing processes of democratization and organizational change.

Despite our goal of comprehensiveness for this review, we must acknowledge its boundaries. First, for the most part, we have had to exclude consideration of other relevant literatures, notably those on new technologies, "diversity" in organizations, and social movements. Second, we have not been able to offer much in the way of historical contexts for the types of organizations and activities we have described and interpreted. Third, despite our intention to "internationalize" the review, we admit to a lack of awareness of much research that no doubt exists about organizations beyond Europe, North America, Russia, Japan, Australia, and New Zealand. We trust that future such reviews will be even more expanded in scope, reflecting both the importance and the dynamism of the theme of democracy, participation, and work.

NOTES

1. Each of these topics has interesting and provocative points of intersection with the discussions in this essay. For example, to what extent do computer-mediated forms of communication allow for new types of democratic participation and perhaps even "community" across geographic borders while perhaps both reflecting and contributing to the loosening of "local" bonds (Rheingold, 1993)? Collins-Jarvis (1997) explains how the media by which members participate in an organization may very well shape the nature and extent of participation. Second, research on the popular topic of "diversity management" raises serious questions about the ultimate outcomes of such organizational programs: a kind of assimilation without uniformity or conformity with the suppression of difference (Allen, 1995; Jackson & Associates, 1992). Third and finally, we should consider the lessons of research on social movements in terms of its implications for organizational democracy, especially with respect to routinization and institutionalization of vibrant, flexible, and democratic patterns of interaction and to how consensus and community can be sustained (Downton & Wehr, 1991). The literatures on all of these topics are growing rapidly.

2. For in-depth and varied discussions of workplace democracy and employee participation, along both historical and international dimensions, consult Crouch and Heller (1983); Davis and Lansbury (1986); Garson and Smith (1976); Lammers and Szell (1989); Lichtenstein and Harris (1993); Naschold, Cole, Gustavsen, and van Beinum (1993); Russell and Rus (1991); Stern and McCarthy (1986); Trist, Murray, and Trist (1993); Tsiganou (1991); University of Piraeus (1994); Wilpert and Sorge (1984); and Wisman (1991).

3. Because of the need to draw some reasonable boundaries around the scope and length of this essay, we have deliberately not considered, in any substantial way, the complex interrelationships of economic and social factors in workplace democratization. However, we wish to mention several relevant points here. First, we have tried to consider issues relevant to a variety of types of organizations—in the public, private, and independent sectors—although in many cases when we comment on research on "organizations" the entities are in fact primarily large, for-profit corporations (and this is reflective of extant studies). Second, in reviewing literatures

on worker cooperatives and organized labor, we have sought to acknowledge explicitly that the material "connections" between the individual and the organization or between the organization and its environment are crucially relevant to democratization in a full sense (see Ellerman, 1992, on the interrelations of property and democracy). Third, although we have been unable to offer a detailed treatment of the role or fate of workplace democracy within the context of "globalizing" corporate capitalism, we have indicated profound concerns about the "democratic" nature of the current form of the market economy: that is, market interaction may represent both democratic possibilities for consumer choice and democratic constraints for the citizen-employee (Mander & Goldsmith, 1996). Finally, we stress the complexity of the interrelations of the economic and the social and the material and the symbolic. For example, it is important to attend to the limits of rhetorical exercises—such as labor campaigns and corporate policies—that largely ignore objective material differences between groups, but it is also true that even some economic "force" that is seemingly solid, such as "the Market" (often referred to as a supreme or sovereign agent in public discourse today), has powerful symbolic dimensions in its taken-for-grantedness (see Aune, 1996; Cloud, 1996; McCloskey, 1985; McMillan & Cheney, 1996; Whalen, 1997). We therefore urge the reader to consider deeply the communication-related aspects of economic and material constraints on democratic social systems.

4. Although we recognize the tremendous theoretical and practical complexities surrounding the matter of "interests," we cannot explore that problem in much depth here. Nevertheless, at several points in this essay we acknowledge the difficulties associated with (a) *knowing* persons' authentic interests, (b) *representing* persons' interests, (c) *accounting for* expressed and unexpressed interests, (d) *handling* competing interests, and (e) *promoting* a plurality of interests (cf. Lukes, 1974; Scott, 1990).

REFERENCES

Abell, P. (1988). *Establishing support systems for industrial cooperatives: Case studies from the Third World.* London: Avebury.

Alinsky, S. D. (1971). *Rules for radicals: A practical primer for realistic radicals.* New York: Vintage.

Allen, B. J. (1995). "Diversity" and organizational communication. *Journal of Applied Communication Research, 23,* 143-155.

Alvesson, M. (1996). *Communication, power, and organization.* Berlin: Walter de Gruyter.

Arterton, F. C. (1987). *Teledemocracy: Can technology protect democracy?* Newbury Park, CA: Sage.

Aune, J. A. (1996, November). *Inevitability and perversity: The loci of capitalist arguments about labor.* Paper presented at the annual meeting of the Speech Communication Association, San Diego, CA.

Bachrach, P., & Botwinick, A. (1992). *Power and empowerment: A radical theory of participatory democracy.* Philadelphia: Temple University Press.

Bahr, M. (1989). Mobilizing for the '90s. *Labor Research Review, 14,* 59-65.

Banks, A., & Metzgar, J. (1989). *Participating in management: Union organizing on a new terrain.* Chicago: Midwest Center for Labor Research.

Barber, B. R. (1984). *Strong democracy.* Berkeley: University of California Press.

Barker, J. R. (1993). Tightening the iron cage: Concertive control in self-managing teams. *Administrative Science Quarterly, 38,* 408-437.

Barker, J. R., & Cheney, G. (1994). The concept and practices of discipline in contemporary organizational life. *Communication Monographs, 61,* 19-43.

Barker, J. R., & Tompkins, P. K. (1994). Identification in the self-managing organization: Characteristics of target and tenure. *Human Communication Research, 21,* 223-240.

Barry, D. (1991, Summer). Managing the bossless team: Lessons in distributed leadership. *Organizational Dynamics, 20,* 31-47.

Batstone, E. (1983). Organization and orientation: A life cycle model of French cooperatives. *Economic and Industrial Democracy, 4,* 139-161.

Baudrillard, J. (1983). *In the shadow of the silent majorities, or the end of the social, and other essays.* New York: Semiotext(e).

Bellah, R. N., Madsen, R., Sullivan, W. M., Swidler, A., & Tipton, S. M. (1985). *Habits of the heart: Individualism and commitment in American life.* Berkeley: University of California Press.

Benhabib, S. (Ed.). (1996). *Democracy and difference: Contesting the boundaries of the political.* Princeton, NJ: Princeton University Press.

Berggren, C. (1992). *Alternatives to lean production: Work organization in the Swedish auto industry.* Ithaca, NY: International Labor Relations Press.

Bernstein, P. (1976). Necessary elements for effective worker participation in decision making. *Journal of Economic Issues, 10,* 490-522.

Bluestone, B. (1989). Goodbye to the management rights clause. *Labor Research Review, 14,* 66-72.

Bluestone, B., & Bluestone, I. (1992). *Negotiating the future: A labor perspective on American business.* New York: Basic Books.

Braverman, H. (1974). *Labor and monopoly capital: The degradation of work in the twentieth century.* New York: Monthly Review Press.

Brody, D. (1992, Winter). The breakdown of labor's social contract: Historical reflections, future prospects. *Dissent,* pp. 32-41.

Bullis, C. (1991). Communication practices as unobtrusive control: An observational study. *Communication Studies, 42,* 254-271.

Bullis, C., & Bach, B. (1996). Feminism and the disenfranchised: Listening beyond the "other." In E. B. Ray (Ed.), *Communication and disenfranchisement: Social health issues and implications* (pp. 3-28). Mahwah, NJ: Lawrence Erlbaum.

Burawoy, M. (1979). *Manufacturing consent: Changes in the labor process under monopoly capitalism.* Chicago: University of Chicago Press.

Burke, K. (1969). *A rhetoric of motives.* Berkeley: University of California Press.

Burns, J. M. (1978). *Leadership.* New York: Harper & Row.

Buzzanell, P. M. (1994). Gaining a voice: Feminist organizational communication theorizing. *Management Communication Quarterly, 7,* 339-383.

Chamberlain, N. (1951). *Collective bargaining.* New York: McGraw-Hill.

Cheney, G. (1995). Democracy in the workplace: Theory and practice from the perspective of communication. *Journal of Applied Communication Research, 23,* 167-200.

Cheney, G. (1997a). *Managed democracy: The shape of employee participation in the consumer-driven firm.* Manuscript in preparation.

Cheney, G. (1997b). The many meanings of "solidarity": The negotiation of values in the Mondragón worker-cooperative complex under pressure. In B. D. Sypher (Ed.), *Contemporary case studies in organizational communication* (pp. 68-83). New York: Guilford.

Cheney, G., & Brancato, J. (1993). *Scientific management's rhetorical force and enduring impact.* Unpublished manuscript, University of Colorado, Boulder.

Cheney, G., & Carroll, C. E. (in press). The person as object in discourses in and around organizations. *Communication Research.*

Cheney, G., & Christensen, L. T. (in press). Identity at issue: Linkages between "internal" and "external" organizational communication. In F. M. Jablin & L. L. Putnam (Eds.), *The new handbook of organizational communication.* Thousand Oaks, CA: Sage.

Clair, R. P. (1993). The use of framing devices to sequester organizational narratives: Hegemony and harassment. *Communication Monographs, 60,* 114-136.

Clay, E. (1994, Spring). Neither democracy nor equity is sufficient for engagement. *Participatory Communication Research Network Newsletter,* pp. 1-8.

Clegg, S. R. (1988). *Frameworks of power.* London: Sage.

Clement, R. W. (1994). Culture, leadership, and power: The keys to organizational change. *Business Horizons, 37,* 33-39.

Cloud, D. (1996, November). *Fighting for words: The limits of symbolic power in the Staley Lockout, 1993-1996.* Paper presented at the annual meeting of the Speech Communication Association, San Diego, CA.

Coleman, J. S. (1974). *Power and the structure of society.* New York: W. W. Norton.

Collins-Jarvis, L. (1997). Participation and consensus in collective action organizations. *Journal of Applied Communication Research, 25,* 1-16.

Commission on the Future of Worker Management Relations. (1994, December). *Report and recommendations.* Washington, DC: U.S. Department of Labor.

Conte, M. A. (1986, March-April). Participation and performance. *Society, 23,* 44-49.

Cooke, W. N. (1990). Factors influencing the effect of joint union-management programs on employee-supervisor relations. *Industrial and Labor Relations Review, 43,* 587-603.

Cornforth, C. (1995). Patterns of cooperative movement: Beyond the degeneration thesis. *Economic and Industrial Democracy, 16,* 487-524.

Cotton, J. L. (1993). *Employee involvement: Methods for improving performance and work attitudes.* Newbury Park, CA: Sage.

Crouch, C., & Heller, F. A. (Eds.). (1983). *International yearbook of organizational democracy: Vol. 1. Organizational democracy and political processes.* Chichester, England: John Wiley.

Dachler, H. P., & Wilpert, B. (1978). Conceptual dimensions and boundaries of participation in organizations: A critical evaluation. *Administrative Science Quarterly, 23,* 1-39.

Dahl, R. A. (1961). *Who governs? Democracy and power in the American city.* New Haven, CT: Yale University Press.

Dahl, R. A. (1985). *A preface to economic democracy.* Berkeley: University of California Press.

Davis, E., & Lansbury, R. (Eds.). (1986). *Democracy and control in the workplace.* Melbourne: Longman.

Deetz, S. A. (1992). *Democracy in an age of corporate colonization: Developments in communication and the politics of everyday life.* Albany: State University of New York Press.

Deetz, S. A. (1995). *Transforming communication, transforming business: Building responsive and responsible workplaces.* New York: Hampton.

Deming, W. E. (1986). *Out of the crisis.* Cambridge: MIT Center for Advanced Engineering Study.

Downton, J. V., & Wehr, P. E. (1991). Peace movements: The role of commitment and community in sustaining member participation. *Research in Social Movements, Conflict, and Change, 13,* 113-134.

Edwards, R. (1979). *Contested terrain: The transformation of the workplace in the twentieth century.* New York: Basic Books.

Edwards, R. (1981). The social relations of production at the point of production. In M. Zey-Ferrell & M. Aiken (Eds.), *Complex organizations: Critical perspectives* (pp. 152-181). Glenview, IL: Scott, Foresman.

Eisenberg, E. (1984). Ambiguity as strategy in organizational communication. *Communication Monographs, 51,* 227-242.

Elden, J. M. (1981). Political efficacy at work: The connection between more autonomous forms of workplace organization and more participatory politics. *American Political Science Review, 75,* 43-58.

Elkouri, F., & Elkouri, E. (1980). *How arbitration works* (3rd ed.). Washington, DC: Bureau of National Affairs.

Ellerman, D. P. (1992). *Property and contract in economics: The democratic alternatives to capitalism and socialism.* Malden, MA: Blackwell.

Elshtain, J. B. (1995). *Democracy on trial.* New York: Basic Books.

Evered, R. D., & Selman, J. C. (1989, Autumn). Coaching and the art of management. *Organizational Dynamics, 18,* 16-32.

Ewing, D. (1977). *Freedom inside the organization: Bringing civil liberties to the workplace.* New York: Dutton.

Fairhurst, G. T., & Sarr, R. A. (1996). *The art of framing.* San Francisco: Jossey-Bass.

Fairhurst, G. T., & Wendt, R. F. (1993). The gap in total quality. *Management Communication Quarterly, 6,* 441-451.

Fantasia, R., Clawson, D., & Graham, R. (1988). A critical view of worker participation in American industry. *Work and Occupations, 15,* 468-488.

Ferguson, K. (1984). *The feminist case against bureaucracy.* Philadelphia: Temple University Press.

Ferree, M. M., & Martin, P. Y. (Eds.). (1995). *Feminist organizations: Harvest of the new women's movement.* Philadelphia: Temple University Press.

Foucault, M. (1984). *The Foucault reader* (P. Rabinow, Ed.). New York: Pantheon.

Freeman, R., & Medoff, J. (1984). *What do unions do?* New York: Basic Books.

Gamson, Z., & Levin, H. (1984). Obstacles to the survival of democratic workplaces. In R. Jackall & H. Levin (Eds.), *Worker cooperatives in America* (pp. 219-244). Berkeley: University of California Press.

Gardell, B. (1977). Autonomy and participation at work. *Human Relations, 30,* 515-533.

Garson, G. D., & Smith, M. P. (Eds.). (1976). *Organizational democracy: Participation and self-management.* Beverly Hills, CA: Sage.

Giddens, A. (1984). *The constitution of society: Outline of the theory of structuration.* Berkeley: University of California Press.

Gillespie, R. (1991). *Manufacturing knowledge: A history of the Hawthorne experiments.* Cambridge: Cambridge University Press.

Glaser, H. (1994). *Structure and struggle in egalitarian groups: Reframing the problems of time, emotion, and inequity as defining characteristics.* Unpublished doctoral dissertation, University of Illinois, Urbana-Champaign.

Gorden, W. I. (1988). Range of employee voice. *Employee Responsibilities and Rights Journal, 1,* 283-299.

Gottfried, H., & Weiss, P. (1994). A compound feminist organization: Purdue University's Council on the Status of Women. *Women and Politics, 14,* 23-43.

Gould, C. (1988). *Rethinking democracy: Freedom and social cooperation in politics, economy, and society.* Cambridge: Cambridge University Press.

Graham, L. (1993). Inside a Japanese transplant: A critical perspective. *Work and Occupations, 20,* 147-173.

Greenberg, E. (1986). *Workplace democracy: The political effects of participation.* Ithaca, NY: Cornell University Press.

Greenwood, D. (1992). *Industrial democracy as process: Participatory action research in the Fagor cooperative group of Mondragón.* Van Gorcum, Netherlands: Swedish Center for Working Life.

Grenier, G. J. (1988). *Inhuman relations: Quality circles and anti-unionism in American industry.* Philadelphia: Temple University Press.

Grimaldi, W. M. A. (1972). *Studies in the philosophy of Aristotle's Rhetoric.* Wiesbaden: Franz Steiner Verlag.

Grunig, J. E. (Ed.). (1992). *Excellence in public relations and communication management.* Hillsdale, NJ: Lawrence Erlbaum.

Grunig, L. A. (1993). Image and symbolic leadership: Using focus group research to bridge the gaps. *Journal of Public Relations Research, 5,* 95-125.

Gustavsen, B. (1992). *Dialogue and development.* Stockholm: Swedish Center for Working Life.

Habermas, J. (1989). The public sphere: An encyclopedia article. In S. E. Bronner & D. M. Kellner (Eds.), *Critical theory and society: A reader* (pp. 136-142). New York: Routledge.

Hackman, J., & Oldham, G. (1980). *Work redesign.* Reading, MA: Addison-Wesley.

Hansmann, H. (1990). When does worker ownership work? ESOPs, law firms, codetermination, and economic democracy. *Yale Law Journal, 99,* 1749-1816.

Harrison, T. M. (1992). Designing the post-bureaucratic organization: Toward egalitarian social structure. *Australian Journal of Communication, 19,* 14-29.

Harrison, T. M. (1994). Communication and interdependence in democratic organizations. In S. A. Deetz (Ed.), *Communication yearbook 17* (pp. 247-274). Thousand Oaks, CA: Sage.

Haskins, W. A. (1996). Freedom of speech: Construct for creating a culture which empowers organizational members. *Journal of Business Communication, 33,* 85-97.

Hater, J. J., & Bass, B. M. (1988). Superiors' evaluation and subordinates' perceptions of transformational and transactional leadership. *Journal of Applied Psychology, 73,* 695-702.

Heckscher, C., & Donnellon, A. (Eds.). (1994). *The post-bureaucratic organization: New perspectives on organizational change.* Thousand Oaks, CA: Sage.

Hegstrom, T., & Kassing, J. (1996, November). *Organizational democracy and democratic communication.* Paper presented at the annual meeting of the Speech Communication Association, San Diego, CA.

Herman, E. E., Kuhn, A., & Seeber, R. (1987). *Collective bargaining and labor relations* (2nd ed.). Englewood Cliffs, NJ: Prentice Hall.

Herzberg, F. (1966). *Work and the nature of man.* New York: World.

Hirokawa, R. Y., & Keyton, J. (1995). Perceived facilitators and inhibitors of effectiveness in organizational work teams. *Management Communication Quarterly, 8,* 424-446.

Hirschman, A. O. (1970). *Exit, voice, and loyalty: Responses to decline in firms, organizations, and states.* Cambridge, MA: Harvard University Press.

Huspek, M., & Kendall, K. E. (1991). On withholding political voice: An analysis of the political vocabulary of a "nonpolitical" speech community. *Quarterly Journal of Speech, 77,* 1-19.

Iannello, K. P. (1992). *Decisions without hierarchy: Feminist interventions in organization theory and practice.* London: Routledge.

Jackson, S. E., & Associates. (Eds.). (1992). *Diversity in the workplace: Human resources initiatives.* New York: Guilford.

Kanter, R. M. (1982, Summer). Dilemmas of managing participation. *Organizational Dynamics, 11,* 5-27.

Kassing, J. (1996, November). *A model of organizational dissent.* Paper presented at the annual meeting of the Speech Communication Association, San Diego, CA.

Katzenbach, J. R., & Smith, D. K. (1993). *The wisdom of teams.* New York: HarperCollins.

Kelley, M., & Harrison, B. (Eds.). (1991). *Unions and economic competitiveness.* Armonk, NY: M. E. Sharpe.

Klingel, S. (1993). *From revolution to evolution: Development of the social councils at Mondragón.* Unpublished master's thesis, Cornell University.

Knights, D., & Willmott, H. C. (1987). Organizational culture as management strategy. *International Studies of Management and Organization, 17,* 40-63.

Kornbluh, H. (1984). Workplace democracy and quality of worklife: Problems and prospects. *Annals of the American Academy of Political and Social Science, 473,* 88-95.

Korten, D. (1995). *When corporations rule the world.* West Hartford, CT/San Francisco: Berrett-Koehler/Kumarian.

Kotter, J. P. (1995). Leading change: Why transformational efforts fail. *Harvard Business Review, 73*(4), 59-67.

Kouzes, J. M., & Posner, B. Z. (1987). *The leadership challenge.* San Francisco: Jossey-Bass.

Krimerman, L., & Lindenfeld, F. (1992). *When workers decide: Workplace democracy takes root in America.* Philadelphia: New Society.

Kuhn, T. (1996, November). *A structurational perspective on alternative organizations.* Paper presented at the annual meeting of the Speech Communication Association, San Diego, CA.

Kunda, G. (1992). *Engineering culture: Control and commitment in a high-tech corporation.* Philadelphia: Temple University Press.

Lammers, C. J., & Szell, G. (1989). *International handbook of participation in organizations: Vol. 1. Organizational democracy: Taking stock.* Oxford: Oxford University Press.

Larson, C. E., & LaFasto, F. M. J. (1989). *Teamwork: What must go right/what can go wrong.* Newbury Park, CA: Sage.

Laufer, R., & Paradeise, C. (1990). *Marketing democracy: Public opinion and media formation in democratic societies.* New Brunswick, NJ: Transaction.

Lawler, E. E., III (1986). *High-involvement management: Participative strategies for improving organizational performance.* San Francisco: Jossey-Bass.

Lawler, E. E., III, Mohrman, S. A., & Ledford, G. E., Jr. (1995). *Creating high-performance organizations.* San Francisco: Jossey-Bass.

Lefort, C. (1988). *Democracy and political theory* (D. Macey, Trans.). Minneapolis: University of Minnesota Press.

Levering, R., & Moskowitz, Z. M. (1993). *The 100 best companies to work for in America.* New York: Doubleday/Currency.

Lewin, K. (1947). Frontiers in group dynamics: Concept, method, and reality in social science; social equilibria and social change. *Human Relations, 1,* 5-41.

Likert, R. (1961). *New patterns of management.* New York: McGraw-Hill.

Lichtenstein, N., & Harris, H. J. (Eds.). (1993). *Industrial democracy in America: The ambiguous promise.* Cambridge: Cambridge University Press.

Lindenfeld, F., & Rothschild-Whitt, J. (Eds.). (1982). *Workplace democracy and social change.* Boston: Porter Sargent.

Locke, E. A., & Schweiger, D. M. (1979). Participation in decision-making: One more look. In B. M. Staw & L. L. Cummings (Eds.), *Research in organizational behavior* (Vol. 1, pp. 265-339). Greenwich, CT: JAI.

Lukes, S. (1974). *Power: A radical view.* London: Macmillan.

March, J. G., & Olsen, J. P. (1995). *Democratic governance.* New York: Free Press.

Maguire, M., & Mohtar, L. R. (1994). Performance and the celebration of a subaltern counterpublic. *Text and Performance Quarterly, 14,* 238-252.

Mandel, E. (1975). Self-management: Dangers and possibilities. *International, 2*(3), 3-9.

Mander, J., & Goldsmith, E. (Eds.). (1996). *The case against the global economy: And a turn toward the local.* San Francisco: Sierra Club Books.

Mansbridge, J. (1973). Time, emotion, and inequality: Three problems of participatory groups. *Journal of Applied Behavioral Science, 9,* 351-368.

Mansbridge, J. (1983). *Beyond adversary democracy.* Chicago: University of Chicago Press.

Mantovani, G. (1994). Is computer-mediated communication intrinsically apt to enhance democracy in organizations? *Human Relations, 47,* 45-62.

Manz, C. C., & Angle, H. (1987). Can group self-management mean a loss of personal control? Triangulating a paradox. *Group and Organization Studies, 11,* 309-334.

Manz, C. C., & Sims, H. P., Jr. (1980). Self-management as a substitute for leadership: A social learning theory perspective. *Academy of Management Review, 5,* 361-367.

Manz, C. C., & Sims, H. P., Jr. (1984). Searching for the unleader: Organizational member views on leading self-managed groups. *Human Relations, 37,* 409-424.

Manz, C. C., & Sims, H. P., Jr. (1987). Leading workers to lead themselves: The external leadership of self-managing work teams. *Administrative Science Quarterly, 32,* 106-128.

Markham, A. (1996). Designing discourse: A critical analysis of strategic ambiguity and workplace control. *Management Communication Quarterly, 1,* 389-421.

Marks, M. L., Hackett, J. E., Mirvis, P. H., & Grady, J. F., Jr. (1986). Employee participation in a quality circle program: Impact on quality of worklife, productivity, and absenteeism. *Journal of Applied Psychology, 71,* 61-69 .

Marshall, A. A., & Stohl, C. (1993). Participating as participation: A network approach. *Communication Monographs, 60,* 137-157.

Martin, P. Y. (1990). Rethinking feminist organizations. *Gender & Society, 4,* 182-206.

Mason, R. M. (1982). *Participatory and workplace democracy: A theoretical development in the critique of liberalism.* Carbondale: Southern Illinois University Press.

Mathews, J. A. (1989). *Age of democracy: The politics of post-Fordism.* Melbourne: Oxford University Press.

McCloskey, D. N. (1985). *The rhetoric of economics.* Madison: University of Wisconsin Press.

McLagan, P. A., & Nel, C. (1995). *The age of participation: New governance for the workplace and the world.* San Francisco/Eugene, OR: Berrett-Koehler/Hulogosi.

McMillan, J. J., & Cheney, G. (1996). The student as consumer: Implications and limitations of a metaphor. *Communication Education, 45,* 1-15.

McPhee, R. D. (1985). Formal structure and organizational communication. In R. D. McPhee & P. K. Tompkins (Eds.), *Organizational communication: Traditional themes and new directions* (pp. 149-178). Beverly Hills, CA: Sage.

Mehan, H. (1987). Language and power in organizational process. *Discourse Processes, 10,* 291-301.

Metzler, M. (1996, November). *Organizations, democracy, and the public sphere: The effects of democratic (r)evolution at a nuclear weapons facility.* Paper presented at the annual meeting of the Speech Communication Association, San Diego, CA.

Michels, R. (1962). *Political parties: A sociological study of the oligarchical tendencies of modern democracy* (E. Paul & C. Paul, Trans.). New York: Collier.

Miller, K. I., & Monge, P. R. (1986). Participation, satisfaction, and productivity: A meta-analytic review. *Academy of Management Journal, 29,* 727-753.

Monge, P. R. (1995). Global network organizations. In R. Cesaria & P. Shockley-Zalabak (Eds.), *Organization means communication* (pp. 131-151). Rome: Sipi Editore.

Monge, P. R., & Miller, K. I. (1988). Participative processes in organizations. In G. M. Goldhaber & G. A. Barnett (Eds.), *Handbook of organizational communication* (pp. 213-229). Norwood, NJ: Ablex.

Mulder, M., & Wilke, H. (1970). Participation and power equalization. *Organizational Behavior and Human Performance, 5,* 430-448.

Mulgan, G. J. (1991). *Communication and control.* New York: Guilford.

Mumby, D. K. (1988). *Communication and power in organizations: Discourse, ideology, and domination.* Norwood, NJ: Ablex.

Mumby, D. K. (1993). Feminism and the critique of organizational communication studies. In S. A. Deetz (Ed.), *Communication yearbook 16* (pp. 155-166). Newbury Park, CA: Sage.

Mumby, D. K. (1997). Modernism, postmodernism, and communication studies: A rereading of an ongoing debate. *Communication Theory, 7,* 1-28.

Mumby, D. K. (in press). Power and organizational communication. In F. M. Jablin & L. L. Putnam (Eds.), *The new handbook of organizational communication.* Thousand Oaks, CA: Sage.

Mumby, D. K., & Putnam, L. L. (1992). The politics of emotion: A feminist reading of bounded rationality. *Academy of Management Review, 17,* 465-486.

Mumby, D. K., & Stohl, C. (1991). Power and discourse in organizational studies: Absence and the dialectic of control. *Discourse and Society, 2,* 313-332.

Mumby, D. K., & Stohl, C. (1996). Disciplining organizational communication studies. *Management Communication Quarterly, 10,* 50-72.

Naschold, F., Cole, R. E., Gustavsen, B., & van Beinum, H. (1993). *Constructing the new industrial society.* Van Gorcum, Netherlands: Swedish Center for Working Life.

Newman, K. (1980). Incipient bureaucracy: The development of hierarchies in egalitarian organizations. In G. M. Britain & R. Cohen (Eds.), *Hierarchy and society: Anthropological perspectives on bureaucracy* (pp. 143-163). Philadelphia: Institute for the Study of Human Values.

Obradovic, J. (1975). Workers' participation: Who participates? *Industrial Relations, 14,* 33-44.

O'Connor, E. S. (1995). Paradoxes of participation: Textual analysis of organizational change. *Organization Studies, 16,* 769-803.

Pacanowsky, M. (1988). Communication in the empowering organization. In J. A. Anderson (Ed.), *Communication yearbook 11* (pp. 356-379). Newbury Park, CA: Sage.

Papa, M., Auwal, M. A., & Singhal, A. (1995). Dialectic of control and emancipation in organizing for social change: A multitheoretic study of the Grameen Bank in Bangladesh. *Communication Theory, 5,* 189-223.

Pardo, M. (1995). Doing it for the kids: Mexican American community activists, border feminists? In M. M. Ferree & P. Y. Martin (Eds.), *Feminist organizations: Harvest of the new women's movement* (pp. 356-371). Philadelphia: Temple University Press.

Parker, M. (1985). *Inside the circle: A union guide to QWL.* Boston: South End.

Parker, M. (1993). Industrial relations myth and shop-floor reality: The "team concept" in the auto industry. In N. Lichtenstein & H. J. Harris (Eds.), *Industrial democracy in America: The ambiguous promise* (pp. 249-274). New York: Cambridge University Press.

Parker, M., & Slaughter, J. (1988). *Choosing sides: Unions and the team concept.* Boston: South End.

Parker, M., & Slaughter, J. (1989). Dealing with good management. *Labor Research Review, 14,* 73-79.

Parker, M., & Slaughter, J. (1994). *Working smart: A union guide to participation programs and reengineering.* Detroit, MI: Labor Notes.

Pateman, C. (1970). *Participation and democratic theory.* London: Cambridge University Press.

Pearson, R. (1989). Business ethics as communication ethics: Public relations practice and the idea of dialogue. In C. H. Botan & V. Hazleton, Jr. (Eds.), *Public relations theory* (pp. 111-134). Hillsdale, NJ: Lawrence Erlbaum.

Phillips, K. R. (1996). The spaces of public dissension: Reconsidering the public sphere. *Communication Monographs, 63,* 231-248.

Plas, J. M. (1996). *Person-centered leadership: An American approach to participatory management.* Thousand Oaks, CA: Sage.

Powell, W. (1990). Neither market nor hierarchy: Network forms of organization. *Research in Organizational Behavior, 12,* 295-336.

Putnam, L. L., Phillips, N., & Chapman, P. (1996). Metaphors of communication and organization. In S. R. Clegg, C. Hardy, & W. Nord (Eds.), *Handbook of organization studies* (pp. 375-408). London: Sage.

Putnam, R. D. (1993). *Making democracy work: Civic traditions in modern Italy.* Princeton, NJ: Princeton University Press.

Putnam, R. D. (1995). Bowling alone: America's declining social capital. *Journal of Democracy, 6,* 65-76.

Ray, E. B. (Ed.). (1996). *Communication and the disenfranchised: Social health issues and implications.* Mahwah, NJ: Lawrence Erlbaum.

Redding, W. C. (1972). *Communication in organizations.* New York: Industrial Communication Council.

Remland, M. S. (1981). Developing leadership skills in nonverbal communication: A situational perspective. *Journal of Business Communication, 18,* 17-29.

Remland, M. S. (1984). Leadership impressions and nonverbal communication in a superior-subordinate interaction. *Communication Quarterly, 32,* 41-48.

Rheingold, H. (1993). *Virtual community: Homesteading on the electric frontier.* Reading, MA: Addison-Wesley.

Richmond, V. P., Wagner, J. P., & McCroskey, J. C. (1983). The impact of perceptions of leadership style, use of power, and conflict management style on organizational outcomes. *Communication Quarterly, 31,* 27-36.

Rifkin, J. (1995). *The end of work.* Los Angeles: Jeremy Tarcher/Putnam.

Rock, C. R. (1991). Workplace democracy in the United States. In J. D. Wisman (Ed.), *Worker empowerment: The struggle for workplace democracy* (pp. 37-58). New York: Bootstrap.

Rodriguez, N. M. (1988). Transcending bureaucracy: Feminist politics at a shelter for battered women. *Gender & Society, 2,* 214-227.

Roethlisberger, F., & Dickson, W. (1939). *Management and the worker.* New York: John Wiley.

Rosen, C. M., Klein, K. J., & Young, K. M. (1986). *Employee ownership in America: The equity solution.* Lexington, MA: Lexington.

Rosner, M. (1984). A search for "coping strategies" or forecasts of cooperative "degeneration." *Economic and Industrial Democracy, 5,* 391-399.

Rothenburg, H. I., & Silverman, S. B. (1973). *Labor unions: How to avert them, beat them, out-negotiate them, live with them, unload them.* Elkins Park, PA: Management Relations.

Rothschild, J., & Whitt, J. A. (1986). *The cooperative workplace: Potentials and dilemmas of organizational democracy and participation.* Cambridge: Cambridge University Press.

Rus, V. (1975). Influence structure in Yugoslav enterprise. *Industrial Relations, 9,* 148-160.

Russell, R. (1984). Using ownership to control: Making workers owners in the contemporary United States. *Politics and Society, 13,* 253-294.

Russell, R. (1985). *Employee ownership.* Albany: State University of New York Press.

Russell, R. (1996, November). *Workplace democracy and organizational communication.* Paper presented at the annual meeting of the Speech Communication Association, San Diego, CA

Russell, R., & Rus, V. (Eds.). (1991). *International handbook of participation in organizations: Vol. 2. Ownership and participation.* Oxford: Oxford University Press.

Sashkin, M. (1984, Spring). Participative management is an ethical imperative. *Organizational Dynamics, 12,* 5-22.

Schiller, B. (1991). Workplace democracy: The dual roots of worker participation. In D. Hancock, J. Logue, & B. Schiller (Eds.), *Managing modern capitalism: Industrial renewal and workplace democracy in the United States and Western Europe* (pp. 109-120). New York: Praeger.

Schonberger, R. J. (1994). Human resources management lessons from a decade of total quality management and reengineering. *California Management Review, 36*(4), 109-123.

Sclove, R. E. (1995). *Democracy and technology.* New York: Guilford.

Scott, J. C. (1990). *Domination and the arts of resistance: Hidden transcripts.* New Haven, CT: Yale University Press.

Seashore, S. (1954). *Group cohesiveness in the industrial work group.* Ann Arbor: University of Michigan, Institute for Social Research.

Seibold, D. R. (1995). Developing the "team" in a team-managed organization: Group facilitation in a new-design plant. In L. Frey (Ed.), *Innovations in group facilitation techniques: Case studies of applications in naturalistic settings* (pp. 282-298). Creskill, NJ: Hampton.

Seibold, D. R., & Shea, B. C. (in press). Participation and decision making. In F. M. Jablin & L. L. Putnam (Eds.), *The new handbook of organizational communication.* Thousand Oaks, CA: Sage.

Senge, P. M. (1990). The leader's new work: Building learning organizations. *Sloan Management Review, 32*(1), 7-23.

Sewell, G., & Wilkinson, B. (1992). "Someone to watch over me": Surveillance, discipline, and the just-in-time labor process. *Sociology, 26,* 271-289.

Sheeran, M. J. (1983). *Beyond majority rule: Voteless decisions in the Religious Society of Friends.* Philadelphia: Religious Society of Friends.

Simons, R. (1995). Control in an age of empowerment. *Harvard Business Review, 73*(4), 80-88.

Sinclair, A. (1992). The tyranny of a team ideology. *Organization Studies, 13,* 611-626.

Slaughter, J. (1983). *Concessions—and how to beat them.* Detroit, MI: Labor Notes.

Smith, R. C. (1993, May). *Images of organizational communication: Root metaphors of the organization-communication relationship.* Paper presented at the annual meeting of the International Communication Association, Washington, DC.

Snyder, N. H., & Graves, M. (1994, January-February). Leadership and vision. *Business Horizons,* pp. 1-7.

Sproull, L., & Kiesler, S. (1991). *Connections: New ways of working in the networked organization.* Cambridge: MIT Press.

Stern, R. N., & McCarthy, S. (Eds.). (1986). *The international yearbook of organizational democracy: Vol. 1. The organizational practice of democracy.* Chichester, England: John Wiley.

Stewart, L. P. (1981). Whistleblowing: Implications for organizational communication. *Journal of Communication, 30,* 90-101.

Stohl, C. (1986). Quality circles and changing patterns of communication. In M. L. McLaughlin (Ed.), *Communication yearbook 9* (pp. 511-531). Beverly Hills, CA: Sage.

Stohl, C. (1987). Bridging the parallel organization: A study of quality circle effectiveness. In M. L. McLaughlin (Ed.), *Communication yearbook 10* (pp. 416-430). Newbury Park, CA: Sage.

Stohl, C. (1993). European managers' interpretations of participation. *Human Communication Research, 20,* 97-117.

Stohl, C. (1995a). *Organizational communication: Connectedness in action.* Thousand Oaks, CA: Sage.

Stohl, C. (1995b). *Paradoxes of employee participation.* Unpublished research proposal, Purdue University.

Stohl, C., & Cheney, G. (1997). *Paradoxes and contradictions of employee participation and workplace democracy.* Manuscript in preparation, Purdue University and University of Montana.

Stohl, C., & Coombs, W. T. (1988). Cooperation or cooptation: An analysis of quality circle training manuals. *Management Communication Quarterly, 2,* 63-89.

Strauss, G. (1982). Workers' participation in management: An international perspective. *Research in Organizational Behavior, 4,* 173-265.

Stryjan, Y. (1989). *Impossible organizations: Self-management and organizational reproduction.* Westport, CT: Greenwood.

Stuart, P. (1993). Labor unions become business partners. *Personnel Journal, 72*(8), 54-63.

Swinney, D. (1989). Broadening the area for participation and control. *Labor Research Review, 14,* 92-98.

Tannenbaum, A. S. (1983). Employee-owned companies. *Research in Organizational Behavior, 5,* 235-268.

Tannenbaum, A. S. (1986). Controversies about control and democracy in organization. In R. N. Stern & S. McCarthy (Eds.), *International yearbook of organizational democracy: Vol. 2. The organizational practice of democracy* (pp. 279-303). Chichester, England: John Wiley.

Taylor, J. R. (1995). Shifting from a heteronomous to an autonomous worldview of organizational communication: Communication theory on the cusp. *Communication Theory, 5,* 1-35.

Thompson, R. (1991). The changing character of employee relations. *Journal of Labor Research, 12,* 320-336.

Thompson, V. A. (1961). *Modern organization.* New York: Knopf.

Tichy, N. M., & Ulrich, D. O. (1984). SMR Forum: The leadership challenge: A call for the transformational leader. *Sloan Management Review, 26*(1), 59-68.

Tompkins, P. K., & Cheney, G. (1985). Communication and unobtrusive control in contemporary organizations. In R. D. McPhee & P. K. Tompkins (Eds.), *Organizational communication: Traditional themes and new directions* (pp. 179-210). Beverly Hills, CA: Sage.

Trist, E. L. (1963). *Organizational choice: Capabilities of groups at the coal factory under changing technologies: The loss, re-discovery, and transformation of a work tradition.* London: Tavistock.

Trist, E. L., & Banforth K. (1951). Some social and psychological consequences of the longwall method of coal getting. *Human Relations, 4,* 3-38.

Trist, E. L., Murray, H., & Trist, B. (Eds.). (1993). *The social engagement of social science: Vol. 2. The socio-technical perspective.* Philadelphia: University of Pennsylvania Press.

Tsiganou, H. (1991). *Worker participative schemes: The experience of capitalist and plan-based societies.* Westport, CT: Greenwood.

University of Piraeus. (Ed.). (1994). *Participation, organizational effectiveness, and quality of work life in the year 2000.* Frankfurt: Peter Lang.

Walker, J. (1996, November). *Embracing paradox as a means to democratization in organizations.* Paper presented at the annual meeting of the Speech Communication Association, San Diego, CA.

Warner, M. (1984). Organizational democracy: The history of an idea. In B. Wilpert & A. Sorge (Eds.), *International yearbook of organizational democracy: Vol. 2. International perspectives on organizational democracy* (pp. 5-21). New York: John Wiley.

Weber, M. (1978). *Economy and society: An outline of interpretive sociology* (Vols. 1-2) (G. Roth & C. Wittich, Trans.). Berkeley: University of California Press.

Wendt, R. F. (1994). Learning to "walk the talk": A critical tale of the micropolitics at a total quality university. *Management Communication Quarterly, 8,* 5-45.

Westenholz, A. (1991). Democracy as "organizational divorce" and how postmodern democracy is stifled by unity and majority. *Economic and Industrial Democracy, 12,* 173-186.

Westenholz, A. (1993). Paradoxical thinking and change in the frames of reference. *Organization Studies, 14,* 37-58.

Whalen, S. (1997). *Working for words: Rhetoric, interests and the eclipse of the contemporary American worker.* Manuscript in preparation, University of Colorado, Boulder.

White, W. (1989). Value of joint programs underestimated. *Labor Research Review, 14,* 87-91.

Whitten, M. (1993). Narrative and the culture of obedience in the workplace. In D. K. Mumby (Ed.), *Narrative and social control: Critical perspectives* (pp. 97-118). Newbury Park, CA: Sage.

Whyte, W. F., & Whyte, K. K. (1991). *Making Mondragón: The growth and dynamics of the worker cooperative complex.* Ithaca, NY: International Labor Relations Press.

Willis, P. (1977). *Learning to labor: How working-class kids get working-class jobs.* New York: Columbia University Press.

Wilpert, B., & Sorge, A. (Eds.). (1984). *International yearbook of organizational democracy: Vol. 2. International perspectives on organizational democracy.* Chichester, England: John Wiley.

Wisman, J. D. (Ed.). (1991). *Worker empowerment: The struggle for workplace democracy.* New York: Bootstrap.

Zorn, T. (1997). The uncooperative cooperative: Attempting to improve employee morale at Weaver Street Market. In B. D. Sypher (Ed.), *Contemporary case studies in organizational communication* (pp. 312-336). New York: Guilford.

Zuboff, S. (1988). *In the age of the smart machine: The future of work and power.* New York: Basic.

CHAPTER CONTENTS

3 Reconceptualizing Organizational Change Implementation as a Communication Problem: A Review of Literature and Research Agenda

LAURIE K. LEWIS
Pennsylvania State University

DAVID R. SEIBOLD
University of California, Santa Barbara

Organizational scholars have acknowledged the importance of communication processes in explanations for organizational change processes, but have focused primarily on the invention, design, adoption, and responses to planned changes. Communication perspectives have largely ignored the means by which change programs are installed and by which users come to learn of such programs. The goal of this chapter is to demonstrate how a communication perspective can enhance understanding of implementation activities. Factors that influence when and how innovations are utilized in organizations are examined. Six major areas of literature in implementation of planned organizational change are reviewed: (a) general approaches to implementation, (b) strategies and tactics for change implementation, (c) characteristics and factors related to change agents, (d) contingencies that affect implementation, (e) strategic planning and implementation, and (f) themes and recommendations in the practitioner literature. In the final section of the chapter, a research agenda for communication scholars in this area of organizational science is proposed. The agenda focuses on interaction during implementation and communication-related structures regarding implementation. Further, it is argued that these foci should be investigated within both formal and informal implementation activities.

IN 1979, Kotter and Schlesinger observed, "Today, more and more managers must deal with new government regulations, new products, growth, increased competition, technological developments, and a changing work force. In response, most companies . . . find that they must undertake moderate

Correspondence and requests for reprints: Laurie K. Lewis, Department of Speech Communication, University of Texas, Austin, TX 78712; e-mail lklewis@mail.utexas.edu

Communication Yearbook 21, pp. 93-151

organizational changes at least once a year and major changes every four or five" (p. 106). This trend has only increased in the past decade and a half (Cushman & King, 1994), and rapid change likely will continue to be a cornerstone of organizational life into the 21st century. The implementation of change programs is costly in terms of financial resources, employee time investment, managerial time, and often in terms of employee morale (Kotter & Schlesinger, 1979). An organization's survival also may hinge on its success in implementing many large-scale changes (e.g., reorganization, downsizing, major production technologies).

Further, planned change implementation efforts often fail. In the case of some technologies, for example, implementation failure rates are as high as 50-75% (Majchrzak, 1988). And as Tornatzky and Johnson (1982) note, the implementation process is "almost always difficult and rarely proceeds as planned" (p. 193). Human and organizational factors are commonly identified as causes and contributors to failures and difficulties in implementation efforts. For example, Miller, Johnson, and Grau (1994) suggest that resistance that may occur during change efforts—reduction of output, quarreling and hostility, work slowdowns, and pessimism regarding goal attainment—can be attributed to numerous political, cultural, normative, and individual causes. Indeed, Bikson and Gutek (1984) found that less than 10% of the failures in the companies they studied were due to technical problems. Understanding just how implementation of change programs is accomplished, and how communication affects the process, appears increasingly central to our understanding of and ability to predict the outcomes of planned change efforts.

Communication is fundamental to organizing (Farace, Monge, & Russell, 1977). Organizing entails the exchange of symbolic representations of ideas, events, emotions, and information in order to overcome problems related to uncertainty, identity, and interdependence. Researchers and theorists have conceptualized numerous organizing phenomena as communicative, including leadership (Eisenberg & Riley, 1988), management behavior (Pfeffer, 1981; Trujillo, 1983), climate (Redding, 1972), socialization (Jablin, 1987b), attitude formation (Salancik & Pfeffer, 1978), control systems (Barker & Tompkins, 1994), and maintenance of organizational image and legitimacy (Elsbach & Sutton, 1992). These reconceptualizations have led to new understandings of how structures and processes in organizations are created, maintained, and changed. Similarly, we argue in this chapter for a reconceptualization of the implementation of planned organizational change as a communication-related phenomenon and offer a framework from which such a reconceptualization may be created. Toward that end, we first explicate constructs central to this review and to the reconceptualization of planned change. We then turn to a more explicit rationale for examining organizational change and implementation as a communication process. That section concludes with an overview of the structure of the remainder of this chapter.

Tornatzky and Johnson (1982) define *implementation* as "the translation of any tool or technique, process, or method of doing, from knowledge to practice. It encompasses that range of activities which take place between 'adoption' of a tool or technique (defined as a decision or intent to use the technology) and its stable incorporation into on-going organizational practice" (p. 193). Lewis and Seibold (1993) conceptualize *structured implementation activities* as "designed and enacted by internal or external change agents to specify usage of innovations and influence users' innovation-role-involvement, their formal (prescribed) and emergent patterns of interactions with and concerning the innovation" (p. 324). Such activities might include the formation of goals, selection and training of users, development of performance criteria, and assessment of implementation outcomes.

COMMUNICATION SCHOLARSHIP ON ORGANIZATIONAL CHANGE AND IMPLEMENTATION

Organizational scholars have acknowledged the importance of communication processes in explanations of organizational change processes (Albrecht & Ropp, 1984; Fairhurst & Wendt, 1993; Fulk, Schmitz, & Steinfield, 1990; Lewis & Seibold, 1993, 1996; Rogers, 1995; Van de Ven, Angle, & Poole, 1989). However, their efforts have focused primarily on the invention, design, adoption, and responses to planned organizational change, as well as outcomes of change efforts. Rogers and his colleagues (Rice & Rogers, 1980; Rogers, 1983, 1995; Rogers & Shoemaker, 1971) and the Minnesota Innovation Research Project (Van de Ven et al., 1989), among others, have made important contributions to our understanding of (a) "triggers" of innovation processes, (b) critical internal factors and organizational processes that are involved during intraorganizational adoption, (c) the role of opinion leaders and change agents in creating acceptance of innovations within organizations, (d) the causes and means by which innovations are "reinvented" or modified during early stages of implementation, and (e) the "routinization" or "institutionalization" of change programs.

Researchers have noted the importance of communication variables in predicting the creation of innovative ideas and perceptions of innovativeness (Albrecht & Hall, 1981; Albrecht & Ropp, 1984; Cheney, Block, & Gordon, 1986; Ebadi & Utterback, 1984; Johnson, Meyer, Berkowitz, & Ethington, 1995; Monge, Cozzens, & Contractor, 1992), the diffusion and adoption of innovations (Bach, 1989; Dearing & Meyer, 1994; Hoffman & Roman, 1984; Rogers, 1983, 1995), the formation of attitudes regarding planned changes (Ellis, 1992; Miller & Monge, 1985; Miller et al., 1994), resistance to change programs (Fairhurst, Green, & Courtright, 1995), behavioral coping responses of innovation users (Lewis & Seibold, 1996), and outcomes of organizational change programs (Johnson & Rice, 1987; Rice & Contractor, 1990). However, central communication processes involved in the installation of planned changes within organizations have received far less attention from communication scholars. Communication processes are inherently a part of these *implementation activities,* including announcement of change programs, training of users, and users' interaction and feedback regarding change programs, to name only a few. Unfortunately, communication scholars have been noticeably silent in this area of the organizational change literature.

One of our goals in this chapter is to demonstrate how a communication perspective can enhance understanding of implementation activities and strategies, and of the factors that influence when and how they are utilized in organizations. In the following sections, we review major areas of research on implementation of planned organizational change and develop a blueprint for a communication-related research agenda. In short, this review demonstrates the lack of a communication perspective on change implementation, illustrates the importance of such a perspective for furthering understanding of implementation activities, and sets forth a research agenda for communication scholars in this area of organizational science.

In the sections below we discuss six areas of implementation literature that have not yet benefited from any single integrative conceptual or theoretical framework and present categories of "topics" from this literature. In the final section, we present a framework that may serve as a potential integrative mechanism. We explore seven research areas within contexts of structure and agency and formality and informality. The process/structure distinction, although theoretically problematic, is analytically useful for exploring how interaction is enabled (and constrained) by structures endemic to innovation implementation and for examining the recursiveness of interactional practices and structure. The formality/informality distinction serves to highlight both "top-down" implementation efforts and "bottom-up" influences on change programs.

AREAS OF THE IMPLEMENTATION
LITERATURE: AN OVERVIEW

The six areas of the change implementation literature reviewed in this essay are as follows:

- General approaches to implementation
- Strategies and tactics for change implementation
- Characteristics and factors related to change agents
- Contingencies that affect implementation
- Strategic planning and implementation
- Themes and recommendations in the practitioner literature

Although the distinctions made here are not formal within the literature, and in some cases single works may cross areas, these areas serve an organizing and descriptive purpose. We treat the research in these six areas in turn, and each section of the chapter includes a table that presents representative works and notes the prevalent constructs under consideration. Each table also notes the presence or absence of communication variables and indicates the focus (case study, conceptual, empirical, review, theoretical) of each of the categorized works. To have been included in this review, works must be focused primarily on implementation (as defined above) as opposed to "adoption" (the selection of innovations) or responses to outcomes of planned change, and they must have been published or presented within the past three decades. Although the review is not exhaustive, the nearly 150 works we have surveyed are representative of the types, quality, and foci of the implementation literature.

GENERAL APPROACHES TO IMPLEMENTATION

Table 3.1 summarizes works that outline general approaches to change implementation. An overarching debate within the implementation literature concerns approaches to change processes as either "rule-bound" or "autonomous" in nature. Rule-bound approaches "involve central direction and highly programmed tasks" (Marcus, 1988, p. 235), whereas autonomous approaches accept "that people in the lowest echelons of an organization exhibit autonomy by redefining policies during the course of implementation" (p. 237). Writing primarily about the implementation of public policy, Linder and Peters (1987) refer to this distinction in terms of "top-down" and "bottom-up" perspectives. In another approach, Johnson (1993) discusses important implications of "formally" and "informally" generated innovations.

Although both of these approaches deal primarily with externally induced change programs (such as those imposed by governmental bodies on local agencies), other scholars have adopted this distinction as important in exploring intraorganizational implementation approaches. For example, in their approach to strategy implementation, Bourgeois and Brodwin (1984) distinguish between the "commander" model, which favors a highly centralized approach to implementation, and the "crescive" model, which "draws on managers' natural inclinations to want to develop new opportunities as they see them in the course of their day-to-day management" (p. 242). The crescive model casts "the role of the CEO from the designer to that of premise-setter and judge" (p. 254). The CEO encourages lower-level employees to derive and propose strategy, and the focus for the CEO becomes one of "prodding, nurturing, and nudging . . . [rather than] shaping, controlling, and restraining" (p. 255).

TABLE 3.1
General Approaches to Implementation of Organizational Changes

Approach	Study	Communication Variables?	Focus
Rule-bound versus autonomous	Baronas & Louis, 1988		empirical
	Bourgeois & Brodwin, 1984		conceptual
	Linder & Peters, 1987		conceptual/review
	Marcus, 1988		empirical
Adaptive versus programmed	Berman, 1980		conceptual
	Roberts-Gray & Gray, 1983		theoretical
	Roberts-Gray, 1985		empirical/conceptual
	Zaltman & Duncan, 1977		conceptual/review
Political	Egri & Frost, 1989		conceptual/case study
	Frost & Egri, 1990a, 1990b		conceptual/case study
	Frost & Egri, 1991		conceptual/case study
	Schein, 1977	yes	conceptual
	Schein, 1985		conceptual
Incrementalism versus radicalism	Dunphy & Stace, 1988		review/theoretical
Breadth versus depth	Lindquist & Mauriel, 1989		empirical
Incremental versus transformation	Lovelady, 1984		conceptual
Collaborative versus coercive	Dunphy & Stace, 1988	yes	review/theoretical
Task technology versus end user	Blackler & Brown, 1986	yes	conceptual

Authors making the rule-bound/autonomous distinction tend to argue in favor of more autonomous approaches. Marcus (1988) argues that rule-bound approaches may lead to resistance from local agencies or "bad-faith" compliance on the part of managers forced to implement policies without the ability to make adaptations. He suggests that "middle managers who believe that their self-interest is being compromised can redirect a strategy, delay its implementation, or reduce the quality of implementation" (p. 237). He cites evidence suggesting that employees of decentralized organizations make more helpful contributions to implementation than do those of highly centralized bureaucratic organizations. Although Bourgeois and Brodwin (1984) acknowledge that the crescive implementation model may be inappropriate for less diversified and less complex organizations, they too favor this more autonomous approach.

Tests of the relative effectiveness of these approaches suggest that autonomous approaches tend to produce better results. In his study of the implementation of nuclear power plant safety review innovations, Marcus (1988) found that poor safety records were associated with rule-bound approaches, whereas plants with strong safety records tended to retain their autonomy. Baronas and Louis's (1988) field experiment concerning users' involvement in the implementation of a statewide payroll system revealed that groups who had been given more control over the process reported significantly higher ratings of the implementation schedule, the implementation teams, and their own satisfaction with user information, and comparatively lower ratings of the previous system (after 2 months).

Whether implementation is "adaptive" or "programmatic" in nature is a second important distinction made concerning general approaches to implementation, and centers on whether implementation of change programs should be modified or adapted. Programmed implementation "assumes that implementation problems can be made tolerable, if not eliminated, by careful and explicit preprogramming of implementation procedures" (Berman, 1980, p. 205), whereas adaptive implementation "holds that policy execution can be improved by processes that enable initial plans to be adapted to unfolding events and decisions" (pp. 205-206). For the "adaptive" implementer, implementation problems "arise because of the overspecification and rigidity of goals, the failure to engage relevant actors in decision-making, and the excessive control of deliverers" (p. 210). For the "programmatic" implementer, difficulties in implementation are attributed to ambiguity in policy goals, participation of too many actors, overlapping authority, and the resistance, ineffectiveness, or inefficiency of implementers.

Roberts-Gray and Gray (1983) and Roberts-Gray (1985) suggest that the choice of an adaptive or programmed approach to implementation depends on whether the implementer wishes to adapt the innovation to fit the organization (adaptive) or to alter the organization to accommodate the innovation (programmed/facilitative). Their model for programmed implementation requires that organizations make changes that render the user capable of using the innovation *and* that commit the user to the innovation. Roberts-Gray and Gray (1983) draw upon Zaltman and Duncan's (1977) strategies in their prescriptive model for facilitating programmed change and the reduction of users' resistance to change. Their strategies include assistance (provision of technical support), education (provision of information and training to users), power (establishment of rules and sanctions to control and enforce innovation use), and persuasion (the shaping of users' values and attitudes to form commitment to the innovation).

Fidelity of the innovation, or the match between the designer's intent and the actual model-in-use, is the goal of a programmed approach. Although writers who favor a programmed approach sometimes acknowledge the prevalence and inevitability of "reinvention," they appear to suggest that this dysfunctional loss of fidelity is a process that can and should be managed. Roberts-Gray (1985) proposes implementation monitoring "as the strategy the developer can apply to support healthy reinventions and mitigate unacceptable adaptations" (p. 265). Successful adaptation is considered to be the goal of an adaptive approach to implementation (Berman, 1980). This distinction points to the important difference between these approaches regarding the role of feedback. Feedback in the programmed model focuses on tracking the obtainment of outcomes (relative to preformulated goals), whereas feedback in the adaptive model is concerned "primarily about the adaptive process and secondarily about outcomes" (Berman, 1980, p. 212).

Another prominent approach to the implementation of planned change focuses on political aspects of the process. As Egri and Frost (1989) observe, "Innovation and change are often the focal point of political struggles" (p. 586). In their view, successful political gamesmanship is necessary for successful implementation—as well as at other points in the design, development, and adoption of change programs. Frost and Egri (1991) also note that implementation is the "most vulnerable time of the innovation process . . . when the dysfunctional nature of organizational politics is most often highlighted" (p. 243). Politics may be responsible for unnecessary delays, excessive conflict, compromised outcomes, and sometimes ultimate failure (Frost & Egri, 1991). The political perspective also highlights the resistance tactics faced by implementers of organizational change—reactions rooted in threats to current power distribution (Frost & Egri 1991; Schein, 1985). In order to counter such resistance tactics, Schein (1985) contends, implementers need to develop counterstrategies: "One needs to develop both power bases and skill in strategically using the resources one has developed. The two key components of the politics of change and implementation are power bases and power strategies" (p. 88). These power bases include expertise, control over information, political access and sensitivity, assessed stature, and group support (Schein, 1977, 1985), as well as tradition and credibility (Schein, 1985). Tactics include the presentation of a nonthreatening image, diffusion of opposition, alignment with powerful others, development of liaisons, negotiation, and quick action, among others (Schein, 1985). Case studies are the prevalent form of empirical research in this area of literature.

A third general distinction in approaches to planned change implementation concerns the time period for change and the scope of change (Dunphy & Stace, 1988; Lindquist & Mauriel, 1989; Lovelady, 1984). For example, Lindquist and Mauriel (1989) compare two common "strategies" that differ based on the scope and spread of the implementation. In the "breadth" strategy the innovation is implemented across all organizational units simultaneously, and in the "depth" strategy the innovation is implemented and "debugged" in a demonstration site before it is generalized to other units in the organization. In Lindquist and Mauriel's study of site-based management programs in two public school districts, the breadth strategy was more successful than the depth strategy. The researchers suggest that political resistance to an innovation can be countered more effectively when the innovation is implemented widely and top-level managers stay in control than when the program is isolated within a demonstration site. Both Lovelady (1984) and Dunphy and Stace (1988) identify a number of factors that can affect whether incremental or radical (transformational) approaches to change are likely or appropriate, including environmental conditions, the nature of the change, the urgency of the change needed, and the location of the implementer (internal or external to the organization).

Other general approaches to the implementation of planned change have made distinctions between "collaborative" and "coercive" models (Dunphy & Stace, 1988) and between "task-technology" approaches and "end-user" approaches (Blackler & Brown, 1986). Like those discussed above, each of these approaches reflects a bipolar conceptualization of implementation options. In general, implementation debates have tended to juxtapose such extremes, and have usually been derived from examination of limited sets of cases or from in-depth analyses of single cases of implementation. Examination of Table 3.1 reveals a high ratio of conceptual works and case studies compared with non-case study, empirical works.

STRATEGIES AND TACTICS FOR IMPLEMENTATION OF ORGANIZATIONAL CHANGE

In addition to general conceptual and empirical treatments of implementing planned change, much of the literature on change implementation in organizations has detailed the strategies and specific tactics available to implementers (see Table 3.2). *Strategy* refers to the general thrust, direction, and focus of the activities that make up the implementation effort. *Tactics* entails the more specific actions, messages, and events constructed and carried out in service of some general strategy or goal. In all the articles and book chapters

TABLE 3.2
Strategies and Tactics for Implementation of Organizational Change

Strategies/Tactics	Study	Communication Variables?	Focus
Strategies			
intervention	Nutt, 1986		empirical/conceptual
participation	Nutt, 1987		empirical/conceptual
persuasion			
edict			
education and communication	Kotter & Schlesinger, 1979		conceptual
participation and involvement			
facilitation and support			
negotiation and agreement			
manipulation and co-optation			
explicit and implicit coercion			
facilitation	Zaltman & Duncan, 1977		conceptual/review
education	Roberts-Gray & Gray, 1983		theoretical
persuasion			
power			
commander	Bourgeois & Brodwin, 1984		conceptual
change			
collaborative			
cultural			
crescive			
political	Frost & Egri, 1990a, 1990b		conceptual/case study

persuasive communication	Armenakis et al., 1993		conceptual/empirical
management of external information			
active participation			
Strategy foci	Beckhard, 1975		conceptual
relationship with environment			
managerial strategy			
organizational structures			
work processes			
Specific tactics			
announcing change	Smeltzer, 1991	yes	empirical
training	Griffith & Northcraft, in press		empirical

on implementation that we examined, very little has been written at the tactical level. Most of what falls within this area of the implementation literature can be construed as comparative "models" of implementation strategy (i.e., ideal types of strategies).

Nutt (1986, 1987) has developed four models of implementation strategy that he terms "tactics"—a coherent set of steps used by managers to elicit support for the planned change. The models are derived from interviews that Nutt conducted with key informants in multiple organizations that had implemented change. Nutt argues that examination of a large case study database avoids the disadvantages of the more limited in-depth case study approaches of previous research: "Using data bases with few cases may fail to discover important implementation-related steps or fail to recognize the idiosyncratic nature of the steps" (p. 233). He derived four models of implementation (intervention, participation, persuasion, and edict), and then tested their relative frequency of use and success. In his study of 91 service organizations, these four models represented 93% of the cases studied (Nutt, 1986). Implementation by "persuasion" (marked by little management review, experts' control of development, and independence of experts) was the most frequently utilized model, followed by implementation by "edict" (marked by sponsors' control and personal power, avoidance of participation, and low expert and user power). The third most common tactic was "intervention" (marked by a problem-solving orientation, "selling of the change," and utilization of users in development), and the least-used tactic was "participation" (marked by high-level goal-setting, low-level decision making, and high user involvement).

The success rates of the different models (defined as final change "adoption") suggest that intervention is the most likely to bring about final adoption, followed by participation, persuasion, and edict. Thus the two most commonly utilized models produced the least successful results. Nutt also identifies a number of important contextual factors that may mediate selection of implementation strategy, such as budgets for change processes and staff support. In his 1987 study, Nutt focused on the use of these models in the implementation of strategic planning. He examined the efforts of 68 organizations to introduce strategic planning projects and classified 91% of the cases studied as using one of his implementation models. In this study, as in Nutt's 1986 work, persuasion was the most frequently utilized model, followed by intervention, edict, and participation. The most highly rated strategic plans had employed an intervention model, followed by plans implemented by persuasion, by participation, and by edict.

Other strategy models have been developed by Kotter and Schlesinger (1979), Zaltman and Duncan (1977), and Bourgeois and Brodwin (1984). These authors have developed their models based on examination of the literature concerning planned change and on their own conceptualizing of relationships among important factors. For example, Armenakis, Harris, and

Mossholder (1993) discuss "readiness interventions," which are designed to get organizational members ready to accept change. They suggest that implementers design persuasive communication, management of external information, and active participation strategies to cope with (a) effects of unplanned media information about change, (b) existing organizational conditions, and (c) significance of change. Several other strategy models also present contingencies that should affect the selection of strategies and their relative effectiveness (e.g., Bourgeois & Brodwin, 1984; Kotter & Schlesinger, 1979; Zaltman & Duncan, 1977), including the context of the change, characteristics of the users, and characteristics of the implementers (i.e., change agents).

Political strategies for implementing change also have been studied empirically. Frost and Egri (1990a, 1990b) examined a number of product, social, and administrative innovations, noting evidence of political strategy and tactics during implementation efforts. They found that "asking for forgiveness is a strategy that can only be successful in the early stages of product innovation" (1990b, p. 9), and that "once the product innovation reaches the stage of acceptance and diffusion, permission to proceed must be sought" (1990b, p. 9). For the social administrative innovation, the only viable political strategy was one of "seeking and securing permission" (1990b, p. 11).

Smeltzer's (1991) study of the elements associated with effective and ineffective announcements of planned changes and Griffith and Northcraft's (in press) comparative study of technology training methods are among the few studies that focus on specific actions, events, and messages undertaken by implementers in introducing planned change within organizations. Although each of these works is narrowly focused on one type of innovation and one tactic choice, both move toward specifying the enactment of implementation strategy. Smeltzer (1991) found, in his interview study in 43 organizations, that what most differentiated between effective and ineffective strategies in announcing organizationwide change were (a) a large number of inaccurate rumors about the change and (b) employees' learning about the change from sources other than management. Griffith and Northcraft (in press) found that users' satisfaction with and feelings of expertise concerning a new technology were related to their perceptions of having enough time to learn and work with the innovation.

CHARACTERISTICS AND FACTORS
RELATED TO CHANGE AGENTS

Table 3.3 summarizes representative works that discuss change agents' importance during implementation and identifies personal characteristics and other factors that affect their performance. Although some scholars do not distinguish explicitly among the roles of the change agent as innovator (e.g.,

TABLE 3.3
Characteristics and Factors Related to Effectiveness of Change Agents

Change Agent Characteristics and Factors	Study	Communication Variables?	Focus
Importance of change agent	Curley & Gremillion, 1983		conceptual/case study
	Kanter, 1983		conceptual/case study
	Maidique, 1980		review
	Ottaway, 1983		review
	Rogers & Shoemaker, 1971		conceptual/empirical
	Schon, 1963		conceptual
	Zaltman & Duncan, 1977		conceptual/review
Characteristics			
openness			
responsiveness	Hamilton, 1988	yes	empirical
comfort with ambiguity			
comfort with oneself			
transformational leadership			
risk taking	Howell & Higgins, 1990	yes	empirical
innovativeness			
initiating influence attempts			
variety of influence tactics			
credibility			
trustworthiness	Armenakis et al., 1993		conceptual/case study
sincerity			
expertise			

Factor	Reference		Type
technical qualifications administrative ability relationship skills job orientation (motivation, commitment, acceptance of constraints) leadership	Zaltman & Duncan, 1977	yes	conceptual/review
homophily versus heterophily	Zaltman & Duncan, 1977 Rogers & Shoemaker, 1971		conceptual/review review
Factors			
internal versus external agents	Case et al., 1990 Zaltman & Duncan, 1977		empirical conceptual/review
inside change agents	Hunsaker, 1985		conceptual
humanistic versus nonhumanistic approach	Case et al., 1990		empirical
internal/external team	Gluckstern & Packard, 1977		conceptual/case study
costs to the change agent	Brimm, 1988		conceptual/case study
individual versus team	Zaltman & Duncan, 1977		conceptual/review
choosing change agent forming task force	Lippitt et al., 1985 Zaltman & Duncan, 1977		conceptual/case study conceptual/review
Effort of change agent client orientation compatibility of program with client needs working with opinion leaders agent's perceived credibility increasing ability to assess change	Rogers & Shoemaker, 1971 Rogers, 1995		review

creating and developing innovations), as diffusion agent (e.g., bringing about formal adoption of innovations), and as implementer (e.g., installing, introducing, and encouraging use), many do make such role distinctions. Ottaway (1983) and Maidique (1980) provide historical reviews of the term *change agent* and related terms (e.g., *idea champion, business innovator, internal entrepreneur, sponsor*) and of various contexts in which change agents may play a significant role. In their extensive research on change agents, Rogers and Shoemaker (1971) draw distinctions between external change agents and internal change agents (opinion leaders) and offer conclusions concerning these roles based on a large database. At times, it is difficult to discern which role particular authors are addressing, but we attempt here to focus on those works that concentrate on the implementer role. Additionally, authors in this area have worked within various contexts in discussing change agents. Some have focused on social change, some on technological change, and still others on organizational change. Because most of their arguments appear to apply equally well to intraorganizational settings, we have chosen to include them here.

Numerous authors have pointed to the significance of the role of the change agent in implementation (Curley & Gremillion, 1983; Kanter, 1983; Maidique, 1980; Ottaway, 1983; Rogers & Shoemaker, 1971; Schon, 1963). As Kanter (1983) argues, "Any new strategy, no matter how brilliant or responsive, no matter how much agreement the formulators have about it, will stand a good chance of not being implemented fully—or sometimes, at all—without someone with power pushing it" (p. 296). The relative success of different implementers, with different characteristics and with different perspectives on change programs, has been the subject of a fair amount of literature. A variety of change agent characteristics have been proposed as important for promoting success during implementation efforts. Hamilton (1988) has developed a list of 37 characteristics and behaviors from a review of relevant literature. She categorizes these into the following groupings: openness and responsiveness, comfort with ambiguity, and comfort with oneself. Findings from her empirical study of 105 organizational development consultants indicate significant differences in characteristics between effective and ineffective change agents (Hamilton, 1988). Specifically, effective consultants expect sensitivity, empathy, and compassion from themselves and others; have a large capacity for ambiguity; are self-reliant; and are friendly, cooperative, venturesome, trusting, and imaginative. Effective consultants also tended to score as "intuitive" on Myers-Briggs.

Zaltman and Duncan (1977) include technical qualifications, administrative ability, interpersonal relations, job orientation, and leadership among their favored characteristics of good change agents. They also outline a number of attitudes, values, areas of knowledge, and skills that change agents should possess. They develop several generalizations concerning change agent effectiveness, including "Change agent success is positively related to his credibility in the eyes of his clients" (p. 203) and "Change agent success is positively related to his client orientation, rather than to change agency orientation" (p. 201).

Howell and Higgins (1990) focus on "project champions" who "distill creative ideas from information resources and then enthusiastically promote them within the organization" (p. 318). They examined the personality characteristics, leadership behaviors, and influence tactics of 25 pairs of technology champions and nonchampions and found that "champions manifest the personality characteristics of risk-taking propensity and innovativeness" and that "fundamental components of a champion's capacity to introduce innovations successfully are the articulation of a compelling vision of the innovation's potential for the organization, the expression of confidence in others to participate effectively in the initiative, and the display of innovation actions to achieve goals" (p. 336). Other authors have argued for other valuable characteristics of change agents, including trustworthiness, sincerity, expertise (Armenakis et al., 1993), and homophily (Rogers & Shoemaker, 1971; Zaltman & Duncan, 1977).

A number of factors that constrain or enhance change agents' effectiveness in implementation efforts seem to dominate the literature (second to discussions of agents' characteristics such as those above). A key concern is whether internal or external change agents do better in implementing change. Case, Vandenberg, and Meredith (1990) define internal change agents as "those who are full time employees of organizations undergoing change" and external agents as independent consultants "whose association with changing organizations is fleeting" (p. 4). Hunsaker (1985) notes that there are relative advantages and disadvantages for both internal and external change agents: External change agents are more independent and tend to have more objective, fresher perspectives, but are strangers to the organization, may lack inside understanding, and may not be able to identify with the problems of the organization; internal change agents are more intimately familiar with the organization, know who the opinion leaders are, speak the language of the organization, understand the norms of the organization, and have greater personal motivation to bring about the success of change programs. However, internal agents may lack objective perspectives, have inadequate skills or technical knowledge associated with the change, lack an adequate power base to invoke compliance with the change program, or be hindered by past images or previous failures.

Case et al.'s (1990) research revealed that external change agents tend to possess more humanistic and democratic values than do internal change agents. Internal change agents were found to be more likely to use techno-structural interventions (aimed at short-term improvement in bottom-line performance) and less likely to use human procedural interventions (aimed toward improving communication, human relations, and climate). Also, internal change agents were found to be more concerned with "hard" evaluation criteria than were external agents.

In a separate vein of the literature on external and internal change agents, Gluckstern and Packard (1977) discuss teams made up of internal and external agents. In their case study of a county jail, they demonstrate how internal and external change agents, working together in the same implementation effort, both bring contributions and liabilities. Each team member can be distinguished in terms of what he or she can offer concerning legitimacy, power, knowledge of the organization, expertise in change processes, rewards, and sanctions among others. Gluckstern and Packard further discuss the reciprocity of roles in such teams. They present a three-phase model that includes building trust, leadership training, and trading bases of credibility of the team relationship.

In other areas of the change agent literature, Brimm (1988) addresses the potential dangers to career health of individuals' taking on the role of change agent. Change agents may threaten other power holders by acquiring control over new or scarce resources, may attract increased attention and scrutiny to their own departments and operations, and may be perceived as critics of previous procedures or processes that are associated with powerful others. Lippitt, Langseth, and Mossop (1985) and Zaltman and Duncan (1977) outline criteria for selecting change agents and for forming and managing task forces (Lippitt et al., 1985). Rogers and Shoemaker (1971) and Rogers (1995) review the factors that affect the abilities of change agents, including effort, client orientation, and perceived credibility. Zaltman and Duncan (1977) discuss the relative advantages of individual implementers and implementation teams.

CONTINGENCIES THAT AFFECT IMPLEMENTATION

Perhaps the predominant area of the literature dealing with implementation of organizational change consists of writings concerning those contingencies that enable successful change and those that lead to failure. The works listed in Table 3.4 are representative of the number and types of contingencies discussed in the literature. Probably the greatest contingency affecting implementation processes is the political context of the change effort. As we noted earlier, innovation and change programs often serve as lightning rods for political battles. DeLuca (1984) states that the sociopolitical context—the power, political activity, and informal social network among actors—is a major factor in any large-scale organizational change.

Most authors who address the political context of change also discuss "resistance" to change efforts. Markus (1983) defines resistance as "behaviors intended to prevent the implementation or use of a system or to prevent system designers from achieving their objectives" (p. 433). However, the term has been used to indicate nonuse of a system even when that nonuse may be due to ignorance of the system's existence, inadequate training, or personal

TABLE 3.4
Contingencies That Affect Innovation Implementation

Contingent Factor	Study	Communication Variables?	Focus
Political context, power, and resistance	DeLuca, 1984		theoretical
	Egri & Frost, 1989		conceptual
	Fidler & Johnson, 1984	yes	conceptual
	Frost & Egri, 1990a, 1990b, 1991		conceptual/theoretical
	Gray & Hay, 1986		conceptual/empirical
	Guth & Macmillan, 1986		conceptual/empirical
	Kotter & Schlesinger, 1979		conceptual
	Kumar & Thibodeaux, 1990		conceptual
	Leonard-Barton, 1987a		empirical
	Markus, 1983	yes	theoretical
	Schein, 1977, 1985		conceptual
	Zaltman & Duncan, 1977		conceptual/review
Nature of the change (type, scope, features)	Berman, 1980		conceptual
	Ettlie et al., 1984		conceptual/empirical
	Ettlie & Rubenstein, 1980		empirical
	Fidler & Johnson, 1984		conceptual
	Leonard-Barton, 1987b	yes	case study
	Mankin et al., 1984	yes	conceptual/review
	Nord & Tucker, 1987		conceptual/review
	Roberts-Gray, 1985		empirical/conceptual
	Van de Ven, 1993		review
	Zaltman & Duncan, 1977		conceptual/review

(continued)

TABLE 3.4
Continued

Contingent Factor	Study	Communication Variables?	Focus
Time	Leonard-Barton, 1987a	yes	case study
	Smeltzer, 1991	yes	empirical
	Tyre & Orlikowski, 1994		empirical
	Van de Ven, 1993		review
	Zaltman & Duncan, 1977		conceptual/review
User participation	Baronas & Louis, 1988	yes	empirical
	Cameron et al., 1993	yes	empirical/case study
	Leonard-Barton, 1987a, 1987b	yes	case study/conceptual
	Leonard-Barton & Sinha, 1993	yes	empirical
	Mankin et al., 1984	yes	conceptual/review
	Zaltman & Duncan, 1977	yes	conceptual/review
Managers' expectations, interpretations, and influence	Cameron et al., 1993		empirical/case study
	Isabella, 1990		theoretical/empirical
	King, 1974		empirical
	Leonard-Barton & Deschamps, 1988	yes	conceptual/empirical
Organizational structure, communication structure, and size of organization	Berman, 1980		conceptual
	Fidler & Johnson, 1984	yes	conceptual
	Nord & Tucker, 1987		conceptual/review
	Spender & Kessler, 1995		theoretical
Dismantling of old ideology	Biggart, 1977		empirical
History and concurrent events	Nord & Tucker, 1987		conceptual/review
Culture	Zaltman & Duncan, 1977		conceptual/review

Variable	References		Type
Goals and decision making	Berman, 1980		conceptual
	Dean et al., 1990		conceptual/review
	Zaltman & Duncan, 1977		
Divisibility of implementation	Leonard-Barton, 1988b		conceptual/case study
Interdependence among users	Nord & Tucker, 1987		conceptual/review
Resources and technical support	Nord & Tucker, 1987		conceptual/review
	Zaltman & Duncan, 1977		conceptual/review
Cognitive frames	Griffith & Northcraft, 1993		theoretical
	Sproull & Hofmeister, 1986	yes	theoretical/empirical
Characteristics of users	Leonard-Barton, 1987b		case study
	Roberts-Gray, 1985		empirical/theoretical
	Griffith, 1995		theoretical
Information provided (positive only, balanced)	Griffith & Northcraft, in press		empirical
Information	Fidler & Johnson, 1984	yes	conceptual
Implementation by-products (morale, learning)	Nord & Tucker, 1987		conceptual/review
Transferability	Leonard-Barton, 1988b	yes	conceptual/case study
Implementation complexity	Leonard-Barton, 1988b	yes	conceptual/case study
Stability of environment	Berman, 1980		conceptual
Reward systems	Griffith, 1995		theoretical
	Leonard-Barton, 1987b		case study
	Mainiero & DeMichiell, 1986		case study

fear of the system. Markus suggests that resistance—even when intentional and conscious—"can also be functional for organizations, by preventing the installation of systems whose use might have on-going negative consequences" (e.g., stress, turnover, reduced performance; p. 433). Markus presents three theories that implementers may have for why users resist organizational change (concerning management information systems, or MIS, technologies): (a) "the person or subunit may be believed to have resisted because of factors internal to the person or group" (p. 431), (b) "because of factors inherent in the application or system being implemented" (p. 431), or (c) "because of an interaction between characteristics related to the people and characteristics related to the system" (p. 431).

In their study of interorganizational change efforts, Gray and Hay (1986) found that the keys to successful implementation of a national coal mining policy were the establishment of the perceived legitimacy of the project and the inclusion of all key stakeholders. "A stakeholder is viewed to have legitimacy when this individual or group is perceived by others to have the right and the capacity to participate. The right derives from one's being influenced by the issues under consideration; the capacity of a legitimate stakeholder refers to one's possessing some degree of power over the domain" (p. 96).

A second major contingency in implementation processes appears to be the nature of the change. Different authors have attended to the type of change (Ettlie, Bridges, & O'Keefe, 1984; Ettlie & Rubenstein, 1980; Nord & Tucker, 1987; Van de Ven, 1993), the scope of the change (Berman, 1980; Van de Ven, 1993), and specific features of change programs (Roberts-Gray, 1985). The type of change noted most often concerns the "radical" or "routine" nature of the change. Ettlie et al. (1984) define one aspect of this distinction as whether the change involves components that represent "a clear risky departure from existing practice" (p. 683). The scope of the change refers to "the kind and amount of change in the standard behavior of members of the implementing system" (Berman, 1980, p. 214). Although conventional wisdom may suggest that changes smaller in scope can be implemented more simply, Berman (1980) presents evidence to support the opposite conclusion. He cites the findings of a RAND Corporation study of educational innovations, in which "projects demanding little change in teacher behavior were likely to be implemented in a pro forma fashion, whereas ambitious change efforts that engaged the sense of professionalism among teachers could be made to work with appropriate implementation strategies" (p. 215).

In a third area, a set of contingent factors relates to the timing of implementation activities. Tyre and Orlikowski (1994) found that a relatively brief window of opportunity exists for the adaptation of change programs before "the technology and its context of use tend to congeal, often embedding unresolved problems into organizational practice" (p. 98). They found that "even when project members recognized the need for ongoing process modifications and incorporated that into their schedules, opportunities for change narrowed over time" (p. 104). A number of factors militate against lengthy implementation programs, including production pressure, the formation and strengthening of new work norms, and erosion of implementing team membership and enthusiasm. Van de Ven (1993) contends that "interest and commitment wane with time. Thus, after the honeymoon period, innovations terminate at disproportionately higher rates, in proportion to the time required for their implementation" (p. 286). In a separate vein, Smeltzer (1991) has found that timing is a critical factor in the announcement of planned organizational change. He observed that in several organizations, delays in making announcements of downsizing resulted in the development of leaks and rumors. Many employees reported feelings of resentment as a result of hearing about the change from rumors.

Fourth, user participation has been noted as important in the implementation process. Although authors have commented on the potential importance of involving users in development and implementation decisions, there is much that is unknown about just what the outcomes of that involvement will be. "Not only is there debate about the ultimate utility of involving users in design, but there is considerable ignorance as to the mechanics of user involvement" (Leonard-Barton, 1987a, p. 9). Leonard-Barton and Sinha (1993) suggest that recent research has not specified the correct amount of user involvement in organizational change. In their study of the relationship between user involvement in the design and implementation of technologies and subsequent user satisfaction, they found that the interaction between developers and users is critical to user satisfaction. However, they did not find a strictly linear relationship between involvement of users and user satisfaction. They found that "although extensive user involvement does not necessarily predict user satisfaction, . . . very low levels [of involvement] are associated with dissatisfaction" (p. 1125). Cameron, Freeman, and Mishra (1993) found evidence for the efficiency of involving users at the lowest levels of the organization during planned change. In their study of implementation of organizational downsizing, effective downsizing strategies were recommended and designed by lower-level employees. "In effective downsizing, employees themselves analyzed job-by-job and task-by-task the operations of the firm. . . . Members identified redundant jobs and partial tasks, found ways to eliminate organizational fat and improve efficiency, and planned ways in which the changes could be implemented" (p. 51).

In attempting to account for the reasons that user involvement affects user acceptance of and satisfaction with change, Baronas and Louis (1988) propose that "system introduction is perceived by the user as a period of transition during which the normal level of personal control is threatened . . . [and] that activities that restore a user's perception of personal control during system implementation will contribute to user acceptance and other aspects of system success" (p. 111). In their exploratory field study, they examined the effects of three forms of personal control—decision choice, behavioral choice, and predictability—on users' responses to the new system being implemented. Increased perceptions of personal control were positively related to increased satisfaction with the new system being implemented. However, due to restrictions on their experimental design, they were not able to untangle the effects of "perceived control" from possible effects of "experienced support."

In a fifth set of contingency factors, managers' expectations, interpretations, and influence have been found to have significant impact on the results of implementation. King (1974) conducted a field experiment in which managers' expectations for the success of a new innovation were manipulated. Findings revealed that implementation results were related more to the managers' expectations than to qualities of the innovation itself. Isabella (1990) tracked the shifts in managers' interpretations of key stages of change events to demonstrate how their role is altered as the change unfolds. Leonard-Barton and Deschamps (1988) found that managers' influence in encouraging use of new technologies is mediated by characteristics of the users: "Employees whose characteristics incline them to adopt an innovation will do so without management support or urging if it is simply made available. Employees low on these characteristics will await a managerial directive before adopting" (p. 1252).

Numerous other factors on which the outcomes of planned organizational change are contingent, as listed in Table 3.4, have emerged from conceptual development by some authors and from case study review by others. Very few of these contingencies have been empirically investigated in a variety of settings, or with different planned changes. Additionally, there seems to be much less consensus about these remaining contingencies than there is about the contingencies in the areas discussed above.

STRATEGIC PLANNING
AND IMPLEMENTATION

Much of the conceptual and empirical literature we have reviewed in the preceding sections concerning implementation of organizational change is rooted—directly or indirectly—in a larger literature on strategic planning. Broadly speaking, strategic planning entails processes related to organizations' efforts to envision their future and to develop and implement procedures and operations necessary to achieve that future (Goodstein, Nolan, & Pfeiffer, 1993). Hence a considerable amount of planned organizational change emanates *directly* from such strategic processes. Indeed, strategic planning traditionally has been bifurcated into subprocesses leading to strategy "formulation" and subsequent subprocesses entailed in strategy "implementation" (for notable critiques of this dichotomy, see Bourgeois & Brodwin,

1984; Mintzberg, 1994). Alternatively, organizations may use their strategic plans as warrants during processes leading to formal adoption of innovations. For example, organizational innovations concerning production (e.g., total quality management) and human resources (e.g., self-directing work teams, variable incentive pay programs) may never have been part of a strategic plan, but may be adopted because they can be legitimated as "strategic thrusts" that will help an organization achieve its overall strategic goal (Goodstein et al., 1993). Viewed this way, ensuing efforts to implement organizational changes related to such innovations can also be considered to flow *indirectly* from organizations' strategic planning processes. In this section we examine basic and applied scholarship in the first area for the most part: implementation of organizational change resulting directly from strategic planning processes.

Different from long-range planning, which merely forecasts current organizational commitments into the future, strategic planning entails envisioning that future and moving toward it (Goodstein et al., 1993). As Mintzberg (1994) has proposed, strategic planning generally answers three questions: Where should we be going? What is our environment? How shall we get there? Traditional strategic planning subprocesses fit neatly within this trichotomy. Envisioning the future entails planning to plan, conducting value scans, and mission formulation. Determining the environment requires the establishment of monitoring mechanisms and development of methods for integrating them into the planning process. Deciding how the organization will attain its goals requires planning in the areas of business modeling, performance auditing, gap analyses, action and contingency planning, and implementation (see Table 3.5). As should also be apparent from Table 3.5, "implementation" is but one aspect of a series of strategic planning subprocesses focusing primarily on strategy formulation and content (Lyles & Thomas, 1988; Stone & Crittenden, 1993) and anticipating the management of strategic change. Furthermore, the implementation of strategic change typically receives the least attention (Hill & Jones, 1992) because it is so often seen as "following."

The implementation of a strategic plan is generally conceived as involving development of (organizationwide) corporate structure controls, (divisional) business unit controls, and (departmental/managerial) functional controls (Hill & Jones, 1992). More specifically, as Goodstein et al. (1993) conclude, strategic plan implementation of organizational change entails (a) creating a subplan for communicating/reinforcing the strategic plan with all stakeholders, (b) creating/modifying management control systems (e.g., in the areas mentioned by Hill & Jones, 1992) to support the strategic plan, (c) creating/modifying motivation and reward systems for employees that will support the strategic plan, (d) creating/modifying information systems to support the plan, and (e) supplying organizational members with tools and training needed to manage strategically and to act consistently with the plan.

TABLE 3.5
Strategic Planning Perspectives With Special Attention to Implementation

Conceptual Focus	Study	Processes/Subprocesses Specified	Communication Variables?
Framework for analysis of strategic management	Stone & Crittenden, 1993	strategy formulation: mission, goals, initiators, information comprehensiveness, contingencies, formalization	yes
		strategy content: typologies, contingencies	yes
		strategic implementation: communication, structure, contingencies	yes
		organizational performance: governance boards, managers	
Approaches to strategic problem formulation: rational, avoidance, adaptive, political, decisive	Lyles & Thomas, 1988	criteria process biases assumptions evidence performance outcomes	
Strategy implementation	Hill & Jones, 1992	corporate structure business unit functional structure	yes

Managing strategic change	Quinn, 1985	formal-analytic processes: identifying objectives, specification of alternatives, optimizing	yes
		power-behavior processes: multiple goals, politics of strategic decisions, bargaining, satisficing, incrementalism	
Applied strategic planning	Goodstein et al., 1993	planning to plan	
		values scan	yes
		environmental monitoring	yes
		mission formulation	yes
		strategic business modeling	
		performance auditing	
		group analysis	
		integrating action plans	
		contingency planning	
		implementation	yes

PRACTITIONER-ORIENTED LITERATURE

Works that target actual organizational implementers as the primary audience, which we term *practitioner-oriented* literature, are presented in Table 3.6. These works are notable for taking an applied perspective, and generally are dominated by the writers' experienced-based advice for actual implementers. Found primarily in business and management journals that have both academic and practitioner readerships (e.g., *Organizational Dynamics, Harvard Business Review,* and *Sloan Management Review*), these works include themes and recommendations that indicate there is little consensus concerning what practitioners should be doing to implement planned changes. However, there are some commonalities.

One common theme concerns the keys to successful implementation of change in organizations. Authors in this area discuss the "essential elements" for organizational change, including the use of effective champions (Beatty, 1990, 1992); use of cross-functional teams (Beatty, 1990; Beatty & Gordon, 1990); adoption of broader guidelines, such as reconceptualization of the organization (Barczak, Smith, & Wilemon, 1988); pervasive education and training (Beddick, 1983); and proper allocation of organizational resources in an "incremental, goal-oriented, interactive learning process" (Quinn, 1985, p. 82). Unfortunately, much of what has been written in this area has addressed only one type of change, new technologies. Of the 18 works examined for this area of review, 11 address the implementation of new technologies and 7 address manufacturing technologies specifically. This trend may be due to the increased importance and prevalence of new technologies in the workplace, but such advice may be less useful for implementers of other types of planned changes.

A second theme concerns the possible barriers to successful change. Beer, Eisenstat, and Spector (1990) assert that "most change programs don't work because they are guided by a theory of change that is fundamentally flawed" (p. 159). Beer et al. suggest that rather than changes in attitudes bringing about changes in behavior, the opposite is true. Brown (1991) argues that the representation of "change" as an indicator that "they are or have been doing something wrong" (p. 23) can act as a barrier. Blasingame and Weeks (1981) and Bevis (1976) relate first- and secondhand experiences in implementation of manufacturing planning systems in manufacturing organizations. They suggest a variety of potential barriers, including technical inadequacies, ineffective organization, and lack of total commitment. They contend that such barriers can jeopardize the success of a planned change due to a lack of organizational readiness, and can be even more problematic than the change itself. Finally, Leonard-Barton and Kraus (1985) and Mainiero and DeMichiell (1986) discuss factors that can lead to resistance to change, including fear of loss of skills, power, or personal benefit and fear of displacement, incompetence, or helplessness.

TABLE 3.6
Themes in the Practitioner Literature

Foci and Recommendations	*Study*
Themes	
keys to successful change	Argote et al., 1983
	Barczak et al., 1988
	Beatty, 1990, 1992
	Beatty & Gordon, 1990
	Beddick, 1983
	Larkin & Larkin, 1994, 1996
	Quinn, 1985
barriers to successful change	Beer et al., 1990
	Bevis, 1976
	Blasingame & Weeks, 1981
	Brown, 1991
	Larkin & Larkin, 1994, 1996
	Leonard-Barton & Kraus, 1985
	Mainiero & DeMichiell, 1986
models and philosophies	Beer et al., 1990
	DeSanctis & Courtney, 1983
	Goodstein & Burke, 1991
	Larkin & Larkin, 1994
	Lawler, 1995
	Leonard-Barton, 1987a, 1987b
	Leonard-Barton & Kraus, 1985
Recommendations	
Get clear support of management.	Ackerman, 1982
	Argote et al., 1983
	Beatty & Gordon, 1990
	Beddick, 1983
	Blasingame & Weeks, 1981
	DeSanctis & Courtney, 1983
	Quinn, 1985
Join diagnosis and development steps.	Beatty & Gordon, 1990
	Beer et al., 1990
	DeSanctis & Courtney, 1983
	Goodstein & Burke, 1991
	Leonard-Barton & Kraus, 1985
Be responsive and make adjustments.	Ackerman, 1982
	Beddick, 1983
	Beer et al., 1990
	Quinn, 1985
Prepare and train users for new roles.	Argote et al., 1983
	Beatty & Gordon, 1990
	Beddick, 1983
	Goodstein & Burke, 1991

(continued)

TABLE 3.6
Continued

Foci and Recommendations	Study
Anticipate the needs of workers.	Argote et al., 1983
	Beatty & Gordon, 1990
	Blasingame & Weeks, 1981
	Mainiero & DeMichiell, 1986
Communicate the status of the implementation.	Ackerman, 1982
	Beatty & Gordon, 1990
	Brown, 1991
Anticipate potential problems/effects.	Argote et al., 1983
	Beatty & Gordon, 1990
	Mainiero & DeMichiell, 1986
Create interfunctional teams.	Beatty, 1990, 1992
	Beatty & Gordon, 1990
	Beddick, 1983
Implement incrementally.	Beatty & Gordon, 1990
	Mainiero & DeMichiell, 1986
	Quinn, 1985
Ensure the adequacy of existing resources.	Beatty, 1990, 1992
	Beddick, 1983
	Blasingame & Weeks, 1981
Maximize the fit of workers to new roles.	Argote et al., 1983
	Leonard-Barton & Kraus, 1985
	Mainiero & DeMichiell, 1986
Involve users in implementation.	Argote et al., 1983
	Brown, 1991
	Mainiero & DeMichiell, 1986
Utilize a "champion."	Beatty, 1990, 1992
	Beatty & Gordon, 1990
Develop reward programs.	Ackerman, 1982
	Mainiero & DeMichiell, 1986
	Quinn, 1985
Foster cooperation of support personnel.	Argote et al., 1983
	Beatty & Gordon, 1990
	Leonard-Barton, 1987a
Break old patterns.	Barczak et al., 1988
	Goodstein & Burke, 1991
Make a commitment to success.	Bevis, 1976
	Quinn, 1985
Demonstrate the value of innovation.	Argote et al., 1983
	Beatty & Gordon, 1990
Create a shared vision.	Beddick, 1983
	Beer et al., 1990

TABLE 3.6
Continued

Foci and Recommendations	Study
Shift ownership to users.	Beddick, 1983
	Leonard-Barton & Kraus, 1985
Develop change in conjunction with immediate need.	DeSanctis & Courtney, 1983
	Quinn, 1985
Ensure the availability of resources.	Quinn, 1985
Set realistic goals.	Beatty & Gordon, 1990
Create a favorable environment.	Goodstein & Burke, 1991
Involve key stakeholders.	Leonard-Barton, 1987a
Communicate face-to-face.	Larkin & Larkin, 1994, 1996
Communicate "facts" about the change.	Larkin & Larkin, 1994, 1996
Communicate change through immediate supervisors.	Larkin & Larkin, 1994, 1996
Revive employees' "personal compacts" with the organization.	Strebel, 1996

A third major theme in the practitioner-oriented literature on implementing planned change frames the change process according to a particular model or philosophy. For example, Leonard-Barton (1987a, 1987b) and Leonard-Barton and Kraus (1985) characterize change implementation as an "internal marketing campaign." They attribute the success of a change to users' reactions to change and suggest that implementers should introduce change as a new commercial product to improve users' readiness and morale. "Perhaps the easiest way to accomplish [the integration of developer and user needs] is to think of implementation as an internal marketing, not a selling, job. The distinction is important because selling starts with a finished product; marketing with research on user needs and preferences" (p. 103). Beer et al. (1990) suggest that "task realignment" is critical to the success of change: "Companies avoid the shortcomings of programmatic change by concentrating on . . . reorganizing employee roles, responsibilities, and relationships to solve specific business problems" (p. 161). They propose six steps to effective change that are consistent with Leonard-Barton and Kraus's (1985) internal marketing framework, including developing a shared vision of change and fostering commitment through joint diagnosis of business problems. We highlight next some specific recommendations that arise out of the general themes.

An examination of Table 3.6 underscores the wide variety of recommendations in the practitioner literature. Three clusters emerge from the recommendations made for implementers: (a) goals and vision, (b) environment and support, and (c) action steps. Goals and vision recommendations concern creating shared meaning, the joining of diagnosis and development steps, involvement of users in implementation, and breaking old patterns. Recommendations focused on environment and support address managerial support of change and other considerations. Among others, action step recommendations suggest that implementers should be responsive, communicate the status of the implementation, and utilize a "champion."

Several generalizations can be made concerning the recommendations. First, among the nearly 20 articles included in this area of the review, only a few recommendations are shared by more than a few authors. Second, as we noted earlier, most recommendations address the implementer/manager's perspective, whereas very little is said about the means by which other stakeholders participate in the change process. Third, there is a noticeable absence of nontechnology changes (e.g., policy changes, program changes, administrative changes). Fourth, only a handful of the articles make any reference to specific communicative tactics of implementation. For example, an author may suggest "involving key stakeholders" without offering specific tactics for accomplishing this end. These "metarecommendations" offer legitimate areas of interest without providing concrete plans of action.

IMPLEMENTATION LITERATURE:
A REPRISE OF CRITICAL THEMES

The existing literature concerning implementation of planned change is wanting in three important ways. First, although discussions of general approaches to implementation and general types of implementation strategy are numerous, there have been few systematic empirical studies of specific activities that implementers utilize. Studies rarely concentrate on implementers' actual actions in installing planned change programs, such as formation of implementation teams, goal setting, presentation of written documents concerning the change, training methods utilized in preparing users for change, means of gathering feedback and monitoring change responses, practices of incorporating change agents and opinion leaders, negotiation of the parameters of change programs, and assessment of change efforts. Where such topics are present in the literature, they tend to appear in isolation or in small subsets and tend to focus on one type of planned change (e.g., MIS technologies, educational policies) or one specific case of change (see Table 3.7). These empirical limitations inhibit generalization or comparison of findings across types of organizations, types of changes, environmental sectors, and types of implementers. Further, the absence of data concerning the specific activities of implementers precludes theoretical understanding of the critical step of strategy enactment.

TABLE 3.7
Studies of Specific Cases of Planned Changes

Type of Planned Change	Study	Communication Variable?
Technologies		
robot	Argote et al., 1983	yes
computer-aided design system	Beatty & Gordon, 1988	
computer-based production system	Beddick, 1983	
production technology	Ettlie & Rubenstein, 1980	
computer-based vision system	Goodman & Griffith, 1991	yes
expert system	Leonard-Barton, 1987a	yes
structured software	Leonard-Barton, 1987b	yes
word processing system	Mainiero & DeMichiell, 1986	
computer-based office information systems	Mankin et al., 1984	
technology-based training system	Roberts-Gray, 1985	
word processing and office systems	Johnson & Rice, 1987	yes
Administrative programs and changes		
reorganization	Biggart, 1977	
restrictive work-site smoking	Gottlieb et al., 1992	yes
national coal mining policy	Gray & Hay, 1986	
role definition	Gross et al., 1970	yes
management by objectives	Sproull & Hofmeister, 1986	
educational management program	Lindquist & Mauriel, 1989	
downsizing	Cameron et al., 1993	
health care units	Salem & Williams, 1992	yes
Work procedures and practices		
educational curriculum	Leithwood, 1981	
safety review procedures	Marcus, 1988	

Second, much of the literature moves quickly to recommendations of "effective strategies" for implementing planned organizational change without offering thorough descriptions of what implementers actually do and why. The literature is replete with factors that will lead to success—or if ignored lead to failure—but much less is said about why implementers choose the "strategies" or activities they choose, or if they are even conscious of their "strategy" choices. Although some general approaches arguably have been found to be disproportionately successful or unsuccessful, without an understanding of the implementer's perspective it may be premature to give advice. Investigation of implementation activities by different types of implementers (e.g., internal versus external, teams versus individuals, expert versus administrative appointee, voluntary versus involuntary) and by implementers in different types of organizations (e.g., bureaucratic, innovative, dynamic, high energy, highly structured), and of different forms of planned changes, would likely be useful for making practitioner recommendations and providing reasons for the relative success of various implementation approaches.

Third, much like other organizational processes that have been cast as "top-down," the implementation process is most often depicted from a managerial perspective. Similar to socialization models that favor explanations of "shaping," "absorbing," and "breaking in" relatively passive newcomers (Jablin, 1984), researchers in the implementation area have focused on how implementers overcome the resistance of users, or persuade, coerce, or cajole users into adopting change programs as the designers intend. In light of ample evidence suggesting that users will often "reinvent" innovations during the process of internal adoption (Glaser & Backer, 1977; Rice & Rogers, 1980; Rogers, 1983, 1995), and of theoretical models that suggest the prevalence and importance of adaptations, alterations, and modifications during implementation (Dornblaser, Lin, & Van de Ven, 1989; Leonard-Barton, 1988a; Lewis & Seibold, 1993), a more dynamic perspective that highlights the active agency of all organizational members in implementation activities appears most appropriate. The impact of "informal implementers" may be as influential as the efforts of formal implementation teams, if not more so. Just as organizational members have been shown to be active seekers of performance feedback (Ashford, 1986; Ashford & Cummings, 1983), active in "individualizing" work roles during socialization (Jablin, 1984; Wanous, 1980), and active in attempting upward influence (Porter, Allen, & Angle, 1981), they also are likely to be active in their participation in implementation processes, and to be more than passive recipients of implementers' events and messages. This perspective deserves more attention than it has received in the literature.

A RESEARCH AGENDA FOR
COMMUNICATION SCHOLARSHIP

Clearly, a comprehensive communication agenda for the study of implementation of planned organizational change would encompass numerous questions, potential hypotheses, theoretical perspectives, and methodological alternatives. It is not feasible to construct such a comprehensive agenda here. Rather, we propose several targeted communication foci for research in the implementation area (see Table 3.8). We propose that a useful research agenda for communication scholars will focus on (a) interaction surrounding implementation and (b) communication-related structures regarding implementation. Further, we believe that these foci should be investigated both within (c) formal and (d) informal implementation activities.

We highlight these four general foci for three reasons. First, we seek to emphasize the tension between structure and agency. As Reed (1996) has argued, this distinction is one of the most fundamental among social theorists

TABLE 3.8
Communication Agenda for the Study of
Implementation of Planned Organizational Change

	Formal Implementation Activities	*Informal Implementation Activities*
Interaction surrounding implementation	**A**	**B**
information sharing	How are innovations announced? What channels are utilized to provide information about change? What type of information is provided about change? To whom? By whom? In what context?	How do users share understandings/ interpretations of formal information? With whom do they share these impressions? What makes information credible? How is additional information sought out? From whom?
vision and motivation	How is vision for planned change communicated? What formal "campaign" tactics are utilized to set goals and to motivate users?	Do supporters or resisters reframe vision of change? Does interaction among users produce informal vision?
social support	What is said to address fears and anxiety of users? How do implementers monitor reactions to change? Should users encourage "social support" among users?	How is supportive and comforting communication accomplished during change? Is evaluative information about the change communicated during social support? With what effects for users and for change programs?
evaluation/ feedback	How is evaluation and feedback sought from and given to users? What means are utilized to address areas of weakness both in users' performance and in change programs? How do implementers cope with upward feedback that negatively evaluates change programs?	Do users draw upon peer feedback more or less than supervisory feedback? Does informal evaluation of change get transmitted to formal implementers? Does informal evaluation lead to "reinvention"? If so, how does communication aid/deter this process?
Communication-related structures	**C**	**D**
reward structures	What systems are utilized for distribution of rewards and disincentives regarding participation in change? What communication channels are created to maintain reward systems? How do users respond?	How do organizational members informally punish or reward participants or nonparticipants? How are consequences for participation communicated informally?

(continued)

TABLE 3.8
Continued

	Formal Implementation Activities	Informal Implementation Activities
participatory structures	What structures do implementers utilize to involve lower-level employees in change implementation? When are implementation decisions made unilaterally, and when are they participatory in nature? What forms of participation are most productive during change implementation?	What channels do users/nonusers create to participate in implementation of change? How do non-implementation team members gain access to and influence in implementation decision making? How do informal "champions" and "assassins" gain status and influence? What forms of participation best address users' effective and cognitive needs?
role structures	How are users/implementers selected and socialized? What formal role status is accorded to change agents? What support is given to users who experience significant role transitions?	What informal socialization do change agents and users receive? What affects the process by which users adopt new roles? What affects the evaluation of users' roles in terms of informal status and influence?

in general: "Those who emphasize agency focus on an understanding of the social and organizational order that stresses the social practices through which human beings create and reproduce institutions. Those located on the structure side highlight the importance of the objectified external relations and patterns that determine and constrain social interaction within specific institutional forms" (p. 46). In organizational communication scholarship, this tension is evident in the juxtaposition of studies aimed primarily at examination of discourse and communicative practices (e.g., Fairhurst, 1993; Fairhurst et al., 1995; Stohl, 1986) and functions of talk (e.g., Pacanowsky, 1988; Tompkins & Cheney, 1985). This also is true of others that have concentrated on communication structures (e.g., Farace et al., 1977; Monge & Eisenberg, 1987) and organizational structures (e.g., Jablin, 1987a; McPhee, 1985) that give rise to, act as barriers to, or provide frames for discourse. Underlying this juxtaposition is a theoretical fault line between structure and interaction; "between a concept of organization that refers to deterministic structures which condition individual and collective behavior, and a concept that is a theoretical short-hand for consciously fabricated interactional networks through which such structures are generated and reproduced" (Reed, 1996, p. 46). This process/structure distinction is analytically useful for exploring how interaction is enabled (and constrained) by structures endemic to innovation implementation, and for examining the recursivity of interactional practices and structure. In analytically separating interaction from structure, we run the risk, as Whittington (1994) observes, of either individual reductionistic or collectivist deterministic accounts of innovation implementation. More fundamentally, analytically separating the literature in this way obscures the mutually constituted and constituting character of interactional processes and institutional structures in producing and reproducing organization. As Giddens (1979, 1984) has argued in his analysis of structuration, production and reproduction of social systems inheres in actors' use of structural resources within the streams of their interactive practices. Unfortunately, none of the studies we have reviewed reflects this duality. Hence, and ultimately, theoretical and empirical treatments that simultaneously examine structure and process will be the *most* productive course in this area.

A second reason we have developed these specific foci is related to the need to direct attention toward specific tactics and implementation behaviors that implementers utilize when enacting planned organizational change. We have developed seven subtopics within the process and structure categories: information sharing, vision and motivation, social support, evaluation/feedback, reward structures, participatory structures, and role structures. These subtopics direct our attention to very specific arenas for action. As we suggested earlier, this "action orientation" is lacking in the majority of the implementation literature to date. Certainly, communication scholars are well equipped to address questions concerning behavioral adaptations, strategies, and tactics. These subtopics are meant as suggested starting points for this new orientation within the literature on implementation of planned change.

Third, as we noted earlier, the implementation literature has reflected top-down, managerial initiatives and strategies to the near exclusion of lower-level employees' active role in implementation in an informal vein. To highlight the separate issues and concerns that might be important regarding "planned, official" implementation and those having to do with "unplanned, unofficial, spontaneous" implementation, we include the "formal" and "informal" categories as the other dimension of this research agenda. We hope that our highlighting of this dichotomy will encourage exploration of both "worlds" of implementation and investigation of the interplay between them.

Interaction Surrounding Implementation

The questions in quadrants A and B of Table 3.8 represent potential topics of inquiry for communication researchers concerned with interaction during both formal and informal implementation activities. Research questions in quadrant A focus on the formal interaction surrounding organizational implementers' introduction of planned change, monitoring of reactions to change, promotion of planned change, and adjustments to users of planned change. The proposed questions are concerned with what implementers talk about, when, with whom, why, and with what results. The quadrant B questions focus on how informal implementation occurs through the day-to-day "unplanned" and "spontaneous" interactions of those who promote, evaluate, make sense of, and resist planned change efforts.

Information Sharing

Uncertainty has been noted by communication scholars, both within and beyond the planned change literature, as a key concern in organizations (Eisenberg & Riley, 1988; Feldman & March, 1981; Redding, 1972). Staw (1980) argues that in attempting to gain a sense of rationality and justification, individuals have expectations of and seek control over the environment. Goals of control and predictability, Staw notes, direct much of organizational members' efforts. Also, theory and empirical studies of newcomer behavior (Comer, 1991; Miller & Jablin, 1991; Morrison, 1993) and feedback and impression management (Ashford, 1986; Ashford & Cummings, 1983; Ashford & Tsui, 1991) suggest that organizational members are persistent and intentional seekers of information.

Previous studies underscore the importance of addressing members' information needs during organizational change. For example, Covin and Kilmann (1990) compiled a list of 900 issues that most affect the success or failure of large-scale organizational change. They found that "failure to share information or to inform people adequately of what changes are necessary and why they are necessary were viewed as having a highly negative impact. Secrecy, dishonesty, and the failure to assess dysfunctional rumors were also issues of concern" (p. 239). Other empirical work has established the role of information in reducing anxiety about change (Miller & Monge, 1985; Smeltzer, 1991) and in increasing willingness to participate in planned change (Miller et al., 1994). Information concerns can sometimes be so strong that any information, even that which negatively evaluates the change, is considered more helpful than no information (Miller & Monge, 1985). In another study, Lewis and Seibold (1996) found that negative evaluation of implementation information was related to users' being more "other-focused" in their behavioral responses to the presence of change programs. This may be due to users' need to talk to others informally to compensate for poor formal information.

Some scholars have distinguished between formal and informal sources and channels for reducing uncertainty during organizational change (Johnson, 1990; Miller et al., 1994; Papa & Papa, 1990). In their study of the effects of messages about change, Papa and Papa (1990) conclude that more research is needed into the relative weight and importance of informal and formal information about change: "It may be possible that employees form perceptions of a change as soon as they hear about it from management or through the grapevine. If this is true, it may be important for managers or trainers to consider how they initially spread information about a change" (p. 37). Papa and Papa found that employees' receiving task-related messages and receiving negative evaluations of the new technology were the strongest predictors of employee productivity with a new technology.

Both Papa and Papa (1990) and Miller et al. (1994) imply that more information-sharing opportunities for users should be created and encouraged by formal implementers. Because employees are "active participants who seek additional information about change and discuss it among themselves instead [of] being passive recipients who must decide whether or not to support change" (Miller et al., 1994, pp. 72-73), perhaps "employees should be encouraged to interact with one another to clarify directions given during training, and overcome problems related to using a new computer on the job. Managers can help by making it easier for employees to find time to talk to one another" (Papa & Papa, 1990, p. 37).

Questions in quadrant A of Table 3.8, then, are aimed at incorporating into studies of implementation of planned change what we know about the importance of information. We can begin by asking how formal implementers actually disseminate information to users and potential users, how they announce change programs of various sorts, and what types of information they perceive to be necessary to share with users. Questions in quadrant B give us insight into the information gathering and dissemination of informal networks and channels. How formal information is translated on the organizational grapevine and how individuals become influential in convincing other users or would-be users to participate in change programs or resist them are of concern here. What counts as "quality" and "useful" information or "credible" information sources may also be a valuable set of investigative questions in this quadrant.

Vision and Motivation

Several authors in the planned change literature have noted the importance of vision and motivation (Fairhurst, 1993; Ford & Ford, 1995; King, 1974). Ford and Ford (1995) argue that one of the key breakdowns in planned change efforts is the "failure to create a shared understanding among participants to produce a clear statement of the conditions of satisfaction for the change" (p. 557). There is also evidence to suggest that leaders' expectations for success, once translated into action by subordinates, are strongly and positively related to successful change. When managers' expectations for the success or failure of change programs were manipulated in King's (1974) field experiment, higher expectations were found to be related to higher productivity. King opines: "These managers transmitted their own strong feelings about the efficacy of the innovation to their employees, created mutual expectancy of high performance, and greatly stimulated productivity. There is the implication, then, that a unique characteristic of these managers was their ability to *communicate* high performance expectancy that subordinates fulfilled" (p. 228; emphasis added). Finally, Cameron et al. (1993) found that downsizing efforts were most effective in organizations that had "dynamic, competent, knowledgeable leaders who articulated a clear, motivating vision of the future . . . [and when leaders] (1) excited and motivated employees, (2) praised them, (3) used symbolic means to provide a vision of future possibilities for them, and (4) remained accessible and visible to them" (pp. 49-50).

Fairhurst (1993) notes the importance of grassroots involvement in creating and promoting "vision" around organizational change programs. In a discourse analysis of an organization implementing a total quality program, she highlights how leaders may fail to serve as good resources for organizational members in providing information that would help them make sense of the vision or reduce conflict: "As such, the discourse gives us a unique look as to how visions may be cast aside. Specifically, it does not appear that individuals abandon the vision in a single, momentous decision. Rather, it takes place in a series of interactional moments where a specific problem at a specific point in time is poorly addressed" (p. 365). One implication of Fairhurst's findings may be that vision is as much a matter of daily informal interaction among organizational members as of formal "organized" informational campaigns.

The research questions proposed in quadrant A of Table 3.8 concern the means that implementers utilize to create and communicate formal goals and vision to users and potential users of change programs. As the studies reviewed above suggest, this is a key function of successful implementation efforts. However, there are likely to be important differences in how various types of organizations, implementers, and stakeholders attempt to communicate vision and to motivate users. Do these strategies differ systematically by type of planned change? By organizational features? By implementer characteristics (e.g., internal versus external change agents)? Investigation of both the intended strategies and the actual communicative behavior of implementers are important arenas for research. The comparison of strategies to behavior may be helpful in accounting for implementation failures and successes.

Questions in quadrant B encourage investigators to examine how vision is framed by users of change programs. Extension of Fairhurst's work within different organizational contexts, with various types of planned change, and with an assortment of user types could be important starting points. Does interaction among users produce "alternative visions" of planned change? What are the techniques and behaviors of supporters and resisters of change with regard to framing the goals of change programs? Is informal "propaganda" a means that "innovation assassins" (Leonard-Barton, 1987a) utilize to reframe or resist the efforts of formal implementers? What role does interaction play in the "translation" of formally created vision into the day-to-day actions of users?

Social Support

Miller (1995) distinguishes among three functions of social support: emotional support, informational support, and instrumental support. Each helps organizational members to cope with uncertainty, conflict, stress, and workload demands. Evidence within the organizational change literature suggests the importance of social support, especially from peers, in effective coping with change programs. In Ashford's (1988) study of coping during organizational transitions, "sharing worries and concerns" appeared to be the most effective strategy serving as a buffer against stress. Ashford concludes that "this may be one strategy individuals use to gain the social support found to be so helpful in stressful situations" (p. 31). She further suggests that "managers can promote the use of this coping mechanism by deliberately creating norms that encourage employees to share their worries and concerns" (p. 31). In contrast, although Papa and Papa (1990) acknowledge that complaining or venting can serve an important function in the workplace, they caution that "it can also lead to motivation problems and poor performance with a new system" (p. 36). They conclude that "managers may wish to discourage employees from making the types of evaluations that are likely to negatively influence the motivation of coworkers trying to adapt to a new technology" (p. 36).

Clearly, opinion is divided on the appropriate application of research on communication of social support during adjustment to change. However, there is little doubt that social information, which may be communicated while users convey social support, may have important effects on users' attitudes and emotions about change (Ashford, 1988; Miller & Monge, 1985), willingness to participate in change programs (Miller et al., 1994), and productivity within change programs (Papa & Papa, 1990).

Questions raised in quadrant A of Table 3.8 propose some tentative steps in investigating the role of formal implementation in providing social support mechanisms. We know very little about the context and manner in which implementers may be able to provide or encourage supportive communication among new participants in change programs. Although organizational members' needs for training, skills acquisition, and informational needs are addressed in the implementation literature somewhat, the potential importance of addressing their emotional needs has not been recognized. How implementers should monitor users' reactions to change programs, and then how best to address users' fears and anxieties, is unclear.

Questions in quadrant B address the need to learn more about how social support functions within informal networks. Does supportive communication during change necessarily or predominantly involve "gripe sessions" that may overemphasize negative information about change? Or do users attempt to focus on the positive points when empathizing with coworkers? What are the relative effects of evaluative information that is conveyed in this comforting context? Does this information have effects similar to evaluative information given outside of a comforting context? Research seeking answers to these questions would aid in identifying the functional and dysfunctional consequences of group and peer support among users.

Evaluation/Feedback

Strikingly little has been written within the planned organizational change literature regarding the communication of evaluation and feedback. Research reveals that feedback serves a number of needs for individuals and for organizations, including improvement of performance, reduction of uncertainty, enhancement of worker self-image, and management of self-presentation goals (Ashford & Cummings, 1983). We also know that individuals actively seek feedback within organizational contexts (Ashford, 1986, 1993; Ashford & Cummings, 1983; Ashford & Tsui, 1991).

Individuals vary in their frequency of feedback-seeking behavior. Ashford (1986) argues that those who lack self-confidence may be less likely to seek feedback; such individuals are "more likely to fear receiving negative evaluations and to regard their social environments as threatening" (p. 470). There also may be risks attached to seeking feedback, including the potential for embarrassment, loss of face, portrayal of self as weak and uncertain, subjection to ego-deflating evaluative information, and loss of energy and time in seeking feedback (Ashford, 1986, p. 471). Further, Ashford found that organizational members with long tenure seek feedback less frequently than do those with shorter tenure. She speculates that the former individuals may fear that seeking feedback can undermine their "standing as confident and self-assured veterans in the eyes of others" (p. 478).

Members may seek feedback from different sources within organizations and may attend to feedback information differently. Ashford (1993) found that individuals reported emphasizing positive feedback over negative feedback, and "company/supervisor" feedback over other sources of feedback (coworkers, self/task, other/unspecified). In a second study, Ashford (1993) found that when asked about their use of feedback with respect to a specific goal—that of career advancement—a sample of managers reported that the most important cues were those representing negative consequences (i.e., being denied a raise), transmitted by their superiors and companies, and indirect negative cues from coworkers. Of least importance were positive coworker cues. How these results may have been affected by the narrow context of the question (i.e., career advancement) is unclear, but the evidence is suggestive that both types and sources of feedback may vary in salience and usefulness depending on the context in which the feedback is sought and given.

Evaluation and feedback can be viewed from at least two perspectives within the context of planned change. First, users' performance with new technologies, techniques, and programs is likely to be evaluated, and feedback may be given to correct deficiencies and/or to praise preferred performance models. Second, users may develop informal evaluations of change programs and may upwardly communicate those evaluations to implementers in the form of feedback. Both of these evaluation/feedback processes should be examined by communication researchers in the context of planned change. Questions in quadrant A ask how evaluation and feedback is sought from, and given to, users of planned change programs. How is performance feedback received by users? What are the factors that most influence perceptions of it as credible and useful feedback? How do implementers address concerns that users raise about change programs, and what are the most effective ways to do so? It is likely that many implementers hear of the complaints and frustrations of users, and then are offered suggestions for improving change programs. How are such evaluations communicated, and who among users are most likely to come forward with feedback of a negative and positive nature?

In quadrant B we raise questions concerning the consequences of informal evaluation of change programs and the use of feedback-seeking strategies by users. For example, does "reinvention" occur more often in organizations where informal evaluation is embraced, or where it is ignored by upper management? What sources of evaluation are considered by users to be most credible and useful? And do users rely most on the feedback of peers, supervisors, experts, or implementers in adjusting performance during planned change?

Communication-Related Structures

The questions in quadrants C and D of Table 3.8 represent potential topics of inquiry for communication researchers concerned with both formal and informal communication structures related to implementation. The research questions within quadrant C focus on the formal structures related to distribution of rewards, organization and maintenance of participation, and creation of roles as they are invoked and designed by *implementers* during introduction of planned change. Quadrant D questions are concerned with the emergent structures that may be created by *users* to compensate for lapses in formal structures or to augment existing formal structures.

Reward Structures

Both expectancy theory and equity theory have been utilized to explain the effects of motivation, rewards, and punishments within organizations. "Expectancy Theory states that an individual's effort on the job can be predicted from his or her beliefs about the effects of job performance and his or her value for organizational rewards. Equity Theory suggests that individuals look to others in determining whether their own input/outcome ratio is fair" (Miller, 1995, p. 174). Although communication scholarship has made considerable effort to explore and explain processes of feedback giving and motivation in organizational settings, far less attention has been paid to formal structures that organizations utilize to create, allocate, and challenge rewards and sanctions (e.g., promotional systems, bonus programs, appraisal systems, grievance procedures) and the communication channels manifested within those structures.

There is some evidence suggesting the importance of formal reward systems in predicting the success or failure of implementation of planned change. For example, formal reward systems have been found to affect the ways in which individuals react to new technologies (Leonard-Barton, 1987b; Mainiero & DeMichiell, 1986). Also, findings reveal that intrinsic rewards (e.g., increased accuracy, reliability) may have different effects from extrinsic rewards created by formal reward systems (Davis, Bagozzi, & Warshaw, 1992). Further, Griffith (1995) proposes that outcomes such as pay, recognition, type of work, and satisfaction are balanced against what users believe they will get in terms of change outcomes, and that this calculation affects their participation in planned change.

In view of the potential motivational effects of reward structures during implementation, and given the paucity of investigations into communication channels associated with reward structures, several questions for addressing formal and informal reward structures are posed for researchers. Questions in quadrant C focus researchers' attention on the creation and maintenance of formal systems for distributing rewards and disincentives to users and non-users. How are rewards and disincentives communicated to users? What characteristics of these systems are related to fairness? To equity? To effectiveness? To motivation? What upward, downward, and/or lateral communication channels are created in the enactment of rewards and punishments? Are rewards and punishments distributed by implementers, supervisors, peers, or experts most effective in reinforcing desired behavior?

Questions in quadrant D concern users' informal reward structures. Do users develop informal means of punishing or rewarding others for participation in change programs? Do these informal reward/punishment structures outweigh the effects of formal systems? How are informal rewards and sanctions communicated? Can implementers counteract the negative impacts of "innovation assassins" who wield influence through such informal structures?

Participatory Structures

Increasingly, organizations are implementing meaningful employee involvement in matters that affect their work and organizational practices for financial, philosophical, contractual, and other reasons (see Appelbaum & Batt, 1994; Lawler, 1995; Seibold & Shea, in press). Concerning employee involvement during organizational change, Cotton (1993) argues, "A highly involved workforce is essential to implementing many of the new technologies, techniques, and practices used in organizations today. Employees must be involved if they are to understand the need for the innovations and how they operate; they must be involved if they are to be committed to changing their behaviors to work in new, improved ways" (pp. vii-viii). Miller and Monge's (1986) meta-analysis of employee participation studies reveals a strong relationship between employee satisfaction and participative climate. Other research indicates that participation has positive effects on job involvement and organizational commitment (Monge & Miller, 1988). Some research has found support for a link between participation and productivity (Cotton, Vollrath, Froggatt, Lengnick-Hall, & Jennings, 1988; Miller & Monge, 1986), although the relationship may be contingent on the form of participation (Cotton, 1993).

Participation within organizations comes in varying degrees (Cotton, 1993; Cotton et al., 1988; Monge & Miller, 1988). Monge and Miller (1988) caution against assuming that more participation is always better: "Like theorists advocating contingency models of participation, we should look carefully at the situations and individuals for which participation is most appropriate" (p. 224). For example, Marshall and Stohl (1993) found that the communication individuals have with managers is of particular importance, because "those individuals who cultivate communicative relationships with managers are more likely to acquire relevant information" (p. 397).

Opportunities to participate, however, are not always seized by employees. Neumann (1989) identifies several factors that militate against participation. For example, she argues that "frequently, primary organizational decision-making processes have little connection with an enterprise's participative efforts. Most participative schemes run parallel to the decision-making processes of the organization" (p. 185). This "parallel structure" that operates alongside the formal bureaucracy may discourage employees from participation. "As long as the real decisions of the organization get made via the chain-of-command, then the participative effort will be perceived as less important than daily operations" (p. 186). Neumann suggests that in order for employees to embrace change, truly empowering participative structures must be in place. However, "most participative efforts invite subordinates to try to influence those who have the authority to exercise power, that is, those who make the important, substantive decisions" (p. 187; see Stohl, 1995, for an analysis of this participation "paradox").

The literature on employee involvement and participation is voluminous indeed. What even this brief outline of some important findings suggests is that simplistic advice to implementers to "involve users in decisions about planned change" is imprecise at best and inappropriate at worst. Literature addressing the need for user participation during change efforts (see Baronas & Louis, 1988; Cameron et al., 1993; Leonard-Barton, 1987a, 1987b; Leonard-Barton & Sinha, 1993; Zaltman & Duncan, 1977) has not yet thoroughly investigated the relative advantages and disadvantages of various forms of participation, the influence of organizational structures on the perceived effectiveness of participatory programs, or the specific contingencies that most affect users' willingness to participate in change implementation. Communication scholars are well positioned to contribute to questions of how participation may hinder or help during organizational planned change.

Several questions within quadrants C and D address how implementers create and maintain participatory structures and how users informally gain access to decision making concerning planned change. For example, when are implementation decisions made unilaterally and when are participatory structures likely to be used? What forms of participation are most productive and which are responded to most positively by users? As a discipline, communication has much to contribute in specifying the means by which participative interaction takes place, both formally and informally, and in identifying the important contingencies that affect the impacts that participation has on individuals, organizations, and change programs (see Seibold & Shea, in press).

Role Structures

Planned organizational change often involves temporary and/or permanent alteration of job duties, role relationships, required skills, and status of users and implementers alike. Activities undertaken by implementers to introduce planned changes are directed at shaping attitudes and values concerning the innovation and at specifying appropriate behavior regarding the innovation. Research on organizational socialization suggests that management of intergroup role conflicts and acquisition of work group norms and values are critical in the socialization of members to new roles (Feldman, 1981). Introduction of planned change also may alter formal and informal networks and role relationships within organizations. Barley's (1990) study of the introduction of new technology revealed that innovations "initially modify tasks, skills, and other nonrelational aspects of roles. These modifications, in turn, shape role relations. Altered role relations either transform or buttress the social networks that constitute occupational and organizational structure" (p. 70).

In Lewis and Seibold's (1993) study of a program innovation in a large manufacturing plant, a line technician position was created in which previously separated functions of production (quality control, mechanical repair, and mechanical maintenance) were combined into one role. Adoption of the "line technician program" made two other positions obsolete. The subsequent necessity of reassignment, retraining, and reskilling of numerous employees became a great source of tension in the organization and posed significant problems for implementers of the program. All of the transitioning employees and many of their coworkers needed to adapt to new roles.

Lewis and Seibold (1993) have identified two factors that may moderate the effects of socialization and lead to lessened homogeneity in attitudes about planned change: (a) variation in exposure to socialization processes and

(b) congruency between informal and formal socialization strategies. They found that "variation in exposure to structured implementation activities resulted in creation of several in-groups and out-groups (e.g., those with mechanical expertise and those without; those who were involved in designing implementation activities and those who were not)" (p. 341). Lack of formal socialization for many transitioning "users" of the line technician program also led to confusion and inconsistencies in role performance. "The line technicians created their own roles based upon what they thought was intended, what they wanted to have as their role, or what they observed as the norm within their significant peer group" (p. 341). Line technicians coped with apparent inconsistencies between informal and formal expectations by "avoiding confrontations with other out-group users who were unhelpful . . . and recruited new sources of in-group support" (p. 342). These coping strategies led to rampant inconsistencies in job performance, skill acquisition, training, and evaluation of new line technicians.

When socialization of users into change programs constitutes significant role transition, there may be added stress on the users. The literature addressing intraorganizational role transitions indicates a clear connection between this form of career change and the negative consequences of increased anxiety, uncertainty, and stress (Ashford & Taylor, 1990; Feldman & Brett, 1983). In addition, research has found that job changers (intraorganizational transitioners) have different reactions during socialization and use coping strategies that are different from those of new hires, and that job changers try harder to control and change their job situations than do new hires (Feldman & Brett, 1983). Ashford and Taylor (1990) argue that transitioning employees negotiate their roles during the change process: "The nature of individuals' negotiations to change organizational demands appears to be a function of the power they perceive themselves to have at the time of negotiation. Negotiations conducted around transition points will tend to be formal and direct [simple requests]. . . . At other times, negotiations are likely to be informal and indirect [ignoring unacceptable job duties, excelling in desirable ones]" (p. 21). Unresolved negotiation of unacceptable demands may result in the exit of transitioners.

The contexts of transitions also may be significant. Lewis (1996) argues that the context of a role transition (e.g., as a group or individual event; the direction of the transition as a promotion, demotion, or lateral move; the desirability of the transition) can have significant impacts both for the individual making the move and for others within the organization who witness it. Lewis points to the important differences between temporary workers and permanent workers, and between new hires, promoted, and demoted individuals in comparable positions as examples of context that matters: "These examples serve to remind us that organizational positions are more than the sum of their job descriptions and official place in the organizational chart. Expectations of positional occupants are made both from the skills and abilities of individual occupants and from the organizational expectations of role senders around them. . . . Further, expectations for occupants are made from the history of the position and the trends of occupancy" (p. 2). Planned change programs may trigger important context variables that can alter the ways in which new roles are perceived by users.

To date, theoretical and empirical evidence strongly supports the importance of socialization of users during change implementation. Simple orientation sessions and formal training programs are likely to be incomplete in addressing the complex needs of new users and, in some cases, may be misguided and useless. Informal work group socialization, and the strong social bonding that often occurs there, has powerful potential to influence attitudes about any program, policy, or technology that affects individuals' work or work unit. Research provides evidence for the strong influence of peers during socialization (Comer, 1991). Further, the context in which users are asked or forced to make significant role transitions may create great stress for them and for coworkers, supervisors, and subordinates.

Questions raised in quadrants C and D of Table 3.8 concern the means by which role transitions and socialization for new role occupants are managed formally and informally. Communication is a primary vehicle through which transitioners learn of new role behaviors, new values, and new norms and develop self-image within new positions in organizations. How these processes are affected by the context of planned organizational change and how they come to have significant impacts on planned change programs are important issues for communication scholars. How change agents, implementers, and users come to have roles communicated to them and how they "negotiate" role expectations may have great significance for the ultimate success or failure of change programs.

Planning Processes, Implementation, and Communication

The literature reviewed in the section on implementation of strategic plans highlights the critical tasks entailed in the implementation of strategic change, including developing a plan for the process of reaching stakeholders; creating information, control, motivation, and reward systems that support the plan; and supplying organizational members with the appropriate tools and training they need to act in accord with the plan (Goodstein et al., 1993). In turn, this suggests the plethora of communication-related issues we have sketched above: information sharing, feedback, support, influence, participation, and collaboration. Indeed, *planning* is so integral to organizational change that it can be thought of as a third dimension to the agenda proposed in Table 3.8. However, as reflected in Table 3.5, more attention has been given to the role of communication in prior steps in the planning of strategic change (scanning, mission formulation, and bargaining surrounding key organizational services and initiatives). Even then, exacting analyses by communication scholars of the "processes" embedded in planning routines, especially top management team effects on the formulation and implementation of planned strategic change, are needed.

Increasingly, empirical research is underscoring the likelihood that an organization's top management "team" may have a greater effect on the organization's change than its CEO (Finkelstein & Hambrick, 1990). Top management teams are the locus for the filtering of information vital to the organization, for development of interpretive frames, and for strategic change, innovation, diversification, decision making, and persistence (Bantel, 1994; Hurst, Rush, & White, 1989). These findings are consistent with, indeed grow from, organizational researchers' long-standing interest in the effects of top management teams on organizational performance (Hambrick & Mason, 1984). Underpinning that research, as well as more specific work on the role of top management teams in influencing organizations' strategic planning, is the implicit question of what makes top management teams effective or ineffective in fostering and facilitating organizational change (O'Reilly, Snyder, & Boothe, 1993). Unfortunately, from the standpoint of communication, organizational behavior researchers in this area— consistent with their disciplinary roots in sociology and social psychology—have looked no further than characteristics of the teams' composition. Couched within demography theory (Pfeffer, 1983), studies have examined management team heterogeneity (O'Reilly, Caldwell, & Barnett, 1989), age (Bantel, 1994), and tenure (Finkelstein & Hambrick, 1990), among other features. Studies of communication processes in top management teams are virtually nonexistent, even in light of proposals that the effects of demographic traits on organizational planning and performance are mediated by members' cognitive processing abilities, experiences together as a team, and interpersonal dynamics, such as communication, conflict, and ability to reach consensus (e.g., O'Reilly et al., 1993). In particular, investigations of factors commonly associated with group influence (Seibold, Meyers, & Sunwolf, 1996)—and linking such "process" studies with important "outcomes" (Gouran, 1990; Jarboe, 1988) related to planning performance—would make important contributions to the communication literature as well as the research on planning for organizational change. What are the formal and emergent patterns of leadership in team planning processes, and are they reflective of other leadership dynamics in the organization? How do decision-making structures in the planning process interpenetrate (Poole, Seibold, & McPhee, 1996) other organizational structures in general, and other planned change structures in particular? To what degree are decision-making processes concerning planning affected by the nature of the change being planned, organizational factors, and those responsible for implementing the change? In what ways do organizational members not formally involved with the implementation of change influence implementation decision making?

CONCLUSION

Our central goal in this chapter has been to demonstrate how a communication perspective can enhance our understanding of implementation activities and strategies, as well as the factors that influence when and how they are utilized in organizations. We have reviewed major areas of research on implementation of planned organizational change and attempted to demonstrate the lack of a communication perspective on change implementation in the current literature in six areas: (a) general approaches to implementation, (b) strategies and tactics for change implementation, (c) characteristics and factors related to change agents, (d) contingencies that affect implementation, (e) strategic planning and implementation, and (f) themes and recommendations in the practitioner literature. In general, the literature offers little empirical evidence of implementers' specific activities, prematurely moves to recommendations without empirical evidence, and represents an overly "top-down" orientation that ignores the informal "bottom-up" influences of lower-level employees during planned change.

Communication researchers are well positioned to make a significant contribution to the change implementation literature, as they have in many other areas of the change and innovation literature. Research efforts of communication scholars have proven insightful in explaining invention, design, adoption, and responses to planned organizational change. Communication is fundamental in the introduction and enactment of planned change efforts in organizations—implementation—as well as in the other areas of the change process. We have proposed a set of research targets for communication scholars in the area of planned change implementation: (a) interaction during implementation, (b) communication-related structures, and (c) formal and (d) informal implementation activities. These four foci, and the questions they may be used to generate, direct communication scholars to areas where they are likely to be able to make significant contributions to the implementation literature. Research within this framework, aimed at investigating information sharing, vision and motivation, social support, evaluation/feedback, reward structures, participatory structures, role structures, and planning, will significantly enhance the planned change implementation literature by addressing the weaknesses raised above and by specifying how change really "happens"—through the communicative processes that are requisite to organizing.

REFERENCES

Note: Asterisks indicate studies included only in the tables.

*Ackerman, L. S. (1982, Winter). Transition management: An in-depth look at managing complex change. *Organizational Dynamics, 11,* 46-66.

Albrecht, T. L., & Hall, B. (1981). Relational and content differences between elites and outsiders in innovation networks. *Human Communication Research, 7,* 535-561.

Albrecht, T. L., & Ropp, V. A. (1984). Communicating about innovation in networks of three U.S. organizations. *Journal of Communication, 4,* 78-91.

Appelbaum, E., & Batt, R. (1994). *The new American workplace: Transforming work systems in the U.S.* Ithaca, NY: Cornell University Press.

*Argote, L., Goodman, P. S., & Schkade, D. (1983). The human side of robotics: How workers react to a robot. *Sloan Management Review, 24*(3), 31-41.

Armenakis, A. A., Harris, S. G., & Mossholder, K. W. (1993). Creating readiness for organizational change. *Human Relations, 46,* 681-703.

Ashford, S. J. (1986). Feedback-seeking in individual adaptation: A resource perspective. *Academy of Management Journal, 29,* 465-487.

Ashford, S. J. (1988). Individual strategies for coping with stress during organizational transitions. *Journal of Applied Behavioral Science, 24,* 19-36.

Ashford, S. J. (1993). The feedback environment: An exploratory study of cue use. *Journal of Organizational Behavior, 14,* 201-224.

Ashford, S. J., & Cummings, L. L. (1983). Feedback as an individual resource: Personal strategies of creating information. *Organizational Behavior and Human Performance, 32,* 370-398.

Ashford, S. J., & Taylor, M. S. (1990). Adaptation to work transitions: An integrative approach. In K. M. Rowland & G. R. Ferris (Eds.), *Research in personnel and human resources management* (Vol. 8, pp. 1-39). Greenwich, CT: JAI.

Ashford, S. J., & Tsui, A. S. (1991). Self-regulation for managerial effectiveness: The role of active feedback seeking. *Academy of Management Journal, 34,* 251-280.

Bach, B. W. (1989). The effect of multiplex relationships upon innovation adoption: A reconsideration of Rogers' model. *Communication Monographs, 56,* 133-150.

Bantel, K. A. (1994). Strategic planning openness: The role of top team demography. *Group and Organization Management, 19,* 406-424.

Barczak, G., Smith, C., & Wilemon, D. (1988, Autumn). Managing large-scale organizational change. *Organizational Dynamics, 17,* 23-35.

Barker, J. R., & Tompkins, P. K. (1994). Identification in the self-managing organization: Characteristics of target and tenure. *Human Communication Research, 21,* 223-240.

Barley, S. R. (1990). The alignment of technology and structure through roles and networks. *Administrative Science Quarterly, 35,* 61-103.

Baronas, A. M. K., & Louis, M. R. (1988, March). Restoring a sense of control during implementation: How user involvement leads to system acceptance. *Management Information Systems Quarterly, 12,* 111-124.

Beatty, C. A. (1990). Implementing advanced manufacturing technology. *Business Quarterly, 55*(2), 46-50.

Beatty, C. A. (1992). Implementing advanced manufacturing technologies: Rules of the road. *Sloan Management Review, 33*(4), 49-60.

*Beatty, C. A., & Gordon, J. R. M. (1988). Barriers to the implementation of CAD/CAM systems. *Sloan Management Review, 29*(4), 25-33.

Beatty, C. A., & Gordon, J. R. M. (1990). Advanced manufacturing technology: Making it happen. *Business Quarterly, 54*(4), 46-53.

*Beckhard, R. (1975). Strategies for large system change. *Sloan Management Review, 16*(2), 43-55.

Beddick, J. F. (1983). Elements of success: MRP implementation. *Production and Inventory Management, 24,* 26-32.

Beer, M., Eisenstat, R. A., & Spector, B. (1990). Why change programs don't produce change. *Harvard Business Review, 68*(6), 158-166.

Berman, P. (1980). Thinking about programmed and adaptive implementation: Matching strategies to situations. In H. M. Ingram & D. E. Mann (Eds.), *Why policies succeed or fail* (pp. 205-227). Beverly Hills, CA: Sage.

Bevis, G. E. (1976). A management viewpoint on the implementation of an MRP system. *Production and Inventory Management, 17,* 105-116.

*Biggart, N. W. (1977). The creative-destructive process of organizational change: The case of the post office. *Administrative Science Quarterly, 22,* 410-426.

Bikson, T., & Gutek, B. (1984). *Implementation of office automation.* Santa Monica, CA: RAND Corporation.

Blackler, F., & Brown, C. (1986). Alternative models to guide the design and introduction of the new information technologies into work organizations. *Journal of Occupational Psychology, 59,* 287-313.

Blasingame, J. W., & Weeks, J. W. (1981). Behavioral dimensions of MRP change: Assessing your organization's strengths and weaknesses. *Production and Inventory Management, 22,* 81-95.

Bourgeois, L. J., & Brodwin, D. R. (1984). Strategic implementation: Five approaches to an elusive phenomenon. *Strategic Management Journal, 5,* 241-264.

Brimm, M. (1988, Autumn). Risky business: Why sponsoring innovations may be hazardous to career health. *Organizational Dynamics, 17,* 28-41.

Brown, R. J. (1991). Cooperatives in managerial transition: What is the least disruptive way to introduce change? *Management Quarterly, 32,* 22-24.

Cameron, K. S., Freeman, S. J., & Mishra, A. K. (1993). Downsizing and redesigning organizations. In G. P. Huber & W. H. Glick (Eds.), *Organizational change and redesign* (pp. 19-63). New York: Oxford University Press.

Case, T. L., Vandenberg, R. J., & Meredith, P. H. (1990). Internal and external change agents. *Leadership and Organizational Development Journal, 11*(1), 4-15.

Cheney, G., Block, B. L., & Gordon, B. S. (1986). Perceptions of innovativeness and communication about innovations: A study of three types of service organizations. *Communication Quarterly, 34,* 213-230.

Comer, D. R. (1991). Organizational newcomers' acquisition of information from peers. *Management Communication Quarterly, 5,* 64-89.

Cotton, J. L. (1993). *Employee involvement: Methods for improving performance and work attitudes.* Newbury Park, CA: Sage.

Cotton, J. L., Vollrath, D. A., Froggatt, K. L., Lengnick-Hall, M. L., & Jennings, K. R. (1988). Employee participation: Diverse forms and different outcomes. *Academy of Management Review, 13,* 8-22.

Covin, T. J., & Kilmann, R. H. (1990). Participant perceptions of positive and negative influences on large-scale change. *Group and Organizational Studies, 15,* 233-248.

Curley, K. F., & Gremillion, L. L. (1983). The role of the champion in DSS implementation. *Information and Management, 6,* 203-209.

Cushman, D. P., & King, S. S. (1994). *High speed management.* Albany: State University of New York Press.

Davis, F. D., Bagozzi, R. P., & Warshaw, P. R. (1992). Extrinsic and intrinsic motivation to use computers in the workplace. *Journal of Applied Social Psychology, 22,* 1111-1132.

*Dean, J. W., Susman, G. I., & Porter, P. S. (1990). Technical, economic and political factors in advanced manufacturing technology implementation. *Journal of Engineering and Technology Management, 7,* 129-144.

Dearing, J., & Meyer, G. (1994). An exploratory tool for predicting adoption decisions. *Science Communication, 16,* 43-57.

DeLuca, J. R. (1984). Managing the socio-political context in planned change efforts. In A. Kakabadse & C. Parker (Eds.), *Power, politics, and organizations: A behavioral science view* (pp. 127-147). New York: John Wiley.

*DeSanctis, G., & Courtney, J. F. (1983). Toward friendly user MIS implementation. *Communications of the ACM, 26,* 732-738.

Dornblaser, B. M., Lin, T., & Van de Ven, A. H. (1989). Innovation outcomes, learning and action loops. In A. H. Van de Ven, H. L. Angle, & M. S. Poole (Eds.), *Research on the management of innovations* (pp. 193-217). New York: Ballinger.

Dunphy, D. C., & Stace, D. (1988). Transformational and coercive strategies for planned organizational change: Beyond the O.D. model. *Organizational Studies, 9,* 317-334.

Ebadi, Y. M., & Utterback, J. M. (1984). The effects of communication on technological innovation. *Management Science, 30,* 572-585.

Egri, C. P., & Frost, P. J. (1989). Threats to innovation; roadblocks to implementation: The politics of the productive process. In M. C. Jackson, P. Keys, & S. A. Cropper (Eds.), *Operational research and the social sciences* (pp. 585-590). New York: Plenum.

Eisenberg, E. M., & Riley, P. (1988). Organizational symbols and sense-making. In G. M. Goldhaber & G. A. Barnett (Eds.), *Handbook of organizational communication* (pp. 131-150). Norwood, NJ: Ablex.

Ellis, B. H. (1992). The effects of uncertainty and source credibility on attitudes about organizational change. *Management Communication Quarterly, 6,* 34-57.

Elsbach, K. D., & Sutton, R. I. (1992). Acquiring organization legitimacy through illegitimate actions: A marriage of institutional and impression management theories. *Academy of Management Journal, 35,* 699-738.

Ettlie, J. E., Bridges, W. P., & O'Keefe, R. D. (1984). Organization strategy and the structural differences for radical versus incremental innovation. *Management Science, 30,* 682-695.

Ettlie, J. E., & Rubenstein, A. H. (1980). Social learning theory and the implementation of production innovation. *Decision Sciences, 11,* 648-668.

Fairhurst, G. T. (1993). Echoes of the vision: When the rest of the organization talks total quality. *Management Communication Quarterly, 6,* 331-371.

Fairhurst, G. T., Green, S., & Courtright, J. (1995). Inertial forces and the implementation of a socio-technical systems approach: A communication study. *Organization Science, 6,* 168-185.

Fairhurst, G. T., & Wendt, R. F. (1993). The gap in total quality: A commentary. *Management Communication Quarterly, 6,* 441-451.

Farace, R. V., Monge, P. R., & Russell, H. M. (1977). *Communicating and organizing.* New York: Random House.

Feldman, D. C., & Brett, J. M. (1983). Coping with new jobs: A comparative study of new hires and job changers. *Academy of Management Journal, 26,* 258-272.

Feldman, M. S. (1981). The multiple socialization of organizational members. *Academy of Management Review, 6,* 309-318.

Feldman, M. S., & March, J. G. (1981). Information in organizations as sign and symbol. *Administrative Science Quarterly, 26,* 171-186.

*Fidler, L. A., & Johnson, J. D. (1984). Communication and innovation implementation. *Academy of Management Review, 9,* 704-711.

Finkelstein, S., & Hambrick, D. (1990). Top management team tenure and organizational outcomes: The moderating role of managerial discretion. *Administrative Science Quarterly, 35,* 484-503.

Ford, J. D., & Ford, L. W. (1995). The role of conversations in producing intentional change in organizations. *Academy of Management Review, 20,* 541-570.

Frost, P. J., & Egri, C. P. (1990a). Influence of political action on innovation (Part I). *Leadership and Organizational Development Journal, 11*(1), 17-25.

Frost, P. J., & Egri, C. P. (1990b). Influence of political action on innovation (Part II). *Leadership and Organizational Development Journal, 11*(2), 4-12.

Frost, P. J., & Egri, C. P. (1991). The political process of innovation. In L. L. Cummings & B. M. Staw (Eds.), *Research in organizational behavior* (Vol. 13, pp. 229-295). Greenwich, CT: JAI.

Fulk, J., Schmitz, J. A., & Steinfield, C. W. (1990). A social influence model of technology use. In J. Fulk & C. W. Steinfield (Eds.), *Organizations and communication technology* (pp. 117-140). Newbury Park, CA: Sage.

Giddens, A. (1979). *Central problems in social theory: Action, structure and contradiction in social analysis.* Berkeley: University of California Press.

Giddens, A. (1984). *The constitution of society: Outline of the theory of structuration.* Berkeley: University of California Press.

Glaser, E. M., & Backer, T. E. (1977). Innovation redefined: Durability and local adaptation. *Evaluation, 4,* 131-135.

Gluckstern, N. B., & Packard, R. W. (1977). The internal-external change-agent team: Bringing change to a "closed institution." *Journal of Applied Behavioral Science, 13,* 41-52.

*Goodman, P. S., & Griffith, T. L. (1991). A process approach to the implementation of new technology. *Journal of Engineering and Technology Management, 8,* 261-285.

*Goodstein, L. D., & Burke, W. W. (1991). Creating successful organization change. *Organization Dynamics, 19*(4), 5-17.

Goodstein, L. D., Nolan, T. M., & Pfeiffer, J. W. (1993). *Applied strategic planning: A comprehensive guide.* New York: McGraw-Hill.

*Gottlieb, N. H., Lovato, C. Y., Weinstein, R., Green, L. W., & Eriksen, M. P. (1992). The implementation of a restrictive worksite smoking policy in a large decentralized organization. *Health Education Quarterly, 19,* 77-100.

Gouran, D. S. (1990). Exploiting the predictive potential of structuration theory. In J. A. Anderson (Ed.), *Communication yearbook 13* (pp. 313-322). Newbury Park, CA: Sage.

Gray, B., & Hay, T. M. (1986). Political limits to interorganizational consensus and change. *Journal of Applied Behavioral Science, 22,* 95-112.

Griffith, T. L. (1995). *Negotiating successful technology implementation: A motivation perspective.* Unpublished manuscript, University of Arizona, Tucson, College of Business and Public Administration.

*Griffith, T. L., & Northcraft, G. B. (1993). Promises, pitfalls and paradox: Cognitive elements in the implementation of new technology. *Journal of Managerial Issues, 5,* 465-482.

Griffith, T. L., & Northcraft, G. B. (in press). Cognitive elements in the implementation of new technology: Testing whether less is more. *Management Information Systems Quarterly.*

*Gross, N., Giacquinta, J. B., & Bernstein, M. (1970). Failure to implement a major organizational innovation. In M. B. Miles & W. W. Charters (Eds.), *Learning in social settings: New readings on the social psychology of education* (pp. 691-705). Boston: Allyn & Bacon.

*Guth, W. D., & Macmillan, I. C. (1986). Strategy implementation versus middle management self-interest. *Strategic Management Journal, 7,* 313-327.

Hambrick, D., & Mason, P. (1984). Upper echelons: The organization as a reflection of its top managers. *Academy of Management Review, 9,* 193-206.

Hamilton, E. E. (1988). The facilitation of organizational change: An empirical study of factors predicting change agents' effectiveness. *Journal of Applied Behavioral Science, 24,* 27-59.

Hill, C. W. L., & Jones, G. R. (1992). *Strategic management: An integrated approach* (2nd ed.). Boston: Houghton Mifflin.

Hoffman, E., & Roman, P. M. (1984). Information diffusion in the implementation of innovation process. *Communication Research, 11,* 117-140.

Howell, J. M., & Higgins, C. A. (1990). Champions of technological innovation. *Administrative Science Quarterly, 35,* 317-341.

Hunsaker, P. (1985). Strategies for organizational change: Role of the inside change agent. In D. Warrick (Ed.), *Contemporary organizational development* (pp. 123-137). Glenview, IL: Scott, Foresman.

Hurst, D. K., Rush, J. C., & White, R. E. (1989). Top management teams and organizational renewal. *Strategic Management Journal, 10,* 87-105.

Isabella, L. A. (1990). Evolving interpretations as a change unfolds: How managers construe key organizational events. *Academy of Management Journal, 33,* 7-41.

Jablin, F. M. (1984). Assimilating new members into organizations. In R. N. Bostrom (Ed.), *Communication yearbook 8* (pp. 594-626). Beverly Hills, CA: Sage.

Jablin, F. M. (1987a). Formal organizational structure. In F. M. Jablin, L. L. Putnam, K. H. Roberts, & L. W. Porter (Eds.), *Handbook of organizational communication* (pp. 389-419). Newbury Park, CA: Sage.

Jablin, F. M. (1987b). Organizational entry, assimilation, and exit. In F. M. Jablin, L. L. Putnam, K. H. Roberts, & L. W. Porter (Eds.), *Handbook of organizational communication* (pp. 679-739). Newbury Park, CA: Sage.

Jarboe, S. (1988). A comparison of input-output, process-output, and input-process-output models of small group problem-solving effectiveness. *Communication Monographs, 55,* 121-142.

Johnson, B. M., & Rice, R. E. (1987). *Managing organizational innovation: The evolution from word processing to office information systems.* New York: Columbia University Press.

Johnson, J. D. (1990). Effects of communicative factors on participation in innovations. *Journal of Business Communication, 27,* 7-24.

Johnson, J. D. (1993). *Organizational communication structure.* Norwood, NJ: Ablex.

Johnson, J. D., Meyer, M., Berkowitz, J., & Ethington, C. (1995, May). *Tests of a model of perceived organizational innovativeness in a contractual network of health services organizations.* Unpublished manuscript, Michigan State University.

Kanter, R. M. (1983). *The change masters.* New York: Simon & Schuster.

King, A. S. (1974). Expectation effects in organizational change. *Administrative Science Quarterly, 19,* 221-230.

Kotter, J. P., & Schlesinger, L. A. (1979). Choosing strategies for change. *Harvard Business Review, 57*(2), 106-114.

*Kumar, K., & Thibodeaux, M. S. (1990). Organizational politics and planned organization change. *Group and Organization Studies, 15,* 357-365.

*Larkin, T. J., & Larkin, S. (1994). *Communicating change: Winning support for new business goals.* New York: McGraw-Hill.

*Larkin, T. J., & Larkin, S. (1996). Reaching and changing front-line employees. *Harvard Business Review, 74*(5), 95-104.

Lawler, E. E., II (1995). *Creating high-performance organizations.* San Francisco: Jossey-Bass.

*Leithwood, K. A. (1981). Managing the implementation of curriculum innovations. *Knowledge: Creation, Diffusion, Utilization, 2,* 341-360.

Leonard-Barton, D. (1987a). The case for integrative innovation: An expert system at Digital. *Sloan Management Review, 29*(1), 7-19.

Leonard-Barton, D. (1987b). Implementing structured software methodologies: A case of innovation in process technology. *Interfaces, 17,* 6-17.

Leonard-Barton, D. (1988a). Implementation as mutual adaptation of technology and organization. *Research Policy, 17,* 251-267.

*Leonard-Barton, D. (1988b). Implementation characteristics or organizational innovations. *Communication Research, 15,* 603-631.

Leonard-Barton, D., & Deschamps, I. (1988). Managerial influence in the implementation of new technology. *Management Science, 34,* 1252-1265.

Leonard-Barton, D., & Kraus, W. A. (1985). Implementing new technology. *Harvard Business Review, 63*(6), 102-110.

Leonard-Barton, D., & Sinha, D. K. (1993). Developer-user interaction and user satisfaction in internal technology transfer. *Academy of Management Journal, 36,* 1125-1139.

Lewis, L. K. (1996, November). *The plum job and the lame duck: Positional histories and the impact of occupancy patterns on individuals' influence in organizations.* Paper presented at the annual meeting of the Speech Communication Association, San Diego, CA.

Lewis, L. K., & Seibold, D. R. (1993). Innovation modification during intra-organizational adoption. *Academy of Management Review, 18,* 322-354.

Lewis, L. K., & Seibold, D. R. (1996). Communication during intraorganizational innovation adoption: Predicting users' behavioral coping responses to innovations in organizations. *Communication Monographs, 63,* 131-157.

Linder, S. H., & Peters, B. G. (1987). A design perspective on policy implementation: The fallacies of misplaced prescription. *Policy Studies Review, 6,* 459-475.

Lindquist, K., & Mauriel, J. (1989). Depth and breadth in innovation implementation: The case of school-based management. In A. H. Van de Ven, H. L. Angle, & M. S. Poole (Eds.), *Research on the management of innovation: The Minnesota studies* (pp. 561-582). New York: Ballinger/Harper & Row.

Lippitt, G. L., Langseth, P., & Mossop, J. (1985). *Implementing organizational change.* San Francisco: Jossey-Bass.

Lovelady, L. (1984). Change strategies and the use of OD consultants to facilitate change. *Leadership and Organizational Development Journal, 5,* 2-12.

Lyles, M. A., & Thomas, H. (1988). Strategic problem formulation: Biases and assumptions embedded in alternative decision-making models. *Journal of Management Studies, 25,* 131-145.

Maidique, M. (1980). Entrepreneurs, champions, and technological innovation. *Sloan Management Review, 21*(2), 59-76.

Mainiero, L. A., & DeMichiell, R. L. (1986, July). Minimizing employee resistance to technological change. *Personnel,* pp. 32-37.

Majchrzak, A. (1988). *The human side of factory automation.* San Francisco: Jossey-Bass.

*Mankin, D., Bikson, T. K., & Gutek, B. (1984). Factors in successful implementation of computer-based office information systems: A review of the literature with suggestions for OBM research. *Journal of OB Management, 6,* 1-20.

Marcus, A. A. (1988). Implementing externally induced innovations: A comparison of rulebound and autonomous approaches. *Academy of Management Journal, 31,* 235-256.

Markus, M. L. (1983). Power, politics, and MIS implementation. *Communications of the ACM, 26,* 430-444.

Marshall, A. A., & Stohl, C. (1993). Being "in the know" in a participative management system. *Management Communication Quarterly, 6,* 372-404.

McPhee, R. D. (1985). Formal structure and organizational communication. In R. D. McPhee & P. K. Tompkins (Eds.), *Organizational communication: Traditional themes and new directions* (pp. 149-178). Beverly Hills, CA: Sage.

Miller, K. I. (1995). *Organizational communication: Approaches and processes.* Albany, NY: Wadsworth.

Miller, K. I., & Monge, P. R. (1985). Social information and employee anxiety about organizational change. *Human Communication Research, 11,* 365-386.

Miller, K. I., & Monge, P. R. (1986). Participation, satisfaction, and productivity: A meta-analytic review. *Academy of Management Journal, 29,* 727-753.

Miller, V. D., & Jablin, F. M. (1991). Information seeking during organizational entry: Influences, tactics, and a model of process. *Academy of Management Review, 16,* 92-120.

Miller, V. D., Johnson, J. R., & Grau, J. (1994). Antecedents to willingness to participate in a planned organizational change. *Journal of Applied Communication Research, 22,* 59-80.

Mintzberg, H. (1994). *The rise and fall of strategic planning.* New York: Free Press.

Monge, P. R., Cozzens, M. D., & Contractor, N. S. (1992). Communication and motivational predictors of the dynamics of organizational innovation. *Organizational Science, 3,* 250-274.

Monge, P. R., & Eisenberg, E. M. (1987). Emergent communication networks. In F. M. Jablin, L. L. Putnam, K. H. Roberts, & L. W. Porter (Eds.), *Handbook of organizational communication* (pp. 304-342). Newbury Park, CA: Sage.

Monge, P. R., & Miller, K. I. (1988). Participative processes in organizations. In G. M. Goldhaber & G. A. Barnett (Eds.), *Handbook of organizational communication* (pp. 213-229). Norwood, NJ: Ablex.

Morrison, E. W. (1993). Newcomer information seeking: Exploring types, modes, sources and outcomes. *Academy of Management Journal, 36,* 557-589.

Neumann, J. E. (1989). Why people don't participate in organizational change. In R. W. Woodman & W. A. Pasmore (Eds.), *Research in organizational change and development* (Vol. 3, pp. 181-212). Greenwich, CT: JAI.

Nord, R., & Tucker, S. (1987). *Implementing routine and radical innovations.* Lexington, MA: Lexington.

Nutt, P. C. (1986). Tactics of implementation. *Academy of Management Journal, 29,* 230-261.

Nutt, P. C. (1987). Identifying and appraising how managers install strategy. *Strategic Management Journal, 8,* 1-14.

O'Reilly, C. A., III, Caldwell, D. F., & Barnett, W. P. (1989). Work group demography, social integration, and turnover. *Administrative Science Quarterly, 34,* 21-37.

O'Reilly, C. A., III, Snyder, R. C., & Boothe, J. N. (1993). Effects of executive team demography on organizational change. In G. P. Huber & W. H. Glick (Eds.), *Organizational change and redesign* (pp. 147-175). New York: Oxford University Press.

Ottaway, R. N. (1983). The change agent: A taxonomy in relation to the change process. *Human Relations, 36,* 361-392.

Pacanowsky, M. (1988). Communication in the empowering organization. In J. A. Anderson (Ed.), *Communication yearbook 11* (pp. 356-379). Newbury Park, CA: Sage.

Papa, M. J., & Papa, W. H. (1990). Perceptual and communicative indices of employee performance with new technology. *Western Journal of Speech Communication, 54,* 21-41.

Pfeffer, J. (1981). Management as symbolic action: The creation and maintenance of organizational paradigms. In L. L. Cummings & B. M. Staw (Eds.), *Research in organizational behavior* (Vol. 3, pp. 1-52). Greenwich, CT: JAI.

Pfeffer, J. (1983). Organizational demography. In L. L. Cummings & B. M. Staw (Eds.), *Research in organizational behavior* (Vol. 5, pp. 299-357). Greenwich, CT: JAI.

Poole, M. S., Seibold, D. R., & McPhee, R. D. (1996). The structuration of group decision making. In R. Y. Hirokawa & M. S. Poole (Eds.), *Communication and group decision making* (2nd ed., pp. 114-146). Thousand Oaks, CA: Sage.

Porter, L. W., Allen, R. W., & Angle, H. L. (1981). The politics of upward influence in organizations. In L. L. Cummings & B. M. Staw (Eds.), *Research in organizational behavior* (Vol. 3, pp. 109-149). Greenwich, CT: JAI.

Quinn, J. B. (1985). Managing innovation: Controlled chaos. *Harvard Business Review, 63*(3), 73-84.

Redding, C. (1972). *Communication within the organization: An interpretive review of theory and research.* New York: Industrial Communication Council.

Reed, M. (1996). Organizational theorizing: A historically contested terrain. In S. R. Clegg, C. Hardy, & W. R. Nord (Eds.), *Handbook of organization studies* (pp. 31-56). Thousand Oaks, CA: Sage.

Rice, R. E., & Contractor, N. (1990). Conceptualizing effects of office information systems: A methodology and application for the study of alpha, beta, and gamma changes. *Decision Sciences, 21,* 301-317.

Rice, R. E., & Rogers, E. M. (1980). Re-invention in the innovation process. *Knowledge: Creation, Diffusion, Utilization, 1,* 499-514.

Roberts-Gray, C. (1985). Managing the implementation of innovations. *Evaluation and Program Planning, 8,* 261-269.

Roberts-Gray, C., & Gray T. (1983). Implementing innovations: A model to bridge the gap between diffusion and utilization. *Knowledge: Creation, Diffusion, Utilization, 4,* 213-232.

Rogers, E. M. (1983). *Diffusion of innovations* (3rd ed.). New York: Free Press.

Rogers, E. M. (1995). *Diffusion of innovations* (4th ed.). New York: Free Press.

Rogers, E. M., & Shoemaker, F. F. (1971). *Communication of innovations: A cross-cultural approach* (2nd ed.). New York: Free Press.

Salancik, G. R., & Pfeffer, J. (1978). A social information processing approach to job attitudes and task design. *Administrative Science Quarterly, 23,* 224-256.

*Salem, P., & Williams, M. L. (1992, May). *Communication factors influencing the success of new health units: Applying a theory of organizational change.* Paper presented at the annual meeting of the International Communication Association, Miami, FL.

Schein, V. (1977). Political strategies for implementing change. *Group and Organization Studies, 2,* 42-48.

Schein, V. (1985). Organizational realities: The politics of change. In D. Warrick (Ed.), *Contemporary organizational development* (pp. 86-97). Glenview, IL: Scott, Foresman.

Schon, D. A. (1963). Champions for radical new inventions. *Harvard Business Review, 41*(4), 78-86.

Seibold, D. R., Meyers, R. A., & Sunwolf. (1996). Communication and influence in group decision making. In R. Y. Hirokawa & M. S. Poole (Eds.), *Communication and group decision making* (2nd ed., pp. 242-268). Thousand Oaks, CA: Sage.

Seibold, D. R., & Shea, B. C. (in press). Participation and decision making. In F. M. Jablin & L. L. Putnam (Eds.), *The new handbook of organizational communication.* Thousand Oaks, CA: Sage.

Smeltzer, L. R. (1991). An analysis of strategies for announcing organization-wide change. *Group and Organization Studies, 16,* 5-24.

*Spender, J. C., & Kessler, E. H. (1995). Managing the uncertainties of innovation: Extending Thompson (1967). *Human Relations, 48,* 35-55.

*Sproull, L. S., & Hofmeister, K. R. (1986). Thinking about implementation. *Journal of Management, 12,* 43-60.

Staw, B. M. (1980). Rationality and justification in organizational life. In B. M. Staw & L. L. Cummings (Eds.), *Research in organizational behavior* (Vol. 2, pp. 45-80). Greenwich, CT: JAI.

Stohl, C. (1986). The role of memorable messages in the process of organizational communication. *Communication Quarterly, 34,* 231-249.

Stohl, C. (1995). Paradoxes of participation. In R. Cesaria & P. Schockley-Zalabak (Eds.), *Organization means communication: Making the organizational communication concept relevant to practice* (pp. 199-215). Rome: Sipi Editore.

Stone, M. M., & Crittenden, W. (1993). A guide to journal articles on strategic management in nonprofit organizations, 1977 to 1992. *Nonprofit Management and Leadership, 4,* 193-213.

Strebel, P. (1996). Why do employees resist change? *Harvard Business Review, 74*(5), 86-92.

Tompkins, P. K., & Cheney, G. (1985). Communication and unobtrusive control in contemporary organizations. In R. D. McPhee & P. K. Tompkins (Eds.), *Organizational communication: Traditional themes and new directions* (pp. 179-210). Beverly Hills, CA: Sage.

Tornatzky, L. G., & Johnson, E. C. (1982). Research on implementation: Implications for evaluation practice and evaluation policy. *Evaluation and Program Planning, 5,* 193-198.

Trujillo, N. (1983). Mintzberg's roles: The nature of managerial communication. In L. L. Putnam & M. E. Pacanowsky (Eds.), *Communication and organizations: An interpretive approach* (pp. 73-98). Beverly Hills, CA: Sage.

Tyre, M. J., & Orlikowski, W. J. (1994). Windows of opportunity: Temporal patterns of technological adaptation in organizations. *Organization Science, 5,* 98-118.

Van de Ven, A. H. (1993). Managing the process of organizational innovation. In G. P. Huber & W. H. Glick (Eds.), *Organizational change and redesign* (pp. 269-294). New York: Oxford University Press.

Van de Ven, A. H., Angle, H. L., & Poole, M. S. (1989). *Research on the management of innovations.* New York: Ballinger.

Wanous, J. P. (1980). *Organizational entry: Recruitment, selection and socialization of newcomers.* Reading, MA: Addison-Wesley.

Whittington, R. (1994). Sociological pluralism, institutions and managerial agency. In J. Hassard & M. Parker (Eds.), *Towards a new theory of organizations* (pp. 53-74). London: Routledge.

Zaltman, G., & Duncan, R. (1977). *Strategies for planned change.* New York: John Wiley.

CHAPTER CONTENTS

4 The Business of Business Negotiation: Intercultural Perspectives

DEBORAH A. CAI
University of Maryland

LAURA E. DRAKE
Northwestern University

Although focused primarily on the goal of transacting business, the intercultural negotiation literature is highly interdisciplinary, drawing not only from business and management, but also from psychology, international relations, law, and linguistics. The common factor connecting this literature is the need to communicate effectively across cultures. To address communication's role in international negotiation, this chapter offers a model for organizing extant research into four quadrants based on two axes: (a) works that range from culture specific to culture general and (b) works that range from applied to theoretical. The two axes cross to create four quadrants of research with distinct aims and assumptions. The authors offer conceptualizations of communication, culture, and negotiation, and then review the aims, assumptions, and various works representing each quadrant. To develop key issues and questions facing future research, the authors draw from communication and traditional negotiation literature to illustrate gaps in intercultural negotiation knowledge.

IN the 1990s, international business activity is flourishing. These joint ventures, mergers, multinational corporations, and buying and selling of international products and services involve negotiation. As Adler (1991) notes, "Negotiation is one of the single most important international business skills" (p. 182). Among U.S. corporations, 74% of those surveyed reported that the type of training most needed for their employees was in negotiation skills to be used with foreign businesses and governments (Harris & Moran, 1991). The importance of negotiation as an international activity is evidenced in the plethora of "how-to" articles and books available on negotiating with

Correspondence and requests for reprints: Deborah A. Cai, Department of Speech Communication, 2110 Skinner Building, University of Maryland, College Park, MD 20742; e-mail debcai@wam.umd.edu

Communication Yearbook 21, pp. 153-189

people of other cultures. In this chapter we organize the literature currently available on cross-cultural and intercultural negotiation by examining trends in the literature and proposing future directions for research. We provide a framework for integrating the intercultural communication and negotiation literature to shed light on the critical issues facing intercultural negotiation research.

Although focused primarily on the goal of transacting business, and thus very practically oriented, the intercultural negotiation literature is highly interdisciplinary, drawing not only from the business and management fields, but also from psychology, international relations, law, and linguistics. The common factor connecting this literature is the need to communicate effectively across cultural boundaries. As Reardon and Spekman (1994) have observed, communication is crucial in developing cooperation, forming alliances, and de-escalating conflict in the hopes of fostering healthy business relations. In Husted's (1994) analysis of U.S.-Mexico trade negotiations, communication tops the list of factors crucial to success. Ineffective communication in negotiation negates trust and interferes with joint problem solving. Because culture affects communication, a primary responsibility of scholars of intercultural business negotiation lies in distinguishing effective from ineffective communication processes.

Our goal in this chapter is to provide a framework for integrating three literatures: those of intercultural communication, negotiation, and international business. The purpose of this integration is to illuminate critical issues for research. Weiss (1996) asserts that "it is the richness of the phenomenon, coupled with the diversity of the parties and conditions, that makes international business negotiation a fascinating subject to explore" (p. 209). We suggest a synergistic approach, because this review reveals that the diversity of participants in international business negotiation has been well documented. Diverse conditions have received relatively less attention. But conspicuously lacking in this area is a thorough investigation of the "richness" of this phenomenon in terms of communicative interactions among the parties involved.

To address communication's role in international negotiation, we offer a model for organizing the extant research into four quadrants based on two axes: (a) works that are either culture specific or culture general and (b) works that are applied or theoretical. Crossing the two axes creates four quadrants of research, each with distinct aims and assumptions. In the following sections, we offer conceptualizations of communication, culture, and negotiation and then review the aims and assumptions as well as various works representative of each quadrant. Then, to develop key issues and questions facing future research, we draw from communication and traditional negotiation literatures to illustrate the gaps in intercultural negotiation knowledge.

CONCEPTUALIZING CULTURE,
COMMUNICATION, AND NEGOTIATION

Culture includes the socially transmitted beliefs, behavior patterns, values, and norms of a collection of individuals, which evolve from the rules, concepts, categories, and assumptions the individuals use to interpret their surroundings and guide their interactions (Salacuse, 1991). This view of culture is predominant in cross-cultural comparisons, which generally consider culture to be the culmination of "knowledge, experiences, beliefs, values, attitudes, meanings, . . . concepts of the universe, and material objects and possessions acquired by a large group of people in the course of generations through individual and group striving" (Samovar, Porter & Jain, 1981, p. 25). From this perspective, culture becomes an overarching explanation for modes of behavior, thought, and communication that varies more between than within groups, defined by their geographic, religious, racial, and/or political characteristics (Haas, 1974).

Communication and Culture

The intercultural communication literature is replete with conceptualizations of culture (Dodd, 1991; Geertz, 1973; Gudykunst & Ting-Toomey, 1988; Trompenaars, 1993). Janosik (1987) provides a useful summary of the various perspectives offered by these conceptualizations in a typology of four categories: (a) "culture as learned behavior" assumes communicative responses are automatic and the result of social conditioning, (b) "shared values" focuses on how the value system in a culture produces responses that are consistent with culturewide beliefs, (c) "dialectic" emphasizes the potentially conflicting values in a single culture, and (d) "culture in context" emphasizes local over global effects of culture. Although culture may predispose the individual to favor some communicative responses over others, situational requirements may interact with or override such predispositions (see Wilson, Cai, Campbell, Donohue, & Drake, 1995).

Dodd (1991) argues that culture is in large part identified by unique communication patterns. Cultural groups have developed distinctive "styles" for handling conflict (Ting-Toomey, 1988), affect displays (Trompenaars, 1993), superior-subordinate relationships (Lee & Rogan, 1991), argumentation (Walker, 1990), persuasion (Johnstone, 1989), work behaviors (Hofstede, 1980), priorities of the group versus the individual (Triandis, Bontempo, Villareal, Asai, & Lucca, 1988), systems of logic (Acuff, 1993; Chu, 1991; Hsu, 1981, Macleod, 1988; Northrop, 1953; Svenkerud, 1993), uncertainty reduction (Gudykunst & Nishida, 1984), and negotiation (Harris & Moran, 1991). Communication functions as reinforcement in the form of positive feedback for individuals who adhere to cultural norms or as punishment in the form of negative feedback for members who deviate from cultural norms (Dodd, 1991). Communication and culture are therefore inextricably tied, so that the presence of differing cultural factors in the process of encoding and decoding verbal and nonverbal messages constitutes intercultural communication (Gudykunst & Kim, 1992).

Negotiation

Fisher, Ury, and Patton (1991) define negotiation as "a process of communicating back and forth for the purpose of reaching a joint decision" (p. 32). Similarly, Pruitt (1981) views negotiation as "a process by which a joint decision is made by two or more parties. The parties first verbalize contradictory demands and then move toward agreement by a process of concession making or search for alternatives" (p. 1). Inherent in these and related definitions of negotiation is the need for communication (Fisher et al., 1991; Jönsson, 1990). Furthermore, most definitions note that conflicting interests are the basis for the need to negotiate and that common interests create the impetus to negotiate (Walton & McKersie, 1965; Ways, 1979).

Few of the studies reviewed for this chapter include clear conceptual definitions of negotiation, much less of intercultural or international negotiation. Implied in most of the literature is that intercultural negotiation is doing business, or simply "negotiating," with people from foreign countries (Adler, 1991; Graham & Andrews, 1987; Kennedy, 1985a, 1985b). In contrast, McCall and Warrington (1984) and Weiss (1993) provide conceptual definitions that consider the essential elements of intercultural negotiation: purpose of negotiation, cultural considerations, and commercial considerations. Their definitions focus on transactions in which at least one party is a business entity, thus specifying a particular context in which this type of communication takes place. Adapting their definitions, we define intercultural negotiation as any communication process whereby parties of both common and conflicting commercial interests and of differing cultural backgrounds attempt to define or redefine the terms of their interdependence.

MAKING SENSE OF THE LITERATURE

Selection of the Literature

Since early anthropological work, business in international settings has been of scholarly interest (Graham & Gronhaug, 1989). We examine here the literature dealing particularly with issues of communication related to business negotiation and cultural difference. The works reviewed include studies of culture's effects on communication and culture's role in business negotiation and/or communication processes in negotiation. We include articles that compare negotiation across cultures (cross-cultural), that describe negotiation within a single culture (intracultural), and that examine face-to-face interaction between negotiators of disparate cultures (intercultural).

Works excluded from the review are those dealing with political and governmental negotiations or power relationships in negotiations between multinational enterprises and host governments (see Weiss, 1996). We excluded these studies because they describe the process of negotiating particular policies or treaties, such as GATT or NAFTA, or macrostrategies, such as a multinational corporation's level of technology or access to foreign markets.

We have also excluded studies that deal with crisis negotiations and hostage taking involving perpetrators from diverse cultures (Hammer, in press; Hammer, Rogan, Van Zandt, & Laffon, 1993; Weaver, in press) because crisis negotiation differs from business negotiation in important respects. First, reducing tension is the primary focus during crises (Hammer, in press), because perpetrators in crisis negotiations frequently suffer from psychological disturbances (such as paranoia; Holmes & Fletcher-Bergland, 1995), often due to their being former victims of abuse (Weaver, in press). Second, perpetrators in hostage situations are typically less rational than are business negotiators, due to heightened emotions (Donohue & Roberto, 1993). Third, crisis negotiations typically pit a single perpetrator (or small group) against an extended and ultimately more powerful team of law enforcement officials and psychologists. Therefore, an enormous power differential exists between bargainers, representing a power play between the perpetrator and police (Donohue & Roberto, 1993).

In contrast to these works, in the current review we examine, from a communication perspective, the literature that Weiss (1996) characterizes as "comparative, microbehavioral":

> The focus of this research paradigm has been face-to-face interaction between individual negotiators, which adherents view as the point of contact in negotiation. . . . the "mutual movement" that characterizes negotiation can occur only through interaction, usually—if not necessarily—face-to-face. Thus, what negotiators do (e.g., making offers, disclosures, threats) defines the process and determines the negotiation outcome. (p. 214)

This focus is consistent with our goal of providing a review of theoretical and substantive as well as methodological approaches to intercultural business negotiation. However, this perspective calls up an interpersonal communication lens through which to view intercultural negotiation. Our perspective is congruent with Weiss's (1996) "microbehavioral" perspective. We argue that interpersonal interaction—that is, face-to-face communication across the negotiation table—constitutes negotiation processes. Although organizational or institution-level perspectives provide valuable insights and are not inconsistent with an interpersonal perspective, they de-emphasize the direct relevance of interpersonal interaction to negotiation outcomes and are not within the purview of this chapter. Here we offer an overview of the substantive issues relevant to communication in hopes of pinpointing areas ripe for further development and theory building.

An Organizing Model

To date, the work on intercultural negotiation can be categorized into four groups that are divided by two axes. The first axis divides the literature according to its focus: from culture specific to culture general. The second axis divides the literature according to its purpose: from applied to theoretical. Four quadrants, designating four different perspectives toward intercultural negotiation, emerge when these two axes are crossed: Quadrant I, prescriptive/descriptive; Quadrant II, guiding principles; Quadrant III, variable analytic; and Quadrant IV, global theory (see Figure 4.1). We chose these two axes with inclusiveness and comprehensiveness in mind. They seem to constitute the least cumbersome and still useful means for compiling vastly different approaches and purposes into a single literature review. First, a theoretic-methodological organizing scheme provides the most inclusive and comprehensive representation of work in intercultural business negotiation. Second, comparisons among the four quadrants provide a view of the directions from which traditional issues in conflict management and negotiation have, and have not, been examined interculturally. Finally, this scheme allows us to highlight the methodologically based and most prominent weakness in current intercultural business research: Our current knowledge is overwhelmingly based on generalizations from intra- rather than intercultural negotiation data.

Quadrant I combines applied, qualitative methods with a focus on specific cultures and examines behaviors typical of negotiators within a given culture. This large, coherent body of qualitative work has been useful for organizing the thinking about and shaping of subsequent research. Through anecdotal accounts of those who have worked overseas, this conceptual lens focuses on specific communication behaviors. Quadrant I represents a vast proportion of the intercultural negotiation literature. During the past two decades in particular, much attention has been given to prescriptive/descriptive accounts. It is precisely this overrepresentation of applied, culture-specific research that prompted us to undertake this review. Our aim is to focus on the need for global theory in intercultural business negotiation.

Quadrant II combines applied, qualitative methods with a broad focus on cultural differences and discusses cultural variances relevant to negotiation and general skills necessary for effective international negotiators. This work differs from that in Quadrant I in terms of being culture general, addressing issues related to overall intercultural competence. Literature in this quadrant argues that culture affects the negotiation process in significant ways, but listing cultural differences does more to promote stereotyping and negotiator judgment error than to improve the effectiveness of intercultural negotiators.

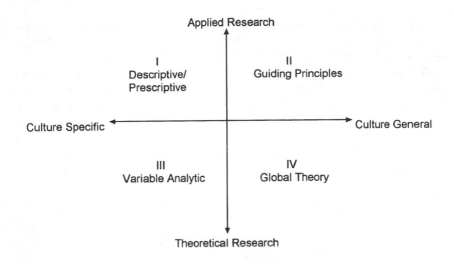

Figure 4.1. An Organizing Model of the Intercultural Negotiation Literature

Quadrant III combines theoretically driven research, conducted in laboratory or naturalistic settings, with a focus on specific cultures. These articles compare negotiating behaviors using cultures or cultural dimensions such as individualism-collectivism as independent variables. Negotiation processes and outcomes are the dependent variables. For example, integrativeness, the concern for maximizing both negotiators' own and their partners' outcomes (Fisher et al., 1991; Pruitt, 1981, 1983), has been addressed by Cai, Wilson, and Drake (1996), who found that a dyad's joint collectivism affects integrativeness in the form of information sharing. When both negotiators were highly collectivistic, the dyad exchanged more information about goals and priorities than when either negotiator was highly individualistic. Negotiation outcomes such as profit and partner's satisfaction (Adler, Graham, & Gehrke, 1987; Campbell, Graham, Jolibert, & Meissner, 1988) and time to reach settlement (Graham, 1985) are commonly investigated.

Quadrant IV encompasses a small but important body of work that is both culture general and theoretically based, rather than applied. Like the works that make up Quadrant II, these works focus on overall competence in international negotiation interaction. However, unlike those in Quadrant II, these works are theoretically driven, borrowing theory from several arenas to model the universal process of negotiating across cultural boundaries. These works are also distinct from those in Quadrant III. Although both groups offer theoretical explanations for negotiating difference, Quadrant IV works move beyond specific differences to explain how any cultural differences may affect processes and outcomes. Work in this category represents scholars' efforts to provide predictive power based on a broader theoretical understanding of the issues involved in examining culture and communication in business negotiation settings. Though small, this literature provides the impetus for further research and theory development in intercultural business negotiations.

We see a wide division between the two "applied" quadrants (I and II) and the "theoretical" quadrants (III and IV) that represents the classical division between research and practice. However, we see the work in Quadrant IV as a means for bridging this chasm in future investigations. Although the category scheme may be somewhat forced, it is crucial (a) to bring this division in the literature to light so that each side, applied and theoretical, can inform the other, and (b) to illustrate the historical development of intercultural negotiation research.

A SUMMARY OF RESEARCH
ACROSS THE FOUR QUADRANTS

Quadrant I: Descriptive/Prescriptive

U.S. corporations lose money each year when their managers or negotiators are unable to deal with cultural issues overseas (Tung, 1991). It has been suggested that the cultures of countries such as Japan and China are so vastly different from U.S. culture that negotiators must understand the differences or suffer frustration and failure (Acuff, 1990; Blaker, 1977a, 1977b; Corne, 1992; Graham & Sano, 1989). If Westerners are not savvy in negotiating with Asian countries, their economic base will suffer (Pye, 1992). Thus the primary focus of literature in this quadrant is to provide practical knowledge that U.S. negotiators can use to assess unusual or unexpected behaviors and adjust their own behaviors and attitudes when encountering negotiators from other cultures (Hall, 1960). These works recommend that American business executives adopt native behaviors and values when negotiating outside the United States, assuming that "doing as the Romans do" will ensure success by increasing perceived similarity and understanding (Cahn, 1983).

The majority of descriptive/prescriptive literature focuses on the Pacific Rim, with particular emphasis on Japan and China (e.g., Acuff, 1990; Chen, 1993; Chu, 1991; Corne, 1992; Davidson, 1987; De Mente, 1981, 1987; DePauw, 1981; Downing, 1992; Eiteman, 1990; Goldman, 1994; Graham & Sano, 1989; Hu & Grove, 1991; Huang, 1990; Lee & Lo, 1988; Macleod, 1988; March, 1985, 1988; Pye, 1982, 1992; Scott & Renault, 1995; Shenkar & Ronen, 1987; Solomon, 1985, 1987; Stewart & Keown, 1989; Tung, 1982, 1984a, 1984b, 1991; Van Zandt, 1970; Walters, 1991; Wilhelm, 1994; Zhang & Kuroda, 1989). Only a handful of remaining articles and books provide descriptions of negotiation in other specific cultures (Soviet Union—Beliaev, Mullen, & Punnett, 1985; Rajan & Graham, 1991; Islamic markets—Wright, 1981) or across a variety of cultures (Acuff, 1993; Burt, 1984; Frank, 1992a,

1992b; Harris & Moran, 1991; Kennedy, 1985a, 1985b; Moran & Stripp, 1991).

This literature takes one of two approaches. First, the descriptive approach implies that knowing common behaviors provides negotiators with an appropriate model for achieving negotiation goals. For example, Frank (1992a, 1992b) recommends that when negotiating in Germany, Austria, and Switzerland, Americans should be prompt and efficient, but when negotiating in Mexico, Americans should "grant concessions that support the ego of the decision maker" (p. 66) and handle problems in a personal rather than a business manner. Building trust and friendship is important when negotiating with Scandinavians. Similar kinds of specific suggestions are made for negotiating with the British (Burt, 1984), in Chinese and Korean cultures (Acuff, 1990; Tung, 1991), and with Russians (Rajan & Graham, 1991).

Second, the prescriptive approach suggests that by understanding cultural values, negotiators may plan proactively. That is, the negotiator can predict likely cultural behaviors and thus plan appropriate, effective responses for negotiating. For example, some key values of Japanese culture include the maintenance of social harmony, protection of "face," enactment of social status within the organization, and the pursuit of long-term relationships.

To illustrate these two perspectives toward cultural behaviors across the descriptive and prescriptive literature, we examine more closely some works that describe negotiating with the Japanese.

Descriptions of Japanese Behavior

Several Japanese cultural behaviors are frequently cited. Japanese negotiators have very specific prenegotiation rituals in which business cards are exchanged and prenegotiation relationships are developed (Corne, 1992; Kennedy, 1985b; Moran & Stripp, 1991; Walters, 1991). Japanese dislike saying no and dislike confrontation and open conflict because of their concern with "saving face" (Corne, 1992; Tung, 1984b; Van Zandt, 1970). Japanese negotiators prepare thoroughly, proceed cautiously, and are known for attention to detail and persistence (Corne, 1992). They maintain high concern for long-term relationships (Corne, 1992; Graham & Sano, 1989; Kennedy, 1985b; Van Zandt, 1970). They are more aware of and bound by hierarchies—both within their own organizations and toward opposing sides' agent(s)—than are Westerners, noting the status of foreign negotiators within their organizations. Attention to hierarchy means that Japanese teams make decisions by consensus and take longer to make decisions than Americans are accustomed to (Corne, 1992; Graham & Sano, 1989; Tung, 1984a, 1984b; Van Zandt, 1970). More than one author has noted that Japanese are said to feign language difficulties as a tactic for their own benefit against their foreign counterparts (Corne, 1992; Walters, 1991). The frequent use of silence and apparent lack of emotion among Japanese negotiators may be disconcerting for visitors (Graham & Sano, 1989; Moran & Stripp, 1991).

Predicting Japanese Behavior

In contrast, several works tie negotiation behaviors to specific values underlying Japanese culture, showing how knowledge of the Japanese value system allows visitors to predict and understand ensuing behaviors. For instance, the emphasis on harmony (*wa*) means that Japanese companies desire not only a profitable agreement, but a business relationship that encompasses both moral and practical obligations. Thus the Japanese possess a different understanding of contracts and the commitments inherent in them (Chen, 1993; Corne, 1992; Graham & Sano, 1989; March, 1985; Zhang & Kuroda, 1989). Similarly, Hofstede (1980) points out that Japanese values toward collectivism make the "we" more important than the "I" (Acuff, 1990). As a result, the corporation is seen as a "paternalistic, cooperative effort of many employees for the collective good" (Zhang & Kuroda, 1989, p. 109) and conducts business differently from corporations in the individualistically oriented United States.

The value of "order" also drives Japanese behavior (March, 1985; Moran & Stripp, 1991; Van Zandt, 1970; Zhang & Kuroda, 1989). This need for order results in attention to hierarchies (*ringi-sho*) that affects negotiation rituals and results in rigid decision-making processes that must progress up through the ranks of the organization. Individual negotiators have no autonomy in making decisions.

Overall, differences in the ways Japanese and Americans view the world in general, and thus the specific problems and issues they are negotiating, result in vastly different ways of approaching negotiation. As March (1985) points out, awareness of cultural differences between Japan and the United States "should alert you to the fact that many of the Japanese you face do not think about problems in the way you do" (p. 26).

Prescriptions for Americans

The studies that fall into Quadrant I generally provide prescriptions for how Americans can negotiate effectively with people from other given cultures. There are several behaviors recommended for Americans when encountering Japanese. For instance, some authors recommend that Americans should consider hiring cultural experts or interpreters to facilitate negotiations (Burt, 1984; Corne, 1992; Van Zandt, 1970; Zhang & Kuroda, 1989); should make extra effort to be prepared, giving special attention to learning as much as possible about Japanese customs and business practices (Chen, 1993; Corne, 1992; Tung, 1984a, 1984b; Van Zandt, 1970; Walters, 1991); should expect negotiations with Japanese to take longer than might be expected in the United States (Burt, 1984; Chen, 1993; Kennedy, 1985b; Walters, 1991); should not expect immediate responses to proposals (Corne, 1992); and should be careful to avoid confrontation and any show of anger (Acuff, 1990; Burt, 1984; Chen, 1993; Corne, 1992; Walters, 1991). In addition, Americans need to be aware of their own cultural assumptions about nonverbal behaviors and not allow superficial interpretations of Japanese silence, gestures and expressions, and indirect verbal communication to mislead them (Corne, 1992; Walters, 1991).

Summary

A common theme in Quadrant I is that cultural awareness will lead to more effective negotiating and higher likelihood of success. This assumption is valuable for guiding research. However, the descriptive approach in Quadrant I suffers the same limitations as most exploratory investigation. The observations are not systematic and not generalizable to intercultural contexts. Nonetheless, although aimed at the practical and applied level, these works give researchers valuable fodder for investigation because they lay out a host of assumptions about cultural behaviors and how the values of those cultures are likely to be enacted at the negotiation table.

Thus cultural assumptions, underlying values, expectations, and supposed appropriate responses on the part of visiting negotiators are phenomena that can be examined more closely in future research. Empirical investigation of the effectiveness of adaptation is particularly important given the emerging evidence that too much adaptation, or "acting the part" of a host culture member when one is merely a visitor, may be detrimental to effectiveness (Francis, 1991). Hammer (in press) asserts that a visitor is likely to be forgiven for cultural taboos because he or she is not expected, as an outsider, to be familiar with all practices in the host culture. This argument is validated in Marriott's (1995) analysis of linguistic deviations in Japanese-Australian negotiation. Although negative evaluation of linguistic deviations was expected, two of three deviation types were evaluated neutrally, indicating that in intercultural interaction, the participants may relax their expectations about communicative interaction.

Quadrant II: Guiding Principles

In direct contrast to the works in Quadrant I, those in Quadrant II avoid culture-specific analyses and advice. Instead, these works highlight issues of general concern for international negotiators. The basis for this approach is summarized by Salacuse (1988), who argues that books and articles that stress different negotiating styles across cultures promote cultural stereotypes. Rubin and Sander (1991) echo this concern about stereotyping, and propose that cultural stereotypes create self-fulfilling prophecies in intercultural negotiation, so that "what passes for [cultural/national] differences may well be the result of expectations and perceptions" (p. 252). Griffin and Daggart (1990) maintain that "what is needed is a skill and not an exhaustive compilation of generalizations. Indeed, generalizations . . . reinforce and exacerbate a negotiator's tendency to make false assumptions" (p. 3). Therefore, the literature in Quadrant II approaches the problem of negotiating across cultures in two ways: (a) by explaining negotiation factors on which cultures may vary, and (b) by proposing a "toolbox" of global attitudes and abilities for successful international negotiators.

Global Variations

Salacuse (1991) urges traveling negotiators to ask the right questions before taking action at the negotiation table. These "right" questions have to do with culture, political systems, and the negotiating environment. The effective negotiator must determine the consequences of his or her behavior after assessing such factors as home advantage, time delays, language and interpreters, bureaucracy, and political ideologies. Salacuse argues that culture affects business negotiations in 10 ways: through the negotiating goal, the negotiating attitude, the negotiator's personal style, the directness of communication, the negotiators' sensitivity to time, emotionalism, the expected form of agreements, how agreements are built (bottom-up or top-down), the organization of negotiating teams, and risk taking. Similarly, Weiss (1994a) and Moran and Stripp (1991) provide lists of cultural characteristics that can affect negotiations. These and other aspects of culture likely to affect the negotiation are echoed by various authors who take a global view of intercultural negotiation (for a summary of these characteristics, see Table 4.1).

Global Attitudes and Abilities

Schwartz (1993) defines an "international mind-set" as an "open-minded, empathic attitude toward conducting business in countries and cultures different from our own" (p. 1282). To develop this empathic and open-minded attitude, researchers have identified numerous skills, such as building rapport and trust (Le Poole, 1989; Reardon & Spekman, 1994), planning for and anticipating the other's goals and expectations, coordinating alliances (Reardon & Spekman, 1994), and managing power within a negotiator's own party and with the other party's negotiators (Elgström, 1990; Reardon & Spekman, 1994). An international mind-set includes flexibility, open-mindedness, patience, and a long-term perspective, as well as knowledge of and appreciation for one's host culture (Casse & Deol, 1985; Donohue, 1992; Elgström, 1990; Le Poole, 1989; Moran & Stripp, 1991; Salacuse, 1988, 1991; Schwartz, 1993).

Summary

Salacuse (1988) argues that the knowledge, skills, and attitudes necessary for international business negotiation are not those generally found in U.S. executives. It is wrong to assume that to be successful interculturally, negotiators must do *outside* as they do *within* the United States. However, one

TABLE 4.1
Areas of Cultural Variation Relevant to Intercultural Negotiation

- Understanding of what *negotiation* means and accomplishes
- Importance of relationship
- View of "profit"
- Understanding of *individual, individual rights,* and *group*
- Perspectives toward time
- How trust is established and maintained
- Customs and norms, including importance of protocol and etiquette
- Makeup of the negotiation team
- View of hierarchies
- Use of interpreter and/or go-between
- Levels of risk
- Values, perceptions, and philosophies underlying the language—not just vocabulary
- Differences in interpreting nonverbal communication
- Manner of communicating information and proposals
- Decision-making processes and styles
- Use of emotions
- Need to save face
- Differences in thinking processes, logic, and reasoning
- Communication styles, including persuasive and conflict styles, use of small talk
- View of what "contract" represents and form of final agreement

weakness in the guiding principles literature is that although the authors assert that certain skills are necessary for contract procurement, none describes exactly how negotiators should enact these skills. Exactly how will a negotiator who has adopted efficient principles for international negotiating communicate, verbally and nonverbally, with his or her counterpart? For example, Schwartz (1993) argues, "When in Rome, Tokyo, Moscow, Cairo, Rio, etc., one should do as the natives do. This does not mean that we should try to become them. Rather, for Americans it is important to remain in character, to be 'authentic' " (p. 1285). Communicatively, how to balance "doing as the natives do" and "remaining authentic" remains vague (Frank, 1992b), however compelling this idea may be intuitively. One notable exception is McCall and Warrington's (1984) explication of communication strategies for establishing intercultural understanding. For example, "flagging" is accomplished by forecasting one's behaviors, as in, "May I ask a question?" or "May I make a suggestion?"

It is our primary argument in this chapter that communication provides the vital link between culture and negotiation (Elgström, 1990). This is reflected in our perspective that interpersonal communication at the negotiation table determines success because it exhibits, or fails to exhibit, these attitudes and principles. Therefore, despite its shortcomings, this body of work is a rich resource for further research because its assumptions can be transformed into hypotheses about (a) the essential elements of effective negotiation that are grounded in communication, such as attitudes, and (b) how cultures vary along negotiation-relevant dimensions, such as "view of profit."

Quadrant III: Variable Analytic

Works in the third quadrant are culture specific, like those in Quadrant I, but are theoretically driven, based on propositions and axioms emerging from research in cultural values and worldviews. As such, these works, rather than merely cataloging negotiators' communication behaviors, move toward explaining what these behaviors mean, culturally and interculturally—a move recommended by Roberts (1970) in her early review of the intercultural negotiation literature. Research in this quadrant focuses on the continuing debate about the local versus global impacts of culture. Scholars on one side argue that culture profoundly influences negotiators' perceptions and preferences. Rubin and Sander (1991) believe that culture is a "powerful organizing prism" through which stimuli are interpreted. Negotiation, as a process of interaction and information gathering, is shaped by culture (Bangert & Pirzada, 1992; Trompenaars, 1993). Researchers on this side treat culture as a global and pervasive factor that drives negotiator behavior in all contexts. On the other side, scholars suggest that negotiation is a universal phenomenon, such that culture has only a minimal impact (At-Twaijri, 1992). Researchers on this side examine the locally managed impact of culture, or how culture influences negotiation behavior within the constraints of role and context, such as intra- versus intercultural interaction, time pressures, and constituent pressures.

Quadrant III comprises two groups. Group A studies (global influence) treat culture as a determinant of negotiation processes and/or outcomes (Fant, 1989; Francis, 1991; Graham, Mintu, & Rodgers, 1994; Grindsted, 1990; Husted, 1994). In addition, many of these studies examine relationships between process and outcome variables. Cultures and dependent variables represented in this group are vast, but these studies share a common implied logic that intracultural behaviors indicate intercultural negotiation tactics. Group B research treats culture as a complex, potentially nonadditive force that affects negotiation processes in conjunction with contextual features and interpersonal propensities (Porat, 1970). This assumption is consistent with Elgström's (1990) argument that culture influences negotiation in complex ways because negotiation is a specific context requiring certain behaviors, regardless of cultural membership. For example, concessions and refusals are fundamental elements of negotiation (Cai et al., 1996; Drake, 1994, 1995;

Wilson, Cai, & Drake, 1995). Thus, though persons from Culture A may be typically avoidant in conflict style, negotiation as a unique context may require more direct refusals than the Culture A negotiator would employ in everyday circumstances (Cai & Donohue, in press). Group B studies suggest that simply understanding cultural values and customs is insufficient for effective intercultural negotiation. Instead, understanding how culture affects a range of communication processes, such as reciprocity and conflict style, or contextual features, such as roles and framing, is imperative.

Group A

Various researchers have taken the global approach to testing hypotheses theorized from cultural differences in individualism-collectivism, approaches to negotiation, and business practices (At-Twaijri, 1992; Graham, 1985; Grindsted, 1990; Husted, 1994; Porat, 1970). For example, Kirkbride, Tang, and Westwood (1991) relate Chinese negotiating behavior to cultural values toward collectivism. Stress on harmony, conformity, face, and power distance (Hofstede, 1980) has been tied to preference for compromising, avoiding, and accommodating; extreme initial demands; low verbal posturing and position taking; and vague and ambiguous language in negotiation. In a representative series of studies, Graham and colleagues (Graham, 1983, 1985; Graham, Evenko, & Rajan, 1992; Graham, Kim, Lin, & Robinson, 1988) have compared Brazilian, Japanese, U.S., Russian, Chinese, and Korean negotiation. Findings across the studies were relatively consistent. No differences emerged for profit. Graham (1983) found the relationship between attractiveness and profit varied across cultures, as did the relationship between impression formation accuracy and profit. Graham (1985) found Brazilian negotiators saying no more often, interrupting and touching more, using more facial gaze, implementing less silence, and making more extreme initial offers than Japanese or U.S. negotiators. Most important, Graham et al. (1988) found that increased use of problem-solving tactics, a measure of integrative bargaining, resulted in increased profits for U.S. negotiators. For both U.S. and Korean negotiators, problem-solving tactics increased partner satisfaction. U.S., Korean, and Japanese negotiators reciprocated problem-solving approaches (Graham et al., 1988), as did Russians (Graham et al., 1992). Campbell et al. (1988) found in their comparison of British, French, German, and U.S. negotiators that a problem-solving approach by buyers increased profits for sellers. These findings provide some empirical support for the links proposed in Quadrant II between positive outcomes and principled negotiation, establishing trust, and communicating proposals. However, because Group A studies represent only cross-cultural comparisons, the generalizability of this link to intercultural contexts is limited.

Other studies in Group A provide empirical support for observed differences reported in Quadrant I. Adler and her colleagues (1987), in a cross-cultural comparison of Anglo-Canadian, Franco-Canadian, Mexican, and U.S. negotiators, found that Mexican negotiators scored highest on partner satisfaction and attractiveness. Franco-Canadians perceived themselves to be the least cooperative. No differences emerged for profit. Fant (1989) found that Spanish negotiators interrupted more, held more face gaze, and used more self-linked coherence markers than did Swedish negotiators. Adler, Brahm, and Graham (1992) found that Chinese negotiators asked more questions, issued fewer hard-line tactics (Allen, Donohue, & Stewart, 1990), interrupted more, and used *no* and *you* less often than did U.S. negotiators. Again, although they provide valuable support for anecdotal accounts, these intracultural findings are not generalizable to intercultural settings.

Quadrant III is heavily influenced by a separate literature comparing conflict styles across cultures. Wilson and his colleagues (1995) review 10 such studies from 1965 through 1991. Conflict resolution preferences have been found to differ across "high- and low context" cultures (Hall, 1976); across superior, peer, and subordinate relationships; in high- versus low-stakes circumstances; and across "in-group" and "out-group" disputants (Triandis et al., 1988).

Although closely related, conflict management studies do not address negotiation behavior per se. Rather, cultural conflict styles include patterned responses across varied communication events (Ting-Toomey et al., 1991). These patterned responses may include children's responses to competition (Kagan, Knight, & Martinez-Romero, 1982), superior-subordinate relationships (Lee & Rogan, 1991), organizational management (Adler, Campbell, & Laurent, 1989), and interpersonal struggles over task or affective issues (McGinn, Harburg, & Ginsburg, 1965; Ohbuchi & Takahashi, 1994; Ting-Toomey et al., 1991; Wolfson & Norden, 1984). The intercultural business negotiation literature is more specified, examining the enactment of roles typical to the business environment (Adler et al., 1992; Cai & Donohue, in press; Drake, 1994; Fant, 1989; Graham & Gronhaug, 1989; Grindsted, 1990; Husted, 1994).

Summary of Group A

Group A studies have systematically investigated many of the intracultural negotiating behaviors reported in Quadrant I and provide qualified support for principles advocated in Quadrant II. However, they bring to light significant questions about the extent to which intracultural negotiating modes predict intercultural interaction (Adler et al., 1989; Bochner & Perks, 1971; Graham & Gronhaug, 1989; Roberts, 1970; Wilhelm, 1994). Adler and Graham (1989) found significant differences between *intra*cultural (Japanese, American, Francophone Canadian, Anglophone Canadian) and *inter*cultural (American-Japanese, Anglo-Francophone Canadian) negotiations. Americans reported more satisfaction, Japanese achieved lower profit,

Francophones reported more cooperation, and Anglophones required longer settlement time in intercultural as opposed to intracultural dyads. Thus there remains much to learn about face-to-face negotiations between disparate cultural representatives.

Group B

Studies in Group B begin to address the intra- versus intercultural question. Two basic assumptions serve as the springboard for these studies. First, because negotiation is dynamic and interactive, processes and outcomes are mutually determined (Gulliver, 1979; Jönsson, 1990; Putnam & Wilson, 1989; Weiss, 1993). Interdependence characterizes negotiation interaction (Deutsch, 1973) so that negotiators must obtain the opponent's cooperation to reach a suitable agreement. Therefore, intercultural negotiators implicitly understand that insistence on their own negotiating style may jeopardize agreement. To avoid that consequence, each will adapt somehow to his or her opponent (Kim & Rubin, 1988; McCall & Warrington, 1984).

Second, negotiators are not only members of national cultures but are also members of political and diplomatic cultures (Weiss, 1993). According to Jönsson (1990), many aspects of verbal and nonverbal communication are more likely to be shared than dissimilar among international travelers, especially diplomats. Diplomatic culture has its own rules and norms (Walker, 1990). Thus negotiators (especially those with experience) may have more in common than others might presume (Limaye & Victor, 1991).

As Bangert and Pirzada (1992) so aptly point out, acknowledging the role of culture in negotiation is not to attribute all differences to culture. Other factors shape negotiation interaction as well. Porat (1970) argues that in labor-management negotiations, a negotiator is constrained by such organizational considerations as operational goals, societal pressures, a preplanned strategy, and perceived role. Similarly, Kirkbride and his colleagues (1991) argue that the assertiveness or cooperativeness exhibited by Chinese negotiators depends on both cultural values (*guanxi,* face, power distance, or reciprocity) and contextual factors (perceived differences in authority, power, and status).

Testing contextuality requires a complex system of controls and experimental conditions. The task is a daunting one. However, studies that make up Group B begin to make progress in this direction. For example, Cai and Donohue (in press) found that in face-to-face interaction, culturally anticipated facework strategies did not emerge in U.S.-Taiwanese negotiation simulations. Rather, these researchers found strong reciprocity of facework and buyer/seller differences, suggesting that role and the norm of reciprocity were stronger influences than culture.

Drake (1994) has also examined American-Taiwanese negotiation simulations based on Harris and Moran's (1991) description of culturally variant reasoning about negotiation. She found only one of four cultural negotiation styles resilient; the three others were reciprocated evenly. Again, strong reciprocity of negotiation styles was found. Wilson and his colleagues (1995), in their examination of intercultural interactions among representatives of 21 cultures, found that collectivism positively affected negotiators' profits. However, contextual features moderated the effects of collectivism, such that only in cases of high partner collectivism were joint profits increased. Cai et al. (1996) extended this previous study and constructed a path model representing the effects of cultural collectivism on negotiation processes and outcomes. Again, contextual features mediated the effects of culture, in that buyers, but not sellers, in high joint collectivism dyads used fewer distributive tactics. In terms of fostering integrative negotiation processes, joint collectivism was less influential than buyers' refusals. Thus role-related behavior overrode the influence of culture.

Graham (1993) took a stimulated recall approach in comparing American-American, Japanese-Japanese, and Japanese-American negotiating dyads. The findings included a change in behavior for Japanese dyads when opponents were well acquainted or when one negotiator was older and more experienced than the other. These findings indicate that authority and hierarchy are important modifiers of expected negotiation behavior (Graham & Andrews, 1987). In an examination of negotiators from 32 countries, Drake (1995) also found role (buyer/seller) a more significant influence on negotiation processes than collectivism. Buyers engaged in fixed-sum thinking (Thompson & Hastie, 1990) at nearly twice the rate of sellers.

Role as a moderator is well documented in that the disparity between buyer and seller profits increases in collectivist cultures such as Japan (Graham, 1983), Korea (Graham et al., 1988), and Mexico (Adler et al., 1987). Graham and Sano (1989) argue that this effect may be due to cultural conceptualizations of buyer-seller relationships. In the United States, buyers and sellers expect to be treated as equals. In Japan, the buyer is afforded more deference.

Summary of Group B

Though relatively few in number, studies in Group B point to the heuristic potential of the investigation of the contextual intricacies of intercultural business negotiation. As we begin to understand the contingencies affecting culture-based negotiation behaviors, we progress toward a fully inclusive theory of intercultural business negotiation. For example, other contextual features should be investigated, such as team size and makeup, power relationships within and across negotiation parties, constituency relationships (Roloff & Campion, 1987), prior knowledge, preparation and training of the parties (Eliashberg, Gauvin, Lilien, & Rangaswamy, 1992), number and importance of the issues to be negotiated, time constraints, language abilities

(Bell, 1988; Marriott, 1995), type of prenegotiation agreements (Klein & Bachechi, 1994), translation, interpretation, use of computer or other technologies, levels of trust (Graham et al., 1994), and negotiator age (Davis & Triandis, 1965).

Studies in Group B, however, also highlight a potential pitfall of this line of research—generalizability. The phenomena in this category are studied in laboratory settings using student subjects who are typically inexperienced in business negotiations. Adler and Graham (1989) cite support for significant differences between the negotiation behavior of students and that of businesspeople. Thus, although these studies may have adequately assessed cultural influences, the representativeness of negotiating strategies is called into question. Nevertheless, the tradition continues as researchers have great difficulty obtaining naturalistic data due to unavailability and issues of confidentiality (Bangert & Pirzada, 1992; Kale & Barnes, 1992), as well as the high monetary and time investments involved in gaining access (Limaye & Victor, 1991; Pruitt & Carnevale, 1993). An initial and obvious challenge for future research is to pursue naturalistic data, and thus gain insight into the development and emergence of issues rather than reactions to researcher-generated scenarios.

Quadrant IV: Global Theory

The remaining quadrant contains works that are culture general and theoretical; broad, overarching propositions about intercultural business contexts are forwarded. The primary difference between the works in this quadrant and those in Quadrant II is their ontological and epistemological tie to traditional negotiation and communication theory (though not explicitly recognized). The works in Quadrant IV build on prior theory and research to develop models and explanations that confront the why and how of effective negotiation principles and attitudes; thus they move beyond the assertions offered in Quadrant II. Early theorizing produced models of the intercultural negotiation process. For example, Fayerweather and Kapoor (1976) offer a concentric-rings model that portrays negotiation interaction as the central event (or inner circle). Interaction is "contextualized" by surrounding events, all represented by surrounding circles and each a set of constraints to be considered as the negotiator selects strategies. The most immediate ring encompasses the "four Cs": criteria, compromise, conflicting interests, and common interests. The next ring represents environmental factors, such as economic character and governmental controls. The outer ring represents the individual perspective.

Next, various "phase models" of negotiation dominated the literature (Habeeb, 1988; Hendon & Hendon, 1990). Gulliver (1979) offered an early model of patterned progression toward success, including eight stages: (a) search for the arena of confrontation, (b) agenda compilation and definition of issues, (c) exploring limits and differing emphases, (d) narrowing differences and reducing issues, (e) preliminaries to bargaining, (f) final bargaining to an outcome, (g) symbolic affirmation of agreement, and (h) execution of terms. A number of similar phase models are found in the literature (for reviews, see Holmes, 1992; McCall & Warrington, 1984). Phase models offer a diagnostic perspective, suggesting that negotiators who can progress through a predictable series of steps will forge satisfying agreements.

Both the early models and phase models offer the strengths of visual and conceptual illustrations of the links between direct and indirect negotiation influences on interaction. Conversely, both suffer a constraint presented by models in general—lack of explanatory power. Weiss (1996) reviews six such models of intercultural business negotiation. Although useful and heuristic (Littlejohn, 1996; Wood, 1997), models make little headway in explaining why or how such influences lead to success or failure. Whereas models occupy the domain of discovery by functioning as heuristic devices, theories occupy the domain of validation by offering empirically testable generalizations (Roberts, 1970). Without explanatory theory, it is difficult to break out of the exploratory mode so well represented in Quadrant I (Graham & Gronhaug, 1989; Limaye & Victor, 1991).

Recently, scholars have taken explanatory approaches to intercultural negotiation theory. Kale and Barnes (1992) propose that three constructs help to determine intercultural negotiation interaction: (a) national culture, including dimensions of culture from Hofstede's seminal work (1980)—power distance, individualism/collectivism, uncertainty avoidance, and masculinity/femininity; (b) organizational culture, including external versus internal emphasis, task versus social focus, conformity versus individuality, and safety versus risk; and (c) negotiator personality, as evidenced through such instruments as the MMPI and the Myers-Briggs Type Indicator. Ranking and comparing negotiators' standings in these three categories permits prediction of negotiation processes and outcomes. Two axioms form the basis for prediction making. First, greater similarity in these areas increases communication compatibility (Sheth, 1983). Second, increased communication compatibility increases the likelihood of success.

This theoretical perspective provides a well-defined framework for studying intercultural business negotiation. Its heuristic value lies in making explicit the underlying assumption present in Quadrants I and II: Similarity fosters liking and improves the odds of mutually satisfactory agreements (Johnson & Tims, 1985). One weakness is that the theory does not account for situational/circumstantial influences, such as political and economic constraints. Rather, these factors receive only brief mention. As yet, the theory has not received empirical support.

Weiss's (1994a, 1994b) theory explicitly addresses the issue of negotiator adaptation. That is, should an international negotiator adopt a native negotiator's typical negotiation practices? Determining each negotiator's familiarity with the other party's culture dictates an appropriate strategy. When neither negotiator has familiarity with the other's culture, an agent, adviser, or mediator should be employed to help the negotiators understand and appropriately interpret offers, counteroffers, and refusals. A negotiator who has moderate familiarity with the other negotiator's culture should adapt to his or her partner's scripted negotiation behaviors. When both negotiators are extremely familiar with their counterparts' cultures, they should have sufficient flexibility to improvise an approach and create their own negotiation rules. This theory is consistent with the notion that international negotiators may share much in the way of specialized, diplomatic protocol.

Bangert and Pirzada (1992) offer a context-dependent theory, proposing that culture's effects at every stage of negotiation differ in intra- versus intercultural contexts. In intracultural negotiation, the process of negotiating may be comparatively easy, because culture does not breed miscommunication. However, agreement may be more difficult to reach because of competing goals. In intercultural negotiation, process becomes more difficult, because culture creates communication barriers. However, a satisfying outcome is more likely due to differing cultural emphases and issue utilities. This theory ignores the important relationship between negotiation processes and outcomes. In any context suffering from miscommunication, barriers to the process of negotiation may have dire consequences for the final outcome. However, the theory does begin to explain the lack of consistent results across intra- and intercultural negotiations (e.g., Adler & Graham, 1989; Francis, 1991). This is consistent with Bonham's (1993) notion that culture's effects are found in the ways that culture affects the perceptions and interpretations of negotiators. He theorizes that cognitive maps can help represent negotiators' substantive knowledge of an issue as well as negotiators' assumptions and goals regarding process.

Finally, Weiss (1993) presents a return to modeling as a theoretical perspective. The RBC model represents links among the three basic components of international business negotiations across relevant levels (i.e., interpersonal, interorganizational, and intraorganizational). The R refers to "relationships," symmetric or asymmetric connections between negotiators, members of a negotiation team, or organizations who negotiate through agents. Encompassed in the relationship category are common interests, power, trust, and perceptions. B refers to "behaviors," actions directed toward or affecting another party. Included in this category are perceptions, information processing, judgment and decision making, planning, verbal styles, concession making, integrativeness, and proposals. C represents "conditions," the circumstances surrounding, stimulating, restricting, or modifying the negotiation. This category includes physical (location) as well as social (cultural) features of the negotiation, such as events, contexts, actions of third parties, capabilities of the negotiators, available communication channels, presence of interpreters, resources available to each side, traits of the negotiators, political and economic environments, and legal systems.

The RBC model is parsimonious in its ability to represent a complex system of influences under only three major headings. As a result, the model is highly flexible; it is equally suitable for application to international and intracultural negotiation situations. However, the RBC model fails to represent some potentially important relationships. For instance, outcome is not treated in this model, although negotiator relationships affect processes and outcomes (McCall & Warrington, 1984). In addition, this model does not represent reciprocal influence between relationships and behaviors. Additionally, it lacks sufficient focus on communication to represent fully the range of influences on negotiation processes and outcomes. Communication is not explicitly addressed in the model, but is an implied aspect of the "relationship" and "behavior" categories. Given our introductory discussion of communication's inseparability from culture, this oversight is not a trivial one.

Cultural dimension theory has proven a powerful heuristic in driving intercultural communication research relevant to international negotiation. This perspective identifies the social-psychological factors common across cultural groups, then notes the variance in these factors from culture to culture. Most popular among the dimensions studied is the collectivism-individualism continuum (Hofstede, 1980; Hui, 1988; Triandis et al., 1988). Hofstede (1980) proposes additional dimensions, including masculinity-femininity, high-low uncertainty avoidance, and high-low power distance. Also popular are Hall's (1976) distinctions between high- and low-context cultures and between monochronic and polychronic time.

However, any discussion of culture's effects must address the question of which cultural dimensions are contextually relevant. Are only work-related values important in intercultural business negotiation (Kale & Barnes, 1992; Limaye & Victor, 1991)? Other dimensions have been proposed, such as McClelland's work on economic growth as an indicator of need achievement resulting from core religious values (Roberts, 1970). In addition, varying dimensions of cognition (sequential, abstract, representational logic versus intuitive, sense based, concrete logic) have been studied (McCall & Warrington, 1984), as well as emphases on history and tradition (Jönsson, 1990).

A basic premise behind dimension theory is that particular psychological characteristics predominate in a given culture, and the culture's social structure permits ongoing expression of that psychology. For example, Sheth (1983) takes a dimensional approach to understanding the impact of culture on "task-oriented" versus "tradition-oriented" negotiation styles. He theorizes that individualism/collectivism, resource/need orientation, traditionalism/modernity, and safety/esteem needs create culturally preferred negotiation styles.

Summary

Eliashberg et al. (1992) argue that effective intercultural negotiation requires both descriptive knowledge and strategic knowledge. Skillful negotiators must not only know negotiation strategies but also when to use those strategies. Their observation is an apt summary of the current state of intercultural business negotiation research. As scholars, we find the descriptive and prescriptive knowledge gained from the works in Quadrants I and II to be a necessary but not sufficient step in the process of theory development. Gaining "strategic knowledge" by contextualizing culture's influence in intercultural negotiation is the function of the works in Quadrants III and IV. As a result, we have some understanding that roles influence culturally expected negotiation behaviors, and adaptation is likely. The remaining task is the construction of comprehensive explanations answering not only the when and why questions, but the how questions as well.

Weiss (1993) advocates a broad understanding of international negotiation and an inclusive theoretical perspective by incorporating major features of existing theories. Contextual (Janosik, 1987) approaches like those of Wilson et al. (1995), Cai et al. (1996), and Drake (1995) begin such incorporation. More work along these lines, particularly methodologies that incorporate face-to-face interaction, has been suggested (McCall & Warrington, 1984). For this reason, we propose that Quadrant IV holds the greatest potential for expanding our insights into intercultural business negotiation. During its next decade of development, intercultural negotiation research will be best served by more scholarly focus on falsification and revision of the theories available. In our estimation, this task is best approached through a careful synthesis of concepts and theories from communication and traditional negotiation research.

A SUMMARY OF KNOWLEDGE AND SYNTHESIS OF LITERATURES

Since Sawyer and Guetzkow (1965) developed their model of negotiation, researchers have devoted much effort to the delineation of the five model components: (a) background factors, (b) antecedent goals, (c) processes, (d) conditions, and (e) outcomes. Although it suffers the same drawbacks as models discussed earlier, Sawyer and Guetzkow's model has been highly popular and is the most familiar to researchers from the various disciplines studying intercultural business negotiation (Weiss, 1996). Based on this rationale, in this section we will use the model as a means to summarize knowledge gained from work reviewed in the four quadrants, highlight the gaps in knowledge, and pinpoint specific areas in which constructs and theories from intercultural communication and traditional negotiation can inform our search for knowledge.

Background Factors

Background factors include preexisting characteristics of the negotiators, including their cultures, national characters, attitudes toward other cultures, prior relations between cultures, and personalities. In Sawyer and Guetzkow's model, such background factors influence goals and processes. Across the intercultural business negotiation literature, culture is the primary background factor, and to date it is presumed to have a powerful influence on goals and processes. Empirical work has not supported this presumption in face-to-face negotiations between divergent cultural representatives.

From works in Quadrant I, we have learned that culture and national character comprise a range of values, preferences, and behaviors that differ across cultures. Values range from emphasis on hierarchy to equality, from high to low power distance, and from individualism to collectivism. Preferences range from relationship building to deal making, from vague to precise language, and from assertive to compromising conflict handling. Behaviors range from timeliness to timelessness and from high to low levels of touch and gaze. In addition, cultures differ in their interpretations of the concepts of "compromise," "contract," "profit," and "negotiation."

We know relatively little about attitudes toward other cultures, prior relations between cultures, and personalities of the negotiators. However, works in Quadrant II suggest that an empathic attitude and basic understanding of an opponent's culture are important factors in intercultural negotiation success, as are trust and friendship between negotiators. In addition, it is suggested that personality traits such as patience and high tolerance of ambiguity will also enhance success. Again, no empirical support exists for these suggested relationships. However, theoretical works in Quadrant IV incorporate the notion that personality similarity helps culturally diverse negotiators to work together successfully.

Communication concepts such as homophily and attraction inform these perspectives (Johnson & Tims, 1985). Communication accommodation theory (Gallois, Franklyn-Stokes, Giles, & Coupland, 1988; Giles, Mulac, Bradac, & Johnson, 1987) speaks to the ability of participants to create interpersonal similarity within their communicative interaction by "converging" to approximate the verbal and nonverbal behavior of the opponent. Unfortunately, communication accommodation theory has not been applied to international negotiation research, therefore we know little about the extent to which negotiators converge or about the relationship between convergence and successful outcomes. Negotiation research on cognitive predispositions to logical error may also inform this area (Jönsson, 1990). This research would include such concepts as the fixed-sum error (Thompson & Hastie, 1990) and risk aversion (Kahneman & Tversky, 1979).

Goals

Goals are antecedent intentions that influence the negotiation process, presumably as negotiators orchestrate negotiating behaviors to meet aims. In the model, goals are influenced by background and, in turn, shape processes. Research from the four quadrants muddies our understanding of the link between background and goals. Specifically, many works treat culture as synonymous with goals. For example, priorities on deal making versus relationship building may serve as indicators of culture, yet may also serve as goals (Davis & Triandis, 1965).

The works in Quadrants I and II suggest additional goals in intercultural business negotiations: long- versus short-term agreements, adherence to constituents' criteria, maintenance of consistency with organizational reputation, and avoidance of psychological traps. Empirically, we know little about goals in intercultural business negotiation. One notable exception is Cai's (1994) investigation of negotiator goals in American-Taiwanese dyads, in which the results indicated that the Americans formed more specific goals and more contingency plans.

Traditional negotiation research speaks to the issue of goals in terms of preplanning (Roloff & Jordan, 1992), setting target and resistance points (Lax & Sibenius, 1986), courting alternatives to negotiation (Bacharach & Lawler, 1981), levels of goal setting, and bargaining range (Bazerman, Magliozzi, & Neale, 1985; Ben-Yoav & Pruitt, 1984). In communication, rules theories such as coordinated management of meaning (Cronen, Chen, & Pearce, 1988) and constructivism (Delia & Clark, 1977; Delia, Kline, & Burleson, 1979; Wood, 1997) may also inform this area, providing insight into goal setting and enactment. Integrating these concepts with intercultural contexts will yield testable hypotheses, and thus seems a reasonable route to pursue in building our knowledge base.

Processes

Processes include interactive aspects such as procedures, agenda construction, exploration of alternatives and preferences, threats, promises, commitments, creative problem solving, and communication aimed at altering the opponent's perceptions. In the model, processes are influenced by background, goals, and conditions. In turn, processes affect outcomes.

The works in Quadrants I and III suggest that intracultural differences exist in face-saving, direct confrontation, direct refusals, use of silence, expression of emotion, explicit versus implicit language, emphasis on protocol, individual versus group decision making, cooperative tactics, attraction, problem solving, interruptions, backchannels, facial gaze, use of coherence markers, question asking, threats and hard-line tactics, touch, extremity of initial offer, argumentative exchange formats, and emphasis on logrolling. Again, despite massive anecdotal and empirical support for differences cross-culturally, we still know little about the resilience of these process differences interculturally. A growing database in Quadrant III points to a relative decrease in process differences interculturally.

Communication theories and constructs are especially well suited to addressing issues of process. For example, face negotiation theory (Ting-Toomey, 1988) may be profitably applied to threats, promises, commitments, and other face techniques. Affective-neutral orientations deal with emotional expression (Trompenaars, 1993). High and low context also holds implications for modes of indirect over direct communication. Nonverbal expectancy violations theory (Burgoon & Hale, 1988) offers avenues for investigating competing approach and avoidance needs. In addition, theories and constructs useful in both communication and traditional negotiation research, such as game theory (Pruitt & Kimmel, 1977) and reciprocity (Cialdini, 1993; Putnam & Jones, 1982), offer avenues for hypothesis testing. For example, work by Kelley and Stahelski (1970) suggests that collaboration/cooperation may be abandoned when the negotiator is faced with a highly competitive opponent. Issues of mediator effectiveness (Kressel & Pruitt, 1989) are also relevant. Finally, social exchange theories might be employed, especially where cultural differences in obligation and social debt are presumed to exist. Traditional negotiation concepts such as target and resistance points (Lax & Sibenius, 1986) may explain extremity of initial offers. In fact, the range of negotiation phenomena described by Bazerman and Neale (1992) lays out a host of topics for investigation in intercultural contexts.

Conditions

Conditions are specific situational constraints on the negotiation, including the physical setting, number of negotiators, number of "sides," and information available. In the model, conditions are another determinant of process. Works in Quadrants I, II, and III suggest that intracultural differences exist in the number of members employed on a negotiation team, governmental restraints on business practices, organizational goals, societal pressures, and degree of information actively pursued from a visiting negotiator.

This is the least-investigated portion of the model, as evidenced by the comparatively small pool of empirical work in Quadrant III examining the effects of culture relative to other conditional factors. Perhaps the most intriguing question for scholars is how intra- versus intercultural conditions affect negotiation processes. Indeed, Quadrant III (subset B) suggests that cultural composition is a crucial constraint. For instance, what are the relative effects of culture in "home" versus "away" cultures? Do negotiation tactics change when the opponent is perceived as "superior"? Are cultural effects more prevalent or less prevalent in the presence of negotiating teams, as opposed to individuals? How does the cultural profile of those teams affect negotiation processes? What happens when more than two parties, representing more than two cultures, meet at the negotiating table?

Other contextual questions are relevant when we consider concepts from communication and negotiation studies. For instance, Davis and Triandis (1965) point out that perceptions of the negotiation task as structured or unstructured profoundly affect process, as does the clarity of procedural rules. From communication, uncertainty reduction theory (Berger & Calabrese,

1975) seems especially apt for addressing these questions. Scholars commonly recognize that whatever the variables involved in intercultural interface, most serve to increase uncertainty (Graham & Gronhaug, 1989). Because interactants are unfamiliar with the communicative enactments of culture in negotiation, reducing uncertainty seems a fundamental task in intercultural communication and negotiation (Gudykunst & Kim, 1992). Interactional or systems theories (Littlejohn, 1996; Wood, 1997) also provide means for explaining the effect of various conditions on negotiation relationships (Donohue & Ramesh, 1992).

Outcomes

Outcomes are final agreements between the parties, whether formal or informal, clearly delineated or vague. In the model, outcomes are driven by processes. The works in Quadrants I and II suggest that cultures differ in their preferences for the form and specificity of final agreements. The works in Quadrant III yield no group differences in profits obtained, but occasional group differences in satisfaction with the negotiation process, profits for buyers as opposed to sellers, time to settle, specificity of final contract, and joint profits. As in other areas, more is known about intracultural than about intercultural negotiation outcomes. Deutsch's (1973) notions of integrative and distributive outcomes help explain the relationship of processes to outcomes. Thibaut and Kelley's (1959) theory of social interdependence helps to explain the stability of final agreements as well as the motivation to construct such agreements. Outcome variables such as time to settle could be profitably explored using cultural dimension theory. In particular, polychronic versus monochronic orientations toward time (Hall, 1976) could be applied.

Summary

The foregoing discussion indicates three major weaknesses present in intercultural negotiation research. First, most work is not, in fact, *inter*cultural. Rather, much of our knowledge of intercultural negotiation is presumed from intracultural investigations. Such presumptions are problematic, given the findings in Quadrant III. Thus far, empirical evidence suggests that negotiators' approach and interaction modes change significantly from intra- to intercultural contexts.

Second, little is understood about the impact of conditions on intercultural negotiation processes. In terms of creating a more complete picture of intercultural business negotiation and fostering theory development, future research must endeavor to study the moderating effects of contextual features in conjunction with background and goals effects.

Third, little is known about intercultural negotiation outcomes. Given that successful and satisfying outcomes are the goals for practitioners and scholars alike, this shortage seems a particularly crippling one for the field. In part, this weakness is a function of the first two. It is also indicative of present theoretical limitations. As the works in Quadrant IV reveal, researchers have several models but few theories on which to formulate hypotheses about outcomes.

Lack of theory is the weakness that can be most profitably addressed by communication scholars. A synthesis of intercultural business negotiation, traditional negotiation, and intercultural communication theories should produce a more coherent body of knowledge about intercultural interaction, conditional contingencies, and business negotiation outcomes (Graham & Gronhaug, 1989). For example, Johnson and Tims (1985) have tested the effects of homophily (measured by perceived common interests) on attraction (represented as a desire for contact between cultural groups) in U.S.-Mexican negotiation. They conceptualize negotiation as the enactment of desire for contact.

CONCLUSION

A core component of these interdisciplinary approaches to understanding intercultural business negotiation is communication. Communication research has laid much of the groundwork for further investigation and theory development in intercultural negotiation. Future research and theorizing must be aimed at addressing intercultural negotiation as a unique context that interacts with culture to yield results that are not yet fully explained by either negotiation or communication concepts. This review should convince researchers of the work yet to be accomplished in this regard.

In the main, research has focused on the Pacific Rim cultures (especially Japan and China). Only recently, as economic interests have grown due to NAFTA and the breakdown of the Soviet Union, has more attention been devoted to negotiating with companies in Eastern Europe and South America. Thus, as we advance into the 21st century, broader knowledge of cultural negotiating behaviors has both heuristic and pragmatic value.

This review reveals the following conclusions regarding literature across the four quadrants (for a summary, see Table 4.2). Quadrant I literature reports observed negotiation styles of various cultures (Soviet, Arab, German, Swiss, and so on). This literature forwards the assumption that cultural awareness leads to successful ends because it allows visitors to adapt to their cultural counterparts. More research is needed to examine the effects of such adaptation. Quadrant II literature asserts the principles and attitudes internationals may rely upon for successful negotiation with persons from any culture, without focusing on the enactment of such principles in any specific culture. These principles can be transformed into a number of testable hypotheses about effective intercultural negotiating.

TABLE 4.2
Summary of Findings Across the Four Quadrants

Quadrant I: Descriptive/Prescriptive

a. Describes negotiation behaviors of cultures such as Japanese, Chinese, Russian, Arab.

b. Cultural awareness leads to effective negotiating.

c. Cultural awareness leads to successful outcomes.

d. Propositions about relationship between cultural values and negotiation behaviors.

Conclusion: More research is needed about the effects of adaptation.

Quadrant II: Guiding Principles

a. Identifies attitudes and behaviors that are helpful for cultural effectiveness.

b. Features of negotiation vary among cultures.

Conclusions: Needs empirical support.
                    Limited focus on communication.
                    No explication of enacting attitudes or behaviors.

Quadrant III: Variable Analytic

a. Specific cultures shown to differ in the following: partner satisfaction, partner attractiveness, integrative bargaining, interruptions, face gaze, coherence markers, questioning, hard-line tactics, use of *no*, use of *you*, touch, silence, extreme offers, time to settle, argument structure, logrolling.

b. Relationships among variables integrative bargaining, similarity, attractiveness, and impression accuracy lead to higher profits; integrative bargaining leads to higher partner satisfaction.

c. Reciprocity found in integrative bargaining, facework.

d. Interactions examined between the following: own and partner's collectivism, collectivism and role, culture and intimacy levels, culture and age.

Conclusions: Support for differences between intra- and intercultural contexts.
                    Support for moderators of cultural effects in intercultural negotiating.
                    Limits to generalizability.

Quadrant IV: Global Theory

a. Descriptive models of process.

b. Phase models of progression toward successful outcomes.

c. Theories: Three levels of culture.
                    Adaptation is based on familiarity.
                    Intra- versus intercultural logrolling and communication potential.
                    Cognitive maps of culture's role in negotiation.
                    Cultural dimension theory.

Conclusions: Visual representations offer descriptive knowledge.
                    Theories offer explanatory propositions.
                    Propositions can be explored by integrating communication and negotiation theories.

Quadrant III literature undertakes empirical investigation of cultural negotiating styles and explicates differences among negotiators from Canada, Mexico, Brazil, Japan, and other cultures in cooperation, interruptions, refusals, face gaze, silence, and integrative approaches. These studies offer some support for the link between integrative bargaining and positive outcomes. They also indicate that reciprocity is a strong force in intercultural as well as intracultural negotiating, thus implying some significant differences between these two contexts. Quadrant IV literature synthesizes the various forces at work in negotiation with an intercultural approach. Various models of the intercultural negotiation process are offered as well as a few explanatory propositions about the relative contributions and effects of culture, personality, organizational structure, and mutual adaptation by negotiators. Among these, cultural dimension theory has been most productively explored. However, from a communication perspective, other theories may prove equally heuristic if integrated with suggested concepts and theories from traditional negotiation and intercultural communication research.

The prescriptive/descriptive and guiding principles literatures provide an advantage not afforded by the variable analytic work in that most of the works in Quadrants I and II have been developed from naturalistic negotiations within and between cultures. The variable analytic literature is largely based on laboratory data and often uses students as "negotiators." There is an obvious gap, then, between these areas of research. Thus the job for intercultural business negotiation scholars is twofold. Integration of theory represents one task; obtaining results in naturalistic intercultural settings is the other.

The study of intercultural business negotiation has grown and matured significantly since Prosser's (1977) first review for the *Communication Yearbook*. Similar intercultural communication issues will only receive greater attention as global markets and intercultural contacts continue to expand. Seeing our evolution and assessing its impact provides communication scholars the opportunity to regroup and set a course for further study in this fascinating arena.

REFERENCES

Acuff, F. L. (1990). Negotiation in the Pacific Rim. *International Executive, 31,* 20.
Acuff, F. L. (1993). *How to negotiate anything with anyone, anywhere in the world.* New York: American Management Association.
Adler, N. J. (1991). *International dimensions of organizational behavior* (2nd ed.). Boston: Kent.
Adler, N. J., Brahm, R., & Graham, J. L. (1992). Strategy implementation: A comparison of face-to-face negotiations in the People's Republic of China and the United States. *Strategic Management Journal, 13,* 449-466.
Adler, N. J., Campbell, N., & Laurent, A. (1989). In search of appropriate methodology: From outside the People's Republic of China looking in. *Journal of International Business Studies, 20,* 61-74.

Adler, N. J., & Graham, J. L. (1989). Cross-cultural interaction: The international comparison fallacy. *Journal of International Business Studies, 20,* 515-537.

Adler, N. J., Graham, J. L., & Gehrke, T. S. (1987). Business negotiations in Canada, Mexico, and the United States. *Journal of Business Research, 15,* 411-429.

Allen, M., Donohue, W., & Stewart, B. (1990). Comparing hardline and softline bargaining strategies in zero-sum situations using meta-analysis. In M. A. Rahim (Ed.), *Theory and research in conflict management* (pp. 86-103). New York: Praeger.

At-Twaijri, M. I. (1992). The negotiating style of Saudi industrial buyers: An empirical investigation. *International Journal of Value Based Management, 5,* 1-15.

Bacharach, S. B., & Lawler, E. J. (1981). *Bargaining: Power, tactics, and outcomes.* Greenwich, CT: JAI.

Bangert, D. C., & Pirzada, K. (1992). Culture and negotiation. *International Executive, 34,* 43-64.

Bazerman, M. H., Magliozzi, T., & Neale, M. A. (1985). Integrative bargaining in a competitive market. *Organizational Behavior and Human Decision Processes, 35,* 294-313.

Bazerman, M. H., & Neale, M. A. (1992). *Negotiating rationally.* New York: Free Press.

Beliaev, E., Mullen, T., & Punnett, B. J. (1985). Understanding the cultural environment: USA-USSR trade negotiations. *California Management Review, 27*(2), 100-112.

Bell, D. V. J. (1988). Political linguistics and international negotiation. *Negotiation Journal, 4,* 233-246.

Ben-Yoav, O., & Pruitt, D. G. (1984). Resistance to yielding and the expectation of cooperative future interaction in negotiation. *Journal of Experimental Social Psychology, 34,* 323-335.

Berger, C. R., & Calabrese, R. J. (1975). Some explorations in initial interaction and beyond: Toward a developmental theory of interpersonal communication. *Human Communication Research, 1,* 99-112.

Blaker, M. (1977a). *Japanese international negotiating style.* New York: Columbia University Press.

Blaker, M. (1977b). Probe, push, and panic: The Japanese tactical style in international negotiations. In R. Scalapino (Ed.), *The foreign policy of modern Japan* (pp. 55-101). Berkeley: University of California Press.

Bochner, S., & Perks, R. W. (1971). National role evocation as a function of cross-cultural interaction. *Journal of Cross-Cultural Psychology, 2,* 157-164.

Bonham, G. M. (1993). Cognitive mapping as a technique for supporting international negotiation. *Theory and Decision, 34,* 255-273.

Burgoon, J., & Hale, J. (1988). Nonverbal expectancy violations. *Communication Monographs, 55,* 58-79.

Burt, D. N. (1984). The nuances of negotiating overseas. *Journal of Purchasing and Materials Management, 20,* 2-8.

Cahn, D. D. (1983). Relative importance of perceived understanding in initial interaction and development of interpersonal relationships. *Psychological Reports, 52,* 923-929.

Cai, D. A. (1994). *Planning in negotiation: A comparison of U.S. and Taiwanese cultures.* Unpublished doctoral dissertation, Michigan State University.

Cai, D. A., & Donohue, W. (in press). Determinants of facework in intercultural negotiation. *Asian Journal of Communication.*

Cai, D. A., Wilson, S. R., & Drake, L. E. (1996, June). *Individualism/collectivism and joint gain: Illuminating the paths to integrative bargaining agreements.* Paper presented at the annual meeting of the International Association for Conflict Management, Ithaca, NY.

Campbell, N. C. G., Graham, J. L., Jolibert, A., & Meissner, H. G. (1988). Marketing negotiations in France, Germany, the United Kingdom, and the United States. *Journal of Marketing, 52,* 44-62.

Casse, P., & Deol, S. (1985). *Managing intercultural negotiation: Guidelines for trainers and negotiators.* Washington, DC: Sietar International.

Chen, M. (1993). Understanding Chinese and Japanese negotiating styles. *International Executive, 35,* 147-159.

Chu, C. N. (1991). *The Asian mind game.* New York: Rawson.

Cialdini, R. B. (1993). *Influence: Science and practice* (3rd ed.). New York: HarperCollins.

Corne, P. H. (1992). The complex art of negotiation between different cultures. *Arbitration Journal, 47,* 46-50.

Cronen, V., Chen, V., & Pearce, W. B. (1988). Coordinated management of meaning: A critical theory. In Y. Y. Kim & W. B. Gudykunst (Eds.), *Theories in intercultural communication* (pp. 66-98). Newbury Park, CA: Sage.

Davidson, W. H. (1987). Creating and managing joint ventures in China. *California Management Review, 29*(4), 77-94.

Davis, E. E., & Triandis, H. C. (1965). *An exploratory study of intercultural negotiations* (Tech. Rep. No. 26). Urbana, IL: Group Effectiveness Research Laboratory.

Delia, J. G., & Clark, R. A. (1977). Cognitive complexity, social perception, and the development of listener-adapted communication in six-, eight-, ten-, and twelve-year old boys. *Communication Monographs, 44,* 326-345.

Delia, J. G., Kline, S. L., & Burleson, B. R. (1979). The development of persuasive communication strategies in kindergarteners through twelfth-graders. *Communication Monographs, 46,* 241-256.

De Mente, B. L. (1981). *The Japanese way of doing business: The psychology of management in Japan.* Englewood Cliffs, NJ: Prentice Hall.

De Mente, B. L. (1987). *How to do business with the Japanese.* Lincolnwood, IL: NTC Business Books.

DePauw, J. W. (1981). *U.S.-Chinese trade negotiations.* New York: Praeger.

Deutsch, M. (1973). *The resolution of conflict: Constructive and destructive processes.* New Haven, CT: Yale University Press.

Dodd, C. H. (1991). *Dynamics of intercultural communication* (3rd ed.). Dubuque, IA: William C. Brown.

Donohue, C. D. (1992, May-June). Negotiating international joint ventures: A test of character. *New Jersey Lawyer,* pp. 26-29.

Donohue, W. A., & Ramesh, C. N. (1992). Negotiator-opponent relationships. In L. L. Putnam & M. E. Roloff (Eds.), *Communication and negotiation* (pp. 209-232). Newbury Park, CA: Sage.

Donohue, W. A., & Roberto, A. J. (1993). Relational development as negotiated order in hostage negotiation. *Human Communication Research, 20,* 175-198.

Downing, R. W. (1992). The continuing power of cultural tradition and socialist ideology: Cross-cultural negotiations involving Chinese, Korean, and American negotiators. *Journal of Dispute Resolution, 1992,* 105-132.

Drake, L. E. (1994). Negotiation styles in intercultural communication. *International Journal of Conflict Management, 6,* 72-90.

Drake, L. E. (1995). *To err is human: Cultural orientation as a source of judgment errors and integrative processes in international negotiation.* Unpublished doctoral dissertation, Michigan State University.

Eiteman, D. K. (1990). American executives' perceptions of negotiating joint ventures with the People's Republic of China: Lessons learned. *Columbia Journal of World Business, 25,* 59-67.

Elgström, O. (1990). Norms, culture, and cognitive patterns in foreign aid negotiations. *Negotiation Journal, 6,* 147-159.

Eliashberg, J., Gauvin, S., Lilien, G. L., & Rangaswamy, A. (1992). An experimental study of alternative preparation aids for international negotiations. *Group Decision and Negotiation, 1,* 243-267.

Fant, L. (1989). Cultural mismatch in conversation: Spanish and Scandinavian communicative behavior in negotiation settings. *Hermes: Journal of Linguistics, 3,* 247-265.

Fayerweather, J., & Kapoor, A. (1976). *Strategy and negotiation for the international corporation*. Cambridge, MA: Ballinger.

Fisher, R., Ury, W., & Patton, B. (1991). *Getting to yes* (2nd ed.). New York: Penguin.

Francis, J. N. P. (1991). When in Rome? The effects of cultural adaptation on intercultural business negotiations. *Journal of International Business Studies, 22,* 403-425.

Frank, S. (1992a). Avoiding the pitfalls of business abroad. *Sales and Marketing Management, 144,* 48-52.

Frank, S. (1992b). Global negotiating: Vive les differences! *Sales and Marketing Management, 144,* 64-69.

Gallois, C., Franklyn-Stokes, A., Giles, H., & Coupland, N. (1988). Communication accommodation in intercultural encounters. In Y. Y. Kim & W. B. Gudykunst (Eds.), *Theories in intercultural communication* (pp. 157-185). Newbury Park, CA: Sage.

Geertz, C. (1973). *The interpretation of cultures: Selected essays.* New York: Basic Books.

Giles, H., Mulac, A., Bradac, J. J., & Johnson, P. (1987). Speech accommodation theory: The first decade and beyond. In M. L. McLaughlin (Ed.), *Communication yearbook 10* (pp. 13-40). Newbury Park, CA: Sage.

Goldman, A. (1994). The centrality of "Ningensei" to Japanese negotiating and interpersonal relationships: Implications for U.S.-Japanese communication. *International Journal of Intercultural Relations, 18,* 29-40.

Graham, J. L. (1983). Brazilian, Japanese, and American business negotiations. *Journal of International Business Studies, 14,* 47-61.

Graham, J. L. (1985). Cross-cultural marketing negotiations: A laboratory experiment. *Marketing Science, 4,* 130-146.

Graham, J. L. (1993). The Japanese negotiation style: Characteristics of a distinct approach. *Negotiation Journal, 9,* 123-140.

Graham, J. L., & Andrews, D. (1987). A holistic analysis of cross-cultural business negotiations. *Journal of Business Communication, 24,* 63-77.

Graham, J. L., Evenko, L. I., & Rajan, M. N. (1992). An empirical comparison of Soviet and American business negotiations. *Journal of International Business Studies, 23,* 387-415.

Graham, J. L., & Gronhaug, K. (1989). Ned Hall didn't have to get a haircut: Or why we haven't learned much about international marketing in twenty-five years. *Journal of Higher Education, 60,* 152-187.

Graham, J. L., Kim, D. K., Lin, C., & Robinson, M. (1988). Buyer-seller negotiations around the Pacific Rim: Differences in fundamental exchange processes. *Journal of Consumer Research, 15,* 48-54.

Graham, J. L., Mintu, A. T., & Rodgers, W. (1994). Explorations of negotiation behaviors in ten foreign cultures using a model developed in the United States. *Management Science, 40,* 72-95.

Graham, J. L., & Sano, Y. (1989). *Smart bargaining: Doing business with the Japanese.* New York: Harper & Row.

Griffin, T. J., & Daggart, W. R. (1990). *The global negotiator.* New York: HarperCollins.

Grindsted, A. (1990). Argumentative exchange formats in Spanish and Danish negotiations. *Merino, 8,* 1-11.

Gudykunst, W. B., & Kim, Y. Y. (1992). *Communicating with strangers* (2nd ed.). New York: McGraw-Hill.

Gudykunst, W. B., & Nishida, T. (1984). Individual and cultural influences on uncertainty reduction. *Communication Monographs, 51,* 23-36.

Gudykunst, W. B., & Ting-Toomey, S. (1988). *Culture and interpersonal communication.* Newbury Park, CA: Sage.

Gulliver, P. (1979). *Disputes and negotiations: A cross-cultural perspective.* New York: Academic Press.

Haas, M. (1974). *International conflict.* New York: Bobbs-Merrill.

Habeeb, W. M. (1988). *Power and tactics in international negotiation*. Baltimore: Johns Hopkins University Press.

Hall, E. T. (1960). The silent language in overseas business. *Harvard Business Review, 38*(3), 1-3.

Hall, E. T. (1976). *Beyond culture*. Garden City, NY: Anchor/Doubleday.

Hammer, M. R. (in press). Negotiating across the cultural divide: Intercultural dynamics in crisis incidents. In R. G. Rogan, M. R. Hammer, & C. R. Van Zandt (Eds.), *Dynamic processes of crisis negotiation: Theory, research and practice*. Westport, CT: Praeger.

Hammer, M. R., Rogan, R. G., Van Zandt, C. R., & Laffon, A. (1993, November). *Communication dynamics in a crisis situation: Negotiating the Talladega Prison take-over*. Paper presented at the annual meeting of the Speech Communication Association, Miami, FL.

Harris, P. R., & Moran, R. T. (1991). *Managing cultural differences: High-performance strategies for a new world of business*. Houston, TX: Gulf.

Hendon, D. W., & Hendon, R. A. (1990). *World-class negotiating*. New York: John Wiley.

Hofstede, G. (1980). *Culture's consequences: International differences in work-related values*. Beverly Hills, CA: Sage.

Holmes, M. E. (1992). Phase structures in negotiation. In L. L. Putnam & M. E. Roloff (Eds.), *Communication and negotiation* (pp. 83-108). Newbury Park, CA: Sage.

Holmes, M. E., & Fletcher-Bergland, T. S. (1995). Negotiations in crisis. In A. M. Nicotera (Ed.), *Conflict and organizations: Communicative processes* (pp. 239-258). Albany: State University of New York Press.

Hsu, F. L. K. (1981). *Americans and Chinese*. Honolulu: University of Hawaii Press.

Hu, W., & Grove, C. (1991). *Encountering the Chinese: A guide for Americans*. Yarmouth, ME: Intercultural Press.

Huang, Z. D. (1990). Negotiation in China: Cultural and practical characteristics. *China Law Reporter, 6*, 139-145.

Hui, C. H. (1988). Measurement of individualism-collectivism: A study of cross-cultural researchers. *Journal of Cross-Cultural Psychology, 17*, 225-248.

Husted, B. W. (1994). Bargaining with the gringos: An exploratory study of negotiations between Mexican and U.S. firms. *International Executive, 36*, 625-644.

Janosik, R. J. (1987). Rethinking the culture-negotiation link. *Negotiation Journal, 3*, 385-395.

Johnson, J. D., & Tims, A. R. (1985). Communication factors related to closer international ties. *Human Communication Research, 12*, 259-273.

Johnstone, B. (1989). Linguistic strategies and cultural styles for persuasive discourse. In S. Ting-Toomey & F. Korzenny (Eds.), *Language, communication, and culture* (pp. 139-156). Newbury Park, CA: Sage.

Jönsson, C. (1990). *Communication in international bargaining*. New York: St. Martin's.

Kagan, S., Knight, G. P., & Martinez-Romero, S. (1982). Culture and the development of conflict resolution style. *Journal of Cross-Cultural Psychology, 13*, 43-58.

Kahneman, D., & Tversky, A. (1979). Prospect theory: An analysis of decision under risk. *Econometrica, 47*, 263-291.

Kale, S. H., & Barnes, J. W. (1992). Understanding the domain of cross-national buyer-seller interactions. *Journal of International Business Studies, 23*, 101-132.

Kelley, H. H., & Stahelski, A. J. (1970). Social interaction basis of cooperators' and competitors' beliefs about others. *Journal of Personality and Social Psychology, 16*, 66-91.

Kennedy, G. (1985a). *Doing business abroad*. New York: Simon & Schuster.

Kennedy, G. (1985b). *Negotiate anywhere!* London: Business Books.

Kim, Y. Y., & Rubin, B. D. (1988). Intercultural transformation: A systems theory. In Y. Y. Kim & W. B. Gudykunst (Eds.), *Theories in intercultural communication* (pp. 299-321). Newbury Park, CA: Sage.

Kirkbride, P. S., Tang, S. F. Y., & Westwood, R. I. (1991). Chinese conflict preference and negotiating behavior: Cultural and psychological influences. *Organization Studies, 12*, 365-386.

Klein, J., & Bachechi, C. (1994). Precontractual liability and the duty of good faith negotiation in international transactions. *Houston Journal of International Law, 17,* 1-25.

Kressel, K., & Pruitt, D. G. (Eds.). (1989). *Mediation research.* San Francisco: Jossey-Bass.

Lax, D., & Sibenius, J. (1986). *The manager as negotiator.* New York: Free Press.

Lee, H. O., & Rogan, R. G. (1991). A cross-cultural comparison of organizational conflict management behavior. *International Journal of Conflict Management, 2,* 181-199.

Lee, K. H., & Lo, T. W. C. (1988). American businesspeople's perceptions of marketing and negotiating in the People's Republic of China. *International Marketing Review, 5*(2), 41-51.

Le Poole, S. (1989, October). Negotiating with Clint Eastwood in Brussels. *Management Review, 78,* 58-60.

Limaye, M. R., & Victor, D. A. (1991). Cross-cultural business communication research: State of the art and hypotheses for the 1990's. *Journal of Business Communication, 28,* 277-299.

Littlejohn, S. W. (1996). *Theories of human communication* (5th ed.). New York: Wadsworth.

Macleod, R. (1988). *China, Inc.: How to do business with the Chinese.* New York: Bantam.

March, R. (1985, April). East meets West at the negotiating table. *Winds,* pp. 55-57.

March, R. (1988). *The Japanese negotiator: Subtlety and strategy beyond Western logic.* New York: Kodansha.

Marriott, H. E. (1995). "Deviations" in an intercultural business negotiation. In A. Firth (Ed.), *The discourse of negotiation: Studies of language in the workplace* (pp. 247-268). London: Pergamon.

McCall, J. B., & Warrington, M. B. (1984). *Marketing by agreement: A cross-cultural approach to business negotiation.* Chichester, England: John Wiley.

McGinn, N. F., Harburg, E., & Ginsburg, G. P. (1965). Responses to interpersonal conflict by middle-class males in Guadalajara and Michigan. *American Anthropologist, 67,* 1483-1494.

Moran, R. T., & Stripp, W. G. (1991). *Dynamics of successful international business negotiations.* Houston, TX: Gulf.

Northrop, F. S. C. (1953). *The meeting of East and West.* New York: Macmillan.

Ohbuchi, K. I., & Takahashi, Y. (1994). Cultural styles of conflict management in Japanese and Americans: Passivity, covertness, and effectiveness of strategies. *Journal of Applied Social Psychology, 24,* 1345-1366.

Porat, A.M. (1970). Cross-cultural differences in resolving union-management conflicts through negotiations. *Journal of Applied Psychology, 54,* 441-451.

Prosser, M. H. (1977). Intercultural communication theory and research: An overview of major constructs. In B. D. Ruben (Ed.), *Communication yearbook 2* (pp. 235-343). New Brunswick, NJ: Transaction.

Pruitt, D. G. (1981). *Negotiation behavior.* New York: Academic Press.

Pruitt, D. G. (1983). Achieving integrative agreements. In M. H. Bazerman & R. J. Lewicki (Eds.), *Negotiating in organizations* (pp. 35-50). Beverly Hills, CA: Sage.

Pruitt, D. G., & Carnevale, P. J. (1993). *Negotiation in social conflict.* Pacific Grove, CA: Brooks/Cole.

Pruitt, D. G., & Kimmel, M. J. (1977). Twenty years of experimental gaming: Critique, synthesis, and suggestions for the future. *Annual Review of Psychology, 28,* 363-392.

Putnam, L. L., & Jones, T. S. (1982). Reciprocity in negotiations: An analysis of bargaining interaction. *Communication Monographs, 49,* 277-297.

Putnam, L. L., & Wilson, S. R. (1989). Argumentation and bargaining strategies as discriminators of integrative outcomes. In M. A. Rahim (Ed.), *Managing conflict: An interdisciplinary approach* (pp. 121-141). New York: Praeger.

Pye, L. W. (1982). *Chinese commercial negotiating style.* Santa Monica, CA: RAND Corporation.

Pye, L. W. (1992). The Chinese approach to negotiating. *International Executive, 34,* 463-468.

Rajan, M. N., & Graham, J. L. (1991). Nobody's grandfather was a merchant: Understanding the Soviet commercial negotiation process and style. *California Management Review, 33*(3), 5-12.

Reardon, K. K., & Spekman, R. E. (1994). Starting out right: Negotiation lessons for domestic and cross-cultural business alliances. *Business Horizons, 37,* 71-79.

Roberts, K. H. (1970). On looking at an elephant: An evaluation of cross-cultural research related to organizations. *Psychological Bulletin, 74,* 327-350.

Roloff, M. E., & Campion, D. E. (1987). On alleviating the debilitating effects of accountability on bargaining: Authority and self-monitoring. *Communication Monographs, 54,* 145-164.

Roloff, M. E., & Jordan, J. M. (1992). Achieving negotiation goals: The "fruits and foibles" of planning ahead. In L. L. Putnam & M. E. Roloff (Eds.), *Communication and negotiation* (pp. 21-45). Newbury Park, CA: Sage.

Rubin, J. Z., & Sander, F. E. A. (1991). Culture, negotiation, and the eye of the beholder. *Negotiation Journal, 7,* 249-253.

Salacuse, J. W. (1988). Making deals in strange places: A beginner's guide to international business negotiations. *Negotiation Journal, 4,* 5-13.

Salacuse, J. W. (1991). *Making global deals.* Boston: Houghton Mifflin.

Samovar, L. A., Porter, R. E., & Jain, N. C. (1981). *Understanding intercultural communication.* Belmont, CA: Wadsworth.

Sawyer, J., & Guetzkow, H. (1965). Bargaining and negotiation in international relations. In H. Kelman (Ed.), *International behavior* (pp. 464-520). New York: Holt, Rinehart & Winston.

Schwartz, S. L. (1993). International computer technology transactions: Fundamental principles in negotiation and conflict management. *Michigan Bar Journal, 72,* 1282-1287.

Scott, D., & Renault, O. (1995). Advice for the PRC joint venturer. *Asialaw, 7,* 24-27.

Shenkar, O., & Ronen, S. (1987). The cultural context of negotiations: The implications of Chinese interpersonal norms. *Journal of Applied Behavioral Science, 23,* 263-275.

Sheth, J. (1983). Cross cultural influences on buyer-seller interaction/negotiation. *Asia Pacific Journal of Management, 1,* 46-55.

Solomon, R. H. (1985). *Chinese political negotiating behavior.* Santa Monica, CA: RAND Corporation.

Solomon, R. H. (1987). China: Friendship and obligation in Chinese negotiating style. In H. Binnendijk (Ed.), *National negotiating styles* (pp. 1-16). Washington, DC: U.S. State Department.

Stewart, S., & Keown, C. F. (1989). Talking with the dragon: Negotiating in the People's Republic of China. *Columbia Journal of World Business, 24,* 68-72.

Svenkerud, P. J. (1993, April). *Spiral and linear logic of argument: The road not taken.* Paper presented at the annual meeting of the Central States Communication Association, Lexington, KY.

Thibaut, J. W., & Kelley, H. H. (1959). *The social psychology of groups.* New York: John Wiley.

Thompson, L., & Hastie, R. (1990). Social perception in negotiation. *Organizational Behavior and Human Decision Processes, 51,* 176-197.

Ting-Toomey, S. (1988). Intercultural conflict styles: A face negotiation theory. In Y. Y. Kim & W. B. Gudykunst (Eds.), *Theories in intercultural communication* (pp. 213-235). Newbury Park, CA: Sage.

Ting-Toomey, S., Gao, G., Trubisky, P., Yang, Z., Kim, H. S., Lin, S. L., & Nishida, T. (1991). Culture, face maintenance, and styles of handling interpersonal conflict: A study in five cultures. *International Journal of Conflict Management, 2,* 275-296.

Triandis, H. C., Bontempo, R., Villareal, M. J., Asai, M., & Lucca, N. (1988). Individualism-collectivism: Cross-cultural perspectives on self-ingroup relationships. *Journal of Personality and Social Psychology, 54,* 323-338.

Trompenaars, F. (1993). *Riding the waves of culture.* London: Economist Books.

Tung, R. L. (1982). U.S.-China trade negotiations: Practices, procedures, and outcomes. *Journal of International Business Studies, 13,* 25-37.

Tung, R. L. (1984a). *Business negotiations with the Japanese.* Lexington, MA: Lexington.

Tung, R. L. (1984b). How to negotiate with the Japanese. *California Management Review, 26*(4), 62-77.

Tung, R. L. (1991, Winter). Handshakes across the sea: Cross-cultural negotiating for business success. *Organizational Dynamics, 19,* 30-40.

Van Zandt, H. F. (1970). How to negotiate in Japan. *Harvard Business Review, 49*(2), 45-56.

Walker, G. (1990). Cross-cultural argument in international negotiation: Values and reasoning at the Law of the Sea Conference. In F. H. Van Eemeren, R. Grootendorst, J. A. Blair, & C. A. Willard (Eds.), *Proceedings of the Second International Conference on Argumentation* (pp. 734-745). Amsterdam: SICSAT.

Walters, R. J. (1991). "Now that I ate the sushi, do we have a deal?": The lawyer as negotiator in Japanese-U.S. business transactions. *Northwestern Journal of International Law and Business, 12,* 335-356.

Walton, R. E., & McKersie, R. B. (1965). *A behavioral theory of labor negotiations: An analysis of a social interaction system.* New York: McGraw-Hill.

Ways, M. (1979, January 15). The virtues, dangers, and limits of negotiation. *Fortune,* pp. 86-90.

Weaver, G. R. (in press). Psychological and cultural dimensions of hostage negotiation. In R. G. Rogan, M. R. Hammer, & C. R. Van Zandt (Eds.), *Dynamic processes of crisis negotiation: Theory, research and practice.* Westport, CT: Praeger.

Weiss, S. E. (1993). Analysis of complex negotiations in international business: The RBC perspective. *Organization Science, 4,* 269-300.

Weiss, S. E. (1994a). Negotiating with "Romans": Part I. *Sloan Management Review, 35*(2), 51-61.

Weiss, S. E. (1994b). Negotiating with "Romans": Part II. *Sloan Management Review, 35*(3), 85-99.

Weiss, S. E. (1996). International negotiations: Bricks, mortar, and prospects. In B. J. Punnett & O. Shenkar (Eds.), *Handbook for international management research* (pp. 209-265). Cambridge, MA: Basil Blackwell.

Wilhelm, A. D., Jr. (1994). *The Chinese at the negotiating table: Style and characteristics.* Washington, DC: National Defense University Press.

Wilson, S. R., Cai, D. A., Campbell, D., Donohue, W., & Drake, L. (1995). Culture and communication processes in intercultural business negotiations. In A. M. Nicotera (Ed.), *Conflict and organizations: Communicative processes* (pp. 201-237). New York: State University of New York Press.

Wilson, S. R., Cai, D. A., & Drake, L. (1995). *Culture in context: Individualism/collectivism, negotiator role, framing, and integrative bargaining outcomes.* Paper presented at the annual meeting of the Academy of Management, Vancouver.

Wolfson, K. & Norden, M. F. (1984). Measuring responses to filmed interpersonal conflict: A rules approach. In W. B. Gudykunst & Y. Y. Kim (Eds.), *Methods for intercultural research* (pp. 155-166). Beverly Hills, CA: Sage.

Wood, J. T. (1997). *Communication theories in action: An introduction.* Belmont, CA: Wadsworth.

Wright, P. (1981). Doing business in Islamic markets. *Harvard Business Review, 59*(3), 34-40.

Zhang, D., & Kuroda, K. (1989). Beware of Japanese negotiation style: How to negotiate with Japanese companies. *Northwestern Journal of International Law and Business, 10,* 195-215.

CHAPTER CONTENTS

5 Constructing a Theoretical Framework for Evaluating Public Relations Programs and Activities

SHERRY DEVEREAUX FERGUSON
University of Ottawa

The growing demand for accountability in organizations places public relations units under pressure to justify their functions. The lack of a solid theoretical framework in the academic literature on evaluation of public relations makes it difficult for practitioners to respond to these demands. This deficit in the literature has resulted, in large part, from the lack of agreement on "what is to be measured" and "who is to do the measuring." This chapter argues that evaluation of public relations activities is a shared responsibility—the domain of program evaluation groups, communication managers, line managers, and internal audit units (where such units exist). CEOs and other top executives engage in management reviews that assess the relevance of public relations functions. Several groups become involved in evaluating role performance (outcomes, processes, efficiency of operations, impact, and outputs). Program evaluation units have the objectivity and expertise to evaluate outcomes. They also have the resources and broader experience with the organization to measure processes. Internal audit groups are well equipped to assess efficiency of operations. The communication manager, working in cooperation with line managers, has the requisite knowledge in public relations to evaluate outputs and impacts of specific products and activities. However, program evaluation teams join with communicators in assessing the impacts of large-scale campaigns, which require greater investment of human and financial resources. Social critics, academics, and practitioners become engaged in evaluating the ethics of public relations practices. The importance of evaluating ethical practices means that organizations should not scale down their evaluation of processes or outputs, even if they choose to put greater emphasis on outcomes and impact.

COMMUNICATION scholars continue to identify the need for more research into evaluation of public relations activities and practices (e.g., Hiebert & Devine, 1985; McElreath, 1989; Pavlik, 1987; Synnott & McKie, 1997). Synott and McKie reported a 1994 study in which 88% of public relations practitioners and academics called for more emphasis

Correspondence and requests for reprints: Sherry Devereaux Ferguson, P.O. Box N-7, Old Chelsea, Quebec, Canada J0X 2N0; e-mail ferguson@uottawa.ca

Communication Yearbook 21, pp. 191-229

on evaluation. Evaluation ranked first in number of mentions. Professional associations in a number of countries—including the United States, Great Britain, Canada, Australia, and Germany—also have called for more research in this area. Examples include the U.S.-based Institute for Public Relations Research and Education and the International Public Relations Association, which recently published a Gold Paper on this topic (Pritchitt et al., 1994). The Gold Paper reports the results of a 1989 survey by Lindenmann that indicates that practitioners talk about evaluation more than they do it. The International Association of Business Communicators (IABC) acknowledged the importance of evaluation research when it awarded funding in 1985 to the largest public relations research project undertaken to date—the Excellence Project. The IABC Research Foundation sponsored the 10-year, $400,000 project in an effort to answer questions about the effectiveness of public relations practices and to determine how best to measure these activities (Dozier, Grunig, & Grunig, 1995). The initial project, which examined evaluation practices in 300 organizations, identified a scarcity of research in the evaluation domain.

Content analysis of the *Public Relations Journal* and *Public Relations Review* (1975-1982)—two journals judged to be "the most accurate barometers of the field"—revealed a lack of "substantive content dealing with research in . . . evaluation of public relations programs" (Broom, Cox, Krueger, & Liebler, 1989, p. 154). Despite the fact that the period 1975-1982 was the heyday of program evaluation research (Patton, 1986; Rossi & Freeman, 1989), only 3% of the total number of articles published in the *Public Relations Journal* and 5% of the articles in *Public Relations Review* during that period were devoted to evaluation research (Broom et al., 1989). Between 1989 and 1991, the *Public Relations Research Annual* published only two articles (6% of the total number) on this topic: articles by Jeffers (1989) and by Piekos and Einsiedel (1990).

Broom and Dozier (1990) claim that this "no research" approach finds its way into the organization, where the goals and objectives of communication become simply "to communicate." The endless recycling of communication activities from former years means that the subsequent year's communication budget becomes "an incremental adjustment of last year's budget . . . institutionalized and routine" (Dozier & Ehling, 1992, p. 161). Budgetary commitments are "historically driven" (Broom, 1986, p. 9). Sometimes, completing the task becomes the goal (Grunig & Hunt, 1984; Pavlik, 1987; Weiss, 1972).

Bissland (1986; cited in Pavlik, 1987) argues that although the amount of evaluation has increased, the quality has not. He says that few evaluation efforts satisfy Lazarsfeld's (1959) criteria for establishing causality. Too often, practitioners measure impact in pounds of press clippings and outcomes by the number of products generated or materials placed in the media. Dozier and Ehling (1992) say that "until professional communicators integrate evaluation research into the routine operation of programs . . . linkage between managed communication and program impact will remain elusive" (p. 176).

The results of many evaluation studies never make it into the academic literature—for instance, the evaluation of social marketing campaigns. Research that is commissioned and sold for commercial gain rarely is shared with the general public (Gillespie, 1992; Leiss, Kline, & Jhally, 1986; Wilde, 1993). With the current emphasis on health communication studies, this situation may be changing somewhat for the better, as governments fund much of the research in this area. Nonetheless, Wilde (1993) and Atkin and Freimuth (1989) assert that many health information campaigns—even large and costly ones—go untested.

Flay (1992) and Johnson (1992) allege deficits in the areas of both formative and summative evaluation. According to Kaufman (1992), *formative* (or interim) evaluation involves ongoing progress checks against objectives for purposes of revision. Formative evaluation is undertaken at any stage of a project that produces results. Many researchers have stressed its importance (e.g., Anderson, 1989; Atkin & Freimuth, 1989; Rice & Atkin, 1989); however, some caution that the costs outweigh the benefits in programs of two or fewer years' duration (Fink, 1993). Patton (1990) warns that ongoing evaluation needs "some discrete stopping places to figure out what has happened over time" (p. 113). *Summative* (or year-end) evaluation is conducted at the end of a program or phase of a project (Kaufman, 1992). Like formative evaluation, summative research evaluates results against objectives. The program may be continued or discontinued on the basis of answers to such questions as "Did we accomplish what we wished to accomplish? Was it worth doing? Were our methods and techniques efficient and valuable?" (Kaufman, 1992, p. 281). *Goal-free* evaluation is terminal evaluation of a situation; however, it does not entail decisions as to whether the goals or objectives of the program or project have been met. Goal-free evaluation involves answering questions such as "What happened that was useful? What happened that was not useful?" (Kaufman, 1992, p. 281). Evaluation purposes and circumstances dictate which of the three forms of evaluation (formative, summative, or goal-free) is most appropriate in a given case. Some researchers assert that evaluation efforts are especially weak in the formative research domain (e.g., Flay, 1992; Freimuth, 1992; Kincaid, 1992; Rice, 1992).

In this chapter I will discuss how the present deficit of research is influencing organizations' abilities to meet demands for accountability, propose a theoretical framework for organizing literature relevant to evaluation of public relations, and suggest directions for future research in this area.

GROWING DEMANDS FOR ACCOUNTABILITY

Public relations practitioners face growing pressure to justify their activities and products on the basis of fit with the organization's strategic objectives.

The simultaneous drive toward client-centered organizations increases pressures to establish and meet acceptable standards of service to the public (Canada, Government, 1990; Canada, Service to the Public Task Force, 1990; Canada, Treasury Board, 1992b) and to show impacts and cost-effectiveness (Eggleton, 1995b, 1995c). Like Canada, the U.S. government is presently focusing on accountability issues in its National Performance Review. Synnott and McKie (1997) report a recent study in which accountability emerged as a critical new concern in 13 African, Australian, and Asian countries.

For many years, evaluation of public relations tended to fall between the cracks, and communicators employed in these areas operated almost without accountability. Even today, large numbers of organizations fail to evaluate their communication efforts—but not without liability. When funds become limited or budgets strained, public relations units typically are the first to experience cuts, and communication managers find it difficult to mount a credible defense with so little evidence to prove the value of the activities under their administration (Pritchitt et al., 1994). Also, when public relations practitioners fail to measure the effects of their efforts, communication becomes an output function that executives exclude from strategic planning and decision making (Broom, 1986; Broom & Dozier, 1983, 1985; Dozier, 1992; Piekos & Einsiedel, 1990; Steiner, 1983; Troy, 1989). Despite this obvious need to evaluate their activities and programs, many practitioners express a fear of having their work evaluated (Pavlik, 1987).

Eggleton (1995b, 1995c) addresses concerns related to program evaluation in general. He says that many managers accept the importance of review processes; however, the deficit of qualified personnel generates problems. He urges external participation in review processes to alleviate the problem. Ormala (1994), on the other hand, speaks of growing professionalism among European evaluators and the emergence of evaluation teams in which members have different backgrounds and experiences but rely on common methodologies. Having come into vogue in the 1960s, program evaluation was firmly ensconced in the operations of most large organizations (especially governments) by the 1970s. However, the growing demand for accountability to legislative groups, funding bodies, program managers, shareholders, and the general public (Miller, 1991) is undoubtedly the driving force behind the present high level of interest in evaluation research.

CONSTRUCTING A THEORETICAL FRAMEWORK: DECIDING "WHAT" AND "WHO"

Further progress in the area of evaluation of public relations requires some agreement on *what should be measured* and *who should be doing the measuring*. As Pavlik (1987) has observed, agreement on what should be measured is lacking at present. However, an examination of existing literature demonstrates that evaluators typically tend to judge the following areas: the relevance of public relations functions, role performance (outcomes, process decisions, efficiency of operations, outputs, and impact of communication activities), and the ethics of public relations activities.

Agreement is also lacking on who should be doing the measuring, yet further progress in articulating an evaluation model requires definition of areas of responsibility. How public relations fits on the organizational chart creates much of the confusion associated with delegation of evaluation responsibilities. Communication managers head public relations units in organizations; in that sense, they have their own program. At the same time, they offer advice and services to other line managers. These multiple reporting obligations create a situation in which communication managers and line managers share responsibility for monitoring and evaluating communication elements in the delivery of specific programs. That is, communication managers evaluate their own programs; however, the line managers that they service also evaluate the communication components in these programs. The work of communication groups also becomes subject to periodic reviews by program evaluators, who look at the performance of line and communication managers. At other times, the heads of organizations conduct management reviews of public relations functions to determine if the functions are appropriate and necessary. Thus the evaluation of communication becomes a shared responsibility, involving the following groups at different points in time: line managers, communication managers, program evaluation teams and audit groups, and upper-management committees. Program managers and communication managers often delegate responsibility for evaluation tasks to individuals under their supervision.

A 1985 Treasury Board (Canada) document addressed this matter of shared responsibility:

> Measuring the impact of the communication activities is . . . a joint responsibility, with both parties [line managers and communication managers] using the results of the measurement. . . . The line manager is interested to know the extent to which the communication efforts are helping the program to achieve its results, and the communication specialist wants to know if the communication has been effective. Both are looking to the future to see what works and what is possible, albeit from slightly differing perspectives. Particularly when programs are not working, it is important to be able to distinguish poor program design from poor communication. In such cases, involvement of the corporate evaluation group with the evaluation of individual communication campaigns is probably useful. (p. 23)

Revenue Canada has recently generated a review continuum that incorporates the possibility for management-led reviews, ongoing monitoring at the program level, and independent reviews by third parties. The continuum also "gives managers a choice of review approaches, ranging from self-assessments to joint audits and evaluations with other jurisdictions" (Eggleton, 1995c, p. 9). Treasury Board President Arthur Eggleton (1995a) has concluded that there is "an extensive amount of review activity in departments" (p. 16489). However, the lack of an evaluation framework has stymied attempts to coordinate and share those efforts. Eggleton (1995c) calls for electronic access to performance data, improved analysis, and better synthesis of data. He also calls for shared responsibilities between program managers (including public relations managers) and internal audit and evaluation groups in the area of impact assessment. Most critical, he argues, is the creation of a management culture that is "fact-based, results-oriented, open and accountable" (p. 1). Others have called for similar types of coordination and sharing (e.g., Canada, Treasury Board, 1992a, p. 20).

In this chapter I propose a logical division of responsibilities in the evaluation of the relevance of public relations functions, role performance (outcomes, process decisions, efficiency of operations, outputs, and impact of communication activities), and the ethics of public relations activities. This model draws its logic from existing structures in organizations and the most common topics referenced in the literature. Governments offer a particularly good basis for study, as they are highly accountable to their publics. I suggest below that evaluation of public relations should be a shared responsibility, involving upper management, program evaluation and audit groups, public relations managers, line managers, and sometimes social critics. Further progress in the delineation of evaluation models and systems requires that these organizational linkages be taken into account.

Relevance of Public Relations Functions:
Evaluation Concerns of Top-Level Administrators

Responsibility for evaluating the relevance of program functions (including public relations) and program rationale resides ultimately with top management. Does the program make sense? Are the functions appropriate? Upper management may delegate this responsibility to subordinates or special committees, who are asked to report back on their findings (Canada, Treasury Board, 1992a).

At the 1990 annual meeting of the Speech Communication Association, a panel of experts considered the direction that public relations should take in the coming decades. In a position paper presented to this group, Heath (1990) argued that any decisions on the future of public relations should be based on a careful analysis of the functions performed by public relations practitioners: "Conceptualization of the discipline requires that a few key functions be empirically verified as core to the activities, interests and motives of all the stakeholders joined inside and outside of each system" (pp. 6-7). In an attempt to delineate these functions, Heath and Cousino (1990) discussed the importance of planning, strategic management of issues, evaluation, and monitoring and analysis of public opinion.

Similarly, the Public Relations Society of America (PRSA) Task Force (cited in Heath, 1990) took a functional approach in its attempt to determine the core concerns addressed in the public relations literature. The task force members emerged with a list of functions that included organizing and managing, communicating, establishing relationships, processing information, informing and persuading, researching and analyzing, identifying stakeholders, planning and implementing, designing messages, selecting channels for the messages, setting goals and objectives, and evaluating. Like Heath and Cousino (1990), the PRSA stressed the importance of social responsibility in undertaking all these functions.

Popular textbooks in public relations show a commitment to these same functions. For example, Cutlip, Center, and Broom (1994) and Baskin and Aronoff (1992) discuss the importance of monitoring and analyzing public opinion, planning, communicating, and evaluating. The standard definition of public relations functions through the 1980s derived from Marston's (1963) RACE (research, action, communication, and evaluation) formula.

Higher-level executives hold ultimate responsibility for evaluating the fundamental appropriateness of all organizational functions. Sometimes they undertake what is called a *management review.* A management review of public relations functions, for example, asks questions such as the following: Are the public relations functions appropriate? Should they be modified in order to respond more effectively to clients and customers? Are the functions socially responsible, conforming to some ethical code of behavior? Some say that a management perspective should be applied to all reviews of public relations activities and products (Dozier & Repper, 1992; Rutman & Mowbray, 1983).

The process that took place in Canada in 1987-1988 demonstrates the kind of review that high-level executives can initiate. In January 1987, the government of Canada launched a management review of federal communication roles. As part of the 1987 review, the evaluators undertook an occupational analysis to identify the day-to-day functions being performed by government communicators. Results showed that communicators were involved in writing, editing, publishing, generating audiovisual materials, designing and executing exhibits and displays, promoting policies and programs, generating publicity and advertising, acting in liaison functions, carrying out community relations work, answering inquiries, and interacting with the media. In other words, the functions were *service-oriented* rather than *management-oriented.*

The researchers concluded that few communication specialists had the time, organizational linkages, or depth of expertise to provide advice to management. They also concluded that government communicators were weak in their ability to carry out the planning and research and analysis functions. The first comprehensive federal policy on communication—and subsequent training initiatives—emerged from this management review. The new policy represented a major effort to rethink the traditional role of the public relations practitioner; the consequence was to shift government public relations from a service to a management function. The 1988 policy defined four functional roles: research and analysis, planning, advising, and managing communication. Subsequent Treasury Board policies have added evaluating and consulting as additional functions of the government communicator (Canada, Treasury Board, 1992a).

A second review is underway in 1997-98, aimed at rewriting the 1988 policy. This review aims to establish a vision of government communications for the new century. Evaluation will almost certainly be part of this vision.

Still another management review, currently under way in Canada, has been concerned with establishing a stronger evaluation component in the government as a whole. As part of the review, 30 department heads were asked to describe how they manage and use review processes. Public affairs units have also been subject to this governmentwide review process. In the United States, the Clinton administration has launched a similar review process called the National Performance Review. Some states, such as Oregon, are also taking steps toward performance-based management systems (Wye, 1994).

The specific terminology for public relations functions—and the number listed—vary .from organization to organization. However, some terms that appear repeatedly in the literature and practices of modern organizations include *research and analysis, planning, advising, communicating, negotiating, consulting,* and *evaluating.*

Research and Analysis

The research and analysis function has received an increasing amount of attention in recent years. A 1992 survey of Fortune 500 companies found that 5 out of 15 respondents reported the presence of a continuous scanning and monitoring system (future-oriented), 2 reported a periodic system (present-oriented), and 2 said that they had an irregular operation (reactive) (Ferguson, 1994). (See Aguilar, 1967, for further description of what is implied by this terminology.) Most communicators believe that research and analysis lay the foundation for good strategic advice and communication planning. The IABC Excellence Project team found that research and analysis functions tended to be present in public relations programs headed by managers, not by technicians (Grunig, 1992). Broom and Dozier (1986) and Dozier (1992) also discovered that those involved in technician roles rarely engage in research and analysis. Others have argued that the viability of research and analysis units depends upon the support of upper management (Herring, 1991; Piekos & Einsiedel, 1990; Reid, 1988).

Planning

A growing number of organizations have called for the involvement of communicators in strategic and operational planning processes (see Ferguson, 1994; Heath, 1990; Heath & Nelson, 1986; Kinkead & Winokur, 1992; Rabin & Franzen, 1981). The volatility of the issue environments of many organizations necessitates the presence of a strong communication component in corporate plans (Ferguson, 1994; Heath & Associates, 1988; Sawaya & Arrington, 1988; Stroup, 1988). Ideally, communicators work with senior managers to produce or update a communication component to the annual or multiyear corporate plan. Then they work with middle managers to produce or update a communication component to the multiyear or annual operational plan. Senior management approval of these plans enables communication planners to progress to more detailed and specific planning at the level of work plans and limited-scope plans (plans for specific activities, campaigns, and initiatives), for which communication units hold ultimate responsibility. Higher levels of management typically approve budgets for these communication activities, campaigns, and initiatives.

Planning should be a participatory exercise, involving all hierarchical levels and parts of the organization (Burkhart & Reuss, 1993). Different people and groups participate at different stages of planning, which—much like a set of Ukrainian nesting dolls—are nestled one inside the other. The first and highest level of planning is strategic planning. Operational plans flow out of strategic planning, and work plans flow out of operational plans. Finally, limited-scope plans, which link back to the strategic and operational planning stages, emerge from work planning. Later evaluation of these planning efforts provides the rationale for adjustment of strategies (Bennett, Canning, & Landry, 1988).

The weight currently attached to the planning function is greater than at any time in the past. Organizations are calling for continuous planning to facilitate ongoing adaptation to changes in volatile issue environments (e.g., Redding & Catalanello, 1994). Distinctions in the management literature among *long-term, middle-term,* and *short-term* planning have all but disappeared, as terms such as *continuous planning, learning organization, strategic readiness, institutionalization of change,* and *proactivity* have come to dominate discussions (Kaufman, 1992; Morgan, 1992; Redding & Catalanello, 1994).

Advising

The growing concern in the public relations field with defining public relations as a management rather than a service or technician function dates from the early 1980s. Dozier (1990) explains the distinction:

> Public relations *managers* make communication policy decisions and are held accountable for the success or failure of public relations programs. . . . Public

relations *technicians,* on the other hand, implement communication programs planned by others. Removed from the dominant coalition, such practitioners crank out communications about the organization in isolation from management decision making, a low-level output function. (p. 9)

Broom (1982), Broom and Center (1983), and Dozier et al. (1995) present this same view.

An advisory role is at the heart of any public relations program with a managerial focus. In such a program, public relations advisers sit on executive committees and report to the CEO. A 1994 survey (part of the IABC Excellence Project) found that 76% of top communicators in the "most excellent" organizations reported directly to the CEO, as opposed to 57% of the top communicators in the "least excellent" organizations (Dozier et al., 1995, p. 84). In other words, in the former instance, the top communicators hold membership in what has been labeled the *dominant coalition.*[1]

Negotiating

The rationale for negotiation as a public relations function relates to the much-discussed concept of coorientation. *Coorientation* refers to the extent to which parties are willing to change to accommodate the position of persons or groups with opposing viewpoints. Newcomb (1953) defines coorientation as "perceived consensus" in systems "straining toward symmetry" (p. 393). He discusses a situation in which cognitive imbalance results when two people who like and respect each other disagree on some issue. In such a circumstance, the desire to maintain the relationship can stimulate attitudinal shifts on the parts of both people. The final position will be somewhere in between the two original positions. A number of more recent researchers have embedded the idea of coorientation in their public relations models. Grunig and Hunt (1984) discuss the mutual adjustment processes that take place at the organizational level; they say that the public should be "just as likely to persuade the organization's management to change their attitudes or behavior as the organization is likely to change the public's attitude or behavior" (p. 23). Thus organizations should use the results of public opinion research to initiate dialogue with publics, to build understanding and relationships, and to manage conflict (Grunig & White, 1992). Dozier and Ehling (1992) say that "communication managers are more successful moving two parties closer together than converting one party (publics) over wholly to the other party's (dominant coalition) perspective" (p. 178).

Cheney and Dionisopoulos (1989) argue that the organization should represent its interests in a way that will allow mutual persuasion processes to occur. Cutlip et al. (1994) incorporate the basic principles of coorientation into their public relations model when they advocate "action strategies" (p. 383). Action strategies assume that the need for public relations results from "something *done,* not something *said*" (p. 380). Such strategies imply more than rhetorical responses to public relations problems; they imply changes in organizational policies, procedures, products, services, and behavior—corrective actions aimed at eliminating the source of the problem. For example, when the Roman Catholic Church learned that some of its priests and brothers had been abusing children under their care, the church hierarchy faced a public relations problem. However, solving the problem implied the need for action first and words later. The organization had to take action to ensure that this situation did not recur in the future; then its leaders had to inform the public on the actions planned or implemented.

In discussing coorientation, it is important to note, however, that movement for the sake of movement will not always be defensible. Some social critics would argue that flexibility and compromise are inappropriate in a dialogue with the tobacco industry or toxic polluters, or even large economic monopolies. Nor is middle ground necessarily the most satisfying position for those involved in a dispute (Keltner, 1994). The negotiation literature contrasts *integrative agreements* (those that reconcile the interests of parties in conflict to achieve high joint benefit) with *compromise agreements* (characterized by concessions that result in both parties moving to middle ground, but with lower joint benefits). Fisher and Ury (1981) describe a situation in which two sisters quarrel over an orange. A compromise agreement results in the girls' splitting the orange in half. An integrative agreement would have given the juice of the orange to the first sister and the peel to the second, who wishes to make a cake. Parties in conflict assign different values to different aspects of issues. Any evaluation instrument designed to measure successful coorientation must measure more than just movement. It must also measure the quality of, and satisfaction with, the solution (see also the discussions in Bazerman & Neale, 1983; Pruitt, 1983). Adding an ethical dimension to this evaluation process requires looking at the ethics of the solution.

Consulting

It may be, in fact, that the act of involvement is more important than the phenomenon of movement. Decision theory tells us that consensus does not imply universal agreement with a decision. Consensus does imply that people are committed to making a decision work, and commitment grows out of engagement in the decision-making process (Hall, 1971). The harmonious relations within Japanese organizations have been attributed to the emphasis placed on consensual decision making (Chao & Gorden, 1979; De Mente, 1972; Kostoff, 1979).

Whereas negotiation places an emphasis on mutual persuasion processes, consultation focuses upon involvement in decision-making processes. Appropriate levels of consultation can help to eliminate the need for negotiation (that is, resolution of conflicts). A growing number of public, private, and nonprofit organizations have accepted the importance of consultation as a public relations function. For example, in 1992, the Privy Council Office and the Treasury Board of Canada established a coordination committee on consultation training to oversee the development of curricula for instructing government communicators on how to conduct consultations. Successful consultations build consensus among stakeholders (Salter & Leiss, 1989). For that reason, a large number of private sector, public sector, and nonprofit organizations have been engaged in developing consultation frameworks. Governments have been particularly active in expanding the consultation function (Bryden, 1982; Canada, Treasury Board, 1995; Canadian-American Committee, 1981; Crispo, 1984; Lindquist, 1991; Salter, 1985; Smith, 1982). Consultation is closely related to the concepts of partnership and coalition building, some of the most established trends of the 1990s (Aleo, 1992; Anderson & Narus, 1991; Ferguson, 1994; Goldhar & Lei, 1991; Hirschhorn & Gilmore, 1992; Lewis, 1990, 1992; Lynch, 1990; Sonnenberg, 1992).

Consultation has been defined as "the basis for a variety of procedures referred to by such terms as *public participation* and *public involvement*" (Dispute Resolution Core Group, n.d., p. 8). Methods can range from "public hearings and requests for written submissions to more interactive techniques such as workshops and advisory committees conducted by public agencies, developers, or their consultants" (p. 8). A characterizing feature of consultation is that the ultimate decision on how much power to hand over to stakeholders remains with the decision maker (Dispute Resolution Core Group, n.d.). Figure 5.1 presents a normative model of consultation that suggests the range of possibilities for stakeholder involvement in organizational decision making. This consultation model owes its logic to Tannenbaum and Schmidt (1958), who have contributed a continuum of leadership behavior. The model assumes the existence of an organizational culture that places a value on appropriate levels of stakeholder participation in decision-making processes. However, management has the final say on how much to involve stakeholders in particular decisions.

Management's decision to consult or not to consult will depend on situational, organizational, and stakeholder variables. Situational variables include the nature of the problem (e.g., a threat to the safety of the population) and perceived level of urgency (the immediacy of the threat). Organizational variables include the availability of resources (human and financial) and the will to carry out the consultation process. Consulting with large numbers of stakeholders is a costly and time-consuming process, unlikely to be undertaken on low-impact issues or decisions of a minor nature. Stakeholder interest in, knowledge of, and support for the issues are other significant factors. It could be speculated that issues that rank high on the private agendas of stakeholders necessitate higher levels of consultation than do issues that

1. Management makes decision and acts on it.
2. Management seeks input from stakeholders, makes decision, and acts on it.
3. Management consults with stakeholders and acts on joint decision.
4. Management seeks instruction on course of action from stakeholders and acts on their instructions.

Figure 5.1. Stakeholder Involvement Continuum

are low on private agendas. For example, health care, employment, and pension issues are always important to Americans. However, audience interest in foreign news is lower than interest in local and national news, sports, or even comics (Graber, 1980). A study by Rubin (1979) provides further evidence for relatively low levels of interest in foreign affairs. A 1986 Decima poll in Canada showed that domestic issues such as abortion policies, gas prices, and smoking in the workplace ranked higher on the agendas of Canadians than did foreign affairs policies. In other words, these latter issues appear to have relatively low priority on people's private agendas—implying a lesser need for consultation on these issues. Moreover, consulting the general public on highly technical issues (e.g., trade initiatives) is inappropriate if those who are consulted do not have the expertise to make meaningful contributions. Finally, a popular initiative will require less consultation than a more controversial one.

At Position 1 on the stakeholder involvement continuum depicted in Figure 5.1, management makes a unilateral decision and acts on it. The Ryobi Tool Company exemplified this position when it responded to a crisis situation involving a new woodcarving tool. An introductory advertising campaign had emphasized the efficiency of and ease in using the new tool. In practice, however, the tool did not allow for adequate safety guard protection. After discovering the tool's inherent dangers, Ryobi made a unilateral decision to withdraw it from the market. The company also advertised its decision in the trade magazines most likely to be read by the tool's users and offered refunds to those buyers who returned the tool to sales outlets. In this case, the immediate unilateral action was appropriate on grounds of ethical obligation and social responsibility. Time delays could have threatened the safety of consumers. In crisis situations, public relations and legal advisers will often encourage an immediate management response, reserving the right to consult at a later point in time. At the other extreme, minimal or no consultation can also be appropriate for many types of routine decisions in which stakeholders have low levels of interest (Dispute Resolution Core Group, n.d.). Despite the trend in organizations toward placing more emphasis on consulting with internal stakeholders (Ferguson, 1994), legal considerations can prompt less consulting and sharing in crisis situations, even at the internal level. In such situations, organizations may limit their internal consultation process to upper management, legal advisers, high-level public relations advisers, and scientific or technical experts (as required).

At Position 2 on the stakeholder involvement continuum, management invites stakeholder input before deciding on a course of action. Management has the option of limiting consultations to elite opinion leaders or experts on the topic or engaging larger numbers of stakeholders. Sometimes members of the general public will not have the knowledge to contribute viewpoints on highly technical matters. However, specific interest groups or professional organizations may have gathered large amounts of information on the topic. Organizations tend to assume a Position 2 stance when (a) they do not perceive the need for immediate action or (b) they want to buy time to work out an acceptable course of action. The suggestion box and the restaurant questionnaire offer vehicles for leisurely change and good customer relations. Governments, on the other hand, often establish commissions of inquiry in order to buy time to develop policy. In this way they demonstrate a commitment to act but postpone binding decisions to a later date.

A Position 3 approach suggests that management perceives the issue to be sufficiently salient to warrant larger-scale involvement of stakeholders. For example, a state government decides to consult with seniors on decisions related to subsidized housing. The bureaucracy commits itself to arriving at a mutually agreeable solution through processes of consultation with opinion leaders and the general population of stakeholders. Partnering contracts sometimes result from such consultations. At Position 3, management grants stakeholders a higher level of decision-making power than they are accorded at Position 1 or Position 2 on the continuum.

Position 4 implies that the organization has granted full decision-making power to stakeholders. A government that calls for a referendum or plebiscite assumes this position. Private sector organizations rarely move to Position 4 on the stakeholder involvement continuum.

A contingency approach to stakeholder involvement assumes that no one option or position on the continuum is appropriate all of the time—a stance that would be credible to public relations practitioners. A number of different variables (organizational, stakeholder, and situational) influence decisions on when and how much to involve stakeholders. No one position has inherent merit over the others; for example, no one would suggest that we should turn decisions on criminal law over to the most obvious stakeholders—the criminals themselves. It is the place of program evaluators to judge the appropriateness of positions assumed by the organization. The extent to which public relations personnel participate in the consultation process varies at different positions on the continuum. However, they are likely to play an advisory role at all points.

Communicating

The traditional role of a public relations practitioner entails communicating—that is, performing the duties of a technician. Tasks include writing (e.g., speeches, press releases, backgrounders, and articles for newsletters and magazines), acting as liaison with the media and community groups (e.g., answering inquiries from the media and providing information as required), and producing publicity and advertising. These public relations functions are service-oriented, providing support as required. Textbooks from the 1980s reflect this emphasis (e.g., Cantor, 1984; Seitel, 1984). These duties remain central to the functions of many public relations practitioners. The IABC Excellence Project team found that "even the most strategically managed department still must possess the expertise to implement communication programs, using the technical expertise within the department" (Dozier et al., 1995, p. 55). Moreover, my own experience demonstrates that although academics argue for a shift in roles, many practitioners fail to share their zeal. Most communicators enter the public relations field because they enjoy the "hands-on" creative aspects of technical functions.

Despite the importance of negotiating and consulting, any evaluation model based solely on the assumption of need to negotiate conflict and to consult with stakeholders would be inappropriate. Not every organization endures a crisis a day; many groups never know what it is like to be thrust into the spotlight in the fashion of Dow Corning, the manufacturer of Tylenol, or the builders of nuclear reactors. Although nonprofit organizations such as the Red Cross and the United Way experience leadership or credibility crises from time to time (e.g., the tainted blood scandal), the large majority utilize their public relations capacity to educate the public on their mandate and mission, to inform the public on social issues, and to seek goodwill and support. These situations do not necessitate the negotiation of differences. As Mulholland (1991) notes, "Negotiation is only necessary when there are differences among people" (p. 67).

Evaluating

The seventh commonly accepted function (at least in theory) of the public relations professional is evaluation. Because this function is the subject of this chapter, it requires no further definition.

Role Performance: A Shared Responsibility

Assessing role performance implies judging the following areas: outcomes, process decisions, efficiency of operations, outputs, and impact of communication activities. Three or four different organizational groups tend to interact in evaluating these areas: line managers, communication managers, auditors, and program evaluation professionals. Auditors and program evaluators may come from inside the organization (but outside the public relations group), or they may enter the organization on a consultancy basis to perform the evaluation. The involvement of external evaluators helps to alleviate problems of bias that can occur when programs evaluate their own performance (Eggleton, 1995c). However, external evaluators often utilize data collected by line managers and communication managers.

A growing number of organizations have ceased to make a distinction between program evaluation and internal audit functions (Canada, Treasury Board, 1992a). However, where organizations separate the efforts of internal audit and program evaluation units, they usually ask program evaluation teams to evaluate effectiveness and impacts and internal audit groups to evaluate adherence to internal administrative procedures and efficiency of operations.[2] For additional clarity, I maintain this distinction in the discussion that follows—recognizing at the same time the overlap that can occur between audit and program evaluation functions (Canada, Treasury Board, 1981).

The broad concerns of program evaluation and audit personnel lead them to examine not only what is happening in the public relations department, but also interactions of public relations professionals with other parts of the organization. For that reason, program evaluators and auditors may interview managers in other functional areas served by public relations. This familiarity with other organizational units gives these specialists the ability to make recommendations based on wider experiences. After reviewing all available data, the program evaluation or audit team makes recommendations concerning the effectiveness and efficiency of communication activities. They may recommend changes to improve the public relations program. The involvement of other evaluation units does not absolve communication or line managers from responsibility. Cutlip et al. (1994) note that communication groups should keep complete records regarding what worked and what failed to work. Evaluations undertaken by the communication or line managers will constitute part of the documentation made available to program evaluators and auditors at a later point in time.

Evaluating Outcomes and Overall Effectiveness:
The Responsibility of Program Evaluation Teams

A primary function of program evaluation is to judge the outcomes of public relations programs. Judging outcomes requires measuring the extent to which the public relations group has met its program objectives, as set out in the multiyear or annual planning process (Berk & Rossi, 1990; Kaufman, 1992). These program objectives reflect the objectives of the larger organization. Thus, ideally, program evaluators should use the multiyear or annual strategic plan of the public relations group as their reference document (Ferguson, 1994). If a plan does not exist or the plan does not specify linkages to the objectives of the larger organization, the program evaluation report must point to this deficit. Organizations that fail to plan have difficulty evaluating outcomes (Hornik, 1992; Ireland & Hitt, 1992).

Evaluating the extent to which a program has *achieved* its objectives is also difficult, because program objectives (even when they are articulated in a strategic plan) tend to be broad (Berk & Rossi, 1990; Fink, 1993; Rutman & Mowbray, 1983). For example, program objectives for a public relations group in an environmental agency might include the following: to contribute to public understanding of major environmental concerns; to assess levels of public knowledge, awareness, and interest in environmental issues; to communicate existing legislative support for environmental initiatives; and to encourage partnerships among all levels of government, the private sector, and special interest groups (Ferguson, 1994).

Wye (1994) complains that organizations tend to generate performance indicators that are focused only on *input/output*. He asserts that they need to place equal stress on identifying performance indicators for impacts and *outcomes*. Performance indicators help to overcome problems associated with vague program objectives (Rutman & Mowbray, 1983). Referring to the example of public relations objectives written for an environmental agency, researchers could look for indicators of increased awareness in the form of larger numbers of telephone calls, greater volume of correspondence, more numerous references to an issue on talk shows, or more frequent discussion in the media. Indicators of increased interest in partnerships could be the number of different contributors to projects, joint submissions to funding agencies, conferences cosponsored, organizations in attendance at events, amounts of contributions, and/or hours of service rendered by volunteers.

Evaluating Process: The Responsibility
of Program Evaluation Teams

Judging role performance also implies looking at process—for example, the appropriateness and adequacy of techniques employed in research and analysis, planning, negotiating, consulting, communicating, advising, and other activities, given the resources and expertise of the public relations group. The organization must measure the *extent* to which these public relations functions are being performed, how *well* they are being performed, and the appropriateness of decisions on *timing*. For example, when is it appropriate to negotiate instead of persuade?

Program evaluators must establish criteria for the judging process early in the planning stages of a project—that is, standards for judging the way in which the research and analysis, planning, advising, consulting, and evaluating functions are implemented. Criteria can be normative (i.e., how PR *should be* practiced) or operational (based on how PR *is* practiced) (Dozier & Ehling, 1992). Governments, in particular, are placing increasing emphasis on setting normative criteria for program performance (i.e., standards for effectiveness) and identifying performance indicators to suggest when those standards have been met (Allen, 1994; Astles & Nurski, 1994; Fink, 1993; Rice, 1992; Smith, 1994; Wye, 1994). For example, the U.S. Congress has passed a law called the *Government Performance and Results Act,* which addresses the matter of performance indicators (Wye, 1994). Canada also has been establishing standards for service to the public (Canada, Government, 1990; Eggleton, 1995c).

A program evaluation can seek to determine the extent to which public relations planning has been integrated into the institution's larger corporate planning structures. Such a review can also look for degree of coordination of communication efforts within the organization or levels of participation in the organization (Canada, Treasury Board, 1992a). The reviewers judge the extent to which the communication program efforts have been linked to corporate planning processes and the extent to which operational communication planning efforts have been linked to strategic communication planning. Alternatively, they might ask whether pretesting of prototype or pilot messages occurred (Atkin & Freimuth, 1989)

Berk and Rossi (1990) note that effectiveness is a relative concept. Compared to what? they ask. The best or the worst of all possible scenarios? One aspect of program evaluation concerns itself with the exploration of alternative approaches for accomplishing the same aims (Rist, 1990). Issues of cost-effectiveness become relevant in the consideration of alternatives (Berk & Rossi, 1990; Canada, Treasury Board, 1989).

Evaluating Efficiency of Operations:
The Responsibility of Audit Teams

Traditionally, internal audit groups have answered questions about procedural matters and the efficiency of operations. For example, audit teams answer the following kinds of procedural questions: Were appropriate authorizations obtained and requests channeled through the right parties? Were appropriate individuals involved and notified on matters relevant to their position? Did these same individuals receive the necessary background materials? Were responsible parties adequately briefed? Were appropriate editing and proofreading procedures followed in the preparation of written materials? Were consultation processes conducted in conformity with organizational norms and procedures? Did language reviews (e.g., to ensure politically correct and plain language) conform to procedures? Did publications conform to pricing criteria? Were publications adequately displayed and distributed? Did organizational members receive updated lists of publications? Were the results of public opinion research reviewed for contradictions and anomalies? Were research and reporting procedures clearly set and understood by all responsible parties? Were the results of opinion research communicated? Were the reporting procedures understood by all parties? Did surveys solicit the responses of users to products and services?

Administrative questions include the following: Were adequate resources available to public relations practitioners? Were personnel used in an efficient and effective way? Is the size and mix of personnel appropriate to the anticipated volume and complexity of communication activities? Audit teams may evaluate the extent to which the organizational structures facilitate effective performance by the public relations groups and the extent to which allocation of human resources to the function are sufficient to enable the group to meet its objectives (Canada, Treasury Board, 1992a).[3] Like program evaluators, auditors must establish criteria for efficiency.

Evaluating Outputs: The Responsibility of Communication Managers and Line Managers

Communication managers generally share the responsibility for assessing outputs with line managers. Program evaluation personnel may review these data, but they will probably not participate in the data collection—unless a major campaign is involved.

Typical outputs of public relations groups include *products* such as brochures and pamphlets, corporate magazines, employee newsletters, press kits, display and exhibit materials, advertising products, media analyses, backgrounders, briefing notes, speeches, public service announcements, and communication plans. Measuring product outputs implies tracking the number of press releases generated, brochures distributed, letters posted, public service announcements aired, or messages picked up by the media. Content analysis of the media can reveal the manner in which stories have been covered or events reported. Organizations contract out much of this work to publicity tracking firms, which sometimes generate computerized psychographic profiles of audiences reached by messages. By suggesting where campaigns are falling short in reaching their target groups or how other media might be better conduits for messages, this type of knowledge contributes to the organization's strategic planning capability. Some tracking systems assign a monetary value to the publicity and weigh that value against comparable advertising costs. (Some challenge the underlying assumption that people respond in the same way to publicity as they do to advertising.)

Outputs can also take the form of *services rendered*—for example, advising on strategies, planning, researching and analyzing the public opinion environment, coordinating a public event, giving a speech, or conducting a media interview. Measuring these services implies documenting the number of times the services were performed. Quantification of outputs can contribute to the organization's ability to decide workloads and assess efficiencies (Rutman & Mowbray, 1983). Assessment of outputs can contribute to the organization's understanding of the quality of its products and services. For example, evaluators examine communication plans to identify the presence or absence of required elements: objectives, audiences, messages, requirements for supplemental materials such as backgrounders and briefing notes, identification of primary spokespersons, responsibilities for producing materials and performing services, distribution deadlines and target dates, timing and sequence for events, coordination mechanisms, evaluation criteria, and methodologies for determining effectiveness. There is a fine line between evaluating *process* and *outputs* in the form of services rendered. However, in the first instance, the evaluator is assessing means for achieving a goal; in the second case, the person is assessing the results of those efforts.

Finally, outputs can relate to *people served*: number of clients contacted, consultation sessions scheduled, telephone calls answered, or audience members at speech events. Systems can be established to quantify the number of people who visit an exhibit, request a brochure, or ask a question about a product or service.

Although measurement of outputs occurs predominantly at the implementation phase of a project (Cutlip et al., 1994), most evaluation researchers agree that assessment also should take place at the preparatory stages. For example, evaluators should assess the quality of data accumulated on audience characteristics to facilitate decisions on the medium, the message, and the occasion.

Evaluating Impacts: The Responsibility of Communication Managers, Line Managers, and Program Evaluation Teams

Typically, communicators measure impacts of specific communication activities, campaigns, and initiatives. Backer, Rogers, and Sopory (1992) say that impact can be evaluated at any point along a continuum that includes exposure, awareness, learning, persuasion, intent to change behavior, actual change in behavior, and maintenance of behavior change. In essence, questions such as the following are asked: How many learned the message content? How many changed their opinions? How many experienced attitude change? How many behaved as desired? How many repeated the behaviors? At the most abstract level, evaluators may be asking, "What kind of long-term social and cultural change occurred?" Atkin and Freimuth (1989) propose a continuum that includes exposure to a message, information processing, cognitive learning, yielding (in terms of forming or changing beliefs, saliences, values, attitudes, and behavioral intentions), and utilization (e.g., taking action). Not all agree that such continua should be the basis for evaluation efforts; some researchers assert that change does not always occur in such a linear fashion (Hornik, 1992; Salmon, 1992). Moreover, these models tend to look at impacts in terms of individuals. Yet impacts can occur at an *individual* level (e.g., changes in levels of awareness, attitudes, values, behavior), at an *interpersonal* level (changes in relationships and degrees of liking for the other party), and at a *societal* level.

Some argue that we should be devoting more resources to measuring the impacts of public relations activities on society (e.g., Ashley, 1992; McDonald, 1992) and on relationships (e.g., Brown & Einsiedel, 1990; Dozier et al., 1995; Grunig, Grunig, & Ehling, 1992). Assessing relationships implies asking questions such as the following: What is the quality of relations among public relations groups, clients within the organization, and stakeholders external to the organization? Does the public relations group enjoy good relations with the dominant coalition? How can these relationships be improved? Ferguson (1984; cited in Grunig et al., 1992) suggests that the quality of an organization's relationship with its publics can be assessed on the following dimensions: dynamism, openness, satisfaction, power distribution, and understanding/agreement. Aldrich (1979) suggests the need to evaluate interorganizational relationships on four dimensions: (a) formalization (the extent to which the organization recognizes the relationship and assigns liaisons to manage it), (b) intensity (the extent to which the organization invests time and money in the relationship), (c) reciprocity (the extent to which other organizations also invest in the relationship), and (d) standardization (the extent to which the interaction becomes established).

Some authors say that impact assessments also should measure client satisfaction (Rutman & Mowbray, 1983). A recent Canadian government publication titled *Measuring Client Satisfaction* (Canada, Treasury Board, 1992b) articulates the need to evaluate client expectations against perceived and actual levels of service. The intent is to determine gaps between client expectations and perceived quality of service, as well as gaps between client *perceptions* of service and other more objective measures of quality of services provided. The publication speaks of the need to identify indicators related to promptness and quality of service, relevance of procedures, ease of access to offices, staff responsiveness, clarity of signage, appropriateness of procedures, and other satisfaction indicators. Canadian Treasury Board President Eggleton (1995b) stresses that program review within government is placing a greater emphasis on the establishment of service standards and measurement of performance. An impact assessment also could measure client perceptions of social or educational benefits of a program or quality of relationships.

As noted earlier, all evaluation efforts seek to measure achievement of objectives. However, confusion arises when people fail to differentiate among the various levels of planning. Program evaluators typically judge the success of public relations units at meeting *program objectives*. They refer back to the objectives that appeared in the multiyear or annual strategic plan. They examine the *cumulative* efforts of the communication group in working toward achieving these broad program objectives. Thus they measure success on the basis of the impacts of a number of different activities and initiatives that contribute to each program objective. Thus assessment of program outcomes grows out of assessment of many smaller activities and initiatives. The communication manager will have been responsible for the evaluation of many of these activities and initiatives, on which ultimately the program is judged. That is, communication managers typically evaluate the extent to which the PR group has met the *more limited objectives set out in communication plans for specific activities, campaigns, and initiatives*. The communication managers use the "limited-scope" plans (Ferguson, 1994, pp. 300-316) as their reference point for evaluation efforts, rather than the multiyear or annual strategic plan used by program evaluators. Objectives appearing in these limited-scope plans state the desired impacts of specific activities or campaigns, such as increased awareness, changed attitudes, or the adoption of new value sets or behaviors. Examples of communication objectives that might appear in a limited-scope plan are as follows: to publicize company initiatives in the area of biodegradable detergents, to increase public knowledge of toxic chemical issues, to encourage community leaders to sponsor environmental awareness days, and to create awareness of the availability of publications and other materials on recycling. These kinds of objectives are specific, concrete, and measurable. Unified planning requires that all communication objectives—even those in the "limited-scope plan"—use broader organizational (corporate or business) objectives as their common reference point.

Ferguson (1984; cited in Grunig et al., 1992) has noted that the coorientation model offers useful concepts that can be translated into communication objectives, which later become the basis for evaluation efforts. Broom and Dozier (1990) suggest ways to set objectives based on the concept of coorientation and to evaluate the success of the organization in achieving those objectives. These objectives will relate to negotiation processes.

To be useful in impact assessments, communication objectives must be clearly articulated, relevant, measurable, cost-efficient, and socially and ethically acceptable (Dozier & Repper, 1992; Ehling & Dozier, 1992; Pritchitt et al., 1994). The objectives must also be realistic (Coleman, 1992; Deutchman, 1992; Hornik, 1992; Rice & Atkin, 1989), operationally distinct from other organization objectives (Ehling, 1987; Ehling & Dozier, 1992), and verifiable (Koontz, O'Donnell, & Weirich, 1982). The framing of broad, fuzzy objectives (e.g., to achieve goodwill or to achieve understanding) is inappropriate (Pavlik, 1987).[4]

The writing of appropriate communication objectives requires identification of target publics. Yet many publics are latent or passive, and thus difficult to identify (Dozier & Ehling, 1992); others are high risk and difficult to reach (Berk & Rossi, 1990; Ferguson, Valenti, & Melwani, 1991). Deciding upon criteria for success with such publics can be problematic (Kelly, 1992; Pentz, criteria for success with such publics can be problematic (Kelly, 1992; Pentz, 1992). Commercial marketers increase the likelihood that they will meet their objectives by setting low goals and targeting those who are easiest to persuade (Rice & Atkin, 1989; Salmon, 1992). Some communication objectives are easier than others to achieve. For example, it is widely accepted that it is easier to achieve cognitive change than behavioral change (Anderson, 1989; Bettinghaus, 1973; Brown & Einsiedel, 1990; Flavier, 1992, p. 79; Gallion, 1992, p. 94; Pavlik, 1992; Pentz, 1992; Rice & Atkin, 1989; Salmon, 1992). Also, it is easier to secure verbal agreement than to effect behavior change (DeFleur & Westie, 1958). Some behavioral changes are easier than others to achieve (Pentz, 1992), and those that are achieved may be short-lived, as alternative behaviors are "ingrained over a lifetime" and "reinforced by individuals' lifestyles, reference groups and family structure" (Salmon, 1989, p. 28). Effects achieved with children may be equally transient (Atkin, 1992).

Sometimes, there may be *no* notable effects, or the effects may be in the opposite direction from what is anticipated or desired (Cutlip, Center, & Broom, 1985; Dozier & Repper, 1992; Hornik, 1992; McDonald, 1992; Wilde, 1993). Dozier and Ehling (1992) argue that there is only a .04% chance that any communication initiative will achieve its intended effects. Rogers (1992) says that there is a .03-.05% chance of success, but only over several years. Setting objectives to achieve 40% to 50% change in behavioral patterns is unrealistic if change tends to occur in increments of 3% to 5% (Rogers, 1992). The chances of success may be even slimmer with high-risk populations who have deep-seated, long-term psychological and emotional barriers to some campaign messages (Gallion, 1992). Pavlik (1987) notes that it may be necessary to specify conditions under which effects will occur.

Some effects are also easier than others to *measure*. For example, it is easier to measure concrete short-term effects than more abstract long-term effects (Dozier & Ehling, 1992). This generates problems in organizations such as those providing public services, where objectives are often long-term, involving considerable resources and time to achieve broad social and cultural changes. At other times, effects can be masked by general societal trends, large-scale changes that make it difficult to discern the more limited effects of persuasion (Pavlik, 1992) or other catalysts (Kostoff, Averch, & Chubin, 1994). For example, if society is already moving in a specific direction, it may be difficult to discern the effects of an information campaign related to some aspect of that general societal trend. Evaluators now emphasize the importance of studying political, economic, and social contexts in which policies, programs, and institutions operate (Ormala, 1994). Brown and Einsiedel (1990) point to the importance of documenting, in process evaluations, what else occurred in the audience's environment during the period being evaluated. These records will enable the evaluators to take other factors into account at a later date when they evaluate the impact of a public relations initiative.

Many believe that the most valuable measurement takes place over time (Ashley, 1992; McDonald, 1992) and includes a consideration of systemic changes—that is, changes in economic and social systems (Gallion, 1992; Wallack, 1992). For example, the United Nations now recognizes that successful health prevention campaigns need to address economic, gender, and other health determinants. Success at achieving improved health care practices may occur only after changes take place in the larger systems. Some researchers claim that the most significant effects may occur years after the initial evaluation research is conducted. Evaluators also emphasize the importance of identifying indirect effects. Classical persuasion studies suggest that opinion leaders may play a significant role in persuasion (Berelson, Lazarsfeld, & McPhee, 1954; Lazarsfeld, Berelson, & Gaudet, 1948; Katz & Lazarsfeld, 1955; Merton, 1949; Star & Hughes, 1950). Therefore, some public relations campaigns focus on these opinion leaders or even journalists, who can influence the larger environment in which individuals make decisions (Wallack, 1992). In this case, the evaluator must determine (a) the extent to which the opinion leaders were influenced and (b) the extent to which the opinion leaders influenced others. In brief, some say that the easier variables are to measure, the less relevant the measures are for decision making (Dozier & Ehling, 1992; Montgomery & Urban, 1969).

Salmon (1992) argues that we must distinguish between *effects* and *effectiveness*. The evaluator of communication must decide whether it is appropriate to measure success by the achievement of some communication effect or whether success should be judged against some "ultimate criterion" that relates to effectiveness. In other words, a communication campaign may succeed in getting people to wear safety belts, but wearing safety belts may not reduce traffic fatality rates (Wilde, 1993). Often, ultimate criteria will relate to strategic objectives of the organization (see the earlier section on outcomes).

The process of evaluation is made more complex by the need to consider intermedia influences (Danielian & Reese, 1989; Rogers, 1992), interaction between messages and media (Ehling & Dozier, 1992; Miller & Starr, 1961), and interaction between media and interpersonal contact (Anderson, 1989; Ashley, 1992, p. 42; Brown & Einsiedel, 1990; Deutchman, 1992; Dyak, 1992; Grunig & Ipes, 1983; Salmon, 1992). Attitude or behavior change may result from a number of different influences, originating in many different sectors of the environment. Evaluation is also made more complex by the need to incorporate interdisciplinary insights ranging from marketing to public health and sociology into thinking processes (McDonald, 1992; Neff, 1989; Rogers, 1992; Rossi & Wright, 1991; Salmon, 1992).

Methodological problems also abound. Scholars and practitioners hotly debate the merits of quantitative versus qualitative methodologies (e.g., Patton, 1986; Rossi & Wright, 1991). Different types of evaluation (e.g., formative, summative, or goal-free) may call for the use of different methodologies. Pavlik (1992) warns that methodologies that rely on averages for behavior change may be missing the mark. Impact assessment is the most difficult of all evaluation chores. To attempt to measure impact is to swim in the same murky waters as other social scientists. Measuring impact implies determining cause-effect relationships—a task that is never easy (and sometimes close to impossible), given the evaluation budgets of most public relations groups. Assessing impact is both time- and money-intensive. Complicating the situation is the fact that few public relations specialists are trained to conduct evaluation research. For these reasons, many organizations expect that communication and line managers will cooperate in evaluating communication components in programs. They also anticipate that program evaluation units will assume responsibility for assessments that require sophisticated methodologies and financial investment—for example, the evaluation of a major campaign undertaken by the communication group.

Coming to grips with the challenges of evaluating impacts on individuals and groups requires (a) a cooperative effort on the part of all parties with relevant expertise and (b) consideration of the costs and benefits of adopting different approaches to impact assessment. The construction of a cost-benefit matrix would be a useful contribution to evaluation research. As Rossi and Freeman (1989) note, "The design of impact evaluations needs to take into account two competing pressures: on the one hand, evaluations should be undertaken with sufficient rigor that firm conclusions can be reached; on the other hand, practical considerations of time, money, cooperation, and protection of human subjects limit the design options and methodological procedures that can be employed" (p. 225). Outside reviewers may later pass judgment on the appropriateness of evaluation designs and methodologies selected by the communication and line managers.

Although evaluations tend to have a retrospective focus (Kaufman, 1992; Rist, 1990), measuring impacts entails setting benchmarks at the early stages of projects and evaluating at all life stages of a program or policy (Cutlip et al., 1994; Pritchitt et al., 1994; Rist, 1990). Collecting baseline data is especially critical to successful large-scale impact assessment (Fink, 1993; Pritchitt et al., 1994).

Ethics of Public Relations Practices: Evaluation Concerns of Social Critics, Academics, and Practitioners

The dual themes of ethics and social responsibility appear frequently in the public relations literature. For example, the 1988 PRSA Task Force expounded upon the necessity for organizations to act in a socially responsible fashion, as did the International Association of Business Communicators in describing the results of its Excellence Project. Numerous scholars have argued for an ethical imperative to guide public relations (Cutlip et al., 1994; DuVernet, 1988; Garnett, 1992; Gibson, 1990; Grunig, 1992; Heath & Cousino, 1990; Pearson, 1989a, 1989b).

The positions assumed by social critics fall along a continuum. The most radical argue that our basic political and economic systems and structures are corrupt—serving power elites who do not have the good of the population at heart. These critics question the most fundamental structures of the society (e.g., Foucault, 1970, 1972; Gandy, 1982; Habermas, 1973; Marcuse, 1964; Schiller, 1989). By extrapolation, any practices that serve those systems, including public relations, must be bad. Authors such as Schiller (1989) speak of the "corporate takeover of public expression." Proponents of this school of thought could be categorized as "lateral" deviants (Bowers & Ochs, 1971), groups or individuals who dispute the value system itself.

A second group of individuals and groups fall into the category of "vertical" deviants (Bowers & Ochs, 1971). These persons subscribe to the value system of the establishment but dispute the distribution of benefits or power within the system. For example, they question the motives (mandate, mission, and strategic objectives) of certain organizations operating in that system. They view the goals of these organizations and/or their leaders (e.g., large multinational corporations, big government, Wall Street entrepreneurs) as being in conflict with the interests of the larger society. Because they regard the organizational goals as illegitimate, they question any efforts at proselytizing or seeking support for those goals (Ginsberg, 1986; Herman & Chomsky, 1988; Olasky, 1985, 1989). Still others accept the trend toward globalization, the necessity for bureaucracies, and the contributions of business to the economy; however, they question the legitimacy and value of specific public relations practices. Boorstin (1971), Nimmo and Combs (1990), and Combs and Nimmo (1993) criticize public relations practitioners for their role in helping to construct political fantasies and for selling candidates as though they are products. They include public relations activities among the new forms of propaganda that dominate our lives. Mitroff and Bennis (1989) complain that public relations departments generate 70% of all the information that we call "news." They say that the celebrity/PR industry has created a vast infrastructure that produces and distributes "partial or slanted truths at best and outright untruths at worst" (p. 108).

Public relations scholars have spent the past decade debating the relative merits of symmetrical and asymmetrical models of public relations. Grunig and Hunt (1984) argued that many organizations follow a two-way asymmetrical model in which the organization researches the public opinion environment but applies the results of the research to persuasive purposes. Grunig (1989) has discussed the implications of this model for ethical communication practices: "In spite of the good intentions of practitioners—it is difficult, if not impossible, to practice public relations in a way that is ethical and socially responsible using an asymmetrical model" (quoted in Grunig & White, 1992, p. 40).

Miller (1989), on the other hand, claims that public relations and persuasion are "two Ps in a pod" (p. 45). Backer et al. (1992) include persuasion as one of the components in their model of public relations practices. A number of rhetorical scholars have entered the fray on the side of Miller, asserting that persuasive practices can be ethical or unethical, manipulative or nonmanipulative. They present the view that dialectic and persuasion are interrelated and inextricably linked to the workings of a democratic society. In the introduction to their edited volume *Rhetorical and Critical Approaches to Public Relations,* for example, Toth and Heath (1992) speak of the need to reconsider the assumption that "objectivity is inherently superior to persuasion, as if persuasion cannot be objective and information unobjective" (p. xiv). Others have gone further to equate the act of communication with persuasion, saying that all communication has some persuasive content. As Hiebert (1981) stated in the period preceding the debate over symmetry, "We normally communicate because we have some purpose in mind" (p. 13). In a study of 22 utilities companies, Gaudino, Fritch, and Haynes (1989) found that, even though the managers perceived their goals to be "mutual understanding among the organization, regulators, interveners, and the customer publics" (pp. 307-308), their strategies suggested an underlying persuasive intent. Springston and Leichty (1990) note that "in order for the process of mutual understanding to take place, both parties would have to have a point of view on a given subject" (pp. 4-5). Miller (1989) argues for a broader interpretation of persuasion: "To say that people seek to control their environments recognizes the patently obvious fact that people (or at least, people who are normatively defined by society as healthy, functioning individuals) have a preference for certain environmental outcomes over others" (p. 46). In another context, Jamieson and Campbell (1988) express the view of most rhetorical scholars: "We presume that rhetoric is an essential part of human action. No one can avoid imposing a perspective when selecting what is to be communicated; no one can avoid making arguments and appeals; no one can avoid shaping content to reach and affect a desired audience" (p. 282). Stewart, Smith, and Denton (1989) concur: "*Persuasion* is not something that one does to another or has done to oneself. It is a *process of mutual adjustment in which people and societies engage*" (p. 116).

A number of scholars have disputed the "either/or" approach that splits behaviors into two discrete categories. Hellweg (1989; cited in Grunig & Grunig, 1992) suggests, for example, that organizations should be registered on a symmetry continuum, rather than being stamped as *symmetrical* or *asymmetrical.* Murphy (1991) likewise questions the appropriateness of dichotomies: "By splitting public relations behavior into only two modes, we tend to polarize undesirable behavior in one (asymmetric) and desirable behavior in the other (symmetric)" (p. 127). Murphy suggests a third, mixed-motive category. Turk (1986) and Reagan, Anderson, Sumner, and Hill (1992; cited in Grunig & Grunig, 1992) have reported that they were unable to find operational distinctions between the two-way symmetrical and two-way asymmetrical models. By 1992, Grunig and White had modified the two-way symmetric and two-way asymmetric models to arrive at a "mixed-motive" model. Dozier et al. (1995) elaborate on this new model, equating the mixed-motive position with a "win-win symmetric zone." They say that negotiation and compromise allow people with "separate and sometimes conflicting interests" (p. 48) to find this common win-win zone.

The new model raises a new set of questions for the evaluator of public relations programs and activities. Dozier et al. (1995) state, for example, that "short-term use of asymmetrical practices within the context of a broad symmetrical philosophy" (p. 51) can provide the basis for ethical public relations practices. But from the point of view of the evaluator, how do you determine what constitutes "short-term use of asymmetrical practices"? More important, how can you know if the public relations practitioners are operating from a "broad symmetrical philosophy"? By examining the mission statement of the organization? By reviewing the program's actions? By judging the outcomes? Grunig and White (1992) argue that an organization's worldview will be deemed ethical if it results in "caring—even loving—*relationships* with other individuals and groups they affect" (p. 38). This latter basis for judging an organization's philosophy—and, by extension, the ethics of its communication practices—raises questions of a pragmatic nature. Sometimes people (and organizations) try hard but do not succeed in their efforts to establish relationships. The quality of a relationship depends on two parties. Should the evaluation of ethics depend on the cooperation of a second party?

Grunig and White (1992) suggest that asymmetrical public relations can be ethical if practitioners are able to demonstrate that their behavior does not harm anyone. But sometimes the most altruistic of persuasive campaigns can result in harm. Consider the public service announcements that sought to persuade parents to buckle their children into car seat belts designed for adults— a practice that has resulted in the loss of many children's lives. Should these persuasive efforts be judged unethical on the basis of outcomes? Murphy (1991) summarizes the dilemma in using symmetry as a criterion for ethical public relations practices: "In two-way symmetric communication we have an attractive model for an effective, ethical relationship between senders and receivers that is elusive in practice" (p. 120).

At the beginning of this chapter, I pointed to the fact that much of the difficulty in arriving at evaluation models derives from the lack of agreement over what should be measured. Evaluation criteria must be capable of capturing the essence of what is important in the public relations process—whether that be distinguishing ethical from unethical communication or differentiating conflict with positive outcomes from conflict with negative outcomes. As DuVernet (1988) has stated: "There are definite ethical parameters to public affairs conduct. Such parameters shift with time, are difficult to define, and are largely unarticulated" (p. 246). Nonetheless, evaluation demands that criteria and performance indicators for ethical conduct of public relations be clearly specified. Some governments are attempting to specify such parameters, including standards for fair practices and service to the public. The Canadian government, for example, is asking the following kinds of questions: "To what extent is the communications function providing the public with necessary and requested information in an accessible, fair and equitable manner?" (Canada, Treasury Board, 1992a, p. 19). Criteria for assessing success include the extent to which the communication group (a) provides the public with prompt, courteous, impartial service; (b) assesses these efforts; (c) answers inquiries from the public in a timely, complete manner; (d) monitors client and media satisfaction with the level of service provided; (e) consults with the public to capture public/client concerns on an ongoing basis; (f) provides service in both official languages and uses plain language in its communications; (g) avoids sexual stereotyping; (h) fairly depicts people in relation to race, ethnic origin, and disability; (i) makes a special effort to reach persons with disabilities and other special circumstances; and (j) ensures that information is provided to multicultural communities (Canada, Treasury Board, 1992a). Additional criteria have impacts on the communication group but involve other levels of management.

Brown and Einsiedel (1990) emphasize the importance of judging social relevance in evaluating public relations efforts. They also suggest performance indicators that would confirm social relevance—for example, the level of community involvement in a campaign, the stages at which the community was engaged in the process, and the value and significance community members attached to the process. An excellent example of this point is the Cape Breton Corporation, Nova Scotia, which engages the whole community each year in writing its annual strategic plan. The planning takes place in an open forum, announced in advance. Likewise, the Canadian government has mentioned the need to evaluate client perceptions of program relevance as well as the fairness and equity of the program (Canada, Treasury Board, 1992b).

IMPLICATIONS FOR FUTURE RESEARCH

As public relations programs have become increasingly management-oriented, practitioners have faced the need to learn new job functions. Their roles have shifted in ways that require them to acquire skills in such areas as research and analysis, planning, advising, and consulting. Evaluation research must place a greater stress on performance indicators for these functions. For example, what indicates successful performance in an advisory role? What are the indicators of good media analyses? What defines successful consultations with target publics? What are the indicators of good relations with stakeholders?

Evaluation researchers could also profit from learning more about best practices in organizations. A typology of evaluation systems in different kinds of organizations could help to sort out some of the confusion over divisions of responsibility in the evaluation area. What are the most common systems? The most effective ones? On what basis are they judged to be so? Where do evaluation functions reside in different kinds of organizations? With specialized evaluation units? Public affairs or other communication units? Advertising or marketing units? To whom do evaluators report? What is their relationship to other units within the organization? What are their reporting obligations? What is their level of cooperation?

The failure of organizations to establish evaluation systems relates, in large measure, to the costs associated with evaluation and the lack of personnel who have had appropriate training. Further research in this domain should attempt to identify the costs and benefits attached to different methodological options and the training required to support the evaluation function. Other studies could survey organizations to determine the most creative approaches currently being used to overcome the prohibitive costs of evaluation.

A major contradiction in the public relations literature relates to processes and outputs. A number of scholars argue that we should de-emphasize the measurement of processes and outputs and emphasize the measurement of outcomes. In other discussions, however, these same scholars argue just as strongly for the importance of ethical procedures, discourse, and symmetrical interactions with publics. Yet these expressed concerns relate to processes and outputs. If we accept the importance of appropriate and ethical processes and outputs, then our evaluation models must continue to include a stress on evaluation of processes and outputs.

Evaluation of public relations in society demands operationalizing some of the philosophical discussions related to ethics. Drawing on Habermas's (1970) discussion of symmetry, Burleson and Kline (1979; cited in Pearson, 1989b) describe a situation in which both parties have a chance to initiate and maintain discourse; challenge, explain, and interpret; interact free of domination or control; and enjoy equal power. The five dimensions on which an evaluator could judge the ethics of a communication act include the degree of communicator understanding of and satisfaction with rules governing (a) the beginning and ending communicative interaction, (b) the length of time separating messages or separating a question from the answer, (c) opportunity for suggesting topics and initiating topic changes, (d) channel selection, and (e) evidence that a partner in communication has produced a response that counts as a response (Pearson, 1989a). Springston and Leichty (1990) say that those concerned about the ethics of public relations practices should be concerned with "whether the ends being promoted involve the enlightened interests of all parties involved, whether the arguments adhere to the standards of fairness: competition within mutually negotiated and agreed-upon rules" (p. 4). This level of specificity is critical to successful evaluation of public relations. In closing, I would like to suggest that the field of public relations may be best served in the coming decade by placing less emphasis on debates over terminology and more stress on delineating indicators of ethical performance, whether that performance be in the area of negotiation or persuasive discourse.

NOTES

1. Dozier et al. (1995, p. 15) note that the term *dominant coalition* originated in the management science and organizational literature. It refers to formal or informal alliances of people with the power to define an organization's mission, set its course, and affect its structure. Hierarchy is only one of the determinants of membership in this dominant coalition. Other bases of power may derive from control of a scarce or valued resource or occupation of a central position in a decision-making network.

2. Program evaluation has been defined as "the periodic independent and objective review and assessment of a program to determine . . . the adequacy of its objectives, its design and its results, both intended and unintended. Evaluations will call into question the very existence of the program. Matters such as the rationale for the program, its impact on the public, and its cost effectiveness as compared with alternative means of program delivery are reviewed" (Canada, Treasury Board, 1981, p. 19). Internal audit has been defined as the "systematic, independent review and appraisal of all departmental operations, including administrative activities, for purposes of advising management as to the efficiency, economy, and effectiveness of the internal management practices and controls" (Canada, Treasury Board, 1981, p. 19).

3. The possibility for overlap between the audit and program evaluation functions can be problematic.

4. It should be noted, however, that the objectives that appear in annual strategic plans are typically broad and fuzzy. This characteristic of "big picture" planning makes program evaluation difficult.

REFERENCES

Aguilar, F. J. (1967). *Scanning the business environment.* New York: Macmillan.

Aldrich, H. E. (1979). *Organizations and environments.* Englewood Cliffs, NJ: Prentice Hall.

Aleo, J. P., Jr. (1992). Redefining the manufacturer-supplier relationship. *Journal of Business Strategy, 13*(5), 10-14.

Allen, J. R. (1994, June). *Using performance indicators in government.* Paper presented at the Conference on Public Sector Performance Measurement and Reporting, Ottawa, ON.

Anderson, J. C., & Narus, J. A. (1991). Partnering as a focused market strategy. *California Management Review, 33*(3), 95-113.

Anderson, R. B. (1989). Reassessing the odds against finding meaningful behavioral change in mass media health promotion campaigns. In C. H. Botan & V. Hazleton, Jr. (Eds.), *Public relations theory* (pp. 309-321). Hillsdale, NJ: Lawrence Erlbaum.

Ashley, W. J. (1992). Interview. In T. E. Backer, E. M. Rogers, & P. Sopory (Eds.), *Designing health communication campaigns: What works?* (pp. 40-46). Newbury Park, CA: Sage.

Astles, D. J., & Nurski, J. (1994). *Performance measurement: Moving IRAP from theory to practice.* Paper presented at the Conference on Public Sector Performance Measurement and Reporting, Ottawa, ON.

Atkin, C. K. (1992). Interview. In T. E. Backer, E. M. Rogers, & P. Sopory (Eds.), *Designing health communication campaigns: What works?* (pp. 46-50). Newbury Park, CA: Sage.

Atkin, C. K., & Freimuth, V. (1989). Formative evaluation research in campaign design. In R. E. Rice & C. K. Atkin (Eds.), *Public communication campaigns* (2nd ed., pp. 131-150). Newbury Park, CA: Sage.

Backer, T. E., Rogers, E. M., & Sopory, P. (1992). Part one: Overview. In T. E. Backer, E. M. Rogers, & P. Sopory (Eds.), *Designing health communication campaigns: What works?* (pp. 1-28). Newbury Park, CA: Sage.

Baskin, O., & Aronoff, C. (1992). *Public relations* (3rd ed.). Dubuque, IA: William C. Brown.

Bazerman, M. H., & Neale, M. A. (1983). Heuristics in negotiation: Limitations to effective dispute resolution. In M. H. Bazerman & R. J. Lewicki (Eds.), *Negotiating in organizations* (pp. 51-67). Beverly Hills, CA: Sage.

Bennett, J. H., Canning, J. E., & Landry, M. R. (1988). Corporate affairs and strategic planning: The organization. In W. J. Wright & C. J. DuVernet (Eds.), *The Canadian public affairs handbook: Maximizing markets, protecting bottom lines* (pp. 147-172). Toronto: Carswell.

Berelson, B., Lazarsfeld, P. F., & McPhee, W. N. (1954). *Voting: A study of opinion formation during a presidential campaign.* Chicago: University of Chicago Press.

Berk, R. A., & Rossi, P. H. (1990). *Thinking about program evaluation.* Newbury Park, CA: Sage.

Bettinghaus, E. P. (1973). *Persuasive communication* (2nd ed.). New York: Holt, Rinehart & Winston.

Bissland, J. H. (1986). *The effort to upgrade public relations evaluation practices: What the record shows.* Unpublished manuscript.

Boorstin, D. J. (1971). *The image: A guide to pseudo-events in America.* New York: Atheneum.

Bowers, J. W., & Ochs, D. J. (1971). *The rhetoric of agitation and control.* Reading, MA: Addison-Wesley.

Broom, G. M. (1982). Comparison of sex roles in public relations. *Public Relations Review, 8*(3), 17-22.

Broom, G. M. (1986). *Public relations roles and systems theory: Functional and historicist causal models.* Paper presented at the meeting of the Public Relations Interest Group, International Communication Association, Chicago.

Broom, G. M., & Center, A. H. (1983). Evaluation research. *Public Relations Quarterly, 28*(3), 2-3.

Broom, G. M., Cox, M. S., Krueger, E. A., & Liebler, C. M. (1989). Horizontal structure in public relations: An exploratory study of departmental differentiation. In J. E. Grunig & L. A. Grunig (Eds.), *Public relations research annual* (Vol. 1, pp. 141-154). Hillsdale, NJ: Lawrence Erlbaum.

Broom, G. M., & Dozier, D. M. (1983). An overview: Evaluation research in public relations. *Public Relations Quarterly, 28*(3), 5-8.

Broom, G. M., & Dozier, D. M. (1985). *Determinants and consequences of public relations roles.* Paper presented at the meeting of the Public Relations Division, Association for Education in Journalism and Mass Communication, Memphis, TN.

Broom, G. M., & Dozier, D. (1986). Advancement for public relations role models. *Public Relations Review, 12*(1), 47.

Broom, G. M., & Dozier, D. M. (1990). *Using research in public relations: Applications to program management.* Englewood Cliffs, NJ: Prentice Hall.

Brown, J. D., & Einsiedel, E. F. (1990). Public health campaigns: Mass media strategies. In E. B. Ray & L. Donohew (Eds.), *Communication and health: Systems and applications* (pp. 153-170). Hillsdale, NJ: Lawrence Erlbaum.

Bryden, K. (1982). Public input into policy-making and administration: The present situation and some requirements for the future. *Canadian Public Administration, 25*(1), 81-107.

Burkhart, P. J., & Reuss, S. (1993). *Successful strategic planning.* Newbury Park, CA: Sage.

Burleson, B. R., & Kline, S. L. (1979). Habermas' theory of communication: A critical explication. *Quarterly Journal of Speech, 65,* 412-428.

Canada, Government. (1990). *Public Service 2000: The renewal of the public service of Canada* (Supply and Services Canada Catalog No. BT74-1/3-1990). Ottawa, ON: Minister of Supply and Services Canada.

Canada, Service to the Public Task Force. (1990). *Service to the Public Task Force report: For discussion.* Ottawa, ON: Public Service 2000.

Canada, Treasury Board Secretariat. (1995). *The federal government as "partner": Six steps to successful collaboration* (Supply and Services Canada Catalog No. BT22-40/5-1995). Ottawa, ON: Planning and Communications Directorate, Treasury Board of Canada Secretariat.

Canada, Treasury Board Secretariat and Office of the Comptroller General. (1981). *Guide on the program evaluation function* (Supply and Services Canada Catalog No. BT32-16/1981). Ottawa, ON: Treasury Board Secretariat, Communications Division.

Canada, Treasury Board Secretariat and Office of the Comptroller General. (1985). *Evaluating departmental communications/information programs.* Ottawa, ON: Office of the Comptroller General, Program Evaluation Branch.

Canada, Treasury Board Secretariat and Office of the Comptroller General. (1989). *Working on standards for the evaluation of programs in federal departments and agencies.* Ottawa, ON: Office of the Comptroller General, Program Evaluation Branch.

Canada, Treasury Board Secretariat (Information Management Practices Group of the Administrative Policy Branch) and Office of the Comptroller General (Evaluation and Audit Branch). (1992a). *A guide to good communications management* (Supply and Services Canada Catalog No. BT32-36/3-1992). Ottawa, ON: Information Management Partnership.

Canada, Treasury Board Secretariat (Information Management Practices Group of the Administrative Policy Branch) and Office of the Comptroller General (Evaluation and Audit Branch). (1992b). *Measuring client satisfaction.* Ottawa, ON: Information Management Partnership.

Canadian-American Committee. (1981). *Improving bilateral consultation on economic issues* [Policy statement]. Montreal/Washington, DC: C. D. Howe Institute of Canada/National Academy of Public Administration.

Cantor, B. (1984). *Inside public relations.* New York: Longman.

Chao, K., & Gorden, W. I. (1979). Culture and communication in the modern Japanese corporate organization. *International and Intercultural Communication Annual, 5,* 27-33.

Cheney, G., & Dionisopoulos, G. N. (1989). Public relations? No, relations with publics: A rhetorical-organizational approach to contemporary corporate communications. In C. H. Botan & V. Hazleton, Jr. (Eds.), *Public relations theory* (pp. 135-158). Hillsdale, NJ: Lawrence Erlbaum.

Coleman, P. C. (1992). Interview. In T. E. Backer, E. M. Rogers, & P. Sopory (Eds.), *Designing health communication campaigns: What works?* (pp. 60-65). Newbury Park, CA: Sage.

Combs, J. E., & Nimmo, D. (1993). *The new propaganda.* New York: Longman.

Crispo, J. (1984). *National consultation: problems and prospects* (Policy Commentary No. 5). Toronto: C. D. Howe Institute.

Cutlip, S. M., Center, A. H., & Broom, G. M. (1985). *Effective public relations* (6th ed.). Englewood Cliffs, NJ: Prentice Hall.

Cutlip, S. M., Center, A. H., & Broom, G. M. (1994). *Effective public relations* (7th ed.). Englewood Cliffs, NJ: Prentice Hall.

Danielian, L. H., & Reese, S. D. (1989). A closer look at intermedia influences on agenda setting: The cocaine issue of 1986. In P. J. Shoemaker (Ed.), *Communication campaigns about drugs: Government, media, and the public* (pp. 47-66). Hillsdale, NJ: Lawrence Erlbaum.

DeFleur, M. L., & Westie, F. R. (1958). Verbal attitudes and overt acts: An experiment on the salience of attitudes. *American Sociological Review, 23,* 667-673.

De Mente, B. L. (1972). *How to do business in Japan: A guide for international businessmen.* Los Angeles: Center for International Business.

Deutchman, L. (1992). Interview. In T. E. Backer, E. M. Rogers, & P. Sopory (Eds.), *Designing health communication campaigns: What works?* (pp. 65-71). Newbury Park, CA: Sage.

Dispute Resolution Core Group of the British Columbia Round Table on the Environment and the Economy. (n.d.). *Reaching agreement: Consensus processes in British Columbia* (Vol. 1). Victoria, BC: Round Table on the Environment and the Economy.

Dozier, D. M. (1990). The innovation of research in public relations practice: Review of a program of studies. In L. A. Grunig & J. E. Grunig (Eds.), *Public relations research annual* (Vol. 2, pp. 3-28). Hillsdale, NJ: Lawrence Erlbaum.

Dozier, D. M. (1992). The organizational roles of communication and public relations practitioners. In J. E. Grunig (Ed.), *Excellence in public relations and communication management* (pp. 327-355). Hillsdale, NJ: Lawrence Erlbaum.

Dozier, D. M., & Ehling, W. P. (1992). Evaluation of public relations programs: What the literature tells us about their effects. In J. E. Grunig (Ed.), *Excellence in public relations and communication management* (pp. 159-184). Hillsdale, NJ: Lawrence Erlbaum.

Dozier, D. M., Grunig, L. A., & Grunig, J. E. (1995). *Manager's guide to excellence in public relations and communication management.* Hillsdale, NJ: Lawrence Erlbaum.

Dozier, D. M., & Repper, F. C. (1992). Research firms and public relations practices. In J. E. Grunig (Ed.), *Excellence in public relations and communication management* (pp. 185-215). Hillsdale, NJ: Lawrence Erlbaum.

DuVernet, C. J. (1988). The parameters of persuasion: Legal and ethical restrictions on public affairs practice. In W. J. Wright & C. J. DuVernet (Eds.), *The Canadian public affairs handbook: Maximizing markets, protecting bottom lines* (pp. 215-246). Toronto: Carswell.

Dyak, B. (1992). Interview. In T. E. Backer, E. M. Rogers, & P. Sopory (Eds.), *Designing health communication campaigns: What works?* (pp. 71-74). Newbury Park, CA: Sage.

Eggleton, A. (1995a). House of Commons debates. *Hansard, 133*(259), 16489.

Eggleton, A. (1995b, June 14). [Notes for a speech presented at the meeting of the Canadian Evaluation Society, Toronto].

Eggleton, A. (1995c). *Strengthening government review: Annual report to Parliament by the president of the Treasury Board* (Supply and Services Canada Catalog No. BT1-10/1995). Ottawa, ON: Planning and Communications Directorate, Treasury Board of Canada, Secretariat.

Ehling, W. P. (1987, May). *Public relations functions and adversarial environments.* Paper presented at the annual meeting of the International Communication Association, Montreal.

Ehling, W. P., & Dozier, D. M. (1992). Public relations management and operations research. In J. E. Grunig (Ed.), *Excellence in public relations and communication management* (pp. 251-284). Hillsdale, NJ: Lawrence Erlbaum.

Ferguson, M. A. (1984, August). *Building theory in public relations: Interorganizational relationships.* Paper presented at the annual meeting of the Association for Education in Journalism and Mass Communication, Gainesville, FL.

Ferguson, M. A., Valenti, J. M., & Melwani, G. (1991). Communicating with risk takers: A public relations perspective. In L. A. Grunig & J. E. Grunig (Eds.), *Public relations research annual* (Vol. 3, pp. 195-224). Hillsdale, NJ: Lawrence Erlbaum.

Ferguson, S. D. (1994). *Mastering the public opinion challenge.* New York: Irwin.

Fink, A. (1993). *Evaluation fundamentals.* Newbury Park, CA: Sage.

Fisher, R., & Ury, W. (1981). *Getting to yes.* Boston: Houghton Mifflin.

Flavier, J. M. (1992). Interview. In T. E. Backer, E. M. Rogers, & P. Sopory (Eds.), *Designing health communication campaigns: What works?* (pp. 78-81). Newbury Park, CA: Sage.

Flay, B. (1992). Interview. In T. E. Backer, E. M. Rogers, & P. Sopory (Eds.), *Designing health communication campaigns: What works?* (pp. 81-84). Newbury Park, CA: Sage.

Foucault, M. (1970). *The order of things: An archaeology of the human sciences.* New York: Pantheon.

Foucault, M. (1972). *The archaeology of knowledge* (A. M. S. Smith, Trans.). New York: Pantheon.

Freimuth, V. (1992). Interview. In T. E. Backer, E. M. Rogers, & P. Sopory (Eds.), *Designing health communication campaigns: What works?* (pp. 89-93). Newbury Park, CA: Sage.

Gallion, K. J. (1992). Interview. In T. E. Backer, E. M. Rogers, & P. Sopory (Eds.), *Designing health communication campaigns: What works?* (pp. 93-99). Newbury Park, CA: Sage.

Gandy, O. H. (1982). *Beyond agenda setting: Information subsidies and public policy.* Norwood, NJ: Ablex.

Garnett, J. L. (1992). *Communicating for results in government.* San Francisco: Jossey-Bass.

Gaudino, J. L., Fritch, J., & Haynes, B. (1989). "If you knew what I knew, you'd make the same decision": A common misperception underlying public relations campaigns? In C. H. Botan & V. Hazleton, Jr. (Eds.), *Public relations theory* (pp. 299-308). Hillsdale, NJ: Lawrence Erlbaum.

Gibson, D. C. (1990, November). *The communication continuum: A theory of public relations.* Paper presented at the annual meeting of the Speech Communication Association, Chicago.

Gillespie, R. W. (1992). Interview. In T. E. Backer, E. M. Rogers, & P. Sopory (Eds.), *Designing health communication campaigns: What works?* (pp. 99-102). Newbury Park, CA: Sage.

Ginsberg, B. (1986). *The captive public.* New York: Basic Books.

Goldhar, J. D., & Lei, D. (1991). The shape of twenty-first century global manufacturing. *Journal of Business Strategy, 12*(2), 37-41.

Graber, D. A. (1980). *Mass media and American politics.* Washington, DC: Congressional Quarterly Press.

Grunig, J. E. (1989). Symmetrical presuppositions as a framework for public relations theory. In C. H. Botan & V. Hazleton, Jr. (Eds.), *Public relations theory* (pp. 17-44). Hillsdale, NJ: Lawrence Erlbaum.

Grunig, J. E. (1992). Communication, public relations, and effective organizations: An overview of the book. In J. E. Grunig (Ed.), *Excellence in public relations and communication management* (pp. 1-28). Hillsdale, NJ: Lawrence Erlbaum.

Grunig, J. E., & Grunig, L. A. (1992). Models of public relations and communication. In J. E. Grunig (Ed.), *Excellence in public relations and communication management* (pp. 285-326). Hillsdale, NJ: Lawrence Erlbaum.

Grunig, J. E., & Hunt, T. (1984). *Managing public relations.* New York: Holt, Rinehart & Winston.

Grunig, J. E., & Ipes, D. A. (1983). The anatomy of a campaign against drunk driving. *Public Relations Review, 9*(3), 36-53.

Grunig, J. E., & White, J. (1992). The effect of worldviews on public relations theory and practice. In J. E. Grunig (Ed.), *Excellence in public relations and communication management* (pp. 31-64). Hillsdale, NJ: Lawrence Erlbaum.

Grunig, L. A. (1992). Toward the philosophy of public relations. In E. L. Toth & R. L. Heath (Eds.), *Rhetorical and critical approaches to public relations* (pp. 65-92). Hillsdale, NJ: Lawrence Erlbaum.

Grunig, L. A., Grunig, J. E., & Ehling, W. P. (1992). What is an effective organization? In J. E. Grunig (Ed.), *Excellence in public relations and communication management* (pp. 65-90). Hillsdale, NJ: Lawrence Erlbaum.

Habermas, J. (1970). Toward a theory of communication competence. *Inquiry, 13,* 360-375.

Habermas, J. (1973). *Legitimation crisis.* Boston: Beacon.

Hall, J. (1971). *Toward group effectiveness.* Conroe, TX: Teleometrics International.

Heath, R. L. (1990, November). *Position paper for the workshop on public relations research and education: Agendas for the 1990s.* Paper presented at the annual meeting of the Speech Communication Association, Chicago.

Heath, R. L., & Associates. (Eds.). (1988). *Strategic issues management.* San Francisco: Jossey-Bass.

Heath, R. L., & Cousino, K. R. (1990). Issues management: End of first decade progress report. *Public Relations Review, 16*(1), 6-18.

Heath, R. L., & Nelson, R. A. (1986). *Issues management: Corporate public policymaking in an information society.* Beverly Hills, CA: Sage.

Hellweg, S. A. (1989, May). *The application of Grunig's symmetry-asymmetry public relations models to internal communication systems.* Paper presented at the annual meeting of the International Communication Association, San Francisco.

Herman, E. S., & Chomsky, N. (1988). *Manufacturing consent.* New York: Pantheon.

Herring, J. P. (1991). Senior management must champion business intelligence programs. *Journal of Business Strategy, 12*(2), 48-53.

Hiebert, R. E. (1981). A model of the government communication process. In L. M. Helm, R. E. Hiebert, M. R. Naver, & K. Rabin (Eds.), *A public affairs handbook: Informing the people* (pp. 3-13). New York: Longman.

Hiebert, R. E., & Devine, C. M. (1985). Government research and evaluation gap. *Public Relations Review, 11*(3), 47-56.

Hirschhorn, L., & Gilmore, T. (1992). The new boundaries of the "boundaryless" company. *Harvard Business Review, 70*(3), 104-115.

Hornik, R. (1992). Interview. In T. E. Backer, E. M. Rogers, & P. Sopory (Eds.), *Designing health communication campaigns: What works?* (pp. 102-107). Newbury Park, CA: Sage.

Ireland, R. D., & Hitt, M. A. (1992, May-June). Mission statements: Importance, challenge and recommendations for development. *Business Horizons,* pp. 34-42.

Jamieson, K. H., & Campbell, K. K. (1988). *The interplay of influence.* Belmont, CA: Wadsworth.

Jeffers, D. W. (1989). Using public relations theory to evaluate specialized magazines as communication channels. In J. E. Grunig & L. A. Grunig (Eds.), *Public relations research annual* (Vol. 1, pp. 115-124). Hillsdale, NJ: Lawrence Erlbaum.

Johnson, C. A. (1992). Interview. In T. E. Backer, E. M. Rogers, & P. Sopory (Eds.), *Designing health communication campaigns: What works?* (pp. 110-114). Newbury Park, CA: Sage.

Katz, E., & Lazarsfeld, P. F. (1955). *Personal influence.* New York: Free Press.

Kaufman, R. (1992). *Strategic planning plus: An organizational guide.* Newbury Park, CA: Sage.

Keltner, J. W. (1994). *The management of struggle: Elements of dispute resolution through negotiation, mediation and arbitration.* Cresskill, NJ: Hampton.

Kelly, M. (1992). Interview. In T. E. Backer, E. M. Rogers, & P. Sopory (Eds.), *Designing health communication campaigns: What works?* (pp. 114-120). Newbury Park, CA: Sage.

Kincaid, L. (1992). Interview. In T. E. Backer, E. M. Rogers, & P. Sopory (Eds.), *Designing health communication campaigns: What works?* (pp. 120-123). Newbury Park, CA: Sage.

Kinkead, R. W., & Winokur, D. (1992, October). How public relations professionals help CEOs make the right moves. *Public Relations Journal, 48,* 18-23.

Koontz, H., O'Donnell, C., & Weirich, H. (1982). *Essentials of management* (3rd ed.). New York: McGraw-Hill.

Kostoff, L. E. (1979). *A yen for harmony: Japanese managers try their style in North America* [Videotape]. Toronto: Ontario Educational Communications Authority.

Kostoff, R. N., Averch, H. A., & Chubin, D. E. (1994). Research impact assessment: Introduction and overview. *Evaluation Review, 18*(1), 3-10.

Lazarsfeld, P. F. (1959). Problems in methodology. In R. K. Merton, L. Broon, & L. S. Cottrell (Eds.), *Sociology today: Problems and prospects* (pp. 39-78). New York: Basic Books.

Lazarsfeld, P., Berelson, P. B., & Gaudet, H. (1948). *The people's choice.* New York: Columbia University Press.

Leiss, W., Kline, S., & Jhally, S. (1986). *Social communication in advertising.* Toronto: Methuen.

Lewis, J. D. (1990). Using alliances to build market power. *Planning Review, 18*(5), 4-9, 48.

Lewis, J. D. (1992). The new power of strategic alliances. *Planning Review 20*(5), 45-46.

Lindquist, E. A. (1991). *Public managers and policy communities: Learning to meet new challenges.* Toronto: Canadian Centre for Management Development.

Lynch, R. P. (1990). Building alliances to penetrate European markets. *Journal of Business Strategy, 11*(1), 4-8.

Marcuse, H. (1964). *One-dimensional man.* Boston: Beacon.

Marston, J. E. (1963). *The nature of public relations.* New York: McGraw-Hill.

McDonald, J. E. (1992). Interview. In T. E. Backer, E. M. Rogers, & P. Sopory (Eds.), *Designing health communication campaigns: What works?* (pp. 128-133). Newbury Park, CA: Sage.

McElreath, M. P. (1977). Public relations evaluative research: Summary statement. *Public Relations Review, 3*(4), 129-136.

McElreath, M. P. (1989, November). *Priority research questions in the field of public relations for the 1990s: Trends for the past ten years and predictions for the future.* Paper presented at the annual meeting of the Speech Communication Association, San Francisco, California.

Merton, R. (1949). *Social theory and social structure.* New York: Free Press.

Miller, D. C. (1991). The future of evaluation research: An addendum. In D. C. Miller (Ed.), *Handbook of research design and social measurement* (5th ed., pp. 94-95). Newbury Park, CA: Sage.

Miller, D. W., & Starr, M. K. (1961). *Executive decisions and operations research.* Englewood Cliffs, NJ: Prentice Hall.

Miller, G. R. (1989). Persuasion and public relations: Two "Ps" in a pod. In C. H. Botan & V. Hazleton, Jr. (Eds.), *Public relations theory* (pp. 45-66). Hillsdale, NJ: Lawrence Erlbaum.

Mitroff, I. I., & Bennis, W. (1989). *The unreality industry.* New York: Oxford University Press.

Montgomery, D. B., & Urban, G. L. (1969). *Management science in marketing.* Englewood Cliffs, NJ: Prentice Hall.

Morgan, G. (1992). Proactive management. In D. Mercer (Ed.), *Managing the external environment: A strategic perspective* (pp. 24-37). London: Open University Press/Sage.

Mulholland, J. (1991). *The language of negotiation.* New York. Routledge.

Murphy, P. (1991). The limits of symmetry: A game theory approach to symmetric and asymmetric public relations. In L. A. Grunig & J. E. Grunig (Eds.), *Public relations research annual* (Vol. 3, pp. 115-131). Hillsdale, NJ: Lawrence Erlbaum.

Neff, B. D. (1989). The emerging theoretical perspective in PR: An opportunity for communication departments. In C. H. Botan & V. Hazleton, Jr. (Eds.), *Public relations theory* (pp. 159-172). Hillsdale, NJ: Lawrence Erlbaum.

Newcomb, T. M. (1953). An approach to the study of communicative acts. *Psychological Review, 60,* 393-404.

Nimmo, D., & Combs, J. E. (1990). *Mediated political realities.* New York: Longman.

Olasky, M. N. (1985). Inside the amoral world of public relations: Truth molded for corporate gain. *Business and Society Review, 53,* 52-55.

Olasky, M. N. (1989). The aborted debate within public relations: An approach through Kuhn's paradigm. In J. E. Grunig & L. A. Grunig (Eds.), *Public relations research annual* (Vol. 1, pp. 87-96). Hillsdale, NJ: Lawrence Erlbaum.

Ormala, E. (1994). Impact assessment: European experience of qualitative methods and practices. *Evaluation Review, 18,* 41-51.

Patton, M. Q. (1986). *Utilization-focused evaluation* (2nd ed.). Beverly Hills, CA: Sage.

Patton, M. Q. (1990). Interview. In M. C. Alkin, *Debates on evaluation.* Newbury Park, CA: Sage.

Pavlik, J. V. (1987). *Public relations: What research tells us.* Newbury Park, CA: Sage.

Pavlik, J. V. (1992). Interview. In T. E. Backer, E. M. Rogers, & P. Sopory (Eds.), *Designing health communication campaigns: What works?* (pp. 134-138). Newbury Park, CA: Sage.

Pearson, R. (1989a). Beyond ethical relativism in public relations: Coorientation, rules, and the idea of communication symmetry. In J. E. Grunig & L. A. Grunig (Eds.), *Public relations research annual* (Vol. 1, pp. 67-86). Hillsdale, NJ: Lawrence Erlbaum.

Pearson, R. (1989b). Business ethics as communication ethics: Public relations practice and the idea of dialogue. In C. H. Botan & V. Hazleton, Jr. (Eds.), *Public relations theory* (pp. 111-134). Hillsdale, NJ: Lawrence Erlbaum.

Pentz, M. A. (1992). Interview. In T. E. Backer, E. M. Rogers, & P. Sopory (Eds.), *Designing health communication campaigns: What works?* (pp. 138-144). Newbury Park, CA: Sage.

Piekos, J. M., & Einsiedel, E. F. (1990). Roles and program evaluation techniques among Canadian public relations practitioners. In L. A. Grunig & J. E. Grunig (Eds.), *Public relations research annual* (Vol. 2, pp. 95-113). Hillsdale, NJ: Lawrence Erlbaum.

Pritchitt, J., Sherman, B., Hocking, C., Walker, G., Jordan, J., Macleod, S., Honnibal, A. M., & Macnamara, J. (1994). *Public relations evaluation: Professional accountability.* Geneva: International Public Relations Association.

Pruitt, D. G. (1983). Achieving integrative agreements. In M. H. Bazerman & R. J. Lewicki (Eds.), *Negotiating with organizations* (pp. 35-50). Beverly Hills, CA: Sage.

Rabin, K., & Franzen, R. (1981). Increasing the role of planning. In L. M. Helm, R. E. Hiebert, M. R. Naver, & K. Rabin (Eds.), *A public affairs handbook: Informing the people* (pp. 191-201). New York: Longman.

Reagan, J., Anderson, R., Sumner, J., & Hill, S. (1989, August). *Using Grunig's "indices" for models of public relations to differentiate job functions within organizations.* Paper presented at the annual meeting of the Association for Education in Journalism and Mass Communication, Washington, DC.

Redding, J. C., & Catalanello, R. F. (1994). *Strategic readiness.* San Francisco: Jossey-Bass.

Reid, A. (1988). Public affairs research: Quantitative and qualitative. In W. J. Wright & C. J. DuVernet (Eds.), *The Canadian public affairs handbook: Maximizing markets, protecting bottom lines* (pp. 117-146). Toronto: Carswell.

Rice, R. E. (1992). Interview. In T. E. Backer, E. M. Rogers, & P. Sopory (Eds.), *Designing health communication campaigns: What works?* (pp. 145-149). Newbury Park, CA: Sage.

Rice, R. E., & Atkin, C. K. (Eds.). (1989). *Public communication campaigns* (2nd ed.). Newbury Park, CA: Sage.

Rist, R. C. (1990). Managing of evaluation or managing by evaluation: Choices and consequences. In R. C. Rist (Ed.), *Program evaluation and the management of government: Patterns and prospects across eight nations* (pp. 3-17). New Brunswick, NJ: Transaction.

Rogers, E. M. (1992). Interview. In T. E. Backer, E. M. Rogers, & P. Sopory (Eds.), *Designing health communication campaigns: What works?* (pp. 149-153). Newbury Park, CA: Sage.

Rossi, P. H., & Freeman, H. F. (1989). *Evaluation: A systematic approach* (4th ed.). Newbury Park, CA: Sage.

Rossi, P. H., & Wright, J. D. (1991). Evaluation research: An assessment. In D. C. Miller (Ed.), *Handbook of research design and social measurement* (5th ed., pp. 87-97). Newbury Park, CA: Sage.

Rubin, B. (1979). International news and the American media. In D. B. Fescell (Ed.), *International news: Freedom under attack.* Beverly Hills, CA: Sage.

Rutman, L., & Mowbray, G. (1983). *Understanding program evaluation.* Beverly Hills, CA: Sage.

Salmon, C. T. (1989). Campaigns for social "improvement": An overview of values, rationales, and impacts. In C. T. Salmon (Ed.), *Information campaigns: Balancing social values and social change.* Newbury Park, CA: Sage.

Salmon, C. T. (1992). Interview. In T. E. Backer, E. M. Rogers, & P. Sopory (Eds.), *Designing health communication campaigns: What works?* (pp. 153-158). Newbury Park, CA: Sage.

Salter, L. (1985). Observations on the politics of assessment: The Captan case. *Canadian Public Policy, 11*(1), 64-76.

Salter, L., & Leiss, W. (1989). *Guide to consultation and consensus building.* Paper prepared for a course on the management of policy development, as material for course participants at the Canadian Centre for Management Development, and as a reference work.

Sawaya, R. N., & Arrington, C. B., Jr. (1988). Linking corporate planning with strategic issues. In R. L. Heath & Associates (Eds.), *Strategic issues management* (pp. 73-86). San Francisco: Jossey-Bass.

Schiller, H. I. (1989). *Culture Inc.* New York: Oxford University Press.

Seitel, F. P. (1984). *The practice of public relations* (2nd ed.). Toronto: Charles E. Merrill.

Smith, L. G. (1982). Mechanisms for public participation at a normative planning level in Canada. *Canadian Public Policy, 8,* 561-572.

Smith, W. (1994). *Establishing meaningful organizational objectives and performance measures.* Paper presented at the Conference on Public Sector Performance Measurement and Reporting, Ottawa, ON.

Sonnenberg, F. K. (1992). Partnering: Entering the age of cooperation. *Journal of Business Strategy, 13*(3), 49-52.

Springston, J. K., & Leichty, G. (1990, November). *Position paper for the workshop on public relations research and education.* Paper presented at the annual meeting of the Speech Communication Association, Chicago.

Star, S., & Hughes, H. (1950). Report of an educational campaign: The Cincinnati plan for the United Nations. *American Journal of Sociology, 55,* 389-400.

Steiner, G. A. (1983). *The new CEO.* New York: Macmillan.

Stewart, C. J., Smith, C. A., & Denton, R. E. (1989). *Persuasion and social movements.* Prospect Heights, IL: Waveland.

Stroup, M. A. (1988). Identifying critical issues for better corporate planning. In R. L. Heath & Associates (Eds.), *Strategic issues management* (pp. 87-98). San Francisco: Jossey-Bass.

Synnott, G., & McKie (1997). International issues in PR: Researching research and prioritizing priorities. *Journal of Public Relations Research, 9*(4), 259-282.

Tannenbaum, R., & Schmidt, W. H. (1958). How to choose a leadership pattern. *Harvard Business Review, 36*(2), 95-101.

Toth, E. L., & Heath, R. L. (1992). Introduction. In E. L. Toth & R. L. Heath (Eds.), *Rhetorical and critical approaches to public relations.* Hillsdale, NJ: Lawrence Erlbaum.

Troy, K. (1989). Internal communication restructures for the '90s. *Communication World,* pp. 28-31.

Turk, J. V. (1986). Forecasting tomorrow's public relations. *Public Relations Review, 12*(3), 12-21.

Wallack, L. (1992). Interview. In T. E. Backer, E. M. Rogers, & P. Sopory (Eds.), *Designing health communication campaigns: What works?* (pp. 161-166). Newbury Park, CA: Sage.

Weiss, C. H. (1972). *Evaluation research: Methods of assessing program effectiveness.* Engle wood Cliffs, NJ: Prentice Hall.

Wilde, G. J. S. (1993). Effects of mass media communication on health and safety habits: An overview of issues and evidence. *Addiction, 88,* 983-996.

Wye, C. (1994, June 26). *Rising with the tide* [draft]. Speech presented at the Institute for International Research, Ottawa, ON.

CHAPTER CONTENTS

6 Communication, Organization, and Crisis

MATTHEW W. SEEGER
Wayne State University

TIMOTHY L. SELLNOW
North Dakota State University

ROBERT R. ULMER
Wayne State University

Communication is increasingly recognized as an important process in organizational crisis and crisis management. The Three Mile Island incident, the Bhopal Union Carbide accident, the crash of Northwest Airlines Flight 255, and the *Exxon Valdez* oil spill can all be described as specific, unexpected, and nonroutine events or series of events that created high levels of uncertainty and threat or perceived threat to an organization's high-priority goals. Crises disrupt employees and communities, damage corporate reputations, and cost hundreds of millions of dollars. Crises also serve as the impetus for investigations and organizational change. This review organizes a dynamic and growing body of communication and organizational literature dealing with crisis, including various developmental approaches used to describe crisis, decision making, public relations, rhetorical approaches, organizational legitimacy, and methodologies for crisis communication research. Research themes and new directions are identified. Weick's concept of enactment, stakeholder theory, and chaos theory are discussed as frameworks for emerging research directions.

F EW events are as dramatic or have impacts as profound as organizational crises. The Three Mile Island and Chernobyl incidents, the Bhopal Union Carbide explosion, the Tylenol poisonings, the *Challenger* space shuttle disaster, Wall Street's Black Monday, the dangerous design problems of the Ford Pinto and A. H. Robins's Dalkon Shield, the asbestos scandal, the crashes of Northwest Airlines Flight 255 and ValuJet Flight 592, and the *Exxon Valdez* oil spill can all be described as organizational crises. Each disrupted the lives of employees, executives, members of

Correspondence and requests for reprints: Matthew W. Seeger, Department of Communication, Wayne State University, Detroit, MI 48202; e-mail Matthew_Seeger@wayne.edu

Communication Yearbook 21, pp. 231-275

the community, and customers; cost hundreds of millions of dollars; damaged the reputations of companies and industries; and affected the psychological and physical health of workers and community members. Each served as the impetus for investigations and created social and organizational changes. In the following review, we organize the dynamic and growing body of communication and organizational literature dealing with crisis, including decision making, public relations, rhetorical approaches to organizational crisis, and organizational legitimacy. We define organizational crisis, examine the role of communication in crisis, and explore the various developmental approaches used to describe crisis. We also review the methodologies used and problems encountered in the investigation of communication and organizational crisis. Finally, we identify research themes and propose new directions for research.

ORGANIZATIONAL CRISIS

Concern with organizational crisis has magnified with society's increasing dependence on large and diverse technological and corporate structures. The media have also given increased attention to these events. Perrow (1984) has noted that "human-made catastrophes appear to have increased with industrialization as we build devices that could crash, burn or explode" (p. 9). Among the consequences of large and diverse systems are the diminished capacity of individuals to comprehend the systems, more centralized decision making, limited public access, growing control by experts, system rigidity, and enhanced probability of crises. The complexity of these systems is compounded by unanticipated, unknown, and often unobserved interactions. Perrow argues that in the past 50 years, society has added interactive complexity as a possible cause of crisis.

Pauchant and Mitroff (1992) see organizational crises "as normal events triggered by the complexity of the system itself and by faulty decisions as well by the interrelationship between technological systems and the humans who attempt to manage them" (p. 20). Meyers and Holusha (1986) have identified several potentially positive outcomes of crisis: Heroes are born, change is accelerated, latent problems are faced, people are changed, new strategies evolve, new warning systems are developed, and new competitive edges appear. Crisis, from this view, is a natural stage of organization grounded in the duality and paradox of deconstruction and construction, organization and disorganization, chaos and "business as usual." These notions, although paradoxical, are linked. Disorganization is necessary to organization, and the chaos of crisis is linked to the routines of business as usual. In discussing the role of chaos theory in our understanding of organizational crisis, Murphy (1996) argues that crises act as "bifurcation points that permanently redefine an organization in a new and unexpected light" (p. 106).

In this way, crisis is part of the natural organizational process, purging elements of the system that are outdated and inappropriate and creating new, unexpected opportunities for growth and change.

Defining Organizational Crisis

We define an organizational crisis as a specific, unexpected, and nonroutine event or series of events that create high levels of uncertainty and threaten or are perceived to threaten an organization's high-priority goals. Organizational crises are conceptually distinct from disasters, which are usually defined in the research literature as non-organizationally based events generated by natural or mass technological forces (Quarantelli, 1988). Disasters (e.g., hurricanes, earthquakes, floods, tornadoes) are usually viewed as large-scale community-based events that affect society or its subunits and that are managed by community, government, or social groups (Kreps, 1984, p. 312). Organizational crises are also more likely to be precipitated by mistakes, oversights, or system deficiencies, whereas disasters tend to be associated with natural phenomena.

Weick (1988) describes crises as "low probability/high consequence events that threaten the most fundamental goals of the organization. Because of their low probability, these events defy interpretations and impose severe demands on sensemaking" (p. 305). Williams and Treadaway (1992) characterize an organizational crisis as a situation that "is marked by a sense of urgency" and "close observation by the media," and that "interrupts normal business operations with a potential loss of revenues and credibility" (p. 57). Hermann's (1963) model of crisis includes three conditions: "(1) threatens high priority values of the organization goals, (2) presents a restricted amount of time in which a decision can be made, and (3) is unexpected or unanticipated by the organization" (p. 64). These three components are widely used to examine organizational crisis (Billings, Milburn, & Schaalman, 1980; Gouran, 1982; Seeger & Bolz, 1996).

Threat

A component universal to crisis is the perception of threat arising from an extreme discrepancy between desired and existing states (Billings et al., 1980, p. 306). A trigger event—some dramatic occurrence such as consumer harm caused by product failure, dramatic disruption of operations, an explosion, or a media report—signals the threat (Billings et al., 1980). These events take the form of a stimulus, such as a message, that calls attention to new crisis circumstances or possibilities. Often, managers are notified of a trigger event by a subordinate or by someone outside the organization. There have been several cases, such as the Union Carbide Bhopal incident, in which failure on the part of managers to interpret a stimulus as indicative of crisis has led to escalation (Seeger & Bolz, 1996). Often, the first person to perceive a trigger event must convince others that a crisis exists. Until agreement about the crisis is reached, a coordinated organizational response is unlikely (Billings et al., 1980).

The severity of the perceived threat is related to the nature of the organizational goals that are compromised and the probability of loss (Billings et al., 1980). In some instances, a crisis may reduce profitability slightly, but has a high probability of occurring. In other instances, the organization's viability is at risk, but the crisis is a low probability. In almost all instances, the exact nature and implications of the threat are not immediately evident. Managers must sort through various possible outcomes and responses before they have some sense of the severity the problem. At any time during the crisis, the nature of the response, the probabilities, and the values of a loss may change as new information becomes available. The threat may also evolve into a secondary crisis, caused by the weakening of the organization, diversion of managers' attention, and scrutiny of outside agencies. In addition, crisis increases the chances of a hostile takeover while management's attention is diverted and stock values are low. Crisis investigation often reveals additional organizational problems or improprieties (Perrow, 1984, p. 16).

Short Response Time

One of the immediate uncertainties produced by crisis concerns the availability and efficacy of organizational responses (Gouran, 1982). Responses are usually critical in reducing, offsetting, and containing harm. In the case of an industrial spill, for example, the organization must quickly provide specific information about the compounds involved so that appropriate treatments can be made available (Seeger & Bolz, 1996). When airplanes crash, it is necessary for airlines to reassure other passengers immediately about safety (Ray, 1991). Decision makers usually must respond to these situations in a very short period of time, often with inadequate information about the causes and consequences of the crisis and with inadequate resources to offset the harm (Sellnow & Ulmer, 1995). They select from among three general sets of crisis responses: inaction, routine responses, and novel, original responses (Billings et al., 1980). When inaction is seen as the appropriate response to alleviate the threat (i.e., the problem will solve itself), the perception of crisis is usually low. When the perception of crisis is stronger, novel responses—that is, untried and unfamiliar responses—may be required.

Crisis is also a public event that creates media scrutiny and pressure for immediate explanations. Although an organization may postpone making any response on the grounds that all the facts are not available, media pressure is likely to continue until the organization offers an adequate explanation (Ray, 1991; Sellnow & Ulmer, 1995). Such an explanation involves a description of the cause of the crisis, dissemination of information that may help reduce harm, identification of the responsible agents, an outline of the steps taken to mitigate the effects of the crisis, and an outline of the changes necessary to ensure that a similar crisis does not occur again (Ice, 1991; Seeger, 1986; Turner, 1976). An incomplete or dishonest explanation may prompt further media and third-party investigation, create additional situations of threat and uncertainty, and damage the organization's credibility and image.

Surprise

Organizational decision makers are almost universally surprised and caught off guard by trigger events, even when the organization has planned for crisis. Surprise is a consequence of being suddenly confronted with circumstances seen as unlikely and inconsistent with routine, familiar activities. Crisis theorists note that humans are creatures of routine and habit; we operate on the expectation that things will continue pretty much as they have in the past. A crisis is by definition nonroutine and outside of familiar, predictable patterns of day-to-day life (Billings et al., 1980; Gouran, Hirokawa, & Martz, 1986). Decision makers faced with crisis are confronted with nonroutine decision situations, unanticipated sources of uncertainty, confusing and incomplete messages, and participants who do not share the organization's values and assumptions (Turner, 1976). Pauchant and Mitroff (1992) argue that one defining characteristic of crisis is this fundamental challenging of basic assumptions that must be either defended or abandoned. This need to examine, reassess, and defend core beliefs may shake accepted guidelines for action during a crisis.

Types of Crisis

Crises have been categorized according to similarities in the locus, source, and cause of the threat (Coombs, 1995; Egelhoff & Sen, 1992; Marcus & Goodman, 1991). Meyers and Holusha (1986), for example, identify nine types. First is crisis in public perception, in which public confidence in the organization or industry is threatened (e.g., the failure of savings and loan institutions). A crisis in public perception is enhanced by extended media reports and inadequate organizational responses. The second kind of crisis is the sudden market shift, such as the changing of consumers' preferences to small, fuel-efficient foreign cars that followed the 1979 oil embargo. The unexpected nature of such shifts precludes organizations from planning or adapting. The third kind of crisis is product failure, which includes product recalls for minor defects and failures that harm consumers. In some instances, such as happened in the Tylenol case, product failure is induced by sabotage. The fourth category of crisis is top management succession. A sudden death, or even a planned retirement, often results in power conflicts, uncertainty, and a loss of organizational direction. Robert Stemple's removal as CEO of General Motors in 1992 created unrest among workers and diverted attention from the day-to-day activities of producing cars. The fifth kind of crisis is the cash crisis, which is usually a sign of other organizational problems. Problems with industrial relations, the sixth category of crisis, may result in strikes and job actions. The seventh form of crisis is the hostile takeover, which can lead to a jarring battle for organizational control. The eighth kind of crisis, the adverse international event (e.g., the 1992 invasion of Kuwait), may disrupt a specific company and cause general unrest in raw materials, personnel, and markets. The ninth kind of crisis involves regulation and deregulation, which can create high levels of uncertainty.

Mitroff, Pauchant, and Shrivastava (1988) have developed a more discrete system by grouping crises according to their underlying structural similarities. These categories include (a) breakdowns or defects in products, plants, packages, equipment, and people; (b) extreme antisocial acts directed at corporations, products, consumers, executives, employees, and employees' families; (c) external economic attacks such as extortion, bribery, boycotts, and hostile takeovers; (d) external informational attacks, such as copyright infringement, loss of information, counterfeiting, and rumors; and (e) environmental accidents. Only in breakdowns or defects in products, plants, products, packages, and people are crises largely within the organization's control. The remaining kinds of crises involve factors that are mostly or entirely beyond the organization's control; outside environmental factors are the primary precipitating agents. The environment is a frequent locus for the development of organizational crisis (Meyer, 1982). Smart (1985) and Smart and Vertinsky (1977) argue that uncertainty and the inability to monitor and communicate with the environment completely are the central elements in most organizational crises.

COMMUNICATION AND ORGANIZATIONAL CRISIS

The study of organizational communication and the study of organizational crisis intersect at a number of points. Communication, for example, is associated with the development of organizational crisis through various stages (Fink, 1986; Turner, 1976; Weick, 1988). The role of communication in crisis decision making has also been explored (Gouran, 1982; Gouran et al., 1986; Janis, 1972). The crisis management literature draws on public relations to clarify the ways in which organizations should communicate with constituencies, including the media (Benson, 1988; Fink, 1986; Katz, 1987). Communication scholars have examined organizational responses to crisis rhetorically using the genre of apologia (Benoit, 1995; Hearit, 1995; Schultz & Seeger, 1991; Sellnow & Ulmer, 1995). Theories of organizational legitimacy have been used to examine accounts of crisis and the threats to image and reputation faced by organizations in crisis (Allen & Caillouet, 1994; Seeger, 1986). These approaches are examined in more detail below.

Communication and Crisis Development

The relationship between communication and crisis development is grounded in a view of organizational communication as epistemic. Weick (1988) takes an enactment-based approach to crisis, arguing that action, including communication, defines, frames, and influences subsequent action. Communication allows members to interpret the informational environment collectively, including the potential for and development of crisis. Researchers can examine organizational crisis developmentally to understand how this enactment occurs using stages or phases (Fink, 1986; Meyers & Holusha, 1986; Pauchant & Mitroff, 1992; Shrivastava, Mitroff, Miller, & Miglani, 1988; Sturges, 1994; Turner, 1976). These approaches are helpful for comparing and contrasting the elements and characteristics of crises. Developmental approaches can also clarify how dynamic and interactive sequences of events and interpretations may, through long and unanticipated cause-effect linkages, result in crisis. Three of these developmental approaches are outlined below. Fink (1986) and Turner (1976) identify stages or phases of crisis development, whereas Weick (1988) offers a more dynamic view of crisis based on the principles of organizational enactment.

Fink (1986) equates crisis to a "dynamic, unstable, and fluid" illness and proposes a medical-based model with the following four stages: (a) prodromal, (b) acute, (c) chronic, and (d) crisis resolution. The prodromal stage is a warning or precrisis stage, which may or may not include signs of the impending crisis. Fink argues that, in some instances, it is possible to avoid a crisis if warning signs exist and decision makers attend to them appropriately. This stage is where crisis begins and serious damage accumulates. In the acute stage, a crisis has erupted and nothing can be done to avoid at least some damage, although effective management may limit damage. The chronic stage is characterized as a postmortem of the crisis events. It is a "period of recovery, self analysis and self-doubt and healing" (p. 24). Fink argues that the chronic crisis phase may become a time of celebration for success and further crisis preparation and planning. During the postcrisis period, the patient is well and able to sense the development of new prodromal stages. Crisis, according to this view, is cyclical, with repeated prodromal, acute, chronic, and resolution stages. Fink's model is also prescriptive in the sense that effective sensing during the prodromal stage allows the organization to move directly to resolution. Often, the signs of impending disaster are obscure and unstructured, so as to preclude sensing. It is only in hindsight that complex interactions, beliefs, and structures related to a crisis are revealed, and even then they may be subject to a variety of competing interpretations.

Turner (1976) proposes a comprehensive developmental sequence of six stages of crisis. He argues that crises may be understood as "large scale intelligence failures" or "failures in foresight" (p. 381). "A disaster occurs because of some inaccuracy or inadequacy in the accepted norms and beliefs"

(p. 381). These beliefs about the world, its hazards, and what constitute reasonable precautions allow organizations to manage many problems. In fact, most are effectively resolved with little or no attention. One difficulty lies in how to determine which problems can be safely ignored, which should be attended to, and what the acceptable level of safety and precaution is. Failures in foresight, then, represent a fundamental "collapse of precautions which have hitherto been regarded culturally as adequate" (p. 380). Crisis often involves problems that had previously been judged unimportant interacting with precautions that were considered adequate.

Crisis, then, is the result of widespread and dramatic failure in shared belief systems rather than of short-term failure in technology, momentary lapse in managerial or operator vigilance, or flawed decision making. Turner (1976) begins with the assumption that a crisis represents a "radical departure from the pattern of normal operations" (p. 381). In Stage I, a point of normal operations and procedures, members have (a) a set of culturally accepted beliefs about the world and its hazards and (b) associated precautionary norms set out in laws, codes, practice, mores, and folkways generally considered adequate (p. 381). Accepted beliefs, policies, and procedures, for example, may govern the handling of dangerous chemicals. These beliefs and norms are interdependent, such that a change in Belief A would necessitate a change in Belief B. In the 1930s and 1940s, for example, it was widely believed that asbestos was a safe, convenient, and technologically superior product. Its flame-retardant and insulating character made it useful in building materials for reducing the risk of fire. Subsequent changes in the belief structures surrounding asbestos, however, have resulted in dramatic changes in the accompanying precautionary norms, codes, and practices. Asbestos itself is now considered to be a major hazard, with accompanying norms, codes, and practices for its safe handling and disposal.

In Turner's Stage II, the incubation period, events that are outside the parameters of and/or at odds with the accepted beliefs about hazards and the norms for their avoidance accumulate unnoticed. Turner argues that the events are either unknown or known but not fully understood. In some instances, however, the events are known and understood, but are not communicated in meaningful ways that garner the attention and action of decision makers. A collective blindness that allows minor problems to grow to overwhelming proportions often occurs in Stage II. The tragedy that took place in Bhopal, India, was precipitated, in part, by a collective blindness regarding both the hazards of the chemicals produced in Union Carbide's plant there and the decay of the plant's safety systems. Turner suggests that incubation often occurs because a problem or issue is poorly structured or defined and, consequently, cannot be easily attended to. The problems in Bhopal were both difficult for Union Carbide to define because of intercultural barriers and easy to ignore because of proximity.

In Stage III, the crisis is first sensed through a precipitating or trigger event that signals the inadequacy of accepted beliefs about hazards and the norms for avoidance. The crisis, although still difficult to define, cannot be ignored. During Stage III, interpretations of earlier stages are modified so that decision makers can define and structure the problem. Formal decision systems are made aware of the crisis-precipitating network of events and agents and its potential for crisis. This is an important first step in the readjustment of beliefs about hazards and avoidance. Stage III, with its trigger event, is followed by Stage IV, the onset of the crisis and its immediate, direct, and unanticipated consequences. Damage varies in intensity and scope from crisis to crisis. Stage V is rescue and salvage, where the immediate collapse of beliefs about the world, its hazards, and avoidance norms are recognized. This recognition allows for initial and rapid ad hoc adjustments and the initiation of rescue and salvage efforts. At this point, the organization may activate its crisis plan and begin to manage the crisis. As the immediate effects of the disaster dissipate, more time is available for a comprehensive and carefully thought-out assessment. This involves untangling the "incubating network of events" associated with the crisis (Turner, 1976, p. 382). In Stage VI, full cultural adjustment takes place in beliefs about the world, its hazards, and avoidance norms, so that they are again compatible with the new insights and understandings. Like Fink (1986), Turner suggests that organizational crises are cyclical, with Stage VI, full cultural readjustment, leading back to Stage I.

A less discrete view of crisis development is grounded in organizational enactment, where actions taken by members toward a crisis-related event influence subsequent developments. Weick (1988) describes three forms of enactment related to organizing and crisis: enactment from capacity to perceive, enactment from expectations, and enactment from public commitment. Organizations have limited capacities to monitor, attend to, and act toward events and activities in their informational environment. Elements that are out of the way or difficult to access and interpret do not call for management's actions or attention. Circumstances that strain the organization's information systems, such as crisis, further reduce information-processing capacity. Weick (1988) argues, "If people think they can do lots of things, then they can afford to pay attention to a wider variety of elements because, whatever they see, they will have some way to cope with it" (p. 311). Highly centralized decision systems, bureaucratic rules and procedures, automated controls, staff cuts, turnover, time pressure, reduction in the channels of communication, and lack of diversity in members' backgrounds, experiences, values, and skills all limit the capacity to perceive and the available repertoire of responses.

Organizations also require sets of expectations about the environment that influence perceptions and guide subsequent enactments in ways not unlike self-fulfilling prophecy (Weick, 1988). This enactment from expectation may derive from the background of management, technology, past experiences, or similar influences on beliefs and assumptions. Because humans expect the future to look much like the past, new developments in the environment may be overlooked or ignored. Previous enactments may have created high levels of specialization that tend to preclude new perspectives. Management may also approach a crisis from a particular set of assumptions and biases based on a particular background, such as legal assumptions about liability. These assumptions may focus crisis enactments and selections toward a set of calculated responses designed to avoid litigation and away from responses that may reflect more humane values of concern and support. Often, expectations develop from previous experiences with similar problems. This process is often one of "We had this problem 10 years ago and we dealt with it in this way." This retained response from earlier experience, Weick argues, influences subsequent crisis organizing.

Finally, the organization's public commitments, justifications, and actions are frequently difficult to undo, deny, or even amend (Weick, 1988). During crises, spokespersons often make public statements and commitments. These statements usually concern interpretations of responsibility, harm, and repair of the damage, including cleanup and aid to victims. Once these statements are made and disseminated through the media, the organization often feels compelled to support and defend them vigorously. When a statement is communicated widely and with certainty, it is difficult if not impossible to retract or reinterpret it. Weick (1988) indicates that in some instances, such public statements and commitments become "tenacious justifications" to which the organization adheres rigorously for its own sake (p. 310).

Although no single developmental model has yet emerged as most useful, these approaches to crisis are valuable for capturing process characteristics and for demonstrating the influences of communication variables and activities on crisis (Seeger, 1986; Sellnow, 1994; Sturges, 1994). Several studies, for example, have demonstrated that communication deficiencies are related to the onset of organizational crisis. Tompkins and Anderson (1971), for example, examined the role of communication in the Kent State University crisis. They concluded that the crisis was at least facilitated by organizational communication deficiencies, including inadequate two-way communication, failures in managerial communication, and divisional and student isolation. Cushing (1994) has examined the role that communication plays in airline disasters. He identifies several basic communication breakdowns related to these disasters, including communication between pilots and air traffic controllers. Ambiguity, misunderstandings based on accents, and technical jargon have been identified as factors in dozens of aircraft disasters. Cushing proposes a variety of technological fixes, including visual communication systems, computerized touch screens, and feedback mechanisms.

Although these and other studies suggest that communication deficiency is related to crisis onset, specific processes and variables remain unclear. Existing evidence points to deficiencies in communication climate that constrain open communication about problems and breakdowns as well as disruptions of coordination as the most common communication-based causes of crisis. Comparative analyses of the development of crises in different industries and of different types would be fruitful in extending this research. Shrivastava et al. (1988), for example, developed an industrial crisis model by comparing the *Challenger* explosion, the Tylenol tampering case, and the Bhopal tragedy on several dimensions. They conclude that although crises are quite variable in terms of causes, manifestations, harms, and social costs, commonalities can be observed. For example, they note: "A common form of interaction in which failure occurs is communication between organizational decision-makers and outsiders. At NASA, and to a lesser extent, at Union Carbide, communication failures played a primary role in causing the crisis" (p. 269). Questions also remain about the role of organizational communication in other crisis stages, including the initial sensing of crisis, initial message-based interpretations of crisis, and the negotiating of crisis resolution. As this body of literature expands, other patterns will likely become manifest. Finally, developmental approaches are linked to other work in group decision making and public relations, discussed below.

CRISIS AND GROUP DECISION MAKING

A small but important body of research has focused on communication and crisis decision making. Grounded in functional decision theory (Gouran, Hirokawa, Julian, & Leathman, 1993; Poole, 1990), this work has three distinct themes unified by an interest in understanding how communication contributes to the maintenance of decisional vigilance. The first theme concerns decision making and crisis development. Janis's (1972) and Janis and Mann's (1977) work on governmental policy disasters, for example, focuses on how the breakdown of vigilance leads to crisis. A second theme is more prescriptive and focuses on the ways decisional vigilance is maintained during crisis-induced threat, surprise, and short response time (Gouran, 1982). This form of crisis decision making is often seen as part of the crisis management function (Nudel & Antokol, 1988). Finally, principles of decision making have utility for the examination of postcrisis investigations (Ray, 1991).

Janis (1972) developed his groupthink thesis from an analysis of government policy fiascoes. He was interested in the internal group process that leads to a fundamental breakdown in decision quality. Groups are generally believed to make more effective and more cautious decisions than are individuals, and consequently groups are favored in many decisional contexts. Janis's analysis focused on cases such as the Bay of Pigs fiasco and the military command responsible for Pearl Harbor immediately prior to the Japanese bombing. Janis concludes that groupthink is a general concurrence-seeking tendency that develops in some decisional groups. This tendency is enhanced by strong group cohesion, the status of the group, and strong leadership, and is characterized by eight symptoms. These include activities that cut the group off from important sources of information and encourage members to discount negative information, encourage consensus, and discourage dissent. Janis argues that these conditions lead to a breakdown in vigilance and often to the development of a crisis.

The principles of groupthink have also been extended to other contexts (Bernthal & Insko, 1993; Callaway & Esser, 1984). Gouran's (1984) analysis illustrates how a failure of collective judgment by President Nixon and his associates led to the Watergate crisis. Faulty inferential judgments by decision makers, partly attributed to the pressure of the situation, played a role in creating the Watergate cover-up. Gouran et al. (1986) sought to understand how NASA's "decisional structure," designed to prevent unwise and unsafe potential launches, failed in the case of *Challenger* (p. 121). By examining testimony given before the Rogers Commission, Gouran et al. identify five factors associated with the failure: (a) perceived pressure to launch *Challenger*; (b) rigid observation of role boundaries; (c) questionable reasoning patterns among managers; (d) ambiguous and misleading language, allowing for risk minimization; and (e) failure to ask important and relevant questions (p. 121). Gouran et al. conclude that a carefully constructed decision system's "effective utilization is still reliant on the social, psychological, and communication environment in which responsible parties function" (p. 133). In their study of the *Exxon Valdez* oil spill, Williams and Olaniran (1994) identify hypervigilance as the decision-making flaw that accounted for Exxon's failed postcrisis response. The stress and pressure of crisis situations, these authors argue, often makes sound decision making difficult.

This second theme of crisis decision making is related to work on public relations and crisis management. Gouran (1982), also drawing on functional decision theory, offers principles for maintaining decisional vigilance during the threat, surprise, and short response time of a crisis situation. These variables affect decision makers and serve to constrain the actions of organizations seeking to manage and respond to crises. Gouran (1982) contends that the uncertainty of crisis, combined with the extra pressure crisis brings to make good decisions, renders effective decision making difficult. Due to the threat, decision makers during a crisis are pressured to make decisions concerning an event that is characterized by low probability and high uncertainty. Janis and Mann (1977) explain that individuals in such situations often fall prey to hypervigilance. The threat is often so severe that decision makers become frozen in inactivity or are compelled to respond quickly to resolve the crisis by choosing the most readily available option. Such quick, impulsive responses can result in an intensification of the crisis.

In addition, due to the factor of surprise, organizational decision makers are constrained in their "ability to identify and marshal the decisional resources" needed (Gouran, 1982, p. 177). As discussed above, decision makers are often conditioned by the efficiency and comfort of routine decisions. Gouran (1982) suggests that the trauma and limited resources available during a crisis often cause decision makers to react rather than reflect about the situation. This type of response often "results in considerable damage before more rational forces can take hold" (p. 177). The limited and equivocal nature of the information available during crisis serves as an important constraint. Gouran posits two conditions that arise due to short response time: confusion of appropriate responses and incapacity to respond. First, limited time can "blur the distinctions among alternative courses of action or constrain a group's ability to compare their strengths and weaknesses" (p. 176). Second, the extreme conditions and stress of a crisis may cause some decision makers to freeze. In addition, Quarantelli (1988) suggests that crisis decision making is inherently characterized by conflict. Four common problems include (a) loss of "higher echelon personnel," (b) conflicts over authority, (c) conflict between emergent and organizational groups regarding domains, and (d) organizational jurisdictional differences (p. 380). In short, the characteristics inherent to crisis situations severely complicate decision makers' ability to reach effective decisions.

One such condition is the need for an early, public, and candid response to crisis (Benoit & Brinson, 1994; Crable & Vibbert, 1985; Schuetz, 1990; Seeger, 1986). Schuetz (1990) summarizes this position by explaining, "The primary objective of crisis management is to provide 'accurate information as quickly as possible' to external publics affected by the crisis" (p. 282). As discussed earlier, research suggests that threat, surprise, and short response time severely constrain an organization's ability to respond appropriately. Consequently, tension arises for the organization as it tries to meet the information demands of the environment while managing the uncertainty, confusion, and stress of a crisis. Crisis management seeks to address this problem in three ways: planning for contingencies, creating as many preset decisions as possible, and using established crisis decision-making methodologies to protect decisional vigilance (Connor, 1985). Crisis decision makers are almost inevitably forced to act with inadequate information and not enough time.

Finally, principles of decision making have utility for the examination of postcrisis investigations. Ray (1991), for example, examined the National Transportation Safety Board's investigation of three major airline disasters. Decision groups such as boards and commissions in postcrisis situations serve to "collect, synthesize, summarize, and disseminate information; identify causes and associated factors; suggest ways in which future crises may be avoided; assign blame and responsibility; and serve as a symbol that something is being done" (pp. 189-190). In other words, the primary responsibilities of organizational decision makers are to reduce the uncertainty concerning the crisis and to communicate the results to external publics. Uncertainty, in this case, involves questions "of what happened, how, who to blame, and what responses should be made" (p. 190). In short, postcrisis decision makers serve to reduce uncertainty and respond to the situation. Seeger (1986) examined the role of the Rogers Commission in repairing NASA's legitimacy following the *Challenger* explosion. He concludes that the commission's inclusion of highly credible, independent members, the use of public hearings, and a systematic and thorough investigation helped move NASA past the crisis. Seeger and Bolz (1996) examined the importance of objective decision systems for the reduction of postcrisis uncertainty in the Union Carbide Bhopal incident. They suggest that Union Carbide's refusal to deny, confirm, or comment on the incident meant that "determinations of cause, blame, responsibility and liability were left to the courts" (p. 262).

The limited research available suggests that decision making is relevant to all stages of crisis development. In precrisis stages, loss of decisional vigilance may contribute to crisis. During crisis, decisions must be made about how to manage the crisis, allocate resources, interpret information, and respond. Postcrisis, decisions are made about reducing uncertainty, future avoidance, and assigning blame. If decision makers do not adequately reduce the uncertainty regarding blame, cause, and harm, they may be unlikely to create an effective postcrisis response. This work is also closely related to public relations approaches to crisis and the practice of crisis management. Effective decision making, usually involving teams, is generally seen as a hallmark of effective crisis management.

Research in decision-making approaches, although contributing much to understanding of crisis and crisis management, is very uneven. Work in functional decision theory, for example, is well developed, whereas postcrisis decision making has received comparatively little attention. Similarly, few efforts have been made to examine systematically the communication and decision making of crisis management teams. As this body of research expands to incorporate more cases of organizational crisis, the relationship of decision making to crisis development, including postcrisis investigation, and the role of specific decision-making groups and teams may become clearer.

PUBLIC RELATIONS AND CRISIS MANAGEMENT

The field of public relations has developed specific practitioner guidelines for effective crisis communication. These guidelines, along with principles for effective crisis decision making, are usually seen as part of the crisis management process. Principles of crisis public relations are drawn largely from the experiences of practitioners (Katz, 1987; Reinhardt, 1987) and from case studies such as Small's (1991) and Williams and Treadaway's (1992) critiques of the *Exxon Valdez* crisis, Benson's (1988) and Snyder and Foster's (1983) analyses of the Tylenol poisonings, and Ice's (1991) examination of

Bhopal. The goal of this literature is to develop communication models and frameworks that inform practice and that help limit and alleviate the damage to both the organization and other crisis stakeholders, such as the community, victims, and their families.

Wilcox, Ault, and Agee (1986), in discussing the role of public relations in crisis, observe that the first instinct of many companies facing crisis is to "deny that a crisis exists, refuse to answer media questions, and resist involvement by appropriate government agencies" (p. 310). A second common response is for organizations to try to manage and control the development of the crisis, "releasing partial, often inaccurate and delayed information while concealing unfavorable facts" (p. 310). In both instances, the organization risks creating an adversarial relationship with the media and further damaging its reputation. Finally, Wilcox et al. note, the organization may adopt a policy of open and accurate communication and maintain channels of communication with outside sources. This quick and complete disclosure, although damaging in the short run, reduces the risk of rumors, leaks, drawn-out media coverage, and the perception of dishonesty (Burson, 1995). A candid, prompt, honest, and complete response may also bolster an organization's reputation and integrity in the long run (Small, 1991). Maintaining open communication is a fundamental tenet of crisis management (Lau, 1987; Newsom, Scott, & Turk, 1989; Pinsdorf, 1987). This openness allows the organization to be proactive in presenting its view of the crisis to the media, but it is often at odds with legal strategies designed to limit organizational liability (Fitzpatrick & Rubin, 1995).

This orientation to crisis, then, informs the specific strategies employed by public relations practitioners in both the planning and the implementation of crisis communication strategies. These strategies include (a) identification and development of a crisis management team; (b) appointment of an appropriate crisis spokesperson; (c) identification of areas of high risk; and (d) the structuring, implementation, and maintenance of an overall crisis communication plan, including contact lists and checklists (Allan, 1990; Gonzalez-Herrero & Pratt, 1995; Katz, 1987; Lau, 1987; Newsom et al., 1989; Reinhardt, 1987; Small, 1991).

A crisis management team is a coordinating structure that brings together participants who have the expertise and resources necessary to manage the crisis (Andriole, 1985; Littlejohn, 1983). Teams are usually constituted in advance and meet regularly to review plans and contingencies. Both the team structure itself and the familiarity of members with one another are seen as important timesaving steps (Burson, 1995). Team members should also know their individual responsibilities and be familiar with the crisis chain of command and crisis policies. Mitroff (1988) argues that crisis teams should be trained to deal effectively with the stress and emotional arousal that accompany crisis. He notes that the surprise and stress of the crisis itself is often paralyzing to decision makers. Typically, a crisis team includes public relations practitioners, legal counsel, members of top management, and a crisis spokesperson. Other organizational areas, such as human resources, security, operations, and marketing, may be represented on the team depending on the nature of the crisis and the organization (Dilenschneider & Hyde, 1985). In some instances, teams may include members from outside the organization.

The public relations literature suggests that in most cases a single designated spokesperson, usually the CEO, should be the primary source for all crisis-related messages (Burson, 1995; Dilenschneider & Hyde, 1985; Hearit, 1995; Small, 1991). A single formal source helps to ensure consistency of message and reduces the chance of rumors. The CEO, as the organization's final authority, is in most instances the most credible crisis spokesperson. Although the designated spokesperson may have other members of the team respond to technical questions, he or she should retain final authority for the message. Because the crisis spokesperson will often deal with an aggressive press, he or she should also have extensive training (Katz, 1987). Small (1991) also suggests that, when feasible, the CEO should travel to the scene of the crisis to signal concern and to collect information firsthand. This strategy, however, should be approached cautiously within the constraints of the specific crisis. In the Bhopal incident, for example, Union Carbide CEO Warren Anderson was arrested upon his arrival in India. Union Carbide, deprived of its top decision maker, was unable to respond effectively (Seeger & Bolz, 1996). Benson (1988) also asserts that the spokesperson should be willing to confront the media when their portrayal of the crisis is unfair or overly sensational. He notes that in the Tylenol tampering case Johnson & Johnson's CEO praised the media and acknowledged their role in disseminating information about the risks associated with Tylenol capsules.

The role of public relations in crisis management also has a proactive dimension in the identification of high-risk areas faced by the organization. According to Newsom et al. (1989), crisis communication management requires ongoing activities, which include assessment of the environment and development of plans and "pro-actions" to limit risk (p. 436). Through such activities, organizations seek to anticipate possible crises and to prepare by changing the conditions of crisis. They do so either by avoiding crisis altogether, if sufficient time and resources are available, or by mitigating its impact. Risk assessment also allows public relations practitioners to develop several response repertoires for different crisis scenarios, what Mitroff (1988) calls a crisis portfolio. This view of public relations as a crisis-sensing activity is similar to the environmental monitoring activities in the precrisis stage. In both cases, communication with elements in the environment may enhance the ability of the organization to sense and avoid threats (Gonzalez-Herrero & Pratt, 1995).

Finally, systematic crisis planning may mitigate some of the psychological stress and arousal of the crisis through a process of emotional inoculation, and allows for the development of preset decisions and contingencies (Fink, 1986). When decision makers engage in crisis planning, for example, they anticipate the resources and information necessary to deal with a crisis without the time constraints usually associated with an actual event (Phelps, 1986). Many of the structures that need to be in place for handling a crisis, such as committees, lists of emergency agencies, locations and types of various emergency supplies, and names of appropriate officials, are established in advance (Gigliotti & Jason, 1991). These plans can be invaluable in reducing response uncertainty and stress, giving decision makers valuable time during a crisis. Contact lists indicate which agencies decision makers should notify in various situations, such as police and fire departments, the Red Cross, insurance companies, hospitals, hazardous waste management agencies, federal and state disaster agencies, and other appropriate local, federal, and state agencies (Lukaszewaki, 1987). Such lists speed coordinated efforts to contain damage and ensure consistency with overall crisis management goals and other organizational policies. Finally, lists should be developed and maintained regarding the availability of various crisis management resources, including containment technology and hazardous materials handling equipment for chemical spills, heavy equipment for transportation accidents, psychological and social services agencies, and medical or other technical expertise. Exxon, for example, made extensive use of biologists, veterinarians, and animal rescue experts following the *Valdez* oil spill (McGill, 1994).

Although observers of crises almost universally advocate the development and maintenance of crisis plans, several studies suggest that many organizations fail to take these basic steps. Fink (1986) found that only 50% of the Fortune 500 firms he examined had such plans. In the *Exxon Valdez* case, elaborate crisis plans were in place, but had not been adequately maintained (McGill, 1994). Spill containment systems at Union Carbide's Bhopal plant had been cannibalized for parts (Seeger & Bolz, 1996). In a survey of public relations practitioners, Guth (1995) found a general lack of adequate planning for crises. He concludes that a relationship exists between an organization's experience with crisis and the tendency to view public relations as a management function, and that larger organizations are more prone to crisis. By definition, crisis is always an uncertain and surprising event. Although crisis planning can help reduce some of the time pressures on decision makers during crisis, by offsetting some of the fundamental decisions and procedures, it cannot alleviate crisis. Moreover, little empirical evidence exists to suggest that crisis planning or experience in crisis management reduces harm. Quarantelli (1988) has suggested that planning is only indirectly related to good crisis management. Benson (1988) argues that Johnson & Johnson's successful management of the second Tylenol tampering was in part a function of the company's experience with the first episode. In addition, the emergence of new types of crises, the development of new technologies of communication, and the globalization of organizations and crises have created new practitioner contingencies.

Public relations has articulated a well-developed set of practitioner principles for managing, containing, and limiting the damage of a crisis. These principles are largely situationally insensitive, however. Openness, for example, is advocated in all crisis circumstances. Moreover, little empirical evidence exists regarding the effectiveness of these principles. Finally, the emphasis on crisis management suggests that crisis can be influenced, contained, and controlled in structured, predictable, and rational ways. As such, public relations shares many of the assumptions that functional decision theory brings to crisis. Nonetheless, this work provides a rich set of anecdotal lessons regarding crisis communication.

RHETORICAL APPROACHES TO CRISIS

Rhetorical approaches to organizational crises emphasize understanding of the communication strategies open to an organization and its spokespersons in the aftermath of a crisis. Most often, these efforts draw on the rhetorical genre of apologia (see Downey, 1993; Ware & Linkugel, 1973). Ware and Linkugel (1973) define apologia as "the recurrent theme of accusation followed by apology" (pp. 273-274). Organizational researchers have expanded this tradition in two important ways. First, organizational responses are examined as distinct from those offered by individuals in terms of their structure, purposes, and audiences. Second, three typologies of crisis response strategies have been developed. We present in this section a discussion of corporate apologia, a review of theoretical advancements, and an examination of the implications of these advancements for the study of crisis communication.

Much of the early work on corporate apologia sought to differentiate corporate discourse from that associated with individual speakers. For example, Schultz and Seeger (1991) contend that organizational discourse "must be understood in part as corporate responses, with corporate sources, corporate purposes and corporate audiences" (p. 51). These distinct properties of organizations have implications concerning both how they respond to crisis and their ability to respond to crisis. Each property is discussed below, along with its implications for crisis communication research.

Researchers have argued that, unlike individual communicators, organizations are composed of complex internal variables and structures, including hierarchical and divisionalized components that constitute corporate sources (Cheney, 1991; Dionisopoulos & Vibbert, 1988). For example, Schultz and Seeger (1991) suggest that the hierarchical nature of organizations "creates the opportunity to deny or diffuse responsibility in ways which may be unique to corporate centered discourse" (p. 52). Cheney (1991) explains that organizations tend to " 'decenter' the self, the individual, the acting subject" (p. 5). In such cases, organizations are able to deflect blame from specific individuals and diffuse responsibility to the organization as a whole (Schultz, 1996). For this reason, determining responsibility for an organizational crisis is often very confused, equivocal, and subject to multiple interpretations. Consequently, organizations often strategically interpret issues of responsibility for crisis in ways that allow them to share, diffuse, and avoid responsibility.

Organizations also communicate with their environment for purposes of satisfying stakeholder needs and expectations (Allen & Caillouet, 1994). These purposes are grounded in a desire to return to profitability, secure market share, maintain autonomy of operation, and create system stability following a crisis. The purposes of organizations during crises, therefore, are often different from those of individuals. For example, following the recent ValuJet crash, the company's stock lost value. Part of ValuJet's postcrisis purpose, then, was to add value to its stock. Another goal was to illustrate appropriate systemwide safety precautions to the National Transportation Safety Board. These purposes are different from those manifested by individual speakers, who, during a crisis, may be concerned primarily about personal safety, level of threat, and damage to their image.

Other researchers attribute the greatest difference between organizational and single-speaker apologia to the diversity of corporate audiences (Allen & Caillouet, 1994; Ice, 1991; Schuetz, 1990; Schultz & Seeger, 1991). Although both single speakers and organizations speak to diverse audiences, Schultz and Seeger (1991) argue, "the modern corporation is unique in the degree of audience diversity and nature of their interests" (p. 51). Much of the literature suggests that the selection of particular strategies to repair relationships with some audiences often alienates others. Sellnow and Ulmer (1995) contend that in circumstances where an organization must address divergent audiences with varying needs, "they can address both audience groups simultaneously by interjecting some form of ambiguity into their public arguments" (p. 148). This strategy is particularly important given the repercussions of alienating an external audience. In addition to arguing that corporate messages in crisis are distinct from those offered by individuals, several researchers have developed typologies of postcrisis responses.

The rhetorical tradition of apologia is grounded in the identification and evaluation of strategies open to communicators during crisis, to repair an image and to respond to criticism or to accusations of wrongdoing. Organizational theorists have synthesized much of this work with the organizational impression management literature in order to create more comprehensive typologies of organizational apologia (Benoit, 1995; Hearit, 1995). Others have adopted impression management literature directly to postcrisis communication (Allen & Caillouet, 1994; Coombs, 1995). Within this area, there is

considerable overlap in the various postcrisis strategies critics have described. Three of the most prominent typologies of organizational apologia
are described below.

Benoit (1995), in a comprehensive work on image restoration, provides a
synthetic typology of strategies for both organizational and individual speakers. He identifies five image restoration strategies: denial, evasion of responsibility, reduction of the offensiveness of the event, corrective action, and
mortification. Benoit also describes two types of denial: simple denial and
shifting the blame. The former consists of the denial of an undesirable act;
the latter is a variant of denial because it seeks to move the guilt from one
person to another. Evasion of responsibility is achieved through four strategies: provocation, defeasibility, accident, and good intentions. Provocation
suggests that the action was a legitimate response to another provoking act.
Defeasibility concerns "pleading lack of information about or control over
important factors in the situation" (p. 76). Accident involves issues of intent
and control. Good intention strategies defend an action in terms of motives
and intentions. Benoit also identifies bolstering, minimization, differentiation, transcendence, attacking the accuser, and compensation as techniques
used to reduce the offensiveness of the event. Bolstering involves "strengthening the audience's positive affect for the rhetor" (p. 77). Minimization is
an attempt to reduce or downplay the negative effects of the offensive act.
Differentiation "attempts to distinguish the act performed from other similar
but less desirable actions" (p. 77). The strategy of transcendence seeks to
reframe the act, placing it in a different context. Attacking the accuser entails
the apologist's reducing the credibility of the accusers. Compensation "offers
to remunerate the victim to help offset the negative feeling arising from the
wrongful act" (p. 78). Benoit explains that accusers also may offer to correct
the problem by returning conditions to their original state or promising the
act will never happen again. Finally, mortification arises as a strategy when
an actor "may admit responsibility for the wrongful act and ask for forgiveness" (p. 79).

Benoit's typology has been widely applied. For example, Benoit and
Brinson's (1994) analysis of AT&T's long-distance service interruption illustrates both the inherent difficulties and the goals that organizations have in
responding in the aftermath of a crisis. AT&T's strategy of consistent bolstering throughout the crisis was designed to silence competitors. Benoit and
Brinson suggest that AT&T's corrective posture was directed at customers
who were asking "what will be done to prevent the problem from recurring"
(p. 85). One factor that made the crisis complex was that AT&T had to worry
not only about local audiences (those directly affected by the crisis) but about
customers across the United States.

At the outset of the crisis, AT&T pinned the blame on lower-level union
workers, who then lashed back at management. AT&T later "acknowledged
that 'no AT&T technicians were at fault' and that 'if all appropriate proce-

dures had been followed by management personnel, the problem could have been averted' " (quoted in Benoit & Brinson, 1994). This illustrates how organizational goals or purposes designed to maintain legitimacy with some audiences can result in alienation of other constituents. The composite audience can often create constraints for an organization responding to a crisis. Moreover, diverse corporate goals and purposes can often put severe pressure on some organizational constituents during crisis.

A second typology of corporate apologia was articulated by Hearit (1994, 1995), who suggests that in apologia, organizations employ three "prototypical appearance/reality disassociations." These include (a) efforts to deny guilt through "opinion/knowledge disassociation," (b) differentiation of guilt by scapegoating through "individual/group disassociation," and (c) distancing of the organization from guilt through "act/essence disassociation" (Hearit, 1995, pp. 121-122). The appearance/reality disassociation involving opinion/knowledge is available to organizations when the facts are contested. This strategy is a form of denial whereby the organization disputes facts and associated claims. Opinion/knowledge disassociation is probably more available to organizations because they often control the technology of fact-finding. Dupont, for example, claimed that it was best able to judge the potential harm of its product Freon because it had the appropriate technological expertise (Szwapa & Seeger, 1988). Differentiation of guilt by scapegoating through individual/group disassociation represents a responsibility avoidance strategy commonly employed in organizational apologia. The individual/group disassociation strategy outlined by Hearit is similar to Schultz and Seeger's (1991) argument regarding structural elements in organizational apologia. Finally, in act/essence disassociation, the organization distances itself by arguing that although the transgression did occur, it is not representative of the organization's true essence. Act/essence is a transcendent strategy grounded in good intentions. Hearit (1995) suggests that such strategies are usually undertaken as a last resort.

Coombs (1995) has constructed a third typology of image restoration strategies based on the work of Allen and Caillouet (1994) and Benoit (1995). Coombs merges the impression management literature with the rhetorical apologetic research to delineate five primary crisis response strategies: nonexistence, distance, ingratiation, mortification, and suffering. The goal of nonexistence strategies is "to show that there is no link between the fictitious crisis and the organization" (Coombs, 1995, p. 450). Coombs identifies four such strategies. Denial involves the simple statement that there is no crisis. Clarification "extends the denial strategy with attempts to explain why there is no crisis" (p. 450). Attack focuses on those who wrongly reported a crisis. Intimidation involves a threat to use organizational power, such as legal action, against the accuser.

The second set of strategies open in the aftermath of an organizational crisis, according to Coombs's (1995) typology, are distance strategies. These tactics acknowledge the crisis but weaken the link between the crisis and the organization. Distance strategies are composed of excuses and justifications. Excuses often deny intention or volition and place blame outside the organization: "An organization cannot control an event if some third party is responsible for the crisis" (p. 451). Justifications involve persuading audiences that the crisis is not as bad as similar events. Coombs suggests that an organization uses justification tactics in "denying the seriousness of an injury, claiming that the victim deserved what happened, and claiming that the crisis even has been misrepresented" (p. 451).

Ingratiation strategies, according to Coombs, are used to gain public approval through linkages between the organization to positive values and outcomes. Ingratiation strategies include bolstering, transcendence, and praising others. Bolstering strategies emphasize the organization's positive features. Transcendence strategies position the crisis, its cause and harm, in a larger, usually more favorable, context. Praising others is a strategy designed to win approval and goodwill among important publics.

Mortification strategies are designed "to win forgiveness of the publics and to create acceptance for the crisis" (Coombs, 1995, p. 452). These strategies include remediation, repentance, and rectification. Remediation tactics involve offering compensation to victims. Repentance strategies include the organization's apologizing for the crisis and asking forgiveness. Rectification entails actions that prevent future recurrence of the crisis. The final strategy that Coombs describes is suffering, which is the depiction of "the organization as an unfair victim of some malicious, outside entity" (p. 453).

Organizational scholars have been successful in delineating a wide range of apologetic and image restorative strategies available to organizations in the aftermath of a crisis. Recently, apologia has moved beyond the description and evaluation of strategies. First, organizational theorists have begun to create predictive models to determine which strategies are most useful given the context of a crisis. Coombs (1995) provides response flowcharts based on four common crises: faux pas, accidents, transgressions, and terrorism. Organizational practitioners can follow the decision-making flowcharts based on the crisis evidence (true, false, ambiguous), damage (major, minor), victim status (victim, nonvictim), and performance history of the organization (positive, negative) to select appropriate strategies. Second, research has emerged on how an organization can use impression management strategies to satisfy multiple stakeholders (Allen & Caillouet, 1994; Ice, 1991; Sellnow & Ulmer, 1995). Stakeholder theory illustrates the importance of meeting the multiple, and often competing, demands of internal and external constituents. Studies in this area argue for both clear and ambiguous communication on the part of the organization in order to meet the complex demands of organizational stakeholders (Ulmer & Sellnow, 1996). Further research should investigate situations in which both types of communication are useful.

The study of the messages that organizations produce following crisis has produced a small but growing body of work. The primary foci of this work are message strategies and the development of typologies for postcrisis communication. Few efforts to develop predictive models exist beyond the work of Coombs (1995). Greater attention should be directed toward matching strategies to crisis conditions. Opportunities also exist to link this work more closely to public relations and crisis management. Critiques of organizational crises also illustrate how inadequate postcrisis responses can produce additional threats to an organization's legitimacy (Hearit, 1995; Seeger, 1986; Williams & Treadaway, 1992). In these cases, crises can endure and maintain their place on the public agenda until affected constituents are satisfied with the organization's response. Beyond concentrating on organizational responses to crisis, more work is needed to differentiate clearly between single-speaker and corporate apologia. The differences between them may help account for the relatively few successful apologetic responses and help shed light on the inherent difficulties in responding to organizational crises.

LEGITIMACY AND ORGANIZATIONAL CRISIS

At the outset of this essay, we described the proliferation of organizational crises that have occupied increasingly dominant positions in the mass media's agenda. Because of the high profiles they generate, crises place organizations "on the defensive to show the legitimacy of themselves or their actions" (Brummer, 1991). The peril of this situation for organizations is made clear by Boulding (1978, p. 89) when he argues that for social systems, legitimacy is probably the major element in survival. Several scholars have argued that it is vital for organizations to regain or maintain their social legitimacy in the wake of crises (Epstein & Votaw, 1978; Finet, 1994; Hearit, 1995; Kerninsky, 1994; Seeger, 1986; Singh, Tucker, & House, 1986). In this section, we first define organizational legitimacy as it applies to crisis situations. We then characterize the role of communication in organizations' maintaining or regaining legitimacy. We conclude the section with a review of representative examples from the literature investigating the communication strategies used by organizations seeking to maintain or regain legitimacy in crisis situations.

Much of the current research regarding organizations and legitimacy is based on the seminal work of Max Weber. Weber's view of legitimacy focuses on the organization's larger social role and justification. Systems theorists have borrowed and expanded on this concept of legitimacy to argue that organizations are always dependent on society for resources. Consequently, society also makes judgments about the appropriate use of those resources (Pfeffer & Salancik, 1978). Dowling and Pfeffer (1975) explain that organizations are viewed as legitimate when they "establish congruence between the social values associated with or implied by their activities and the norms of acceptable behavior in the larger social system of which they are a part" (p. 122).

Similar to systems theory, institutional theory focuses on the relationships between organizations and their environments. In the institutional perspective, the legitimacy of an organization is based upon a "full range of economic, legal, moral, and social responsibilities as determined by its environment" (Brummer, 1991, p. 95). Environments demand that organizations justify their activities according to the environments' "prevailing norms" (Oliver, 1990). Consequently, organizations become "impregnated with community values" (Perrow, 1972, p. 191). However, organizations are not necessarily passive reflectors of societal values. On the contrary, Finet (in press) argues that organizations can "influence, with varying degree of conscious intent, the direction of [sociopolitical] change." This influence can create a more favorable environment for the organization (Perrow, 1972). Ironically, organizations can also use the attention generated by crisis events to mold public policy issues that have impacts on their profitability (Crable & Vibbert, 1985). For example, Johnson and Sellnow (1995) argue that Exxon used the investigation of the *Valdez* disaster to advance its argument that government regulation of oil transportation is harmful to the oil industry and the U.S. economy.

To be viewed as socially legitimate, then, it is "not enough for an organization to be profitable; rather some larger social purpose or value [is] required" (Seeger, in press). Moreover, legitimacy is not "coextensive with, nor is it defined by," legality (Epstein & Votaw, 1978, p. 76). A crisis is likely to occur if an organization violates a deeply established social norm or value regardless of whether or not the organization has technically broken a law. In short, organizations seek to identify their goals and actions visibly with those that are valued by the larger social system.

Having a noble purpose, however, is no guarantee that an organization will be perceived as legitimate (Hearit, 1995). As Smith (1994) explains, "The public has been known to grant legitimacy to organizations involved in completely illegal activities and deny this essential element to totally above board organizations" (p. 1). For example, drug use, generally seen as illegitimate, may run rampant in a community that refuses to support legitimate institutions such as school systems through a tax increase. Legitimacy may also suffer if an organization with appropriate goals fails to achieve those goals (Seeger, 1986). Certainly, legitimacy is a highly complex, but typically essential, quality for any organization seeking to maintain system stability and support from members of its relevant environment.

Ideally, an organization and the larger social system establish "mutual expectations" through their communication (Turkel, 1982, p. 166). When organizations violate their norms of legitimacy, they no longer meet "certain expectations on the part of citizens with regard to the policies of the official order and its personnel" (Friedrichs, 1980, p. 549). To overcome such incongruity, organizations must engage in sustained discourse with their publics that provides adequate justification for whatever actions are under scrutiny (Strauss, 1982; Turkel, 1982). Seeger (1986) argues that for organizations, the process of securing or regaining legitimacy is "in part rhetorical and involves offering adequate justifications within a consensus producing dialogue concerning the value of the institution and its activities" (p. 148). Several efforts have been made to examine the rhetorical strategies of organizations seeking to regain legitimacy, including Seeger's (1986) analysis of NASA following the *Challenger* explosion and Hearit's (1995) evaluation of the efforts of Domino's Pizza and the Exxon Corporation to purify their images after their policies were blamed for highly publicized crises.

Seeger (1986) views the *Challenger* disaster as a crisis in legitimacy for NASA. The sudden destruction of the space shuttle forced NASA, a traditionally valued institution in U.S. society, to review and justify its goals and processes publicly. At stake was an argument regarding the substantial financial support provided to NASA by Congress and whether this funding was being used in appropriate ways. Seeger sees the Rogers Commission, appointed by President Reagan to investigate the crisis, as a means to "help recreate the perception of NASA as a rational organization pursuing worthy goals with success" (p. 155). With the aid of the commission, NASA worked to reestablish its social legitimacy by holding open hearings, shifting authority, creating an impression of a renewed rationality, and limiting performance goals. Seeger concludes that NASA's "long-term legitimacy is dependent upon goals which correspond to values within the environment" rather than upon mere technical expertise (p. 155).

Hearit (1991) identifies both negative and positive strategies employed by Exxon following the *Valdez* oil spill and by Domino's Pizza after claims that the company's pizza delivery policy had put employees and the public at risk. He identifies dissociation as a negative rhetoric that "diffuses hostility through redefinition" (p. 11). For example, an organization may shift the blame to individual employees in an effort to deny responsibility for a crisis. If the organization cannot deny responsibility, it may choose to dissociate itself from the crisis by claiming that the crisis is an inconsistent exception to the organization's typical performance. If, however, the organization wishes to demonstrate "organizational adherence to the values that the critics have charged it to have transgressed," it must engage the positive strategies of corrective action and reaffirmation (p. 10). Corrective action involves correcting the immediate problem and instituting "controls to ensure that it will not happen again" (p. 10). This form of long-term correction is essential in the relegitimation process, because routine solutions such as blaming and firing responsible individuals may salvage an organization's reputation, but do little to avert fears that similar crises will occur in the future (Sellnow, 1994).

Conversely, original solutions that signal change within an organization can often "enhance a perception of preventive, long-term change and renewed social legitimacy" (Sellnow & Seeger, 1989). Hearit suggests that these corrective actions should be followed by "a form of epideictic, value-oriented discourse" in which the organization reaffirms its allegiance to the same values it is accused of violating (p. 11). Hearit cautions that reaffirmation requires a sustained effort if relegitimation is to occur.

Another body of rhetorically based work regarding legitimacy is derived from Jürgen Habermas's (1971) critique of capitalism. Burleson and Kline (1979) summarize Habermas's work in their development of four types of validity claims found in legitimating discourses. These include (a) intelligibility (claims should be understandable), (b) truth (based on accurate information), (c) truthfulness (involving the sincerity of the speaker), and (d) appropriateness of response (communication that is consistent with socially accepted norms). The application of these ideas to organizational legitimacy, however, has been limited (Szwapa & Seeger, 1988).

Impression management theory has also served as the basis for analysis of the messages of organizations seeking to regain legitimacy. Schlenker (1980) provides a conceptual framework for impression management that details a variety of strategies organizations may enact to regain legitimacy. Much like apologia, impression management theory was originally applied to individuals but has been expanded to the analysis of corporate messages designed to regain legitimacy for troubled organizations (Elsbach & Sutton, 1992). Several studies have used impression management as a perspective for analysis, including Ashforth and Gibbs' (1990) identification of the potential pitfalls associated with seeking to regain legitimacy; Marcus and Goodman's (1991) focus on image restoration following harmful accidents; Ginzel, Kramer, and Sutton's (1993) work on the audience in impression management; and Allen and Caillouet's (1994) development of a typology of impression management strategies employed by a reuse-recycle facility whose legitimacy was threatened.

Ashforth and Gibbs (1990) observe that research regarding the efforts of organizations to seek or maintain legitimacy has disproportionately focused on successful organizations. Thus they claim that "previous work has implicitly assumed that the means indeed produce the desired effects" (p. 177). Ashforth and Gibbs reviewed a variety of impression management strategies used by organizations seeking to acquire legitimacy. They found that when organizations seek to establish legitimacy in difficult periods, such as crises, their messages are more likely to be scrutinized by a skeptical public. Consequently, organizations lacking legitimacy are more likely to employ tactics that, in turn, face a greater probability of rejection. In short, Ashforth and Gibbs conclude, "the very need for legitimacy may trigger events which prevent the realization of the need" (p. 191).

Marcus and Goodman (1991) have analyzed the uneasy relationships that can emerge among an organization's multiple audiences during crisis situations. The various response strategies available to an organization's leadership may create favorable impressions within particular audiences and yet may anger other relevant groups. Marcus and Goodman's review of the managerial policies employed by organizations involved in more than a dozen recent crises reveals several differences among crisis types. For example, accommodative signals tend to serve both shareholders and victims in crises involving scandals. However, in crises involving accidents, shareholders are best served by defensive messages whereas victims are best served by accommodative messages. To resolve this dilemma, Marcus and Goodman assert, managers "should adopt a rigorous ethical position in which they lay prudence aside and sacrifice profits for the sake of the victims of crisis" (p. 300). In short, these authors suggest that acting on the basis of moral conviction is most likely to garner favorable response from constituents.

Ginzel et al. (1993) focus on the audience in impression management processes. They suggest that impression management involves negotiation and reciprocal influence between audiences and management. Top management is responsible for providing accounts and interpreting meaning for organizational audiences. The account-giving process, according to Ginzel et al., occurs in three phases: (a) an initiation phase, in which an image-protecting or -enhancing account is given; (b) a phase of member reactions to the account; and (c) a negotiation phase, in which discrepancies between organizational accounts and member interpretations are resolved (p. 237). Accounts fail, these authors argue, because of psychological factors, organizational factors, or multiple audience effects.

Like Marcus and Goodman (1991) and Ginzel et al. (1993), Allen and Caillouet (1994) explain that the relegitimation process for organizations is complicated by the fact that their environments are composed of "multiple stakeholders" (p. 46). The needs of various stakeholder groups often conflict. Allen and Caillouet found that in the case of the reuse-recycle organization they studied, "different strategies appeared in messages directed toward the various stakeholders" as the organization attempted to communicate with its diverse audiences (p. 51). For example, the most frequently used strategy was ingratiation. Government and regulatory agencies were key targets of ingratiating messages, due to the influence of these groups on the organization's legitimacy. Denouncements, the second most frequent strategy, were directed toward competitors and included for purposes of clarification in messages to suppliers. Allen and Caillouet also found elements of intimidation contained in the organization's messages to the special interest groups with which it clashed. These researchers ultimately create a typology of impression management strategies available to organizations as they seek to reestablish their legitimacy.

To date, relatively few research efforts have involved the application of legitimacy to crisis and crisis communication. This may be due to the fact that organizational legitimacy as a concept is very difficult to operationalize.

Organizational impression management may be a more pragmatic way to examine legitimacy. Existing applications such as those discussed above have promise, however, for linking crisis to general social values, normative evaluation, the rhetorical construction of the organization's social value, and an institutional effort toward effective impression management. The legitimation process following crisis is closely associated with apologia and image restoration and with the relative success of crisis management processes. Work in this area should explore and expand these links. Beyond this, however, legitimacy is associated with the normative evaluation of the organization's noncrisis state. It is logical to assume that organizations with more positive assessments of legitimacy are better able to withstand the jolts of crisis. No empirical evidence is currently available, however, to support this claim. Substantial research will be required before a clear relationship is established between legitimacy and successful crisis management. History suggests that at least some organizations that most observers would conclude lack legitimacy (e.g., tobacco companies) have an impressive capacity to withstand crisis.

METHODOLOGICAL STANCES IN
COMMUNICATION AND CRISIS

Selection of a methodological stance for the study of crisis communication is, to a large extent, dependent upon characteristics inherent in organizational crises. As discussed above, an organization's survival during crisis often depends upon its responses to its relevant audiences or stakeholders. These responses are encumbered by the threat and surprise associated with the particular crisis and the duration of the crisis. Although audience complexity and the durations of crises vary, they remain consistent factors to consider in the selection of a methodology. The unique situational demands of a given crisis also produce important ethical questions concerning treatment and respect of victims, privacy, and the urgency and stress of the situation. The duration of the crisis, stakeholder needs and characteristics, and ethical considerations all combine to constrain and complicate the study of communication and organizational crises. In this section, we review and describe various methods employed in the study of organizational crisis communication.

Our classification of the types of methods used in the study of crises is based on the work of Redding and Tompkins (1988) and Wert-Gray, Center, Brashers, and Meyers (1991). Building on the categories established by Habermas (1971), these researchers have defined three categories of organizational communication research: modernistic, naturalistic, and critical. *Modernistic* research adheres to "the linear model of inferential statistics" (Wert-Gray et al., 1991). Because such research requires a good deal of control, modernistic approaches are rare in the study of communication and crisis, although they may be useful in the examination of crisis decision-making models and crisis plans. Most of the literature examining organizational crisis favors naturalistic and critical approaches. For purposes of this discussion, *naturalistic* research is divided into two categories: research that has at its base an emphasis on the frequency of message types and research based on description and exploration of an organization in its natural setting. *Critical* research efforts are those studies that interpret and evaluate an organization's communication using primarily rhetorical perspectives. We present discussion of each approach in turn below, along with a representative summary of the literature.

Frequency-Based Approaches

Measures of frequency in crisis communication research have focused primarily on survey and content analysis methodologies (Beaver & Jandt, 1973; Danowski & Edison-Swift, 1985; Dionisopoulos & Vibbert, 1988; Fink, 1986; Fitzpatrick & Rubin, 1995; Guth, 1995; McGill, 1994; Millar & Irvine, 1996; Pettey, Perloff, Neuendorf, & Pollick, 1986). Researchers using these approaches generally seek to quantify the moods and strategies that are evident during organizational crisis. Because the survey approach requires response time, the urgency of the crisis situation complicates this method, and the involvement of multiple audiences poses challenges. Additionally, the inherent threat to the organization and its employees may diminish respondents' willingness to share information honestly on a survey. Similarly, organizations are often simply too preoccupied to grant approval for researchers to conduct surveys during crises.

Despite these challenges, Beaver and Jandt (1973) were able to survey an industrial plant with 400 hourly employees at the onset of a crisis. Before the survey was conducted, employees were informed that the plant would not be the producer of a new product line. A nearby metropolitan newspaper signaled a potential crisis for employees by reporting that "an estimated fifty to sixty hourly employees would be laid off and that production of one of the major lines would be cut by fifty percent" (p. 106). Although actions on the part of the plant manager limited the survey's response rate, Beaver and Jandt conclude that the "ambiguity and apprehension" in the plant made it a "perfect situation for rumor propagation and transmission" (pp. 112-113). They also note that the inability or unwillingness of management personnel to deter such feelings made them "somewhat ineffective" in dealing with the crisis (p. 113).

Guth (1995) used a survey to examine the crisis communication function in organizations, thereby avoiding the complications of urgency and complexity of crisis conditions. Guth surveyed the membership of the Public Relations Society of America and the International Association of Business Communicators to measure the relationship between previous experiences with organizational crisis and the managerial level of the public relations practitioner

(p. 128). He also investigated the influence of organizational size on crisis experience and assessed the degree of organizational preparedness. Guth found a "link between an organization's crisis experiential level and the managerial role of its public relations function" and that "more experienced and better-paid practitioners gravitate toward the organizations with the highest crisis experiential levels" (p. 133). He also found that larger organizations were more prone to experience crisis than were smaller organizations. Guth expresses concern regarding "the lack of planning for crises" found in his study (p. 135). He contends that this lack of planning is an ethical issue, and that crises that are perceived as "preventable" result in "moral outrage" (p. 135).

Pettey et al. (1986) focused exclusively on external stakeholders in their study of the public's reaction to the space shuttle *Challenger* disaster. They surveyed 119 undergraduate students in an attempt to examine the feeling, learning, and diffusion effects of the crisis. Those undergraduate students who followed the crisis on television "possessed the most accurate knowledge about the crisis," and were also better able to "recall accurately the 'visual details' of the crisis" (p. 178). Feelings of pride and shame were the best predictors of the facts recalled. Those who heard about the tragedy soon after it occurred were more saddened than were those who learned of it later. Knowing an individual involved with NASA also heightened interest and retention. Pettey et al. overcame the concern related to the duration of a crisis by conducting their survey repeatedly over consistent time intervals. Because the study concerned an external audience with no direct link to NASA, questions of ethics and audience complexity were not paramount.

Danowski and Edison-Swift (1985) were able to capture actual internal messages exchanged during a change in a private electronic mail system as news of a merger came to the company. These authors note that they saw the merger as a crisis because of "the kinds of environmental changes" that it produced (p. 252). They found that the numbers of messages and communicators increased as the crisis developed, although the length of the messages decreased. Messages returned to their previous levels a month after the merger was announced. Danowski and Edison-Swift had access to all electronic messages throughout the crisis, which allowed them to track the crisis over time. By their own admission, their study created "ethical problems" (p. 260). To compensate for the employees' potential loss of privacy, the researchers used numbers rather than names and relied on word frequency as opposed to detailed analysis of individual messages. Regardless of these measures, studies using this method pose serious threats to the privacy of employees.

In addition to survey research, investigators have conducted content analysis of crisis messages. Because content-analytic methods most often focus on public messages, they avoid many of the privacy issues raised by other forms of research. McGill (1994) content analyzed 117 press releases produced by Exxon following the *Valdez* oil spill, employing four categories initially developed by Garrett, Bradford, Meyer, and Becker (1989) in the study of managers' responses to accusations of wrongdoing. These responses included denials, excuses, justifications, and concessions. McGill determined that almost half the releases were issued from Exxon corporate headquarters in Houston rather than from the crisis site. In addition, the releases focused on (a) the costs of the spill, (b) the failed cleanup, (c) portrayals of responsibility, and (d) the diverse parties involved in the crisis (p. 94). McGill concludes that Exxon's efforts to diffuse responsibility for the crisis alienated some crisis constituencies and enhanced the overall level of animosity directed toward the company.

Fitzpatrick and Rubin (1995) conducted a content analysis of news reports concerning charges of sexual harassment following the Clarence Thomas-Anita Hill hearings. Within an 18-month period, they found 39 news reports of cases involving sexual harassment in a range of organizations in various industries. Fitzpatrick and Rubin examined these reports for communication strategies based in legal considerations, public relations considerations, or some combination of the two. Legal strategies dominated, followed by combined legal and public relations strategies. Public relations strategies were used in a very small proportion of these cases.

Survey and content-analytic methods are typically limited to a single audience group. Researchers using these methods have, however, found various means of evaluating crises as they develop over time. When dealing with internal audiences, researchers must be careful to preserve the ethical integrity of their research. An element of risk is always present when the words of employees are evaluated, but this risk is intensified by the threat that is inherent in crisis situations.

Descriptive/Exploratory Approaches

Putnam and Stohl (1990) point out that "some researchers treat naturalistic studies as synonymous with descriptive or exploratory methods" (p. 249). They contend that, despite their naturalistic setting, such studies can "be experimental when the researcher takes advantage of naturally occurring events" (p. 249). In the genre of crisis communication, however, such descriptive/exploratory studies have generally taken a case study approach. The characteristics of crisis situations make this orientation necessary. Crises occur with little perceived warning, hence manipulation of the contexts in which they occur is at best unreasonable and at worst unethical. The study of communication in naturalistic settings contributes to theory development when "we can generalize findings across . . . divergent settings" (Cragan, Shields, & Wright, 1994). Because the emphasis in case studies is on description, researchers face few limitations. Consequently, such studies are not necessarily limited in terms of time or audience. Similarly, ethical considerations must be evaluated on a case-by-case basis. Despite these limitations, a good deal of theoretical development in crisis communication has been based on descriptive or exploratory research (Calloway, 1991; Gouran et al., 1986; Heath, 1995; Ice, 1991; Kerninsky, 1994; Marcus & Goodman, 1991; Seeger & Bolz, 1996; Sellnow, 1993; Small, 1991; Snyder & Foster 1983; Weick, 1988).

Gouran et al. (1986), for example, have explored the ill-fated decision-making process that led to the launching of the space shuttle *Challenger.* They provide a detailed examination of the testimony given by key figures who appeared before the Rogers Commission as it sought to determine the cause of the disaster. Gouran et al. trace this investigation in an effort to understand "the climate in which informed judgment ostensibly was either precluded or sacrificed to interests of expediency by intelligent, experienced, and seemingly safety-conscious decision-makers" (p. 120). They identify five influences that may lead to flawed decision making: (a) perceived pressure, (b) rigid conformity to perceived role requirements, (c) questionable reasoning, (d) ambiguous use of language, and (e) failure to ask important relevant questions. The descriptive nature of their study clarifies a series of decision-making influences that may be generalizable to other crises.

Ice (1991) offers a detailed description of the distinct needs of the multiple audiences that Union Carbide faced in response to its gas leak in Bhopal, India, which resulted in the deaths of more than 2,000 people and injuries to countless others. In the wake of this massive crisis, Union Carbide was "called to justify itself in order to repair its damaged reputation" (p. 341). To do so, however, the corporation had to respond to the Indian government, the U.S. government, stockholders, Union Carbide employees, consumers, other corporations in the chemical industry, and the general public. Ice concludes that the corporation demonstrated public responsibility in addressing scientific and financial issues, but failed to address the more human needs raised by the crisis. He also offers the generalizable observation that "the rhetorical strategies a corporation chooses to emphasize can repair certain public relationships, while alienating other publics" (p. 360).

In conducting their studies, Gouran et al. (1986) and Ice (1991) capitalized on the descriptive or exploratory nature of the case study approach to observe crises over time. In particular, Ice's report is inclusive of the diverse audiences involved in his case study. Both studies made use of data from the public domain and avoided ethical constraints. One challenge in such descriptive studies involves the identification of conclusions that are generalizable. Gouran et al. and Ice both meet this challenge by offering conclusions that admonish organizations to compensate for external pressures and adapt to distinct audience needs when facing crisis situations.

Critical Approaches

Cheney and McMillan (1990) contend that organizations are "understood intuitively by lay persons as persuasive enterprises," and that the "prevalence and power of organizational persuasion make it an important and exciting subject for communication inquiry" (pp. 93-94). Thus they see rhetoric as having an "inevitable" presence in the organizational persuasion process (p. 94). Crable (1990) sees organizations as "the true rhetors of the latter half of the twentieth century" (p. 127). Studies of organizational rhetoric, however, must take into account the distinction between individual and organizational rhetors (Cheney, 1991; Schuetz, 1990; Schultz & Seeger, 1991). Cheney (1991) states that organizations "tend to 'decenter' the self, the individual, the acting subject" (p. 5). Consequently, messages are attributed to the organization that "obscure matters of authorship, attribution and responsibility" (Schultz & Seeger, 1991). Still, rhetorical criticism of organizational crisis messages is vital, for, as Elwood (1995) explains, "rhetoric constitutes the core component to public relations" (p. 12). Benoit (1995) contends that criticism, unlike descriptive/exploratory case studies, must "go beyond describing options" to advance our knowledge of apologetic discourse (p. 32). A host of studies have sought to advance understanding of image restoration theories by providing criticisms of the external rhetoric offered by organizations during crisis (Benoit, 1995; Benoit & Brinson, 1994; Benoit & Lindsey, 1987; Elwood, 1995; Johnson & Sellnow, 1995; Mister, 1986; Schuetz, 1990; Schultz & Seeger, 1991; Sellnow & Seeger, 1989; Sellnow & Ulmer, 1995).

Mister (1986) provides a criticism of Reagan's tribute to those who died aboard the space shuttle *Challenger.* To do so, he delineates "the generic constraints and specific situational demands laid upon the President following the shuttle tragedy" and offers judgments regarding the degree to which Reagan's speech met "the expectations that led up to the televised address" (p. 161). As president, Reagan served as the ultimate spokesperson for NASA. He faced the demands of consoling the public while reviving commitment to the NASA program. Mister asserts that Reagan "constructed a speech that fulfilled the nation's rhetorical expectations for a Presidential eulogy and its human needs of the moment" (p. 164). Mister's conclusions expand the genre of eulogy to consider the secondary need of affiliated organizations—in this case, NASA. Reagan's speech did as much to bolster the need for space exploration as it did to honor the individuals who died aboard *Challenger.*

Schultz and Seeger (1991) note the use of apologia in their critical analysis of a speech delivered by Lee Iacocca at a press conference concerning the closing of the Kenosha, Wisconsin, Chrysler assembly plant. Iacocca and Chrysler met with condemnation from employees and Wisconsin legislators when they announced that the Kenosha plant would be closed. This closing came in spite of a recent $200 million investment and pledge by Chrysler to keep the plant open. Schultz and Seeger found that Iacocca used nondenial and transcendence while offering concessions to the employees in an effort to counter accusations of mendacity, insensitivity, and greed. The decentered nature of organizations makes strategies of transcendence and nondenial plausible. Schultz and Seeger also emphasize that corporate rhetoric "must be understood within a larger social context" that includes any unique factors of the organization's history.

The critical approach is typically reserved for messages directed toward external audiences. This approach does not prohibit the analysis of internal messages, but the preference of communication scholars appears to be the study of messages designed for wide consumption outside the organization. If critics choose to focus on one or only a few such messages, the understanding of crisis development may be limited. Focusing on external audiences, however, limits much of the ethical constraint for the critic.

In summary, all three methodological approaches outlined above are applicable to both internal and external audiences. The descriptive/exploratory approach appears best suited for the study of the messages addressed to multiple stakeholders in a crisis situation. Frequency-based studies provide an efficient means of analyzing the attitudes of various audiences, either at a single point or throughout the evolution of a crisis. The critical approach appears to be most efficient in contributing to theory development, although all three methods have this potential. All three approaches can create ethical issues for the researcher, but such issues are most apparent in the evaluation of internal messages.

OTHER APPROACHES TO CRISIS COMMUNICATION

In this section we explore related bodies of literature and other approaches to crisis. Several authors have examined specific aspects of crisis not directly related to those discussed above, whereas other work has focused on technical and applied aspects of crisis. Additionally, crisis communication is related to two other substantial bodies of communication research: risk communication and issue management.

Calloway (1991), for example, has explored the role of communication technologies, including the Internet, in crisis management. The speed of information dissemination over the Internet, he argues, may be valuable in crisis management. Pinsdorf (1991) asserts that intercultural influences are important factors in how a crisis is perceived. This area is particularly noteworthy as organizations are becoming increasingly multinational. Lacey and Llewellyn (1995) examined the Alar apple scare, in which public relations contributed to the development of a crisis. A large technical body of research focuses on hazardous waste, hazardous waste management, spill response, pollution prevention, and related topics (Blackman, 1996; Cheremisinoff, 1995; Lieberman, 1994). A diverse body of literature also exists in business trade publications such as *Hotel & Motel Management, Employee Relations Today, Hospital Management, U.S. Banker, Progressive Grocer, Air Transportation World,* and *Beverage World.* This work generally focuses on industry-

specific crises, such as the outbreak of food-borne illness, workplace violence, product tampering, transportation risks, technical issues, and infec-
tious disease. Most often, this work takes a heavily applied approach in
describing principles of crisis management, planning, risk avoidance, and
public relations, drawing on anecdotes and practitioner experience. This work
also tends to focus on context-specific crisis contingencies (e.g., industry-
specific regulations, experiences, practices, technologies, and risks and
changes in these various contingencies).

Crisis communication is conceptually related to two other important bodies
of research. Risk communication is a developing area of communication
research that is related directly to crisis perception. According to Heath
(1995), "Risk communication deals with risk estimates, whether they are
appropriately tolerable, and risk consequences" (p. 257). Covello (1992)
defines risk communication as "the exchange of information among interested parties about the nature, magnitude, significance, or control of a risk"
(p. 359). Risk communication is most closely associated with crisis sensing
and threat assessment in early stages of crisis. This work also focuses on
media reporting of environmental hazards associated with industrial activities
(Nelkin, 1988), and with messages regarding health (Covello, 1992). Crisis
communication is also conceptually related to issue management (Crable &
Vibbert, 1985; Jones & Chase, 1979). Gaunt and Ollenburger (1995) suggest
that although the two are not entirely distinct, issue management tends to be
more proactive in its efforts to create and influence public policy regarding
relevant issues. Crisis communication is more reactive in the sense that it
responds to trigger events after initial damage has occurred. The threats
associated with crisis tend to be direct and immediate, and occur within a
relatively restricted time frame. A crisis may, however, become a public issue,
particularly in the latter stages of development, and in some cases, issues
escalate into crises (Grunig, 1992).

THEMES IN THE STUDY OF CRISIS COMMUNICATION

The crisis communication literature is diverse yet integrative, reaching
across traditional boundaries in the communication discipline and using a
variety of approaches and perspectives. It is increasingly an interdisciplinary
area of study, with contributions from organizational theory, public relations,
and mass communication. Although we want to avoid making sweeping
generalizations regarding this body of work, three general themes are evident:
(a) the centrality of communication to organizational crisis, (b) an external
audience-centered focus, and (c) interest in both application and theory.

This body of theory and research consistently identifies communication as
a defining variable in crisis development. Unlike many other areas of communication research, organizational crisis is also a context in which the

effects of communication are often very direct, immediate, and self-evident. Work in crisis development (Fink, 1986; Turner, 1976) and in crisis decision making (Gouran et al., 1986) suggests that failure to communicate effectively is often directly related to the onset of crisis. In public relations and crisis management, communication is a fundamental coordinating and organizing process in efforts to contain crisis and limit damage (Mitroff, 1988). Finally, developmental approaches and work in organizational apologia suggest that postcrisis responses may reduce the duration and severity of a crisis (Hearit, 1994). These responses may help move the crisis off the mass media agenda more quickly. Communication researchers, then, should view crisis as an organizational phenomenon in which such variables as message, climate, frequency, audience, timing, and width of diffusion are integral to all stages of crisis development, including resolution. Crisis should also be viewed as a context in which the effects of communication can often be directly observed.

One promising model for exploring this theme is Karl Weick's (1969, 1979, 1988, 1995) concept of enactment. According to Weick's model, communication is the fundamental input to the organizing process. Through communication, members create, and continually re-create, organization in their efforts to reduce equivocality of informational inputs through enactment, selection, and retention. Enactment occurs when an individual acts toward something, "says" something, or chooses to notice some informational input. Selection is the process of choosing a sensible interpretation of the input. Retention involves using the interpretation for subsequent sense making (Weick, 1979, p. 134). Weick (1979) sums up this view as, "How can I know what I think until I see what I say?" (pp. 5, 133). Crisis, due to its intensity and high equivocality, is well suited to enactment-based approaches, including interpretation and sense making (see Ginzel et al., 1993; Weick, 1988). Moreover, these approaches allow researchers to focus on how messages and retained interpretations influence crisis development. One explanation for the value of immediate and complete communication following a crisis, for example, is that it provides all the necessary informational inputs for crisis stakeholders to engage in sense making.

A second theme running through this work concerns the need to examine external communication from audience-centered perspectives. Although it is tempting to focus on internal organizational processes and messages in order to understand crisis and its development, a number of scholars point to the organization's larger environment as the source for this understanding (Smart & Vertinsky, 1977). Developmental approaches (Turner, 1976) suggest that the environment is the source of crisis threats. Failure to perceive, sense, or interact with the environment accurately is usually the larger failure that leads to crisis. Theorists in public relations and decision making argue that organizations must be open to their environments during crisis (Gouran, 1982; Newsom et al., 1989). Finally, the work on apologia and legitimacy emphasizes the need for organizations to communicate to external audiences following crisis (Benoit, 1995). The stakeholder model is one externally oriented perspective that may be useful for the examination of crisis audiences.

Organizational theorists have argued that specific constituent stakeholders are likely to be "directly affected by the decisions of the corporation or [to] have an explicit contractual relationship with it" and to have "an interest in the corporation" (Brummer, 1991, p. 144). Freeman (1984, p. 52) notes that stakeholders are not only groups affected by the company, but also groups that can affect the organization. Stakeholders may choose to withhold resources and support, limit access to new markets, and/or actively campaign against the organization. Stakeholder proponents argue that the organization should take the interests, needs, and concerns of these constituencies into account in its decision-making and problem-solving processes (Freeman & Gilbert, 1987, p. 397). The stakeholder model has been adapted by Shrivastava (1987) in his analysis of the Union Carbide Bhopal industrial accident. Shrivastava discusses "crisis stakeholders" as those groups and individuals who were affected by the crisis and had a vested interest in its resolution. These included the local and national governments, the victims and their families, and Union Carbide and its Indian subsidiary. Shrivastava suggests that failures to reach consensus among these crisis stakeholders, due to blame shifting and scapegoating, resulted in a prolonged crisis and increased harm. The concept of stakeholders may be particularly useful in the study of communication and organizational crisis when the focus is on specific external messages, audiences, and linkages at various stages of crisis development (Coombs, 1995). Stakeholder perspectives may also be useful in the assessment of an organization's communicative links to environments before crisis and threats are manifested. Finally, stakeholder approaches may be helpful in the evaluation of the degree of organizational openness following crisis and in assessment of the effectiveness of particular message strategies.

The third theme in the crisis communication literature concerns the link between theory and application. This literature has two distinct branches. The first is heavily grounded in practitioner experience, goal-directed messages, and strategies designed to create instrumental outcomes. Public relations and group decision making, as part of the crisis management process, are most representative of this emphasis on communication as a way to avoid crisis or mitigate its effects. Planning is seen as the primary method of avoiding harm. Communication is a tangible action that managers can take during crisis to help exert control over events. A second branch of this literature focuses on crisis as a random and inevitable organizational and social force. Murphy's (1996) work on chaos theory and crisis and Perrow's (1984) thesis regarding the normalness of accidents in technology-intensive systems are most representative of this second branch. Organizational crisis, from these systems-based views, is inevitable within large, complex, technology-intensive systems functioning within disturbed-reactive environments. Crisis is a force of systemic change that inserts randomness, disorder, and chaos into the organization's stability and order. Planning is largely futile. In fact, the ability to manage strategically and exert control over these events and the associated crisis stakeholders is highly limited (Murphy, 1996, p. 110). Crisis prediction is also problematic, although patterns can be observed in crisis and organizations can adjust to the conditions of crisis as they become manifest.

Although these branches initially appear irreconcilable, their differences are largely functions of the perspectives from which they view crisis. Practitioners interested in managing crisis through communication take a microscopic approach, usually focusing on a relatively narrow segment of the crisis, its impact on the organization, and steps to reduce or control that impact in postcrisis conditions. Theorists interested in understanding crisis as a social force usually take a macroscopic perspective, and do so over a relatively expansive time frame that includes precrisis events. This broader perspective may help researchers to identify heretofore unidentified patterns in crisis. Researchers using both perspectives should work to bridge the gap between these two branches as they expand the crisis communication literature.

DIRECTIONS FOR RESEARCH

The themes discussed above suggest a number of issues and directions for future research. From a developmental perspective, communication research that follows crisis over time may be particularly valuable for clarifying crisis development stages and identifying new patterns in organizational crisis. To date, most research has focused only on the very short time intervals immediately following crisis trigger events. Most often, researchers concentrate on a single case. Many important questions also remain about the efficacy of particular crisis management techniques. The relationship of crisis experience to effective crisis management, for example, has not been explored. Research that follows an organization, such as an airline, through several successive crises may provide insights regarding an organization's capacity to learn from crisis. Both approaches would also contribute to our understanding of how crisis is enacted through communication.

Related to the need for longitudinal investigation of crisis development is the need for examination of crisis management successes. With only a few exceptions, most investigations of organizational crisis have focused on crisis management failures, such as the *Exxon Valdez* accident, Union Carbide's Bhopal explosion, and the NASA *Challenger* disaster. Crisis management successes, such as management's response to the recent fire at Malden Mills, might prove more instructive in identifying effective strategies and processes.

Related to the theme of external focus is the need to investigate audience responses to crisis messages. Examination of how perceptions of risk are created in audiences would also provide a link to risk communication.

Another direction for communication scholars interested in communication and crisis involves investigation of crisis-prone and crisis-proof organizations. Pauchant and Mitroff (1992) argue that some organizations—by virtue of structure, management style, technology, markets, and environment—appear to be prone to crisis. It is reasonable to assume that some communication variables, such as climate, might also be related to crisis vulnerability.

Many opportunities exist for the examination of crisis decision making, particularly in postcrisis investigations. Analysis of agencies such as the National Transportation Safety Board would help clarify how crisis is understood and ultimately resolved. Little if any communication research has focused on the personal and interpersonal effects of organizational crisis, although sociology has a well-developed body of work in this field (Kreps, 1984).

Chaos theory seems particularly well suited to macroscopic investigations of organizational crisis. Similarly, the metaphor of postmodernity, with its emphasis on situated meanings, multiple audiences, counterrationality, and competing narratives, may prove useful for our understanding of organizational crisis.

Finally, we believe that efforts to understand organizational crisis will benefit from multiple methods. Intensive study of one crisis, such as an airline disaster, might involve content analysis of press releases, rhetorical analysis of postcrisis explanations, investigation of postcrisis decision making by the National Transportation Safety Board, and surveys of crisis stakeholders. Such intensive study would help reveal the communicative complexities and interdependencies of crisis.

CONCLUSION

We began this review by listing a number of dramatic organization-based crises and suggesting that technological dependence and intensity as well as greater system interdependence and complexity increase the probability of such large-scale crises. The increased risk of crisis and the central role of communication in crisis sensing, avoidance, development, and resolution suggest that communication researchers should view this area of investigation as an opportunity for the development of both theory and practice. Although researchers are often reticent to sift through the artifacts of organizational crises, such research may ultimately help to ensure that these crises remain relatively rare events.

REFERENCES

Allan, M. J. (1990). Quake '89 observations from the front. *Public Relations Journal, 46*(3), 25-26.

Allen, M. W., & Caillouet, R. H. (1994). Legitimation endeavors: Impression management strategies used by an organization in crisis. *Communication Monographs, 61*, 44-62.

Andriole, S. J. (Ed.). (1985). *Corporate crisis management.* Princeton, NJ: Petrocelli.

Ashforth, B., & Gibbs, B. W. (1990). The double-edge of organizational legitimation. *Organizational Science, 1,* 177-194.

Beaver, C. D., & Jandt, F. E. (1973). A pilot study on alienation and anxiety during a rumored plant closing. *Journal of Applied Communication Research, 1,* 105-114.

Benoit, W. L. (1995). *Accounts, excuses, and apologies.* Albany: State University of New York Press.

Benoit, W. L., & Brinson, S. L. (1994). AT&T: "Apologies are not enough." *Communication Quarterly, 42,* 75-88.

Benoit, W. L., & Lindsey, J. J. (1987). Argument strategies: Antidote to Tylenol's poisoned image. *Journal of the American Forensic Association, 23,* 136-146.

Benson, J. A. (1988). Crisis revisited: An analysis of strategies used by Tylenol in the second tampering episode. *Central States Speech Journal, 39,* 49-66.

Bernthal, P. R., & Insko, C. A. (1993). Cohesiveness without groupthink: The interactive effects of social and task cohesion. *Group and Organizational Management, 18,* 66-87.

Billings, R. S., Milburn T. W., & Schaalman, M. L. (1980). A model of crisis perception: A theoretical and empirical analysis. *Administrative Science Quarterly, 25,* 300-316.

Blackman, W. C. (1996). *Basic hazardous waste management* (2nd ed.). Boca Raton, FL: CRC.

Boulding, K. E. (1978). The legitimacy of the business institution. In E. E. Epstein & D. Votaw (Eds.), *Rationality, legitimacy, responsibility: Search for new directions in business and society* (pp. 83-98). Santa Monica, CA: Goodyear.

Brummer, J. J. (1991). *Corporate responsibility and legitimacy: An interdisciplinary analysis.* Westport, CT: Greenwood.

Burleson, B. R., & Kline, S. I. (1979). Habermas' theory of communication: A critical explication. *Quarterly Journal of Speech, 65,* 412-428.

Burson, H. (1995, December). Damage control in a crisis. *Management Review, 84,* 42-45.

Callaway, M. R., & Esser, J. K. (1984). Groupthink: Effects of cohesiveness and problem solving procedures on group decision making. *Social Behavior and Personality, 12,* 157-164.

Calloway, L. J. (1991). Survival of the fastest: Information technology and corporate crisis. *Public Relations Review, 17*(1), 85-92.

Cheney, G. (1991). *Rhetoric in an organizational society: Managing multiple identities.* Columbia: University of South Carolina Press.

Cheney, G., & McMillan J. J. (1990). Organizational rhetoric and the practice of criticism. *Journal of Applied Communication Research, 18,* 93-114.

Cheremisinoff, N. P. (1995). *Hazardous materials and waste management: A guide for the professional hazards manager.* Park Ridge, NJ: Noyes.

Connor, M. F. (1985). Methodology for corporate crisis decision making. In S. J. Andriole (Ed.), *Corporate crisis management* (pp. 239-258). Princeton, NJ: Petrocelli.

Coombs, W. T. (1995). The development of guidelines for the selection of the "appropriate" crisis response strategies. *Management Communication Quarterly, 4,* 447-476.

Covello, V. T. (1992). Risk communication: An emerging area of health communication research. In S. A. Deetz (Ed.), *Communication yearbook 15* (pp. 359-373). Newbury Park, CA: Sage.

Crable, R. E. (1990). "Organizational rhetoric" as the fourth great system: Theoretical, critical and pragmatic implications. *Journal of Applied Communication Research, 18,* 115-128.

Crable, R. E., & Vibbert S. L. (1985). Managing issues and influencing public policy. *Public Relations Review, 11*(2), 3-16.

Cragan, J. F., Shields, D. C., & Wright, D. W. (1994). Revitalizing the study of small group communication: A thematic critique. *Communication Studies, 45,* 92-96.

Cushing, S. (1994). *Fatal words: Communication clashes and aircraft crashes.* Chicago: University of Chicago Press.

Danowski, J. A., & Edison-Swift, P. (1985). Crisis effects on intraorganizational computer-based communication. *Communication Research, 12,* 251-270.

Dilenschneider, R. L., & Hyde, R. C. (1985, January-February). Crisis communications: Planning for the unplanned. *Business Horizons, 28,* 35-38.

Dionisopoulos, G. N., & Vibbert, S. L. (1988). CBS vs. Mobil Oil: Charges of creative bookkeeping in 1979. In H. R. Ryan (Ed.), *Oratorical encounters: Selected studies and sources of twentieth-century political accusations and apologies* (pp. 241-252). Westport, CT: Greenwood.

Dowling, J., & Pfeffer, J. (1975). Organizational legitimacy: Social values and organizational behavior. *Pacific Sociological Review, 18,* 122-130.

Downey, S. D. (1993). The evolution of the rhetorical genre of apologia. *Western Journal of Communication, 57,* 42-64.

Egelhoff, W. G., & Sen, F. (1992). An information processing model of crisis management. *Management Communication Quarterly, 5,* 433-484.

Elsbach, K. D., & Sutton, R. I. (1992). Acquiring organizational legitimacy through illegitimate actions: A marriage of institutional and impression management theories. *Academy of Management Journal, 35,* 699-738.

Elwood, W. N. (1995). Public relations is a rhetorical experience: The integral principle in case study analysis. In W. N. Elwood (Ed.), *Public relations inquiry as rhetorical criticism: Case studies of corporate discourse and social influence* (pp. 3-12). Westport, CT: Praeger.

Epstein, E. E., & Votaw, D. (Eds.). (1978). *Rationality, legitimacy, responsibility: Search for new directions in business and society.* Santa Monica, CA: Goodyear.

Finet, D. (1994). Interest advocacy and the transformation in organizational communication. In B. Kovacic (Ed.), *New approaches to organizational communication* (pp. 169-190). Albany: State University of New York Press.

Finet, D. (in press). Sociopolitical environments and issues. In F. M. Jablin & L. L. Putnam (Eds.), *The new handbook of organizational communication.* Thousand Oaks, CA: Sage.

Fink, S. (1986). *Crisis management planning for the inevitable.* New York: AMACOM.

Fitzpatrick, K. R., & Rubin, M. S. (1995). Public relations vs. legal strategies in organizational crisis decisions. *Public Relations Review, 21*(1), 21-33.

Freeman, R. E. (1984). *Strategic management: A stakeholder approach.* Marshfield, MA: Pitman.

Freeman, R. E., & Gilbert, D. R. (1987). Managing stakeholder interests. In S. P. Sethi & C. M. Fable (Eds.), *Business and society: Dimensions of conflict and cooperation* (pp. 397-422). Lexington, MA: Lexington.

Friedrichs, D. O. (1980). The legitimacy crisis in the United States: A conceptual analysis. *Social Problems, 27,* 540-553.

Garrett, D. E., Bradford, J. E., Meyer, R. A., & Becker, J. (1989). Issue management and organizational accounts: An analysis of corporate responses to accusations of unethical business practices. *Journal of Business Ethics, 8,* 507-520.

Gaunt, P., & Ollenburger, J. (1995). Issues management revisited: A tool that deserves another look. *Public Relations Review, 21,* 199-210.

Gigliotti, R., & Jason, R. (1991). *Emergency planning for maximum protection.* Boston: Butterworth-Heinemann.

Ginzel, L. E., Kramer, R. M., & Sutton, R. I. (1993). Organizational impression management as reciprocal influence process: The negotiated role of the organizational audience. In L. L. Cummings & B. M. Staw (Eds.), *Research in organizational behavior* (Vol. 15, pp. 227-266). Greenwich, CT: JAI.

Gonzalez-Herrero, A., & Pratt, C. B. (1995). How to manage a crisis before—or whenever—it happens. *Public Relations Quarterly, 40*(1), 25-29.

Gouran, D. S. (1982). *Making decisions in groups.* Glenview, IL: Scott, Foresman.

Gouran, D. S. (1984). Communicative influences on decisions related to the Watergate coverup: The failure of collective judgment. *Central States Speech Journal, 35,* 260-269.

Gouran, D. S., Hirokawa, R. Y., Julian, K. M., & Leathman, G. B. (1993). The evolution and current status of the functional perspective on communication in decision-making and problem-solving groups. In S. A. Deetz (Ed.), *Communication yearbook 16* (pp. 573-600). Newbury Park, CA: Sage.

Gouran, D. S., Hirokawa, R. Y., & Martz, A. E. (1986). A critical analysis of factors related to decisional processes involved in the *Challenger* disaster. *Central States Speech Journal, 37,* 119-135.

Grunig, J. E. (1992). *Excellence in public relations and communication management.* Hillsdale, NJ: Lawrence Erlbaum.

Guth, D. W. (1995). Organizational crisis experience and public relations roles. *Public Relations Review, 21*(2), 123-136.

Habermas, J. (1971). *Knowledge and human interests.* Boston: Beacon.

Hearit, K. M. (1991, November). *Organizations and legitimacy.* Paper presented at the annual meeting of the Speech Communication Association, Atlanta, GA.

Hearit, K. M. (1994). Apologies and public relations crises at Chrysler, Toshiba, and Volvo. *Public Relations Review, 20*(2), 113-125.

Hearit, K. M. (1995). From "We didn't do it" to "It's not our fault": The use of apologia in public relations crises. In W. N. Elwood (Ed.), *Public relations inquiry as rhetorical criticism: Case studies of corporate discourse and social influence* (pp. 117-134). Westport, CT: Praeger.

Heath, R. L. (1995). Corporate environmental risk communication: Cases and practices along the Texas gulf coast. In B. R. Burleson (Ed.), *Communication yearbook 18* (pp. 255-277). Thousand Oaks, CA: Sage.

Hermann, C. F. (1963). Some consequences of crisis which limit the viability of organizations. *Administrative Science Quarterly, 8,* 61-82.

Ice, R. (1991). Corporate publics and rhetorical strategies. *Management Communication Quarterly, 4,* 341-362.

Janis, I. (1972). *Victims of groupthink: A psychological study of foreign decisions and fiascoes.* Boston: Houghton Mifflin.

Janis, I., & Mann, L. (1977). *Decision making: A psychological analysis of conflict, choice and commitment.* New York: Free Press.

Johnson, D., & Sellnow, T. (1995). Deliberative rhetoric as a step in organizational crisis management: Exxon as a case study. *Communication Reports, 8*(1), 54-60.

Jones, B. L., & Chase, W. H. (1979). Managing public policy issues. *Public Relations Review, 5*(2), 3-23.

Katz, A. R. (1987). Ten steps to complete crisis planning. *Public Relations Journal, 43*(11), 46-47.

Kerninsky, D. A. (1994, May). *A critical analysis of the ethicality of organizational legitimation strategies: Dow Chemical's issues management bulletins—1979-1990.* Paper presented at the National Communication Ethics Conference, Gull Lake, MI.

Kreps, G. A. (1984). Sociological inquiry and disaster research. In R. E. Turner & J. F. Short, Jr. (Eds.), *Annual review of sociology* (Vol. 10, pp. 309-330). Palo Alto, CA: Annual Reviews.

Lacey, J. P., & Llewellyn, J. T. (1995). The engineering of outrage: Mediated constructions of risk in the Alar controversy. In W. N. Elwood (Ed.), *Public relations inquiry as rhetorical criticism: Case studies of corporate discourse and social influence* (pp. 47-68). Westport CT: Praeger.

Lau, B. (1987). Crisis communication planning for organizations: Part II. *Management Quarterly, 28,* 25-28.

Lieberman, J. L. (1994). *A practical guide for hazardous waste management, administration, and compliance.* Boca Raton, FL: Lewis.

Littlejohn, R. F. (1983). *Crisis management: A team approach.* New York: AMA.

Lukaszewaki, J. E. (1987). Anatomy of a crisis. *Public Relations Journal, 43*(11), 45-47.

Marcus, A. A., & Goodman, R. S. (1991). Victims and shareholders: The dilemmas of presenting corporate policy during a crisis. *Academy of Management Journal, 34,* 281-305.

McGill, T. (1994). *Corporate public discourse: Exxon's accounts following the Valdez oil spill of March 24, 1989.* Unpublished doctoral dissertation, Wayne State University.

Meyer, A. D. (1982). Adapting to environmental jolts. *Administrative Science Quarterly, 27,* 515-537.

Meyers, G. C., & Holusha, J. (1986). *When it hits the fan: Managing the nine crises of business.* Boston: Houghton Mifflin.

Millar, D. P., & Irvine, R. B. (1996, November). *Exposing the errors: An examination of the nature of organizational crisis.* Paper presented at the annual meeting of the Speech Communication Association, San Diego, CA.

Mister, S. (1986). Reagan's *Challenger* tribute: Combining generic constraints and situational demands. *Central States Speech Journal, 37,* 158-165.

Mitroff, I. I. (1986). Teaching corporate America to think about crisis prevention. *Journal of Business Strategy, 6*(4), 40-48.

Mitroff, I. I. (1988). Crisis management: Cutting through the confusion. *Sloan Management Review, 29*(2), 15-19.

Mitroff, I. I., Pauchant, T. C., & Shrivastava, P. (1988). Conceptual and empirical issues in the development of a general theory of crisis management. *Technological Forecasting and Social Change, 33,* 83-107.

Murphy, P. (1996). Chaos theory as a model for managing issues and crises. *Public Relations Review, 22*(2), 95-113.

Nelkin, D. (1988). Risk reporting and the management of industrial crises. *Journal of Management Studies, 24,* 342-351.

Newsom, D., Scott, A., & Turk, J. V. (1989). *This is PR* (4th ed.). Belmont, CA: Wadsworth.

Nudel, M., & Antokol, N. (1988). *The handbook for effective crisis and emergency management.* Lexington, MA: D. C. Heath.

Oliver, C. (1990). Determinants of interorganizational relationships: Integration and future directions. *Academy of Management Review, 15,* 241-265.

Pauchant, T. C., & Mitroff, I. I. (1992). *Transforming the crisis-prone organization.* San Francisco: Jossey-Bass.

Perrow, C. (1972). *Complex organizations: A critical essay.* Glenview, IL: Scott, Foresman.

Perrow, C. (1984). *Normal accidents.* New York: Basic Books.

Pettey, G. R., Perloff, R. M., Neuendorf, K. A., & Pollick, B. (1986). Feeling and learning about a critical event: The shuttle explodes. *Central States Speech Journal, 37,* 166-179.

Pfeffer, J., & Salancik, G. R. (1978). *The external control of organizations.* New York: Free Press.

Phelps, N. L. (1986). Setting up a crisis recovery plan. *Journal of Business Strategy, 6*(4), 5-8.

Pinsdorf, M. (1987). *Communicating when your company is under siege.* Lexington, MA: Lexington.

Pinsdorf, M. (1991). Flying different skies: How cultures respond to airline disasters. *Public Relations Review, 17*(1), 37-56.

Poole, M. S. (1990). Do we have any theories of group communication? *Communication Studies, 41,* 237-247.

Putnam, L. L., & Stohl, C. (1990). Bona fide groups: A reconceptualization of groups in context. *Communication Studies, 41,* 248-265.

Quarantelli, E. I. (1988). Disaster crisis management: A summary of research findings. *Journal of Management Studies, 25,* 273-385.

Ray, S. (1991). *Post crisis investigations: The National Transportation Safety Board and the airline industry.* Unpublished doctoral dissertation, Wayne State University, Detroit, MI.

Redding, W. C., & Tompkins, P. D. (1988). Organizational communication: Past and present tenses. In G. M. Goldhaber & G. A. Barnett (Eds.), *Handbook of organizational communication* (pp. 5-34). Norwood, NJ: Ablex.

Reinhardt, C. (1987). How to handle a crisis. *Public Relations Journal, 43*(11), 43-45.

Schlenker, B. R. (1980). *Impression management: The self concept, social identity, and interpersonal relations.* Monterey, CA: Brooks/Cole.

Schuetz, J. (1990). Corporate advocacy as argumentation. In R. Trapp & J. Schuetz (Eds.), *Perspectives on argumentation* (pp. 272-284). Prospect Heights, IL: Waveland.

Schultz, P. D. (1996). The morally accountable corporation: A postmodern approach to organizational responsibility. *Journal of Business Communication, 33,* 165-184.

Schultz, P. D., & Seeger, M. W. (1991). Corporate centered apologia: Iacocca in defense of Chrysler. *Speaker and Gavel, 28,* 50-60.

Seeger, M. W. (1986). The *Challenger* tragedy and search for legitimacy. *Central States Speech Journal, 37,* 147-157.

Seeger, M. W. (in press). *Communication, organizations and ethics.* Cresskill, NJ: Hampton.

Seeger, M. W., & Bolz, B. (1996). Technological transfer and multinational corporations in the Union Carbide Crisis Bhopal, India. In J. Jaksa & M. Pritchard (Eds.), *Ethics of technological transfer* (pp. 245-265). Cresskill, NJ: Hampton.

Sellnow, T. L. (1993). Scientific argument in organizational crisis communication: The case of Exxon. *Argumentation and Advocacy, 30,* 28-41.

Sellnow, T. L. (1994). Speaking in defense of Chrysler: Lee Iacocca's crisis communication. In M. W. Seeger (Ed.), *"I gotta tell you": Speeches of Lee Iacocca* (pp. 97-108). Detroit, MI: Wayne State University Press.

Sellnow, T. L., & Seeger, M. W. (1989). Crisis messages: Wall Street and the Reagan administration after Black Monday. *Speaker and Gavel, 26,* 9-18.

Sellnow, T. L., & Ulmer, R. R. (1995). Ambiguous argument as advocacy in organizational crisis communication. *Argumentation and Advocacy, 31,* 138-150.

Shrivastava, P. (1987). *Bhopal: Anatomy of a crisis.* Cambridge, MA: Ballinger.

Shrivastava, P., & Mitroff, I. I. (1987). Strategic management of corporate crisis. *Columbia Journal of World Business, 22,* 5-11.

Shrivastava, P., Mitroff, I. I., Miller, D., & Miglani, A. (1988). Understanding industrial crises. *Journal of Management Studies, 25,* 285-301.

Singh, J. V., Tucker D. J., & House, R. J. (1986). Organizational legitimacy and the liability of newness. *Administrative Science Quarterly, 31,* 171-193.

Small, W. (1991). *Exxon Valdez*: How to spend billions and still get a black eye. *Public Relations Review, 17*(1), 9-26.

Smart, C. F. (1985). Strategic business planning: Predicting susceptibility to crisis. In S. J. Andriole (Ed.), *Corporate crisis management* (pp. 9-21). Princeton, NJ: Petrocelli.

Smart, C. F., & Vertinsky, I. (1977). Designs for crisis decision units. *Administrative Science Quarterly, 22,* 640-657.

Smith, D. A. (1994). *An ethical examination of the A. H. Robins legitimizing strategies during the 21 year Dalkon Shield crisis.* Paper presented at the National Communication Ethics Conference, Gull Lake, MI.

Snyder, L., & Foster, L. G. (1983). An anniversary review and critique: The Tylenol crisis. *Public Relations Review, 9*(3), 24-34.

Strauss, A. (1982). Social worlds and legitimation processes. *Studies in Symbolic Interaction, 4,* 171-190.

Sturges, D. L. (1994). Communicating through crisis a strategy for organizational survival. *Management Communication Quarterly, 7,* 297-316.

Szwapa, C., & Seeger, M. W. (1988). *Legitimizing strategies in the chemical industry: A case study of DuPont deNemoires and the Dow Chemical company.* Paper presented at the annual meeting of the International Communication Association, San Francisco.

Tompkins, P. K., & Anderson, E. V. B. (1971). *Communication crisis at Kent State.* New York: Gordon & Breach.

Turkel, G. (1982). Situated corporatist legitimacy: The 1980 Chrysler loan guarantee. *Research in Law, Deviance and Social Control, 4,* 165-189.

Turner, B. (1976). The organizational and interorganizational development of disasters. *Administrative Science Quarterly, 21,* 378-397.

Ulmer, R. R., & Sellnow, T. L. (1996). *Responsibility and organizational communication: Environmental uncertainty and crisis communication.* Paper presented at the Fourth National Conference on Communication Ethics, Gull Lake, MI.

Ware, B. L., & Linkugel, W. A. (1973). They spoke in defense of themselves: On the generic criticism of apologia. *Quarterly Journal of Speech, 59,* 273-283.

Weick, K. (1969). *The social psychology of organizing.* Reading, MA: Addison-Wesley.
Weick, K. (1979). *The social psychology of organizing* (2nd ed.). New York: Random House.
Weick, K. (1988). Enacted sensemaking in a crisis situation. *Journal of Management Studies,* 25, 305-317.
Weick, K. (1995). *Sensemaking in organizations.* Thousand Oaks, CA: Sage.
Wert-Gray, S., Center, C., Brashers, D. E., & Meyers, R. (1991). Research topics and methodological orientations in organizational communication: A decade of review. *Communication Studies, 42,* 141-154.
Wilcox, D. L., Ault, P. H., & Agee, W. K. (1986). *Public relations strategies and tactics.* New York: Harper & Row.
Williams, D. E., & Olaniran, B. A. (1994). Exxon's decision making flaws: The hypervigilant response to the *Valdez* grounding. *Public Relations Review, 20*(1), 5-18.
Williams, D. E., & Treadaway, G. (1992). Exxon and the *Valdez* accident: A failure in crisis communication. *Communication Studies, 43,* 56-64.

CHAPTER CONTENTS

7   Old Wine in a New Bottle: Public Journalism, Developmental Journalism, and Social Responsibility

SHELTON A. GUNARATNE
Moorhead State University

The emerging concept of public journalism in the United States is very similar to the concept of developmental journalism that the West had denounced in the past in debates concerning the New World Information and Communication Order (NWICO). Many of the ideas of the International Commission for the Study of Communication Problems, as well as those regarding the social responsibility theory of the press associated with the Commission on Freedom of the Press, have appeared in the writings of those who advocate public journalism. Just as during the NWICO debates, scholars are questioning the validity of conventional news values based on what Galtung and Vincent call "occidental cosmology." Participatory communication and cultural identity appear to be vital components of both public journalism and developmental journalism. How can one explain the philosophical similarities of these three movements—social responsibility, NWICO, and public journalism— that have influenced our thinking on journalism during the second half of the 20th century? This essay argues that all three were responses to the effects of different stages of capitalism on the press, and that their similarities are a consequence of evolutionary thinking.

T HE First Amendment to the U.S. Constitution, which became effective December 15, 1791, proclaims: "Congress shall make no law respecting an establishment of religion, or prohibiting the free exercise thereof; or abridging the freedom of speech, or of the press; or the right of the people peaceably to assemble, and to petition the Government for a redress of grievances." The framers of the Constitution thus recognized the indispensability of freedom of thought and expression for the healthy growth of a democracy. The libertarianism reflected in the First Amendment—an

Correspondence and requests for reprints: Shelton A. Gunaratne, 3215 Village Green Drive, Moorhead, MN 56560; e-mail gunarat@mhd1.moorhead.msus.edu

Communication Yearbook 21, pp. 277-321

outgrowth of the political tradition reflected in the writings of Milton, Locke, Mill, and others—was ideally suited to the late-18th-century capitalist environment of the 13 states that made up the United States of America, with a population of fewer than 4 million.

Two centuries after the adoption of the Bill of Rights, the United States faced a different phase of capitalist growth. The constitutionally guaranteed media libertarianism no longer seemed adequate to propel people into democratic participation. The original press, which had evolved into a multifaceted mass media—print, broadcast, and electronic (cyberspace)—reflected the people's predilection for entertainment rather than for knowledge of public affairs and political participation. Thus emerged the public/civic/communitarian journalism movement (J. Black, 1996) to critique the performance of the conventional media.

The scenario had become more complex even by the mid-20th century, leading to the call for a new libertarianism, a concept that came to be called *social responsibility*. T. Peterson describes the change:

> The framers of the constitution were children of the Enlightenment, and their assumptions about the nature of man and the relationship of man to government were implicit in the instrument they drafted. Government was the chief foe of liberty, they believed, and the press must be free to serve as a guardian against governmental encroachments on individual liberty. If the press were free, men would speak. True, they might lie, vilify, distort. But the wonderful invisible hand envisioned by Adam Smith and the self-righting process discerned by John Milton would set things right. Man would seek truth amidst the welter of ideas that swarmed in the market place; and being rational, he would separate truth from falsehood, good from bad. But somewhere along the way, faith diminished in the optimistic notion that a virtually absolute freedom and the nature of man carried built-in correctives for the press. (in Siebert, Peterson, & Schramm, 1956, pp. 76-77)

In this essay, I propose that the constituent elements of public journalism—also known as civic, communitarian, or conversational journalism—are not new. These elements have emerged from time to time as reactions to different stages of capitalism.[1] For instance, the social responsibility theory of the press was an obvious reaction to the state of capitalism in the United States that emerged after World War II. So was the movement for a New World Information and Communication Order (NWICO) that promoted the concept of developmental journalism at the end of the era of Western colonialism. All three movements targeted the lapses in the libertarian press concept implicit in the First Amendment.

Furthermore, although I will examine here the similarities of these three movements, I will pay greatest attention to the latest—public journalism—in my literature review. Because scholars have already thoroughly examined the large body of literature on the social responsibility and NWICO (developmental) journalism concepts (e.g., Golding & Harris, 1997; Hasim, 1996a, 1996b; Jayaweera & Amunugama, 1987; Mehra, 1989; Nerone, 1995; Nordenstreng, Manet, & Kleinwachter, 1986), the present endeavor, in relation to these two, will refer only to those sources that pertain to the thrust of this essay.

PUBLIC JOURNALISM

The Poynter Institute for Media Studies's (1996) compilation of the public journalism bibliography covering the period 1990-1996 lists 31 books and reports, 74 articles, and 9 on-line resources.[2] An annotated bibliography compiled by Lee (1996) lists 47 publications about public journalism, 10 related to public journalism, and 7 useful background sources.[3] Lambeth (1996) also has attempted to cover all the relevant resources, including Web sites, available to readers on public journalism. Because the writings of some authors in various publications tend to be repetitious, my focus in the present literature review on public journalism (also known as civic or communitarian or conversational journalism) will be on those works that expand on this concept in different ways, so that I may extract their commonalities.

A Loose Definition

In 1996, the on-line source Democracy Forum USA defined civic journalism as "an effort by print and broadcast journalists to reach out to the public more aggressively in the reporting process, to listen to how citizens frame their problems and what citizens see as solutions to those problems. And then to use that information to enrich their newspaper or broadcast report" (http://soundprint.org:80/democracy/civicjdf.html). Fishkin (1995) defines public/civic journalism as a movement "to create a more active and engaged public by self-consciously giving voice to the people's agenda" (p. 156). McKnight (1997) describes it as a movement "to steer journalism towards reinvigorating public life, which many see as excluding ordinary citizens and devaluing the need to inform them" (p. 1).

Charity (1995) mentions Rosen as an early promoter of the concept. In Rosen's view, "public journalism worries about becoming properly *attached*" and "getting the *connections* right," unlike traditional journalism, which values detachment. Whereas traditional journalism seeks to inform and to act as a watchdog over government, public journalism "tries to strengthen the community's *capacity*—to recognize itself, to converse well, and make choices. The guiding image behind public journalism is a vision of the well-connected community, where everything that should connect does connect. Where everyone who should be talking is, in fact, talking" (Rosen, 1994 speech; quoted in Charity, 1995, p. 159).

Rosen (1992c) asserts that the terms *objectivity, fairness, balance,* and *accuracy* have left journalists bereft of any philosophy of action, and that journalists should present themselves as advocates for the kind of serious talk a mature polity requires. Rosen (1994a) says that the identifying features of public journalism include a willingness to break with old routines, a desire to "reconnect" with citizens and their true concerns, an emphasis on serious discussion as the primary activity in democratic politics, and a focus on citizens as actors within, rather than spectators to, the public drama. Rosen (1995b) also says that public journalism—derived from academic theory based on the work of Habermas, Dewey, and Carey—means at least three things: an argument about the proper task of the press, a set of practices that is slowly spreading through American journalism, and a movement of people and institutions.

The proponents of public journalism have deliberately avoided aiming at a standard definition of the concept. Merritt (1995b) says that "for any one editor or institution to define public journalism concretely would also mean limiting the possibilities" (p. 114). Rosen clarifies: "Public journalism is not a settled doctrine or a strict code of conduct but an unfolding philosophy about the place of the journalist in public life" (in Rosen & Merritt, 1994, p. 6). Rosen (1995a), therefore, calls public journalism "a work in progress," because no one can say what it will be in 5 or 10 years (p. v).

However, Merritt (1995c) provides a clarification: "Public journalism seeks to define and learn a different set of reflexes, one that has a purpose beyond telling the news. It seeks to break away from the concept of One Journalism, with its idea that the rules and conventions of the profession are pervasive and inflexible" (p. 127). He goes on to say that public journalism involves "learning to report and write about public life beyond traditional politics" and, among other things, reporting "the very important news of civic life—including civic successes" (p. 130). Moreover, Merritt says that public journalism, which is the antithesis of "One Journalism," "seeks to define another set of five Ws and H" (pp. 131-132). He adds, "Public life, according to the values of public journalism, requires shared information and shared deliberation; people participate in answering democracy's fundamental question of 'What shall we do?' " (p. 131).

Merritt (1995b) also says that "public journalism is additive. It builds on telling the news by recognizing (a) the fundamental connection between democracy and journalism, (b) the need for public life to go well, for democracy to fulfill its historic promise, and (c) journalism's rational self-interest, both economic and intellectual, in public life's going well" (p. 114). Accordingly, Merritt sees the public journalist as "a fair-minded participant in a community that works" (quoted in Charity, 1995, p. 150; see Merritt, 1995b, p. 94).

According to Charity (1995), public journalism arose out of the conviction that something essential was lacking in American life right now: rational talk, community-based approaches, participatory discussions, communal glue, a proper emphasis on activity (p. 151). And, unlike "most forms of self-styled newer, better journalism," public journalism provided what economists would call *added value*: the ability to help the audience conduct an ongoing conversation in depth (pp. 157-158). Public journalism, Charity says, "is nothing more than the conviction that journalism's business is about making citizenship work" (p. 9). Three interlocking metaphors describe who public journalists are: They are "experts in public life," "civic capitalists," and "full-time citizens"; they are not "radicals departing from the canons of their profession, but traditionalists attempting a return to first principles" (pp. 11-12). Practitioners of the concept have learned that "telling ordinary people's stories and dramatizing the community's struggle to solve its problems both roots people in an issue and helps them keep perspective on it over time" (p. 17). Public journalists aim to print "all the news that citizens want to know" (p. 19). Charity (1996) also says that public journalism is only one part of a much larger story: the democratic renewal going on in a lot of professions and communities all at once.

More recently, Rosen (1996a) has formulated two overlapping propositions to capture the essence of public journalism. He says that public journalism reverses two traditional assumptions in the following manner: (a) "People have to participate, so that they'll want and need to become informed," and (b) "information is what we have—in the media age, information is everywhere—and democracy is what we need" (p. 83).

Anderson, Dardenne, and Killenberg (1994), who coined the term *conversational journalism,* start with the view that "the prime role of journalism, and the only way by which it can survive as a viable institution in the pubic arena, is to take the responsibility to stimulate public dialogue on issues of concern to a democratic public" (pp. xix-xx). Their radical platform calls for a de-emphasis on the reliance of current news values and the attempt to project objectivity, a shift from the heavy reliance on the inverted pyramid format of presenting news to the much more natural narrative (storytelling) format, a change from the linear transmission of news as a commodity to a communication mode that entails interactive feedback, as well as a reconceptualization of ethics to encompass multicultural and feminine perceptions (summarized in Gunaratne, 1996b).

Anderson et al. (1994) explain that conversational journalism is a pluralistic journalism based on the triangular interaction of *news, communication,* and *community*—the three touchstones that produce "people-to-people communication that ranges far beyond the printed page or newscast script" (p. 2). Far from being radical, this concept merely brings back an earlier community-based narrative style of journalism. Anderson et al. argue that the definition of news must include a broader range of what happens to people, so that news becomes a cocreative activity that depends on community participation. They suggest dumping the linear transfer models of *communication*—the source-message-channel-receiver models—in favor of the notion of the informational commons, where "people can learn, mature, agree, and dis-agree—and from which social change can occur" (p. 6). Furthermore, they argue that because a *community* exists not through agreements but through communication, journalism can legitimate the "conversational commons" that links previously disconnected people, groups, and places (p. 12).

In an interview with Bishop (1997), Campbell has noted that he sees public journalism as the third leg of a three-legged model of journalism. The first is the fact-finding, investigative leg. The second is the storytelling leg, which represents the literary tradition of journalism. The third is the leg of conver-sation, wherein the "journalist helps engage the reader not as a client, and not as an audience member, but as a partner in coming to some understanding of life" (p. 10). This partnership, which represents public journalism, helps "explore what is relevant in the experience of the readers" and "adds depth to our understanding of what's happening in the world" (p. 10). Thus Campbell, who, like Merritt, is a key practitioner of public journalism, endorses the metaphor of "conversation" that Anderson et al. (1994) use to define the so-called third leg of the craft.

Lauterer (1995) notes, "Call it whatever you will—community journalism, public journalism, relentlessly local coverage—it's not a new idea" (p. 184). He says that community journalism satisfies a basic human craving: "the affirmation of the sense of community, a positive and intimate reflection of the sense of place, a stroke for our us-ness, our extended family-ness and our profound and interlocking connectedness" (p. 9).

Weichelt (1995) asserts that public journalism has two goals: to make news organizations listen more closely to their audiences and to make them play more active roles in their communities. Stepp (1996) explains that public journalism offers many specific antidotes to today's nonpublic journalism: involving citizens in the news agenda, divorcing coverage from officialdom and grounding it in people's lives, and clearing away some of the snideness and smugness that have infiltrated the media. Parisi (1995) argues that public journalism advances understanding of news as a coherent narrative of the world that serves certain interests, rather than as a mirror image of truth. He suggests that journalists can best develop public journalism by acknowl-edging more public news narratives, drawing on the insights of media criti-cism, and addressing creatively the limitations of objectivity as a narrative framework for serving the public interest.

E. Black (1996) says that "public journalism is hard to define succinctly. It has arisen in response to various signals warning that democracy and public life are in trouble and that journalism is in disrepute, and in response to the belief that certain bad habits of conventional journalism have contributed to these problems" (p. A8). He points out that public journalism is designed to "invite ordinary citizens back into public life by making their concerns the starting point of the debate," to "overcome journalistic cynicism and ac-knowledge the possibility that citizens working together might be able to solve some of society's problems," and to "modify the rules of detachment by accepting that journalists have an interest in and responsibility for raising the level of public discourse and helping society find solutions to its problems" (p. A8).

According to Merritt (1995b), public journalism involves at least five mental shifts on the part of the conventional journalist: Moving "beyond the limited mission of telling the news to a broader mission of helping public life to go well, and act[ing] out that imperative" (p. 113); moving "from detachment to being a fair-minded participant in public life" (p. 113); moving "from worrying about proper separations to concerns with proper connections" (p. 113); moving "beyond only describing what is 'going wrong' to also imagining what 'going right' would be like" (p. 113); and moving "from people as consumers . . . to seeing them as a public, as potential actors in arriving at democratic solutions to public problems" (p. 114).

Lambeth (1994) argues that the new forms of civic journalism constitute some combination of the following: careful, timely, and sensitive listening to public needs; systematic consultation of the public by means of polls and focus groups; journalist-organized dialogue with panels of resource specialists chosen for their differing expertise and perspectives; media-sponsored public forums designed to deliberate on key issues; continuity of in-depth reporting on issues chosen independently by journalists for their fidelity to citizen concerns; and occasional cooperative projects undertaken by newspaper, radio, and/or television newsrooms. Lambeth and Craig (1995) define civic journalism as an effort to probe beneath the surface of events and cover all issues, as well as to have experts speak clearly to the public. Lambeth (1992b) and Lambeth and Aucoin (1993) have further elaborated on the relationship between the news media and democracy and the role of the journalist as a leader in community action.

McMillan, Guppy, Kunz, and Reis (1996) have attempted to flesh out the meaning of public journalism through textual analysis in which they have sought denotative and connotative meanings and associated metaphors. They group the explicit definitions into two primary categories: those that define public journalism philosophically and those that define its practices. These researchers have analyzed the implicit definitions in terms of two factors: use of metaphor and other literary devices and use of opposition in defining the concept. Their analysis provides "a picture of public journalism that is based on a new, or at least revitalized, relationship between news organizations and citizens"—a relationship that changes "the practice of journalism by focusing more on connections than detachment and by looking to citizens rather than 'officials' to define the public agenda" (p. 27). They found that "images of a quest, often with religious and reformist overtones," have inspired much of the literature (p. 27). Many writers have used sports analogies to sketch the performance of public journalism. The literature uses "both health and creation metaphors" to "suggest a model for healing or fixing the sick and broken relationship between news organizations and citizens" (p. 28). Changes in journalistic practice, "most notably the abandonment of objectivity and the breaking of a co-dependency relationship with the 'official' sources of traditional journalism," characterize this new relationship (p. 28). McMillan et al. conclude that although no unified model has yet evolved for public journalism, three models have emerged: "one based on changes to news coverage, a second based on community activism, and a third driven by financial concerns" (p. 28).

Intellectual Antecedents

Fishkin (1995) traces the start of public journalism to suggestions put forth by Broder (1990) and Rosen (1992c). Broder called for an effort to "help reconnect politics and government," and Rosen argued that journalists must use the press to alter and improve political debate. Both Broder and Rosen pointed out the efforts of the *Ledger-Enquirer* of Columbus, Georgia, in 1988 to foster "public politics"—a politics based on citizen engagement and serious dialogue between citizens and leaders (cited in Fishkin, 1995, pp. 156-158). The *Wichita* (Kansas) *Eagle* and the *Charlotte* (North Carolina) *Observer* followed suit with a citizens' agenda. All three newspapers belonged to the Knight-Ridder chain.[4]

The public journalism movement generally associates itself with a wider movement to address the central question of what makes democracy work or fail. That wider movement mirrors the writings of political scientist Barber (1984); journalist Dionne (1991); former federal cabinet officials Gardner (1990) and Mathews (1994); researchers Harwood, Perry, and Schmitt, who constitute the Harwood Group (1993); Putnam (1993), who investigated the success and failure of modern Italian governments; and others. These writers have put forth the view that democracy is fixable and that journalists can play a role in the process.

Barber (1984), who argues that the old liberal ideals of democracy are too "thin," calls for a "strong" democracy that involves all people in making common choices and taking common action. The detachment of the press does not fit into such a framework. Dionne (1991) argues that the bifurcation of politics into "liberalism" and "conservatism" has provided a deeply false choice that is inimical to public life. He spells out the wisdom of involving the public by getting back to consensual politics. Gardner (1990) points out that good leaders do not so much command, proclaim, or manage as empower their constituents to work toward a common purpose—a goal of public journalism. Mathews (1994) refers to a "politics that is not called politics"— citizens getting together to talk about problems such as drugs in their neighborhood schools or decay in their housing projects, so they can find solutions and build personal bonds along the way—that could provide the framework for a more successful democratic life (quoted in Charity, 1995, p. 174). The

Harwood Group (1993) identifies the main factors that draw people into a public issue and sustain their engagement. These researchers found that the people they studied sought emotional involvement rather than detachment, ambivalence rather than certainty, and big, interconnected issues rather than narrow, easily digestible fragments. These findings contradict the media's attitude of detachment and preference for simplicity and news atoms. Putnam (1993), who studied a new layer of 15 regional bodies that Italy introduced in 1970, found that the most successful of them were in those areas with the densest, most egalitarian, and most honest civic associations. Based on this research, he has identified the sorts of social organizations that can create the most productive civic (or social) capital in U.S. settings. Public journalism emphasizes the nurturing of civic capital.

Although the writers cited above, and others, have stimulated the public journalism movement, the writer who has influenced the operational framework of the new concept is Yankelovich (1991), who describes "how insights into the way people make decisions can be turned into concrete newsroom goals for making those decisions easier" (Charity, 1995, pp. 3-4). Yankelovich (1991) outlines three steps that the public has to pass through to travel from mass opinion to public judgment:

1. The *consciousness-raising* stage, "in which the public learns about an issue and becomes aware of its existence and meaning" (p. 63): Journalists can help the public if they choose more judiciously where to focus public attention and present the news in user-friendly forms.

2. The *working-through* stage, when "people must abandon the passive-receptive mode" (of the consciousness-raising stage) and become "actively engaged and involved" (p. 64): Journalists can improve the chances of keeping the process on track by reducing issues to choices, plumbing to core values, spelling out the costs and consequences of each choice, bridging the expert-public gap, facilitating deliberation, and promoting civility.

3. The *resolution* stage, which shows "the result of successful consciousness raising and working through" (p. 65): Journalists can shore up people's motivation by prodding action on the public's choice.

Thus Yankelovich has set out the framework for journalists' engagement. However, others have pointed out that the theory behind public journalism has evolved from the work of several scholars: Arendt (1958, 1961/1987, 1963/1990, 1970), Carey (1969, 1975, 1982, 1985, 1987, 1988, 1989, 1993, 1995), Dewey (1916, 1927, 1929, 1938), Habermas (1962/1989, 1975, 1979, 1987, 1990, 1992, 1993), Mead (1934, 1956), and Park (1940, 1955), in particular.

Anderson et al. (1994) state that "Dewey envisioned a society of conversationalists who encounter and respond to messages as participants, not as news consumers" (p. 21), that Mead regarded conversation as "the essence of human endeavor" (p. 23), that Park asserted "the newspaper's role in maintaining a Jeffersonian democracy" (p. 102), and that Carey looked at conversation as the mechanism that "connects people to memory" (p. 29).

Heikkila and Kunelius (1996) assert that although a number of thinkers have influenced public journalism, perhaps two of the major sources of inspiration have been Dewey and Arendt, who share some fundamental features as social theorists. Heikkila and Kunelius argue that Dewey's contribution lies in answering the question, "What is a public?" and Arendt's in answering the question, "What is done in the public?" Heikkila and Kunelius rely heavily on Dewey's *The Public and Its Problems* (1927) and Arendt's *The Human Condition* (1958) to show the relevance of these two thinkers to the building of a theory of public journalism.

Dewey (1927) views *public problems* in two ways: first, in the sense of the troubled state of *the public* as an organ of democratic life; second, in the sense of the social formation of *the publics* when problems appear. Heikkila and Kunelius (1996) say that Dewey is most relevant to public journalism in the latter sense. Lippmann's (1923) reliance on detached "experts" was, for Dewey, "the greatest indictment of democracy yet written" (Carey, 1987, p. 7).

Arendt (1958, 1961/1987) defines her notion of *action* (i.e., what is done in the public) as taking the initiative through speech: the means of actualizing oneself as well as the means of causing consequences beyond one's personal life. The consequences of action, which have the qualities of unpredictability and futility, remain unknown to the actor. Thus action is also the most dangerous of human abilities. "Out of this conceptualization of action, three ideas appear particularly challenging for public journalism: ontological motivation for action, 'public happiness,' and web of relationships created in action" (Heikkila & Kunelius, 1996, p. 86).

Coleman (1996) says that the roots of public journalism go back to Dewey's notion of a free press in a democracy. However, both American mass communication practice and American mass communication research have failed to follow the cultural approach that Dewey's work advocates (Carey, 1975, 1982, 1985). Coleman points out that Dewey's theory of mass media is inseparable from his theory of democracy: "the idea of community life itself" (Dewey, 1927, p. 148). For Dewey, individuals are incomplete without a community; therefore, individuals owe a social debt to advance the common good. Coleman says that central to Dewey's vision is a belief in the problem-solving powers of groups. Communication is Dewey's answer to the problems of American democracy, and he envisaged a more active role for the press. Carey (1989) interprets Dewey's hope for mass communication as transforming "the great society into the great community" to "create or restore public life on a scale matching that of industry and politics" (quoted in Coleman, 1996, p. 7). Coleman sees striking similarities between Arendt's and Dewey's ideas. Arendt (1963/1990) makes a distinction between negative freedom (i.e., "being liberated") and positive freedom (i.e., "being free"). Arendt

(1958) also sees individuality as possible only within a public sphere. These concepts are related to public journalism.

Dykers (1995) claims that public journalism's rhetorical roots are sunk into 300 years of Western intellectual history. She sees connections between public journalism and (a) 17th-, 18th-, and 19th-century development of the idea of a "liberal" democracy and (b) the concept of the *public sphere.* Habermas (1962/1989), who elaborates on the latter concept, says that public discussion is the means through which citizens in a democracy achieve "consensus about what [is] practically necessary in the interest of all" (p. 83). Habermas notes that the successive enfranchisement of different groups as "citizens" means the involvement of a greater range of perspectives in the conversation. Dykers points out that for Habermas, public life encompasses two key spheres of society: (a) civil society, which involves all those who qualify as citizens, whose consent is necessary to form the apparatus of government for handling collective affairs; and (b) the public sphere, the public space within civil society where citizens meeting as equals take part in rational discussions about shared concerns. Coleman (1996) draws attention to Habermas's (1962/1989) assertion that today the public sphere has lost interest in public debate and has become a vehicle for facts, expert opinion, and advertising.

The concept of *discourse ethics* that Habermas (1987, 1990, 1993) theorizes in relation to communication in modern life also fits into the Dewey-inspired stream of democratic theory. The key element of discourse ethics, related to the storytelling approach to journalism, is its "universalization principle" that societal norms are valid only if they win or could win the approval of all participants "in a practical discourse" (Habermas, 1990, p. 93). Furthermore, "all concerned in principle [must] take part, freely and equally, in a cooperative search for the truth, where nothing coerces anyone except the force of the better argument" (p. 198). Discourse ethics models two principles fundamental to Habermas's moral philosophy: "Act with an orientation to mutual understanding, and allow everyone the communicative freedom to take positions on validity claims" (1993, p. 66). Like Dewey, Habermas (1990) argues that society cannot create justice for the individual without assuring his or her community's solidarity (p. 200).

Anderson et al. (1994) argue that Dewey's work had a direct and pervasive influence on Mead (1934, 1956), who has also influenced the philosophy of conversational journalism. Mead sees conversation as the essence of human behavior and uses the term as a key image to explain the interrelated processes of mind, self, and society. Mead envisions the social order as a "conversation of gestures" (1934, p. 135; 1956, p. 212). To have a society is, therefore, to have a conversation. Park (1940, 1955), as much as Dewey, also views communication as the key to public life. He asserts that the press has a role in maintaining a Jeffersonian democracy: "The newspaper must continue to tell us about ourselves. We must somehow learn to know our community and its affairs in the same intimate way in which we know them in the country villages" (1955, p. 93).

Carey is the contemporary cultural theorist who has attempted to reformulate the Deweyan concepts to show their aptness to the public journalism movement. He writes:

> The god term of journalism—the be-all and end-all, the term without which the entire enterprise fails to make sense—is the public. Insofar as journalism is grounded, it is grounded in the public. Insofar as journalism has a client, the client is the public. . . . The canons of journalism originate in and flow from the relationship of the press to the public. The public is totem and talisman, an object of ritual homage. . . . But for all the ritual incantation of the public in the rhetoric of journalism, no one quite knows any longer what the public is, or where one might find it, or even whether it exists any longer. (Carey, 1987, p. 5)

Heikkila and Kunelius (1996), however, point out that if journalism is grounded in the public, then the term *public journalism* sounds "tautological, if not schizophrenic" (p. 81). But public journalism advocates claim that being *public* cannot be taken for granted. Moreover, Heikkila and Kunelius argue that contrary to what Carey (1989) has written, the concept of public is not "unusually abstract," considering that the public in Dewey's theory is an actual phenomenon (p. 83).

Carey (1987) asserts that neither journalism nor public life will improve until journalism is rethought, redescribed, and reinterpreted. His view is that journalism's fundamental task is to bring the public back into existence, and that what is clearly needed is a model of conversation rather than a model of information. Carey (1988) includes in his definition of communication the tie between communication and community. He questions the tradition of focusing on the social and political functions of communication and argues for the examination of the content and purpose of communication. He redefines the goal of communication as an effort "to enlarge the human conversation by comprehending what others are saying" (quoted in Lee, 1996, p. 14).

Merritt (1996) says that the critics of public journalism must examine the concept's intellectual roots for "a truly useful and needed debate to occur," and that critics should stop the "tag-team wrestling match" over early public journalism experiments (p. 30). Drawing from Carey, Merritt says that "public journalism is as much or more about public life than it is about journalism, a fact universally overlooked in the wild thrust and parry over techniques and sacred, uncrossable lines" (p. 30).

Stepp (1996), who assumes the role of referee in this "wrestling match," posits that although public journalism has broken down barriers to change and energized the news community, its intent to "try to be another branch of government" or "to substitute journalism for government" has brought about much skepticism (p. 40). However, he says, to the degree that it seeks to fix journalism, public journalism is a blessing.

The Key Players

The two people most widely recognized as founders of the contemporary public journalism movement are Jay Rosen (1991a, 1991b, 1992a, 1992b, 1992c, 1993a, 1993b, 1994a, 1994b, 1995a, 1995b, 1995c, 1996a, 1996b, 1996c, 1996d), the scholar who heads New York University's Project on Public Life and the Press, and Davis Merritt (1994, 1995a, 1995b, 1995c, 1996), the professional who used the newspaper he edited, the *Wichita Eagle,* to try out the concept. Rosen and Merritt (1994) have had the support of the Kettering Foundation, which, together with the Pew Center for Civic Journalism and the Poynter Institute for Media Studies, has promoted public journalism. Two newspaper chains, Gannett and Knight-Ridder, also have embraced public journalism, with project funding coming from the Gannett Foundation and the Knight Foundation.

Among the other significant players are the members of a circle of communication scholars (e.g., Anderson et al., 1994; J. Black, 1996; Charity, 1995; Christians, 1995; Glasser, 1991; Lambeth, 1992a, 1992b, 1994; Lauterer, 1995; Meyer, 1995), some of whom are actively encouraging younger scholars to promote the movement through civic interest groups. Despite the skeptics (e.g., Case, 1994; Frankel, 1995; Gartner, 1995; Hoyt, 1995; Raines, 1996; Remnick, 1996; Shafer, 1996; Shaw, 1993; Woo, 1995a, 1995b), the number of journalists using the public journalism approach appears to be on the increase (see Albers, 1996; Brewer & McCombs, 1996; Broder, 1992; Campbell, 1995; Clifton, 1994; Conte, 1996; Cripe, 1997; Denton & Thorson, 1995; Fallows, 1996; Fouhy, 1994, 1995; Glaberson, 1994; Jurkowitz, 1996; Peirce, 1994; Peterson, 1996; Reider, 1995; Schaffer & Miller, 1995; Shepard, 1994; Winn, 1993).

The movement's key players have used the terms *public journalism, civic journalism, community journalism,* and *conversational journalism,* for diverse reasons. Christians (1995) says that the term *public journalism,* which Rosen prefers, underscores the concept's legacy in pragmatism—as in Dewey's *The Public and Its Problems* (1927)—and makes a direct lingual connection to current debates about the public sphere that Habermas and others initiated. The term *civic journalism,* which Lambeth (1994) and the Pew Center prefer, reflects the mission of the press and its connection to political theory. The term *community journalism,* which Lauterer (1995) and Christians (1995) prefer, shows the concept's most direct connection to communitarian political philosophy and to the importance of community in social theory and communication studies. The term *conversational journalism,* which Anderson et al. (1994, p. 43) prefer, emphasizes Mead's (1934) point that, given a voice, people become part of the conversation.

Christians, Ferre, and Fackler (1993) recommend a communitarian model that would require changes in mass media institutions' hiring practices and workers' involvement in management, as well as encouragement and implementation of civic involvement. They argue that the "community cannot be resuscitated without the leadership of the press," and that "structural changes are needed in the press' world view" (quoted in Lee, 1996, p. 2). In their view, the media should serve as a forum for debate and discussion over issues until the community reaches consensus.

Glasser (1991) has developed an alternative conception of the democratic community in which politics becomes what private individuals carry out as citizens and public communication also becomes a regulative ideal. He concludes that a publicly told story engages others by creating a shared experience or discovery and works toward consensus and understanding. He applies these concepts to a conversational model of journalism.

Lambeth and Craig (1995) describe civic journalism projects and categorize each into one of three groups that lie along a continuum: Mode 1 involves emphasis on public listening, Mode 2 involves emphasis on initiating dialogue, and Mode 3 involves participation with the public and experts or leaders to solve public problems.

Meyer (1995) points out the need for a well-formed theory of public journalism to prevent abuse of this concept. He sees six elements as vital for public journalism's success: a desire to rebuild a community's sense of itself, a lengthened attention span, a willingness to go into deep explanations of the systems that influence people's lives, increased attention focused on the rational middle ground of issues and decreased attention to the extremes, a preference for substance over tactics in political coverage, and a desire to foster deliberation.

Dykers (1995) points out that today's public or civic journalists are moving Dewey's and Park's (1955) ideas into the 21st century because such journalists, who are attempting to create communication across differences, are creating among citizens a social good called "reciprocity." Ettema and Peer (1995) say that every attempt to redefine the mission of the press in terms of civic or public journalism has boiled down to the theme of a *relationship* with the community that facilitates *dialogue* on substantive issues.

Reaction to the Capitalism of the Late 1980s

A link is clear between the emergence of the public journalism movement and the stage of capitalism that the United States had reached in the late 1980s. One can argue that public journalism responded to the situation of the press in the United States in the late 1980s, particularly the declining political participation, the declining readership of newspapers, and the end of the Cold War.

The profit-motivated mass media were emphasizing entertainment rather than public service in the chase for the advertising dollar. The people were avoiding political participation in large numbers, so much so that Census Bureau data show only 45% of the voting-age population casting their votes in the 1990 congressional elections—a 10% drop over two decades. The end of the Cold War had brought a high degree of complacency. Americans were shunning their daily newspapers and relying more on entertainment-oriented broadcast media for superficial news. The information overload brought about in part by the growth of the Internet was on the verge of takeoff. The daily newspaper circulation per capita had reached an all-time low. Although the U.S. population rose 82.1% from 1946 to 1993, the country's daily newspaper circulation rose a mere 17.4% in the same period. Circulation dropped from 38.2 copies per 100 people in 1946 to 23.3 per 100 in 1993 (Gunaratne, 1996b).

The *Yankelovich Monitor* reported that between 1988 and 1993 people's confidence in television news dropped from 55% to 25%; confidence in newspaper news dropped from 50% to 20%, and in magazine news from 38% to 12% (Merritt, 1995b). Commenting on this phenomenon, Merritt (1995b) reasons that journalism "in all its forms ignored its obligations to effective public life"; such "failure has been a major contributor to the resultant malaise in public life"; "journalism should be—and can be—a primary force in the revitalization of public life"; however, "fundamental change in the profession—cultural, generational change—is necessary for that to occur" (p. 5).

Merritt clearly places the blame for the changes listed above on the traditional practice of journalism, thereby making a case for public journalism. However, what he and other protagonists have overlooked is the broken educational system, which has failed to promote effective public life or competence in reading. A 1992 national adult literacy survey revealed that 21-23% of Americans—or some 40-44 million of the 191 million adults in the United States—"demonstrated skills in the lowest level of prose, document, and quantitative proficiencies" (Kirsch, Jungeblut, Jenkins, & Kolstad, 1993, p. xiv). Merritt's observations, however, reflect the general recognition of the failure of the press to attract a wider audience through other solutions: readership research programs, new promotional programs, and massive redesign efforts, as well as other efforts to mimic television. This state of capitalist growth in the United States was clearly not conducive to the unquestioned acceptance of the libertarian press concept protected by the First Amendment.

Summary

The public journalism movement in the United States has, among other things, sought a redefinition of news values, questioned the value of objectivity and the ethics relating to it, pushed for greater involvement of journalists as active participants in their communities, called on journalism to reflect accurately the multicultural composition of U.S. society, and suggested that journalism should place itself within the discipline of communication. Although the movement has the appearance of an intranational development, the debate relating to it has clear international and global implications.

If one were to put together the ideas emerging from the foregoing review, public journalism would appear as a pluralistic journalism based on the triangular interaction of *news, communication,* and *community* that emphasizes the following:

1. Journalism must redefine the traditional *news* values (e.g., significance/impact, prominence, proximity, timeliness, currency, conflict, and the unusual) and arrive at another set of five Ws and H. The One Journalism that emphasizes objectivity and detachment, as well as related ethics, is no longer adequate. News should become a coherent narrative that produces "added value" for the audience. The linear transmission of news as a commodity is now less appropriate. News on civic life, including civic successes, is extremely pertinent. Journalism ethics needs to recognize and encompass multicultural and feminist perspectives.

2. Journalism fits in more appropriately within the discipline of *communication.* Journalists should listen more closely to their audiences and facilitate dialogue or "conversation," so that everyone who should be talking, is talking. They should promote participatory communication across differences, particularly in a multicultural society, to create "reciprocity."

3. The journalist must be a "fair-minded participant in a *community* that works" (Charity, 1995, p. 150, emphasis added; see Merritt, 1995b, p. 94). The journalist must become a properly attached advocate of serious talk to enable the community to recognize itself and make choices. The affirmation of a sense of community and the recognition of interlocking connectedness are pertinent to journalism.

The above framework stands on a solid intellectual foundation built on the Deweyan concept of the public and its problems. Other intellectuals, including Arendt, Carey, Habermas, Mead, and Park, have contributed to strengthening that foundation. McMillan et al. (1996) say that the current practice of public journalism has resulted in the emergence of three models: "one based on changes to news coverage, a second based on community activism, and a third driven by financial concerns" (p. 28).

In the remainder of this essay I will analyze the relationship of the first two models of public journalism to the developmental journalism concept and the concept of the social responsibility of the press. The concept of developmental journalism took the world stage with the backing of the MacBride Commission (International Commission for the Study of Communication Problems [ICSCP], 1980). The social responsibility theory of the press evolved from the work of the Hutchins Commission (Commission on Freedom of the Press [CFP], 1947).

DEVELOPMENTAL JOURNALISM (AN ASPECT OF NWICO)

Shah (1996) sees a connection between public journalism, which he terms "communitarian journalism," and developmental journalism, which he calls "emancipatory journalism." A few other scholars have also analyzed this connection in various ways (e.g., Gunaratne, 1996b, 1996c; Gunaratne &

Hasim, 1996; Shafer, 1996; Yin, 1996). The key players in the public journalism movement, however, have so far confined themselves only to its Western intellectual roots.

Developmental journalism has its roots in developmental communication, which goes back to the work of agricultural extension carried out by large land-grant state universities in the United States (Stevenson, 1994). A 1964 seminar convened by the East-West Center in Honolulu formalized the concept, which later evolved into a coherent doctrine (Jayaweera & Amunugama, 1987). Journalists became a part of the picture simply because of their crucial role in communication.

The developmental journalism concept caught global attention during the acrimonious NWICO debates of the 1970s and 1980s. It received strength from the MacBride Report as part of its communication philosophy: a *free flow* and a wider and better *balanced* dissemination of information, with the goal of creating a new, more just, and more effective world information and communication order. The concern with *balance* did not find favor with the defenders of undiluted libertarianism, which the First Amendment implicitly espouses, because they feared it would give way to government intervention. That fear became real when politicians of the nonaligned movement took up the cause of developmental journalism. Thus the Western libertarians managed to turn this constructive concept into something no better than the authoritarian and the Communist practice of journalism.

A Loose Definition

The term *developmental journalism* goes back to the Philippines in the 1960s (Stevenson, 1994). In 1968, the Thomson Foundation sponsored the Economic Writers' Training Course, during which the seminar chairman, Alan Chalkley, coined the term *development journalist* (see Chalkley, 1968, 1975, 1980). Chalkley (1968) explained that a journalist's main task is to inform, to give his or her readers the facts. The journalist's secondary tasks are to interpret, to put the facts in their framework, and, where possible, to draw conclusions. According to Chalkley, these are the tasks of political journalists as well as of crime reporters, society-page writers, human interest writers, and every other journalist. The development journalist, however, also has a third task, a positive one that might be called "promotion": not only to give the facts of economic life and to interpret those facts, but also to promote the meaning of the facts and bring them home to the readers. "You must get your readers to realize how serious the development problem is, to think about the problem, to open their eyes to the possible solutions—to punch that hole in the vicious circle," Chalkley (1968) says in his initial definition of developmental journalism (quoted in Gunaratne & Hasim, 1996, p. 98). No concrete definition of the concept has emerged since then, although scholars, practitioners, and politicians have presented their different visions.

Chalkley (1968) also points out at the outset that development journalism is not for the elite but for the ordinary people. Therefore, the development journalist should use simple terms and avoid jargon. Chalkley, the practitioner, clearly did not envisage his construct as "government-say-so journalism," as libertarian defenders later branded it. Its intent, Chalkley (1975) has said, is not the retailing of government rallying cries, but rather "the formation of a new class of newspaper and broadcasting and magazine reporters who were fully trained and informed in the general economic field, as specialists" (p. 27).

Elsewhere, I have described developmental journalism as an integral part of a new journalism that involves "analytical interpretation, subtle investigation, constructive criticism and sincere association with the grass-roots (rather than with the elite)" (Gunaratne, 1978b, p. 5). I have argued that developmental journalism is not compatible with either the libertarian concept, which defines the function of the mass media as providing information and entertainment, or the authoritarian concept, which stifles "criticism of political machinery and the officials in power" and imposes a "top-down approach to problem solving" (p. 5). This view of the construct, however, has fallen on deaf ears among the libertarian defenders.

Aggarwala (1978) has pointed out that Western critics have erroneously equated development-oriented news with government-controlled news. He argues that the development news beat involves reporting on the relevance of development projects to national and local needs, on the differences between planned schemes and their actual implementation, and on the differences between projects' actual impacts on people and the impacts claimed by government officials. Ogan (1982) describes developmental journalism as the critical examination, evaluation, and reporting of the relevance, enactment, and impact of development programs by a mass media independent of the government. Fair (1988) conceptualizes developmental journalism as the reporting of news that relates to the primary, secondary, or tertiary needs of a country's population; that satisfies the needs of a country's population and contributes to self-reliance; and that is related to development or to social, economic, or political problems.

The thrust of developmental journalism embodied in scholarly analyses, or as practiced by alternative news services such as Inter Press Service, Depthnews, Gemini, and South-North News, reflects the Hutchins Commission's view of social responsibility. As Ali (1996) comments, "The concept of development[al] journalism is good, and always was, so it is a pity it became embroiled in the acrimonious debate surrounding the New World Information Order" (p. 30).

Frederick (1993) agrees that developmental journalism does not mean government-controlled news, as some critics maintain. He notes that supporters of NWICO have argued that "the role of journalism and the style of reporting must be different in the Third World because of the difference in the level of development and the dissimilar social and historical conditions" (p. 134). The goal has been to harness communication and information to the needs of economic and social development.

Edeani (1993) makes a distinction between developmental and development journalism. Quoting Ogan (1982), Edeani says that *developmental* journalism is "a government controlled form of communication," whereas *development* journalism is independent, socially responsible, and interpretive. In Edeani's view, all journalists—conventional, developmental, and development—are "engaged in development journalism; the only thing is they are engaged in it in varying degrees in accordance with their different levels of commitment to the values of development journalism and their equally dissimilar orientations to their professional roles" (p. 133). Edeani also attributes his negative definition of *development[al]* journalism to Kunczik (1988), who identifies its function as "spreading government news" (p. 84). In this essay I have elected to disregard such belabored distinctions because of the confusion they have caused. I presume that "government-say-so journalism" belongs to either the Communist or the authoritarian typology.

McKay (1993) traces the origins of developmental journalism to the print media associated with private or nongovernmental organizations in India and the Philippines. Such practice of developmental journalism had started well before it got its name in the mid-1960s. McKay says that the original developmental journalists were "committed to playing a more active role actually pressing for change, and this marked the departure from the Western notion of objective reporting" (p. 239). The work of Depthnews, which the Press Foundation of Asia set up in 1969, and Inter Press Service, the original Third World service set up in 1964, exemplifies the kind of developmental journalism envisaged by the concept's original thinkers and practitioners.

Hachten (1992) and his student Stevenson (1994), however, provide a negative definition of developmental journalism. Both clearly see the development concept as akin to authoritarian and Communist concepts. Hachten (1992) asserts that the development concept entails a situation in which the government mobilizes all the mass media; the media, therefore, cannot challenge authority; information becomes the property of the state; civil liberties, including freedom of expression, are irrelevant; and the government controls the flow of news (p. 35). Stevenson (1994) says that because the government mobilizes the mass media as agents of change under the development concept, developmental journalism is related more closely to the Communist system than to the authoritarian (p. 242). Thus he cites the *China Daily* and the *Pyongyang Times* as examples of purveyors of protocol news, the extreme of development news. Lambeth (1995) simply repeats Hachten's view that a "developmental press is most likely controlled by government or a political party," and that its "stated policies are most often aimed at the development of the nation's economic infrastructure, internal political unification, and the alleviation of hunger, illiteracy, and ill health" (p. 15).

Because of the negative connotations associated with the term *developmental journalism,* Shah (1996) has suggested its replacement with *emancipatory journalism,* a term that would facilitate recognition of the concept as "a role for journalists as participants in a process of progressive social change" (p. 144). He makes this point in the context of his view that "communication can contribute to participatory democracy, security, peace, and other humanistic principles that are at the core of the discourse on modernity" (p. 144). Emancipatory journalism "requires not only provision of socially relevant information but also journalistic activism in challenging and changing oppressive structures" (p. 145). It gives individuals in communities marginalized by modernization "a means of voicing critique and articulating alternative visions of society" (p. 145). Furthermore, it encourages "journalists to abandon the role of neutral observer while reporting in a manner that is thorough, deeply researched, and historically and culturally grounded, and that promotes social change in favor of the dispossessed" (p. 145).

If one were to conceptualize a contemporary framework for developmental journalism, taking into consideration the discussion that has gone on for well over a quarter century, one might take into consideration the 10 proposals for a development-oriented news media put forth by Galtung and Vincent (1992). The task of the journalist, these authors argue, is to unravel the threads of the development drama that takes place both in the center and on the periphery, pick them out of the intricate web of relationships, and "hold them up in the sunlight, and demonstrate the connections to readers, listeners and viewers," as Inter Press Service attempts to do at present (p. 146). Galtung and Vincent point out the inherent drama in development, democracy, and participation, all of which are interconnected. "The problem, however, is that when this drama is written out, the underlying text tends to be about the same in all cases: imperialism, exploitation and other 'leftist' themes" (p. 150). They outline their 10 proposals as follows:

1. *"Whenever there is a reference to development, try to make it concrete in terms of concrete human beings"* (p. 151). Thus they urge journalists to relate development to people. Journalists can discuss the human needs for *"survival, well-being, identity and freedom"* (p. 151) in terms of age, gender, race, class, and nation. They should report people as "subjects, actors, and agents" rather than as objects or victims with "needs deficits" (p. 152). They should "define problems and solutions as clearly as possible," taking into consideration ecological balance as well (p. 152).

2. A "development-oriented mass media should *focus not only on the economics of development, but also on military, political and cultural aspects*" (p. 154). Thus developmental journalism has to focus on more than economics, because all aspects—military power, political power, cultural power, and so on—have to do with development in one way or another. Journalists should get people to "reveal their inner agenda" because that constitutes drama that would make journalism "more similar to literature" (p. 155).

3. *Mere economic growth data are not adequate without accompanying dispersion data.* Journalists must look at the income of the "bottom 50 percent, or 10 percent," as well as of the "top 5 percent, or 1 percent" (p. 156).

4. *"Focus on relations, not only differences; and do so not only within countries, but also between countries"* (p. 156). Thus journalists must cover both differences and relations. They must substantiate the relational aspect between the rich and the poor: how, for instance, wages may be frozen but not prices, so that those who live from movable prices for their goods and services benefit, whereas people on fixed wages do not.

5. *"A development-oriented press would do well to focus on the totality of concrete life situations"* (p. 159). This means focusing on various people's life situations, as when British television took up the development problematic by selecting and reporting on a family unit from each of five world regions to represent the well-to-do, the middle class, the working class, the poor, and the dirt poor.

6. *"A development-oriented journalism would never forget the dimension of democracy"* (p. 160). The media must report what the system is doing. "Democracy can only function when there is a free flow of information between people, the system, and the media. Using the media to *make the people visible,* both as objects and as subjects, becomes one task. Using them to *expose the system* through investigative reporting is the second. Using the media to expose the media that fail to do their job is the third" (p. 160). The development journalist may have to do investigative reporting more subtly where such an activity may antagonize government sources; reporters can contrast government statements "with development reality without necessarily implying that there is a link between the two" (p. 162).

7. "There is always the possibility of *reporting about development, not critically in terms of problems, but constructively in terms of positive programs"* (p. 162). "Success stories may contribute to a general sense of optimism that might generate more momentum for democracy and development" (p. 162). People in similar situations elsewhere can benefit from such success stories if the reports are adequately concrete (p. 162).

8. *Allow the "people" to talk.* This means giving a voice to the people. A useful approach is for journalists to sit down with people from high to low strata and ask them to discuss the meaning of development, thereby generating "an enormous range of visions" as well as "how-to" insights (p. 163). Thus media should give people a voice *as experts* "through talented interviewing, in line with the seven preceding ideas" (p. 164). Community cable television channels in the United States enable this to happen to some extent.

9. "Go one step further, and *let the people to some extent run the media"* (p. 164). This means giving people some media control. Letters to the editor and the op-ed pages have space constraints. The next stage is to let people contribute to much of the newspaper, or produce broadcast television programs, thereby enabling them to use their own knowledge, experience, and expertise. The extent to which this happens can become a criterion of mass media quality in a country.

10. *"Let people run more of society, . . . and then report on what happens"* (p. 164). This is what ought to happen in a democracy. People's movements and organiza-

tions do precisely this. Development-oriented media should report more on what popular movements are doing—not only their successes, but their failures too.

Although no definition of developmental journalism may satisfy everyone, Galtung and Vincent's (1992) 10 proposals, as well as Shah's (1996) thinking on emancipatory journalism, provide a reasonable framework for understanding the essentials of the concept. This framework will enable us to compare developmental journalism with its newborn cousin that calls itself *public journalism.*

Intellectual Antecedents

The practice of developmental journalism in South and Southeast Asia in the 1960s preceded the NWICO debate, which caused the politicization of the concept. The social responsibility theory of the press, resulting from the 1947 Hutchins Commission report (Siebert et al., 1956), is a clear intellectual antecedent of the developmental journalism concept. In fact, the social responsibility theory clearly influenced the philosophy that Schramm (1964) expounds in his seminal book on mass media and national development, which became both a technical manual for communication development and a bully pulpit promoting the use of mass media for development.

The work of Rostow (1960) and Lerner (1958) also coincided with the emergence of the developmental journalism concept. These authors, as well as Schramm, undoubtedly had a contemporaneous influence on the concept. Rostow argued that change in Europe had evolved slowly until a critical mass of people and resources reached a takeoff point, at which time economic growth became self-sustaining. Lerner, who studied the traditional societies in the Middle East, found some of the same patterns that Rostow found in Europe, but with a difference: Mass media seemed to be accelerating the change and replacing some of the traditional agents of cultural influence. Lerner's *dominant paradigm* asserts that the mass media, along with urbanization and literacy, produced the critical mass of *modernity* that brought developing countries to the takeoff point of self-sustaining economic and social growth. Mass media enabled people to develop *empathy,* a key element of Lerner's formulation. Schramm asserted that the mass media could be the "great multiplier" in bringing about modernization (Stevenson, 1994).

The contemporaneous work of Freire (1974), a Brazilian thinker and philosopher, appears also to have influenced the Third World communication scholars engaged in promoting participatory communication in rural societies. Freire's thinking is also consistent with that of developmental or public journalists who take an active role in solving community problems. A Deweyan streak runs through Freire's view of communication: "The world of human beings is a world of communication. As a conscious being . . . the human being acts, thinks and speaks on and about this reality, which is the mediation between him or her and other human beings who also act, think and speak" (p. 137).

Nyirenda (1996) interprets this in relation to how extension agents (for whom we may substitute developmental or public journalists) should choose communication to help solve community problems. First, the journalist must understand the linguistic signs of the community participants for successful engagement in dialogue. Second, the journalist should be aware of the worldview of the community and the realities of community life.

If indeed the proponents of the social responsibility concept were the intellectual precursors of developmental journalism, then one can rightly argue that those who influenced the formulation of the social responsibility concept (and the contemporary public journalism concept) also had an intellectual impact on developmental journalism. This chain of events harks back to the contributions of Dewey, Mead, and Park as well.

We may also justifiably consider the communication principles of the East derived from the philosophic traditions of Buddhism, Hinduism, Confucianism, Taoism, Shintoism, and Islam as having facilitated the concept of developmental journalism in South, Southeast, and East Asia. These principles recognize the following: the central role that emotion plays in communication; the importance of human relationships, including preference for authority; the ultimate wholeness or unity of disparate parts; the collective consequences of action; and reliance on intuitive perception (Gunaratne, 1991).

Reaction to the Capitalism of the 1960s

The NWICO debates were a response to the situation of developing countries in the middle of the Cold War and the information inequalities of the world at large. The nonaligned movement gathered momentum as Western colonialism crumbled across the continents, creating a large number of economically poor nations. These nations realized that the former colonial powers, headed by the United States, continued to dominate the global economic and information structures, thereby making political independence somewhat meaningless. A center-periphery structure of the world had emerged that prompted some scholars to formulate *dependence theory* in the 1960s (Frank, 1993, p. 12). The second global superpower, the Soviet Union, was sympathetic to the plight of the Third World but powerless against the economic and communication might of the West.

Developmental journalism, a significant facet of NWICO, was a reaction to the occidental news values (Gunaratne, 1992) that had created an unbalanced global news flow favoring Western news and views. Those news values emphasized elite nations, elite people, personalization, and negativity (Galtung & Vincent, 1992, p. 50). As Somavia (1976) pointed out in an influential essay, the Western mass media and the giant transnational wire services—Associated Press, United Press International, Reuters, and Agence France-Presse—were treating news as a commodity, not as a social good (Gunaratne, 1978a, 1982). Capitalism, on a global scale, had created a news structure that was inimical to the development aspirations of the majority of humanity. The defenders of the libertarian concept (and the First Amendment), however, saw little merit in the concept of news as a social good, the very justification for developmental journalism. They were more concerned with the free flow of news in the global marketplace.

In the developing countries themselves, concerned scholars, not just politicians, expressed dissatisfaction with the libertarian practice of journalism. For instance, as far back as 1960, A. J. Wilson (1960), a Sri Lankan political scientist, complained about "the vast engines that controlled opinion today." He asserted that "experience of the working of the daily press in this country especially since 1956 has revealed how easy it is to disrupt a government by the pillorying of its leaders, by magnifying completely out of proportion the activities of communal extremists," and noted that "if freedom of the press tends to disrupt national unity, if such freedom is utilized to promote civil commotion and conflict between communities, religious or racial, it might become necessary for the state to introduce restrictions which might help toward restoring order or promoting unity." He was, in effect, calling for a socially responsible developmental journalism against "the wholesale imitation of Western standards by our societies" (all quotes pp. 5-9; quoted in Gunaratne, 1975, p. 17).

On the global front, countries in the nonaligned movement, with the support of the Soviet Bloc, called for a New International Economic Order (NIEO) as well as a concomitant New World Information and Communication Order from the 1960s onward (Galtung & Vincent, 1992, pp. 18, 104). That reaction to the state of global capitalism in the 1960s antagonized the powerful defenders of capitalism, the United States and Great Britain. Both those countries quit their membership in UNESCO in the mid-1980s to protest UNESCO's support for NWICO (Gunaratne, 1987, 1993; Gunaratne & Conteh, 1988). Moreover, the United States reneged on its payment of dues to the United Nations, which adopted the NIEO resolutions in the mid-1970s.

The consensus resolution on NWICO that UNESCO adopted at the 1980 Belgrade conference, following the completion of the controversial MacBride Report, called on developing countries to make "their information and communication media suitable to their needs and aspirations," and to respect "the right of the public, of ethnic and social groups and of individuals to have access to information sources and to participate actively in the communication process." It urged all countries to find "diverse solutions to information and communication problems . . . because social, political, cultural and economic problems differ from one country to another and, within a given country, from one group to another" (Galtung & Vincent, 1992, pp. 99-100). These statements clearly favored the fostering of developmental or public journalism.

Earlier, at the 1978 Paris conference, UNESCO had adopted by acclamation its controversial mass media declaration calling for "a free flow and a wider and better balanced dissemination of information." It called on the mass media to "be responsive to concerns of peoples and individuals, thus promoting the participation of the public in the elaboration of information" (see Gerbner, Mowlana, & Nordenstreng, 1993, pp. 173-178). Its 11 articles implicitly back many of the elements of both developmental and public journalism.

The NWICO debate soured the taste for developmental journalism and the social responsibility concept on the part of the defenders of the libertarian concept. The U.S. National News Council, which criticized the U.S. media for their biased coverage of UNESCO, had to disband in the early 1980s for lack of media support (Gerbner, 1993, p. 115). Some U.S. scholars (e.g., Hachten, 1992; Stevenson, 1994) dropped the social responsibility concept from their press theory schema and adopted a so-called Western concept, which they equated with "a free or independent press" (Hachten, 1992, p. 19). They also confused developmental journalism with the authoritarian or Communist concept (Gunaratne, 1995). The environment was clearly hostile for the proponents of public journalism to claim any links to the Hutchins and MacBride recommendations.

In 1987, UNESCO itself abandoned its support for NWICO and developmental journalism in a failed attempt to entice the United States and Great Britain back to the fold (Gunaratne, 1994). The MacBride Round Table, a private group of concerned individuals, has met annually since 1989 to promote the goals of NWICO (Roach, 1996). The Round Table has chosen to promote two key concepts of the MacBride Report: the right to communicate and the democratization of communications, both vital elements of developmental and public journalism. The Round Table has also stressed the need for the mass media to promote peace, an essential tenet of the UNESCO mass media declaration. It has also taken up the issue of the need to control or provide sound alternatives to the giant transnational media corporations. In 1994, the Round Table constituted itself as a nongovernmental organization, with statutes and a founding seat in Dublin.

Summary

If one were to put together the ideas emerging from the foregoing review, developmental journalism would also appear as a pluralistic journalism based on the triangular interaction of *news, communication,* and *community* that emphasizes the following:

1. Developmental journalism must go beyond the traditional *news* values that Galtung and Vincent (1992) say are based on "occidental cosmology" (p. 13). News values must encompass the "promotion" of developmental issues and possible solutions. News should focus on the primary, secondary, and tertiary

needs of ordinary people rather than the elite. The relevance of development to national and local needs is newsworthy. News includes the critical examination, evaluation, and reporting of the relevance, enactment, and impact of development. This boils down to unraveling the threads of the development drama. Success stories are also newsworthy.

2. The model of *communication* relating to developmental communication ought to be the bottom-up type that allows the "people" at the grass roots to talk. Journalism must give individuals a voice to articulate "alternative visions of society." The linear model of communication is less relevant to the promotion of development, even though Eastern communication philosophy reflects respect for authority.

3. The *community* is what matters in development. Let the "people" run more of society and, to some extent, the media, because the dimension of democracy is so important. The journalist should be an active community participant in social change. He or she cannot be a neutral observer who adheres to objectivity, but should be "committed to playing a more active role actually pressing for change" (McKay, 1993, p. 239). The journalist must relate development to people and focus on relations and the totality of concrete life situations. He or she must go well beyond economics and bring out the inherent drama in development, democracy, and participation.

This summary and the one offered at the end of the preceding section make clear the common elements of developmental journalism and public journalism. However, to gain a holistic view of the historical links of these concepts to the Hutchins Commission (CFP, 1947), one must examine the social responsibility concept in some detail.

THE SOCIAL RESPONSIBILITY CONCEPT

Grosswiler (1995) observes that before the emergence of the Third World, noninternational groups of critics had addressed issues relating to the content, control, and currents of international and intercultural communication. The Hutchins Commission, a brainchild of media magnate Henry Luce, was one such group whose recommendations, though mostly concerned with the U.S. media, also touched on international communication. This group "sought to persuade the media to be more responsible and fair in carrying out their obligations to society, including the preservation of world peace" (p. 110).

Mehra (1986) draws attention to the fact that the Hutchins Commission called for improved communication structures, fewer political and economic obstructions, and more accurate, representative, and higher-quality reports of global information. The commission called for government and media committees to fill the void where commercial media interests failed to present balanced and comprehensive information. It suggested a public service function of private industry, with a government undertaking as a last resort.

Furthermore, it suggested setting up a foreign correspondents' organization that would have authority to implement a binding code of ethics. The commission also suggested the establishment of an independent unit within UNESCO to monitor abuses. These issues became important to the subsequent NWICO debate as well.

Nordenstreng et al. (1986) have pointed out the international aspects of the Hutchins Commission's report, particularly its call for special attention to the need to report the "truth about the fact" (CFP, 1947, p. 22) in international news and the need to project representative pictures of different cultures and nations without stereotyping.

With regard to the U.S. role in international communication, the Hutchins Commission suggested that the U.S. government should use its own media to inform the public of U.S. policies when private media are unwilling to supply U.S. information abroad (CFP, 1947). Stating that the mass media should remain a private industry with a public interest, the commission urged the media to elevate rather than degrade public wants and to accept the responsibilities of common carriers of information and discussion. It urged the public to recognize the crucial role of the media in world crisis and said that adults must "learn to live together in peace" in a "world on the brink of suicide" (CFP, 1947, p. 99) in the aftermath of Word War II. It urged the public to create nonprofit institutions to ensure the needed supply, variety, quality, and quantity of media services. It proposed that a nongovernmental independent agency could report annually on media performance, including minority access and international cooperation regarding the picture of life presented in the U.S. media.

Siebert et al. (1956) point out that the mid-20th-century conditions demanded "of the mass media a new and different kind of social responsibility. This realization came about the time that people began to measure and assess the 'communication revolution' through which they were passing" (p. 4). Thus emerged the new libertarian concept known as the social responsibility theory of the press.

A Loose Definition

The social responsibility theory of the press accepts the six functions that libertarian theory ascribes to the press but, as T. Peterson explains, expresses "dissatisfaction with the interpretation of those functions by some media owners and operators and with the way the press has carried them out" (in Siebert et al., 1956, p. 74). The theory has this major premise: "Freedom carries concomitant obligations; and the press, which enjoys a privileged position . . . , is obliged to be responsible to society for carrying out certain essential functions of mass communication in contemporary society" (p. 74).

The six functions of the press are (a) to service the political system by providing information, discussion, and debate on public affairs; (b) to enlighten the public so as to make it capable of self-government; (c) to safeguard the rights of the individual by serving as a watchdog against government; (d) to service the economic system primarily by bringing together the buyers and sellers of goods and services through the medium of advertising; (e) to provide entertainment; and (f) to maintain its own financial self-sufficiency so as to be free from the pressures of special interests.

The theory of social responsibility asserts that the press has been deficient in performing the first three of its functions. It also says that the fourth function should not take "precedence over such other functions as promoting the democratic processes or enlightening the public" (Siebert et al., 1956, p. 74)—something on which both developmental journalism and public journalism would agree. It further asserts that the fifth function should relate to "good" entertainment. With regard to the sixth function, it "would exempt certain individual media from having to earn their way in the market place" (p. 74).

The Hutchins Commission, whose work T. Peterson (in Siebert et al., 1956) uses to elaborate on the social responsibility theory, called on the media to (a) provide "a truthful, comprehensive and intelligent account of the day's events in a context which gives them meaning" (p. 87); (b) serve as "a forum for the exchange of comment and criticism" (p. 89); (c) project "a representative picture of the constituent groups in society" (p. 91); (d) be responsible for "the presentation and clarification of the goals and values of the society" (p. 91); and (e) provide "full access to the day's intelligence" (p. 91).

Intellectual Antecedents

Coleman (1996) points out that the philosophy behind the social responsibility theory is akin to Dewey's proposal of the role of the press in helping to build a more populist and tolerant society. She says that repeatedly in history, Dewey's path has been the road not taken. Lippmann's (1923) order of the press won the day over Dewey's response to it when it was proposed in the 1920s. Coleman notes: "Dewey's ideas were then revived during the era of social responsibility theory. Some of his ideas were adopted but his theory was not wholeheartedly embraced" (pp. 3-4). McMillan et al. (1996) agree that the American political system has consolidated Lippmann's notion of technocratic expertise while rejecting Dewey's notions of organic involvement, which public journalism (as well as social responsibility theory) clearly espouses.

T. Peterson (in Siebert et al., 1956) mentions that the elements of the social responsibility theory grew out of the ideas of many people, and that the emerging theory was "largely a grafting of new ideas onto traditional theory" (p. 75). Especially important were the work of Hutchins Commission member Hocking (1947) and the contemporaneous work of the Royal Commission on the Press (1949) in Britain. Irwin's (1911) criticism of the press also had a bearing. Among other things, Irwin criticized the commercial nature of the newspaper.

The intellectual climate of the first half of the 20th century also seems to have favored the growth of a theory such as social responsibility. The libertarian theory, which had accommodated itself to the worldview of the Enlightenment, seems to have been at odds with the emergent worldview of the mid-20th century. Jensen (1950) has written that "the revolution in contemporary thought" had precipitously undermined "the philosophical foundations of the traditional concept of freedom of the press" (p. 405). The "idea of evolution and the dynamic concepts of modern physics" had wrecked the Newtonian ideas, while "contemporary economists" had repudiated classical laissez-faire economics, thereby making the Miltonian doctrine of the "self-righting process" also suspect (p. 406).

In the discussion of public journalism above, we saw the complementarity of the thinking of Dewey, Mead, and Park. Therefore, it is reasonable to presume that the latter two also provided intellectual backing for the social responsibility theory. Furthermore, Coleman (1996) points out that the social responsibility theory's view of negative liberty as insufficient also agrees with the philosophies of Arendt, Dewey, and Habermas.

Reaction to the Capitalism of the Late 1940s

The Hutchins Commission report that helped to formulate the social responsibility theory of the press was a response to the immediate postwar situation in the United States and the degree of concentration of the press on the eve of the introduction of television (CFP, 1947).

Siebert et al. (1956) have observed that the state of U.S. capitalism had taken such a turn that "it was no longer easy to enter the publishing business or to operate a newspaper or a radio station" (p. 4). These units had grown larger, requiring huge investments to own and manage the business. Concentration had decimated the small media units that had represented different viewpoints. Less than 7% of the daily newspaper towns in the nation had competing dailies. Three television networks, four radio networks, and three wire services shaped a large part of the information that people received. The few powerful rulers of the press rigorously protected the press against government interference. The "free marketplace of ideas," as defined by Mill and Jefferson, was in danger. The Hutchins Commission observed: "Protection against government is not now enough to guarantee that a man who has something to say shall have a chance to say it. The owners and managers of the press determine which persons, which facts, which versions of these facts, shall reach the public" (quoted in Siebert et al., 1956, pp. 4-5).

Summary

The social responsibility theory of the press, which arose out of the intellectual ferment of the postwar United States, asserted that the power and near-monopoly position of the news media imposed on them "an obligation to be socially responsible" (Siebert et al., 1956, p. 5). Furthermore, it asserted that such responsibility required the media to present all sides fairly, so "the public has enough information to decide" (p. 5). It also asserted that if the media failed to assume such a responsibility, some other agency of the public may have to enforce it.

Analyzed as a pluralistic journalism based on the triangular interaction of *news, communication,* and *community,* the social responsibility concept stands thus:

1. The concept implicitly asks for a redefinition of traditional *news* values when it blames the press for being "deficient" in performing the media's first three functions in preference to the fourth—advertising. It demands "truth about the fact" and more accurate, representative, and higher-quality reporting of different cultures and nations. In short, just as in the cases of developmental and public journalism, this theory pleads with the media to treat news as a social good rather than as a commodity.

2. Although the model of *communication* relating to this theory is not explicit, as it is in the cases of public and developmental journalism, it implores the media "to serve as a forum for exchange of comment and criticism" (Siebert et al., 1956, p. 89), to cherish rather than degrade public wants, to better serve the political system, and to enlighten the public on the democratic process. It also asks for improved communication structures. One can reasonably presume that such exhortations are meant to spur journalists to engage in conversation with the community.

3. The theory is quite clear about the media's relationship with the *community,* just as in the cases of public and developmental journalism. The active promotion of democratic participation receives close attention. The theory calls for a public committee to monitor the media for their *balanced* and comprehensive presentation of information. It demands that the media accurately portray the constituent groups of society, the varying minorities. It calls for an organization to enforce a journalistic code of ethics. It asks the media to clarify and present the goals and values of the community, and to goad the lethargic elements.

COMPARISON AND CONCLUSION

The Hutchins Commission

Parisi (1995) points out that although public journalists do not appear to recognize a connection with the Hutchins Commission's aims, "their work clearly enters similar territory" (p. 12). He says that the Hutchins Commission anticipated public journalism in its call for news reporting that projects "the opinions and attitudes of the groups in society to one another" and offers "a method of presenting and clarifying the goals and values of the society" (CFP, 1947, p. 22). The commission called for news to become "a truthful, comprehensive and intelligent account of the day's events in a context which gives them meaning" (CFP, 1947, p. 20; Siebert et al., 1956, p. 87), a matter of reporting not just "the fact truthfully" but "the truth about the fact" (CFP, 1947, p. 22; Siebert et al., p. 88). The commission's idea of news also focused on "the public good and on broad-based reporting about significant issues of the day" (Christians et al., 1993, p. 38).

The commission's second, third, and fourth recommendations—for the media to serve as "a forum for the exchange of comment and criticism" (Siebert et al., 1956, p. 89), to project "a representative picture of the constituent groups of society" (p. 91), and to be responsible for "the presentation and clarification of the goals and values of society" (p. 91)—are central to the philosophy that drives both developmental journalism and public journalism as well.

Moreover, the social responsibility theory of the press rests on a concept of positive liberty, unlike the libertarian theory, which was born of a concept of "negative liberty" (Siebert et al., 1956, p. 93). Both developmental journalism and public journalism clearly condone positive liberty. The libertarian theory, born at a time when the state was regarded as the chief foe of liberty, and the social responsibility theory differ in the views they take of the nature and functions of government: The latter holds that the "government should help society to obtain the services it requires from the mass media if a self-regulated press and self-righting features of community life are insufficient to provide them" (p. 95). On this matter, developmental journalism seems to be more in agreement with the social responsibility theory than does public journalism.

The social responsibility theory differs from the libertarian theory on the nature of freedom of expression as well. The latter considers freedom of expression a natural right, whereas the former considers it a "moral right" rather than an absolute right (Siebert et al., 1956, p. 96). Both developmental journalism and public journalism would tend to agree that freedom of expression is a moral right.

The social responsibility theory and the libertarian theory differ fundamentally in their views of the nature of humankind. The latter regards man as primarily a moral and rational being who will hunt for, and be guided by, the truth. The social responsibility theory views man as not so much irrational as lethargic. Thus "the more alert elements of the community must goad him into the exercise of his reason" (Siebert et al., 1956, p. 100). Both developmental journalism and public journalism assign to journalists the role of these "alert elements."

Finally, the social responsibility theory "puts far less faith than the libertarian theory in the efficacy of the self-righting process" (Siebert et al., 1956, p. 102). Both developmental journalism and public journalism would agree with that view. Shah (1996), on the other hand, points out that even though the social responsibility theory calls for the provision of socially relevant information, it does not call for "journalistic activism in challenging and changing oppressive structures" (p. 145), a task he associates with his new conceptualization of developmental journalism. However, one may as well argue that the "watchdog" function associated with the theory does not preclude journalists' active participation in the community.

The MacBride Commission

Several recommendations of the MacBride Commission, which espoused developmental journalism, also fit into public journalism (ICSCP, 1980). Whereas the Hutchins Commission addressed the U.S. media, the MacBride Commission addressed the international media. (I have already drawn attention to the international aspects of the Hutchins Commission; thus one cannot doubt the impact of the one on the other.) In previous work, I have pointed out that the *right to communicate* espoused by the MacBride Commission has a remarkable resemblance to the philosophies of both public and developmental journalism (Gunaratne, 1996b). The commission's Recommendation 54 says, "Communication needs in a democratic society should be met by the extension of specific rights such as the right to be informed, the right to inform, the right to privacy, the right to participate in public communication—all elements of a new concept, the right to communicate" (ICSCP, 1984, p. 216; Traber & Nordenstreng, 1992, p. 60).

This right equates with the espousal of a "conversational commons." In fact, this stands out as the major difference between developmental or public journalism and traditional journalism, which relies heavily on elite sources. Participatory democracy is meaningless without the right to communicate. The social responsibility theory implicitly condones it when it calls on the mass media to project "a representative picture of the constituent groups in society."

Among the other most pertinent MacBride Commission recommendations that relate to public or developmental journalism are the following: Recommendation 22, which seeks the "promotion of dialogue for development as a central component of both communication and development policies" (ICSCP, 1984, p. 202; Traber & Nordenstreng, 1992, p. 52); and Recommendation 23, which calls on the media to adapt prevailing news values and practices "to be more receptive to development needs and problems" (ICSCP, 1984, p. 202; Traber & Nordenstreng, 1992, p. 52). These two denote the importance the commission attached to the integration of communication in development. It considered communication to be a "a major development resource, a vehicle to ensure real political participation in decision making, a central information base for defining policy options, and an instrument for creating awareness of national policies" (ICSCP, 1984, p. 201; Traber & Nordenstreng, 1992, p. 52). These recommendations are compatible with the underlying assumptions of the social responsibility theory, as well as with the emphasis on "conversation" in public journalism to promote community problem solving. Just as Chalkley (1968) urges the development journalist to use simple language, the MacBride Commission points out the need for "the use of non-technical language and comprehensible symbols, images and forms to ensure popular understanding" (ICSCP, 1984, p. 202; Traber & Nordenstreng, 1992, p. 52).

The MacBride Commission's Recommendation 31 calls for noncommercial forms of mass communication that are in conformity with "the traditions, culture, development objectives and sociopolitical system of each country" (ICSCP, 1984, p. 205; Traber & Nordenstreng, 1992, p. 54). This too resembles the social responsibility theory, which also recognizes the need to "exempt certain individual media from having to earn their way in the market place" (Siebert et al., 1956, p. 74). Developmental journalism accommodates this view, whereas the concept of public journalism, insofar as its present proponents are concerned, seems content to accomplish its goals within the prevailing marketplace set-up in the United States.

The MacBride Commission's Recommendation 45 says that "conventional standards of news selection and reporting, and many accepted news values, need to be re-assessed if readers and listeners around the world are to receive a more faithful and comprehensive account of events, movements and trends in both developing and developed countries" (ICSCP, 1984, p. 211; Traber & Nordenstreng, 1992, p. 58). Both developmental journalism and public journalism point out the need to go well beyond traditional occidental news values to make the mass media more relevant to readers, viewers, and listeners in a democracy that promotes participation. The Hutchins Commission implicitly attacks these news values when it says that "the press has often paid more attention to the superficial and sensational than to the significant in its coverage of current happenings" (Siebert et al., 1956, p. 78).

Recommendation 63 of the MacBride Commission says that "those in charge of media should encourage their audiences to play a more active role in communication by allocating more newspaper space, or broadcasting time, for the views of individual members of the public or organized social groups" (ICSCP, 1984, p. 219; Traber & Nordenstreng, 1992, p. 63). The MacBride Commission has criticized the mass media for treating their audience members as "passive receivers of information" (ICSCP, 1984, p. 219; Traber & Nordenstreng, 1992, p. 63). Both developmental journalism and public journalism have a major aim: to make the "people" play an active role in communication. This is compatible with the social responsibility theory, which recognizes freedom of expression as a moral right of individuals.

The foregoing analysis confirms that public journalism is clearly a younger cousin of developmental journalism. The two seem to have separate identities because the term *developmental journalism* does not fit the cultural terminology applicable to advanced countries. On the other hand, some researchers have applied the term *development news* to news on race relations and similar matters in rural Georgia newspapers in the United States (e.g., Griswold &

Swenson, 1992; Swenson & Griswold, 1993). Both concepts aim to accomplish similar goals in dissimilar sociocultural environments. Despite pretenses, both have much to do with the ideas that were part of the erstwhile NWICO debates, as exemplified in the MacBride Commission's recommendations.

Public Journalism

This essay has already highlighted the three models of public journalism that have emerged in contemporary practice: those with respective emphasis on news coverage, community activism, and financial concerns (McMillan et al., 1996). Clearly, the last of these models is incompatible with the practice of developmental journalism. Although the social responsibility theory endorses the financial independence of media institutions, the exploitation of civic tactics for profiteering would not receive its nod.

Yin (1996) says that a comparison of the direction, characteristics, and practices of developmental journalism and public journalism shows a trend toward *activist* journalism, *involved* journalism, and journalism for predetermined ends. Such distinctions, however, require greater semantic clarity: How is *activist* different from *involved*? In broad terms, Yin observes, "Both development[al] journalism and public journalism belong to the social responsibility theory of the press as both consciously choose to do some good for the society and neither needs state or authority control of the press as a prerequisite to function." Both approaches, he points out, "undertake greater social responsibilities than the five requirements defined by the Hutchins Commission" (p. 19).

Going back to some of the specific elements of public journalism that E. Black (1996) has listed, one can further discern the similarities between public and developmental journalism and their relationship to social responsibility:

1. Public journalism invites "ordinary citizens back into public life by making their concerns the starting point of the debate" (E. Black, 1996, p. A8). Developmental journalism tries to achieve a similar objective by making the concerns of the large majority of underprivileged people in the backwoods of developing nations known to their national leaders and the world.

2. Public journalism overcomes "journalistic cynicism and acknowledge[s] the possibility that citizens working together might be able to solve some of society's problems" (p. A8). This happens to be the crux of developmental journalism as well. The mass media can and should play an active role in encouraging citizens to work together to solve their rural and urban problems.

3. Public journalism modifies "the rules of detachment by accepting that journalists have an interest in and responsibility for raising the level of public discourse and helping society find solutions to its problems" (p. A8). Again, this looks like the model of the development journalist. Detachment cannot achieve the objectives of developmental journalism; journalists have to play a catalytic role, stirring people up into being active participants in nation building.

Merritt's (1995b) list of the five mental shifts the conventional journalist must make in order to practice public journalism holds true for the practice of developmental journalism as well: moving "beyond the limited mission of telling the news to a broader mission of helping public life to go well, and act[ing] out that imperative" (p. 113); moving "from detachment to being a fair-minded participant in public life" (p. 113); moving "from worrying about proper separations to concerns with proper connections" (p. 113); moving "beyond only describing what is 'going wrong' to also imagining what 'going right' would be like" (p. 113); and moving "from people as consumers . . . to seeing them as a public, as potential actors in arriving at democratic solutions to public problems" (p. 114).

Finally, many of the techniques used in the practice of public journalism (Lambeth, 1994) are relevant also for developmental journalism: careful, timely, and sensitive listening to public needs; systematic consultation of the public by means of polls and focus groups; journalist-organized dialogue with panels of resource specialists chosen for their differing expertise and perspectives; media-sponsored public forums designed to deliberate on key issues; continuity of in-depth reporting on issues chosen independently by journalists for their fidelity to citizen concerns; and occasional cooperative projects by newspaper, radio, and/or television newsrooms. Although some of these techniques pertain to practices useful in advanced societies, development journalists may use them also, depending on the degrees of sophistication particular societies have reached.

Criticism

Public journalism has encountered much skepticism, with reactions such as the following: It endangers the credibility of newspapers because it repudiates the principles of objectivity and fairness that have been the lodestar of American journalism for half a century; it compromises enterprising, sustained, independent reporting; and it involves reader committees in deciding what goes into the newspaper, and thereby replaces objectivity with advocacy (Zang, 1995). One may recall similar accusations against developmental journalism, particularly associating it with the manipulations of authoritarian or Communist governments.

Shafer (1996) asserts that the interventionist nature of developmental journalism has run up against the professional beliefs and values of Filipino journalists. Therefore, he expects the same reaction toward public journalism when U.S. journalists perceive its interventionist nature, which requires practitioners to manipulate mass media messages and their audiences. However, Shafer sees developmental journalism as having "a more structuralist vision" than public journalism, which "appears to be much more micro-oriented" (p. 5). Contrary to my assessment in this essay, Shafer asserts that developmental journalism does "not hold democracy to be a critical or necessary element in the development process" (p. 5). (He does not, however, clarify the abstract term *democracy.*) He laments the lack of theory behind these two interventionist models. (In contrast, in this essay I have summarized the intellectual philosophy behind these models going back to Dewey and others.)

Conclusion

The summaries presented at the ends of the first three main sections of this essay—those dealing with public journalism, developmental journalism, and the social responsibility concept—clearly show the close interrelationships of these concepts. These interrelationships become further apparent when one examines specific points relating to their constituent elements.

First, all three concepts are in agreement that the mass media must go beyond traditional *news* values to provide more useful service to the community. Galtung and Vincent (1992) argue that the prevalent news values have resulted in very little coverage of "how structures are operating to produce . . . unhappy circumstances for poor people" (p. 51). Both public and developmental journalism explicitly aspire to solve this aspect of the "One Journalism," whereas the social responsibility concept does so implicitly.

Second, both public journalism and developmental journalism are founded on the Dewey-Mead-Park-Carey vision of *communication* as conversation. The participatory, bottom-up (nonlinear) model of communication endorsed by scholars who have written on communication and development is integral to both. Although the social responsibility concept is mute on this matter, its exhortation to improve communication structures implies its endorsement for journalists to engage in conversation with the community.

Third, just as public journalism is concerned with *community* building within the framework of democratic ideals, developmental journalism is concerned with public participation in nation building within the same framework. Developmental journalism also envisions a rational self-interest of doing well in political environments that ranges from authoritarianism to varying degrees of democracy. The social responsibility theory of the press, which views human beings as not so much irrational as lethargic, says that the more alert elements of the community must goad man into the exercise of his reason (Siebert et al., 1956, pp. 99-100). Both developmental journalism and public journalism assign to journalists the role of these "alert elements." If one were to place the three concepts—social responsibility, developmental journalism, and public journalism—in their historical context, one might reasonably conclude that the latter two reflect evolutionary extensions of the first, developed to repair the deficiencies of capitalist-oriented libertarianism, either globally or domestically, within the framework of democratic ideals.[5]

Contemporary scholars have critiqued *Four Theories of the Press* (Siebert et al., 1956) on the basis that the theories are founded on Western political theory that discounts the consensual and communal traditions of some societies, or because the theories fail to recognize the communication implications of the current technological revolution (Hasim, 1996a, 1996b; Mehra, 1989; Nerone, 1995).[6] The social responsibility concept has come under criticism as a mere "negotiated position" between Hocking (1947) and Chafee (1947) that inevitably contains inconsistencies and contradictions; Nerone et al. (1995) assert that its impact has been to endorse "the status quo by erecting standards of performance that can make monopoly media seem like the voice of the people, even as the media keep the people silent and stupid" (pp. 78-79).

Such criticism of the social responsibility concept seems too harsh, because those who formulated the concept never intended it as anything more than an experimental, new libertarianism that suited the American intellectual climate of the mid-20th century. They put together in their *developing theory* "all the essentials" that responsible editors and publishers had been advocating long before the Hutchins Commission (Siebert et al., 1956, p. 5). Members of the commission themselves were not in unanimous accord, because "some of them hugged tradition and others stood far from it" (p. 75). T. Peterson makes the following point: "It is important to remember that the social responsibility theory is still chiefly a *theory*. But as a theory it is important because it suggests a direction in which thinking about freedom of the press is heading. Then, too, some aspects of the theory have found their way into practice" (in Siebert et al., 1956, p. 75).

Thus the theory's formulators expected its evolution over time to suit historical circumstances. Developmental journalism and public journalism, which beefed up the rudimentary elements of the social responsibility theory, reflected that evolution at two historical points. These two approaches clarified the new libertarianism's "essentials" and filled the gaps on which the original theory was silent. Viewed in this light, their distinct similarities can be appreciated. The continuum will go on unless we have come to the end of history.

I began this essay with the thesis that the constituent elements of public journalism are not new. In the terms of a striking Persian metaphor, they constitute old wine in a new bottle. Like its two precursors, public journalism has targeted the lapses in the libertarian concept embodied in the First Amendment.

NOTES

1. This approach to the analysis of public journalism was sparked during the review process as I worked on this essay. I am indebted to the reviewer who challenged me to consider adopting this approach.

2. Several of the listed books in the Poynter Institute bibliography, however, do not relate directly to the public journalism concept itself. Of the 74 articles listed for the period 1990-1996, only 31 appeared during 1990-1994. Most of the listed articles are from two newspapers—the *New York Times* and *Washington Post*—and the following professional or other periodicals:

American Journalism Review, ASNE Bulletin, Communication, Communicator, CQ Researcher, Editor & Publisher, IRE Journal, Masthead, New Yorker, Nieman Reports, Presstime, Poynter Report, and *St. Louis Journalism Review.* A handful are from the following professional journals: *Critical Studies in Mass Communications, Journalism & Mass Communication Quarterly, Journalism Educator, Journal of Broadcasting & Electronic Media, Journal of Democracy, Journal of International Affairs,* and *Media Studies Journal.* No unpublished conference papers or articles from foreign publications are listed.

3. In addition to some of the publications mentioned in the Poynter bibliography, this list includes articles published in four other newspapers (*Boston Globe, Los Angeles Times, Miami Herald,* and *Virginian-Pilot*), in seven other magazines (*Center Magazine, Columbia Journalism Review, Forbes Media Critic, The Nation, National Civic Review,* and *National Journal*), and in one other academic quarterly (*Newspaper Research Journal*). It includes additional books as well.

4. According to Corrigan (1997), more than 200 U.S. daily newspapers have implemented public journalism projects; and journalism and communication departments, including those at Stanford University and University of Maryland, are teaching public journalism as a reporting methodology. Corrigan reports the results of a 1996 survey thus: "Survey results confirmed that the public journalism movement has had great success in 'getting on the radar screen' of both daily newspaper editors and professors in journalism and mass communication" (p. 1).

5. Jay Rosen (personal communication, February 13, 1997) asserts that the *movement* of public journalism is distinct because it "is primarily rooted in the efforts of reform-minded journalists around the country who agree that it is time for a change. If there is anything 'radical' or radically 'new' in public journalism, it is this: mainstream journalists are driving the car because they sense something wrong, dangerously adrift, in their craft. . . . the Hutchins and MacBride work did not have this element and neither did developmental journalism. . . . To put it another way, public journalism is not 'new,' but the movement in search of it is. Inherent in the idea is the effort to keep the language and the intellectual work close to the soul of the craft. Equally important is that the debate over the notion has taken place within the culture of the press, with heavyweights as well as ordinary foot soldiers divided in their views of the notion's validity."

6. As I have pointed out in previous work, the contemporary high-tech revolution connecting the estimated 9.4 million computers to an estimated worldwide population of 40 million has touched a mere 0.7% of the world's people (Gunaratne, 1996a). An estimated 60% of these computers are in the United States. Thus rewriting theories of the press to suit the technological revolution is a premature exercise unless those theories are intended to apply to the advanced world alone.

REFERENCES

Aggarwala, N. K. (1978, May-June). A Third World perspective on the news. *Freedom at Issue,* pp. 13-20.
Albers, R. R. (1996, July-August). The year of the voter. *Presstime,* pp. 23-27.
Ali, O. A. (1996). Roundtable. *Media Asia, 23*(1), 30, 32.
Anderson, R., Dardenne, R., & Killenberg, G. M. (1994). *The conversation of journalism: Communication, community and news.* Westport, CT: Praeger.
Arendt, H. (1958). *The human condition.* Chicago: University of Chicago Press.
Arendt, H. (1970). *On violence.* San Diego, CA: Harcourt Brace Jovanovich.
Arendt, H. (1987). *Between past and future.* Dallas: Penguin. (Original work published 1961)
Arendt, H. (1990). *On revolution.* New York: Viking. (Original work published 1963)
Barber, B. R. (1984). *Strong democracy: Participatory politics for a new age.* Berkeley: University of California Press.

Bishop, E. (1997, March). Doing journalism to "public journalism": A conversation with Post editor Cole Campbell. *St. Louis Journalism Review,* pp. 10-11.

Black, E. (1996, April 8). Journalism tests new definition of involvement. *The* (Minneapolis) *Star Tribune,* pp. A1, A8.

Black, J. (Ed.). (1996). *Mixed news: The public/civic/communitarian journalism debate.* Mahwah, NJ: Lawrence Erlbaum.

Brewer, M., & McCombs, M. (1996). Setting the community agenda. *Journalism & Mass Communication Quarterly, 73*(1), 7-16.

Broder, D. (1990, January 3). Democracy and the press. *Washington Post,* p. A15.

Broder, D. (1992, March). Campaign '92. *Quill,* pp. 8-9.

Campbell, C. C. (1995, April 9). We must discuss issues to ensure a stronger and less divisive society. *Virginian-Pilot,* p. A2.

Carey, J. W. (1969). The communications revolution and the professional communicator. *Sociological Review Monograph, 13,* 23-28.

Carey, J. W. (1975). A cultural approach to communication. *Communication, 2,* 1-22.

Carey, J. W. (1982). The mass media and critical theory: An American view. In M. Burgoon (Ed.), *Communication yearbook 6* (pp. 18-33). Beverly Hills, CA: Sage.

Carey, J. W. (1985). Overcoming resistance to cultural studies. In M. Gurevitch & M. R. Levy (Eds.), *Mass communication review yearbook 5* (pp. 23-26). Beverly Hills, CA: Sage.

Carey, J. W. (1987, March-April). The press and the public discourse. *Center Magazine,* pp. 4-16.

Carey, J. W. (1988). *Communication as culture: Essays in media and society.* Boston: Unwin Hyman.

Carey, J. W. (1989). Communication and the progressives. *Critical Studies in Mass Communication, 6,* 264-282.

Carey, J. W. (1993, Summer). The mass media and democracy: Between the modern and the postmodern. *Journal of International Affairs,* pp. 1-21.

Carey, J. W. (1995). The press, public opinion and public discourse. In T. L. Glasser & C. T. Salmon (Eds.), *Public opinion and the communication of consent* (pp. 373-402). New York: Guilford.

Case, T. (1994, November 12). Public journalism denounced. *Editor & Publisher,* p. 14.

Chafee, Z., Jr. (1947). *Government and mass communications* (2 vols.). Chicago: University of Chicago Press.

Chalkley, A. (1968). *A manual of development journalism.* Manila: Thomson Foundation/Press Foundation of Asia.

Chalkley, A. (1975, May). Development journalism is NOT "government-say-so journalism." *Media,* p. 27.

Chalkley, A. (1980). Development journalism: A new dimension in the information process. *Media Asia, 7,* 215-217.

Charity, A. (1995). *Doing public journalism.* New York: Guilford.

Charity, A. (1996, January-February). Reluctant sea change: Resources abound for journalists seeking information about public journalism's role. *Quill,* pp. 23-27.

Christians, C. G. (1995, August). *The common good in a global setting.* Paper presented at the annual meeting of the Association for Education in Journalism and Mass Communication, Washington, DC.

Christians, C. G., Ferre, J. P., & Fackler, P. M. (1993). *Good news: Social ethics and the press.* New York: Oxford University Press.

Clifton, D. (1994, March 6). Creating a forum to help solve community problems. *Miami Herald,* p. C4.

Coleman, R. (1996, August). *The intellectual antecedents of public journalism.* Paper presented at the annual meeting of the Association for Education in Journalism and Mass Communication, Anaheim, CA.

Commission on Freedom of the Press (CFP). (1947). *A free and responsible press.* Chicago: University of Chicago Press.

Conte, C. (1996, September 20). Civic journalism: Can press reforms revitalize democracy? *CQ Researcher,* pp. 817-840.

Corrigan, D. (1997, March). Racial pledges, gang summits, election forums: What actually makes a public journalism project? *St. Louis Journalism Review,* pp. 1, 8-9.

Cripe, D. (1997, Spring). The "new" journalism. *The Dow Jones Newspaper Fund Adviser Update,* pp. 1A-2A.

Denton, F., & Thorson, E. (1995). *Civic journalism: Does it work?* Washington, DC: Pew Center for Civic Journalism.

Dewey, J. (1916). *Democracy and education: An introduction to the philosophy of education.* New York: Free Press.

Dewey, J. (1927). *The public and its problems.* Denver: Allan Swallow.

Dewey, J. (1929). *Individualism, old and new.* New York: Capricorn.

Dewey, J. (1938). *Experience and education.* New York: Collier.

Dionne, E. J. (1991). *Why Americans hate politics.* New York: Simon & Schuster.

Dykers, C. R. (1995, August). *A critical review: Re-conceptualizing the relation of "democracy" to "news."* Paper presented at the annual meeting of the Association for Education in Journalism and Mass Communication, Washington, DC.

Edeani, D. O. (1993). Role of development journalism in Nigeria's development. *Gazette, 52,* 123-143.

Ettema, J. S., & Peer, L. (1995, August). *Good news from a bad neighborhood: A theoretical and empirical approach to civic journalism.* Paper presented at the annual meeting of the Association for Education in Journalism and Mass Communication, Washington, DC.

Fair, J. E. (1988). A meta-research case study of development journalism. *Journalism Quarterly, 65,* 165-170.

Fallows, J. (1996). *Breaking the news: How the media undermine American democracy.* New York: Pantheon.

Fishkin, J. S. (1995). *The voice of the people: Public opinion and democracy.* New Haven, CT: Yale University Press.

Fouhy, E. M. (1994, May). Is "civic" journalism the answer? *Communicator,* pp. 18-19.

Fouhy, E. M. (1995, August). A sense of community. *Communicator,* pp. 15-16.

Frank, A. G. (1993). No end to history! History to no end. In K. Nordenstreng & H. I. Schiller (Eds.), *Beyond national sovereignty: International communication in the 1990s* (pp. 3-27). Norwood, NJ: Ablex.

Frankel, M. (1995, May 21). Fix-it journalism. *New York Times,* sec. 6, p. 28.

Frederick, H. (1993). *Global communication and international relations.* Belmont, CA: Wadsworth.

Freire, P. (1974). *Education for critical consciousness.* London: Sheed & Ward.

Galtung, J., & Vincent, R. C. (1992). *Global glasnost: Toward a new world information and communication order?* Cresskill, NJ: Hampton.

Gardner, J. (1990). *On leadership.* New York: Free Press.

Gartner, M. (1995, November-December). Give me old-time journalism. *Quill,* pp. 66-68.

Gerbner, G. (1993). UNESCO in the U.S. press. In G. Gerbner, H. Mowlana, & K. Nordenstreng (Eds.), *The global media debate: Its rise, fall, and renewal* (pp. 111-121). Norwood, NJ: Ablex.

Gerbner, G., Mowlana, H., & Nordenstreng, K. (Eds.). (1993). *The global media debate: Its rise, fall, and renewal.* Norwood, NJ: Ablex.

Glaberson, W. (1994, October 3). The media business, a new press role: Solving problems. *New York Times,* p. D6.

Glasser, T. L. (1991). Communication and the cultivation of citizenship. *Communication, 12,* 235-248.

Golding, P., & Harris, P. (Eds.). (1997). *Beyond cultural imperialism: Globalization, communication and the new international order.* London: Sage.

Griswold, W. F., & Swenson, J. D. (1992). Development news in rural Georgia newspapers: A comparison with media in developing nations. *Journalism Quarterly, 69,* 580-590.

Grosswiler, P. (1995). Continuing media controversies. In J. C. Merrill (Ed.), *Global journalism: Survey of international communication* (3rd ed., pp. 103-120). White Plains, NY: Longman.

Gunaratne, S. A. (1975). *The taming of the press in Sri Lanka.* Lexington, KY: Association for Education in Journalism.

Gunaratne, S. A. (1978a). The background to the non-aligned news pool: Pros and cons and research findings. *Gazette, 24,* 20-35.

Gunaratne, S. A. (1978b). Media subservience and developmental journalism. *Communications and Development Review, 2*(2), 3-7.

Gunaratne, S. A. (1982). Reporting the Third World in the 1970s: A longitudinal content analysis of two Australian dailies. *Gazette, 29,* 15-29.

Gunaratne, S. A. (1987). Facts and fallacies on the withdrawals from UNESCO. *Australian Journalism Review, 9*(1-2), 65-82, 144.

Gunaratne, S. A. (1991). Asian approaches to communication theory. *Media Development, 38*(1), 53-55.

Gunaratne, S. A. (1992). Invading the privacy of mourners and victims. *Media Development, 39*(4), 11-13.

Gunaratne, S. A. (1993). UNESCO must recover its universality. *Media Development, 40*(2), 41-43.

Gunaratne, S. A. (1994). U.S. and U.K. re-entry into UNESCO (October 1995?): A reportorial description and a theoretical analysis. *Jurnal Komunikasi, 10,* 99-122.

Gunaratne, S. A. (1995). Books on global communication: A philosophical tussle. *Media Development, 42*(2), 44-47.

Gunaratne, S. A. (1996a, December 20). Are we witnessing start of technological imperialism? [Letter to the editor]. *The* (Fargo, ND) *Forum,* p. A4.

Gunaratne, S. A. (1996b). New thinking on journalism and news puts emphasis on democratic values. In Z. Bajka & J. Mikulowski-Pomorski (Eds.), *Valeriana: Essays on human communication* (pp. 182-197). Kraców, Poland: Osrodek Badan Prasoznawczych.

Gunaratne, S. A. (1996c). Old wine in a new bottle: Public versus developmental journalism. *AsiaPacific MediaEducator, 1*(1), 64-75.

Gunaratne, S. A., & Conteh, A. (1988). *Global communication and dependency: Links between NIEO and NWICO demands and the withdrawals from UNESCO.* Moorhead, MN: Moorhead State University.

Gunaratne, S. A., & Hasim, M. S. (1996). Social responsibility theory revisited: A comparative study of public journalism and developmental journalism. *Javnost—The Public, 3*(3), 97-107.

Habermas, J. (1975). *Legitimation crisis* (T. McCarthy, Trans.). Boston: Beacon.

Habermas, J. (1979). *Communication and the evolution of society* (T. McCarthy, Trans.). Boston: Beacon.

Habermas, J. (1987). *The theory of communicative action—lifeworld and system: A critique of functionalist reason* (Vol. 2, T. McCarthy, Trans.). Boston: Beacon.

Habermas, J. (1989). *Structural transformation of the public sphere* (T. Burger, Trans.). Cambridge: MIT Press. (Original work published 1962)

Habermas, J. (1990). *Moral consciousness and communicative action* (C. Lenhardt & S. W. Nicholson, Trans.). Cambridge: MIT Press.

Habermas, J. (1992). *Autonomy and solidarity* (rev. ed., P. Drews, Ed.). London: Verso.

Habermas, J. (1993). *Justification and application: Remarks on discourse ethics* (C. Cronin, Trans.). Cambridge: MIT Press.

Hachten, W. A. (1992). *The world news prism: Changing media of international communication* (3rd ed.). Ames: Iowa State University Press.

Harwood Group. (1993). *Meaningful chaos: How people form relationships with public concerns.* Dayton, OH: Kettering Foundation.

Hasim, M. S. (1996a). *Akhbar dan Kuasa: Perkembangan sistem akhbar di Malaysia sejak 1806* [Newspapers and power: Development of the press system in Malaysia since 1806]. Kuala Lumpur: Penerbit Universiti Malaya.

Hasim, M. S. (1996b, August 18-22). *Press theories and power.* Paper presented at the annual meeting of the International Association for Mass Communication Research, Sydney.

Heikkila, H., & Kunelius, R. (1996). Public journalism and its problems. *Javnost—The Public, 3*(3), 81-95.

Hocking, W. E. (1947). *Freedom of the press: A framework of principle.* Chicago: University of Chicago Press.

Hoyt, M. (1995, September-October). Are you, or will you ever be, a civic journalist? *Columbia Journalism Review,* pp. 27-33.

International Commission for the Study of Communication Problems (ICSCP). (1980). *Many voices, one world: Towards a new more just and more efficient world information and communication order.* Paris: UNESCO.

International Commission for the Study of Communication Problems (ICSCP). (1984). *Many voices, one world: Towards a new more just and more efficient world information and communication order* (condensed ed.). Paris: UNESCO.

Irwin, W. (1911, January 21-July 29). The American newspaper [Series of 15 articles]. *Collier's.*

Jayaweera, N., & Amunugama, S. (1987). *Rethinking development communication.* Singapore: Amic.

Jensen, J. W. (1950). Toward a solution of the problem of freedom of the press. *Journalism Quarterly, 27,* 399-408.

Jurkowitz, M. (1996, April). From the citizen up. *Forbes Media Critic,* pp. 75-83.

Kirsch, I. S., Jungeblut, A., Jenkins, L., & Kolstad, A. (1993). *Adult literacy in America: A first look at the results of the national adult literacy survey.* Washington, DC: U.S. Department of Education.

Kunczik, M. (1988). *Concepts of journalism North and South.* Bonn: Courier-Druck.

Lambeth, E. B. (1992a). *Committed journalism* (2nd ed.). Bloomington: Indiana University Press.

Lambeth, E. B. (1992b). The news media and democracy. *Media Studies Journal, 6*(4), 161-175.

Lambeth, E. B. (1994). [Review of the book *Good news, social ethics and the press*]. *Media Development, 41*(4), 50-51.

Lambeth, E. B. (1995). Global media philosophies. In J. C. Merrill (Ed.), *Global journalism: Survey of international communication* (3rd ed., pp. 3-18). White Plains, NY: Longman.

Lambeth, E. B. (1996). A bibliographic essay on civic/public journalism. *National Civic Review, 85*(1), 18-21.

Lambeth, E. B., & Aucoin, J. (1993). Understanding communities: The journalist as leader. *Journalism Educator, 48*(1), 12-19.

Lambeth, E. B., & Craig, D. (1995). Civic journalism as research. *Newspaper Research Journal, 16*(2), 148-160.

Lauterer, J. (1995). *Community journalism: The personal approach.* Ames: Iowa State University Press.

Lee, E. (1996). *The idea of public journalism: Annotated bibliography.* Unpublished manuscript, Stanford University.

Lerner, D. (1958). *The passing of traditional society; Modernizing the Middle East.* Glencoe, IL: Free Press.

Lippmann, W. (1923). *Public opinion.* New York: Free Press.

Mathews, D. (1994). *Politics for people: Finding a responsible public voice.* Urbana: University of Illinois Press.

McKay, F. J. (1993). Development journalism in an Asian setting: A study of Depthnews. *Gazette, 51,* 236-251.

McKnight, D. (1997, February). Public journalism: A response to the crisis in public life. *Australian Press Council News,* pp. 1-2.

McMillan, S., Guppy, M., Kunz, W., & Reis, R. (1996, August). *A defining moment: Who says what about public journalism.* Paper presented at the annual meeting of the Association for Education in Journalism and Mass Communication, Anaheim, CA.

Mead, G. H. (1934). *Mind, self, and society: From the standpoint of a social behaviorist.* Chicago: University of Chicago Press.

Mead, G. H. (1956). *The social psychology of George Herbert Mead.* Chicago: University of Chicago Press.

Mehra, A. (1986). *Free flow of information: A new paradigm.* Westport, CT: Greenwood.

Mehra, A. (Ed.). (1989). *Press systems in Asian states.* Singapore: Amic.

Merritt, D. (1994, October 30). Public journalism: A movement toward a basic cultural change. *Wichita Eagle,* p. A17.

Merritt, D. (1995a, July 1). The misconception about public journalism. *Editor & Publisher,* pp. 80, 68.

Merritt, D. (1995b). *Public journalism and public life: Why telling the news is not enough.* Mahwah, NJ: Lawrence Erlbaum.

Merritt, D. (1995c). Public journalism: Defining a democratic art. *Media Studies Journal, 9*(3), 125-132.

Merritt, D. (1996, July-August). Missing the point. *American Journalism Review,* pp. 29-31.

Meyer, P. (1995, November-December). Defining public journalism: Discourse leading solutions. *IRE Journal,* pp. 3-5.

Nerone, J. C. (Ed.). (1995). *Last rights: Revisiting four theories of the press.* Urbana: University of Illinois Press.

Nerone, J. C., Berry, W. E., Christians, C., Helle, S. J., Liebovich, L. W., & Rotzoll, K. B. (1995). Social responsibility theory. In J. C. Nerone (Ed.), *Last rights: Revisiting four theories of the press* (pp. 77-124). Urbana: University of Illinois Press.

Nordenstreng, K., Manet, G. E., & Kleinwachter, W. (1986). *New international information and communication order sourcebook.* Prague: International Organization of Journalists.

Nyirenda, J. E. (1996). The relevance of Paulo Freire's contributions to education and development in present day Africa. *Africa Media Review, 10*(1), 1-20.

Ogan, C. L. (1982). Development journalism/communication: The status of the concept. *Gazette, 29,* 3-13.

Parisi, P. (1995, August). *Toward a "philosophy of framing": Narrative strategy and public journalism.* Paper presented at the annual meeting of the Association for Education in Journalism and Mass Communication, Washington, DC.

Park, R. E. (1940). News as a form of knowledge: A chapter in the sociology of knowledge. *American Journal of Sociology, 45,* 669-686.

Park, R. E. (1955). *Society: Collective behavior, news and opinion, sociology and modern society.* Glencoe, IL: Free Press.

Peterson, I. (1996, March 4). Civic-minded pursuits gain ground at newspapers. *New York Times,* p. D5.

Peirce, N. R. (1994, July 2). Civic journalism: A new genre. *National Journal, 26,* 1585.

Poynter Institute for Media Studies. (1996). *Bibliography: Public journalism* (D. B. Shedden, Comp.) [On-line]. Available HTTP://www/poynter.org/research/biblio/bib_pj.html

Putnam, R. (1993). *Making democracy work: Civic traditions in modern Italy.* Princeton, NJ: Princeton University Press.

Raines, H. (1996, February 25). The Fallows fallacy. *New York Times,* sec. 4, p. 14.

Reider, R. (1995, December). Public journalism; Stop the shooting. *American Journalism Review,* p. 6.

Remnick, D. (1996, January 29). Scoop. *New Yorker,* pp. 38-42.

Roach, C. (1996). The MacBride Round Table on communication. *Media Development, 43*(3), 19-20.

Rosen, J. (1991a). Making journalism more public. *Communication, 12,* 267-284.

Rosen, J. (1991b, October). To be or not to be? Newspapers may be our last hope for recreating public life in our communities. *ASNE Bulletin*, pp. 16-19.

Rosen, J. (1992a, March). Community action: Sin or salvation? *Quill*, pp. 30-32.

Rosen, J. (1992b, November-December). Discourse. *Columbia Journalism Review*, pp. 34-35.

Rosen, J. (1992c). Politics, vision and the press: Toward a public agenda for journalism. In J. Rosen & P. Taylor, *The new news v. the old news: The press and politics in the 1990s* (pp. 3-33). New York: Twentieth Century Fund.

Rosen, J. (1993a). *Community connectedness: Passwords for public journalism*. St. Petersburg, FL: Poynter Institute for Media Studies.

Rosen, J. (1993b, November-December). Public life and the press: Building a new house for journalism ethics. *Quill*, pp. 27-28.

Rosen, J. (1994a). Making things more public: On the political responsibility of the media intellectual. *Critical Studies in Mass Communication, 11*, 363-388.

Rosen, J. (1994b). *Public journalism as a democratic art*. Unpublished manuscript, New York University, Project on Public Life and the Press.

Rosen, J. (1995a). Foreword. In A. Charity, *Doing public journalism* (pp. v-vi). New York: Guilford.

Rosen, J. (1995b, May-June). Public journalism: A case for public scholarship. *Change*, pp. 34-38.

Rosen, J. (1995c, November-December). What should we be doing? *IRE Journal*, pp. 6-8.

Rosen, J. (1996a). *Getting the connections right: Public journalism and the troubles in the press*. New York: Twentieth Century Fund.

Rosen, J. (1996b, Winter-Spring). Public journalism is a challenge to you (yes, you). *National Civic Review*, pp. 3-6.

Rosen, J. (1996c). Public scholarship. In D. W. Brown (Ed.), *Higher education exchange* (pp. 23-38). Dayton, OH: Kettering Foundation.

Rosen, J. (1996d, February 19). Take back the campaign. *The Nation*, p. 10.

Rosen, J., & Merritt, D. (1994). *Public journalism: Theory and practice*. Dayton, OH: Kettering Foundation.

Rostow, W. R. (1960). *The stages of economic growth*. Cambridge: Cambridge University Press.

Royal Commission on the Press. (1949). *Report*. London: His Majesty's Stationery Office.

Schaffer, J., & Miller, E. D. (1995). *Civic journalism: Six case studies*. Washington, DC: Pew Center for Civic Journalism.

Schramm, W. (1964). *Mass media and national development: The role of information in developing countries*. Palo Alto, CA: Stanford University Press.

Shafer, R. (1996, August). *Journalists as reluctant interventionists: Comparing development and civic journalism*. Paper presented at the annual meeting of the Association for Education in Journalism and Mass Communication, Anaheim, CA.

Shah, H. (1996). Modernization, marginalization and emancipation: Toward a normative model of journalism and national development. *Communication Theory, 6*, 143-166.

Shaw, D. (1993, April 1). Some papers seek readers' guidance in shaping coverage. *Los Angeles Times*, p. A18.

Shepard, A. C. (1994, September). The gospel of public journalism. *American Journalism Review*, pp. 28-35.

Siebert, F. S., Peterson, T., & Schramm, W. (1956). *Four theories of the press*. Urbana: University of Illinois Press.

Somavia, J. (1976). The transnational power structure and international information: Elements of a Third World policy for transnational news agencies. *Development Dialogue, 2*, 15-28.

Stepp, C. S. (1996, May). Public journalism: Balancing the scales. *American Journalism Review*, pp. 38-40.

Stevenson, R. L. (1994). *Global communication in the twenty-first century*. New York: Longman.

Swenson, J. D., & Griswold, W. F. (1993). Reporting race relations as development news: Case studies of journalism in Georgia. *Howard Journal of Communications, 4*, 358-368.

Traber, M., & Nordenstreng, K. (Eds.). (1992). *Few voices, many worlds: Towards a media reform movement.* London: World Association for Christian Communication.

Weichelt, A. (1995, August). *Public journalism: Leadership or readership? A look at media involvement.* Paper presented at the annual meeting of the Association for Education in Journalism and Mass Communication, Washington, DC.

Wilson, A. J. (1960, September 30). *The press in a democracy.* Paper presented at a Student Christian Movement seminar, Colombo, Sri Lanka.

Winn, B. (1993, Winter). Public journalism: An early attempt. *Nieman Reports,* pp. 54-56.

Woo, W. F. (1995a, February 13). *As old gods falter: Public journalism and the tradition of detachment.* Paper presented at the *Press-Enterprise* Lecture Series, University of California, Riverside.

Woo, W. F. (1995b, July-August). Should the press be an observer or an actor in public affairs? *St. Louis Journalism Review,* pp. 10-12.

Yankelovich, D. (1991). *Coming to public judgment: Making democracy work in a complex world.* Syracuse, NY: Syracuse University Press.

Yin, J. (1996, August). *A trend, imagined or real? A comparative study of development journalism and public journalism.* Paper presented at the annual meeting of the Association for Education in Journalism and Mass Communication, Anaheim, CA.

Zang, B. (1995, August). *Missing voices in the civic/public journalism debates.* Paper presented at the annual meeting of the Association for Education in Journalism and Mass Communication, Washington, DC.

CHAPTER CONTENTS

8 Programming Theory Under Stress: The Active Industry and the Active Audience

SUSAN TYLER EASTMAN
Indiana University

Renewed stress on programming theory has inevitably resulted from escalating competition within the television industry, the audience's increasing ease in choosing programs, and the inescapable threat posed by on-line entertainment services. This historical analysis shows how models of programming theory have been altered over the past 50 years, spurred by changing audience behaviors and industry programming strategies. The persistent theoretical concepts modified by new viewer-control technologies suggest likely directions for future programming research in the on-line era.

PROGRAMS are television's bait. They lure viewers to millions of TV sets, and, in the normal way of things, those viewers are in turn "sold" as rating numbers to advertisers hoping to reach the viewers with commercial messages. According to one network head of research, as little as one-tenth of a rating point over the course of a year can be worth as much as $30 million in revenue.[1] Given programs' incredible value, the business of programming—the choosing and scheduling of programs—is crucial to the television industry, and the networks have developed a panoply of strategies for capturing audiences.

In the past decade, however, conventional ideas about programming have been greatly stressed by three things: escalating competition within the traditional television industry, the audience's augmented ease of program choice, and the inescapable advance of on-line entertainment services. As programming scholars have been pointing out for a decade, network program schedules no longer greatly inhibit viewer choice; scheduling practices no longer funnel unsuspecting viewers from show to show along a narrow

Correspondence and requests for reprints: Susan Tyler Eastman, Department of Telecommunications, Radio-TV Center 203, Indiana University, Bloomington, IN 47405; e-mail eastman@indiana.edu

Communication Yearbook 21, pp. 323-377

pathway (if, indeed, viewers have ever been so naively gullible—they may only have lacked options). The industry's traditional flow strategies have accounted for progressively less variance in ratings and, at the same time, structural models of viewing have been able to account for only a part of conventional viewer behavior. Nonetheless, scheduling practices have continued to be the centerpiece of scholarly programming theory and research.

The fundamental premises behind television (and radio) industry programming theory for nearly six decades have been (a) that audiences watch programs, not channels; (b) that audiences flow into and out of programs; and (c) that the flow from program to program can be affected by scheduling practices. The concern of programming theorists has been to understand the factors that mediate the influence of scheduling practices on television viewing. Early programming scholars looked to program typologies and demographics to define scheduling effects but ultimately found few persistent associations. Some did, however, recognize the importance of adjacent radio programs in creating flow as early as 1941 (see Fishman & Roslow, 1944). By the late 1970s, scholarly exploration of television flow had established the decisive theoretical importance of inherited viewership and repeat viewing measures (the keystones of programming theories). By the mid-1980s, the number and types of competing program options had significant impact on the flow of viewers through an evening. And by the 1990s, new variables such as between-program transitions were being proposed, and researchers were measuring the impacts on ratings of structural variables in on-air promotion.

But do structural flow considerations even matter in an on-line era? To answer this question, I link three elements in this review: technical advances in television reception used by the audience, practitioner strategies in the industry, and scholarly programming models. This analysis contributes a distinctive developmental history of evolving programming theory, focusing on the major contributors to programming and audience research and applying their ideas to digital and on-line television. Webster and Phalen (1997) have provided a thorough analysis of inheritance effects and repeat viewing within the context of mass audience research. The next step is to project some directions for inquiry in the next decade based on current research into television programming. As conventional television converges with on-line communications (an evolving process; see Baldwin, McVoy, & Steinfield, 1996; Fidler, 1997), a half century of presumptions about how audiences can be affected by industry scheduling practices are likely to be challenged. If scholarly interest in programming research appears to have slumped at present, this should be seen as only a brief pause before the outburst of concern that will follow inevitably from the long-anticipated convergence of on-line entertainment and present-day television.[2]

The term *programming theory* refers to a loose body of beliefs—supported by some tested propositions—that the practitioners of programming use to make predictions about the likely success of their efforts. Their assumptions are the starting points of the actual programming practices applied by stations and networks. This body of beliefs has its roots in early studies of radio audiences that flowered with the development of television; at base, its assumptions are about how the mass audience is likely to behave. Programming is a narrow portion of the larger body of effects research that attempts to isolate media's impact. Insofar as the scholarly study of programming is theoretical, it focuses on propositions that can be demonstrated to reach across situations, time, and media. Substantiated models and theories about programming have been, in practice, structural—that is, chiefly concerned with the effects of program placement (scheduling) on audience flow. *Programming strategy,* a term often used virtually interchangeably with programming theory, refers more vaguely to the much larger body of conventional industry practices that depend on assumptions about competitive industry economics and politics as well as audience behavior; *strategies* normally refers to traditional inter- and intranetwork (or station/system) practices in selecting, scheduling, and evaluating programs (see Eastman & Ferguson, 1997). In sum, *strategy* means competitive design or approach—a pragmatic concern—whereas *theory* refers to principles tested in disinterested research. However, even in scholarly writing, the distinction blurs, and a clear separation between theory and strategy is only rarely maintained. In this analysis I will attempt to distinguish theory from strategy by examining the most influential models and concepts used by programming scholars.

CHANGING THE FRAME

The framework underlying this analysis is the definition of *programming* as the study of the contest between the industry and the audience—the tension between how audiences behave and how they have been maneuvered by industry strategies. With regard to television programming, the relationship between industry and audience can be viewed as a tug-of-war in which equilibrium never holds for long; the advantage shifts somewhat first to one side, then to the other, then back again, and so on. Figure 8.1 is a lighthearted depiction of this rubber-band tension in which "viewing" is pulled first one way, then another.[3] The tension is depicted as a tug-of-war using a multi-stranded rope, with each broadcast and cable network tugging on its own strand in one general direction while millions of individual viewers collectively pull various strands in the other direction. Such a conception diverges from such classic models as Schramm's (1965) communicator-message-receiver approach by focusing on dynamism or *activity* as the defining characteristic of the relationship at the end of the 20th century. But the industry's strategies have not remained immobile; the stresses of the 1990s have made it active, too.

Thus the counterpart of the *active audience* is not a *passive audience,* but rather an *active media industry.* Although ratings are supposedly the way the

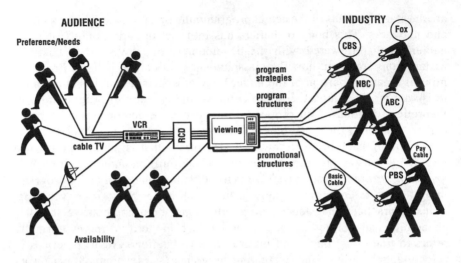

Figure 8.1. Audience and Industry Tensions on Television Viewing

audience tells the industry what it wants, the flaws of ratings as measures of viewer/user interests have been long exposed. Programming scholars normally justify their research on the grounds that it increases understanding of audience behavior, but too often researchers divorce studies of industry programming practices from studies of audience behavior. Indeed, media industry studies have been tarred with the pejorative *applied* when many have really been a missing portion of the single equation of the evolving television viewing process. Television audience activity is best understood in tension with television industry activity, because the two act on each other and yet are continually out of balance. The television industry attempts to manipulate the audience (to make more money, of course) by means of content and scheduling strategies, and the audience reacts by seeking maximal control of its viewing, which in turn leads the industry to attempt new programming strategies.

Although Ang (1991) and others justly point to invidious implications for society in the media's manipulations (see also Neuman, 1991), in this analysis the industry's attempts at control of viewing are not conceived as nefarious warfare, but merely as the normal (self-interested) business practice of seeking to steer viewing in order to achieve greater financial reward for particular media companies. In the view adopted here, the television industry is neither particularly pernicious nor hugely powerful; indeed, as economists such as Owen and Wildman (1992) have noted, competition among media companies (networks, advertisers, ratings firms, pressure groups, government agencies) often negates any momentary big-industry advantage over viewers.[4] Understanding the factors that influence audience decision making is the fabric of a single rope; the factors affecting flow tell the industry how to tug on the rope and help the industry to measure its success in tugging. At the same time, new television technologies give audience members the ability to tug in their own directions. The phrase *locus of power* has been used most commonly to refer to geographic locations—especially in a military context—and second-arily to refer to political groups and individual leaders where power aggre-gates. In this discussion, however, it has a third meaning: It refers to the shifting balance of influence *on viewing* by the programmers of the television industry and the viewers in and out of their homes—both of whom seek their own ends. Although many other scholars have examined the industry's pro-gramming role, the import of an audience/industry duality has remained far in the background and has balkanized the research agenda. However, this duality must become a foreground conception as programming theory adapts to the on-line era. Examined over the historical sweep of four decades, shifts of advantage in the tug-of-war between industry and audience may explain why many proposed programming theories have not held up very well over time.

Table 8.1 illustrates some major parallels among developments in media technologies, industry strategies, and programming theories; it briefly out-lines the historical portion of this analysis. Because viewers have accepted some technological developments and rejected others, *technology* is inter-preted here as an opportunity for audience activity, not as an inevitable cause. In the table, technical developments in television stand as surrogates for audience activity in relation to industry programming strategies and scholarly theory. Explanations for the shorthand terminology for industry strategies appear in the subsequent sections. At the theoretical level, the table implies that the interactions between what audiences do and what the television industry does are pivotal to the explanations generated by programming scholars. The table includes the most influential communication models and the six powerful programming concepts that provide continuing threads through this analysis: flow, inheritance, competition, activity, motivation, and agency.

Within the table, reception-related television technologies are associated horizontally with industry strategies and programming theories/models and exemplary scholars. Although the theories are listed in the table according to the years in which critical publications first appeared, the reader should assume that prior publications occurred in each area and that expanding cones of research arose in each major vertical trajectory. This historical analysis of the most influential scholarly writings about audiences/industry and program-ming converges on three key questions:

1. What is implied by the conceptualization of activity as a shifting struggle for control between audience and industry?
2. Why are previous structural flow theories fading in importance?
3. What relevance has present programming theory for the on-line era?

TABLE 8.1
Parallel Developments in Audience Technologies, Industry Strategies, and Programming Theories

Decade	Audience Technologies	Industry Strategies	Programming Research Models/Theories	
1940s	radio	program typologies	demographics	Lazarsfeld & Stanton, 1944
1950s	television	advertising clout	propaganda tool economics	Hovland et al., 1949 Head, 1956; Steiner, 1952
1960s			intervening factors active audiences	Klapper, 1960; McPhee, 1963 Bauer & Bauer, 1960
1970s		least objectionable program	program preferences program typologies uses and gratifications	Brown, 1971; Klein, 1971a; McQuail et al., 1972 Greenberg & Barnett, 1971 Blumler & Katz, 1974 Owen et al., 1974
	cable TV	counterprogramming stunting blocking	inheritance "laws"	Goodhardt et al., 1975; Headen et al., 1979
1980s	videotex	lead-in program warehousing hammocking/sandwiching	cultivation perspective expectancy value program strategies	Gerbner & Gross, 1976 Ehrenberg & Goodhardt, 1981; Palmgreen et al., 1980 Adams et al., 1983; Bantz, 1982; Barwise et al., 1982; Eastman et al., 1981
	teletext VCRs TVROs subcarriers		media dependency theory audience activity model selective exposure theory competitive choice models	Webster, 1983; Webster & Wakshlag, 1982 Ball-Rokeach, 1985 Levy & Windahl, 1984 Zillmann & Bryant, 1985 Biocca, 1988; Heeter, 1985; Heeter & Greenberg, 1988; Rust & Donthu, 1988; Tiedge & Ksobiech, 1988; Walker, 1988; Webster, 1985; Webster & Newton, 1988

Era	Technology	Concept	References
1990s	RCDs	lead-off	Bryant & Zillmann, 1991; Owen & Wildman, 1992;
	repertoire models		Webster & Lichty, 1991
	blocking by evenings		Ferguson, 1992a
		repeat viewing	Adams, 1993; Cooper, 1993; Webster & Wang, 1992
		interactivity	Walker & Bellamy, 1993
	seamlessness	program transitions	Eastman et al., 1995
	multiplexing	promotional impact	Eastman et al., 1997
	branding		Bellamy & Walker, 1996
	DBS		
	digital TV	new program typologies	Adams, in press; Webster & Phalen, 1997
2000s	smart TVs		
	on-line era	models of agency	

As computer technology creates increasingly intelligent television sets, a nearly unlimited array of program options looms ahead that is likely to change many programming rules for the industry and render moot many common assumptions guiding scholarly research in programming.

EXPLAINING PROGRAM CHOICE IN A STABLE ENVIRONMENT: THE 1970s

Until the latter half of the 1970s, network television in the United States was in a stable competitive situation. Until 1976, ABC was an also-ran and prime-time television was dominated by CBS and NBC, with CBS as ratings leader from the mid-1940s until the mid-1970s. In Great Britain, the situation in the 1960s and most of the 1970s was equally stable, with only two BBC channels and one weak independent. In the period between 1950 and 1975, the rudiments of programming theory deriving from radio research were applied to television, and many of the early presumptions continue to underlie both network strategy and scholarly programming theories in the late 1990s.

Early research in radio in the 1940s, largely masterminded by innovator Paul Lazarsfeld, consisted mostly of field surveys and case studies that sought to understand what listeners valued in radio programs (e.g., Lazarsfeld & Stanton, 1944). Statistical studies separated listeners by demographic groups (e.g., age, sex, education, income, geography) and programs by gross types (e.g., news, talk forums, serious music, popular music). Many of Lazarsfeld's methods and some of his conclusions persist in industry strategy today: Ratings continue to subdivide viewers by age and sex, and programmers reiterate such presumptions as, for example, men listen to (or watch) more news than women; upper-income listeners choose serious content far more often than do lower-income listeners; and rural listeners more often choose personal (country) over formal (classical) formats, just as they did in Lazarsfeld's radio days. During and just after World War II, many scholars conducted research into radio as a propaganda tool, but television's spread in the 1950s greatly boosted government and industry interest in media research of all kinds.

The 1950s left a conceptual legacy of television as an immensely powerful advertising vehicle (Innis, 1950), a frightening tool of mass persuasion (Hovland, Lumsdaine, & Sheffield, 1949), and, at the same time, a means of social escape (Katz & Foulkes, 1962; Pearlin, 1959). The economist Peter Steiner (1952) had previously proposed a model of program choice that posited maximal effectiveness for a monopolistic industry, and critics trumpeted their anxiety about television's presumably enormous (and supposedly monolithic) power over a mass audience (see Schramm, 1957). Taking a moderate position, Sydney Head (1956) spelled out the financial strategies guiding programming in the industry and the social questions they raised. The ideas in his book—in its multiple editions and copycat volumes—influenced generations of future programmers as well as programming researchers. But industry programmers asserted that simple popularity (likability) generally explained the greater viewership of one program over another, assigning the preponderance of control to audiences. Contradictory views of audience and industry power developed right at the start of media research into radio listening, shifted straightaway to television viewing, and persist to this day.

The 1960s commenced with several publications of lasting theoretical influence on programming scholarship. Klapper (1960) attempted a massive summation of the media's direct effects and outlined the crucial idea of "intervening factors" in one-way mass communication, a conceptualization that continues to undergird research into structural effects in programming as increased computing power has become available to test specific variables. Bauer (1963, 1964) promulgated the idea of the *obstinate* audience, referring to viewers' (and listeners') unwillingness to do exactly as the media ordered (through their propaganda, through their commercial messages, and through their structural scheduling practices). Bauer's illuminating idea was the precursor to the active audience perspective that became a cornerstone of uses and gratifications theory.[5]

The Theory of Double Jeopardy

In Great Britain, the first major studies on the structural aspects of programming concluded that program structure was the dominant influence on viewer flow. In other words, the order of the programs increased or decreased the size of the audience as the program schedule progressed through the evening (always allowing for fall-off as the hour grew later). Attributed to McPhee (1963), the clever idea of *double jeopardy* surfaced. McPhee claimed that low-rated programs are in a double bind because they have both low exposure and little chance of getting more exposure, because unpopular programs suffer from fewer and less committed viewers. His assumptions are reflected in the persistent network strategy of quickly canceling weak prime-time shows (see Adams, 1993).

In the late 1960s, the first major scholarly studies of program types in relation to demographic groups appeared in journals. Many of these studies were driven by concern about advertising's potency (see, e.g., Ehrenberg, 1968). After 1965, Schramm's authoritative book *The Process and Effects of Mass Communication* dominated the American research landscape, labeling the basic elements of the communication process (communicator, message, receiver) and supporting complex notions of the intervening factors model of media effects. Also appearing at this time were the first major theoretical conceptualizations of the process of inherited viewership, emphasizing the might of the lead-in program (Ehrenberg & Goodhardt, 1969). Meanwhile, the second volume of Barnouw's (1968) massive history of broadcasting appeared, articulating the economic motive behind most industry programming strategies, a view still widely upheld (see Ettema & Whitney, 1994; Owen & Wildman, 1992).

In the early 1970s, other hints appeared of what was to come: McQuail, Blumler, and Brown (1972) published their collective look at what viewers get from watching television. From the industry activity side, Les Brown's (1971) popular paperback on the television business was widely adopted as a classroom textbook. It gave currency to the industry's financial motives and articulated many of the scheduling strategies that were soon to be fodder for academic study. These included the idea of placing two or more similar short programs in sequence to encourage viewer flow (called blocking and commonly applied to half-hour situation comedies) and selecting programs to attract audiences different from those the main competitors attracted (called counterprogramming). Meanwhile, historical analyses of program types collared academic interest at this time. For example, Robert Bailey (1970) took a 20-year look at television specials, and Greenberg and Barnett (1971) described and analyzed the major program types. Soon thereafter, Owen, Beebe, and Manning (1974) published their authoritative *Broadcast Economics,* and William Wells (1974) published his classic book defining social lifestyles and psychographic research as related to media, which influenced much marketing and advertising research related to television programming.

The Theory of the Least Objectionable Program

In the same period, Paul Klein (1971a, 1971b, 1979), perhaps tongue in cheek, articulated his conception of the *least objectionable program.* His perspective on audience flow drove much of the thinking about programming throughout the late 1960s and the 1970s. What Klein was presumed to think about audience flow had a pervasive effect on network strategy, as he was head of NBC audience measurement and later became head of NBC network programming. Klein theorized that viewers who chose to watch television settled on the program that was the least undesirable to the most viewers in the room. This meant that one viewer might like Program A very much but hate Program B, and another might really dislike A and love B, but because neither felt strongly about Program C, that would be the one they ended up watching. Variations on this theme considered inappropriateness for the youngest or most sensitive member of the group (instead of group members' likes and dislikes). This theory may have made sense in the viewing environment of a shared household television set, but it was challenged a decade later, when the viewing situation had changed drastically (see Adams, Eastman, Horney, & Popovich, 1983). Variations on the least objectionable program theory have continued to influence research into family viewing, but the theory has been undercut by the proliferation of program networks and households with multiple television sets.

By the mid-1970s, scholarly research related to programming could be seen splitting into two strands: One strand looked at audience behavior and motives, and the other looked at industry structure and strategies. The audience perspective was energized by Blumler and Katz's (1974) definitive book about uses and gratifications, which contained influential chapters by Wright on functionalism (which stirred many scholarly passions). This book (accompanied by a flood of research articles) defined, illustrated, and gave rise to wide adoption of the theoretical perspective called uses and gratifications. The central assumptions of this perspective are as follows:

1. Audience behavior is active and purposive (goal directed). Actions have functions and consequences.
2. People use media, rather than solely being used by it.
3. A host of social and psychological variables mediate media behavior.
4. The media compete with other activities for selection, attention, and use.

The Duplication of Viewing Law

Concurrently, there was a creative upsurge in publications focused on the theory behind scheduling practices. In Great Britain, Goodhardt, Ehrenberg, and Collins (1975) produced their instrumental book that promulgated the startling "duplication of viewing law." It attested to a principle of audience duplication that was to undergird much of subsequent structural programming research. Happily, Goodhardt et al.'s "law" moved through the classic stages of theory to model to mathematical embodiment, thought to be the epitome of truly scientific research. Their law even necessitated a mathematical constant that could become the centerpiece of dozens, perhaps hundreds, of subsequent studies.

The duplication of viewing law was as follows: "The proportion of the audience of any TV programme who watch another programme on another day of the same week is directly proportional to the rating of the latter programme (i.e., equal to it times a certain constant)" (p. 11). As a percentage of the whole population, the law can be stated as follows: The percentage of the population who watch both A and B equals the rating of A times the rating of B times a coefficient divided by 100 (Goodhardt et al., 1975, p. 12). That is,

$$\text{(Program A's Rating} \times \text{Program B's Rating} \times \text{Coefficient)}/100$$
$$= \text{Inherited Audience.}$$

For example:

$$(30 \times 20 \times 1.4)/100 = 8.4\%$$

Subsequent research in both the United States and Great Britain immediately focused on specifying the exact size of the constant. For Great Britain,

Goodhardt et al. concluded that "about 55% of viewers of one episode of a programme also watch the following episode" (p. 125) and that television is, indeed, a "mass medium" characterized by "a few very general and simple patterns" (p. 127).

The advent of this single "law" generated enormous excitement among academics in general because it immediately implied the potential for additional "laws of communication" and conferred on communication the status of a "serious science." Bolstered by a rapid upsurge in related publications, the mid-1970s writings of Blumler and Katz and of Goodhardt, Ehrenberg, and Collins can be seen as direct progenitors of two major strands of present-day audience and industry programming research.

In the late 1970s, dozens of scholars began looking at motives and uses of television for particular subgroups. Lawrence Wenner (1976), for example, examined the functions—another term for uses and gratifications (U&G)—of television for older viewers (and later for news viewers). Alan Rubin (1979) analyzed functions of television for adolescents, Mark Levy (1977) applied U&G to news viewing, and David Swanson (1977) wrote an authoritative analysis of U&G's potential misuses. Ellen Wartella's (1979) and Wakshlag and Greenberg's (1979) separate analyses of television's impact on children appeared, as did Jay Blumler's (1979) expanded discussions of viewer gratifications. Berlo (1977) soon articulated the idea of communication as process rather than effects, and Umberto Eco's enormously influential treatise on semiotics appeared in 1979, snowballing interest in programs from critical and cultural perspectives. The 1980s gave rise to another major split, separating critical and cultural perspectives (see Gerbner, Gross, Morgan, & Signorielli, 1986) from effects paradigms.

Prior to the 1970s, the popularity of one or another of the two main networks' programs had seemed to account for most patterns of television viewing. After the rise of ABC, when the idea of testing the effectiveness of television scheduling strategies caught fire in the late 1970s, a great deal of scholarly activity turned to isolating the value of specific industry strategies for manipulating viewing. Headen, Klompmaker, and Rust (1979) were among the first to focus on applying Goodhardt et al.'s repeated viewing principles to American television viewing. In the three-network situation, they demonstrated that channel and ratings explained a whopping 72% of the variance in duplicated audiences, and that program type explained an additional 6%. After 1979, the hunt was on for (a) the size of Goodhardt et al.'s mathematical constants and (b) the variables intervening between industry strategies and viewer behaviors. Pursuit of flow variables and predictive structural models has continued to the present day.

Program Type Effects and Passivity

Meanwhile, the issue of program diversity remained salient. Many critics expressed concern about the diversity of news voices heard by the public, the television industry wanted to be able to track programs by type, and programming scholars wanted to assess effects by program type. By the 1970s, sufficient computing power was readily available for researchers to undertake analyses of very large ratings databases. Dominick and Pearce (1976) and Joel Persky (1977) analyzed trends in prime-time program types over the preceding 20 years, followed shortly thereafter by Barry Litman's (1979) scathing assessment of the methods and theoretical assumptions behind program typing and its lack of usefulness to date. The eventual conclusion of most scholars was that program types are more closely related to program dislikes than to likes or to program choices (Goodhardt, Ehrenberg, & Collins, 1987). However, George Comstock (1980, p. 38) reminded programming scholars of his assertion that *whether* to watch comes before *what* to watch, an assumption reiterated by Webster and Wakshlag (1983), ultimately turning more researchers toward the factors influencing choice.

Examining repeat viewing of stripped programs (i.e., programs carried at the same time every day), Barwise, Ehrenberg, and Goodhardt (1982) concluded that "only about half of those viewing a program one day view it again on any other given day" (p. 22), and that the decision to view "seems to be largely passive" (p. 27). The assumption of initial passivity was subsequently presumed by many researchers to be valid for some or most viewing—until cable's spread and the remote control's arrival. The publication of studies employing ethnographic observations of television viewing in the home (see Lemish, 1983; Lull, 1982) finally wiped away most of passivity's remaining conceptual credibility (see Walker & Bellamy, 1993).

EXPLORING THE IMPACTS OF
RISING COMPETITION: THE 1980s

In the early 1980s, the topic of motives (or gratifications) for the use of media and the choice of particular programs captured much of researchers' attention. Palmgreen, Wenner, and Rayburn (1980) introduced the crucial distinction between "gratifications expected" and "gratifications obtained," ultimately creating the "expectancy value" approach to gratifications, which set the pattern for numerous subsequent studies that focused on audience behavior (see also Palmgreen, 1984; Palmgreen & Rayburn, 1985). While Walter Gantz and I were taking a first scholarly look at how television viewers use program promotion (Gantz & Eastman, 1983) and Charles Bantz (1982) was exploring uses of television in comparison to individuals' favorite types of programs, A. M. Rubin and R. B. Rubin (1982; R. B. Rubin & A. M. Rubin, 1982) were looking closely at the motives of demographic subdivisions of viewers (the old and the young). Still others were exploring the motives common to all media or that distinguished just one medium (see R. B. Rubin & A. M. Rubin, 1982).

Meanwhile, Ehrenberg and Goodhardt (1981) were following up on the purely structural approach to programming. They applied Goodhardt's theories about inherited viewers and loyalty to programs or the sources of programs to the diverse body of U.S. television, and they compared estimates for the mathematical "inheritance constant" across the Atlantic and across program types, dayparts, and audiences (which failed to hold up very well). This kind of analysis estimated the impact of some structural factors on viewer behavior (the type of lead-in program and types of competing programs), thus implying, by extrapolation, that the television industry could manipulate these factors and better lure particular viewers. Adams et al. (1983) seized on this implication to explore the ways the industry was able to manipulate directly the size of ratings—that supposedly "objective" measure of program success or failure—in order to justify the cancellation of specific (probably costly) programs. In a historical analysis, Adams (1993, in press) also demonstrated that moving a program's schedule location (day and time) or placing it on hiatus for more than 2 weeks almost invariably drove its ratings down.

The Concept of Availability

At this time, James Webster (1983, 1985) and Webster and Wakshlag (1982, 1983) cogently delineated the underlying assumptions of the structural approach to programming, concluding that audience *availability* (as measured by shares of audience rather than ratings) was the key to television audience size because it was responsible for the absence of content-based patterns of choice. Their analyses focused variously on loyalty, cable television, news viewing, and group entertainment viewing. In their 1983 study, they were among the first to attempt to integrate both the U&G and effects perspectives through a proposed model of choice. The early Webster and Wakshlag model was illustrated as a triangle, with audience availability, program type preference, and competing program options (the more options, the less impact for lead-in) as the key variables explaining program choice. Other variables such as viewer needs, group viewing, awareness of options, and personal preferences modify or intervene in the choice process. These variables have remained central to subsequent structural programming theory, and Webster and Wakshlag's discerning articulation made clear to subsequent programming researchers why audience shares are much to be preferred to audience ratings as viewership measures.[6]

Initially, Webster and Wakshlag (1983) defined an active audience as "motivated by a desire to access specific television content," and passive audience viewing as "a function of availability and not of specific content" (p. 437). Although widely prevalent in the early 1980s, their conception lost blanket acceptance when content-specific cable channels proliferated, making at least some kinds of content (e.g., music, news, shopping, movies, sports) available at any moment.

The mid-1980s saw an explosion in studies of new technologies—ranging from cable television to subcarriers to home video recorders to computers in schools, homes, and businesses—generally from a uses and gratifications perspective. Influenced by Everett Rogers's (1983) seminal work on the diffusion of innovations, Rice and Associates (1984) held a magnifying glass to economic, group, and individual barriers to the adoption of computers (teleconferencing and the like) in the business world. At this time, Rubin (1984) articulated his dual conceptions of ritual and instrumental motivations, arguing that television viewing motives are a primary signal of audience activity and that they can be either nonselective or selective. In the next year, Sandra Ball-Rokeach (1985) articulated her media dependency theory to explain why individuals turn to a particular medium to fulfill a goal. She concluded that individuals develop relationships of dependency with the media in order to attain goals structured along the dimensions of play, orientation, and understanding. Thus users' orientations have personal as well as social dimensions, reflecting recursive relationships between behavior and the development of dependencies (e.g., watching home shopping shows; see Grant, Guthries, & Ball-Rokeach, 1991).

The functionalist approach to why people choose what they choose to watch was effectively summarized in Rosengren, Wenner, and Palmgreen's (1985) edited volume that looked at viewer needs and the intervening variables, viewing group, and viewer awareness of options as well as the values expected in behavioral outcomes or media attributes (see also Babrow, 1988). In 1986, Rubin and Windahl attempted to merge the two perspectives of gratifications and dependencies by envisioning the specifics of industry programming (such as structure) as only a tiny portion of the composite of functions, uses, and motives on effects.

But by the mid-1980s, cable television had penetrated 30% of homes in the United States, crossing a significant hurdle established by advertising interests, and its penetration was expected to continue at a rapid rate. Although the broadcast networks continued to decry cable's importance—at least publicly—the size (and eventually the type) of the competition was soon accepted as a crucial intervening factor in any structural impacts on television ratings. When cable's sudden proliferation was followed by the rapid consumer acceptance of other new media technologies (e.g., home video recorders, home satellite receivers), scholars everywhere pronounced the end of "massness" and the demise of direct media effects theories. The number of intervening variables seemed to have grown too enormous to be encompassed even by advanced multivariate statistics. Considerable research energy became focused on investigations of seemingly new kinds of audience behavior for subsets of viewers, and this new conceptual posture led to a shift in the direction of researchers' questions. If competition permitted viewers to evade influence by the industry's manipulations, programming scholars wanted to know how and why audiences chose and rejected programs. Attention switched

COMMUNICATION YEARBOOK 21

away from the programs themselves and concentrated on the audiences. Seeking explanations that swept across a variety of technologies, scholars adopted the framework of *activity*, but tended to speak as if activity resided only in audiences, and the industry (its strategies, in other words) was constant and immutable.

In an article of enduring influence on uses and gratifications research, Levy and Windahl (1984) published their innovative six-part model for audience activity. Versions of this model (see Levy, 1987; Levy & Windahl, 1985) succeeded in capturing researchers' imaginations and overshadowed audience activity theory for years to come. Levy and Windahl were concerned with the conceptual basis of how people (television viewers or company employees) used media. They explicated the basic assumption of activity as both *voluntary* and *selective* on the part of the audience and with activity occurring at various times in the process (preexposure, during exposure, and postexposure). They proposed varying degrees of "activeness," conceptualizations that resonated with the views of many programming scholars influenced by U&G and overwhelmed by the spread of new media technologies. However, their model culminated in exposure (usually interpreted as ratings) and ignored the likelihood of activity on the industry side.

The Concept of Selectivity

Two edited books by the prolific team of Jennings Bryant and Dolf Zillmann synthesized the essence of previous research within frameworks that seemed to resolve many issues in media effects. They rejected as too simplistic the previous notions of media exposure that characterized research in the 1970s. First came Zillmann and Bryant's (1985) *Selective Exposure to Communication* and then Bryant and Zillmann's (1986) *Perspectives on Media Effects*. Whereas the second book brings together a wide range of proponents of all the major perspectives in a useful, edited volume, the first book focuses more narrowly; its thesis rejects previous notions of media exposure and draws from psychology the notion of *selectivity* in media consumption and thus exposure. The main features of selectivity theory are as follows:

1. It rejects the direct effects model of exposure (cultivation) on the grounds that it does not explain whether exposure causes behavioral conditions or behavioral conditions cause selective exposure.
2. It argues that selectivity occurs prior to exposure. The key issue concerns *intended* or *accidental* exposure—whether media exposure was the *primary* perceptual activity.
3. It argues that selectivity occurs in all kinds of environments.
4. It redefines the media effects question away from the effects of consumption toward the effects on message selection.

Because there are too many stimuli, Zillmann and Bryant (1985) argue, people reduce their exposure by selectively eliminating some information. They define selective exposure as "behavior that is deliberately performed to attain and sustain perceptual control of some stimulus events" (p. 2) and maintain that selectivity operates in all kinds of environments. But, they point out, selective exposure need not be a "continual, uninterrupted effort at sustaining perceptual control"; it may be "spontaneous and rather mindless" (p. 4). For Zillmann and Bryant, the key issues are whether exposure was intended or accidental and/or whether exposure to a program was the primary perceptual activity. They conceptualize the dependent variable of selective exposure as "the effect *on* message selection for consumption" (p. 6), not the older question of "the effect *of* consumption of selected messages" (p. 6) on audiences. They conclude that exposure to communication is situation and disposition specific.

Zillmann and Bryant (1985) point particularly to the fact that in much direct-effects research, the direction of effects could be reversed: "Instead of exposure causing behavior, behavioral conditions might cause selective exposure" (p. 7). Selective exposure was proposed as an alternative to the effects hypothesis inherent to the cultivation hypothesis, a view with popular acceptance but rejected by many scholars. In a key Zillmann and Bryant example, the question is whether crime drama consumption fosters fear or fear makes crime drama more attractive and thus fosters exposure. In an experimental study, Zillmann and Bryant demonstrated that the relationship between crime and fear is, at least in part, selective exposure.

Looking back to Klapper (1960) and others in the psychology of communication, Zillmann and Bryant's synthesis of previously largely distinct bodies of research (psychology and communication) dynamited any lingering hypodermic or mass audience notions and focused much subsequent research on the activities of viewer subsets. The notion of exposure as selective rather than as a mass phenomenon fundamentally distinguished uses and gratifications from cultivation theories after this time. However, Zillmann and Bryant's theory or paradigm accounted for what audience members did and why (or what they thought they did and why) without paying much attention to what they were reacting to and concurrent changes in industry behavior. Traditional effects models asked how audiences are affected by media, whereas newer (and better) questions consider how audiences engage in different ways with particular forms and genres in different contexts. Although Zillmann and Bryant did not deal directly with structural programming theory, their ideas were picked up by researchers investigating the impacts of new television technologies on audience behavior.

Reconceiving Audience Activity

Ratcheting up inquiry into audience decision making, Carrie Heeter (1985) published her program choice process model of audience behavior in the environment of a large number of competing television channels. Deviating from Webster and Wakshlag's (1983) notion of the central importance of availability, Heeter demonstrated that viewers have (a) small repertoires of frequently viewed channels and (b) imperfect awareness of what is available in situations with many channels. She proposed that viewers conduct orienting searches of different types that may or may not include guide use or channel checking, followed by reevaluation. This process is affected by both channel familiarity and channel repertoire.

Heeter's model proposed that viewers use guides and orienting searches that are substantially influenced by each viewer's familiarity with the available channels and each viewer's personal repertoire of regularly used channels. Searches can be fairly automatic, elaborated, or exhaustive, and, unless automatic, are constantly being reevaluated (for desirable programs). Heeter's model reiterated Comstock's (1980) view that whether to view is a largely passive decision, but what to view is more active. Within the two-step process Heeter delineated, program preference appeared a very weak predictor of viewership. Also during the same period, Heeter and Greenberg (1985) reported a small study about remote control zapping that was to reverberate in a boomlet of remote control studies in the 1990s.[7]

In another key article that year, Webster (1985) reached what is probably the most quoted conclusion in subsequent programming research: "About half of those who viewed one program also viewed the following program" (p. 129). This sustained Goodhardt et al.'s (1975) similar conclusion of a decade before about viewing in Great Britain. Although he has since revised his conclusions (see Webster & Phalen, 1997), at that time Webster analyzed duplicated viewing in prime time and found that the correlation between duplicated viewers and rating/share was as high as 83%. He concluded, in almost offhand fashion, that the average program inherited about 50% of its audience from the preceding program. One weakness of his study was that Webster estimated repeat viewing using a formula adopted from Barwise et al. (1982) in a secondary analysis of Arbitron data. However, the figure of 50% inherited viewers corroborated Headen et al.'s (1979) conclusion about American viewing, and thus powerfully demonstrated the overwhelming importance of lead-in ratings on the next program's ratings. This assumption had been widely held in the industry for more than a decade, but was difficult to demonstrate because of the small program samples in most academic studies. In later studies using different databases, Webster continued to explain audience duplication as a consequence of availability affected by lead-in ratings (which he called a surrogate for audience preference; see Webster & Wang, 1992). In turn, he showed lead-in ratings to be affected by scheduling and program type variables—which he found to be significantly correlated. This second factor contradicted Goodhardt et al.'s earlier conclusion that program type had no impact on audience duplication patterns. Webster (1986) also concluded that structural factors in choice making were becoming *stronger* determinants of exposure.

The second half of the 1980s was another prolific period for both audience and programming research, but most studies were extensions of previous research. On the audience side, studies appeared that tested Levy and Windahl's (1984) degrees of activity (see Rubin & Perse, 1987a, 1987b), and Donohew, Palmgreen, and Rayburn (1987) refocused their attention on the role of lifestyles (and psychographics) in media use. In the second edition of their classic book, Goodhardt et al. (1987) maintained their focus on the structural characteristics of network programming. They concluded that inheritance had the most effect on subsequent episodes of the same program or on adjacent program ratings. In this edition, Goodhardt et al. explicated values for their duplication of viewing law for the United States, finding levels inexplicably lower than their logic had predicted. Whereas they had demonstrated repeat viewing levels of 55% in Great Britain a decade before, the level of repeat viewing in the United States was judged as low as 25%.

Meanwhile, on cable television's theoretical and methodological fronts, Heeter and Greenberg's 1988 edited volume synthesized the impacts of cable and showed what new things could be accomplished by means of finely timed measurement. Among other things, the researchers argued that cable might produce *more* channel loyalty (a) because loyalty to program type aligns with channel loyalty, (b) because people pay for cable channels, and (c) because identification simplifies the choice process. This contrasts with the earlier broadcast-only research finding that channel and program loyalty are not closely tied (Wakshlag, Agostino, Terry, Driscoll, & Ramsey, 1983), but it may explain Goodhardt et al.'s (1975) findings in Great Britain.

Frank Biocca (1988) undertook a razor-sharp historical and projective analysis of audience activity research, rejecting ambiguity and imprecise theoretical bases and ultimately retying audience activity firmly to psychological theory. Implied, however, was massive disdain for whatever the industry was doing. Biocca's analysis of the passive/active dichotomy and its importance to mass communication research deserves detailed attention here because of its insight and comprehensiveness, and because Biocca's conclusions provide a foundation for the discussion central to this review. Biocca began by pointing facetiously to a "theoretical tug-of-war" between the *active* audience, which he saw as individualistic, not able to be influenced, rational, and selective, and the *passive* audience, which he saw as conformist, gullible, anomic, vulnerable, and victims, labeling these different perceptions of social reality (p. 51). Of special relevance here is his reminder that although scholars today tend to say audience *activity,* the original idea was *audience* activity. Biocca attributed the emphasis on *audience* activity to what he called the early "administrative" perspective, but then he dropped the topic, failing to take notice of tension between the audience and industry in present-day research.

Biocca (1988) identified five main theoretical perspectives or processes driving activity research: (a) selectivity (Heeter's funneling, 1985; Klapper's selective attention, perception, and retention, 1960), (b) utility (Palmgreen's expectancy value, 1984), (c) intentionality (Wenner's schema, 1982), (d) involvement (Hawkins & Pingree's cognitive effort, 1986; Levy's affective arousal, 1983), and (e) immunity to influence (Bauer's precursor to the cultivation perspective, 1964). Biocca concluded that the heart of the active/passive debate is a political question of "locus of control" in addition to a scientific question of "cause" (p. 61). He placed the core of the activity concept within cognitive processing and asserted that meaning may largely be constructed outside of consciousness. But, he argued, some evidence shows active, conscious processes influencing viewers' models and schema. It can be deduced, therefore, that examining causes of audience behavior without accounting for the shifting locus of control has resulted in studies that explain little.

Although Biocca went on to refer to activity primarily within human cognition and perception, the concept has application to the shifting balance within the relationships between audience and industry. Thus locus of control can be given an external meaning: Although scholars have endlessly debated how much control resides in the audience, most have failed to articulate that the source of agency moves back and forth between the audience and the industry. Although one must entirely reject the hypodermic notion and the idea of large one-way mass effects (however mediated), programming history reveals an active industry. It constantly attempts to manipulate the mass of viewers—and typically succeeds for a time in affecting how many television viewers behave—until the audience finds ways to reassert a large measure of mastery. As Webster and Phalen (1997) argue, there is a mass audience, and as Ettema and Whitney (1994) contend, it is an artifact created by the media, but it has considerable power to affect what the media does. Applied to structural programming theories, this two-sided selectivity perspective presumes the importance of structural factors about programming itself. It also argues the importance of utility, intention, and involvement on the part of the audience, but envisions them varying in pull at different points in time. Biocca would appear to agree, as he concluded with several related recommendations. Besides giving up on a metaconstruct of audience activity and incorporating a theory of text and semiotic codes in message analysis, he identified the need to define the communicator's objectives, strategies, and perceptions of the audience. The last is vital here if conceptualized as part of an interactive audience/industry duality in relation to programming.

About the same time, Thomas Lindlof (1988) synthesized a hermeneutic/interpretive conception of program type or genre *not* at the moment of generation (by producers) or reception (by viewers), but as evolving "achievements of the interpreting community" (p. 81). As Gunter (1988) explained in his contribution to the same volume, *community* here refers to the "various social, occupational/professional and public groups" (see also Lemish, 1983) that everyone belongs to (p. 117). Like Anderson and Meyer in their 1988 book, Lindlof criticized studies of media audiences that use aggregated measures because they ignore the "socially contingent nature of much mediated communication activity" and the "ever expanding frames of meaning" that people generate as they encounter television (p. 81). He distinguished the "presented meaning" in the content of media from the "constructed meaning" as utilized/interpreted by viewers and concluded that program content has meaning only within specific situations and groups. Called the "social action perspective," its methods are illustrated in James Lull's (1990) *Inside Family Viewing*, published in Great Britain, his second book exploring at-home television use and motives ethnographically, and the premises and claims of social action theory were explicated in a later essay by Schoening and Anderson (1995). This perspective and its associated ethnographic methods may prove useful in the on-line era when audiences (computer or smart TV users) subdivide into splinter groups interested (at least momentarily) in hard-to-identify clusters of content. From the interpretive perspective, it becomes essential to return to viewers to ask *them* about program content (in Q-sorts) or to observe them in relation to content (in ethnographic studies), rather than to continue applying the worn-out typologies of early programming research.

By the late 1980s, the broadcast television industry had become extremely anxious about cable's inroads. The size of network prime-time audiences had fallen from about 90% of viewers two decades before to around 60%, and was predicted to go even lower in the coming decade. Widespread adoption of new technologies, such as cable system feeds, home video recorders, home satellite dishes, and remote control devices, was blamed for the defections. Networks and stations increased their "warehousing" of potentially popular programs, prebuying rights to shows and delaying their airing or even their production in order to deny the shows to competitors. Next, their programmers concentrated on structural solutions to competition. They emphasized the placement of new shows between established programs (hammocking), hoping for strong carryover effect; they stressed the role of 8:00 p.m. lead-off programs in initially capturing viewers for an evening; and they intensified their use of similar types of programs throughout an evening (blocking). Nonetheless, broadcast network ratings continued to slide.

Turning to closer examination of conventional programming assumptions, in the late 1980s programming scholars delved into finer and finer measurement of inheritance and repeat viewing. Rust and Alpert (1984) articulated a mathematical audience flow model that was subsequently used to project the maximization of positioning in cable television (Rust & Donthu, 1988) and flow in broadcast television (Rust & Eechambadi, 1989). The Rust and Alpert mathematical model incorporates the ideas of audience segmentation, program utility, and audience flow, and predicts the probability of an individual's viewing choice (in the three-network situation) given the individual's demographic segment, the program type, and the flow state (presuming that changing channels must have disutility for a viewer). The authors concluded that the model had predictive accuracy of 76%, significant for an initial model but of limited value because of the model's complexity even within the three-network situation it tested.

Meanwhile, Tiedge and Ksobiech (1986, 1987, 1988) remeasured the impacts of lead-in, counterprogramming, and sandwich strategies on prime-time ratings in a series of studies utilizing a 23-year population of programs. They concluded that lead-in is very powerful when programs are new or arranged in same-type blocks, or when there are few competitors. They found counterprogramming usually successful when two competitors blunted each other with similar types of content, but not so effective when opponents were counterprogramming with different types of content. They attributed strength to the lead-out when half-hour programs were sandwiched (i.e., blocked with at least two others of the same type fore and aft). These conclusions have generally held up in subsequent research about broadcast television, despite the permanent evaporation of the "few competitors" situation and the presence of interactions arising from the fact that *new* half-hour series are generally scheduled in blocks. Not examined in the 23-year database were the ebb and flow of ratings over time.

However, Webster and Newton (1988) took note of the two major explanations of television exposure—one group veering toward individual characteristics, the other staying with structural characteristics. Inspecting inheritance effects, Webster and Newton examined the case of newscasts, and Walker (1988) examined inheritance in light of new media technologies. Webster and Newton concluded that the news program's rating, its lead-in rating, and the size of the market combined were able to explain 81% of the variation in local news ratings, but lead-in contributed just 9% of the variance. Walker found a strongly positive correlation between lead-in and program ratings occurring before, but not after, 1985, attributing the decreased correlation to remote control penetration. In a shrewd examination of changing industry economics, Atkins and Litman (1986) showed that although broadcast network ratings have declined, revenue losses to cable have been offset by increased home penetration and higher advertising rates, leading them to conclude that each rating point had become more valuable. However, Barwise (1986) examined repeat viewing and then, rather surprisingly, claimed that new technologies brought no fundamental changes to the way people watch television (see Barwise & Ehrenberg, 1988). This is a claim consistently challenged by the findings of many subsequent studies of the impacts of cable, home video recorders, and remote controls.[8]

SCHEDULING THEORY AND PRACTICE: THE 1990s

In the early 1990s, some scholars rejected the macro-level approach to audiences that typified the 1980s, which utilized such mass audience predictors as exposure, availability, and motives, and increasingly adopted the micro-level perspective advocated by Biocca and others. These researchers concentrated more on cognition and such variables as attention, involvement, and awareness, and interest in qualitative methods increased. Thus a split becomes evident between mass audience "sociological-level" concerns regarding aggregate behaviors and individual-level "psychological" concerns about cognition, affect, and individual behavior.[9] A few researchers continued to cross this divide, however. Elizabeth Perse (1990a, 1990b, 1990c), for example, focused directly on the audience's involvement in programming; Carolyn Lin (1990, 1992) looked conceptually at activity in relation to VCR use, noting a shifting of the "locus of control" between industry programmers and individual viewers (1992, p. 345); and Ferguson (1992b) concluded that the new media enhance selectivity and have a negative effect on inheritance.

Two books appeared in 1991 that epitomized the opposing perspectives of audience and industry in relation to programming: Bryant and Zillmann's (1991) edited volume reported on research into viewers' reactions to and perceptions of television, and Webster and Lichty (1991) published a comprehensive text on industry ratings, analyzing ratings theory and methods. The Bryant and Zillmann book comes from the psychological and experimental perspective; the Webster and Lichty book distinguishes between the individual traits approach to explaining audience behavior (referring to demographics such as sex and age) and structural variables in programming (such as availability or scheduling characteristics). Webster and Lichty conclude that structural factors should be given priority over individual traits in explaining mass audience behavior.

At this time, Owen and Wildman (1992) published their powerful analysis of the economic structure of the broadcasting and cable industries and their huge oligopolist power. Douglas Ferguson (1992a) focused on the problem of channel repertoire (a topic explored again by Ferguson & Perse, 1993). They found that repertoires continued to be inexplicably small, given the large number of channels available through cable, the popularity of many cable networks, and the likely end of novelty effects.[10]

Meanwhile, Webster and Wang (1992) examined the structural determinants of exposure to television in repeat viewing, and concluded that the variables of scheduling, ratings, and continuing versus noncontinuing story lines explained 83% of variance in repeat viewing levels for subsequent episodes. Confirming Goodhardt et al. (1987), Webster and Wang found that repeat viewing varied from 20% to 60% and was highest with daytime soaps. They reported a 79% correlation between scheduling and repeat viewing, and a 50% correlation between program type and repeat viewing.[11] This last finding had not appeared in previous research on program types and was unexpectedly high. Applying the audience/industry frame amid the rise of competition, newly significant findings for program type imply changes in audience behavior over time.

Going beyond the three or four broadcast networks situation, Ferguson (1992b) argued that the new media environment appeared to be enhancing selective exposure—in other words, home videotaping and greater cable penetration were having a negative impact on inheritance scores. He concluded that selectivity could be expected to grow over time as new technologies diffused more thoroughly. He also demonstrated some program type effects for news and called for more by-genre studies as well as for research on the reasons for channel changing, the process of group compromise and preference, and the channel characteristics that affect repertoire (Ferguson, 1992b). Ferguson and Perse (1993) concluded that selectivity may be increasing.

Scheduling Versus Preference

Studies published by Cooper (1993) and Adams (1993) illustrated contrasting perspectives within structural programming research at this time. These authors were trying to explain why programming researchers cannot account for all the statistical variance in ratings or shares (presuming them to be adequate approximations of viewer behavior). Roger Cooper (1993) argued that studies have found many scheduling variables that do a good job of explaining audience choice, while at the same time he challenged linear assumptions about the role of the number of competing options when the total number of such options (from cable) is very large and virtually unmeasurable (see also Litman & Kohl, 1992). Cooper (1993) proposed a structural "effects model of choice" (p. 402), incorporating lead-in and lead-out, network affiliation and frequency band, cable penetration, and market concentration, and tested it on all syndicated first-run and off-network programs aired on weekdays in 50 markets. His analysis traced relationships among traditional programming variables unanticipated by conventional programming theory. The important point here is that Cooper concluded that audience availability accounted for the missing variance.

William J. Adams (1993), on the other hand, claimed that most structural studies look only at the short term (one season), and when the history of programs in relation to ratings is examined over decades, most strategies fail to hold up, leaving the assumptions behind them without statistical or theoretical support. Adams analyzed 20 years of use of such structural strategies as counterprogramming, blunting, defensive scheduling (i.e., placing the strongest shows against the competition's strongest shows), and offensive scheduling (placing the strongest shows against the competition's weakest shows). He found that most strategies had no impact on ratings. He concluded that audience preference as well as a historical variable of habit (operationalized as the preexisting strength of the time slot) must be the keys to audience choice and account for ratings variance. Meanwhile, providing some support for Cooper's claims, Rust and Eechambadi (1989) concluded that "audience flow may be more important than program attractiveness in determining ratings" (p. 15). On the other hand, providing some support for Adams's claims, Rust, Kamakura, and Alpert (1992) illustrated advertisers' belief in audience preference ("small but loyal" audiences; p. 16).

Cooper (1996) concluded that most structural factors are grounded in audience duplication "as a major component of program choice models" (p. 96). He argued that structural factors are fundamental to an understanding of viewing patterns, but noted the difficulty of demonstrating linear relationships between inheritance effects and the number of options and/or program type because small amounts of variance are hidden within such aggregate audience measures as ratings/shares. He defined four different types of "duplication," each of which refers to a "special tendency for the audience of one program to be represented in the audience of another program" (p. 96), and argued that they explain patterns of television viewing. Adams (in press), on the other hand, continued to argue for the demise of network television structural strategies, demonstrating their increased utilization by the industry as their effectiveness declined. He concluded that "strength and type-based scheduling appear to be vastly overrated by programmers," supplying further support for his theory that historical program preferences have become the overriding determinant of audience ratings and shares. In contrast, Cooper concluded that levels of repeated exposure to reruns seemed to be a function of viewer availability and ratings, and suggested that repeat exposure may be greater for nonserialized program types—the opposite of the cultivation perspective that viewing would be greater for story-line programs.

About this time, Massey (1995) reopened the question of passive versus active audiences, concluding that qualitative approaches better address the issues. August Grant (1994) went back to the unfinished topic of diversity on television, seeing it within the context of increasing numbers of cable television networks. Steve Sherman (1995) applied the variables affecting repeat viewing on the commercial networks to public television, and found the double-jeopardy effect in patterns nearly identical to those previously asserted for commercial television. In the same year, Lin (1995) published an article that supports many of the conclusions reached here. Testing four programming strategies using game theory, she found a high correlation between declining viewership and increased use of conservative programming strategies, such as counterprogramming and, more recently, blunting. Presumably, declining viewership is a result of increased competition, and conservative programming strategies are those that maximize revenues. Lin made the point, however, that the traditional goal of the largest audience share has now been transformed into the "optimal audience share attainable" (p. 493). Her theory provides an alternate explanation for previous findings by Tiedge and Ksobiech (1986, 1987) that demonstrated a rank order for programming strategies (in descending order: countering a blunt, blunting, countering, and blunting a counter). In addition, her findings support Adams's (1993) argument that programming preferences are the key to successful ratings.

Interactivity

Of all recent developments in home electronics, the remote control device is widely thought to have had the greatest and most sudden impact on audience behavior. In just a decade, its penetration zoomed from a few homes to 94% of television households (Nielsen Media Research, 1997). The remote control has been seen as the primary agent of declining network shares of audience and as the acme of viewer control over the viewing process. Drawing on insider sources in the industry, Ainslie (1988) placed a magnifying lens on the process of using remote control devices and concluded that the proliferation of remotes signaled radical changes for the television industry. Ainslie riveted scholarly attention with the first comprehensive, insider look at the impact of remote controls. Propelled by the availability of industry reports, programming and new-technology researchers immediately undertook a flood of studies. Walker and Bellamy's edited 1993 volume reported the latest research on viewer motives for, and uses of, the remote itself and the social and industry implications. The advent of the remote control, accompanied by the convergence of computers, telephones, and televisions, has triggered an evolving reconception of *activity* as *interactivity,* emphasizing the two-way nature of media processes. Consistent with earlier television research, research into remotes has appeared to confirm the notion of multiple levels of selectivity among TV viewers and a wide range of TV uses and gratifications. Researchers have also concluded that the remote control led to substantial changes in network strategies and practices (see Eastman & Newton, 1995).

The topic of promotion became prominent in convention panels and in journal articles by the mid-1990s, and a few researchers turned their attention to it. Walker (1993) investigated the role of frequency in network on-air promotion's effectiveness and found little positive impact except on continuing series' ratings. Eastman and Otteson (1994) calculated the effectiveness of on-air promotion for prime-time series carried within coverage of the Olympic Games and found virtually no positive impact for promotion and no correlation between program and lead-in ratings or shares. Meanwhile, Schleuder, White, and Cameron (1993) experimented with promotional bumpers and teasers for news and found some positive impact for priming by teasers on attention and verbal (but not visual) memory. Douglas Ferguson (1994) examined grazing as a "mundane" rather than an exceptional behavior (p. 35) and found *underestimation* of channel flipping frequency. Eastman and Newton (1995), in contrast, found very little non-goal-directed "grazing" among most remote users. They concluded that most channel changing was to get to or from specific channels and occurred during the breaks between programs rather than within programs. Eastman, Neal-Lunsford, and Riggs (1995) examined structural and content means of accelerating viewer flow from program to program and found the networks were removing some breaks between programs ("seamlessness," identified by Davis & Walker, 1990), shortening transitions, and altering program ends and starts. In a follow-up study, they established the presence of a modest positive impact on ratings from flow acceleration and concluded that transitional strategies should be added to models of the traditional lead-in and competitive factors affecting audience flow (Eastman, Newton, Riggs, & Neal-Lunsford, 1997).

Eastman, Newton, and Pack (1996) demonstrated the increased relevance of promotion for programming theory. Their verbal model—incorporating inheritance and five other structural and presentational factors—accounted for only 30% of the total variance, and they attributed just 12% of variance to lead-in (while arguing that sports may be a special case). In a follow-up study, Eastman et al. (1997) found a significant relationship between structural salience for promos and program ratings. The total package of structural variables then accounted for as much as 60% of the overall variance in their study, although lead-in remained the most influential single variable. However, its contribution had diminished to only about one-third of the variance, far less than the half of variance accounted for by lead-in alone a decade earlier.[12]

Bellamy and Walker (1996) analyzed the remote control's impact on television viewing, but they also explored broader issues related to the impact of technology on programming theory. These authors concluded that "the power of television as a unifying cultural force may be waning" (p. 120) and that selectivity may be on the increase. They took note of the rise in studies of captive audiences in airports, schools, stores, and other sited television viewing (also called "place-based media"; see Turow, 1992), and they noted the increased impact that advertising will have to have in order to command viewers' attention. Announcing the advent of the immanent *third generation of television,* they postulated that "the industry will have to conform to the desires of the television user—a complete reversal of the first generation [pre-1980s] and a major change from the transitional second generation [approximately 1980-1995]" (p. 147).

Tables 8.2 and 8.3 summarize the trends in structural programming research. Table 8.2 condenses the results of eight key studies, listed from most recent to earliest, that focused on the effects of lead-in ratings/shares on program ratings/shares using correlational methods. Table 8.3 condenses seven related studies that used multiple regression. Both tables report, for each study, the database used (prime-time or syndicated programs or news), the statistical method, the main conclusions, and, insofar as available, the size of the average correlation between lead-in and following program or, in Table 8.3, the amount of variance accounted for by the variables listed horizontally.

Table 8.2 shows that correlations between lead-in and following programs may have dropped precipitously by the mid-1990s (after the widespread adoption of remote controls), and Table 8.3 shows that both the individual impact of lead-in on program ratings and the combined impact of clusters of variables may have fallen between 1985 and 1996. Because the numbers of

TABLE 8.2
Recent Studies Using Correlations Between Lead-In and Program Ratings/Shares

Study	Database	Statistical Method	Dependent Variable/Outcomes	r
Adams, in press	1,137 new network prime-time series population	PPMC with new program ratings	1. Lead-in had only a weak to moderate r for *new* programs.	.35
			2. Lead-in, follow-up, and time slot measure different aspects of a program's ratings performance.	
			3. Strength- and type-based scheduling strategies may be losing effectiveness.	
Walker, 1993	386 on-air promos for prime-time series carried in 151 prime-time hours on three networks	PPMC with program ratings, controlling for lead-in ratings	1. Promotion frequency was not significantly correlated with program ratings overall.	ns
			2. A modest positive correlation between *continuing* (but not *new*) program ratings and promo frequency appeared.	.25
			3. The relationship between promo frequency per episode and ratings changes for *new programs* appeared curvilinear, moving from moderately negative to weakly positive as ratings increased.	

Study	Sample	Method	Findings	r

Davis & Walker, 1990	Shares for prime-time programs with lead-ins aired in 2 weeks of each year from 1983 to 1988	PPMC, with and without controlling for competing options, type compatibility, and program type	1. Share maintenance effects declined from 1983 to 1985 and then rose again from 1986 to 1988.
			2. New technologies did not have a direct linear impact on network shares.
			3. Lead-in shares had a high positive correlation with program shares:
			  a. lead-in shares in 1988
			  b. lead-in shares controlling for options, type, and compatibility
				.75
				.72

Walker, 1988	1,455 network program shares with lead-ins from 2 weeks in each of 4 months in each of 4 years (1976, 1979, 1982, 1985)	PPMC with mean program shares	1. Correlations between lead-in and program shares were stronger when types were the same. 2. Correlations between lead-in and program shares were stronger when pre/post types were the same and competing options were fewer. 3. Inheritance effects have decreased as new media have increased.	.69
Webster & Newton, 1988	Ratings for local early news for a random sample of 103 stations	PPMC with local news ratings	1. Network news audience size is highly dependent on the size of the local news lead-in audience. 2. The local evening news audience is closely linked to the network news audience but less so than no. 1.	.62
Boemer, 1987	2 years of Arbitron ratings for local late news in one large market	PPMC	1. Ratings declined when late local news came on. 2. Mean lead-in ratings and overall news ratings were correlated at moderate to high rate and varied from .69 to .30: a. lead-in overall r	.58

(continued)

TABLE 8.2
Continued

Study	Database	Statistical Method	Dependent Variable/Outcomes	r
Tiedge & Ksobiech, 1986	1,471 network shares with lead-ins in the 22 years between 1963 and 1985 (total population)	PPMC with mean program shares	1. Programs with strong lead-ins gained nearly 7 share points over programs with weak lead-ins. 2. New series gain almost 3 share points more than established shows from a strong lead-in. 3. Inheritance is more than availability; it also reflects type preference and competing options.	.32 for top third of shows; .26 for bottom third of shows
Webster, 1985	Diary-based ratings for 1 month for 74 program pairs for February 1982 for Portland, Maine	PPMC for paired program ratings	1. Overall, about half of one program's audience is inherited from the preceding program: a. inherited viewership 2. The number of competing program options at an interface is inversely related to the size of duplicated audiences.	.50 est.

published studies reporting these kinds of data are few, any trend must be considered suggestive, not conclusive. But the general idea of diminishing values for traditional structural variables is gaining acceptance among programming scholars and has been reflected in industry programmers' concerns as well. The latter suggests that proprietary industry research has been reaching the same conclusion. Evidence appears in the shift of industry interest toward such new concerns as the transitions between programs, methods of display of opening and end credits, and new on-air promotional strategies (see Eastman et al., 1995, 1996). Davis and Walker (1990) pointed to the networks' increasing focus on program acquisition, promotion, and flow within their schedules, and to increased sex and violence in network promotion. Webster and Wang (1992) concluded that the assumption of double jeopardy no longer holds in the "new media environment"—the term proposed earlier by Webster (1986, p. 77) to describe the differential availability of cable channels, many carrying just a single type of programming. Lin (1995) reexamined trends in prime-time network programming strategies using dilemma theory and concluded that increasing competition had caused gradual alternations in industry strategies "to optimize viewing shares and consolidate any potential risk" (p. 493). In programming, one means of reducing risk is to avoid unknown product and employ such tactics as the spin-off program. Previously, Bellamy, McDonald, and Walker (1990) had weighed the effectiveness of the classic industry spin-off strategy for the preceding 28 seasons and found significantly higher mean ratings for spin-offs than for non-spin-off programs (see Table 8.3).

In Europe, along with a flood of scholarly energy within critical and cross-cultural studies, the availability of new measurement methods via people-meters spurred renewed interest in tracking patterns of use (see Hargrave, 1995; Hasebrink & Krotz, 1994). In the United States, the number of unanswered programming questions—or questions with contradictory answers—appeared on the increase. And then Microsoft materialized on the horizon (see Gates, 1995), and on-line services became a very real threat to broadcasting. Thousands of media-related businesses began devoting financial resources to home pages on the Internet in the late 1990s. The digitization of television became both an advantage and a risk. Digitization reenergized the broadcast television industry (and promised sales of hundreds of millions of new television sets to consumers) while it encouraged satellite-distributed competitors and permitted linkages with other media and database services that might eventually consume much of that audience.

Although the biggest menace to broadcast television comes from unnameable on-line services even science fiction writers can now barely imagine, the near-future reality is that the major television networks and their affiliated stations continue to capture most of the audience's attention. Broadcasters have responded to strong competition in two ways. On one front, they have altered their on-air program structures (e.g., they experimented with seamless

TABLE 8.3
Analysis of Influences on Exposure Using Multiple Regression

Study	Database	Statistical Method	Dependent Variable/Outcomes	R^2 (variance accounted for)
Eastman et al., 1997	Duplicated adult viewers in prime time (custom 4-week Nielsen sample) tracking 240 program transitions	regression	1. Lead-in was not correlated with r/s.	
			2. Combined effect of variables on duplicated viewers:	44%
			a. compatibility of adjacent program types	12% add.
			b. number of competing options	9% add.
			c. transitions (program ends and break length)	65%
			3. Concluded that lead-in ratings/shares did not affect duplicated viewing in prime time.	
			4. Compatible program type, competing options, and transitional strategies affected duplicated viewing.	
			5. Differences between fall and spring viewing can be explained in terms of familiarity, with network strategies having more impact when programs are new than when they are largely known to viewers.	
Sherman, 1995	Average ratings for 42 PTV series aired between 1988 and 1994; repeat viewing estimated using assumed levels of repeat viewing	regression	1. Combined effects of variables on repeat viewing:	
			a. rating	n.a.
			b. story line	n.a.
				60%
			2. Concluded that double-jeopardy effect did not operate for public television because higher viewing associated with more repeat viewing and lower viewing associated with less repeat viewing.	

		3. Stripped programs had higher rates of repeat viewing than programs scheduled once a week. 4. Continuing story lines associated with higher levels of repeat viewing.	
Cooper, 1993	Ratings for stripped non-prime-time syndicated programs aired in 50 randomly selected markets	regression	1. Combined variance in structural and market factors on syndicated programs' rating: a. lead-in b. lead-out 2. Concluded that the combined effects of lead-in and lead-out ratings overwhelmed such other factors as market concentration, cable penetration, network affiliation, and competing options.	n.a. $\frac{\text{n.a.}}{87\%}$
Webster & Wang, 1992	Estimated duplicate viewing from 4 weeks of peoplemeter ratings based on distribution assumption	regression	1. Combined effects of variables on average percentage of estimated viewing: a. scheduling (day/strip-nonstrip) b. ratings c. program type 2. Concluded that repeat viewing was no longer about 55% but was usually much lower, and levels varied from 20% to 60%. 3. Double jeopardy did not operate as repeat viewing could not be predicted from program ratings. 4. Ratings need to be combined with scheduling information to predict exposure.	n.a. n.a. $\frac{\text{n.a.}}{83\%}$

(continued)

TABLE 8.3
Continued

Study	Database	Statistical Method	Dependent Variable/Outcomes	R^2 (variance accounted for)
Bellamy et al., 1990	mean yearly ratings for 59 spin-off series aired between 1955 and 1988	regression	1. Combined effect of variables on yearly average ratings:	
			a. program type/year	17%
			b. channel effects	6% more
			c. status (parent/spin-off)	6% more
			d. inheritance (lead-in)	4% more
				33%
			2. Spin-off series have lower average ratings than their parent series but higher ratings than new series not linked to previously successful series.	
Webster & Newton, 1988	ratings for a random sample of 103 stations	regression	1. Combined effect of variables on early local news:	
			a. network news ratings	67%
			b. lead-in rating	9%
			c. PUT level	5%
				81%
			2. Concluded that within-channel structural factors have a powerful impact on the size of program audiences.	
			3. Availability interacts with individual needs and gratifications and should be studied together.	

Webster, 1985	1-month ratings for 74 program pairs in one small market drawn from 500 women	regression	1. Combined effect of variables on duplicated pairs:	
			a. lead-in program's rating	68%
			b. number of competing options	13%
			c. program rating	3%
			d. program type	1%
				85%
			2. Concluded that the adjacent program inherited 50% of its audience in prime time.	
			3. Patterns of audience flow are largely the result of viewer availability, accompanied by both lead-in and program ratings, scheduling variables, and program type variables.	
			4. Inheritance effects are likely to become increasingly important as cable proliferates.	

transitions from program to program and intensified the blocking of whole evenings with similar programs). But their biggest efforts have gone into domestic and international marketing. They strengthened both their brand identification, through improved on-air promotion and print marketing, and their brand positioning around the world as the preeminent suppliers of original entertainment. As the century shifted, the larger networks, and companies such as Time Warner and AT&T, sought to broaden their array of product offerings under their umbrella identifiers (logos, wordmarks) in the process known as brand clustering.

THE NEXT STEPS

Where does this leave programming scholars? Three questions seem central here: How should programmers conceive of activity and thus selectivity? What is happening to structural flow theories? What are the implications for the on-line era of programming research to date?

Six Decades of Flow Research

What have six decades of programming research shown? Looking back over the more than 40 years of television programming research, one can see how the thrust toward patterns of use (of television) became models of choice and then reappeared as patterns of use in a larger framework of more competing channels. The studies show conceptions of preference shifting to conceptions of structural inheritance, and then preference reappears again. What was first seen as direct inheritance became more complex as lead-in effects were seen to be mediated by such factors as the number of competing program options, the compatibility of adjacent and competing program genres, the types of flow accelerators, and the amount and type of program promotion.

Clearly, then, direct inheritance's importance decreases as viewers' options become very large, and by the 1990s at the broadcast networks, the success of flow strategies had receded in favor of a flood of experimental counterprogramming strategies. However, blocking had resurfaced by the mid-1990s in combination with new strategies for accelerating flow and promoting entire evenings of programming. But despite improvements in researchers' ability to identify and measure more variables accounting for viewer behavior, the collective amount of variance that can be accounted for has shrunk rather than grown. Two explanations are evident: Methodologies may have been improved and thus better reflect conditions as they always were, or audience behaviors may have changed over time and reflect a shifting locus of control. In practice, programming researchers in the 1990s often find they must greatly narrow their focus (for example, to repeat viewing within adjacent series programs only inside prime time) to command significant results.

Just a decade ago, it seemed safe to claim that at least half the prime-time audience was inherited from the preceding program (see Table 8.2). By 1987, only about a quarter of viewing appeared to be a function of lead-in program ratings, probably because of greatly increased program options and the ability to reach those options easily. Although scholars have found that ratings remain fairly steady from week to week, the viewers who make up the percentages change; at least 40% of any original set of viewers are not watching any television at a second point in time. By 1997, several related structural variables—including lead-in as well as competition, program genres, and transitions—could account for only about 60% of variance in viewing (as measured by ratings/shares). Of that, the amount accounted for by lead-in appeared to be diminishing, and the role of program type appeared to be increasing. Of course, ratings are poor measures to begin with, so researchers can never expect to explain most of their variance; there will always be an element of randomness because of unreliable data collection and analysis. The collective total of variance accounted for in the Eastman et al. (1997) study has importance because the study used actual duplicated viewers (as calculated by Nielsen in a customized analysis), not estimated duplicated (or repeat) viewers using a formula. Nonetheless, we can ask why more precisely measured variables do not achieve bigger increments in explanatory power. In the past, explanations have ranged from differences in audience availability to specific scheduling characteristics to promotion's impact to viewers' degree of involvement with programs. Because repeat viewing levels vary with the daypart examined, Cooper (1996) may be right when he says that "popularity (ratings) causes loyalty (repeat viewing)," or it may be the case that repeat viewing causes popularity. But because Cooper also finds it logical that some *types* of programs lend themselves to repeat viewing, he comes closer to Adams's (in press) position on the role of genre, habit, and program preference. Other researchers have found that each program's audience contains a mix of frequent, infrequent, and nonviewers, and that as people are available to view, strong loyalties affect program choice.

In general, programming scholars are likely to concur that program choice—and thus the success of industry strategies as measured in ratings—has been and is influenced by program structure, but not as much as was once expected. The remaining variance may be largely personal preference for programs. Following are a few of the conclusions about program structure that have held up through shifts in research perspectives and models and through innovations in methodology. Far from comprehensive, this list nonetheless suggests that scholarly research has been fruitful—at least for scholars:

1. Lead-in matters more than any other variable, but less as competition becomes greater and stiffer.
2. Flow enhancement strategies matter for new programs, but little for established programs.

3. Variations in availability cause uninterpretable variance in ratings, making shares a better measure for finding the factors affecting exposure.
4. Program choice occurs in stages.
5. The decision of what to watch on television is not always preceded by the decision to watch some television.
6. Both the audience and the industry are active, but the amount and strength of activity vary with the historical moment and with such factors as new technologies, new strategies, and stronger competitive efforts.
7. New technologies that aid audience choice are generally successful with viewers and to some degree undercut previously successful industry strategies.
8. The industry's structural and marketing strategies may account for about one-third of the variance in ratings. The remainder can generally be attributed to preference (although inherent weaknesses in ratings measurement mean that a large portion of variance is always unattributable).
9. Factors such as group or independent viewing, dependency relationships, accessibility of technologies (personal television sets, remote controls), and preselected repertoires of narrowly defined program genres having age, sex, and lifestyle affinity may explain much of program preference.
10. Entropy always prevails eventually.

The Hidden Tug-of-War

Where does the tug-of-war reside? In this analysis, the tug-of-war emerged in the sway of the locus of control between industry and audience. In the period of stability in the 1950s and 1960s, the industry's selection of programs held sway; viewers had very little choice and could only turn off the television set. During the rise of competition in the 1970s, their choices increased somewhat (ABC achieved parity), leading the networks to focus on manipulating viewers through closely monitored scheduling strategies and the orchestration of ratings and program content. During this period, diversity in program types diminished sharply (Wakshlag & Adams, 1985). But it was in the 1980s that the movement of the rope—pulling back and forth—most clearly emerged: As VCRs appeared, viewers could avoid the networks' schedules, yet see the programs; as cable spread widely, viewers could change to more and more channels; as the remote control became common, viewers could change those channels with great ease and convenience, and they discovered the joys (and irritations) of grazing. But the industry was not standing still. When VCRs appeared, the networks intensified their efforts by broadcasting "special live" programs and by making unpredictable last-minute schedule changes (called stunting) that attempted to forestall frequent home recording. All the networks began placing their most attractive programs as evening lead-offs (7:00 or 8:00 p.m.), bracing new programs in hammocks between established programs, and bolstering sagging evening schedules with tent-pole programs or counterprogramming. Until the 1980s, the networks had not put much effort into programming strategies and the research to support them.

Then, as cable penetration swelled, the networks soon multiplied their budgets for program production to outdo whatever financing the fledgling cable networks could muster. In this period, rights fees for sporting events, for example, escalated beyond imagining, and the licensing fees for programs in general rapidly shot upward. Simultaneously, the air filled with cheap-to-produce newsmagazines and real-people series. When remote control use threatened the size of their audiences, advertisers turned to roadblocking (i.e., airing the same ad on several channels at the same time) and the networks turned to such strategies as seamless transitions from program to program (avoiding any impetus toward channel changing). When that proved not enough, the networks invested tremendous sums in program promotion. In the 1990s, a large portion of the industry's attention shifted to vertical integration, with the goal of gaining worldwide market share and instant recognition by potential viewers in countless non-English-speaking countries.

The short history of television programming reflects the audience's periodic tugs on the rope of control and the industry's periodic tugs back. Although industry strategies for gaining and holding viewers are continuous parts of television scheduling, viewer strategies for controlling their own viewing/using situation also operate continuously. But what stands out are bursts of new practices implemented to solve particular loss-of-control problems. The history of programming is not just a history of technology. Indeed, several technologies have failed to appeal to viewers and thus resulted in very little industry attention. Consider, for example, teletext, videotex, and subcarriers as they were first implemented. Even backyard satellite dishes and direct broadcasting were not threats for more than a decade, and their advent cannot be associated with widespread use of new industry strategies because they were not widely adopted by viewers.

But the tug-of-war between industry and audience is not the whole story. Alongside has been a tug-of-war between research perspectives: on one side, a concern for the effects of exposure; on the other, an acknowledgment of the selective nature of effects because of viewers' willingness to participate in those "effects" by using the media in ways that give rise to them. For example, with regard to remote control use, Bellamy and Walker (1996) have distinguished sharply between the "desire for control" and the "locus of control":

> Respondents who believe they are in control of their behaviors and fates seem to exercise more control over the viewing environment by changing channels more frequently. However, those who desire control, but do not necessarily believe they have it, appear to use the [remote control device] less. Perhaps their desire for control is partially the result of their perceived lack of real control. (p. 106)

The Contribution of Two-Sided Activity

In what way is knowledge of the industry essential to studies of audience? Traditional programming theory built on three decades of industry stability was deeply undermined by the rapid spread of cable TV in the 1980s, then made nearly moot by the dispersal of the remote control in the 1990s, and finally nearly eviscerated by the threat of on-line video services before the year 2000. But studies of programming have discovered principles of television audience activity that can illuminate the on-line activity of the future. It is important to recognize, however, that although early adopters give signals that can guide our understanding, they differ in important ways from the bulk of the audience. Inadvertent shifts between samples of early and later adopters may account for much of the fluctuation in audience behaviors that appeared in programming studies throughout the 1980s.

What significance does the "activity" of the industry have? How does it help to reconceptualize the audience/industry relationship as a back-and-forth rope pull? There are several answers: (a) The nondialectical model better accounts for technology's role, which always fell a bit short of the defining position some scholars tried to give it; (b) it places programming theories about structure and preference in the mainstream alongside models of audience choice; (c) it explains the chronological movement of programming theory from a focus on scheduling strategies to models of choice and then to structural factors by tying theories and models to specific historical times; (d) it helps predict the likely directions for research in the on-line era by pinpointing some elements of theory to date that will apply, as well as others likely to fall by the wayside; and (e) it extends the uses and gratifications model into "agency." Summarizing the U&G research, Rubin (1994) has reported five characteristics in recent research: (a) Communication behavior is goal directed, purposive, and motivated, because people are relatively active communication participants with behavior that has functions and consequences; (b) people use media rather than are used by it; (c) a host of social and psychological factors mediate communication behavior; (d) the media compete with other activities for selection, attention, and use; and (e) people are usually more influential than media, but not always. If one adopts the perspective that the industry is as active as the audience, then Rubin's second point becomes inadequate: The "use" is on both sides, continuous, and complementary.

As the crucial factors of diversity, competition, activity, motivation, and selectivity intensify, inheritance will diminish and entropy will increasingly prevail. Flow from lead-in and lead-off programs will recede further, and such structural industry strategies as sandwiching, hammocking, and perhaps blocking will have less effectiveness. Counterprogramming becomes a trivial concept in an environment of, say, 200 or more cable/telephone/computer channels, where more than a few competitors will be targeting every conceivable audience group. And in a virtually unlimited on-line environment, counterprogramming becomes meaningless. But the study of agency and attention should prove fruitful for the immediate on-line future, and these elements should play crucial roles in surviving programming theories.

IMPLICATIONS FOR PROGRAMMING
IN THE COMING DECADE

In the digital era, there are at least three new broad questions to be answered. The broadcast and cable industries will want to know which strategies will be most effective in preserving a strong role for traditional television. A more interesting question is how television programs and programming must change to attract viewing in the digital on-line environment. Finally, the most intriguing question of all, but one that cannot be approached at this early date, is how experiencing television on-line (however it appears) will differentially affect people—in Zillmann and Bryant's (1985) terms, What effects on program choice will consumption of television by means of on-line services have?

Models of choice tended to be too static—good only for particular points in time. Such models were in constant need of revision, not because they were necessarily inadequate at given times, but because what the industry did changed and the audience response changed, and thus the circumstances of viewing were altered. A theory from the biological sciences seems germane to accounting for the fits and starts of the relatively short history of programming. In evolution, scientists have recognized that species undergo rapid periods of change followed by long periods of stability, a process called *punctuated equilibrium.* It follows that programming models that allow for a shifting locus of control become essential. How the audience views (uses/ interacts with) television shifts not only with individuals' circumstances but with the industry's strategies for capturing or recapturing viewing. Although no one can predict the dimensions and uses of new media technologies in the 21st century in detail, several assumptions about the era of smart televisions are likely, such as those discussed below.

Availability will no longer be a meaningful programming fundamental, except on the individual level. Portable digital technology can be expected to utterly reconfigure viewing patterns. Large amounts of television viewing will take place in locations other than the home, undermining the concept of dayparting and the centrality of prime time. Although 8:00-11:00 p.m. will continue to be important, such industry changes as the end of access time and the end of network limits on syndication and financial participation, such technical developments as video on demand, and such societal changes as flextime and telecommuting will eventually spread viewing outside formerly traditional boundaries.

Preference will dominate over structure. Individuals will be inclined to seek both favorite and highly self-relevant media. The sequencing of programs, the transitions between them, and the structural strategies for lead-in, lead-off, blocking, and counterprogramming will become less important than other facets, such as capturing the essence of a program's appeal in brief promotional spots. Indeed, the development of smart agents to help viewers find their preferred programs will be a major endeavor. Eventually, these smart agents within television sets will automatically winnow the plethora of options for viewers and present the few most likely options that match individuals' expressed preferences. (The maximum number of options may fall between 8 and 13, both historically salient quantities that can be encompassed visually by most people with ease.) Self-imposed and wholly individualistic structures of choice will evolve, and most industry scheduling structures larger than the unit of whole entertainment programs will be dispensed with (at least for continuing series; new series and one-time-only shows will necessitate special treatment).

Branding of programs will become an essential ingredient. From the industry's perspective, effective branding will be key to building audiences; from the audience's perspective, branding will be key to awareness of options and thus program choice. Alongside the present-day fixation on international branding of the major services, branding of individual programs through promotion and marketing will become essential within a preference-driven system. As smart cable boxes (or other agents within TV sets) learn what particular viewers like and how to locate those kinds of programs, it will be up to programmers to describe and promote their programs accurately and effectively. Marketing and promotion will encompass user-friendly, menu-driven systems, barker information, interactive indexing of programs, and promotions that reward viewers for watching commercials (and presumably the programs carrying them). Programs without promotion will be invisible. But on-air promotion itself may be invisible unless what is being promoted fits within viewers' predetermined parameters.

Program typologies will generate renewed researcher interest. New ways will be needed to define genre or program type. From the industry side, the goal will be to maximize appeals in fine-tuned promotional efforts targeting very narrow subgroups of viewers/users. From the audience side, researchers will continue to seek to interpret and model audience behavior and program choice. Program types will be crucial identifiers in the menu structures that will precede automated programming.

Interactivity can be expected to play a big role in the process of selecting programs to watch, but only a small role in intraprogram construction. Interactivity, defined as real-time audience feedback other than ratings, will be unimportant to the predominant types of entertainment programs—situation comedies, dramas, and movies. Interactive television has already become successful in hotel rooms. Business travelers are finding that they can use their rooms' television sets to make reservations; to check out; to order food, flowers, and clothes; to send and receive e-mail; and to surf the Internet (Sterngold, 1996). And interactivity has a role to play in audience response to commercials and in programs targeting children and teens. For the bulk of home viewers in the coming decade, however, interactivity is unlikely to be important to entertainment program content directly—at least for programs targeting adults, with the likely exceptions of such activities as home shopping, participating in game shows, and perhaps selecting news topics. Personalized television programs (where viewers select among alternate pathways) will be most useful in educational materials and in games played by younger viewers. Most adults, most of the time, will still want the attributes of convenience, escape, and one-way entertainment demonstrated heretofore in programming and audience research. They will gradually use intelligent computer programs to select a few options, but will have little energy to make decisions about plots or to give elaborate feedback. Interactivity thus appears vital to the commercial side of television and to the search process to locate programs. Viewers' differential degrees of selectivity can be expected to increase. However, children and teens may be more active viewers and may demand a mix of interactive and traditional storytelling programs, and may carry those expectations into adulthood in the subsequent generation.

Understanding the mechanisms of attention and predicting degrees/levels of involvement and engagement with programs will become one of the two main focuses of cognitive theory and research. Research into micro-level characteristics such as attention and involvement has promise for increasing understanding of both audience and industry behaviors. Development of a conceptual understanding of cognition will always rank high among academic concerns, and understanding of cognitive processes may even spin off some practical applications in program conception, design, and implementation. There may be a coming together of the two strands of audience and industry research in studies of—as yet undefined—concepts such as involvement. Certainly, understanding the processes of cognition that operate in individuals' choices among television programs can contribute to the development of agents that will act on behalf of viewers.

Agency as it affects audience flow and behavior will become the other main thrust of research. Digital television lends itself to the incorporation of agents to act for individual viewers. This meaning of *agent* comes from the traditional word for someone who acts for an owner, as in a shipping agent or estate factor. Thus *agent* refers to soon-to-be-practical computer software that can be preprogrammed to search among program options. These agents will become increasingly intelligent, applying more complex directions and ultimately learning from experience about their viewers' preferences. Analysis of the processes of selection represented by viewer use of agent software will become the focus of researchers interested in new technologies and in decision making. Eventually, however, the software will evolve from "black boxes" into "avatars"—electronic representations of users in virtual worlds, representing individual people and understanding and intelligently mimicking human speech and behavior—who will "find" information, programs, or products in virtual space and interact with other avatars in shopping, games, work, and play. At a broader level, research into agency will become the study of the more abstract locus of control of viewing at a given point in time, encompassing a source and its concerns, the users of media and their concerns, and the process of shifting balance between the two. From a communication perspective, the study of interactions within virtual spaces can only gain in strength and importance.

In the near future, researchers focusing on audiences (or "users") will want to know (a) how people construct their television choice parameters and (b) what effectuates changes in those boundaries. Attention will also go to (c) how individuals develop preferences and (d) how groups negotiate decision making. Those researchers focusing on industry practices will want to know (e) what structural and content factors influence programs' being chosen and (f) how relatively effective these factors are (because a single program supplier cannot do all "effective" things at one time with regard to one program). Another area of interest will be (g) comparative analyses, not so much cross-media (as broadcast/cable comparisons were once called) as intramedia and within genre. Studies will examine the comparative strategies across genres—just sports programming, just situation comedies, just movies—and locate their analyses within the socio/economic/cultural complex of technological availability and strategic concerns.

DISCUSSION

One might fairly ask whether the industry has been affected by scholarly programming research. For most of the past three decades, the answer is properly a resounding *no,* as has also been the case with much scholarly policy and technology research, despite purported close ties to the industry in all three areas. Until the end of the 1980s, little communications research was acknowledged by industry executives, a situation that dismayed many neophyte programming (and policy and technology) scholars. However, the peril of competition from such menacing entities as Microsoft and AT&T through on-line services forcefully changed the situation. The threat of competition generated an enormous industry anxiety about "getting a leg up" on these new and tougher competitors. It is important to recognize that competition has grown not only through a greater number of competitors, but also through more powerful competitive practices. By the mid-1990s, the directors of research at some of the largest networks were poring over scholarly programming research for useful tidbits. Even the tiniest advantage can be worth millions of dollars in revenue to a network. Given the woeful underfunding of most academic research, scholars' ideas usually lead not to direct industry impacts but to further research—with bigger databases and more sophisticated analyses—by industry programmers and Nielsen Media Research, which may or may not uphold the original hypotheses and conclusions. But as the merits of the ideas (i.e., likelihood of making money or increasing market share) accrue, those that survive the sifting eventually influence not only the major American broadcast networks but, potentially, the cable networks and the international and foreign national networks. Do scholars' best ideas ever have much impact on local television stations? Probably not. Industry arrogance and shortsightedness are most entrenched there. As Bellamy and Walker (1996) have noted, the big players know enough to worry about other big competitors; the small players rarely recognize their vulnerability.

It is easy to assume a "gee whiz" stance regarding new media technologies. As one considers such innovations as wall-sized plasma screens, soon to be followed by virtual reality holography in the home (so say the optimistic pundits), one is tempted to conclude that one-way network entertainment television will soon be just plain irrelevant. But interactivity takes energy and some self-awareness of needs. Traditional broadcasting allows for less active—but not wholly inactive—viewing. Even the V-chip brings complaints that it represents a loss of control of viewing (DePalma, 1996). A mix of conventional television serial programs, sports, movies, and news on structured one-way channels will continue to find huge mass audiences in prime time. As Eli Noam said when the announcement was made that AT&T will offer some free Internet access to its subscribers, "The Internet is going to take one further step toward being a mass medium" (quoted in Lewis, 1996, p. A-1). Much attention has been focused on the means of delivery—the megamergers, the digital pathways—but the real function of television is mass audience storytelling. Sustained, mass-appeal storytelling requires a complex set of professional skills that are television's forte and will remain the purview of big-budget studios and major program producers.

Recently, Fidler (1997) asked two questions especially pertinent to programming: Will mass entertainment television actually shift to a collaborative, process-oriented mode? Or will it have only the illusion of audience control? Indeed, the submessage of network broadcasting is mass entertainment and information interwoven with commercials, media that were largely encountered passively until the advent of cable and remote controls and preprogramming on increasingly smarter television sets. Scholars are right to refer to the illusion of control, because an imbalance of power persists between content and medium providers. The user-as-program-provider will occur sometimes and in some contexts. Clearly, selecting news topics makes sense; at-home shopping and game playing make obvious sense. But the preponderance of exposure/consumption will continue to be of entire entertainment programs. Selecting from among menu choices makes sense only for types of programs (Do you want movies? News? Sitcoms? Sports?) and subclasses within those categories (If sports, do you want basketball? College or professional? Which geographic region? Men's or women's games?). The features of sports that make events particularly involving have received some research attention, but the characteristics of engagement within entertainment programs need closer study. Predicting megahit programs has remained more art than science.

The tens of millions of television viewers who came to computers in adult life will continue to constitute the bulk of the television audience through the first quarter of the 21st century. They will be reluctant to give up a modest form of activity to become the highly interactive viewers that some scholars imagine. Because *on-line* refers also to smart TV sets or computers that display entertainment television programs (cutely called *telecomputers*), programming scholars should not be distracted by the issues of electronic mail and interactive games and shopping. They should focus on the traditional prime-time entertainment fare that will continue to be the mainstay of audience entertainment. Such entertainment will, however, move out of prime time into all dayparts and seasons as work/school/shop at home, any-season vacations, part-time out-of-house obligations, and frequent lifestyle changes increase. Interactivity, beyond the level of channel changing by remote (or eventually by voice), will not be appealing for most entertainment because adults want to relax in the evenings and, for the most part, absorb, view, watch, and consume undemanding programs that tell stories. Television is the great storyteller, and stories have been central to "entertainment" throughout history.

The topic of program typology has been a thorn in the side of researchers throughout the nearly 50 years of television history. The industry has tended to use just a few types, but their number has grown somewhat over the decades. Nielsen Media Research generally reported just 9 types in the 1960s and 1970s (the quantity Rust & Alpert used in their 1984 research), but reported 40 and utilized as many as 22 groupings in its specialized studies in the early 1990s. Similarly, Adams (1993) found 41 types of programs by asking large numbers of viewers to undertake Q-sorts of representative selections of real programs by title and brief description. Moreover, in his 40-year program population summaries, Shapiro (1989) classified prime time into as many as 69 types, and said that new ones may be emerging in the 1990s. Webster and Wang's (1992) findings of remarkably strong relationships between program scheduling and repeat viewing and between repeat viewing and program type should stimulate further investigation. Definition of program types will require much more care than it has received in the past if it is to be useful for menus and selective software. The very real possibility exists that some classes of programs will be deleted owing to widespread lack of viewer accessing, thus eliminating even the possibility of their accidentally capturing viewers through grazing. Engaging and credible promotion on the air and in other media will become crucial to placing a service's programs among the options for millions of viewers. Barker channels of the future may multiply in order to focus exclusively on programs appealing to narrowly defined audience groups.

Whether one imagines that people will get most of their entertainment through smart television sets or computer screens, scholars can assume the proliferation of individual reception units that can be elaborately preprogrammed to match their particular users' preferences. Already, RCA offers a home satellite dish with a primitive menu-driven system that allows viewers to program some of their preferences. Huge group-viewing sets—with picture-in-picture—have already appeared that family/friends watch together because they choose to watch together. As work, education, and shopping become more convenient and disassociated from particular places, they will occur more in isolation from other people; to fulfill the need for companionship, people will choose more group entertainment and virtual activities. As other scholars have pointed out, media researchers should examine the choice of viewing alone or in a group—the process of compromise essential to group viewing and concomitant increases or decreases in selectivity. Researchers should also evaluate promotion's necessarily greater role amid greater competition and less predetermined flow. And researchers should delve into the role of genre/type in instant preference clues in menu selection. These lines of research will converge as the study of avatars becomes practical. The contrasts between virtual and in-person communication behaviors will provide an extraordinary laboratory for study outside conventional laboratories.

NOTES

1. These figures come from comments made by Horst Stipp, NBC vice president for research, at the Broadcast Education Association meeting held in Las Vegas, April 4, 1997.

2. Distribution of the first generation of digital television sets and the transmission of some digital programming is set for the spring of 1998 (Landler, 1996). Digitization of broadcast television (permitting progressive scanning like computers use rather than only interlace scanning) sets the stage for massive changes in the services television sets can provide for home users. Limited on-line linkages will be one of the first digital services because of its ready marketability. Convergence is finally coming, albeit slowly from the vantage point of the 1990s audience (but immensely swiftly from a historical perspective).

3. Why not a teeter-totter image? One could presume that, over time, if one could quantify all changes at the industry and audience ends, that the overall average *might* balance. But that is somewhat misleading because it necessitates imagining each end swelling or shrinking along with changes in technology and scheduling strategies to tilt the balance—not what commonly happens on your neighborhood teeter-totter.

4. Economic and cultural scholars such as Ien Ang (1991) assume greater industry malevolence by placing media-driven media within a larger sociological perspective. Economists such as Owen and Wildman (1992) recognize many counterbalancing forces and conclude that individual or groups of media companies have only modest influence.

5. About the same time, researchers' attention was galvanized by Gary Steiner's (1963) comprehensive survey in *The People Look at Television,* along with Harold E. Krugman's (1965) classic on how people learn from advertising "without involvement," and Marshall McLuhan's

invigorating conception of the television medium's own vital importance (in *The Gutenberg Galaxy,* 1962, and later books).

6. *Audience shares* refers to the percentages of those using television (and thus available to become part of some audience), whereas *ratings* refers to percentages of all television households (thus everybody, irrespective of whether they are sleeping, working, or doing something other than watching television). Ratings are always smaller than shares, because the size of the total pie is so much larger. Shares are considered the purer programming measure because they show how one network/station does against its competition, not how it does against all other possible activities collectively.

7. Although most programming researchers were concerned with how audiences selected and used television, an old topic also related to television programs resurfaced: content analyses of television shows, epitomized by Greenberg and D'Alessio's (1985) look at sex in soaps. Many such analyses in the late 1980s looked at race and gender roles or specific reactive behaviors, typically deploring low counts of some variable (role models of one kind or another, nonviolent responses to verbal provocations) and then presuming causal effects from the absence of the key group or behavior, despite the problematic nature of that assumption. Although viewing the content of television through a microscope reveals much about its warts and mythologies and can be used to track changes in content, it is of little use for deducing changes in audience behavior or industry manipulations—the foci of this chapter.

8. In 1989, DeFleur and Ball-Rokeach published the fifth edition of their widely used *Theories of Mass Communication,* and Salvaggio and Bryant published an edited volume largely looking back on the new media technologies that had so characterized the 1980s. Also in 1989, Wenner's edited volume on media and sports appeared, signaling an increasingly wider interest in televised sports, a long-ignored aspect of entertainment programming with its own special economics, strategies, and appeals.

9. Two other directions for analyses of program content that were evident by the mid-1990s are not discussed here: Feminist scholars focused on the ways in which gender was created and maintained (and advantaged) in programs, and other scholars began serious exploration of the creation and maintenance of racial stereotypes.

10. Also in the 1990s, considerable American scholarly attention was directed toward the cultural significance of television audience practices and the interpretation of the content of television programs. The influence of David Morley's 1993 criticisms of activity theory was widely felt. The prolific Bryant and Zillmann published an updated volume titled *Media Effects: Advances in Theory and Research* (1994), which contains chapters by advocates of most theoretical perspectives. In it, Gerbner, Gross, Morgan, and Signorielli (1994) explain television as a system of storytelling in which exposure to the total pattern (not specific programs or genres) accounts for the consequences of living with television: "the cultivation of shared conceptions of reality among otherwise diverse publics" (p. 18). Violence is conceived as a demonstration of power in the TV world. The cultivation perspective rejects the "before/after" exposure model because, its proponents argue, television enters infants' lives from the start, and rejects the "intervening variables" model because television affects the formation of the interveners (pp. 18-21).

11. Webster and Wang (1992, p. 128) include an especially useful table summarizing research on repeat viewing of television programs, a topic of particular interest to programming scholars.

12. It will never be possible to account for all variance in ratings because ratings themselves are error filled and some behavior will always appear random. Nonetheless, one must ask what accounts for the remaining 40% or so.

REFERENCES

Adams, W. J. (1993). TV program scheduling strategies and their relationship to new program renewal rates and rating changes. *Journal of Broadcasting & Electronic Media, 37,* 465-474.

Adams, W. J. (in press). Scheduling practices based on audience flow: What are the effects on new program success? *Journalism Quarterly.*

Adams, W. J., Eastman, S. T., Horney, L., & Popovich, M. (1983). Cancellation and manipulation of prime-time programming. *Journal of Communication, 33*(1), 10-28.

Ainslie, P. (1988, September). Confronting a nation of grazers. *Channels: The Business of Communications,* pp. 54-62.

Anderson, J. A., & Meyer, T. P. (1988). *Mediated communication: A social action perspective.* Newbury Park, CA: Sage.

Ang, I. (1991). *Desperately seeking the audience.* New York: Routledge.

Atkins, D., & Litman, B. (1986). Network television programming: Economics, audiences, and the ratings game, 1971-1986. *Journal of Communication, 36*(3), 32-51.

Babrow, A. S. (1988). Theory and method in research on audience motives. *Journal of Broadcasting & Electronic Media, 32,* 471-487.

Bailey, R. L. (1970). The content of network television prime-time special programming: 1948-1968. *Journal of Broadcasting, 14,* 325-336.

Baldwin, T. F., McVoy, S., & Steinfield, C. (1996). *Convergence: Integrating media, information, and communication.* Thousand Oaks, CA: Sage.

Ball-Rokeach, S. (1985). The origins of individual media-system dependency: A sociological framework. *Communication Research, 12,* 485-510.

Bantz, C. R. (1982). Exploring uses and gratifications: A comparison of reported uses of television and reported uses of favorite program type. *Communication Research, 9,* 352-379.

Barnouw, E. (1968). *The golden web: A history of broadcasting in the U.S. from 1933-1953.* New York: Oxford University Press.

Barwise, T. P. (1986). Repeat viewing of prime-time series. *Journal of Advertising Research, 26,* 27-31.

Barwise, T. P., & Ehrenberg, A. S. C. (1988). *Television and its audience.* London: Sage.

Barwise, T. P., Ehrenberg, A. S. C., & Goodhardt, G. J. (1982). Glued to the box? Patterns of repeat-viewing. *Journal of Communication, 32*(4), 22-29.

Bauer, R. A. (1963). The initiative of the audience. *Journal of Advertising Research, 3,* 2-7.

Bauer, R. A. (1964). The obstinate audience: The influence process from the point of view of social communication. *American Psychologist, 19,* 319-328.

Bauer, R. A., & Bauer, A. (1960). America, "mass society," and mass media. *Journal of Social Issues, 16,* 3-66.

Bellamy, R. V., Jr., McDonald, D. G., & Walker, J. R. (1990). The spin-off as television form and strategy. *Journal of Broadcasting & Electronic Media, 34,* 283-297.

Bellamy, R. V., Jr., & Walker, J. R. (1996). *Television and the remote control: Grazing on a vast wasteland.* New York: Guilford.

Berlo, D. K. (1977). Communication as process: Review and commentary. In B. D. Ruben (Ed.), *Communication yearbook 1* (pp. 11-27). New Brunswick, NJ: Transaction.

Biocca, F. A. (1988). Opposing conceptions of the audience: The active and passive hemispheres of mass communication theory. In J. A. Anderson (Ed.), *Communication yearbook 11* (pp. 51-80). Newbury Park, CA: Sage.

Blumler, J. G. (1979). The role of theory in uses and gratifications research. *Communication Research, 6,* 9-36.

Blumler, J. G., & Katz, E. (Eds.). (1974). *The uses of mass communications: Current perspectives on gratifications research.* Beverly Hills, CA: Sage.

Boemer, M. L. (1987). Correlating lead-in show ratings with local television news ratings. *Journal of Broadcasting & Electronic Media, 31,* 89-94.

Brown, L. (1971). *Television: Behind the box.* New York: Harcourt Brace Jovanovich.

Bryant, J., & Zillmann, D. (Eds.). (1986). *Perspectives on media effects.* Hillsdale, NJ: Lawrence Erlbaum.

Bryant, J., & Zillmann, D. (Eds.). (1991). *Responding to the screen: Reception and reaction processes.* Hillsdale, NJ: Lawrence Erlbaum.

Bryant, J., & Zillmann, D. (Eds.). (1994). *Media effects: Advances in theory and research.* Hillsdale, NJ: Lawrence Erlbaum.

Comstock, G. (1980). *Television in America.* Beverly Hills, CA: Sage.

Cooper, R. (1993). An expanded, integrated model for determining audience exposure to television. *Journal of Broadcasting & Electronic Media, 37,* 401-418.

Cooper, R. (1996). The status and future of audience duplication research: An assessment of ratings-based theories of audience behavior. *Journal of Broadcasting & Electronic Media, 40,* 96-111.

Davis, D. M., & Walker, J. R. (1990). Countering the new media: The resurgence of share maintenance in primetime network television. *Journal of Broadcasting & Electronic Media, 34,* 487-493.

DeFleur, M. L., & Ball-Rokeach, S. J. (1989). *Theories of mass communication* (5th ed.). New York: Longman.

DePalma, A. (1996, December 30). Canadian parents test limits on TV access. *New York Times,* pp. B1, B6.

Dominick, J. R., & Pearce, M. C. (1976). Trends in network prime-time programming, 1953-1974. *Journal of Communication, 26*(1), 70-80.

Donohew, L., Palmgreen, P., & Rayburn, J. D., II. (1987). Social and psychological origins of media use: A lifestyle analysis. *Journal of Broadcasting & Electronic Media, 31,* 255-278.

Eastman, S. T., & Ferguson, D. (1997). *Broadcast/cable programming: Strategies and practices* (5th ed.). Belmont, CA: Wadsworth.

Eastman, S. T., Head, S. W., & Klein, L. (1981). *Broadcast programming: Strategies for winning television and radio audiences.* Belmont, CA: Wadsworth.

Eastman, S. T., Neal-Lunsford, J., & Riggs, K. A. (1995). Coping with grazing: Prime-time strategies for accelerated program transitions. *Journal of Broadcasting & Electronic Media, 39,* 92-108.

Eastman, S. T., & Newton, G. D. (1995). Delineating grazing: Observations of remote control use. *Journal of Communication, 45*(1), 77-95.

Eastman, S. T., Newton, G. D., & Pack, L. (1996). Promoting prime-time programs in megasporting events. *Journal of Broadcasting & Electronic Media, 40,* 366-388.

Eastman, S. T., Newton, G. D., Riggs, K. A., & Neal-Lunsford, J. (1997). Accelerating the flow: A transition effect in programming theory? *Journal of Broadcasting & Electronic Media, 41,* 305-323.

Eastman, S. T., & Otteson, J. A. (1994). Promotion raises ratings, doesn't it? The impact of program promotion in the 1992 Olympics. *Journal of Broadcasting & Electronic Media, 38,* 307-322.

Eco, U. (1979). *The role of the reader: Explorations in the semiotics of texts.* Bloomington: Indiana University Press.

Ehrenberg, A. S. C. (1968). The factor analytic search for program types. *Journal of Advertising Research, 8,* 55-63.

Ehrenberg, A. S. C., & Goodhardt, G. J. (1969). Practical applications of the duplication of viewing law. *Journal of the Market Research Society, 11,* 6-24.

Ehrenberg, A. S. C., & Goodhardt, G. J. (1981). Attitudes to episodes and programs. *Journal of the Market Research Society, 23,* 189-208.

Ettema, J. S., & Whitney, D. C. (1994). The money arrow: An introduction to audiencemaking. In J. S. Ettema & D. C. Whitney (Eds.), *Audiencemaking: How the media create the audience* (pp. 1-18). Thousand Oaks, CA: Sage.

Ferguson, D. A. (1992a). Channel repertoire in the presence of remote control devices, VCRs, and cable television. *Journal of Broadcasting & Electronic Media, 36,* 83-91.

Ferguson, D. A. (1992b). Predicting inheritance effects from VCR and cable penetration. *Dowden Center Journal, 1,* 28-40.

Ferguson, D. A. (1994). Measurement of mundane behaviors: Remote control device flipping frequency. *Journal of Broadcasting & Electronic Media, 38,* 35-47.

Ferguson, D. A., & Perse, E. M. (1993). Media and audience influences on channel repertoire. *Journal of Broadcasting & Electronic Media, 37,* 31-47.

Fidler, R. (1997). *Mediamorphosis: Understanding new media.* Thousand Oaks, CA: Pine Forge.

Fishman, S., & Roslow, S. (1944). The study of adjacent listening. In P. F. Lazarsfeld & F. N. Stanton (Eds.), *Radio research: 1942-1943* (pp. 397-406). New York: Duell, Sloan & Pearce.

Gantz, W., & Eastman, S. T. (1983). Viewer uses of promotional media to find out about television programs. *Journal of Broadcasting, 27,* 269-277.

Gates, B., with Myhrvold, N., & Rinearson, P. (1995). *The road ahead.* New York: Viking.

Gerbner, G., & Gross, L. (1976). Living with television: The violence profile. *Journal of Communication, 26*(2), 172-199.

Gerbner, G., Gross, L., Morgan, M., & Signorielli, N. (1986). Living with television: The dynamics of the cultivation process. In J. Bryant & D. Zillmann (Eds.), *Perspectives on media effects* (pp. 17-39). Hillsdale, NJ: Lawrence Erlbaum.

Gerbner, G., Gross, L., Morgan, M., & Signorielli, N. (1994). Growing up with television: The cultivation perspective. In J. Bryant & D. Zillmann (Eds.), *Media effects: Advances in theory and research* (pp. 17-41). Hillsdale, NJ: Lawrence Erlbaum.

Goodhardt, G. J., Ehrenberg, A. S. C., & Collins, M. (1975). *The television audience: Patterns of viewing.* Westmead, England: Saxon House.

Goodhardt, G. J., Ehrenberg, A. S. C., & Collins, M. (1987). *The television audience: Patterns of viewing* (2nd ed.). Westmead, England: Gower.

Grant, A. E. (1994). The promise fulfilled? An empirical analysis of program diversity on television. *Journal of Media Economics, 7,* 51-64.

Grant, A. E., Guthries, K., & Ball-Rokeach, S. (1991). Television shopping: A media system dependency perspective. *Communication Research, 18,* 773-798.

Greenberg, B. S., & Barnett, H. (1971). TV program diversity: New evidence and old theories. *American Economic Review, 61,* 89-93.

Greenberg, B. S., & D'Alessio, D. (1985). Quantity and quality of sex in the soaps. *Journal of Broadcasting & Electronic Media, 29,* 309-321.

Gunter, B. (1988). The perceptive audience. In J. A. Anderson (Ed.), *Communication yearbook 11* (pp. 22-50). Newbury Park, CA: Sage.

Hargrave, A. M. (1995). *The scheduling game: Audience attitudes to broadcast scheduling.* London: John Libby.

Hasebrink, U., & Krotz, F. (1994, May). *Diversity in front of the screen: An analysis of individual patterns of viewing on the basis of people meter data.* Paper presented at the annual meeting of the International Communication Association, Sydney.

Hawkins, R. P., & Pingree, S. (1986). Activity in the effects of television on children. In J. Bryant & D. Zillmann (Eds.), *Perspectives on media effects* (pp. 233-250). Hillsdale, NJ: Lawrence Erlbaum.

Head, S. W. (1956). *Broadcasting in America: A survey of radio-television.* Boston: Houghton Mifflin.

Headen, R. S., Klompmaker, J. E., & Rust, R. T. (1979). The duplication of viewing law and television media schedule evaluation. *Journal of Marketing Research, 16,* 333-340.

Heeter, C. (1985). Program selection with abundance of choice: A process model. *Human Communication Research, 12,* 126-152.

Heeter, C., & Greenberg, B. S. (1985). Profiling the zappers. *Journal of Advertising Research, 25,* 15-19.

Heeter, C., & Greenberg, B. S. (Eds.). (1988). *Cableviewing.* Norwood, NJ: Ablex.

Hovland, C. I., Lumsdaine, A., & Sheffield, F. (1949). *Experiments on mass communications.* Princeton, NJ: Princeton University Press.

Innis, H. (1950). *Empire and communications.* Oxford: Clarendon.

Katz, E., & Foulkes, D. (1962). On the use of the mass media as "escape": Clarification of a concept. *Public Opinion Quarterly, 26,* 377-388.

Klapper, J. T. (1960). *The effects of mass communication.* Glencoe, IL: Free Press.

Klein, P. L. (1971a, January 25). The men who run TV aren't stupid . . . they know us better than you think. *New York,* pp. 20-29.

Klein, P. L. (1971b, July 24). Why you watch what you watch when you watch. *TV Guide,* pp. 6-10.

Klein, P. L. (1979). Programming. In S. Morgenstern (Ed.), *Inside the TV business* (pp. 11-36). New York: Sterling.

Krugman, H. E. (1965). The impact of television advertising: Learning without involvement. *Public Opinion Quarterly, 29,* 349-358.

Landler, M. (1996, November 26). Industries agree on U.S. standards for TV of future. *New York Times,* pp. A1, C6.

Lazarsfeld, P. F., & Stanton, F. N. (Eds.). (1944). *Radio research: 1942-1943.* New York: Duell, Sloan & Pearce.

Lemish, D. (1983). The rules of viewing television in public places. *Journal of Broadcasting, 28,* 757-781.

Levy, M. R. (1977). Experiencing television news. *Journal of Communication, 27*(2), 112-117.

Levy, M. R. (1983). Conceptualizing and measuring aspects of audience activity. *Journalism Quarterly, 60,* 109-114.

Levy, M. R. (1987). VCR use and the concept of audience activity. *Communication Quarterly, 35,* 267-275.

Levy, M. R., & Windahl, S. (1984). Audience activity and gratifications: A conceptual clarification and exploration. *Communication Research, 11,* 51-78.

Levy, M. R., & Windahl, S. (1985). The concept of audience activity. In K. E. Rosengren, L. A. Wenner, & P. Palmgreen (Eds.), *Media gratifications research: Current perspectives* (pp. 109-122). Beverly Hills, CA: Sage.

Lewis, P. H. (1996, February 28). AT&T will offer no-fee Internet. *New York Times,* pp. A-1, C-5.

Lin, C. A. (1990). Audience activity and VCR use. In J. R. Dobrow (Ed.), *Social and cultural aspects of VCR use* (pp. 75-92). Hillsdale, NJ: Lawrence Erlbaum.

Lin, C. A. (1992). The functions of the VCR in the home leisure environment. *Journal of Broadcasting & Electronic Media, 36,* 345-351.

Lin, C. A. (1995). Network prime-time programming strategies in the 1980s. *Journal of Broadcasting & Electronic Media, 39,* 482-495.

Lindlof, T. R. (1988). Media audiences as interpretive communities. In J. A. Anderson (Ed.), *Communication yearbook 11* (pp. 81-107). Newbury Park, CA: Sage.

Litman, B. (1979). The television networks, competition and program diversity. *Journal of Broadcasting, 23,* 393-409.

Litman, B. R., & Kohl, L. S. (1992). Network rerun viewing in the age of new programming services. *Journalism Quarterly, 69,* 383-391.

Lull, J. (1982). How families select television programs: A mass-observational study. *Journal of Broadcasting & Electronic Media, 26,* 801-811.

Lull, J. (1990). *Inside family viewing.* London: Routledge.

Massey, K. B. (1995). Analyzing the uses and gratifications concept of audience activity with a qualitative approach: Media encounters during the 1989 Loma Prieta earthquake disaster. *Journal of Broadcasting & Electronic Media, 39,* 328-349.

McLuhan, M. (1962). *The Gutenberg galaxy.* New York: Signet.

McPhee, W. N. (1963). *Formal theories of mass behavior.* Glencoe, IL: Free Press.

McQuail, D., Blumler, J., & Brown, J. (1972). The television audience: A revised perspective. In D. McQuail (Ed.), *Sociology of mass communications* (pp. 135-165). Harmondsworth, England: Penguin.

Morley, D. (1993). Active audience theory: Pendulums and pitfalls. *Journal of Communication, 43*(4), 13-19.

Neuman, W. R. (1991). *The future of the mass audience.* Cambridge: Cambridge University Press.

Nielsen Media Research. (1997, April 9). National Television Index for November/December, 1996. In PBS Research, *National audience report.* Alexandria, VA: Author.

Owen, B. M., Beebe, J. H., & Manning, W. (1974). *Television economics.* Lexington, MA: Lexington.

Owen, B. M., & Wildman, S. S. (1992). *Video economics.* Cambridge, MA: Harvard University Press.

Palmgreen, P. (1984). Uses and gratifications: A theoretical perspective. In R. N. Bostrom (Ed.), *Communication yearbook 8* (pp. 20-55). Beverly Hills, CA: Sage.

Palmgreen, P., & Rayburn, J. D. (1985). A comparison of gratifications models of media satisfaction. *Communication Monographs, 52,* 334-346.

Palmgreen, P., Wenner, L. A., & Rayburn, J. D. (1980). Relations between gratifications sought and obtained: A study of television news. *Communication Research, 7,* 161-192.

Pearlin, L. J. (1959). Social and personal stress and escape TV viewing. *Public Opinion Quarterly, 23,* 255-259.

Perse, E. M. (1990a). Audience selectivity and involvement in the newer media environment. *Communication Research, 17,* 675-697.

Perse, E. M. (1990b). Involvement with local television news: Cognitive and emotional dimensions. *Human Communication Research, 16,* 556-581.

Perse, E. M. (1990c). Media involvement and local news effects. *Journal of Broadcasting & Electronic Media, 34,* 17-36.

Persky, J. (1977). Twenty years of prime-time. *Television Quarterly, 14,* 50-52.

Rice, R. E., & Associates. (1984). *The new media: Communication, research, and technology.* Beverly Hills, CA: Sage.

Rogers, E. M. (1983). *Diffusion of innovations* (3rd ed.). New York: Free Press.

Rosengren, K. E., Wenner, L. A., & Palmgreen, P. (Eds.). (1985). *Media gratifications research: Current perspectives.* Beverly Hills, CA: Sage.

Rubin, A. M. (1979). Television use by children and adolescents. *Human Communication Research, 5,* 109-120.

Rubin, A. M. (1984). Ritualized and instrumental television viewing. *Journal of Communication, 34*(3), 67-77.

Rubin, A. M. (1994). Media uses and effects: A uses-and-gratifications perspective. In J. Bryant & D. Zillmann (Eds.), *Media effects: Advances in theory and research* (pp. 315-364). Hillsdale, NJ: Lawrence Erlbaum.

Rubin, A. M., & Perse, E. M. (1987a). Audience activity and soap opera involvement: A uses and effects investigation. *Human Communication Research, 14,* 246-268.

Rubin, A. M., & Perse, E. M. (1987b). Audience activity and television news gratifications. *Communication Research, 14,* 58-84.

Rubin, A. M., & Rubin, R. B. (1982). Older persons' TV viewing patterns and motivations. *Communication Research, 9,* 287-313.

Rubin, A. M., & Windahl, S. (1986). The uses and dependency model of mass communication. *Critical Studies in Mass Communication, 3,* 184-199.

Rubin, R. B., & Rubin, A. M. (1982). Contextual age and television use: Reexamining a life-position indicator. In M. Burgoon (Ed.), *Communication yearbook 6* (pp. 583-604). Beverly Hills, CA: Sage.

Rust, R. T., & Alpert, M. I. (1984). An audience flow model of television viewing choice. *Marketing Science, 3,* 113-124.

Rust, R. T., & Donthu, N. (1988). A programming and positioning strategy for cable television networks. *Journal of Advertising, 17*(4), 6-13.

Rust, R. T., & Eechambadi, N. V. (1989). Scheduling network television programs: A heuristic audience flow approach to maximizing audience share. *Journal of Advertising, 18*(2), 11-18.

Rust, R. T., Kamakura, W. & Alpert, M. (1992). Viewer preference segmentation and viewing choice models for network television. *Journal of Advertising, 21*(1), 1-18.

Salvaggio, J., & Bryant, J. (Eds.). (1989). *Media use in the information age: Emerging patterns of adoption and consumer use.* Hillsdale, NJ: Lawrence Erlbaum.

Schleuder, J. D., White, A. V., & Cameron, G. T. (1993). Priming effects of television news bumpers and teasers on attention and memory. *Journal of Broadcasting & Electronic Media, 37,* 437-452.

Schoening, G. T., & Anderson, J. A. (1995). Social action media studies: Foundational arguments and common premises. *Communication Theory, 5,* 93-116.

Schramm, W. (1957). *Responsibility in mass communications.* New York: Harper.

Schramm, W. (1965). *The process and effects of mass communication.* Urbana: University of Illinois Press.

Shapiro, M. E. (1989). *Television network prime-time programming, 1948-1988.* Jefferson, NC: McFarland.

Sherman, S. M. (1995). Determinants of repeat viewing to prime-time public television programming. *Journal of Broadcasting & Electronic Media, 39,* 472-481.

Steiner, G. A. (1963). *The people look at television.* New York: Knopf.

Steiner, P. O. (1952). Program patterns and preferences, and the workability of competition in radio broadcasting. *Quarterly Journal of Economics, 66,* 194-223.

Sterngold, J. (1996, December 23). A room with a cyberview: On-line hotels for the itinerant business traveler. *New York Times,* pp. C1, C9.

Swanson, D. (1977). The uses and misuses of uses and gratifications. *Human Communication Research, 3,* 214-221.

Tiedge, J. T., & Ksobiech, K. (1986). The "lead-in" strategy for prime-time TV: Does it increase the audience? *Journal of Communication, 36*(2), 51-63.

Tiedge, J. T., & Ksobiech, K. (1987). Counterprogramming primetime network television. *Journal of Broadcasting & Electronic Media, 31,* 41-55.

Tiedge, J. T., & Ksobiech, K. (1988). The sandwich programming strategy: A case of audience flow. *Journalism Quarterly, 65,* 376-383.

Turow, J. (1992). *Media systems in society: Understanding industries, strategies, and power.* White Plains, NY: Longman.

Wakshlag, J., & Adams, W. J. (1985). Trends in program variety and the prime time access rule. *Journal of Broadcasting & Electronic Media, 29,* 23-34.

Wakshlag, J., Agostino, D., Terry, H., Driscoll, P., & Ramsey, B. (1983). Television news viewing and network affiliation changes. *Journal of Broadcasting, 27,* 5-68.

Wakshlag, J., & Greenberg, B. S. (1979). Programming strategies and the popularity of television programs for children. *Human Communication Research, 6,* 58-68.

Walker, J. R. (1988). Inheritance effects in the new media environment. *Journal of Broadcasting & Electronic Media, 32,* 391-401.

Walker, J. R. (1993). Catchy, yes, but does it work? The impact of broadcast network promotion frequency and type on program success. *Journal of Broadcasting & Electronic Media, 37,* 197-207.

Walker, J. R., & Bellamy, R. V., Jr. (Eds.). (1993). *The remote control in the new age of television.* Westport, CT: Praeger.

Wartella, E. (1979). Children and television: The development of the child's understanding of the medium. In D. Wilhoit & M. de Bock (Eds.), *Mass communication review yearbook 1* (pp. 516-553). Beverly Hills, CA: Sage.

Webster, J. G. (1983). The impact of cable and pay cable television on local station audiences. *Journal of Broadcasting, 27,* 119-126.

Webster, J. G. (1985). Program audience duplication: A study of television inheritance effects. *Journal of Broadcasting & Electronic Media, 29,* 121-133.

Webster, J. G. (1986). Audience behavior in the new media environment. *Journal of Communication, 36*(3), 77-91.

Webster, J. G., & Lichty, L. W. (1991). *Ratings analysis: Theory and practice.* Hillsdale, NJ: Lawrence Erlbaum.

Webster, J. G., & Newton, G. D. (1988). Structural determinants of the television news audience. *Journal of Broadcasting & Electronic Media, 32,* 381-389.

Webster, J. G., & Phalen, P. F. (1997). *The mass audience: Rediscovering the dominant model.* Mahwah, NJ: Lawrence Erlbaum.

Webster, J. G., & Wakshlag, J. J. (1982). The impact of group viewing on patterns of television program choice. *Journal of Broadcasting, 26,* 445-455.

Webster, J. G., & Wakshlag, J. J. (1983). A theory of television program choice. *Communication Research, 10,* 430-446.

Webster, J. G., & Wang, T. (1992). Structural determinants of exposure to television: The case of repeat viewing. *Journal of Broadcasting & Electronic Media, 36,* 125-136.

Wells, W. D. (1974). *Lifestyle and psychographics.* New York: American Marketing Association.

Wenner, L. A. (1976). Functional analysis of TV viewing for older adults. *Journal of Broadcasting, 20,* 77-88.

Wenner, L. A. (1982). Gratifications sought and obtained in program dependency: A study of network evening news programs and *60 Minutes. Communication Research, 9,* 529-560.

Wenner, L. A. (Ed.). (1989). *Media, sports, and society.* Newbury Park, CA: Sage.

Zillmann, D., & Bryant, J. (Eds.). (1985). *Selective exposure to communication.* Hillsdale, NJ: Lawrence Erlbaum.

CHAPTER CONTENTS

9 Quick Communicators: Editorial Cartoonists in Communication Overdrive

W. BRADFORD MELLO
Trinity College

Political humor, specifically editorial cartooning, is an appropriate communicative response to political situations and can help to construct the political landscape. Editorial cartooning as a medium of political and social communication has been studied by scholars from many disciplines using a variety of methods. This essay reviews studies that deal with mostly single-panel American political cartoons designed for quick consumption. The review indicates that editorial cartoonists give meaning to facts and help to construct social reality, but exactly how they go about this, what messages are embedded in their work, and the impacts they have are not completely understood.

EDITORIAL cartoonist Dennis Renault of the *Sacramento Bee* learned a few years ago that editorial cartoons can influence readership behavior. As Stein (1994) reports, "A Feb. 4 editorial cartoon intended to take a slap at racism backfired on the *Sacramento Bee,* bringing a torrent of criticism of the use of the term 'nigger' in the caption" (p. 9). Stein describes the cartoon, which prompted more than 1,000 people to cancel their subscriptions to the newspaper:

> The cartoon shows two Ku Klux Klansman, one hooded and the other holding up a quote from a statement that Nation of Islam leader, Louis Farrakhan, made at a recent press conference: "You can't be a racist by talking—only by acting." The caption had the unhooded klansman saying, "That nigger makes a lot of sense." (p. 9)

Apologies were offered on the front page of the paper, but many were still deeply offended by the cartoon and argued that it reflected a racist viewpoint on the part of the editorial staff. Similarly, a cartoon that appeared in the

Correspondence and requests for reprints: W. Bradford Mello, Trinity College, 125 Michigan Avenue, NE, Washington, DC 20017-1094.

Communication Yearbook 21, pp. 379-403

December 20, 1991, issue of Chicago's *Reader* was criticized for a racist caricature of a Chicago Alderman. In this case the paper refused to apologize, arguing, "We don't pretend to the objectivity of the Sun-Times. We have free-lancers who are very involved in a story writing about it. It's a different standard, but a lot of things about the alternative press are different" (quoted in Fitzgerald, 1992, p. 15). An advertising boycott of the *Reader* was called for by many local politicians.

In the late 1870s, editorial cartoonist Thomas Nast was instrumental in taking down Boss Tweed, as Tweed indicated in a response to Nast's visual attacks: "I don't care what they write about me, my constituents can't read. But can't you stop those terrible cartoons" (quoted in Maurice & Cooper, 1904, p. 259). Nast's cartoons led not only to Tweed's political downfall, but to his capture in Spain by police, who recognized Tweed from a "likeness Nast had drawn of him as a kidnapper" (Maurice & Cooper, 1904, p. 259). But Nast's cartoons had little to compete with visually at that time. Today, with television, film, and CD-ROMs, it is unusual for an editorial cartoon to have an effect like that of Renault's cartoon in the *Sacramento Bee*. Editorial cartoonists lampoon politicians and social problems ruthlessly, and the politicians they ridicule still win election and reelection, and social problems still persist. However, editorial cartoons are one part of a filtering system that helps individuals to construct their social reality. Nilsen (1990) argues that because politics permeates our lives by influencing the economy, war and peace, and social and research program funding, we must respond to politics in some manner. Political humor, such as that displayed in editorial cartooning, is a useful social response that performs several functions. As Nilsen notes:

> Political humor has many social functions. From the point of view of the politician himself, humor can be used to define political concepts, to disarm critics, to establish detente, to establish a position or make a point, to inbond, to relieve tension, and to provide a substitute for actual physical or military confrontation. From the point of view of the political critic, humor can be used to expose chauvinism, to expose ineptitude, to expose oppression, and to expose pretentiousness. (p. 35)

Taking a broader stance, Boulding (1956) asserts that "for any individual organism or organization, there are no such things as 'facts.' There are only messages filtered through a changeable value system" (p. 14). To extend this argument, the humorous responses to political situations found in political cartoons are media messages that flow through our value system. Edelman (1988) contributes to the argument by noting that the media help to "construct the social reality to which people respond" (p. 34). Political humor, specifically editorial cartooning, is an appropriate response to political situations and can help to construct the political landscape. In their study of the atomic bomb in political cartoons, Gamson and Stuart (1992) note:

The mass media play a central role in the construction of political meaning for the attentive public but they have a second role that is more easily overlooked. Because of their presumed influence, they become, to quote Gurevitch and Levy (1985:19), "a site on which various social groups, institutions, and ideologies struggle over the definition and construction of social reality." The media, in this view, provide a series of arenas in which symbolic contests are carried out among competing sponsors of meaning. (p. 55)

Gamson and Stuart explain that editorial cartoons are just one media arena among many and that "this is a heavily contested arena rather than a hegemonic one. Not only are alternative ways of framing nuclear issues offered but the same specific symbols are used by the competitors, albeit with a different context and meaning" (p. 78). Editorial cartoonists can aid in giving meaning to "facts" and help construct the social reality responded to by those who pay attention to editorial cartoons, but a thorough review of the literature indicates that the magnitude of their influence is questionable and the process of that influence is complicated and not completely understood. As indicated earlier, as visual information, in a dense society such as ours, the editorial cartoon may not be much competition for the latest Oliver Stone film.

Editorial cartooning as a medium of political and social communication has been studied by scholars from many disciplines using a variety of different methods. For this discussion, a definition and brief explanation of the function of the political cartoonist are in order. Generally speaking, political cartoonists are social judges who interpret the news. They are pundits. Political cartoons are a form of journalistic commentary designed to influence viewers regarding events of the day. People often want simple interpretations of events, and cartoonists can fulfill this role. Political cartoons can insinuate subtle messages, and thus sometimes say what others dare not. Humor, albeit often dark humor, concerning serious issues can help to alleviate the painful truth of some situations. The political cartoon is a significant form of political and social communication (Harrison, 1981; Press, 1981; Reeves, 1991).

SCOPE OF THIS REVIEW

Undertaking a review of the literature on editorial cartoons presents two specific problems: a problem of organization and a problem of limits. How does one group and make sense of studies from divergent disciplines, with methods ranging from the presentation of studied opinion to statistical analysis to rhetorical inquiry? First, many scholars have considered the history of editorial cartooning significant and worthy of study. Its history is rich and diverse, with much opportunity for continued research. Beyond the history, there are two broad divisions in the study of cartooning that seem appropriate for review. Scholars (and cartoonists themselves) have tended to concentrate either on the practical aspects of the art or on the work's rhetorical/persuasive functions. Regarding the practical aspects, scholars generally seek to answer such questions as, How do editorial cartoons find their way to the printed page? What influence does the editor or the publisher wield over the artist? The rhetorical/persuasive impact of the cartoons is more difficult to gauge. Using various methods of inquiry, from rhetorical criticism to statistical analysis, scholars have attempted to illuminate the influence and impact of editorial cartoons.

Although I have found it necessary to limit the literature reviewed here to studies focused on editorial cartooning in the United States, editorial cartooning is practiced and studied around the world, and an enormous international body of literature exists on the topic. There are rich editorial cartooning traditions in many countries around the world, and studies about those traditions have appeared in several communication journals. For example, Martin (1987) has focused on Spanish political cartoons. He provides a brief outline of the modern press in Spain and concludes that "one of the most interesting developments of the 'new Spanish press' has been the work of political cartoonists appearing in both national and daily newspapers and news magazines" and that they have contributed "a needed input of humor and reflections as well as critical and in some cases, caustic commentary" (p. 161). Turning to the other side of the globe, Hung (1994) has analyzed the influence of cartoons on public opinion in late republican China, 1945 to 1949. And Mosher (1991) has briefly chronicled the success of Hong Kong cartoonist Mark Yuen, who has been cartooning in Hong Kong for nearly 20 years and has even created his own publication, titled *Rebel*.

Another limit stems from the blurred line between political/editorial cartooning and cartooning in general. The fracture occurs when one attempts to define political cartooning. Press (1981) points to the difficulty of defining political cartooning as different from social commentary cartooning and comic art in general. Simply put, most cartoons fit into more than one of these categories. It is difficult to decide what distinguishes a political cartoon from any other; indeed, Press argues that ultimately the decision is arbitrary. He provides a useful starting point for definition, however, by saying that political cartoons are "drawings with a partisan message for viewers about what they should think or do politically" (p. 16). Cartoonist Garland (1989) offers a more complex description of the components of a political cartoon:

> Political cartoons are not so much rapier thrusts (which they are often called) as they are missiles, which, although quite small, carry at least three explosive warheads. First, caricature—the humorously or maliciously distorted representation of politicians; second, the actual political comment, criticism or stance communicated in the drawing; and third, the vehicle or image chosen to convey the political point. (p. 32)

However, this description does not eliminate strip cartoons. Certainly Opus, the best-known political philosopher/penguin in the country, is political. *Doonesbury* is run on the opinion page in some papers or not at all. Before their creator retired, Calvin and Hobbes often pontificated on the social and political ills of our country. And Charlie Brown still comes up with zinger comments on life in America. Perhaps one reason strip cartoons are often so political is that many strip cartoonists started their careers drawing editorial cartoons (Hess & Kaplan, 1968). However, the success of strip cartoons relies on narrative, and in this they are distinct from standard editorial cartoons. In this review, I consider only studies that deal with mostly single-panel (some editorial cartoonists occasionally split the frame) political cartoons that combine caricature and political commentary, relying on instant image recognition and brief commentary rather than narrative development to communicate their messages.

In preparing this review, I conducted electronic searches of several databases, including Psychlit, Soclit, Humanities Index, ERIC, and a general periodicals index available through the Washington Library Consortium. This process uncovered many articles and books that led to various other sources not indexed on-line. The feedback I received on earlier versions of this essay led to the inclusion of additional sources, specifically historical and popular culture references.

To recap, then, this essay considers the relevant literature on editorial cartooning in the United States. It is organized into three broad categories: the historical, practical, and rhetorical/persuasive aspects of editorial cartoons.

HISTORICALLY SPEAKING

A few significant historical studies provide comprehensive accounts of the development of the political cartoon and the cartoonists who guided that development. Thorkelson (1979) provides a unique Marxist perspective and argues that editorial cartoonists have great potential to focus attention on inequities in society. He also points to the decline of political cartooning because cartoonists "hedge their politics." Harrison (1981), Hess and Kaplan (1968), and Press (1981) have authored comprehensive books that provide detailed overviews of the development of cartooning in the United States, but have some limitations (to be discussed later in this essay). Two other works provide more comprehensive examinations of cartooning in the United States of the 19th century: Maurice and Cooper's *The History of the Nineteenth Century in Caricature* (1904) and Nevins and Weitenkampf's *A Century of Political Cartoons: Caricature in the United States From 1800-1900* (1944). Maurice and Cooper use cartoons to enlighten readers about the historical events of periods such as the Napoleonic era and the Franco-Prussian War.

They argue that the cartoons of those times identified important factors to Americans and reflected the mood of the country. They provide detailed accounts of the development of significant outlets for cartooning, such as the early magazines *Judge, Puck,* and *Punch.* However, the caricatures they present give only one picture of the mood of the country during any given moment, making the book limited in scope. The volume *A Cartoon History of United States Foreign Policy From 1945 to the Present* (King & Editors of the Foreign Policy Association, 1991) tackles different subject matter with similar successes and limitations.

Nevins and Weitenkampf (1944) concentrate on the development of caricature and cartooning in the United States. They define a good cartoon as a caricature that has wit and humor, portrays at least one side of the truth, and demonstrates a moral purpose. They also discuss the pitfalls of intemperate partisanship, overproduction, inadequate artistry, and lack of principle. Nevins and Weitenkampf argue that cartooning flourishes when significant issues and individuals capture the attention of the country. In addition, they note: "Despite their limitations American cartoons are invaluable to the student of political history. They bring us face to face with a vast variety of political maneuverings" (p. 17). And, much like Maurice and Cooper (1904), Nevins and Weitenkampf argue that cartoons can throw light on the national mood, although they qualify their observation somewhat: "Evidently, the political cartoon is a valuable item in the documentary outfit of the historian. The laugh-provoker of yesterday has become a serious contribution to history" (p. 18).

Harrison (1981), Hess and Kaplan (1968), and Press (1981) all review some aspects of the early history of cartooning in the United States and pick up where Maurice and Cooper and Nevins and Weitenkampf leave off, outlining most of the significant contributors to the editorial cartoon page in the 20th century. But like the current essay, they are limited to the American scene. Sheppard (1985) indicates another limitation of these works regarding the exclusion of women cartoonists:

> There is a common belief that women have only recently endeavored to become political cartoonists. Harrison (1981) represents this view in his book, *The Cartoon,* as does Charles Press (1981) in *The Political Cartoon.* The latter concurs, "Almost all until recently have been men" (182). There is no doubt that women political cartoonists remain a minority in the field. Yet, contemporary women artists do not form the vanguard, but represent descendants of a tradition founded early in the century. There were over two dozen women political cartoonists at the time of the most significant social and political effort by women—the struggle for suffrage. (p. 39)

Sheppard focuses on two prosuffragist women cartoonists, Annie "Lou" Rogers and Nina Allender. Her article provides several useful examples of their work, biographical sketches of both artists, a description of the social conditions that influenced their cartooning, and historical accounts of their work.

Caswell (1988) brings to the foreground a woman she claims was the first female editorial cartoonist, Edwina Dumm. Dumm drew editorial cartoons for the *Columbus Daily Monitor* from 1915 to 1917, when she switched her focus to comic strip cartooning. According to Sheppard (1985), however, Rogers and Allender were cartooning as early as 1911 for the *Women's Journal*. Perhaps Caswell bases her claim that Dumm was the first woman editorial cartoonist on the fact that she was apparently the first to draw cartoons for a daily paper. In any case, the editorial cartoons that Rogers penned in 1912 for *Judge*'s feature page titled "The Modern Woman" would qualify Rogers as the first woman editorial cartoonist. The controversy over who was first aside, Caswell (1988) describes Dumm's style well: "Her artistic style was vigorous and she did not produce timid, stereotypically 'feminine' work" (p. 6).

A significant source of historical information about cartoonists is the cartoonists themselves, especially cartoonists of the 20th century. Most popular, successful political cartoonists have written memoirs or autobiographies that provide valuable clues to the development of the political cartoon in the United States. Herbert "Herblock" Block's autobiography, *Herblock: A Cartoonist's Life* (1993), chronicles major historical events of the latter part of this century as well as Herblock's views on the development and influence of political cartoons. His emphasis on the late President Richard M. Nixon is particularly compelling. It is easy to understand why Nixon has been quoted as saying during the 1960 presidential race, "I have to erase the Herblock image" (in Hess & Kaplan, 1968). There were probably many cartoons featuring Nixon that contributed to that "Herblock image," but perhaps most compelling is Herblock's depiction of Nixon arriving in Washington ready for work via a sewer on Pennsylvania Avenue.

Two biographies of Jay Norward "Ding" Darling have chronicled this famous cartoonist's life during the first half of this century (Darling, 1962; Lendt, 1979), and Bill Mauldin's (1971) memoir recalls his famous Willie and Joe characters, who were popular with GIs during World War II. In his book, Mauldin recounts the assertion in a letter he once received, "You probably never thought of yourself in a ministerial light." His response: "The hell I haven't" (p. 11). Cartoonists' biographies and autobiographies often reveal their understanding of their persuasive force as well as provide information on their careers. Other recent works by cartoonists Doug Marlette (1991) and Paul Conrad (1985) have mapped the contemporary landscape well.

Finally, there are many collections of political cartoons available that serve as valuable documentary evidence. Weitenkampf (1953) compiled an annotated list of cartoons and caricatures from 1787 to 1898. The text provides brief descriptions of hundreds of cartoons of that period and represents a valuable research tool for any scholar interested in early cartooning in the United States. Johnson (1958) explains the historical situations that inspired the Pulitzer Prize-winning cartoons from 1922, when the first prize was awarded, through 1958. Block (1984) has captured the early Reagan years in cartoons, and Westin (1979) highlights the work of 14 major cartoonists in *Getting Angry Six Times a Week: A Portfolio of Political Cartoons.* Pelican Publishing Company publishes yearly collections of the best political cartoons, including Pulitzer Prize winners and the winners of various other journalism awards. Also, the original works of political cartoonists are sometimes available for public viewing at exhibits such as the recent celebration of the 200th anniversary of the Bill of Rights held at the National Archives in Washington, D.C. (Ingalls, 1991).

The World Encyclopedia of Cartoons (Horn, 1980) is broader in scope than the works cited above in that it contains information about strip cartooning and animation, but its chronology and history of cartooning, brief biographical entries on many cartoonists, and countless examples of editorial cartoons are valuable resources for anyone interested in this area.

The above accounting of sources of original work is not meant to be comprehensive. Many early cartoonists, such as Clifford Berryman (*Washington Star*, 1907-1949), as well as many contemporary cartoonists have published collections that are valuable resources for the student of editorial cartoons. But not only have many editorial cartoonists published collections of their work that serve as raw historical data, they often have pondered, along with many scholars, the practical aspects of producing editorial cartoons on a daily basis.

PRODUCTION OF THE EDITORIAL CARTOON

> The editorial cartoonist is an anomaly in the newsroom. Employed expressly to provide opinion and critical commentary—directly and, for the most part, without words—the cartoonist differs from the language-oriented news person whose every professional action is purportedly informed by dedication to objectivity. (Riffe, Sneed, & Van Ommeren, 1985, p. 378)

The production of editorial cartoons involves both the artist and the editor. Studies in this arena have focused on editor-artist relations and the format of the editorial cartoon, as well as on specific editorial cartoonists. A few historical accounts of editorial cartooning also provide insights into the production process.

Riffe et al. (1985) surveyed 176 cartoonists and their editors and received a 55% response rate from the cartoonists and 43% from the editors. They asked their respondents to indicate their political preferences, to report how often they turned out cartoons, and to rank the following list of cartoonist roles in terms of importance: critic, artist, opinion leader, entertainer, judge, reporter, teacher. The editors and cartoonists agreed that cartoonists need autonomy, but, contrary to the cartoonists' opinions, the editors did not believe the cartoonists should be free from all editorial constraints. However, both did agree that the central role of the cartoonist is that of a critic. Although this study was somewhat limited by response rate, it provides a useful glimpse into how these artists and their editors view their roles.

Penner and Penner (1994) argue that cartoons that finally make it to the printed page reflect the views of the newspapers in which they appear, and thus can provide insight into dominant power groups in society.

Omitted from these studies are placement and context issues. Why must editorial cartoons be placed on the editorial page most often? Do editors look for cartoons that complement editorial content? Does placement on the editorial page and the prominence or size of the cartoon influence the audience significantly? Is there a difference between a paper like the *Washington Times,* which places political cartoons in various sections rather than on the editorial page, and other papers that place political cartoons only on the editorial page? These questions seem to be natural follow-ups to studies that have focused on the editor's role in the production of editorial cartooning.

Editors are not the only ones seeking a role in the production of cartoon content. Lamb (1995) outlines how the federal government stifled opposing viewpoints presented in editorial cartoons during World War I. Lamb concludes by commenting on what one targeted cartoonist, Robert Minor, represented:

> Minor would earn the dubious distinction of personally witnessing government suppression of civil liberties during one world war after another. His "At Last a Perfect Soldier" remains a graphic indictment of war and an artifact of one of the most repressive periods in American history. The cartoonists either supported World War I or had trouble finding outlets for their drawings. (pp. 23-24)

The government apparently had a different view of what was tasteful and appropriate. According to Lamb, the government freely silenced dissenting viewpoints during World War I.

Using a method similar to the one they employed in their 1985 study, Riffe, Sneed, and Van Ommeren (1987) later tackled questions of taste in editorial cartooning. They argue that although editors tend to be more conservative in what they consider suitable subjects and how they treat subjects, both editors and cartoonists believe that cartoonists should push the barriers with their work. The findings of Riffe et al.'s 1987 study, like those of their earlier one, are limited by response rate (65% for cartoonists and 55% for editors), but, again, the data reported in the brief essay provide valuable insights into how professionals view their craft.

Giobbe (1994) outlines one example in which an editor felt that cartoonist Doug Marlette had delved into tastelessness with his pen. Marlette had satirized Howard Stern's run for the New York governorship by picturing Stern flashing the Statue of Liberty and claiming, "It looks like a challenge to Cuomo's leadership, only smaller" (p. 18). Editor James Klurfeld of *Newsday* opted not to run the cartoon because he believed it crossed the line into poor taste. But, as Platt (1994) argues, cartoonists often walk a thin line between what is and is not tasteful.

Bivins (1984) performed a content analysis of 100 editorial cartoons in order to examine cartoonist format preferences. Of the sample studied, 50 were single-frame cartoons and 50 were multipanel cartoons. Through the data-gathering process, Bivins found that the cartoonists most often preferred to work in the single-panel format. The single-panel cartoons relied more on visual metaphors and less on words, whereas the multipanel cartoons, which contained less white space, relied more on verbal gags than on visual metaphors. Bivins concludes by quoting Bob Gorell of the *Charlotte News*:

> My perception of the editorial cartoon has always been that it derives its power from simple visual imagery. Single panel cartoons, when totally non-verbal, are the most effective way of enveloping that simplicity and imagery. Multi-panels, while no easier to produce, tend to become wordy and verbal in character, with the gag often overwhelming the intended, and properly more important, message. (p. 184)

Editorial cartoonists in the 1950s "saw themselves and other members of the press as 'defenders of the truth' " (Handleman, 1984, p. 137). Handleman's (1984) work is unique in that it presents a picture of cartoonists as both contributors to the social unrest of their time and victims of it: "Although cartoonists of the 1950's proclaimed that they were not afraid to stand up for their vision of democracy as a blending of many voices, many truths, it seems that they themselves became victims of the very anxiety and ambivalence that they recognized" (p. 141). Handleman suggests that political cartoons and the artists that produce them are in decline because of the rise of cartoon syndication. Editorial cartoonist Tim Menees agrees, and argues further that cartoonists too often go for gags rather than hard-hitting commentary (cited in Astor, 1989a). But syndication, as I explain below, represents one of the few ways a cartoonist can make any real money practicing his or her craft. Handleman (1984) does not explain the decision to concentrate on cartoonists' view of themselves in the 1950s; although the article provides insight into that period through archival research, it is also clearly limited in scope. However, it does show that editorial cartoonists believed then, just as they do today, that they depict issues in a simplified fashion and thus frame public opinion.

As Judge and West (1988) point out, syndication is lucrative for cartoonists. Thus many editorial cartoonists may choose to ignore important local issues in their work in favor of commenting on national or international issues. In this way they can appeal to a mass audience, as well as to prize juries, and often enjoy significant monetary payoffs (anywhere from $10,000 to $100,000 per year). Some cartoonists opt to address local issues at the price of fame and fortune but often find different rewards: "Those cartoonists who devote themselves to local cartoons may not find riches and national fame, but they're likely to look at their city or region and feel that the work they've done has made a difference" (Judge & West, 1988, p. 42).

The increased availability and sophistication of modern technology has resulted in the addition of color to some syndicated cartoons. At least one artist, Mike Shelton, believes that his cartoons may receive more reaction because of the use of color. One of his early color cartoons, a commentary on President Bush's change of heart regarding his "no new taxes" pledge, depicted Bush mooning the United States and saying, "Hey tax payers, read this!" The cartoon provoked a great deal of reader response. " 'I really think the volume of the response was because it was in color,' said Shelton. 'More people noticed it because when their eyes went by that page, that big color spot caught their eyes' " (quoted in Lamb, 1991, p. 40).

Syndication may hit a glitch, however, as California attempts "to tax the sale of political cartoons and comics to California newspapers" (Astor, 1995, p. 49), equating political cartoons to similar items, such as painting, that are taxed. Many artists cite the First Amendment in their opposition to such a tax, saying that it is a tax on free expression. Editorial cartoonists also fear a downward trend in their craft. Jobs are scarce, and newspapers are reluctant to take chances with editorial cartoons (Astor, 1994).

In an analysis of the syndication trend published more than 20 years ago, Dennis (1974) states that although syndication did lead to a decline in political cartooning, artists such as Herblock, Conrad, and Mauldin were returning the medium to its glory days, when cartoonists like Nast took "savage swipes at the Tweed ring" (p. 665). Dennis argues that cartoonists' strongly held views, fueled by events such as Watergate, helped to bring cartooning back. Although the works of Herblock, Conrad, and Mauldin are exemplary, Dennis's focus on these three individuals means that he necessarily omits discussion of the contributions of many others. He notes that "the most powerful political cartoons are usually scorching indictments of people and issues" (p. 664), and certainly many politicians on local, national, and international levels have been burned by the pens of a variety of cartoonists. Although Dennis hints that a new wave of practitioners was on the way, he found the influence of the three giants on which he focused to be most significant. No more recent studies have focused on the new wave of editorial cartoonists that Dennis mentions, but considering the growth of the alternative press (e.g., papers such as Chicago's *Reader*), it seems likely that new practitioners are indeed arising, but their work is not finding its way into traditional media outlets.

Contemporary editorial cartoonists sometimes discuss ethical issues related to their profession. In 1989, a panel of practitioners concluded that editorial cartoonists should be free to attack any politician and should permit politicians to attempt to curry favor with cartoonists. However, cartoonists should not offer favors to politicians, nor should a cartoonist concentrate too much on a particular politician, because "readers might think you're supporting him because you're buddies" (Astor, 1989b, p. 140).

There have been few pieces written on the political views of cartoonists themselves, perhaps because, as Riffe et al. (1985) discovered in their survey, most editorial cartoonists consider themselves to be political independents. Articles about politically moderate cartoonists would simply have little appeal. Few fall strictly left or right in their commentary, but one particular cartoonist stands out as leaning defiantly in one direction. Cartoonist Chuck Asay's stated goal is to bring about change, although not in the direction you might expect. According to Lamb (1994), "Asay, 51, is just as interested in changing society as his liberal colleagues, but he wants that change to be conservative" (p. 40). Lamb outlines the origins of Asay's conservative views, his relationship with his editor (they are of similar political mind), and the wealth of material that the Clinton administration and the formerly Democratic Congress have provided him.

Studies of cartoonists' attitudes and beliefs about their profession are limited, and even less has been written on the relationships between cartoonists and their editors. With some cartoonists publishing their e-mail addresses alongside their cartoons and the growth of gatherings such as the Comic Arts Conference, which meets in conjunction with the annual professional conference held by members of the comics community, it is time for researchers to start talking more to the cartoonists themselves. Researchers should also investigate in depth the relationships between editors and editorial cartoonists, to gain greater understanding of how editorial decisions are made in this field. For example, how often do editors overrule cartoonists, as when Bill Mauldin was overruled when he wanted to kill off his famous World War II characters Willie and Joe (Thorkelson, 1979)? When questions of taste arise, whose taste rules most often? How was Doug Marlette able to prevail in the printing of his cartoon of Jesse Helms mooning the Capitol from his office window (Marlette, 1991)?

Is the craft of editorial cartooning dying? Given that jobs in major media outlets are scarce, are cartoonists turning to other outlets? And, although most cartoonists tend to see themselves as political independents, does their work conform to this view? We do know that editorial cartoonists perceive themselves as shapers of public opinion, and that they prefer not to work under editorial constraints, but as the works reviewed in the following section indicate, cartoonists' effectiveness in molding public opinion is debatable.

VISUAL PERSUASION

"A few deft lines, a word or two, and a little drawing . . . can be worth more than a thousand words or a thousand pages of analysis in the *New York Times,* or *Le Monde,* or *Pravda*" (Reeves, 1991, p. xi). Exactly how much a little drawing is worth, or the rate of exchange between words and pictures, is debatable. Scholars are often interested in what editorial cartoonists say about the world with their drawings. Much of the scholarship on editorial cartooning seeks to explain how to critique or understand the persuasive message behind the art, to uncover the artist's position as revealed in the cartoon, or to explain how readers process the image. Originating in a variety of disciplines and using diverse methods, scholars often seem to be saying, Look what the cartoonists are up to now. The literature may be divided into two broad and admittedly oversimplified categories: rhetorical criticism and descriptive studies. A few researchers have attempted to gauge the effects of political cartoons on readers. In this section I review research that addresses two issues: How do readers process the images, and what, if any, persuasive effects do the images have?

Perhaps the most comprehensive rhetorical study of the editorial cartoon is Medhurst and DeSousa's (1981) "taxonomic study of the available means of graphic persuasion as manifested in the art of political cartooning" (p. 197). This seminal article offers a set of graphic rhetorical canons modeled on Cicero's classical rhetorical canons as a method of critiquing and understanding the persuasive messages in political cartoons:

> If caricature is a unique form of visual communication, then one ought to be able to derive an outline of the formal principles utilized by graphic artists in the construction of their persuasive invitation to the reader. This is precisely what we offer: a classificatory scheme for recognizing and analyzing the elements of graphic persuasion as embodied in the political cartoon. (pp. 198-199)

Medhurst and DeSousa argue that the general framework of the classical rhetorical canons for constructing oral arguments is applicable to graphic arguments, although the specific techniques are different. The specific techniques follow along with the canons. Cartoonists consult many commonplaces, or topoi, such as political, literary, and cultural allusions. Medhurst and DeSousa demonstrate "how contrast, commentary and contradiction function as formal organizing principles" (p. 236) and how line, form, and graphic exaggeration constitute a cartoonist's stylistic repertoire. The traditional canon of delivery is treated as the tone or appropriateness of the cartoon, and memory is related to the "art of evocation which draws upon shared cultural symbology to invite completion of an enthymematic chain" (p. 236). This approach to graphic discourse serves the critic well, but, as the authors themselves indicate, it leaves a few questions unanswered. Mainly, how do readers process visual information? How do we best teach others to interpret and understand the visual form?

Bostdorff (1987), while "making light of James Watt," offers a Burkean approach to the criticism of graphic discourse, emphasizing tropes. Bostdorff criticizes Medhurst and DeSousa (1981) for not dealing more directly with the interaction of discursive and nondiscursive elements in the cartoon. Further, Bostdorff notes, the "inventional topoi discussed by Medhurst and DeSousa actually are subservient to tropes which serve 'as organizing principles establishing a point of view by which the viewer reads cartoons' " (p. 44). Bostdorff outlines the use of burlesque in political cartoons, as well as metaphor, irony, synecdoche, and metonymy, employing cartoons of James Watt as examples. Although Bostdorff does not cite Grombrich (1985) for this specific purpose, she appears to be taking her cue from Grombrich. Grombrich outlines the various graphic figures of speech (tropes) available to the political cartoonist, although he does not make use of the Burkean framework that Bostdorff does. Both Bostdorff and Medhurst and DeSousa offer comprehensive approaches, and although Bostdorff criticizes Medhurst and DeSousa, I believe that both methods of criticism can increase our understanding of the message in the frame. These two articles represent the most significant contributions regarding the study of political cartoons that have appeared in major communication journals.

Morris (1991) takes a semiotic/cultural approach to criticism. He relies on a functionalist and Marxist perspective, explaining the goals of the two in the following manner: "A functionalist perspective based on Greimas inductively seeks to display the structure of oppositions around which the drawings were constructed. A Marxist approach, based on Angenot and ultimately Bakhtin, seeks ideologemes about class, gender and linguistic struggles" (p. 228). Morris demonstrates his approach through an analysis of 12 cartoons by one artist concerning bilingualism in Canada. Morris argues that "editorial cartoons are a metalanguage for discourse about social orders. They create imaginary worlds which allow a fresh perspective on the present world by inverting certain of its features" (p. 225). Although the cultural approach has a set of underlying assumptions different from those of the rhetorical approaches outlined above, I believe that none invalidates the others. All are useful methods for criticizing visual discourse in the form of editorial cartoons, but they, like the group of descriptive studies discussed below, do not attempt to answer the questions of how readers process this visual information or what magnitude of influence it may have over them.

Descriptive studies of editorial cartoons abound. Codell (1988) describes in great detail how an 1857 painting by Millais influenced many cartoons of the time, thus demonstrating how two forms of popular art may intersect. Most descriptive studies, however, focus on the portrayals of certain groups in political cartoons. Thibodeau (1989) examined blacks in *New Yorker* cartoons from 1946 to 1987 and found an evolution from racist uses of blacks to their appearance as mere tokens in the cartoon frame or their not appearing at all. As a possible explanation for these changes, Thibodeau suggests that "because norms regarding what in fact constitutes racism (particularly on a subtle level) may not be altogether clear in the post-civil rights era, cartoonists face the risk of inadvertently invoking a stereotype associated with blacks and, thus, may find themselves open to the charge of racism" (p. 492). The editors of the *Sacramento Bee* discovered exactly what Thibodeau means when they lost more than 1,000 subscribers because of the cartoon described at the opening of this chapter: A cartoon intended to condemn racism was seen as racist itself.

Thibodeau's mapping of the changes in portrayals of blacks in *New Yorker* cartoons, although limited to only one group of cartoons that reached a limited audience, provides useful information about how members of a specific minority group have been characterized in an important public forum. Many other researchers have similarly focused on the portrayals of specific groups or cultural objects in political cartoons. Meyer, Seidler, Curry, and Aveni (1980) found that the women in Fourth of July cartoons over a 100-year period evolved from matronly to glamorous and then to a more lifelike portrayal, but were still subordinate to men throughout. Sena (1985) found that cartoonists treated Geraldine Ferraro's run for the vice presidency in a positive fashion for the most part, although there were some sexist jokes in the cartoons. Sena notes that although cartoonists "did not take cheap shots at Ferraro for being a woman, it is also unfortunate that the fact that she was a woman was largely ignored" (p. 11). He suggests that perhaps cartoonists ignored the significant fact that Ferraro is a woman because most major editorial cartoonists in the United States are men. Perhaps, too, as Thibodeau argues regarding the portrayal of blacks in *New Yorker* cartoons, some cartoonists shied away from the gender issue for fear of being labeled sexist. Some, however, clearly flocked to sexist messages. One cartoonist put these words in the mouth of a sailor on shore leave who is seen with a buddy looking at a telephone booth wall: "Wait . . . this looks promising: 'For a good time call Geraldine . . .' "; another portrayed Ferraro as voluptuous and sexually inviting (Sena, 1985).

One symbol that is easily recognized around the world has brought light to cartoonists' use of female figures. In cartoons, Lady Liberty often stands for freedom—a mother welcoming her children (immigrants) or righteous citizens (soldiers). Lady Liberty cries to mourn the death of Martin Luther King, Jr., or in sympathy with the plight of prisoners of war, or in joy at the release of the hostages from Tehran. Fischer (1986) notes that Liberty has been exploited successfully as a national symbol for many years and has metamorphosed "from a novel and controversial oddity into the first lady of American icons and then, in the creations of many of our more creative and iconoclastic current cartoonists, increasingly as a reminder of our more callous deviations from the ideal of an open society rooted in individual liberty and human dignity" (p. 63).

Other researchers have concentrated on specific individuals and the images of the characters that cartoons evoke rather than groups or cultural symbols. Richard Nixon is probably the best recent example of the power of cartoons to portray a negative image. As Fischer (1990) observes, Nixon has evolved into a generic symbol for cartoonists that over the years may either fall "into cartoon oblivion" or live on "as a graphic symbol of sleaze, as useful to cartoonists in portraying the venial sins of the political process as Lucifer and Death have been for the truly apocalyptic horrors" (p. 19). Not as negative as Lucifer, death, or sleaze, but equally damning, cartoonists' depictions of Nixon as Pinocchio held, as Grofman (1989) has noted, because the rich metaphor worked on many levels; Nixon's long nose and stiff, wooden style played to the allusion well.

Two other politicians who did not receive positive portrayal in editorial cartoons were Presidents Carter and Reagan. Blackwood (1989) found that Canadian cartoons portrayed Carter positively and Reagan negatively. In American cartoons, Carter did not fare so well. According to Hill (1978):

> The negative smiles of Carter exhibit connotations of stupidity, cunning, sadism, ghoulishness, greed, and hypocrisy. The positive smiles convey genuine affability and good will. There were many more negative Carters than positive ones in the spring and summer of 1976, which is to be expected of the cartoons of any candidate since the genre is largely satirical, but these caricatures show more detestable personality attributes than the facts of Carter's career could possibly warrant. (p. 330)

"Ronbo" received similar treatment in Canada. One Canadian cartoonist said, "From a Canadian point of view, the fear is that doddering fool is the one that has a finger on the button, and Canadians may unwittingly become involved in world conflict" (quoted in Blackwood, 1989, p. 457). Block's (1984) collection of cartoons of the early Reagan years is equally negative. From failing to balance the budget to poor environmental policy, Herblock lampooned Reagan, sometimes with light jabs, other times with knockout punches.

Oddly, one character and one group (a group that may be thought of as having a collective singular character), according to the studies included in this review, seem to share the title of most negatively portrayed. The character is the Ayatollah Khomeini; the group is psychiatrists. Sharf (1986) found that cartoons during the trial of Reagan would-be assassin Hinckley likened psychiatrists to alchemists dabbling in their craft. DeSousa (1984) reveals how cartoons portrayed the Ayatollah as a madman, religious fraud, and manipulator. The shortcomings of these descriptive studies are that, although they show how a certain group of artists with relatively large access to the public portrays society, they provide no clue as to how readers make use of these cartoons or what influence the cartoons may have. These limitations are similar to those of historical studies that outline the histories of particular periods through the use of cartoons. Such studies simply do not present a complete picture.

The messages embedded in the images of editorial cartoons, whether negative or not, must have some influence on readers. The weakness of descriptive studies as a whole is that they do not examine this influence. Culbertson (1987) argues: "Political cartoons seldom persuade; they do not support their 'arguments' with facts or well turned phrases. That is not their purpose. They create images, which often prove far more devastating than words" (p. 18). Of course, I would argue that the task of creating an image is a persuasive task—maybe not in the traditional sense of a well-developed argument, but at least equally or, as Culbertson indicates, more persuasive. Devastating or persuasive, editorial cartoons wield some influence that is important to consider. They attempt to educate readers about domestic politics or foreign policy (see King & Editors of the Foreign Policy Association, 1991), or they simply provide a chuckle for readers on the way to some other section of the paper. Whether the impacts of editorial cartoons are significant or minor, we must attempt to gauge them. Determining these impacts objectively is difficult, however, as the sparseness of studies available indicates. Researchers have had an easier time determining how readers process editorial cartoons than they have had in measuring how readers are influenced by cartoons. In fact, given that many studies have indicated that readers fail to understand the intended messages of editorial cartoons much of the time, perhaps the cartoons have little impact at all. Researchers have used survey and experimental research designs in attempts to determine the influence of cartoons. Focus group studies, such as those that have been used to gauge the impacts of political commercials (Jamieson, 1992), may represent another useful research method for investigating the influence editorial cartoons wield with readers.

Based on the research conducted to date, the influence of editorial cartoons is difficult to judge. There have been a few quantitative and qualitative research efforts, but the results are inconclusive (Beniger, 1983; Bormann, Koester, & Bennet, 1978; Brinkman, 1968; Carl, 1968; Cerulo, 1984; Morrison, 1969; Zillmann, Bryant, & Cantor, 1974). The quantitative efforts have tended to suggest that the effects of editorial cartoons are minimal, whereas the qualitative studies have shown that these cartoons can influence the images people form of the world. Further, although editorial cartoons make use of many cultural symbols, no research has been conducted to determine whether the cartoons reflect social reality or help create it.

Carl (1968) asserts that editorial cartoons are merely insignificant players on the editorial page. He surveyed a random sample of persons from three different towns and compared their interpretations of editorial cartoons to the intended messages of the cartoons as indicated by the cartoonists themselves. He found that the readers simply misinterpreted cartoons or missed the intended messages too often for the cartoons to have much effect. More than 60% of the time, Carl's respondents failed to concur with the meanings of the cartoons as described by the cartoonists. However, failing to concur with a cartoonist's interpretation may suggest that the reader is not influenced in the manner intended, but it does not mean that no influence occurs. Carl's study is simply not sophisticated enough to answer clearly the question of influence, but it does highlight a significant characteristic of editorial cartoons: They are difficult to interpret, and so different readers often take different meanings from them.

Two more recent studies with elementary and secondary students as subjects found results similar to Carl's (Bedient & Moore, 1985; Hunter, Moore, & Sewell, 1991). Both studies questioned the use of cartoons as a teaching strategy, because students could not correctly interpret the cartoons. The researchers recommend that teachers provide extensive background information on the subject matter of cartoons used in the classroom, as well as instruction in visual literacy, to help students understand and learn from editorial cartoons.

DeSousa and Medhurst (1982) have also reported the problem of incorrect interpretation in a study that employed a college student sample. Some students reported that they simply lacked the political background to understand the cartoons they were shown. The researchers did not attempt to correlate correct interpretations of the cartoons with tests of political knowledge, although such a step may have helped to explain why certain audience groups accurately or inaccurately interpreted the cartoons. Another step that might provide information on how readers process the content of editorial cartoons, investigation of correlations between subjects' political affiliations and the ways they interpret the cartoons, was not attempted in any of the studies reviewed for this essay. Still, as DeSousa and Medhurst (1982) argue, consistent misinterpretation of cartoons by readers supports the notion that it is time for "media researchers to begin examining the premise that the political cartoon is the most clearly understood form of newspaper editorializing. Indeed, instead of clarity we may find it is the essential ambiguity of the cartoon which is the source of its popularity and proliferation" (p. 50).

Brinkman (1968) found that an editorial cartoon combined with a supportive editorial created greater opinion change than an editorial alone, but did not investigate the extent of opinion change caused by an editorial cartoon alone. Through Q-method combined with fantasy theme analysis, Bormann et al. (1978) identified interpretive groups based on how they decoded a cartoon. Although this study indicates that groups may be identified based on how they respond to cartoons, it does nothing to increase our understanding of how the cartoons influence those groups.

Zillmann et al. (1974) discovered that decoders of cartoons found more humor in the cartoons when they depicted minor attacks on political candidates they opposed rather than on those they favored. When the attacks were more brutal, the subjects found the cartoons less humorous when they were directed at a candidate they opposed; the more brutal attacks apparently induced sympathy for the victim. However, the manipulations of brutality in the cartoons used in this study are problematic. For example, one cartoon came in the following versions. The nonbrutal cartoon depicted Nixon approaching a hurdle labeled "negative press." The medium-brutality version was the same as the nonbrutal cartoon, except that it included a few tacks in front of the hurdle and small spikes on the hurdle. The high-brutality cartoon added a spiked pit just beyond the hurdle. It could be argued that the focus of criticism changes in these cartoons rather than the degree of brutality aimed at Nixon. The high-brutality cartoon could be seen as criticizing the press rather than Nixon. This study, however, like Bormann et al.'s (1978), provides some evidence concerning how readers process editorial cartoons based on individual reader characteristics, such as groups they belong to or political viewpoints held.

Prerost (1993) found appreciation of editorial cartoons to be related to self-consciousness and the ability to use humor as a coping mechanism. Individuals in the study who were classified as highly self-conscious appreciated cartoons about the 1992 presidential campaign more than did other subjects, possibly because of "a tendency among high self-consciousness individuals to show views perceived as acceptable on the college campus during the 1992 presidential campaign" (p. 7). Persons who often used humor as a coping mechanism also appreciated the cartoons more than did others.

Finally, although Buell and Maus (1988) lack survey evidence, they conclude their study of cartoons about the 1988 presidential nominating campaigns by arguing that the cartoons appear to have had little influence: "In rough correlational terms, at least, Bush's harsh cartoon treatment was inversely associated with his winning the GOP nomination" (p. 857). This conclusion is weak, however, because of limited participation in primary voting and the researchers' admitted lack of survey evidence. The most interesting finding of Buell and Maus's study is that the cartoons, like the news coverage and editorials of the period studied, appeared to operate from a "horse-race" mentality, giving greater attention to the front-runners in the campaigns.

Political cartoons are presumed to influence those who pay attention to them, but the sparse empirical research available indicates that they have limited influence. It has been shown that individuals often either misinterpret cartoons or respond to them in unintended ways. However, there has not been enough research conducted to support fully the notion that these cartoons have limited influence, and much of the research that has produced such findings is now more than 20 years old. More research is needed on how readers interpret, make use of, and are affected by editorial cartoons before we can conclude that they have limited influence, especially considering that from a qualitative perspective the influence of these cartoons has been described as quite strong. For example, Morrison (1969) argues:

> The political cartoonist wields a potent weapon that can be used to stymie or assist any calculated design to galvanize a fresh godlike image for fickle celebrity-wor-shippers. This graphic communicator is not a harmless jester, providing editorial page fillers, but an effective opinion molder. The cartoonist's pen is mightier than the sword when it is both a sword and pen—a rapier dipped in India ink. (p. 252)

Morrison bases these assertions on an analysis of the images of three politicians: Abraham Lincoln, James G. Blaine, and Robert Kennedy. He qualifies his argument somewhat, stating, "The cartoonist does not father the image, he is the midwife in its birth" (p. 260). In other words, the cartoonist helps to carry images of society and politicians to audiences. The images displayed in cartoons may become the ones that are remembered, but Morrison does not address the process by which the images may influence readers.

Beniger (1983) suggests that other forces may be at work, noting that since the arrival of television, labeling in editorial cartoons has decreased. Television has enhanced the shared symbolic environment by increasing public awareness and recognition of cultural symbols. Cerulo (1984) offers a similar conclusion based on studies of magazine covers. Both Beniger's and Cerulo's studies offer compelling evidence that the onslaught of television has removed the need for cartoonists (and magazine cover artists) to label famous characters, because readers already know what these people look like.

A little humor can go a long way in a political campaign. Former presidential candidate and governor Adlai Stevenson said, "Humor helps to distinguish the really bright and thoughtful, and also the humble, from the self-conscious and the self-righteous presumptuous type" (quoted in Shields, 1987, p. 16). The public stands to learn a great deal through the humor and satire in political cartoons as well as through the responses they inspire. For example, voters certainly learned something about Senator Jesse Helms when he responded to a Doug Marlette cartoon that appeared in the *Charlotte Observer* by refusing to speak with any of that newspaper's reporters (Marlette, 1991).

Clearly, editorial cartoons do wield some influence, but the extent of that influence is little understood. Even though their cartoons provoke flak, death threats, and general reader disgruntlement at times (especially those that go against popular viewpoints, such as those opposed to the Gulf War; Astor,

1991), most cartoonists believe that their influence is minimal. Cartoonist Etta Hulme has said, "I don't think we have any real clout. Maybe some geological drip." Asked why she continues to cartoon, she responded, "We need geological drip" (quoted in Astor, 1989a, p. 60).

More study, especially from an empirical point of view, is needed to gauge the magnitude of influence of editorial cartoons. Progress has been made over the years in that researchers have developed ways of exploring and understanding visual persuasion in the form of editorial cartoons. But, as Medhurst and DeSousa (1981) argue, we need to explore further how readers process cartoons. Bormann et al. (1978) and Zillmann et al. (1974) have begun to approach this issue, but many questions remain unanswered. For example, "What is the role of learning and acculturation in interpretation? Do people who are more familiar with print display markedly better ability to interpret visual information presented through the print media?" (Medhurst & DeSousa, 1981, p. 236). We need to continue mapping out changes in images of groups, such as Thibodeau (1989) has done regarding blacks in *New Yorker* cartoons, but we also need to move beyond studying cartoons to studying what audiences do with cartoons.

CONCLUSION: LOOKING TO THE FUTURE

Coupe (1969), in responding to Streicher's (1967) call for a general theory of political caricature, argues:

> We still do not possess sufficient empirical studies on which such a theory might be based; even in the age of the mass produced Ph.D., the academic study of caricature and political cartooning has suffered from considerable neglect, partly no doubt because it lies in a peculiar no-man's-land where several disciplines meet, and so tends to be scorned by the purists. (p. 79)

It appears that the call still has not been answered. However, it would seem that communication scholars are uniquely qualified to tackle the problem.

Streicher (1967) notes that the words *caricature* and *cartoon* are "often employed interchangeably to refer to a drawing which contains ridicule or denigration" (p. 432). He describes caricature as satire, and says that "satire typically deals with demonstration and exposure of human vices or follies in order to scorn or ridicule humans; graphic caricatures ridicule pictorially" (p. 431). The editorial cartoon is mainly a negative medium, and many editorial cartoonists do not hesitate to point this out. It is a negative form of political and/or social commentary meant for mass production and quick consumption. As Streicher notes, "The caricature does not aim at 'contemplative readers' but at passionate, stand-taking, mass reading publics" (p. 433). According to Streicher, passionate emotion is often an aggressive emotion.

Caricatures are negative definitions, stereotypes, which are aimed at dramatizing aggressive tendencies through the definitions of targets, the collective integration of "private" feelings into public sentiments of "self-defense" and the training of hatred and debunking techniques. Caricature interprets nations, figures and events and helps to supplement the news presentation with statements of "meaning." (p. 438)

Editorial cartoons evoke emotion and give meaning to events, yet their significance and influence are debatable. As Coupe (1969) argues, "The cartoonist is concerned with the creation and manipulation of public opinion, but his actual impact, although often undoubtedly great, has not infrequently been exaggerated" (p. 82). However, as the editor and publisher of the *Sacramento Bee* discovered, the influence of an editorial cartoon can be financially significant. We do not understand the full impact of cartoons, nor do we completely understand the creation of "meaning." Editorial cartoonists give meaning to facts and help construct our social reality, but exactly how they go about it, what messages are embedded, and what impacts they have are not clear. Of these issues, the impacts of editorial cartoons appear to be the least understood. Do audiences gain political knowledge from cartoons? Do readers interpret cartoons based on what they know of the cartoonists? For example, are there certain responses that can be expected from a Republican who is interpreting a Herblock creation? Would the Republican reading Herblock create counterarguments against the message presented? (Such responses have been found in other arenas; see Ball-Rokeach, Grube, & Rokeach, 1981; Frey, 1986.) Or might a Republican consciously choose not to read a Herblock cartoon? A complete theory of political caricature and political cartooning needs to consider the audience in depth, including how readers interpret the cartoons and the political reality or realities the cartoons help readers to construct.

In this essay I have briefly reviewed the historical works on political cartoons, then turned to practical considerations of cartooning, and finally addressed questions of persuasion, influence, and impact. I have attempted to provide some insight into these areas based on the works reviewed, but the sparse research available on some topics has made this discussion incomplete. Further inquiry from diverse perspectives in the field of communication study should continue to focus on all of the areas addressed in this essay, but special attention should be devoted to the subject of how readers process visual information presented in the form of editorial cartoons.

REFERENCES

Astor, D. (1989a, November 18). Are some cartoonists toiling too hard? *Editor & Publisher,* pp. 58-60.

Astor, D. (1989b, June 10). Political cartoonists speak about ethics. *Editor & Publisher,* pp. 138-141.

Astor, D. (1991, May 18). Anti-Gulf War cartoonists got reader flak. *Editor & Publisher,* pp. 44-45.

Astor, D. (1994, June 25). Downbeat look at a profession's future. *Editor & Publisher,* pp. 110-111.

Astor, D. (1995, June 3). Syndicate is fighting California's attempt to levy a tax on cartoons. *Editor & Publisher,* pp. 49-50.

Ball-Rokeach, S. J., Grube, J. W., & Rokeach, M. J. (1981). "Roots: The next generations": Who watched and with what effect? *Public Opinion Quarterly, 45,* 56-68.

Bedient, D., & Moore, D. M. (1985). Student interpretations of political cartoons. *Journal of Visual/Verbal Languaging, 5*(2), 29-35.

Beniger, J. R. (1983). Does television enhance the shared symbolic environment? Trends in labeling of editorial cartoons, 1948-1980. *American Sociological Review, 48,* 103-111.

Bivins, T. H. (1984). Format preferences in editorial cartooning. *Journalism Quarterly, 61,* 182-185.

Blackwood, R. E. (1989). Ronbo and the peanut farmer in Canadian editorial cartoons. *Journalism Quarterly, 66,* 453-457.

Block, H. (1984). *Herblock through the looking glass: The Reagan years in words and pictures.* New York: W. W. Norton.

Block, H. (1993). *Herblock: A cartoonist's life.* New York: Macmillan.

Bormann, E., Koester, J., & Bennet, J. (1978). Political cartoons and salient rhetorical fantasies: An empirical analysis of the '76 presidential campaign. *Communication Monographs, 45,* 317-329.

Bostdorff, D. M. (1987). Making light of James Watt: A Burkean approach to the form and attitude of political cartoons. *Quarterly Journal of Speech, 73,* 43-59.

Boulding, K. E. (1956). *The image: Knowledge in life and society.* Ann Arbor: University of Michigan Press.

Brinkman, D. (1968). Do editorial cartoons and editorials change opinion? *Journalism Quarterly, 45,* 724-726.

Buell, E. H., & Maus, M. (1988). Is the pen mightier than the word? Editorial cartoons and 1988 presidential nominating politics. *PS: Political Science and Politics, 21,* 847-858.

Carl, L. M. (1968). Editorial cartoons fail to reach many readers. *Journalism Quarterly, 45,* 533-535.

Caswell, L. S. (1988). Edwina Dumm: Pioneer woman editorial cartoonist, 1915-1917. *Journalism History, 51*(1), 2-7.

Cerulo, K. A. (1984). Television, magazine covers, and the shared symbolic environment: 1948-1970. *American Sociological Review, 49,* 566-570.

Codell, J. F. (1988). Sir Isumbras, M.P.: Millais's painting and political cartoons. *Journal of Popular Culture, 22*(3), 29-47.

Conrad, P. (1985). *Drawn and quartered: The best political cartoons.* Los Angeles: Abrams.

Coupe, W. A. (1969). Observations on a theory of political caricature. *Comparative Studies in Society and History, 11,* 79-95.

Culbertson, T. (1987, September/October). Political cartoons: Following the laugh track. *Public Opinion,* pp. 18-19, 58.

Darling, J. N. (1962). *Ding's half century.* New York: Duell, Sloan & Pearce.

Dennis, E. (1974). The regeneration of political cartooning. *Journalism Quarterly, 51,* 664-669.

DeSousa, M. A. (1984). Symbolic action and pretended insight: The Ayatollah Khomeini in U.S. editorial cartoons. In M. J. Medhurst & T. W. Benson (Eds.), *Rhetorical dimensions in media: A critical casebook* (pp. 204-230). Dubuque, IA: Kendall/Hunt.

DeSousa, M. A., & Medhurst, M. J. (1982). The editorial cartoon as visual rhetoric: Rethinking Boss Tweed. *Journal of Visual/Verbal Languaging, 2*(2), 43-52.

Edelman, M. (1988). *Constructing the political spectacle.* Chicago: University of Chicago Press.

Fischer, R. A. (1986). Oddity, icon, challenge: The Statue of Liberty in American cartoon art, 1879-1986. *Journal of American Culture, 9,* 63-81.

Fischer, R. A. (1990). The Lucifer legacy: Boss Tweed and Richard Nixon as generic sleaze symbols in cartoon art. *Journal of American Culture, 13,* 1-19.

Fitzgerald, M. (1992, January 25). Controversial caricature: More than a month after publication, debate over Chicago weekly's political cartoon continues to be hot and heavy. *Editor & Publisher,* pp. 14-15.

Frey, D. (1986). Recent advances on selective exposure to information. In L. Berkowitz (Ed.), *Advances in experimental social psychology* (Vol. 19, pp. 41-80). New York Academic Press.

Garland, N. (1989, September 1). Cartoonist's-eye view. *National Review,* pp. 32-33.

Gamson, W. A., & Stuart, D. (1992). Media discourse as a symbolic contest: The bomb in political cartoons. *Sociological Forum, 7*(1), 55-86. '

Giobbe, D. (1994, April 23). A matter of taste. *Editor & Publisher,* pp. 18-19.

Grofman, B. (1989). Richard Nixon as Pinocchio, Richard II and Santa Claus: The use of allusion in political satire. *Journal of Politics, 51,* 165-173.

Grombrich, E. H. (1985). *Meditations on a hobby horse and other essays on the theory of art* (4th ed.). Chicago: University of Chicago Press.

Gurevitch, M., & Levy, M. R. (1985). *Mass communication review yearbook 5.* Beverly Hills, CA: Sage.

Handleman, A. (1984). Political cartoonists as they saw themselves during the 1950's. *Journalism Quarterly, 61,* 137-141.

Harrison, R. P. (1981). *The cartoon: Communication to the quick.* Beverly Hills, CA: Sage.

Hess, S., & Kaplan, M. (1968). *The ungentlemanly art: A history of American political cartoons.* New York: Macmillan.

Hill, A. (1978). The Carter campaign in retrospect: Decoding the cartoons. *Semiotica, 23,* 307-332.

Horn, M. (Ed.). (1980). *The world encyclopedia of cartoons* (Vol. 1). New York: Gale Research.

Hung, C. T. (1994). The fuming image: Cartoons and public opinion in late republican China, 1945-1949. *Comparative Studies in Society and History, 33,* 122-145.

Hunter, J. M., Moore, D. M., & Sewell, E. H. (1991). The effects of teaching strategy and cognitive style on student interpretations of editorial cartoons. *Journal of Visual Literacy, 11*(2), 35-55.

Ingalls, Z. (1991, July 10). Political cartoons at National Archives; Accountants as collectors of American art. *Chronicle of Higher Education, 37,* B2.

Jamieson, K. H. (1992). *Dirty politics: Deception, distraction and democracy.* New York: Oxford University Press.

Johnson, G. M. (1958). *The lines are drawn: American life since the First World War as reflected in the Pulitzer Prize cartoons.* Philadelphia: J. B. Lippincott.

Judge, L., & West, R. S. (1988, September). Why political cartoonists sell out: In the race for fame they ignore what matters at home. *Washington Monthly,* pp. 38-42.

King, N., & Editors of the Foreign Policy Association. (Eds.). (1991). *A cartoon history of United States foreign policy from 1945 to the present.* New York: Pharos.

Lamb, C. (1991, January 19). Color political cartoons being syndicated. *Editor & Publisher,* pp. 40-41.

Lamb, C. (1994, February 26). Political cartoonist with rightist views. *Editor & Publisher,* pp. 40-41.

Lamb, C. (1995, August). *Drawn and quartered: The government and cartoonists during World War I.* Paper presented at the annual meeting of the Association for Education in Journalism and Mass Communication, Washington, DC.

Lendt, D. L. (1979). *Ding: The life of Jay Norwood Darling.* Ames: Iowa State University Press.

Marlette, D. (1991). *In your face: A cartoonist at work.* Boston: Houghton Mifflin.

Martin, W. R. (1987). "Peridis" and political cartoons in post-Franco Spain. *Journal of Popular Culture, 20*(4), 159-173.

Mauldin, B. (1971). *The brass ring.* New York: W. W. Norton.

Maurice, A. B., & Cooper, F. T. (1904). *The history of the nineteenth century in caricature.* New York: Dodd, Mead.

Medhurst, M. J., & DeSousa, M. A. (1981). Political cartoons as rhetorical form: A taxonomy of graphic discourse. *Communication Monographs, 48,* 197-236.

Meyer, K., Seidler, J., Curry, T., & Aveni, A. (1980). Women in July Fourth cartoons: A 100-year look. *Journal of Communication, 30*(1), 21-30.

Morris, R. (1991). Cultural analysis through semiotics: Len Norris' cartoons on official bilingualism. *Canadian Review of Society and Anthropology, 28,* 225-254.

Morrison, M. (1969). The role of the political cartoonist in image making. *Central States Speech Journal, 20,* 252-260.

Mosher, S. (1991, October). In Hong Kong, fear and satire. *World Press Review, 38,* 27-28.

Nevins, A., & Weitenkampf, F. (1944). *A century of political cartoons: Caricature in the United States from 1800-1900.* New York: Charles Scribner's Sons.

Nilsen, D. L. F. (1990). The social functions of political humor. *Journal of Popular Culture, 20*(3), 35-47.

Penner, M., & Penner, S. (1994). Publicizing, politicizing, and neutralizing homelessness: Comic strips. *Communication Research, 21,* 766-781.

Platt, S. (1994, March 18). The right to be offensive: Political cartoonists and political correctness. *New Statesman & Society,* pp. 25-41.

Prerost, F. J. (1993). *Appreciation of presidential editorial cartoons in relation to self-consciousness.* (ERIC Document Reproduction Service No. ED 379 176).

Press, C. (1981). *The political cartoon.* London: Associated University Press.

Reeves, R. (1991). Introduction. In N. King & Editors of the Foreign Policy Association (Eds.), *A cartoon history of United States foreign policy from 1945 to the present* (pp. vii-xi). New York: Pharos.

Riffe, D., Sneed, D., & Van Ommeren, R. L. (1985). Behind the editorial cartoon. *Journalism Quarterly, 62,* 378-383, 450.

Riffe, D., Sneed, D., & Van Ommeren, R. L. (1987). Deciding the limits of taste in editorial cartooning. *Journalism Quarterly, 64,* 607-610.

Sena, J. (1985). A picture is worth a thousand votes: Geraldine Ferraro and the editorial cartoonist. *Journal of American Culture, 8,* 2-12.

Sharf, B. F. (1986). Send in the clowns: The image of psychiatry during the Hinckley trial. *Journal of Communication, 36*(4), 80-93.

Sheppard, A. (1985). Political and social consciousness in the woman suffrage cartoons of Lou Rogers and Nina Allender. *Studies in American Humor, 4*(1-2), 39-50.

Shields, M. (1987, September/October). Political humor: Who are these jokers? *Public Opinion, 10,* 15-17, 57.

Stein, M. L. (1994, February 19). Cartoon's message backfires in California. *Editor & Publisher,* pp. 9-10.

Streicher, L. H. (1967). On a theory of political caricature. *Comparative Studies in Society and History, 9,* 427-445.

Thibodeau, R. (1989). From racism to tokenism: The changing faces of blacks in *New Yorker* cartoons. *Public Opinion Quarterly, 53,* 482-494.

Thorkelson, N. (1979, March/April). Cartooning. *Radical America,* pp. 27-50.

Weitenkampf, F. (1953). *Political caricature in the United States: In separate published cartoons.* New York: New York Public Library/Arno.

Westin, A. F. (1979). *Getting angry six times a week: A portfolio of political cartoons.* Boston: Beacon.

Zillmann, D., Bryant, J., & Cantor, J. R. (1974). Brutality of assault in political cartoons affecting humor appreciation. *Journal of Research in Personality, 7,* 334-345.

CHAPTER CONTENTS

10 The Rhetorical Presidency: Deepening Vision, Widening Exchange

MARY E. STUCKEY
University of Mississippi

FREDERICK J. ANTCZAK
University of Iowa

Research on the rhetorical presidency has been marked by two important sets of theoretical divisions: individual versus institutional approaches to the analytic task and instrumental versus constitutive understandings of the rhetorical enterprise. In both cases, this has led to a situation in which scholars from the differing positions tend to talk past rather than to one another. In keeping with the generally interdisciplinary focus of political communication as it develops as a recognizable subfield with places in both political science and communication studies, this essay is intended to begin pointing the way toward redirecting some of those conversations, such that representatives from the various analytic communities can begin to work with one another rather than on parallel or opposing tracks.

THERE is a long scholarly history dedicated to research on presidential speech (Brigance, 1943; Hochmuth, 1943). The term *the rhetorical presidency* was coined by political scientists James W. Ceaser, Glen E. Thurow, Jeffrey Tulis, and Joseph M. Bessette (1981) and popularized in Tulis's (1987) book of the same name. These researchers have presented analyses of changes in the institution of the presidency in the second half of the 20th century. Following their landmark work, the assumption underlying

AUTHORS' NOTE: We would like to thank Brant Burleson, J. Michael Hogan, Kathleen Hall Jamieson, Kathleen Kendall, Richard Morris, Michael E. Roloff, and the anonymous reviewers for their help and advice. They did all they could to improve the manuscript; any remaining flaws are solely our responsibility. Several of the good ideas incorporated herein were gleaned from a conversation with Michael McGee; we thank him. We are also grateful to Lisa Pemble and Monique Moleon for their bibliographic assistance.

Correspondence and requests for reprints: Mary E. Stuckey, Department of Political Science, University of Mississippi, University, MS 38677; e-mail psmes@olemiss.edu

Communication Yearbook 21, pp. 405-441

much of the research on the rhetorical presidency has been that the role of the president within the national government has changed from emphasizing constitutionally delineated power to power based on the president's relationship with the American public. This research, undertaken primarily by political scientists, has emphasized the institutional position of the presidency within the governmental structure. Scholars have focused on the behavior of individual presidents only insofar as that behavior generated long-term changes in the presidency as an institution.

Other work, by both political scientists and scholars of speech communication, has focused on other implications and permutations of the president's increased public role. The best of this work, most notably by Roderick P. Hart (1984b, 1987) and David Zarefsky (1979, 1980, 1986), has combined scholarship from both political science and rhetorical studies and has yielded groundbreaking insights for both disciplines.

Still, the field in general has been driven by two dichotomies, one more obviously divisive than the other. The more overtly restrictive division pits studies of the institution against studies of the individual; the more subtly subversive division segregates the analysis of instrumental functions of communication from considerations of their more constitutive consequences.

Much of the research on the rhetorical presidency has been divided according to the scholarly orientations of the individual researchers. This division is being ameliorated somewhat by the union of the two disciplines in the study of political communication generally (Nimmo & Sanders, 1981; Swanson & Nimmo, 1990). The tension between the influence of the individual and the influence of the institution, however, remains (Hager & Sullivan, 1994). As political scientist Terry Moe (1993) has said:

> Persuasion and bargaining are essential to presidential leadership. But the activities surrounding them are reflections of their institutional setting. Institutions allocate authority, resources and opportunities—they entail a structure of power. The way this power gets exercised is, to a significant degree, epiphenomenal. It *arises* from structure, and it can be fully appreciated only when its connection to structure is laid bare. . . . The problem is not the relevance of personal factors for presidential behavior. The problem is that the personal side of the presidency lends itself very poorly to theory. (pp. 378-379)

Solid analysis of the rhetorical presidency requires attention to the tools of persuasion and bargaining, the contexts in which these tools are used, and the development of theories that allow generalization beyond the experience of a single president. But such analysis must also include recognition that presidential rhetoric has constitutive as well as instrumental consequences, that—as suggested by scholarship in the tradition of Edelman (1964, 1971, 1977, 1988)—political reality is partly or wholly created from and sustained in rhetoric, and that presidential communication plays a major role in the construction and continuous reconstruction of political perceptions. An exclusive focus on the instrumental functions of presidential rhetoric reinforces the notion that individual presidents exercise a broader range of discretion and control than actually is the case. Each president, as president, intentionally or not, helps to create and maintain specific sorts of rhetorical communities, communities that in turn work to shape and constrain the possibilities of the presidency (Edelman, 1988; Zarefsky, 1980; Zernicke, 1994).

This review is grounded in the assumption that the most promising research on the rhetorical presidency acknowledges these distinctions and opens possibilities for wider intellectual exchange. It is, however, true that more research exists on both sides of the first division, stressing either the individual or the institution. In the latter case, there is considerably more extant scholarship on the instrumental uses of rhetoric than there is on its constitutive functions. This review reflects that balance.

PRESIDENTIAL SCHOLARSHIP BEFORE
THE RHETORICAL PRESIDENCY

Presidents and presidential candidates have always been concerned with the creation and maintenance of favorable public opinion toward themselves personally and toward the policies they have favored. With the institutionalization of the rhetorical presidency (Ceaser et al., 1981), the distinction between campaigning and governing has become increasingly blurred, making the inclusion of campaigning relevant to this review.

Scholars have investigated the impacts of presidential campaigning at least as far back as Andrew Johnson's public speaking tour (Harris, 1989) and William Jennings Bryant's campaign (Koenig, 1980), but have paid particular attention to changes in the institution of the presidency since the turn of the century, as manifested in the presidencies of Woodrow Wilson and Theodore Roosevelt (Gould, 1989), and especially to the developments fostered by changes in campaigning (Broh, 1983; Krasner, 1979; West, 1982) and the inception of television (Just et al., 1996; Miroff, 1982; Schmertz, 1986).

For much of U.S. history, presidential forays into the public arena have been rare and carefully orchestrated. Presidents have traditionally articulated the American values associated with the national civil religion (Fairbanks, 1981; Hart, 1977) and maintained largely ceremonial roles as public speakers. With the presidencies of Woodrow Wilson and Theodore Roosevelt (Tulis, 1987), however, presidents began to assume more aggressive public personas. Franklin Roosevelt's time in office is credited as the beginning of the "modern presidency," which is characterized by (among other things) the emergence of personalized politics (Cronin & Hochman, 1985; Ryan, 1988).

This increased focus on the expansion of presidential power and the attention paid to the person of the president were correlated with an apparent belief that with the right sort of leadership, all of our political problems could be ameliorated, if not eliminated (Corwin, 1940)—that "American history is mainly the history of men rising to the demands of their time" (Stevenson, 1984, p. 19). This "heroic" model of the presidency was reflected in both political science and in speech communication as scholars concentrated on the rhetoric and administrations of individual presidents and largely ignored the development and influences of the political structures of the institution of the presidency.

The scholarly preoccupation with the heroic presidency was largely displaced as the events of Watergate and Vietnam combined to render Americans less than hopeful about the possibilities of presidential leadership and more aware of its potential dangers (Cronin, 1974). Notions of the "imperial" presidency (Schlesinger, 1973) gave way in their turn to notions of an "imperiled" or "impossible" presidency as scholars during the Ford and Carter years strove to find a locus for presidential leadership that was both intellectually satisfying and politically possible (Nelson, 1990).

Ronald Reagan seemed for a time to provide the sort of leadership that represented an apparent return to the "old days" of presidential leadership (albeit with strikingly different political preferences), accomplishing much of his agenda despite a hostile Congress (Pika, 1990). That he appeared to do this through the generation of strong public support for both his persona and his policies fostered an increased interest in the nature of leadership in general and its communicative aspects in particular (Denton & Hahn, 1986; Edwards, 1983; Hart, 1984b, 1987; Kellerman, 1984; Kernell, 1993; King & Schudson, 1987; Ostrom & Simon, 1989).

Scholars agree that since the late 1950s and early 1960s, presidential politics has been increasingly affected by public evaluations of presidential performance (Simon & Ostrom, 1988), and they have consequently devoted increasing attention to systematizing and analyzing the political and institutional consequences of the increased public role in the processes of governance. These studies often stress the contrast of the contemporary office to the designs of the framers of the Constitution (Lawler, 1987), and are not generally sanguine about the consequences for the future of democratic politics, concluding that the American public expects more from the presidency than any individual president can possibly deliver (Buchanan, 1978; Fishel, 1985; Kellerman & Barilleaux, 1991; Lowi, 1985; Roelofs, 1992). In general, the literature thus has two forms: Generally qualitative studies of the office measure the prevailing practices of the presidency against a normative standard of ideal presidential performance, and more quantitative work stresses the creation of models for predicting a president's success in advancing a policy agenda given a specified political environment. Much could be gained if these perspectives and methodologies were combined to produce workable theories of presidential power and the consequences of its exercise. As yet, however, the scholarly communities remain largely distinct.

THE RHETORICAL PRESIDENCY DEFINED

The rhetorical presidency as an analytic construct can be traced back to the publication in 1960 of Richard Neustadt's landmark work *Presidential Power.* Neustadt began the shift away from strictly legal and institutional studies of the presidency, and brought to political science a new understanding of the roles that bargaining and persuasion play in the practice of the presidency (Moe, 1993, Neustadt, 1960, 1990). Although scholars in the field of speech communication had long been interested in these roles, it was not until the 1970s and 1980s that the two fields began to exchange insights systematically. The result has been a burgeoning of literature dedicated to increasing our understanding of both the systemic and the individual effects of the rhetorical presidency.

In 1974, Michael Novak published *Choosing Our King,* in which he described the president as

> *king*—king in the sense of symbolic, decisive, focal point of our power and destiny. He is *prophet*—prophet in the sense of chief interpreter of our national self-understanding, establishing the terms of our national discourse. He is *priest*—priest in the sense of incarnating our self-image, our values, our aspirations, and expressing those through every action he selects, every action he avoids. (p. 52)

Three years later, Roderick P. Hart expanded on that theme in *The Political Pulpit* (1977). In 1980, Walter Fisher's "Rhetorical Fiction and the Presidency" helped to focus attention on the presidency as "an office and a role, an institution and a persona" (p. 119), which depended on ethos, which in turn depended upon the president's relationship to the people (p. 124). The landmark study "The Rise of the Rhetorical Presidency" (Ceaser et al., 1981) and *The Symbolic Dimensions of the American Presidency* (Denton, 1982) signaled the beginning of scholarship on "the rhetorical presidency," as opposed to scholarship dealing with communicative aspects of the presidency or rhetoric and the presidency. Theodore Windt (1986) then outlined the field and suggested methods and approaches for its study.

In general, these early studies, like those that followed throughout the 1980s and into the 1990s (Abbott, 1988; Campbell & Jamieson, 1990; Edwards, 1983; Hart, 1984b, 1987; Kellerman, 1984; Kernell, 1993; Patterson, 1993; Rockman, 1984; Smith & Smith, 1994; Tulis, 1987), were concerned primarily with the institutional effects of the changes they documented in the conduct of the presidency. For all of these researchers, the rhetorical presidency marked a change from the framers' conception of the institution as a deliberative, largely administrative entity and toward a more epideictic, publicly responsive institution.

Although these scholars approached their subject from a wide variety of perspectives, they agreed that the constitutional system as a whole had been weakened by presidents' attempts to build a direct relationship between themselves and the American people and by presidents' dependence upon the mass public rather than the political parties both to govern and to maintain their status as national leaders (Lowi, 1985). These attempts have changed both the presidency and the system in which it is embedded, including an increase in presidential speech (Hart, 1984b, 1987), a change in the nature and meaning of that speech (Campbell & Jamieson, 1990; Hart, 1984a; Stuckey, 1991), an erosion of the traditional means of governance (Kernell, 1993; Lowi, 1985), and an increase in the president's ceremonial rather than substantive role (Kellerman, 1984). These changes in the institution of the presidency took place under the influence of three dramatic developments: (a) the decline of the power and standing of political parties, (b) the growing political and cultural influence of the autonomous institutions of mass communication, and (c) the increasing personalization of politics (Ceaser et al., 1981; Entman, 1989; Hart, 1994; Jamieson, 1988; Lowi, 1985; Manheim, 1991).

Changes in the presidency appeared simultaneously with the growth of mass media (Stuckey, 1991). These changes began with the inception of mass-circulation newspapers during the administrations of Teddy Roosevelt and Woodrow Wilson and extended into the development of mass communications, beginning with radio and Franklin D. Roosevelt and continuing with television and Ronald Reagan (Dallek, 1984; Denton, 1989; Erickson, 1985; Glaros & Miroff, 1983; Rogin, 1987). The new electronic media are changing politics in ways that are as yet poorly understood (Gronbeck, 1995; "The Net," 1996). Without some efficient and reliable way of reaching the mass public, given the weakened mechanism of political parties, the rhetorical presidency would not be possible.

It is important to note that presidents sought the mass public not merely as an audience, but as a tool for governance. As the responsibilities of the national government and the presidency grew as a result of FDR's approach to the Depression and World War II, the president had increased responsibility for policy making on the federal level. But he did not have increased power vis-à-vis the other policy-making institutions to support his attempts to handle those responsibilities (Arnold, 1995). The president's public appeals constituted attempts to gain leverage over the other elements of the national policy-making structure. Nonetheless, the strategy of "going public" is no longer simply an extra option in the president's repertoire. Presidents who fail to meet the expectations of the people and the mass media regarding the institution's public role are presidents who are likely to be excoriated by both audiences. Public character depends partly on policies put forward and implemented—and those left off of the agenda—which scholars have already studied in some detail. Another part of public character concerns the rhetorical battles a president chooses to fight or abandon, the reflection of public concerns, commitments, and character that he embodies.

It is equally important to note that even as presidents sought the mass public as a tool for governance, the effects of presidential persuasive rhetoric also reconstituted that public, rendering them as participants, as spectators, and then as the objects of polling. These renderings have caused considerable concern, but they are as yet undertheorized and underresearched.

The changes that fall under the rubric of the rhetorical presidency thus have affected the president's responsibilities and obligations, as well as his relationships with the mass public and the other institutions of the national government and the nature of the American polity. Consequently, the following sections are organized around the changes and pressures that have altered the president's relationship to the people and the effects those changes have had on presidential relationships with Congress and the mass media, as well as on the president as an individual and as a public official.

The President and the People

Examinations of the myriad relationships between the president and the people, especially those that originate in political science, understand communication as purely instrumental—rhetorical acts are interesting to these researchers as variables that potentially affect polls. Little regard is given to the idea that constituting the "public" as "respondents" is itself a rhetorical move that has potentially important political consequences for the democratic polity. In this area, political scientists could learn much from scholars in other disciplines, even as those who are interested in the constitutive effects of presidential rhetoric have much to learn about the political contexts that constrain that rhetoric.

The roots of the rhetorical presidency can be found in the processes of nominating and electing presidents, and in the failure of other institutions to fulfill the functions they traditionally discharged (Ceaser et al., 1981; Patterson, 1993). Campaigns have been the focus of an enormous amount of research, in both political science and speech communication. Because campaigns are discrete, time-bounded events that generate increases in both media coverage and public attention, they lend themselves to empirical analyses from both behavioral and humanistic perspectives. Much of this scholarship grapples with how the mass media and the other technologies of what was once known as "the new politics" have changed both the nature of campaigns and the methods used to study them (Swanson, 1972).

Considerable work has been done on primaries (Kendall, 1995b, in press) as well as on general elections (Hacker, 1995). A good deal of this research is concerned with the influence of controlled media on electoral processes, such as the legitimation of political advertisements as a tool for voter decision making (Kaid, Gobetz, & Garner, 1993), the nature and persuasive qualities of those advertisements (Cappella & Jamieson, 1994; Hallin, 1992; Jamieson, 1992a, 1992b; Kern, 1989; Pfau & Kenski, 1990; Pfau & Louden, 1994), the interplay between formal electoral structures and the media (Corcoran & Kendall, 1992; Iyengar, 1987; Kendall, 1993; Minow & Mitchell, 1986; Wattenberg, 1989), the rhetorical structures of campaign ads (Gronbeck, 1992; Marvin, 1994), and the relationships between media and voter interest in politics (Garramone, 1985; Newhagen, 1994; Wagner, 1983) and levels of information (Chaffee, Zhao, & Leshner, 1994; Conover & Feldman, 1989; Lowden, Anderson, Dozier, & Lauzen, 1994). Much of this literature is beset by the divisions that arise from the specialization characterizing the academy today; even among those in cognate areas, there is too little generalization across these divisions to promote active theory building outside of a narrowly defined area. Thus there are many strong and viable theories of micro-level significance, and not enough that unite and inform the fields generally, or that help to communicate findings to a broader audience.

There is some commonality, however. For instance, scholars generally point to the promise of television as a medium for reaching a mass, culturally diverse audience, while also finding that controlled media, and advertisements in particular, fail to live up to that promise, offering instead increasingly terse, increasingly negative, and increasingly empty slogans rather than the argumentation that would accomplish the goals of political education as outlined in traditional democratic theory (Antczak, 1985; Entman, 1989). Other scholars have focused their attention on the functions of uncontrolled media in presidential campaigns, especially the role of news coverage (Jacques, Meilinger, Balmoris, Gerns, & Denby, 1993; Meyrowitz, 1994). These researchers have found differences between print and televised news reporting, with television providing less useful information, more coverage of the "horse race," an increased tendency toward "attack journalism" (Sabato, 1991), and more sensationalized and dramatic treatment of campaigns (Fry & Fry, 1986; Jamieson, 1992a, 1992b; Sigelman & Bullock, 1991; Stovall, 1984; Vidich, 1990; West, 1983, 1984), whereas candidates have been found to respond to the exigencies of uncontrolled as well as controlled media (Hart, 1994). In addition, television news coverage of primary races has been accused of contributing to "front loading," the disproportionate influence of early primaries in shaping public perceptions of candidates (Castle, 1991; Graber, 1987; Kaid, Leland, & Whitney, 1992; Roberts, 1981; Ross, 1992).

Considerable research has also been done on the communicative aspects of specific events within a campaign, especially debates. There is evidence that debates both can and do influence vote choice (Geer, 1988; Vancil & Pendell, 1984), that both substance and style affect voter responses to the participants (Carter & Stamm, 1994; Rowland, 1986), that media coverage of debates is focused less on issues than on images (Gadziala & Becker, 1983; Rouner & Perloff, 1988), and that the visuals of television play a particularly important role in structuring viewer reactions to debates (Friedenberg, 1994; Hellweg,

Pfau, & Brydon, 1992; Jamieson & Birdsell, 1988; Morello, 1988). Consequently, media specialists within the various campaigns work hard to affect the coverage of all aspects of political debates (Berquist & Golden, 1981; Lanoue & Schrott, 1991). There is good reason to do so. The first major effort to assess the overall educative value of debates showed that diversity of formats, compressed scheduling, and the inclusion of third-party candidates were all significant aids in learning, but debates are still dominated by the media, and learning is inhibited by the timing, short response times, and overlap of topics that continue to characterize them (Carlin & McKinney, 1994). Debates remain important, and the role of the media in interpreting them for voters continues unimpeded.

Still other campaign-related research has focused on the rhetoric offered by the various candidates. Ronald Reagan has undoubtedly received the bulk of recent attention (Dallek, 1984; Erickson, 1985; Ingold & Windt, 1984; Kiewe & Houck, 1991; Rogin, 1987), but other candidates and other elections have also been studied productively, including Nixon and Kennedy in 1960 (Depoe, 1991; Goldzwig & Dionisopoulos, 1995b), Dan Quayle (Moore, 1992), Mario Cuomo (Henry, 1988), and Jesse Jackson (Merritt, 1986; Washington, 1985). Other scholars have analyzed the collective purposes of campaign dramas (Gronbeck, 1985); specific rhetorical strategies, such as silence (Erickson & Schmidt, 1982); and rhetoric as a tool for agenda setting (West, 1982).

Researchers have also studied the various aspects of campaigns as recurring strategic problems (Denton, 1994; Kendall, 1995a; Trent & Friedenberg, 1991). Among the subjects investigated have been concession speeches (Corcoran, 1994), the role of public opinion polls (Bauman & Herbst, 1994), public and media preferences in candidate characteristics (Trent, Mongeau, Trent, Kendall, & Cushing, 1993), and the problem of dealing with controversial issues (Daughton, 1994; Gregg, 1994).

Finally, there has been considerable research on the relationship between presidential campaigns and governance. Here, there are possibilities for including analyses of the constitutive nature of rhetoric, studying how the nation chooses among visions of itself even as it chooses among the policies and images offered by various candidates (Blumenthal, 1990; Gregg, 1994). Other links, however, have received more attention, with scholars finding that most candidates, most of the time, intend to keep (and do in fact keep) the majority of their campaign promises (Fishel, 1985; Krukones, 1980). Other scholars worry about the link between what they see as debased processes of campaign communication and its relationship to equally debased modes of democratic governance (Andersen & Thorson, 1989; Jamieson, 1988; Kellner, 1990). A good deal of this concern is generated by a belief that the media are not well suited to roles that were once occupied by formal institutions, most notably the political parties (Patterson, 1993).

The electoral reforms of the Progressive Era and the changes mandated by the 1968 McGovern-Fraser Commission, combined with the rise of television as a purveyor of political information, have contributed to a weakening of political parties as institutions, rendering them less viable for attaching individual voters to the political system. Concomitantly, the political parties have become less relevant both to presidential candidates and to presidents who are pursuing specific policy agendas. Consequently, presidents spend more and more of their time attempting to influence public opinion concerning their policies as well as their persons (Edwards, 1990; Kernell, 1976, 1978; Ostrom & Simon, 1984, 1988; Simon & Ostrom, 1988) in an effort to create and maintain support that will translate into legislative success. Much of the literature on this topic deals not with normative concerns about the definitions and consequences of that success, but primarily with our ability to define and predict the conditions for success.

We know, therefore, that presidents have developed several strategies aimed at affecting public opinion, strategies that have constitutive as well as instrumental consequences (Morris & Stuckey, in press), but we continue to know little about the parameters of those consequences. The State of the Union Address has been shown to be an effective presidential tool for influencing the public's issue agenda (Cohen, 1995), and issue salience has in turn been demonstrated to play an indirect role in public approval of the president (Edwards, Mitchell, & Welch, 1995). Other tools for the manipulation of public opinion include polls (Sudman, 1982), travel (Darcy & Richman, 1988; Simon & Ostrom, 1989), speeches (Gilboa, 1990; Ragsdale, 1984; Smith, 1993), silence (Brummet, 1980; Erickson & Schmidt, 1982), and foreign diplomacy (Plischke, 1985).

The best-known example of this sort of manipulation is the "rally effect." In its simplest form, the rally effect is the tendency of presidential approval scores to increase as the public responds to perceived international crises with generalized support for the president. This effect has been found in studies of broad trends in public opinion (Lanoue, 1989; Stoll, 1987) as well as in specific instances, such as the Iranian hostage crisis (Conover & Sigelman, 1982). The assertion that the rally effect exists remains somewhat controversial, however; there is evidence that increases in approval scores may be attributable to the extent and nature of the media coverage and structural factors such as whether the president enjoys bipartisan support, the initial level of approval, and the recency of the last crisis (Lian & O'Neal, 1993; MacKuen, 1983). It seems evident that simple saber rattling will not suffice to affect the level of presidential approval materially and, in the absence of consensus on a clearly defined crisis, may work to the president's detriment (Evensen, 1993).

There is also evidence that presidential approval is affected by structural factors that the president can do little to control directly (Stimson, 1976). Partisan ties greatly affect perceptions of and reactions to presidential decisions and actions (Tatalovich & Gitelson, 1990), as do policy preferences

(Hurwitz, Peffley, & Raymond, 1989; Reilly, 1983) and prior expectations of presidential performance (Sigelman & Knight, 1985).

The strongest evidence for the strength of structural influences on presidential approval comes from the economy. Unemployment levels appear to have little influence, but changes in personal income levels, inflation rates, and both recessions and recoveries have been shown to affect presidential approval ratings (Lanoue, 1987).

Presidential behavior is a response to perceived public opinion as well as an instigator of that opinion. Manheim and Lammers (1981), for example, found that changes in the scheduling of news conferences were correlated with Gallup Poll ratings. West's (1984) study of the 1980 presidential campaign indicates that campaigns are useful to political actors as mechanisms for learning public opinion and that candidates act upon those lessons.

Whether as a response to or a motivator of public opinion, presidential rhetorical behavior is significant both from a policy standpoint and as a symbol of national identity, a voice for our national values, defining the American polity (Campbell & Jamieson, 1985, 1990; Dunn, 1984; Hart, Smith-Howell, & Llewellyn, 1991; Sandman, 1989). Presidents are expected to reflect and enact qualities that at any given point in time are considered emblematic of leadership (Brummet, 1981; Cronin, 1984; Hogan, 1989; Rozell, 1993a), an especially difficult task given an apparent public preference for simple myth rather than the complex reality that political actors face (Hoffman, 1981). Nonetheless, some presidents do accomplish this task. Many studies have been done, for example, on Ronald Reagan and his ability to fulfill public expectations in this regard (Erickson, 1985; King & Schudson, 1987; Smith, 1987; Wills, 1987).

Consequently, the personal characteristics of presidents have become increasingly important (Glass, 1985; Keeter, 1987; McCann, 1990; Norrander, 1986; Thomas & Sigelman, 1984). Researchers have found this to be true regardless of their respondents' levels of education (Miller, Wattenberg, & Malanchuk, 1986). This trend makes the increase in voter negativity and disaffection particularly disturbing, as negative reactions to individuals and to the system as a whole appear to be reinforcing (Gant & Davis, 1984).

Presidents thus exert considerable effort in creating their public images and tailoring them to the exigencies of prevailing circumstances (Bennett, Harris, Laskey, Levitch, & Monrad, 1976; Frankel, 1988; Steele, 1974). Their tactics include innovative uses of the media (Adams, 1985; Barkin, 1986; H. Martin, 1984; M. Martin, 1983); the use of past experiences, such as success in war to support a heroic image (Schwartz, 1983); "wimp-baiting," a tactic aimed at denigrating the opposition as weak (Curtis, 1989); the targeting of specific audiences (Smith, 1993; Spragens, 1984); and, of course, the use of political consultants (Link, 1989). This is one area of research where the union of different research agendas could produce valuable theoretical results, bettering our understanding of how the constitutive and instrumental uses of rhetoric complement and enable one another, thus leading to both policy success and communal unity, or how the failure of one element can contribute to the weakening of the other. Very little such research currently exists.

What we do know is that presidents, feeling constrained by the inherent difficulties of fulfilling the role of the presidency within the limits of the Constitution, have brought the public into the political process in ways that are antithetical to the original constitutional design. This new relationship between the president and the public would not be possible without the technologies of the mass media.

The Mediated President

Scholarship on the media tends to focus on the instrumental uses of rhetoric, as in agenda setting, framing, and so on. We know much less, and have perhaps thought too little, about the issues involved with constituting the public as "audience." Important work has been conducted to examine how television especially has affected the democratic polity, rendering citizens passive and uninvolved, but the exact processes by which this occurs and the precise implications for policy remain poorly understood.

The White House and the media have always had an important relationship, although it has not always been a pleasant one (Zeidenstein, 1983). As Ithiel de Sola Pool has written: "The whole relationship of reporter and politician resembles a bad marriage. They cannot live without each other, nor can they live without hostility. . . . It is conflict within a shared system" (quoted in Linsky, 1986, p. 17). Just as reporters need access to official sources in order to cover the government adequately, members of the government need access to influential reporters in order to communicate with the public adequately. Although both sides often characterize the relationship as "adversarial," it is in fact symbiotic, with each partner receiving benefit from the relationship (Grossman & Kumar, 1981). But as de Sola Pool has pointed out, symbiotic relationships are not necessarily amiable ones. As the national media have become increasingly influential, presidents have exerted more energy trying to control them (Locander, 1983; Rubin, 1981). Although members of the media recognize their dependence on the White House as a source of information, they resist overt control by the White House. It is a complicated arrangement for both participants, and has become more complicated in the wake of Watergate and Vietnam, which, in addition to increasing the cynicism and perceived bias in reporting (Linsky, 1986; Rivers, 1982; Tebbel & Watts, 1985), also encouraged an increase in the number of reporters covering the White House and the national government, for reporters go where they perceive the best sources of news can be found. As the president dominates the national policy scene, the presidency dominates the national news scene (Brennan & Hahn, 1990; Cornfield, 1988; Davis, 1990). The two arenas have come to complement one another, and in a reciprocal relationship, influence in one arena affects influence in the other, not always to the president's advantage.

Presidents thus increasingly orient the institution toward communication and their communication toward television (James, 1988; Kerbel, 1991). This preoccupation with television has been building ever since the early 1950s (Reinsch, 1988), but it reached its peak in what Robert E. Denton, Jr. (1989) has called Ronald Reagan's "primetime presidency." For Denton, Reagan was our first true television president, and he crafted his administration to fit the requirements of the medium. Those requirements include the need to accommodate the preferences of advertisers, maintain profits, increase the audience share, and allow for journalistic efficiency by developing routinized patterns of information gathering (Schudson, 1982; Smoller, 1986).

Because the information relayed via the media is so important to a president's public standing (Iyengar, Kinder, Krosnick, & Peters, 1984; Paletz & Vinegar, 1977-1978; Smoller, 1988), presidents go to extraordinary—and sometimes illegal—lengths to control what information is released (Rozell, 1993b; Winfield, 1981). Information control can be explicit, as in lying and leaking (Erickson, 1989) or withholding information, or it can be a matter of timing, emphasis, or context (Abel, 1987; Graber, 1981; Hinckley, 1990; Lammers, 1981; Manheim, 1991; Orman, 1987; Popkin, 1991; Windt, 1990), phenomena more difficult to capture analytically.

Despite these strategies, presidents are not able to control media interpretations of the political world unilaterally (Iyengar, 1987, 1991; Paletz & Entman, 1980; Pan & Kosicki, 1993; Robinson, 1974). Considerable scholarly attention has been devoted to the media's ability to frame events and thus affect viewers' perceptions of reality (Bormann, 1982; Dobkin, 1996; Iyengar, 1989; Kenski, 1996). Behr and Iyengar (1985), for instance, found that media agenda setting is unidirectional—that media coverage contributes to the level of public concern on an issue. Similarly, Krosnick and Kinder's (1990) study of the media, the president, and events in Nicaragua indicates that the more attention the media pay to an issue, the more citizens will rely on that issue in making judgments concerning presidential performance (Roberts & McCombs, 1994).

Media frames do not always work against the president, despite the presidential faith in negative and unfair media coverage (Zeidenstein, 1983). Cornfield and Yalof (1988) found that the use of the Watergate analogy by the media covering the Iran-contra affair assisted Reagan's political recovery from the scandal by emphasizing issues of law and justice. Further research on how frames work, and how they influence the rhetorical aspects of the presidency, are clearly warranted (Entman, 1993), especially in a post-Cold War context (Norris, 1995).

Presidents seek to influence the media and the public in order to increase their leverage vis-à-vis Congress, the branch of the federal government formally charged with policy-making responsibilities, with more attention to instrumental goals than to constitutive functions. Scholarly attention has followed that of presidents in this regard. In both cases, the results of the attention have been mixed at best.

The President and Congress

The presidential role vis-à-vis Congress is particularly complicated. Public expectations of the president as a legislative agent increased under Franklin D. Roosevelt and have remained high. Yet although presidents are expected to exercise leadership in the legislative arena, they are given neither constitutional nor legal authority to act unilaterally (Bond & Fleisher, 1990). Presidents, as Richard Neustadt (1960) has noted, cannot command; they can only persuade.

Because of the nature of the federal system as one of separated powers, presidents find that persuasive task particularly onerous, as the members of the legislative branch have developed different goals, different priorities, and different perspectives from those of the executive branch (Edwards, 1980; Fisher, 1987; Polsby, 1976; Seligman & Covington, 1989). Although some research indicates that the fact of divided government may not be as inimical as conventional wisdom suggests (Mayhew, 1991), presidents still face enormous challenges in attempting to shepherd their agendas through the legislative process.

"Going public" is one strategy aimed at meeting those challenges. Political scientist Samuel Kernell (1993) describes going public as "a strategy whereby a president promotes himself and his policies in Washington by appealing to the American public for support" (p. 2). This strategy is an attempt to "go over the heads" of members of Congress and to exert indirect pressure on them via their constituents. A president's going public relies on his stature as the only elected official with a national constituency, and its success depends on his ability to speak convincingly for the nation. Kernell (1993) and others (e.g., Simon & Ostrom, 1988) have found this change to be significant for the practice of the contemporary and increasingly rhetorical presidency.

There is evidence that the more popular and the more rhetorically skilled the president, the more influence he can assert over the policy process (Brace & Hinckley, 1992; Ostrom & Simon, 1985; Page & Shapiro, 1984; Rivers & Rose, 1985; Rohde & Simon, 1985). For instance, Chester (1981) found that Ronald Reagan's speeches were successful in creating a climate of opinion that forced Congress to act on his agenda. Even these studies, however, indicate that the links between popularity and legislative success are tenuous. Bond and Fleisher (1990) found that increased popularity increases support only among the president's partisans and actually increases the negativity of his opponents. Similarly, Bond, Fleisher, and Northrup (1988) found that although approval ratings have statistically significant effects on the president's relationship with Congress, the substantive effects are marginal, have slightly more impact on foreign than on economic issues, and are generally stronger on members of the president's party than on members of the opposition party. There is also evidence that presidential popularity declines over the average term in office (Brace & Hinckley, 1991; Sigelman & Knight, 1983). Thus some scholars believe that presidents should "hit the ground running" (Pfiffner, 1988) and act on as much of their agendas as they can as early in their terms as possible.

Other scholars, however, have found little support for the "bank account presidency" (Bond & Fleisher, 1984, 1990; Collier & Sullivan, 1995; Edwards, 1989; Gleiber & Shull, 1992; Sullivan, 1991) and conclude that other factors—such as prestige, the state of the economy, and the degree of focus the administration has concerning its agenda—are more important in the policy process. As Terry Sullivan (1991) says, "Maybe the most important temporal dictum, then, has less to do with a ready agenda and more to do with a focused one; that is, it is not, 'move it or lose it,' but 'concentrate or lose'" (p. 722).

Still more recent evidence indicates that this disagreement may be more methodological than substantive, that there is a difference between a president's attempting to generate support for his policies and his attempting to generate support for his person. Collier (1995) suggests that the way we conceptualize and thus investigate the strategy of going public may need refinement. Analysis of how presidential rhetoric influences and is influenced by the broader public conception of itself and thus the appropriate goals of its policies would contribute significantly to this refining process, as research along these lines indicates (Zarefsky, 1980; Zernicke, 1994).

Whatever the empirical validity to the belief that presidents can influence Congress by influencing and/or mobilizing the mass public, it appears true that presidents continue to believe that the benefits of public politics outweigh the potential risks to themselves and to the system.

Whether or not presidents can influence the outcome of legislation, there is little doubt that they can and do exert enormous influence over the legislative agenda (Moen, 1988). The prime vehicle for presidential agenda setting in Congress is the State of the Union Address. There is some evidence that the president competes with the media for public attention in agenda setting (Wanta, 1991), and that the two have reciprocal influences (Wanta, Stephenson, Turk, & McCombs, 1989). There is other evidence that the media have more ability to set the president's agenda than vice versa (Gilberg, Eyal, McCombs, & Nichols, 1980). Individual members of Congress, as well as Congress as an institution, also compete with the president in setting the national legislative agenda, and structural forces such as the state of the economy play important roles in determining the outcomes of such competition (Verdier, 1988).

There is also evidence that presidents approach the question of legislative agenda setting strategically, considering factors such as long-term political goals, the changing institutional setting, and the risks involved with plebiscitary politics (Mouw & MacKuen, 1992), and are willing to settle for what they think they can get rather than asking for what they would prefer in an ideal world (Zarefsky, 1986). There is little research on the effects this pattern of decision making may have for our understanding of ourselves as a nation committed to the enactment of certain ideals.

There is, however, considerable research on the presidential ability to influence the way Americans respond to political events (Brenders & Fabj, 1993; Daughton, 1993; Dorsey, 1995). On the domestic front, researchers have investigated Reagan's effectiveness in implementing his social agenda (Medhurst, 1984), the comparative levels of symbol and substance in presidential speeches on civil rights (Shull & Ringelstein, 1989), and how presidents use argumentative tactics to deflect criticism of their policies (Crable & Vibbert, 1983; Holland, 1990) and to control the impacts of social movements (Miroff, 1981). In general, these studies furnish information on how particular instances or genres of persuasive speech have functioned, rather than readily generalizable data that apply across and between presidencies. This is indeed valuable work, and it provides considerable illumination concerning particular individual presidents, but it is limited in applicability to a review such as this one, which is focused on more general issues. Such studies do, however, provide an important locus for beginning to understand how instrumental and constitutive rhetorical functions combine.

Rhetorical studies concerning the president and foreign policy have received a great deal more systematic attention. There has been considerable scholarship on the rhetorical construction of foreign policy. This scholarship has focused on (a) the construction of foreign policy rhetoric (Dionisopoulos & Goldzwig, 1992; Hogan, 1985; Hollihan, 1986; O'Loughlin & Grant, 1990; Rushing, 1986; Tetlock, 1983; Wander, 1984), (b) the political uses of crisis (Bostdorff, 1991, 1994; Cherwitz & Zagacki, 1986; Dow, 1989; Heisey, 1986; Kern, Levering, & Levering, 1984; Kiewe, 1994; Klope, 1986; Windt, 1990), (c) presidential constructions of communism and the Cold War (Broadwater, 1989; Goodnight, 1986; Hinds & Windt, 1991; Ivie, 1984; Medhurst, 1987, 1988; Medhurst, Ivie, Wander, & Scott, 1990; Paterson, 1979; Stuckey, 1995; Tetlock, 1988), (d) the rhetoric of war (Depoe, 1988; Ivie, 1974, 1980, 1982, 1987; McPherson, 1991-1992; Steele, 1984, 1985; Stuckey, 1992), and (e) individual case studies (Ball, 1990; Birdsell, 1987; Dowling & Marraro, 1986; Reilly, 1983; Ryan, 1981a, 1981b; Smith, 1986; Stelzner, 1966).

Much of this research sheds light on how the American polity has learned to understand itself and its cultural history through the rhetorical forms of foreign policy (Morris & Ehrenhaus, 1990). Dionisopoulos and Goldzwig (1992), for example, offer a compelling analysis of how George Schultz was able to present a successful revisionary history of the Vietnam War and how the past can be reframed to meet the political exigencies of the present. Rushing (1986) has accomplished a similar goal in her study of Reagan's rhetoric as an exemplar of the continuing myth of the New Frontier. The work of Phillip Wander (1984) and of Thomas Hollihan (1986) provides particularly useful examples of how language use is associated with specific ideological agendas and indicates how critiques of language and its accompanying agenda can best be accomplished. Tetlock (1983) accomplishes a similar aim from a psychological rather than a rhetorical vantage point in his examination of the highly simplified images used by the makers of foreign policy in their endeavors to understand a complicated and elusive world scene. Boynton (1996) offers a similar analysis of the workings of the Senate Foreign Relations Committee.

Other scholars have confined their interest to the Cold War and its aftermath, conducting examinations of how the Cold War affected American elections (Blumenthal, 1990; Broadwater, 1989) or the processes of American politics more generally. Still other scholars have investigated how specific presidents have used rhetorical tactics to advance American interests vis-à-vis the Soviet Union (Medhurst, 1987) or their own interests vis-à-vis the American polity (Goodnight, 1986; Ivie, 1984; Medhurst, 1988; Paterson, 1979).

Scholars have found that among the persuasive devices available to presidents, one of the most effective is the delineation of a national "crisis" (Bostdorff, 1991; Dow, 1989; Heisey, 1986; Klope, 1986; Windt, 1990). Of all crises, of course, none is as effective a rallying cry as war, and significant work has been done on the rhetoric of war, with examinations of the genre as a whole (Campbell & Jamieson, 1990; Ivie, 1974, 1980, 1982, 1987) as well as of specific instances, such as the rhetoric employed by Lincoln (McPherson, 1991-1992), Franklin Roosevelt (Steele, 1984, 1985), Truman (Medhurst, 1988; Paterson, 1979; Ryan, 1981a), Eisenhower (Medhurst, 1988), the Johnson administration (Depoe, 1988; Zarefsky, 1986), Carter (Smith, 1986), Reagan (Birdsell, 1987; Bostdorff, 1991; Dowling & Marraro, 1986; Heisey, 1986; Ivie, 1984; Klope, 1986; Rushing, 1986), Bush (Stuckey, 1992, 1995), and Clinton (Stuckey, 1995). This work examines the justifications for war and how those justifications work as persuasive devices that allow Americans to engage in war while maintaining a belief in the essential nobility of the American mission and in the corresponding nobility of the president, who is charged with the enactment of that mission. This work could be profitably united with the public opinion-based studies of the rally effect, a pairing that could potentially yield valuable insights concerning the processes and consequences of public opinion formation and change.

The Person of the President

In order to survive politically, presidents attempt to control—or appear to control—nearly every aspect of every event that occurs during their administrations. Inevitably, much of what happens to them, much of what they choose to do, is beyond their control. The economy weakens, a war is declared, a famine strikes Africa, the Soviet Union disintegrates, an African American is beaten by police in Los Angeles. Whether or not the president is actually responsible for any of these events, he will be held accountable for our national reaction to them. This cannot but affect the president psychologically (Denton, 1983) as well as rhetorically, presenting an exigency with which he must deal. Indeed, presidential personality and character have been considered key factors in every element of presidential governance, from the nature of the media coverage (Streitmatter, 1985) to economic decisions (Keller & May, 1984), the nature of preferred policy actions (Tetlock, 1988), and legislative success (Hargrove, 1984; Kellerman, 1983).

Presidents have created both individual and institutional responses to the pressures of attempting to control much that is uncontrollable. In response to this pressure, individual presidents give an increasing number of speeches that reflect ever more ceremonial, abstract content (Allen, 1993; Finkelstein, 1981; Hart, 1984b; Jamieson, 1988; Lammers, 1981; McMillan & Ragan, 1983; Seymour-Ure, 1980; Stuckey, 1991). In addition to rhetorical responses, presidents have also derived institutional ways of adapting themselves and the office to the changed expectations that have accompanied the rhetorical presidency. These institutional adaptations include attempts to control information (Winfield, 1984), the development of the White House Office of Communications, and changes in the ways press secretaries function (Grossman & Kumar, 1981; Maltese, 1994; Seymour-Ure, 1980), as well as changes in the overall communicative patterns of the presidency. Among the most important members of the president's staff are the speechwriters, charged with rendering a president's public speech intelligible if not eloquent. Both scholarly studies and insider memoirs attest to the importance of the White House speechwriter (Carpenter, 1989; Noonan, 1990; Speakes, 1988; Witherspoon, 1991).

Scholars have also devoted considerable attention to the question of presidential style and have provided valuable analyses of the political situations and rhetoric of many presidents, including Washington (Edwards, 1991), FDR (Preston, 1984; Ryan, 1981b; Winfield, 1987), Truman (Liebovich, 1989), Eisenhower (Griffin, 1992; Medhurst, 1994), Kennedy (Goldzwig & Dionisopoulos, 1995a; Kern et al., 1984; Osborne, 1980), Carter (Motter, 1992; Orman, 1984; Paletz & Entman, 1980), Reagan (Greenstein, 1990; Lewis, 1987; Scheele, 1984), and Bush (Mullins & Wildavsky, 1992; Stuckey & Antczak, 1992). Presidential candidates such as Edward Kennedy (Devlin, 1982), Jesse Jackson (Merritt, 1986; Washington, 1985), and Pat Robertson (O'Leary & MacFarland, 1989) have also received their share of attention.

These institutional developments that emphasize the person of the president have not come without cost, both for presidents and for the system they help to govern. Not least among these costs for the president is shortened life spans (Gilbert, 1985). There are also costs in terms of the president's personal psychology (Buchanan, 1978), a finding that has led some scholars to endorse close examination of the "presidential character" both prior to and after election (Barber, 1977; Stark, 1992). Other scholars, while finding merit in psychological studies, are less convinced of the voters'—or scholars'—ability to perform adequate analyses based on present theories and the available data (Cohen, 1980; George, 1974; Hoeskra, 1989). In general, psychological studies of presidential character and style are beset by methodological difficulties that detract from the utility of, if not the fascination with, the development of psychologically based predictions of presidential behavior.

Rather than focusing rather narrowly on the psychology of the president, some scholars have had more theoretical success by construing character more broadly, as "image." These scholars understand image as comprising personal and public elements, individual and institutional elements, symbolic activity and policy outcomes, and the institutional structures of the presidency. They have seen this entity as cooperatively constructed by political actors, the electorate, and the media (Hacker, 1995; Harrison, Stephen, Husson, & Fehr, 1991; Hellweg, Dionisopoulos, & Kluger, 1986; Kern & Just, 1995; Sanders & Pace, 1977; Trent et al., 1993). Images are by definition subjective (Boulding, 1956) as well as interactively constructed (Nimmo & Savage, 1976). As a consequence, they are fluid rather than static and involve elements of both rationality and affect. There is tremendous potential in this branch of research into the rhetorical presidency, for it offers a locus for the union of several different strains of existing research.

From whatever perspective the president is studied, this research is valuable because it points out the enduring influence of the personalistic aspects of the presidency and the ways in which those elements intersect with the demands of the office as an institution. The theory informing such studies remains largely undeveloped, and the issue of prediction versus post hoc understanding remains unresolved. This is clearly one area that can benefit from more systematic attention to the ends as well as the means of presidential research.

DIRECTIONS FOR FUTURE RESEARCH

In the relatively short time that the rhetorical presidency has been recognized as a distinct field of endeavor, scholars from various disciplines have generated a prodigious body of research. The idea that presidents speak increasingly often and that this increase begets changes in the institutional practices of the presidency is a deceptively simple one, as the extent and diversity of the scholarly literature on the rhetorical presidency indicate. Although the field is already rich in both insight and applications, it can only profit from the development of a more unified field of vision in which different issues can come into focus without obscuring the whole.

Consider the institutional versus individual tendencies of presidential re-search, a problem with which scholars of the presidency have long struggled. The tendency has been to focus on the person of the president rather than on the institutional influences that act upon him. The corollary is that presidential scholars tend to concentrate on the individual president rather than on the collective institution, which includes the White House staff as well as the entire executive bureaucracy. Both of these tendencies lead to anecdotal rather than theoretical formulations of the presidency. Presidents may exert influence on political contexts and institutional structures, but those structures and contexts also exert enormous influence and constraints upon any president. Attempting to understand presidential behavior without reference to institutional and political factors is likely to perpetuate rather than to challenge error.

Another tendency has been to see communication only in its instrumental aspects, accomplishing short-term, policy-oriented or political goals, or to envision it constitutively, recognizing how political reality itself—including political perceptions, even the options that are plausibly available—is continuously constructed and reconstructed in communication. The implications are that scholars studying rhetorical elements of communication can miss the local constraints that context can impose, whereas scholars seeing communication solely in its instrumental functions can miss the larger implications of those functions. These tendencies lead at worst to misreading of the literature, as the expectations of one school are imposed on the other. More often, they lead to bifurcated rather than unified formulations of the presidency—isolated and inbred research agendas in which scholars cannot thoughtfully reject or integrate ideas because tunnel vision obscures their relevance. Attempting to understand presidential communicative behavior by uniting the instrumental and constitutive notions of rhetoric is more likely to yield a comprehensive view of the office, its communicative dimensions, and their relation to the political and social structures in which they are embedded.

If scholarship on the rhetorical presidency is envisioned less in detached dichotomies and more as a continuous conversation, promising areas of inquiry emerge. The most important of these is the question of whether the rhetorical presidency as a theoretical construct accurately reflects significant changes in the practice of the American presidency. Scholars have been far better at applying and extrapolating the insights of the early work on the rhetorical presidency than they have been at deriving empirical tests of it, whether using qualitative or quantitative methods. Although it seems beyond dispute that contemporary presidents both speak more often and construct different sorts of rhetorics than did previous presidents, it is considerably less clear that these practices necessarily imply significant changes in the presidency as a policy-making institution. This argument needs to be analyzed rather than asserted and assumed, as is too often done currently. There is some evidence, in fact, that the strategy of going public is less viable as an explanation for presidential success in Congress than are the traditional models of bargaining (Bodnick, 1990). More such research that tests the boundaries and defines the limits of the rhetorical presidency as a theoretical tool is necessary.

Add to this the distinct possibility that the concept of the rhetorical presidency may be in need of some refinement. Collier (1995), for instance, distinguishes between presidential uses of the strategy of going public in attempts to garner support for their policies and uses of the same strategy to accrue approval for themselves as leaders. Such distinctions imply different consequences for the presidency as a policy-making institution and for the system as a whole. Public involvement in debate over the merits of specific policy alternatives is less inimical to the framers' design than if the public is construed as the unwitting pawn of increasingly demagogic leaders. Again, more research on the utility of such distinctions can only help the field as a whole, regardless of the theoretical approach of the researcher.

Scholars may also need to examine further the question of how presidents are making appeals to mass audiences. With the American polity increasingly fragmented into a variety of publics, and with the mass media fragmenting as well, scholars interested in the relationship between national institutions and the practice of democracy would do well to examine which of these publics, if any, are granted differential degrees of presidential attention and assess the implications for the policy that is then produced by the national government.

Finally, there is the issue of designing theories and methods appropriate for analyzing the new technologies of communication as they extend and alter the rhetorical possibilities of the presidency. Foremost among these technologies are those involving computer networking. As yet, discussion of the implications of the "information superhighway" are considerably more prevalent in the popular media than in the academic literature. This is particularly true for political science, which has all but ignored the Internet (Fisher, Margolis, & Resnick, 1995; Schaefer, 1995).

Most scholars who seek to analyze the possibilities of computerized communication are generally sanguine, if not optimistic, about those possibilities, seeing in the new technology increased access to the structures of power and thus greater opportunities for the construction of authentic democratic communities (Abramson, Arterton, & Orren, 1988; Benson, 1994, 1996; Hiltz & Turoff, 1993; Jones, 1995; Lanham, 1993; Rheingold, 1994; Splichal & Wasko, 1993). Others are more concerned about such issues as inequality of access (Fisher et al., 1995; Graber, 1995; Morris, 1995). Whatever the consequences computer technologies may have for democracy, scholars of the rhetorical presidency need to develop theories and methods for testing those theories if we are going to understand the rhetorical presidency in an increasingly electronic age (Gronbeck, 1995).

Beyond the vast body of research generated by scholars from various disciplines lies an even broader expanse of emendations, clarifications, and unanswered questions. If researchers from all these disciplines and approaches can welcome what they do not know, the wider possibilities of exchange will broaden scholarly fields of vision and deepen our collective understanding of the rhetorical presidency.

REFERENCES

Abbott, P. (1988). Do presidents talk too much? The rhetorical presidency and its alternative. *Presidential Studies Quarterly, 18,* 347-362.

Abel, E. (1987). *Leaking: Who does it? Who benefits? At what cost?* New York: Priority.

Abramson, J., Arterton, F., & Orren, G., (1988). *The electronic commonwealth: The impact of new media technologies on democratic politics.* New York: Basic Books.

Adams, W. (1985). The power of the right stuff: A quasi-experimental field test of the docudrama hypothesis. *Public Opinion Quarterly, 49,* 330-339.

Allen, C. (1993). News conferences on TV: Ike-age politics revisited. *Journalism Quarterly, 70,* 13-25.

Andersen, K., & Thorson, S. (1989). Public discourse or strategic game? Changes in our conception of elections. *Studies in American Political Development, 3,* 263-278.

Antczak, F. J. (1985). *Thought and character: The rhetoric of democratic education.* Ames: Iowa State University Press.

Arnold, P. (1995). *Strategic resources and policy leadership in the pre-modern presidency: The case of Theodore Roosevelt's naval policy.* Unpublished manuscript.

Ball, M. (1990). A case study of the Kennedy administration's decision-making concerning the Diem coup of November 1963. *Western Journal of Speech Communication, 54,* 557-574.

Barber, J. (1977). *The presidential character: Predicting performance in the White House* (2nd ed.). Englewood Cliffs, NJ: Prentice Hall.

Barkin, S. (1986). Eisenhower's secret strategy: Television planning in the 1952 campaign. *Journal of Advertising History, 9,* 18-28.

Bauman, S., & Herbst, S. (1994). Managing perceptions of public opinion: Candidates' and journalists' reactions to the 1992 polls. *Political Communication, 11,* 133-144.

Behr, R., & Iyengar, S. (1985). Television news, real-world cues, and changes in the public agenda. *Public Opinion Quarterly, 49,* 38-57.

Bennett, W., Harris, P., Laskey, J., Levitch, A., & Monrad, S. (1976). Deep and surface images in the construction of political issues: The case of amnesty. *Quarterly Journal of Speech, 62,* 109-126.

Benson, T. (1994). The first e-mail election: Electronic networking and the Clinton campaign. In S. Smith (Ed.), *Bill Clinton on stump, state, and stage: The rhetorical road to the presidency* (pp. 315-340). Fayetteville: University of Arkansas Press.

Benson, T. (1996). Desktop demos: New communication technologies and the future of the rhetorical presidency. In M. Medhurst (Ed.), *Beyond the rhetorical presidency* (pp. 50-76). College Station: Texas A&M Press.

Berquist, G., & Golden, J. (1981). Media rhetoric, criticism, and the public perception of the 1980 presidential debates. *Quarterly Journal of Speech, 67,* 125-137.

Birdsell, D. (1987). Ronald Reagan on Lebanon and Grenada: Flexibility and interpretation in the application of Kenneth Burke's pentad. *Quarterly Journal of Speech, 73,* 267-279.

Blumenthal, S. (1990). *Pledging allegiance: The last campaign of the Cold War.* New York: HarperCollins.

Bodnick, M. (1990). "Going public" reconsidered: Reagan's 1981 tax and budget cuts, and revisionist theories of presidential power. *Congress and the Presidency, 17,* 13-28.

Bond, J., & Fleisher, R. (1984). Presidential popularity and congressional voting: A re-examination of public opinion as a source of influence in Congress. *Western Political Quarterly, 37,* 291-306.

Bond, J., & Fleisher, R. (1990). *The president in the legislative arena.* Chicago: University of Chicago Press.

Bond, J., Fleisher, R., & Northrup, M. (1988). Public opinion and presidential support. *Annals of the American Academy of Political and Social Science, 499,* 47-63.

Bormann, E. (1982). A fantasy theme analysis of the television coverage of the hostage release and the Reagan inaugural. *Quarterly Journal of Speech, 68,* 133-145.

Bostdorff, D. (1991). The presidency and promoted crisis: Reagan, Grenada, and issue management. *Presidential Studies Quarterly, 21,* 737-750.

Bostdorff, D. (1994). *The presidency and the rhetoric of foreign crisis.* Columbia: University of South Carolina Press.

Boulding, K. (1956). *The image: Knowledge in life and society.* Ann Arbor: University of Michigan Press.

Boynton, G. (1996). How the past is present in writing international affairs: Telling the Cambodian story. In M. E. Stuckey (Ed.), *The theory and practice of political communication research* (pp. 177-195). Albany: State University of New York Press.

Brace, P., & Hinckley, B. (1991). The structure of presidential approval: Constraints within and across presidencies. *Journal of Politics, 53,* 993-1017.

Brace, P., & Hinckley, B. (1992). *Follow the leader: Opinion polls and the modern presidents.* New York: Basic Books.

Brenders, D., & Fabj, V. (1993). Perceived control and the Clinton presidency: Political discourse in an alienated age. *American Behavioral Scientist, 37,* 211-225.

Brennan, R., & Hahn, D. (1990). *Listening for a president: A citizen's campaign methodology.* New York: Praeger.

Brigance, W. (Ed.). (1943). *A history and criticism of American public address* (Vols. 1-2). New York: McGraw-Hill.

Broadwater, J. (1989). Communism and the great crusade: Internal security and the presidential election of 1952. *Maryland Historian, 20,* 40-53.

Broh, A. (1983). Polls, pols, and parties. *Journal of Politics, 45,* 732-744.

Brummet, B. (1980). Toward a theory of silence as a political strategy. *Quarterly Journal of Speech, 66,* 289-303.

Brummet, B. (1981). Gastronomic reference, synecdoche, and political images. *Quarterly Journal of Speech, 67,* 138-145.

Buchanan, B. (1978). *The presidential experience: What the office does to the man.* Englewood Cliffs, NJ: Prentice Hall.

Campbell, K., & Jamieson, K. H. (1985). Inaugurating the presidency. *Presidential Studies Quarterly, 15,* 394-411.

Campbell, K., & Jamieson, K. H. (1990). *Deeds done in words: Presidential rhetoric and the genres of governance.* Chicago: University of Chicago Press.

Cappella, J. N., & Jamieson, K. H. (1994). Broadcast adwatch effects: A field experiment. *Communication Research, 21,* 342-365.

Carlin, D., & McKinney, M. (Eds.). (1994). *The 1992 presidential debates in focus.* New York: Praeger.

Carpenter, R. (1989). Woodrow Wilson as speechwriter for George Creel: Presidential style in discourse as an index of personality. *Presidential Studies Quarterly, 19,* 117-126.

Carter, R., & Stamm, R. (1994). The 1992 presidential campaign and debates: A cognitive view. *Communication Research, 21,* 380-395.

Castle, D. (1991). Media coverage of presidential primaries. *American Politics Quarterly, 19,* 33-42.

Ceaser, J. W., Thurow, G. E., Tulis, J., & Bessette, J. M. (1981). The rise of the rhetorical presidency. *Presidential Studies Quarterly, 11,* 158-171.

Chaffee, S. H., Zhao, X., & Leshner, G. (1994). Political knowledge and the campaign media of 1992. *Communication Research, 21,* 305-324.

Cherwitz, R. & Zagacki, K. (1986). Consummatory versus justificatory crisis rhetoric. *Western Journal of Speech Communication, 50,* 307-324.

Chester, E. (1981). Shadow or substance? Critiquing Reagan's inaugural address. *Presidential Studies Quarterly, 11,* 172-176.

Cohen, J. (1980). Presidential personality and political behavior: Theoretical issues and an empirical test. *Presidential Studies Quarterly, 10,* 588-599.

Cohen, J. (1995). Presidential rhetoric and the public agenda. *American Journal of Political Science, 39,* 87-107.

Collier, K. (1995, April). *The president, the public, and Congress.* Paper presented at the annual meeting of the Midwest Political Science Association, Chicago.

Collier, K., & Sullivan, T. (1995). New evidence undercutting the linkage of approval with presidential support and influence. *Journal of Politics, 57,* 197-209.

Conover, P. J., & Feldman, S. (1989). Candidate perception in an ambiguous world: Campaigns, cues, and inference processes. *American Journal of Political Science, 33,* 912-940.

Conover, P. J., & Sigelman, L. (1982). Presidential influence and public opinion: The case of the Iranian hostage crisis. *Social Science Quarterly, 63,* 249-264.

Corcoran, P. (1994). Presidential concession speeches: The rhetoric of defeat. *Political Communication, 11,* 109-132.

Corcoran, P., & Kendall, K. E. (1992). Communication in the first primaries: The "voice of the people" in 1912. *Presidential Studies Quarterly, 22,* 15-29.

Cornfield, M. (1988). The Watergate audience: Parsing the powers of the press. In J. W. Carey (Ed.), *Media, myths, and narratives: Television and the press* (pp. 180-204). Newbury Park, CA: Sage.

Cornfield, M., & Yalof, D. (1988). Innocent by reason of analogy: How the Watergate analogy served both Reagan and the press during the Iran-contra affair. *Corruption and Reform, 3,* 185-205.

Corwin, E. (1940). *The president, office and powers: History and analysis of practice and opinion.* London: Oxford University Press.

Crable, R. E., & Vibbert, S. L. (1983). Argumentative stance and political faith healing: "The dream will come true." *Quarterly Journal of Speech, 69,* 290-301.

Cronin, T. (1974). The presidency's public relations script. In T. Cronin & R. Tugwell (Eds.), *The presidency reappraised* (pp. 168-186). New York: Praeger.

Cronin, T. (1984). Thinking and learning about leadership. *Presidential Studies Quarterly, 14,* 22-34.

Cronin, T., & Hochman, W. (1985). Franklin D. Roosevelt and the American presidency. *Presidential Studies Quarterly, 15,* 277-286.

Curtis, B. (1989). The wimp factor. *American Heritage, 40*(7), 40-50.

Dallek, R. (1984). *Ronald Reagan: The politics of symbolism.* Cambridge, MA: Harvard University Press.

Darcy, R., & Richman, A. (1988). Presidential travel and public opinion. *Presidential Studies Quarterly, 18,* 85-90.

Daughton, S. (1993). Metaphorical transcendence: Images of the holy war in Franklin Roosevelt's first inaugural. *Quarterly Journal of Speech, 79,* 427-446.

Daughton, S. (1994). Women's issues, women's place: Gender-related problems in presidential campaigns. *Communication Quarterly, 42,* 106-119.

Davis, D. (1990). News and politics. In D. Swanson & D. Nimmo (Eds.), *New directions in political communication: A resource book* (pp. 147-184). Newbury Park, CA: Sage.

Denton, R. E., Jr. (1982). *The symbolic dimensions of the American presidency: Description and analysis.* Prospect Heights, IL: Waveland.

Denton, R. E., Jr. (1983). On "becoming" president of the United States: The interaction of the office with the office holder. *Presidential Studies Quarterly, 13,* 367-382.

Denton, R. E., Jr. (1989). *The primetime presidency of Ronald Reagan: The era of the television presidency.* New York: Praeger.

Denton, R. E., Jr. (Ed.). (1994). *The 1992 presidential campaign: A communication perspective.* New York: Praeger.

Denton, R. E., Jr., & Hahn, D. (1986). *Presidential communication: Description and analysis.* New York: Praeger.

Depoe, S. (1988). Arthur Schlesinger, Jr.'s "middle way out of Vietnam": The limits of "technocratic realism" as the basis for foreign policy dissent. *Western Journal of Speech Communication, 52,* 147-166.

Depoe, S. (1991). Space and the 1960 presidential campaign: Kennedy, Nixon, and "public time." *Western Journal of Speech Communication, 55,* 215-233.

Devlin, I. P. (1982). An analysis of Kennedy's communication in the 1980 campaign. *Quarterly Journal of Speech, 68,* 397-417.

Dionisopoulos, G. N., & Goldzwig, S. (1992). The meaning of Vietnam: Political rhetoric as revisionist cultural history. *Quarterly Journal of Speech, 78,* 61-78.

Dobkin, B. (1996). Video verite: Language and image in the interpretation of power. In M. E. Stuckey (Ed.), *The theory and practice of political communication research* (pp. 89-94). Albany: State University of New York Press.

Dorsey, L. (1995). The frontier myth in presidential rhetoric: Theodore Roosevelt's campaign for conservation. *Western Journal of Communication, 59,* 1-19.

Dow, B. (1989). The function of epideictic and deliberative strategies in presidential crisis rhetoric. *Western Journal of Speech Communication, 53,* 294-310.

Dowling, R., & Marraro, G. (1986). Grenada and the great communicator: A study in democratic ethics. *Western Journal of Speech Communication, 50,* 350-367.

Dunn, C. (1984). The theological dimensions of presidential leadership: A classification model. *Presidential Studies Quarterly, 14,* 61-72.

Edelman, M. (1964). *The symbolic uses of politics.* Urbana: University of Illinois Press.

Edelman, M. (1971). *Politics as symbolic action: Mass arousal and quiescence.* Chicago: Markham.

Edelman, M. (1977). *Political language: Words that succeed and policies that fail.* New York: Academic Press.

Edelman, M. (1988). *Constructing the political spectacle.* Chicago: University of Chicago Press.

Edwards, G. (1980). *Presidential influence in Congress.* San Francisco: W. H. Freeman.

Edwards, G. (1983). *The public presidency: The pursuit of popular support.* New York: St. Martin's.

Edwards, G. (1989). *At the margins: Presidential leadership of Congress.* New Haven, CT: Yale University Press.

Edwards, G., with Gallup, A. M. (1990). *Presidential approval: A sourcebook.* Baltimore: Johns Hopkins University Press.

Edwards, G. (1991). George Washington's leadership of Congress: Director or facilitator? *Congress and the Presidency, 18,* 163-180.

Edwards, G., Mitchell, W., & Welch, R. (1995). Explaining presidential approval: The significance of issue salience. *American Journal of Political Science, 39,* 108-134.

Entman, R. (1989). *Democracy without citizens: Media and the decay of American politics.* New York: Oxford University Press.

Entman, R. (1993). Framing: Toward clarification of a fractured paradigm. *Journal of Communication, 43*(4), 51-58.

Erickson, K. (1989). Presidential leaks: Rhetoric and mediated political knowledge. *Communication Monographs, 56,* 199-214.

Erickson, K., & Schmidt, W. (1982). Presidential political silence: Rhetoric and the rose garden strategy. *Southern Speech Communication Journal, 47,* 402-421.

Erickson, P. (1985). *Reagan speaks: The making of an American myth.* New York: New York University Press.

Evensen, B. (1993). The limits of presidential leadership: Truman at war with Zionists, the press, public opinion, and his own State Department over Palestine. *Presidential Studies Quarterly, 23,* 269-287.

Fairbanks, J. (1981). The priestly functions of the presidency: A discussion of the literature on civil religion and its implications for the study of presidential leadership. *Presidential Studies Quarterly, 11,* 214-232.

Finkelstein, L. (1981). The calendrical rite of ascension to power. *Western Journal of Speech Communication, 45,* 51-59.

Fishel, J. (1985). *Presidents and promises: From campaign pledge to presidential performance.* Washington, DC: Congressional Quarterly Press.

Fisher, B., Margolis, M., & Resnick, D. (1995, April). *Politics and civic life on the Internet.* Paper presented at the annual meeting of the Midwest Political Science Association.

Fisher, L. (1987). *The politics of shared power: Congress and the executive* (2nd ed.). Washington, DC: Congressional Quarterly Press.

Fisher, W. (1980). Rhetorical fiction and the presidency. *Quarterly Journal of Speech, 66,* 119-126.

Frankel, J. (1988). No wonder the ratings are low. *Washington Monthly, 19*(12), 25-27.

Friedenberg, R. (1994). *Rhetorical studies of national political debates, 1960-1992* (2nd ed.). Westport, CT: Praeger.

Fry, D. H., & Fry, V. H. (1986). Language use and political environments in media coverage of "Super Tuesday." *Journalism Quarterly, 63,* 719-727.

Gadziala, S., & Becker, L. (1983). A new look at agenda-setting in the 1976 election debates. *Journalism Quarterly, 60,* 122-126.

Gant, M., & Davis, D. (1984). Negative voter support in presidential elections. *Western Political Quarterly, 37,* 272-290.

Garramone, G. M. (1985). Motivation and selective attention to political information formats. *Journalism Quarterly, 62,* 37-44.

Geer, J. (1988). The effects of presidential debates on the electorate's preferences for candidates. *American Politics Quarterly, 16,* 486-501.

George, A. (1974). Assessing presidential character. *World Politics, 26,* 234-282.

Gilberg, S., Eyal, C., McCombs, M., & Nichols, D. (1980). The state of the union address and the press agenda. *Journalism Quarterly, 57,* 584-588.

Gilbert, R. (1985). Personality, stress, and achievements: Keys to presidential longevity. *Presidential Studies Quarterly, 15,* 33-50.

Gilboa, E. (1990). Effects of televised presidential addresses on public opinion: President Reagan and terrorism in the Middle East. *Presidential Studies Quarterly, 20,* 43-53.

Glaros, R., & Miroff, B. (1983). Watching Ronald Reagan: Viewers' reactions to the president on television. *Congress and the Presidency, 10,* 25-46.

Glass, D. (1985). Evaluating presidential candidates: Who focuses on their personal attributes? *Public Opinion Quarterly, 49,* 517-534.

Gleiber, D., & Shull, S. (1992). Presidential influence in the policy process. *Western Political Quarterly, 45,* 441-467.

Goldzwig, S., & Dionisopoulos, G. N. (1995a). *In a perilous hour: The public address of John F. Kennedy.* Westport, CT: Greenwood.

Goldzwig, S., & Dionisopoulos, G. N. (1995b). Legitimating liberal credentials for the presidency: John F. Kennedy and the Strategy for Peace. *Southern Communication Journal, 60,* 312-331.

Goodnight, T. (1986). Ronald Reagan's re-formulation of the rhetoric of war: Analysis of the "zero option," "evil empire," and "star wars" addresses. *Quarterly Journal of Speech, 72,* 390-414.

Gould, L. (1989). Theodore Roosevelt, Woodrow Wilson, and the emergence of the modern presidency: An introductory essay. *Presidential Studies Quarterly, 19,* 41-50.

Graber, D. (1981). Political languages. In D. Nimmo & K. Sanders (Eds.), *The handbook of political communication* (pp. 195-211). Beverly Hills, CA: Sage.

Graber, D. (1987). Framing election news broadcasts: News context and its impact on the 1984 presidential election. *Social Science Quarterly, 68,* 552-268.

Graber, D. (1995, April). *Potholes along America's information superhighway.* Paper presented at the annual meeting of the Midwest Political Science Association.

Greenstein, F. (1990). Ronald Reagan: Another hidden-hand Ike? *PS: Political Science and Politics, 23,* 7-13.

Gregg, R. (1994). Rhetorical strategies for a culture war: Abortion in the 1992 campaign. *Communication Quarterly, 42,* 229-243.

Griffin, C. (1992). New light on Eisenhower's farewell address. *Presidential Studies Quarterly, 22,* 469-479.

Gronbeck, B. (1985). The presidential campaign dramas of 1984. *Presidential Studies Quarterly, 15,* 386-393.

Gronbeck, B. (1992). Negative narrative in 1988 presidential campaign ads. *Quarterly Journal of Speech, 78,* 333-346.

Gronbeck, B. (1995). The presidency in the age of secondary orality. In M. Medhurst (Ed.), *Beyond the rhetorical presidency* (pp. 30-49). College Station: Texas A&M Press.

Grossman, M., & Kumar, M. (1981). *Portraying the president: The White House and the news media.* Baltimore: Johns Hopkins University Press.

Hacker, K. (1995). *Candidate images in presidential elections.* New York: Praeger.

Hager, G., & Sullivan, T. (1994). President-centered and presidency-centered explanations of presidential activity. *American Journal of Political Science, 38,* 1079-1103.

Hallin, D. (1992). Sound bite news: Television coverage of elections, 1968-1988. *Journal of Communication, 42*(2), 5-24.

Hargrove, E. (1984). The uses and limits of skill in presidential leadership: The case of Jimmy Carter. *Policy Studies Journal, 13,* 287-294.

Harris, W. (1989). Andrew Johnson's first "swing around the circle": His northern campaign of 1863. *Civil War History, 35*(2), 153-171.

Harrison, T., Stephen, T., Husson, W., & Fehr, B. (1991). Images versus issues in the 1984 presidential election: Differences between men and women. *Human Communication Research, 18,* 209-227.

Hart, R. P. (1977). *The political pulpit.* West Lafayette, IN: Purdue University Press.

Hart, R. P. (1984a). The language of the modern presidency. *Presidential Studies Quarterly, 14,* 249-264.

Hart, R. P. (1984b). *Verbal style and the presidency: A computer-based analysis.* Orlando, FL: Academic Press.

Hart, R. P. (1987). *The sound of leadership: Presidential communication in the modern age.* Chicago: University of Chicago Press.

Hart, R. P. (1994). *Seducing America: How television charms the modern voter.* New York: Oxford University Press.

Hart, R. P., Smith-Howell, D., & Llewellyn, J. (1991). The mindscape of the presidency: *Time* magazine, 1945-1985. *Journal of Communication, 41*(3), 6-25.

Heisey, D. (1986). Reagan and Mitterand respond to international crisis: Creating versus transcending appearances. *Western Journal of Speech Communication, 50,* 325-335.

Hellweg, S., Dionisopoulos, G. N., & Kluger, D. (1986, November). *Political candidate image: Concepts and conceptualizations.* Paper presented at the annual meeting of the Speech Communication Association.

Hellweg, S., Pfau, M., & Brydon, S. (1992). *Televised presidential debates: Advocacy in contemporary America.* New York: Praeger.

Henry, D. (1988). The rhetorical dynamics of Mario Cuomo's 1984 keynote address: Situation, speaker, metaphor. *Southern Speech Communication Journal, 53,* 105-120.

Hiltz, S., & Turoff, M. (1993). *The network nation: Human communication via computer* (rev. ed.). Cambridge: MIT Press.

Hinckley, B. (1990). *The symbolic presidency: How presidents portray themselves.* New York: Routledge.

Hinds, L., & Windt, T. (1991). *The Cold War as rhetoric: The beginnings, 1945-1950.* New York: Praeger.

Hochmuth, M. (Ed.). (1943). *A history and criticism of American public address* (Vol. 3). New York: McGraw-Hill.

Hoeskra, D. (1989). Neustadt, Barber, and presidential statesmanship: The problem of Lincoln. *Presidential Studies Quarterly, 19,* 285-299.

Hoffman, S. (1981). Foreign policy transition: Requiem. *Foreign Policy, 42,* 3-25.

Hogan, J. M. (1985). Public opinion and American foreign policy: The case of illusory support for the Panama Canal treaties. *Quarterly Journal of Speech, 71,* 302-317.

Hogan, M. (1989). Theodore Roosevelt and the heroes of Panama. *Presidential Studies Quarterly, 19,* 79-94.

Holland, J. (1990). The great gamble: Jimmy Carter and the 1979 energy crises. *Prologue, 22,* 63-79.

Hollihan, T. (1986). The public controversy over the Panama Canal treaties: An analysis of American foreign policy rhetoric. *Western Journal of Speech Communication, 50,* 368-387.

Hurwitz, J., Peffley, M., & Raymond, P. (1989). Presidential support during the Iran-contra affair: An individual-level analysis of presidential reappraisal. *American Politics Quarterly, 17,* 359-385.

Ingold, B., & Windt, T. (1984). Trying to "stay the course": President Reagan's rhetoric during the 1982 elections. *Presidential Studies Quarterly, 14,* 87-97.

Ivie, R. (1974). Presidential motives for war. *Quarterly Journal of Speech, 60,* 337-345.

Ivie, R. (1980). Images of savagery in American justifications for war. *Communication Monographs, 47,* 279-294.

Ivie, R. (1982). The metaphor of force in prowar discourse: The case of 1812. *Quarterly Journal of Speech, 66,* 240-253.

Ivie, R. (1984). Speaking "common sense" about the Soviet threat: Reagan's rhetorical stance. *Western Journal of Speech Communication, 48,* 39-50.

Ivie, R. (1987). Metaphor and the rhetorical invention of Cold War "idealists." *Communication Monographs, 54,* 165-182.

Iyengar, S. (1987). Television news and citizens' explanations of national affairs. *American Political Science Review, 81,* 815-831.

Iyengar, S. (1989). How citizens think about national issues: A matter of responsibility. *American Journal of Political Science, 33,* 878-900.

Iyengar, S. (1991). *Is anyone responsible? How television frames political issues.* Chicago: University of Chicago Press.

Iyengar, S., Kinder, D. R., Krosnick, J. A., & Peters, M. D. (1984). The evening news and presidential evaluations. *Journal of Personality and Social Psychology, 46,* 778-787.

Jacques, W., Meilinger, F., Balmoris, M., Gerns, C., & Denby, S. (1993). Some aspects of major newspaper coverage of the 1992 presidential debates. *American Behavioral Scientist, 37,* 252-256.

James, D. (1988). Television and the syntax of presidential leadership. *Presidential Studies Quarterly, 18,* 737-739.

Jamieson, K. H. (1988). *Eloquence in an electronic age: The transformation of American political speechmaking.* New York: Oxford University Press.

Jamieson, K. H. (1992a). *Dirty politics: Deception, distraction and democracy.* New York: Oxford University Press.

Jamieson, K. H. (1992b). *Packaging the presidency: A history and criticism of presidential campaign advertising* (2nd ed.). New York: Oxford University Press.

Jamieson, K. H., & Birdsell, D. (1988). *Presidential debates: The challenge of creating an informed electorate.* New York: Oxford University Press.

Jones, S. (Ed.). (1995). *Cybersociety: Computer-mediated communication and community.* New York: Basic Books.

Just, M., Crigler, A., Alger, D., Cook, T., Kern, M., & West, D. (1996). *Crosstalk: Citizens, candidates, and media in a presidential campaign.* Chicago: University of Chicago Press.

Kaid, L., Gobetz, R., & Garner, J. (1993). Television news and presidential campaigns: The legitimation of televised political advertising. *Social Science Quarterly, 74,* 274-285.

Kaid, L., Leland, C., & Whitney, S. (1992). The impact of televised political ads: Evoking viewer responses in the 1988 presidential campaign. *Southern Communication Journal, 57,* 285-295.

Keeter, S. (1987). The illusion of intimacy: Television and the role of candidate personal qualities in voter choice. *Public Opinion Quarterly, 51,* 344-358.

Keller, R., & May, A. (1984). The presidential political business cycle of 1972. *Journal of Economic History, 44,* 265-271.

Kellerman, B. (1983). Introversion in the Oval Office. *Presidential Studies Quarterly, 13,* 383-399.

Kellerman, B. (1984). *The political presidency: The practice of leadership.* New York: Oxford University Press.

Kellerman, B., & Barilleaux, R. (1991). *The president as world leader.* New York: St. Martin's.

Kellner, D. (1990). *Television and the crisis of democracy.* Boulder, CO: Westview.

Kendall, K. E. (1993). Public speaking in the presidential primaries through media eyes. *American Behavioral Scientist, 37,* 240-251.

Kendall, K. E. (Ed.). (1995a). *Presidential campaign discourse: Strategic communication problems.* Albany: State University of New York Press.

Kendall, K. E. (1995b). The problem of beginnings in New Hampshire: Control over the play. In K. E. Kendall (Ed.), *Presidential campaign discourse: Strategic communication problems* (pp. 1-34). Albany: State University of New York Press.

Kendall, K. E. (in press). *Communication in presidential primaries, 1912-1992.* New York: Praeger.

Kenski, H. (1996). From agenda setting to priming and framing: Reflections on theory and method. In M. E. Stuckey (Ed.), *The theory and practice of political communication research* (pp. 67-83). Albany: State University of New York Press.

Kerbel, M. R. (1991). *Beyond persuasion: Organizational efficiency and presidential power.* Albany: State University of New York Press.

Kern, M. (1989). *30-second politics: Political advertising in the eighties.* New York: Praeger.

Kern, M., & Just, M. (1995). The focus group method, political advertising, campaign news, and the construction of candidate images. *Political Communication, 12,* 127-146.

Kern, M., Levering, P., & Levering, R. (1984). *The Kennedy crises: The press, the presidency, and foreign policy.* Chapel Hill: University of North Carolina Press.

Kernell, S. (1976). The Truman doctrine speech: A case study of the dynamics of presidential opinion leadership. *Social Science History, 1,* 20-45.

Kernell, S. (1978). Explaining presidential popularity. *American Political Science Review, 72,* 506-522.

Kernell, S. (1993). *Going public: New strategies of presidential leadership* (2nd ed.). Washington, DC: Congressional Quarterly Press.

Kiewe, A. (Ed.). (1994). *The modern presidency and crisis rhetoric.* New York: Praeger.

Kiewe, A., & Houck, D. (1991). *A shining city on a hill: Ronald Reagan's economic rhetoric, 1951-1989.* New York: Praeger.

King, E., & Schudson, M. (1987). The myth of the great communicator. *Columbia Journalism Review, 26,* 37-39.

Klope, D. (1986). Defusing a foreign policy crisis: Myth and victimage in Reagan's 1983 Lebanon/Grenada address. *Western Journal of Speech Communication, 50,* 336-349.

Koenig, L. (1980). The first hurrah. *American Heritage, 31*(3), 4-11.

Krasner, M. (1979). Why great presidents will become more rare. *Presidential Studies Quarterly, 9,* 367-375.

Krosnick, J. A., & Kinder, D. R. (1990). Altering the foundations of support for the president through priming. *American Political Science Review, 84,* 497-512.

Krukones, M. (1980). Predicting presidential performance through political campaigns. *Presidential Studies Quarterly, 10,* 527-543.

Lammers, W. (1981). Presidential press conference schedules: Who hides and when? *Political Science Quarterly, 96,* 261-278.

Lanham, R. (1993). *The electronic word: Democracy, technology, and the arts.* Chicago: University of Chicago Press.

Lanoue, D. (1987). Economic prosperity and presidential popularity: Sorting out the effects. *Western Political Quarterly, 40,* 237-245.

Lanoue, D. (1989). The "teflon factor": Ronald Reagan and comparative presidential popularity. *Polity, 21,* 481-501.

Lanoue, D., & Schrott, P. (1991). *The joint press conference: The history, impact, and prospects of American presidential debates.* Westport, CT: Greenwood.

Lawler, P. (1987). The federalist's hostility to leadership and the crisis of the contemporary presidency. *Presidential Studies Quarterly, 17,* 711-723.

Lewis, W. (1987). Telling America's story: Narrative form and the Reagan presidency. *Quarterly Journal of Speech, 73,* 280-302.

Lian, B., & O'Neal, J. (1993). Presidents, the use of military force, and public opinion. *Journal of Conflict Resolution, 37,* 277-300.

Liebovich, L. (1989). Failed White House press relations in the early months of the Truman administration. *Presidential Studies Quarterly, 19,* 583-591.

Link, M. (1989). Perception, style, and theme in the Carter-Rafshoon White House. *Proceedings and Papers of the Georgia Association of Historians, 10,* 131-143.

Linsky, M. (1986). *Impact: How the press affects federal policymaking.* New York: W. W. Norton.

Locander, R. (1983). Modern presidential in-office communications: The national, direct, local, and latent strategies. *Presidential Studies Quarterly, 13,* 242-254.

Lowden, N., Anderson, P., Dozier, D., & Lauzen, M. (1994). Media use in the primary election: A secondary medium model. *Communication Research, 21,* 293-304.

Lowi, T. (1985). *The personal president: Power invested, promise unfulfilled.* Ithaca, NY: Cornell University Press.

MacKuen, M. (1983). Political drama, economic conditions, and the dynamics of presidential popularity. *American Journal of Political Science, 27,* 165-192.

Maltese, J. (1994). *Spin control: The White House Office of Communications and the management of presidential news* (2nd ed.). Chapel Hill: University of North Carolina Press.

Manheim, J. (1991). *All of the people all of the time: Strategic communication and American politics.* Armonk, NY: M. E. Sharpe.

Manheim, J., & Lammers, W. (1981). The news conference and presidential leadership of public opinion: Does the tail wag the dog? *Presidential Studies Quarterly, 11,* 177-188.

Martin, H. (1984). President Reagan's return to radio. *Journalism Quarterly, 61,* 817-821.

Martin, M. (1983). Ideologues, ideographs, and "the best men": From Carter to Reagan. *Southern Speech Communication Journal, 49,* 12-25.

Marvin, C. (1994). Fresh blood, public meat: Rituals of totem regeneration in the 1992 presidential race. *Communication Research, 21,* 264-292.

Mayhew, D. (1991). *Divided we govern: Party control, lawmaking, and investigations 1946-1990.* New Haven, CT: Yale University Press.

McCann, J. (1990). Changing electoral contexts and changing candidate images during the 1984 presidential campaign. *American Politics Quarterly, 18,* 123-140.

McMillan, J., & Ragan, S. (1983). The presidential press conference: A study in escalating institutionalization. *Presidential Studies Quarterly, 13,* 231-241.

McPherson, J. (1991-1992). How Lincoln won the war with metaphors. *Chicago History, 20*(3-4), 32-53.

Medhurst, M. (1984). Postponing the social agenda: Reagan's strategy and tactics. *Western Journal of Speech Communication, 48,* 262-276.

Medhurst, M. (1987). Eisenhower's "atoms for peace" speech: A case study in the strategic use of language. *Communication Monographs, 54,* 204-220.

Medhurst, M. (1988). Truman's rhetorical reticence, 1945-1947: An interpretive essay. *Quarterly Journal of Speech, 74,* 52-70.

Medhurst, M. (1994). *Eisenhower's war of words: Rhetoric and leadership.* East Lansing: Michigan State University Press.

Medhurst, M., Ivie, R., Wander, P., & Scott, R. (1990). *Cold War rhetoric: Strategy, metaphor, and ideology.* Westport, CT: Greenwood.

Merritt, B. (1986). Jesse Jackson and television: Black image presentation and affect in the 1984 Democratic campaign debates. *Journal of Black Studies, 16,* 347-368.

Meyrowitz, J. (1994). Visible and invisible candidates: A case study in "competing logics" of campaign coverage. *Political Communication, 11,* 145-164.

Miller, A., Wattenberg, M., & Malanchuk, O. (1986). Schematic assessments of presidential candidates. *American Political Science Review, 80,* 521-540.

Minow, N., & Mitchell, L. (1986). Putting on the candidates: The use of television in presidential elections. *Annals of the American Academy of Political and Social Science, 486,* 146-157.

Miroff, B. (1981). Presidential leverage over social movements: The Johnson White House and civil rights. *Journal of Politics, 43,* 2-23.

Miroff, B. (1982). Monopolizing the public space: The president as a problem for democratic politics. In T. Cronin (Ed.), *Rethinking the presidency* (pp. 218-232). Boston: Little, Brown.

Moe, T. (1993). Presidents, institutions, and theory. In G. Edwards, J. Kessel, & B. Rockman (Eds.), *Researching the presidency: Vital questions, new approaches* (pp. 337-386). Pittsburgh: University of Pittsburgh Press.

Moen, M. (1988). The political agenda of Ronald Reagan: A content analysis of the State of the Union messages. *Presidential Studies Quarterly, 18,* 775-785.

Moore, M. (1992). "The Quayle quagmire": Political campaigns in the poetic form of burlesque. *Western Journal of Speech Communication, 56,* 108-124.

Morello, J. (1988). Argument and visual structuring in the 1984 Mondale-Reagan debates: The medium's influence on the perception of clash. *Western Journal of Speech Communication, 52,* 277-290.

Morris, R. (1995, March). *Computer mediated communication and the practices of liberty: A reply to Thomas Benson.* Paper presented at the Conference on the Future of the Rhetorical Presidency, Texas A&M University.

Morris, R., & Ehrenhaus, P. (Eds.). (1990). *Cultural legacies of Vietnam: Uses of the past in the present.* Norwood, NJ: Ablex.

Morris, R., & Stuckey, M. E. (in press). More rain and less thunder: Substitute vocabularies, Richard Nixon, and the construction of political reality. *Communication Monographs.*

Motter, R. (1992). Jimmy Carter in context. *Mississippi Quarterly, 45,* 467-482.

Mouw, C., & MacKuen, M. (1992). The strategic agenda in legislative politics. *American Political Science Review, 86,* 87-105.

Mullins, K., & Wildavsky, A. (1992). The procedural presidency of George Bush. *Political Science Quarterly, 107,* 31-62.

Nelson, M. (1990). Evaluating the presidency. In M. Nelson (Ed.), *The presidency and the political system* (rev. ed., pp. 5-11). Washington, DC: Congressional Quarterly Press.

The Net [Special issue]. (1996). *Journal of Communication, 46*(1).

Neustadt, R. (1960). *Presidential power: The politics of leadership.* New York: John Wiley.

Neustadt, R. (1990). *Presidential power and the modern presidents: The politics of leadership from Roosevelt to Reagan.* New York: Free Press.

Newhagen, J. (1994). Self-efficacy and call-in political television show use. *Communication Research, 21,* 366-379.

Nimmo, D., & Sanders, K. (Eds.). (1981). *The handbook of political communication.* Beverly Hills, CA: Sage.

Nimmo, D., & Savage, R. (1976). *Candidates and their images: Concepts, methods, and findings.* Pacific Palisades, CA: Goodyear.

Noonan, P. (1990). *What I saw at the revolution: A political life in the Reagan era.* New York: Random House.

Norrander, B. (1986). Correlates of vote choice in the 1980 presidential primaries. *Journal of Politics, 48,* 156-166.

Norris, P. (1995). The restless searchlight: Network news framing of the post-Cold War world. *Political Communication, 12,* 357-370.

Novak, M. (1974). *Choosing our king: Powerful symbols in presidential politics.* New York: Macmillan.

O'Leary, S., & MacFarland, M. (1989). The political use of mythic discourse: Prophetic interpretation in Pat Robertson's presidential campaign. *Quarterly Journal of Speech, 75,* 433-452.

O'Loughlin, J., & Grant, R. (1990). The political geography of presidential speeches, 1946-87. *Annals of the Association of American Geographers, 80,* 504-530.

Orman, J. (1984). Covering the American presidency: Valenced reporting in the periodical press, 1900-1982. *Presidential Studies Quarterly, 14,* 381-390.

Orman, J. (1987). *Comparing presidential behavior: Carter, Reagan, and the macho presidential style.* Westport, CT: Greenwood.

Osborne, L. (1980). Rhetorical patterns in President Kennedy's major speeches: A case study. *Presidential Studies Quarterly, 10,* 332-335.

Ostrom, C., & Simon, D. (1984). Managing popular support: The presidential dilemma. *Policy Studies Journal, 12,* 677-690.

Ostrom, C., & Simon, D. (1985). Promise and performance: A dynamic model of presidential popularity. *American Political Science Review, 79,* 334-358.

Ostrom, C., & Simon, D. (1988). The president's public. *American Journal of Political Science, 32,* 1096-1119.

Ostrom, C., & Simon, D. (1989). The man in the teflon suit? The environmental connection, political drama, and popular support in the Reagan presidency. *Public Opinion Quarterly, 53,* 353-387.

Page, B., & Shapiro, R. (1984). Presidents as opinion leaders: Some new evidence. *Policy Studies Journal, 12,* 649-662.

Paletz, D., & Entman, R. (1980). Presidents, power, and the press. *Presidential Studies Quarterly, 10,* 416-426.

Paletz, D., & Vinegar, R. (1977-1978). Presidents on television: The effects of instant analysis. *Public Opinion Quarterly, 41,* 488-497.

Pan, Z., & Kosicki, G. M. (1993). Framing analysis: An approach to news discourse. *Political Communication, 10,* 55-76.

Paterson, T. (1979). Presidential foreign policy, public opinion, and Congress: The Truman years. *Diplomatic History, 3,* 1-18.

Patterson, T. E. (1993). *Out of order.* New York: Knopf.

Pfau, M., & Kenski, H. (1990). *Attack politics: Strategy and defense.* New York: Praeger.

Pfau, M., & Louden, A. (1994). Effectiveness of adwatch formats in deflecting political attack ads. *Communication Research, 21,* 325-341.

Pfiffner, J. (1988). *The strategic presidency: Hitting the ground running.* Homewood, IL: Dorsey.

Pika, J. (1990). Recent trends in studying the presidency: Reagan and beyond. *American Studies International, 28,* 13-31.

Plischke, E. (1985). The president's image as diplomat in chief. *Review of Politics, 47,* 544-565.

Polsby, N. (1976). *Congress and the presidency* (3rd ed.). Englewood Cliffs, NJ: Prentice Hall.

Popkin, S. (1991). *The reasoning voter: Communication and persuasion in presidential campaigns.* Chicago: University of Chicago Press.

Preston, C. (1984). Reagan's "new beginning": Is it the "new deal" of the eighties? *Southern Speech Communication Journal, 49,* 198-211.

Ragsdale, L. (1984). The politics of presidential speechmaking, 1949-1980. *American Political Science Review, 78,* 971-984.

Reilly, J. (1983). American opinion: Continuity, not Reaganism. *Foreign Policy, 50,* 86-104.

Reinsch, L. (1988). *Getting elected: From radio and Roosevelt to television and Reagan.* New York: Hippocrene.

Rheingold, H. (1994). *The virtual community: Homesteading on the electronic frontier.* Thousand Oaks, CA: Sage.

Rivers, D., & Rose, N. (1985). Passing the president's program: Public opinion and presidential influence in Congress. *American Journal of Political Science, 29,* 183-196.

Rivers, W. L. (1982). *The other government: Power and the Washington media.* New York: Universe.

Roberts, C. (1981). From primary to the presidency: A panel study of images and issues in the 1976 election. *Western Journal of Speech Communication, 45,* 60-70.

Roberts, M., & McCombs, M. (1994). Agenda setting and political advertising: Origins of the news agenda. *Political Communication, 11,* 249-262.

Robinson, M. (1974). The televised Watergate hearings. *Journal of Communication, 24*(2), 17-30.

Rockman, B. (1984). *The leadership question: The presidency and the American system.* New York: Praeger.

Roelofs, M. (1992). The prophetic president: Charisma and the American political tradition. *Polity, 25,* 1-20.

Rogin, M. (1987). *Ronald Reagan, the movie: And other episodes in political demonology.* Berkeley: University of California Press.

Rohde, D., & Simon, D. (1985). Presidential vetoes and congressional response: A study of institutional conflict. *American Journal of Political Science, 29,* 397-427.

Ross, M. (1992). Television news and candidate fortunes in presidential nomination campaigns: The case of 1984. *American Politics Quarterly, 20,* 69-98.

Rouner, D., & Perloff, R. (1988). Selective perception of the outcome of the first 1984 presidential debate. *Journalism Quarterly, 65,* 141-147, 240.

Rowland, R. (1986). The substance of the 1980 Carter-Reagan debate. *Southern Speech Communication Journal, 51,* 142-165.

Rozell, M. (1993a). Carter rehabilitated: What caused the 39th president's press transformation? *Presidential Studies Quarterly, 23,* 317-330.

Rozell, M. (1993b). The limits of White House image control. *Political Science Quarterly, 108,* 453-480.

Rubin, R. (1981). The presidency in the age of television. *Proceedings of the Academy of Political Science, 34,* 138-152.

Rushing, J. (1986). Ronald Reagan's "star wars" address: Mythic containment of technical reasoning. *Quarterly Journal of Speech, 72,* 415-433.

Ryan, H. (1981a). Harry S. Truman: A misdirected defense for MacArthur's dismissal. *Presidential Studies Quarterly, 11,* 576-582.

Ryan, H. (1981b). Roosevelt's fourth inaugural: A study of its composition. *Quarterly Journal of Speech, 67,* 157-166.

Ryan, H. (1988). *Franklin D. Roosevelt's rhetorical presidency.* Westport, CT: Greenwood.

Sabato, L. (1991). *Feeding frenzy: How attack journalism has transformed American politics.* New York: Free Press.

Sanders, K., & Pace, T. (1977). The influence of speech communication on the image of a political candidate: "Limited effects" revised. In B. D. Ruben (Ed.), *Communication yearbook 1* (pp. 465-474). New Brunswick, NJ: Transaction.

Sandman, J. (1989). Winning the presidency: The vision and values approach. *Presidential Studies Quarterly, 19,* 259-256.

Schaefer, R. (1995, May). *The politics of the new mediated communication.* Paper presented at the annual meeting of the International Communication Association, Albuquerque, NM.

Scheele, H. (1984). Ronald Reagan's 1980 acceptance address: A focus on American values. *Western Journal of Speech Communication, 48,* 51-61.

Schlesinger, A. (1973). *The imperial presidency.* Boston: Little, Brown.

Schmertz, H. (1986). The media and the presidency. *Presidential Studies Quarterly, 16,* 11-21.

Schudson, M. (1982). The politics of narrative form: The emergence of news conventions in print and television. *Daedalus, 3,* 97-112.

Schwartz, B. (1983). George Washington and the Whig conception of heroic leadership. *American Sociological Review, 48,* 18-33.

Seligman, L., & Covington, C. (1989). *The coalitional presidency.* Homewood, IL: Dorsey.

Seymour-Ure, C. (1980). Presidential power, press secretaries and communication. *Political Studies, 28,* 253-270.

Shull, S., & Ringelstein, A. (1989). Presidential attention, support, and symbolism in civil rights, 1963-1984. *Social Science Journal, 26,* 45-54.

Sigelman, L., & Bullock, D. (1991). Candidates, issues, horse races, and hoopla: Presidential campaign coverage, 1888-1988. *American Politics Quarterly, 19,* 5-32.

Sigelman, L., & Knight, K. (1983). Why does presidential popularity decline? A test of the expectation/disillusionment theory. *Public Opinion Quarterly, 47,* 310-324.

Sigelman, L., & Knight, K. (1985). Expectation/disillusion and presidential popularity: The Reagan experience. *Public Opinion Quarterly, 49,* 209-213.

Simon, D., & Ostrom, C. (1988). The politics of prestige: Popular support and the modern presidency. *Presidential Studies Quarterly, 18,* 741-759.

Simon, D., & Ostrom, C. (1989). The impact of televised speeches and foreign travel on presidential approval. *Public Opinion Quarterly, 53,* 58-82.

Smith, C. (1986). Leadership, orientation, and rhetorical vision: Jimmy Carter, the "new right," and the Panama Canal. *Presidential Studies Quarterly, 16,* 317-328.

Smith, C. (1987). MisteReagan's neighborhood: Rhetoric and national unity. *Southern Speech Communication Journal, 52,* 219-239.

Smith, C. (1993). The audiences of the "rhetorical presidency": An analysis of presidential-constituent interactions, 1963-1981. *Presidential Studies Quarterly, 13,* 613-622.

Smith, C., & Smith K. (1994). *The White House speaks: Presidential leadership as persuasion.* Westport, CT: Praeger.

Smoller, F. (1986). The six o'clock presidency: Patterns of network news coverage of the president. *Presidential Studies Quarterly, 16,* 31-49.

Smoller, F. (1988). Presidents and their critics: The structure of television news coverage. *Congress and the Presidency, 15,* 75-90.

Speakes, L., with Pack, R. (1988). *Speaking out: The Reagan presidency from inside the White House.* New York: Scribner.

Splichal, S., & Wasko, J. (Eds.). (1993). *Communication and democracy.* Norwood, NJ: Ablex.

Spragens, W. (1984). Kennedy era speechwriting, public relations, and public opinion. *Presidential Studies Quarterly, 14,* 78-85.

Stark, L. (1992). Predicting presidential performance from campaign conduct: A character analysis of the 1988 election. *Presidential Studies Quarterly, 22,* 295-309.

Steele, R. (1974). The pulse of the people: Franklin D. Roosevelt and the gauging of American public opinion. *Journal of Contemporary History, 9,* 195-216.

Steele, R. (1984). The great debate: Roosevelt, the media, and the coming of the war, 1940-1941. *Journal of American History, 71,* 69-92.

Steele, R. (1985). News of the "good war": World War II news management. *Journalism Quarterly, 62,* 707-716.

Stelzner, H. (1966). "War message" December 8, 1941: An approach to language. *Speech Monographs, 33,* 419-437.

Stevenson, A. (1984). The presidency 1984. *Presidential Studies Quarterly, 14,* 18-21.

Stimson, J. (1976). Public support for American presidents: A cyclical model. *Public Opinion Quarterly, 40,* 1-21.

Stoll, R. (1987). The sound of the guns: Is there a congressional rally effect after U.S. military action? *American Politics Quarterly, 15,* 223-237.

Stovall, J. (1984). Incumbency and news coverage of the 1980 presidential election campaign. *Western Political Quarterly, 37,* 621-631.

Streitmatter, R. (1985). The impact of presidential personality on news coverage in major newspapers. *Journalism Quarterly, 62,* 66-73.

Stuckey, M. E. (1991). *The president as interpreter-in-chief.* Chatham, NJ: Chatham House.

Stuckey, M. E. (1992). Remembering the future: Rhetorical echoes of World War II and Vietnam in George Bush's public speech on the Gulf War. *Communication Studies, 43,* 246-256.

Stuckey, M. E. (1995). Competing foreign policy visions: Rhetorical hybrids after the Cold War. *Western Journal of Speech Communication, 59,* 214-227.

Stuckey, M. E., & Antczak, F. J. (1992). Governance as political theater: George Bush and the MTV presidency. In R. Barilleaux & M. E. Stuckey (Eds.), *Leadership and the Bush presidency: Prudence or drift in an era of change?* (pp. 24-36). New York: Praeger.

Sudman, S. (1982). The presidents and the polls. *Public Opinion Quarterly, 46,* 301-310.

Sullivan, T. (1991). The bank account presidency: A new measure and evidence on the temporal path of presidential influence. *American Journal of Political Science, 35,* 686-723.

Swanson, D. (1972). The new politics meets the old rhetoric: New directions in campaign communication research. *Quarterly Journal of Speech, 58,* 31-40.

Swanson, D., & Nimmo, D. (Eds.). (1990). *New directions in political communication: A resource book.* Newbury Park, CA: Sage.

Tatalovich, R., & Gitelson, A. (1990). Political party linkages to presidential popularity: Assessing the "coalition of minorities" thesis. *Journal of Politics, 52,* 234-242.

Tebbel, J., & Watts, S. (1985). *The press and the presidency: From George Washington to Ronald Reagan.* New York: Oxford University Press.

Tetlock, P. (1983). Policy-makers' images of international conflict. *Journal of Social Issues, 39,* 67-85.

Tetlock, P. (1988). Monitoring the integrative complexity of American and Soviet policy rhetoric: What can be learned? *Journal of Social Issues, 44,* 101-131.

Thomas, D., & Sigelman, L. (1984). Presidential identification and policy leadership: Experimental evidence on the Reagan case. *Policy Studies Journal, 12,* 663-675.

Trent, J., & Friedenberg, R. (1991). *Political campaign communication: Principles and practices* (2nd ed.). New York: Praeger.

Trent, J., Mongeau, P., Trent, J., Kendall, K., & Cushing, R. (1993). The ideal candidate: A study of the desired attributes of the public and the media across two presidential campaigns. *American Behavioral Scientist, 37,* 225-239.

Tulis, J. (1987). *The rhetorical presidency.* Princeton, NJ: Princeton University Press.

Vancil, D., & Pendell, S. (1984). Winning presidential debates: An analysis of criteria influencing audience response. *Western Journal of Speech Communication, 48,* 62-74.

Verdier, J. (1988). The president, Congress, and tax reform: Patterns over three decades. *Annals of the American Academy of Political and Social Science, 499,* 114-123.

Vidich, A. (1990). American democracy in the late twentieth century: Political rhetorics and mass media. *International Journal of Politics, Culture, and Society, 4,* 5-29.

Wagner, J. (1983). Media do make a difference: The differential impact of mass media in the 1976 presidential race. *American Journal of Political Science, 27,* 407-430.

Wander, P. (1984). The rhetoric of American foreign policy. *Quarterly Journal of Speech, 70,* 339-361.

Wanta, W. (1991). Presidential approval ratings as a variable in the agenda-building process. *Journalism Quarterly, 68,* 672-679.

Wanta, W., Stephenson, M., Turk, J., & McCombs, M. (1989). How president's state of the union talk influenced news media agendas. *Journalism Quarterly, 66,* 537-541.

Washington, J. (1985). Jesse Jackson and the symbolic politics of black Christendom. *Annals of the American Academy of Political and Social Science, 480,* 89-105.

Wattenberg, M. (1989). When you can't beat them, join them: Shaping the presidential nominating process to the television age. *Polity, 21,* 587-597.

West, D. (1982). Rhetoric and agenda setting in the 1980 presidential campaign. *Congress and the Presidency, 9,* 1-21.

West, D. (1983). Press coverage in the 1980 presidential campaign. *Social Science Quarterly, 64,* 624-633.

West, D. (1984). Cheers and jeers: Candidate presentation and audience reactions in the 1980 presidential campaign. *Presidential Studies Quarterly, 12,* 23-50.

Wills, G. (1987). *Reagan's America: Innocents at home.* Garden City, NY: Doubleday.

Windt, T. (1986). Presidential rhetoric: Definition of a field of study. *Presidential Studies Quarterly, 16,* 102-116.

Windt, T. (1990). *Presidents and protesters: Political rhetoric in the 1960s.* Tuscaloosa: University of Alabama Press.

Winfield, B. (1981). Franklin D. Roosevelt's efforts to influence the news during his first term press conferences. *Presidential Studies Quarterly, 11,* 189-199.

Winfield, B. (1984). The New Deal publicity operation: Foundation for the modern presidency. *Journalism Quarterly, 61,* 40-48, 218.

Winfield, B. (1987). FDR wins (and loses) journalist friends in the rising age of news interpretation. *Journalism Quarterly, 64,* 698-706.

Witherspoon, P. (1991). *Within these walls: A study of communication between presidents and their senior staffs.* New York: Praeger.

Zarefsky, D. (1979). The Great Society as a rhetorical proposition. *Quarterly Journal of Speech, 65,* 364-378.

Zarefsky, D. (1980). Lyndon Johnson redefines "equal opportunity": The beginnings of affirmative action. *Central States Speech Journal, 31,* 85-94.

Zarefsky, D. (1986). *President Johnson's War on Poverty: Rhetoric and history.* Tuscaloosa: University of Alabama Press.

Zeidenstein, H. (1983). White House perceptions of news media bias. *Presidential Studies Quarterly, 13,* 345-356.

Zernicke, P. H. (1994). *Pitching the presidency: How presidents depict the office.* Westport, CT: Praeger.

CHAPTER CONTENTS

11 Attention, Resource Allocation, and Communication Research: What Do Secondary Task Reaction Times Measure, Anyway?

ANNIE LANG
Indiana University

MICHAEL D. BASIL
University of Denver

This chapter refines the conceptual and operational definitions underlying secondary task reaction times (STRTs) in an attempt to clarify exactly what STRTs measure. The intent is to make the measure more useful to researchers studying changes in attention and effort during communication activities. Perusal of the communication literature yields four frequently stated operational definitions of what STRTs measure: (a) the resources required by a message, (b) the resources allocated to the message, (c) the resources available for processing, and (d) the resources remaining in the system. It is demonstrated that these pieces of the resource pie do not always covary. It is suggested that the published research best supports the interpretation of STRTs as available resources. However, interpreting STRTs as available resources cannot explain instances found in the literature where STRTs are fast and memory for messages is slow. A further modification of the model is proposed that involves integrating the limited-capacity approach to television viewing with the four definitions of the STRT. This integration yields a model that interprets STRTs as an index of resources available to the encoding subprocess and interprets memory as an index of resources available at storage. This model is then used to predict the effects of the various independent variables found in the published research on STRTs and memory. The model accurately predicts 16 out of the 20 (84%) of the results of published reaction time studies and 12 out of 14 (85%) of the published tests of memory performance.

Correspondence and requests for reprints: Annie Lang, Department of Telecommunications, Indiana University, 515 North Park Avenue, Bloomington, IN 47405; e-mail anlang@indiana.edu

Communication Yearbook 21, pp. 443-473

WHAT is attention? Can we measure it? How should we measure it? Attention is one of those concepts that are difficult to define, harder to measure, and impossible to do without. Attention is a concept that appears in most areas of communication research (sometimes lurking behind other equally bothersome pseudonyms, such as *involvement, elaborative processing, effort,* and *interest*). Because of its ubiquity, we have become accustomed to dealing with a variety of conceptual and operational definitions of attention. This cornucopia of attention theory and measurement has been well reviewed elsewhere (Grimes & Meadowcroft, 1995) and is not the focus of this essay. Rather, we will examine closely one of these measurement tools, secondary task reaction times (STRTs), and the definitions and theoretical assumptions that accompany it. Our goals in this review are to investigate how STRTs have been conceptualized theoretically, to refine the conceptual definition, and to offer a new interpretation of what STRTs measure based on a limited-resource approach to television viewing.

To achieve these goals, we will first briefly review the development of limited-capacity/resource theories of attention and the development of the STRT measure in the psychology literature. We will then review how this theory and measurement technique has been applied to questions in communication, as well as the conceptual and operational definitions of the STRT used in the communication literature. We will then offer a new interpretation of the STRT using a limited-resource approach to television viewing. Finally, we will "test" this new interpretation of STRTs by comparing the predictions made by this model with the findings in the published literature in the field.

ATTENTION IN PSYCHOLOGY

Speculation among psychologists about attention goes back at least as far as 1890 and William James (Norman, 1976). A primary focus of this research has been on attention as the selection of certain sensory information over other sensory information (Cherry, 1953; Craik & Lockhart, 1972; Harris, 1983; Norman & Bobrow, 1975). Research in this area has addressed two primary questions: (a) How is information selected for attention? (b) How much information can be selected at a given time?

Initial research suggested that the mechanism of selection might be an "attention filter" (Broadbent, 1958; Deutsch & Deutsch, 1963; Triesman, 1960). Later research suggested that selection might be based on various properties of the stimulus, including sensory channel (Allport, 1989; Shiffrin & Schneider, 1977), features (Triesman, 1988), and relevance (Bargh, 1988).

Eventually, limited-capacity models of attention were developed to accommodate the wide variety of selection mechanisms that appear to be operating. These models posit that attention occurs when a person (defined as a limited-capacity information processor) allocates processing resources to a task.

Some tasks involve a great deal of our limited resources, but we can perform other tasks using very few processing resources (Kahneman, 1973). Research within the limited-capacity approach focuses on questions dealing with how resources are allocated to tasks and how much of an individual's capacity (or how many of his or her resources) is used up by various tasks.

Many specific processing models exist within the general class of limited-capacity processing theories. For example, Norman and Bobrow (1975) have proposed a model involving two major processing strategies: "bottom-up" processes, which are data driven and require considerable resources, and "top-down" processes, which automate the attention process and organize incoming material using very few resources. Shiffrin and Schneider (1977) have proposed a "two-process theory" of automatic and controlled processing. According to this model, some attention processes are automatic and require virtually no processing resources, whereas others, called controlled processes, require substantial processing resources.

Limited-resource theories continue to be refined in terms of how resources are allocated and to what resources are being allocated. Some theories now posit that resources are allocated to the various processes involved in attention, such as vigilance or meaning processing (Posner & Raichle, 1994). And Posner (1994) has identified possible neural mechanisms that could be responsible for the executive control over resource allocation.

MEASUREMENT IN PSYCHOLOGY

Measurement of attention in psychology has followed the theoretical development of the concept. Early measurement techniques, aimed at locating the "filter," were based on subjects' ability to detect various stimuli at different stages of processing. In tests involving shadowing tasks, for example, subjects were asked to repeat a message heard in one ear while ignoring a message presented to the other ear (Broadbent, 1958; Cherry, 1953).

With the advent of resource models of attention (Broadbent, 1977; Kahneman, 1973), the secondary reaction task was developed (Posner, 1978). The use of secondary task reaction time is predicated on the assumption that attention is a limited resource (Kahneman, 1973; Posner, 1978). The STRT measure was expected to provide a window into the allocation of these otherwise invisible resources.

To apply the secondary task reaction time measure, researchers ask a subject to perform a primary task at the same time he or she is performing a secondary task. The secondary task typically involves the subject's pushing a button as quickly as possible whenever he or she detects a certain signal (a tone, a flash, color bars, or tactile stimulation). Theoretically, resources that are being used to perform the primary task cannot be used to perform the secondary task. As the primary task consumes more and more resources, there are fewer and fewer resources left over for the subject to perform the secondary task. As a result, the subject performs the secondary task more slowly. Thus, as the primary task requires more resources, STRTs become slower.

THE USE OF THE STRT IN
COMMUNICATION RESEARCH

Prior to about 1980, communication researchers viewed attention largely as a condition that might mediate message effects (McLeod & Reeves, 1980). When these researchers measured attention, they did so usually in one of two ways: (a) by measuring exposure and equating attention and exposure or (b) by measuring memory and inferring increased attention from increased memory. Since 1980, however, communication researchers have begun to consider attention as an important variable in the processing of mediated messages. New definitions of attention have surfaced that reflect the changing conceptions of attention in psychology. Attention has come to be viewed not as a static condition, but rather as a process that could vary both within a communication message (intrastimulus attention) and between communication messages (interstimulus attention) (Reeves et al., 1985). Similarly, definitions of attention have begun to incorporate both long- and short-term components of attention (Lang, 1990) as well as voluntary and involuntary allocation of attention (Lang, 1990; Newhagen & Reeves, 1992).

Along with these new conceptualizations of attention have come new measurement techniques (Lang, 1994). These include continuous response measures (Biocca, 1994), self-report Likert scale questions (Chaffee & Schleuder, 1986), eyes on screen (Anderson & Levin, 1976; Thorson, 1994), alpha blocking (Reeves et al., 1985), heart rate decelerations (Lang, 1990), and secondary task reaction times (Basil, 1994c; Thorson, Reeves, & Schleuder, 1987).

This review focuses on the research that has used STRT as a measure of how much attention television viewers pay to television messages (Basil, 1994a, 1994b, 1994c; Cameron, Schleuder, & Thorson, 1991; Geiger & Reeves, 1993a, 1993b; Gilbert & Schleuder, 1990; Grimes, 1991; Lang, Chaffeur, Davidson, Funabiki, & Reynvaan, 1992; Lang, Dhillon, & Dong, 1995; Lang, Geiger, Strickwerda, & Sumner, 1993; Lang, Sias, Chantrill, & Burek, 1995; Meadowcroft & Reeves, 1989; Meadowcroft & Watt, 1988; Reeves & Thorson, 1986; Reeves, Thorson, & Schleuder, 1986; Schleuder, 1990; Schleuder, Cameron, & Thorson, 1989; Schleuder, Thorson, & Reeves, 1988; Shapiro, 1986; Thorson, Reeves, & Schleuder, 1985, 1987). To date, the STRT measure has been used to investigate how people learn from news and entertainment programming, how children learn from television, and how people learn from print media (both texts and photographs). Though it is a fairly "new" measure in communication research, it is broadly applicable and offers a real-time measure of attention that does not require media consumers to introspect and report on their "attention" to a given activity. On the other hand, certain inconsistencies in the research using STRTs, as well as theoretical concerns over exactly what is being measured, may limit its use. It is our hope that the analysis presented here will help to clarify the uses and interpretations of the STRT and increase its use as a methodological tool for all areas of communication research.

By and large, researchers measuring STRTs have used some version of the limited-capacity/resource model described above. These models assume that people are limited-capacity information processors. Attention is defined as the allocation of processing resources to a message. Attention to a task increases as the number of resources allocated to the task increases. The application of the STRT measure to communication research is fairly straightforward. The primary task is the communication task (e.g., watching, listening, or reading a mediated message), and the secondary task is to push a button as fast as possible in response to some signal (e.g., a tone, a flash, color bars, or tactile stimulation). As in psychology, the basic premise is that when the primary task requires more resources, the subject will have fewer resources left over to perform the secondary task. Performance on the secondary task, therefore, will slow down.

Although this approach has proven useful, it has also produced some counterintuitive results. For example, several studies have shown that television viewers have faster secondary task reaction times while viewing complex video messages than they do when viewing simple video messages (Reeves et al., 1986; Schleuder et al., 1988; Thorson et al., 1985, 1987). Similarly, audio complexity has frequently been observed to have no effect on STRTs (Lang et al., 1992; Reeves et al., 1986; Schleuder et al., 1988; Thorson et al., 1985). On the face of it, these results seem to suggest that increasing the complexity of a television stimulus does not increase the resources the subject must use for processing.

Adding to the difficulty of interpreting these results is the less-than-consistent relationship observed between secondary task reaction times and subjects' memories for the messages contained in the primary task. Because, in the STRT paradigm, subjects are asked to work as hard as they can on the primary task (usually, remembering the message), it is logical to argue that faster reaction times are indicative of fewer resources being required or used up by the primary task (presumably because the primary task is easy). In this case, one might argue that the primary task should be performed "better" (i.e., viewers should have better memory for the messages). Yet this is not necessarily the case. In some instances, faster reaction times are associated with better memory (Cameron et al., 1991; Lang, Sias, et al., 1995); in others, slower reaction times are associated with better memory (Reeves et al., 1986; Thorson et al., 1987).

Although good alternative explanations for these findings have been proposed, the overall pattern of inconsistency has led some researchers to question what STRTs actually measure (Basil, 1994a, 1994b; Grimes, 1991). Here, we offer a reinterpretation of the STRT that better predicts what might otherwise be viewed as an inconsistent pattern of results.

In presenting our reinterpretation, we will do three things: (a) look at the conceptual and operational definitions of attention and secondary task reaction times being used by researchers in communication; (b) construct a model of the "possible" locus of measurement being indexed by STRT within the general resource models being used; and (c) suggest an alternative model for interpretation of STRTs.

Conceptual Definitions of Attention

The communication studies that have employed secondary task measurement have all approached attention using some kind of limited-resource information processing model. In spite of the overall similarity in approach, however, specific definitions of attention have varied from study to study. Although these differences are small and, in some cases, may not have been viewed as differences by the authors of the studies, examining them can lead to insight into exactly what aspect of the resource allocation process is being measured by the STRT.

In some studies, attention is defined simply as the limited resource with a fixed capacity that can be flexibly (and unevenly) distributed across stimuli or tasks (Grimes, 1991; Lang et al., 1992; Schleuder et al., 1989). In other words, attention is the fixed pool of processing resources. Other studies define attention not as the limited resource, but as the process of allocating the limited resource from a fixed-capacity pool of resources or from multiple fixed-capacity resource pools (Basil, 1994a, 1994b; Cameron et al., 1991). In other words, these definitions cast attention not as the resource pool but rather as the process of removing resources from the pool and allocating them to a task. A variation on this definition defines attention as the process of allocating mental resources (Schleuder, 1990). In this view, mental resources are defined as the visual and verbal sensory systems and memory mechanisms involved in message processing.

Another group of researchers defines attention not in terms of the allocation of resources to something, but rather in terms of the resources required by the thing. In these studies, attention is viewed as the resources required to carry out a task (Gilbert & Schleuder, 1990; Shapiro, 1986; Thorson et al., 1987). A somewhat similar definition, proposed by Thorson et al. (1985), conceives of attention as the degree to which a task requires cognitive resources or fills cognitive capacity. This definition adds the notion that a given message requires a certain amount of resources to be processed and that the demand for those resources may be somewhat imperative.

Finally, there is a group of studies that combines these last two approaches (allocating resources to and resources required by), defining attention as both discretionary and automatic allocation of limited resources to the processing of a task (Lang, Dhillon, & Dong, 1995; Lang et al., 1993; Lang, Sias, et al., 1995; Meadowcroft & Reeves, 1989; Meadowcroft & Watt, 1989). In this approach, discretionary allocation is related to the allocation of resources to something (notions of effort, involvement, and so on), whereas automatic allocation of resources is related to the resources required or demanded by a stimulus.

In short, all of these studies define attention as a limited resource existing in a fixed-capacity pool. Attention is defined as the process of allocating resources, whereas the *level* of attention is defined as the amount of resources allocated. Control of the allocation process is at times ignored and at other times given to the message, the person, or a combination of the two.

Generally, the words *resources* and *capacity* seem to be used interchangeably. Some authors refer to allocating capacity and others to the allocation of processing resources. For purposes of this chapter, we conceptualize each individual as having a fixed-capacity pool of processing resources. A person's capacity is the sum total of his or her processing resources.

Operational Definitions of Attention: What Is That STRT?

Not surprisingly, there is also variability in how researchers translate their definitions of attention into interpretations of secondary task reaction times. For example, those who discuss the costs of tasks are more likely to interpret STRTs in terms of task requirements, whereas those who view attention as filled capacity see STRTs as indicators of how much capacity is filled or used up. Generally, there appear to be four different basic definitions of what a secondary task reaction time measures, reflecting four alternative ways of thinking about the resources indexed by the STRT.

Definition 1: This definition is an amalgam of various ways of defining the secondary task reaction time as a measure of the cost of the task or a measure of how many resources are required to perform the task (Gilbert & Schleuder, 1990; Grimes, 1991; Lang et al., 1993; Lang, Sias, et al., 1995; Reeves et al., 1986; Shapiro, 1986; Thorson et al., 1985, 1987). Examples of this kind of definition include the STRT as (a) the capacity required to process a photograph (Gilbert & Schleuder, 1990, p. 751), (b) the attention required to encode and store a message (Grimes, 1991), (c) the amount of capacity required to process a primary task (Lang et al., 1993, p. 13), and (d) the impact of the resources required by the primary task on the performance of a secondary task (Basil, 1994c, p. 87). This definition of STRT implies, to invoke a consumer analogy, that a message or a stimulus has a resource price tag. As the price goes up (that is, as processing the message requires more resources), the STRT gets slower.

Definition 2: The definitions that combine to make up Definition 2 are those that consider the STRT to be a measure of the resources allocated to a task (Cameron et al., 1991; Lang et al., 1992; Lang, Dhillon, & Dong, 1995; Lang, Sias, et al., 1995; Meadowcroft & Reeves, 1989; Meadowcroft & Watt, 1988). Examples of this kind of definition are as follows: (a) Slower reaction times indicate subjects were paying more attention (defined as allocation of resources) to television (Cameron et al., 1991) and (b) "[STRTs index] how much cognitive capacity is being allocated to the primary task" (Lang, Sias, et al., 1995, p. 5). To continue the consumer analogy, this definition regards the STRT as an indicator of how much the person paid for the message. Unlike consumers at a local supermarket, limited-capacity information processors do not have to pay the amount on the price tag. People can pay less than the price (that is, allocate fewer resources to the message than the message requires for complete processing), but they will get only what they pay for. Thus if a person underpays, he or she will only partially process the message. If the STRT measures the allocation of resources, then it would measure how many resources a viewer allocated to the task, irrespective of how many resources the task actually required. Using this definition, the more resources a person allocates to a task, the slower the secondary task reaction time will be.

Definition 3: A third approach found in this literature holds that secondary task reaction times measure available resources (Basil, 1994b; Lang, Dhillon, & Dong, 1995; Shapiro, 1986). Basil (1994b) defines available resources as the resources allocated to a task minus the resources required by a task. Thus this definition is mathematically equivalent to Definition 2 minus Definition 1. Returning to our consumer analogy, if Definition 1 is the price and Definition 2 is what someone pays, this third definition is either the change the individual receives or his or her deficit. If a person allocates exactly the amount of resources a message requires, this number is zero. If a person allocates more resources to a task than it requires, this number is positive. If a person allocates fewer resources to a task than it requires, this number is negative. In this case, the STRT is an indicator of whether a person allocates sufficient or insufficient resources to the task. Response time will get faster the more a person overallocates, and slower the more he or she underallocates.

Definition 4: The definitions that make up Definition 4 are those in which secondary task reaction times are regarded as an index of the resources that are not allocated to the task and are, therefore, remaining, unused, or left over in the system (Basil, 1994a, 1994b; Grimes, 1991; Schleuder et al., 1989). The approaches using this definition sometimes posit the possibility of separate resource pools for different tasks (Wickens, 1980, 1984). Examples of this kind of definition include the following: (a) STRTs index "remaining resources" (Basil, 1994a); (b) "[Reaction time] to the probe measures residual capacity" (Grimes, 1991, p. 272); and (c) Reaction times measure "leftover" capacity (Schleuder et al., 1989, p. 12). In the consumer analogy, this definition may be compared to the money a person leaves in his or her wallet during a transaction. Leftover resources (Definition 4) are equal to available capacity/resources (Definition 3) only when the resources allocated to a task (the amount paid) are equal to all the resources existing in the system (all the money in the person's wallet). If, however, an individual allocates only a portion of total resources to a task (i.e., takes only some of the money out of his or her wallet to pay for something), then the resources not allocated (total resources minus resources allocated to the task) would be the person's leftover resources or unused capacity. In this case, STRTs would measure the resources remaining in the system that have not been allocated to any task. As more of an individual's total resources are allocated to the task, STRTs would get slower.

Do These Differences Matter?

Close examination of these definitions reveals that they are not the same, although most scholars have treated them as such. In fact, they are often used interchangeably. For example, in a single paragraph, Lang et al. (1993) define secondary task measures in three of the above four ways: (a) available resources ("The faster a person responds to the tone, the more capacity is inferred to be available"), (b) resources allocated ("Speed of response can be an accurate index of how hard a person is thinking"), and (c) remaining resources ("The secondary task procedure uses the measurement of how quickly a person responds to a probe to index the amount of processing capacity being used up by the primary task") (p. 13).

Further, in various situations, these four pieces of the resource pool will not always vary together. For example, in a given situation, the resources required by a message (its price for full processing) might go up, but the resources allocated to the message (how much a person pays) might go down. In that case, if STRTs were measuring the resources required by the message, they would get slower, but if they were measuring the resources allocated to the message, they would get faster.

Table 11.1 illustrates how these different methods of dividing up the resource pie result in various-size pieces in different situations. For the purposes of this example, assume that a person's total resource capacity is 100 units. The first three lines of the table illustrate a situation in which a task is difficult. The task requires 75 units of resources to be performed well. The first line of the table illustrates a situation in which a person does not allocate the full resource price to the task, but instead allocates only 50 units to the task. As a result, there is a shortfall of 25 units for the task. On the other hand, there are still 50 resource units elsewhere in the system to perform other tasks. In this case, the four pieces of the resource puzzle described above have the following values: (a) resources required by the message (i.e., the price) is equal to 75 units; (b) resources allocated to the task (i.e., what a person pays) is equal to 50 units; (c) resources available (i.e., a person's change or the

TABLE 11.1
The Pieces of the Capacity Puzzle

Difficulty	Resources Required	Resources Allocated	Capacity Available	Capacity Remaining
Hard task	75	50	–25	50
	75	75	0	25
	75	100	25	0
Medium task	50	50	0	50
	50	75	25	25
	50	100	50	0
Simple task	25	50	25	50
	25	75	50	25
	25	100	75	0

NOTE: Table entries are in arbitrary resource units. This example assumes a limited capacity of 100 arbitrary resource units.

deficit) is equal to resources allocated minus the resources required, in this case –25 units; and (d) remaining resources (i.e., what's left in the person's wallet) is total resources minus resources allocated, in this case 50 units. Thus, in this example, if the STRT were indexing the requirements of the message (75 units), it would be fairly slow. However, if it were indexing the resources allocated (50 units) or the resources remaining (50 units), it would be somewhat faster. In contrast, if it were indexing the available resources (–25) it would be very slow. In other words, the first task would be "resource limited" and not be fully performed, but, because there are unallocated resources remaining in the system, other tasks would not necessarily be limited.

The second line in Table 11.1 shows a situation in which the subject allocates 75 resource units to the 75-unit task. In this case, the resources required by the task and the resources allocated to the task are equal (75 units). This results in zero units of available resources (75 – 75 = 0). In addition, there are 25 units of remaining resources in the system. The third line shows a situation in which a person allocates all 100 units to a 75-unit task. In this case, the task requires 75 units, the person allocates 100 units, the available resources equal 100 – 75, or 25 units, and there are zero unallocated or remaining resource units.

Figures 11.1, 11.2, and 11.3 graphically depict the values of these "pieces" of capacity at various levels of allocation. In Figure 11.1, the person is assumed to be allocating all of his or her resources to the task. Given that the secondary task methodology does involve instructing subjects to pay close attention to the primary tasks because they will be tested, this is not an unreasonable example. Figure 11.2 shows the case where a person allocates 50% of his or her resources to the primary task, and Figure 11.3 shows the

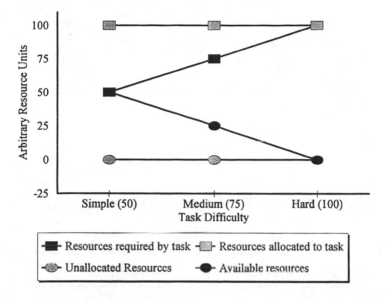

Figure 11.1. 100% Resources Allocated to Task

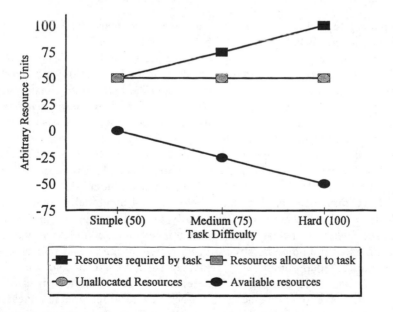

Figure 11.2. 50% Resources Allocated to Task

case where a person allocates 25% of resources to the primary task. It should be clear from these figures and from Table 11.1 that the prediction of whether

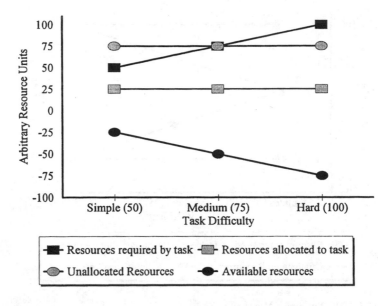

Figure 11.3. 25% Resources Allocated to Task

a secondary task reaction time will increase or decrease depends on which piece of capacity is being measured by the STRT measure.

What are we actually measuring when we use secondary task procedures? One way to begin to answer this question is to look at the independent variables that have been used to manipulate STRT, taking into consideration which piece of capacity is most likely to be affected by these variables. A review of the communication literature on secondary tasks reveals the use of a number of independent variables. These appear to fall into five general categories: (a) audio complexity, (b) video complexity, (c) information channel, (d) cognitive load, and (e) other variables. Table 11.2 provides a list of the specific variables and the studies that have used them.

Audio complexity variables have been looked at globally (that is, as a property of an entire message) and locally (as different points in the same message). Generally, researchers have quantified audio complexity by coding such things as grammatical structure, narrative strength, and rate of audio presentation. Video complexity variables also have global and local variations. Global video complexity has generally been operationalized as the number of cuts, edits, movement, and other structural features in a message. Local complexity has generally been operationalized through comparison of points in messages where visual complexity was high with points in messages where visual complexity was low.

The third category of variables reflects manipulations that move the informational content of the message from one channel to the other (i.e., from

TABLE 11.2
Independent Variables in STRT Studies

Variable Type	Levels	Study
Presentation condition	audio only, video only, audio/video	Reeves et al., 1986 Thorson et al., 1985
Global visual complexity	number of cuts/edits/structural features	Reeves et al., 1986 Schleuder et al., 1988 Thorson et al., 1987 Thorson et al., 1985 Lang et al., 1992
Local visual complexity	related/unrelated cuts	Geiger & Reeves, 1993a Lang et al., 1993
	points without structural features color/B&W photos	Thorson et al., 1987 Gilbert & Schleuder, 1990
Global audio complexity	grammar, words, rate of presentation	Reeves et al., 1986 Schleuder et al., 1988 Thorson et al., 1985
	grammar, words, rate of presentation	Lang et al., 1992
	strength of narrative structure	Lang, Sias, et al., 1995
Local audio complexity	simple points compared with complex ones	Schleuder et al., 1988
Information channel variables	audio/video redundancy issue/image political ads channel of semantic information	Grimes, 1991 Schleuder, 1990 Basil, 1994a
Cognitive load variables	visualization instructions presence of analogy schema development preceding teaser	Shapiro, 1986 Shapiro, 1986 Meadowcroft & Reeves, 1989 Cameron et al., 1991 Schleuder et al., 1989
	instructed focus (audio/video channel)	Basil, 1994a
Other variables	arousal valence local global complexity	Lang, Dhillon, & Dong, 1995 Lang, Dhillon, & Dong, 1995 Thorson et al., 1987

audio to video or video to audio). Examples of these include issue versus image political ads, more or less audio/video redundancy, and audio or video semantic information channel. Cognitive load variables generally reflect something done either to the message or to the viewer to increase the amount of thinking required to process the message. Variables contained in the message have included the presence/absence of analogies and the presence/absence of a news teaser preceding a commercial. Viewer-based variables include the relative development of viewers' schema and instructions to visualize or not visualize the message. The "other" category includes variables such as arousal, valence, and local versus global complexity.

How have researchers proposed that these variables alter viewers' resource allocation? Generally speaking, complexity variables have been described as variables that increase the amount of resources required for processing of the message. This in turn has been thought to result in an increase in the resources allocated by the viewer. Cognitive load variables have generally been thought to reduce remaining resources. Our simple mathematical explanation suggests that these resource pieces are not all the same, however, and that they need not always vary together. If secondary task reaction times always index the same aspect of capacity or resource allocation, which one might it be?

If STRTs always index a specific aspect of resource allocation, then we must conclude that reaction times will slow down when one (or more) of four things happens: (a) The resources required to process the message are increased, (b) the resources allocated to process a message are increased, (c) the resources available to process the message are reduced, or (d) leftover resources are reduced. Does one of these definitions of a secondary task reaction time fit the results published in the literature better than any of the others?

Table 11.3 presents the results of these studies, which suggest that there are five conditions that consistently elicit *slower* reaction times. First, STRTs are slower during *audio/video* presentations compared with *single-channel* presentations (Grimes, 1991; Reeves et al., 1986; Thorson et al., 1985). Second, STRTs are slower during *global video simple* messages than they are during *global video complex* messages (Reeves et al., 1986; Thorson et al., 1985, 1987). Third, STRTs during *local video complex* messages are slower than those evoked during *local video simple* messages (Geiger & Reeves, 1993a; Lang et al., 1993). Fourth, STRTs are slower during messages with *information based in the video channel* compared with messages with *information based in the audio channel* (Basil, 1994b; Grimes, 1991; Schleuder, 1990). Fifth, STRTs are slower during situations with *increased cognitive load* compared with situations with *decreased cognitive load* (Cameron et al., 1991; Meadowcroft & Reeves, 1989; Schleuder et al., 1989; Shapiro, 1986).

By and large, results for audio manipulations are less likely to show significant reaction time effects (Lang et al., 1992; Schleuder et al., 1988; Thorson et al., 1985, 1987). When they do, there is some indication that global simple (Reeves et al., 1986; Lang, Sias, et al., 1995) and local complex (Schleuder et al., 1988) audio messages slow reaction times. This is the same pattern that is seen for the visual independent variables described above.

All this would seem to imply that audio/video messages, locally complex messages, messages with information in the video channel, high cognitive

TABLE 11.3
Results of STRT Studies by Study and Independent Variable

Variable Type	Comparison	Study	Results (fastest to slowest)
Audio/video complexity variables			
presentation channel	audio, A/V	Reeves et al., 1986	not significant
	audio, video, A/V	Thorson et al., 1985	video, audio, A/V
global visual complexity	simple, complex	Reeves et al., 1986	complex, simple
	simple, complex	Thorson et al., 1987	complex, simple
	simple, complex	Schleuder et al., 1988	complex, simple
	simple, complex	Thorson et al., 1985	complex, simple
	simple, complex	Lang et al., 1992	complex, simple
local visual complexity	simple, complex	Geiger & Reeves, 1993a	simple, complex
	simple, complex	Lang et al., 1993	simple, complex
	simple, complex	Thorson ct al., 1987	not significant
	color, B&W (photos)	Gilbert & Schleuder, 1990	color, B&W
global audio complexity	simple, complex	Reeves et al., 1986	complex, simple
	simple, complex	Schleuder, 1990	not significant
	simple, complex	Lang et al., 1992	not significant
	simple, complex	Thorson et al., 1985	not significant
	strong, weak (narrative)	Lang, Sias, et al., 1995	weak, strong
local audio complexity	simple, complex	Schleuder, 1990	simple, complex
channel of information	audio, video	Basil, 1994a	audio, video
	nonredundant, redundant	Grimes, 1991	nonredundant, redundant
	issue, image	Schleuder, 1990	issue, image
Cognitive load variables			
preceding teaser	present, absent	Cameron et al., 1991	absent, present
	present, absent	Schleuder et al., 1989	absent, present
visualization	don't, do visualize	Shapiro, 1986	don't, do visualize
analogy	present, absent	Shapiro, 1986	present, absent
schema development	good, poor	Meadowcroft & Reeves, 1989	good, poor
instructed focus	audio, video	Basil, 1994a	audio, video
Other independent variables			
emotion	negative, positive	Lang, Dhillon, & Dong, 1995	negative, positive

load situations, and globally simple messages all result in some aspect of resources (allocated, required, available, or remaining) going in the same direction. It is difficult to accept logically, however, that global complex messages, compared with global simple messages, require fewer resources, have fewer resources allocated to them, or result in more leftover resources. Several attempts have been made to explain these findings. Thorson et al. (1985) suggest that simple messages fill cognitive capacity more than do complex messages. Reeves et al. (1986) argue that global complex messages are more arousing than simple messages and that arousal might speed reaction time. Others have suggested that people might stop trying when messages are complex, and therefore they allocate fewer resources to the message.

We suggest a more parsimonious explanation of this finding: that complex messages result in more resources being *available.* In other words, increasing global complexity results in more resources being allocated to the message, and this increase in allocated resources is greater than any associated increase in resources required to process the message, resulting in an increase in available resources. According to this view, it is the global complexity of a message that determines how many resources are allocated to the attention task and the content/structure of the message that determines how many of those resources are required to process the message.

In the rest of this chapter, we will use a specific limited-resource approach to television viewing to argue that the extant data in the field best support the interpretation of secondary task reaction time as an indicator of available resources, and specifically of resources available to the cognitive subprocess of encoding the message into short-term memory. We will further suggest that the resources available at encoding are determined by three things: (a) the structural features of the message that elicit automatic allocation of processing resources to encoding, (b) the change in the difficulty of the encoding task, and (c) the concurrent demands for resources made by the ongoing processing and storage of the message content.

THE LIMITED-RESOURCE APPROACH
TO TELEVISION VIEWING

The model used here is a data-based, limited-capacity approach that has been developed specifically to explain how people process mediated messages, in particular, television. Although the roots of this model are firmly grounded in psychological work on attention and cognitive processing, many of the theoretical relationships discussed here were developed directly from work done in communication research laboratories. As a result, this model may be more applicable to the complex (psychologists might say hopelessly complex) stimuli involved in media research than would models borrowed directly from the psychology laboratory.

The limited-resource model of television viewing (Kawahara et al., 1995; Lang, 1995; Lang, Dhillon, & Dong, 1995; Lang et al., 1993; Lang, Sias, et al., 1995) posits that each individual has a fixed and limited capacity of processing resources. These resources are allocated across ongoing tasks as a result of both automatic and controlled processes (Lang, 1995; Shiffrin & Schneider, 1977). Television viewers control some aspects of how their processing resources are allocated through decisions about when to view and how hard to work at it.

Television also controls some aspects of resource allocation, through the elicitation of automatic attention responses, called orienting responses (Lang, 1990; Lynn, 1966). The orienting response, sometimes called the "What is it?" response, is an automatic reaction to a change in the environment or to something (such as hearing one's own name) that "signals" relevant information is about to occur. The orienting response consists of a group of behavioral, physiological, and cognitive changes that occur together following some stimulus (Lynn, 1966). Research suggests that when elements of a mediated message elicit orienting, the orienting response is accompanied by some kind of change in resource allocation, which can be measured using STRTs.

The piece of the resource pie we have defined as resources allocated to the task is under the dual control of the viewer (who decides how much effort to put into the task) and the stimulus (which can call additional resources to itself through the elicitation of orienting responses). Thus a structural feature that elicits an orienting response will result in an automatic increase in the resources allocated to processing a message.

The question is, then, does processing the structural feature require all of the additional resources that it automatically elicits? To answer this, consider the case of related and unrelated cuts, where related cuts are defined as cuts from one camera to another in the same visual scene and unrelated cuts are defined as cuts from one visual scene to another. Both related and unrelated cuts elicit cardiac orienting responses in attentive viewers (Lang et al., 1993). The latency and amplitude of these orienting responses do not differ between related cuts and unrelated cuts. This finding suggests that the same automatic attention response occurs to both of these structural features and, therefore, that the same amount of resources may be allocated to each one. Yet, arguably, the unrelated cut requires more processing resources to be used, because a new visual scene is being introduced. Also, because available resources equals the resources allocated (a constant) minus the amount of resources required (which should be greater for unrelated than for related cuts), available resources should be greater for related cuts than for unrelated cuts. Remaining resources (those not allocated) should remain unchanged. Thus if STRTs measure either the *allocation of resources* or the *remaining resources,* they should show no difference for related and unrelated cuts, because these two pieces of the resource pie should not change as a result of the type of cut.

On the other hand, if they measure either *resources required* by the message (which increases for unrelated cuts) or *available resources* (which decreases for unrelated cuts), they should show slower reaction times for unrelated than for related cuts. Studies show that STRTs measured at the points of related cuts are indeed slower than STRTs measured at the points of unrelated cuts (Geiger & Reeves, 1993a; Lang et al., 1993). These results eliminate from our consideration the first definition (*resources allocated*) and the fourth definition (*resources remaining*).

The results of the Geiger and Reeves (1993a) and Lang et al. (1993) studies suggest that secondary task reaction times measure either the *resources required* by the message or the *available resources*. To choose between these two resource pieces, consider the case of global video complexity. As we have already discussed, global video complex messages result in *faster* reaction times than do global video simple messages. Using the limited-resource model described above, global complex video messages should elicit numerous orienting responses and thus result in a general increase in the resources required by the message. If STRTs are measuring the resources required by the message, then STRTs should slow down as global complexity increases. But research shows that STRTs get faster when global video complexity goes up (Reeves et al., 1986; Schleuder et al., 1988; Thorson et al., 1985, 1987). This result eliminates *resources required by the message* as a possible definition (among the four) of what is being measured by the STRT, leaving only *available resources*. If STRTs are measuring available resources, would they get faster when global video complexity is increased? As discussed above, the resources allocated to the message should increase as video complexity increases. Available resources is equal to the resources allocated to the message (which is increasing) minus the resources required by the message. What happens to the resources required by a message when global video complexity is increased? This question is difficult, but perhaps not impossible, to answer. In the studies cited here, global video complexity is operationalized as the number of cuts, edits, movement, and other structural features contained in a message. Some of these structural features (e.g., related cuts, edits, and movement) may require little or none of the additional resources they elicit through orienting. Others (e.g., unrelated cuts or video graphics) may well require most or all of the additional resources they elicit. Overall, it seems likely that the globally complex messages require more resources than do the globally simple messages. However, the increase in required resources is probably not directly equal to the number of resources automatically allocated to the message by orienting responses. Therefore, to the extent that the resources required are less than the resources allocated, the available resources during global complex video messages may very well increase. In this situation, then, the amount of resources required by the message is increasing, but probably at a slower rate than the resources allocated to the message. Therefore, there should be more available resources during video complex messages than there are during video simple messages. If reaction times index *available resources,* this increase should result in the faster reaction times, which are in fact reported in the literature.

The available resources explanation also predicts the published STRT results for the other categories of independent variables described above. Some of the load variables (e.g., schema development, presence of analogy) reduce the *resources required* to process the message without necessarily changing the *allocation of resources* to the message. When resources required goes down and resources allocated does not change, *available resources* will automatically increase.

Other variables, such as the presence of a preceding news teaser and the instruction to visualize, may reduce the *resources allocated* to message viewing, because resources are also required to perform this competing task (e.g., remembering the news teaser, or visualizing). These manipulations, however, do not change the *resources required* to process the message. When resources allocated goes down and resources required stays the same, available resources will also go down. If STRTs measure the available resources, this should result in the slower STRTs shown in the literature.

STRTs AND MEMORY

Another type of evidence to consider concerns the relationship between STRTs and memory for mediated messages. If faster reaction times indicate more available resources, then when reaction times are fast, viewers are allocating more resources to the primary task than they need to, hence they have resources available. If viewers have more resources allocated to the task than they need, it would seem logical to assume that fast reaction times should be associated with better performance on memory tests. But this is not always the case. For some independent variables (such as global video complexity), faster reaction times are associated with poorer memory performance, but for other independent variables (e.g., local video complexity), faster reaction times are associated with better memory performance (Cameron et al., 1991; Gilbert & Schleuder, 1990; Grimes, 1991; Lang et al., 1993; Meadowcroft & Reeves, 1989; Reeves et al., 1986; Thorson et al., 1987). Can the "available resources" model be modified to match these data?

Lang and her colleagues (Kawahara et al., 1995; Lang, 1995) have offered an explanation for this phenomenon that is consistent with STRTs being a measure of available resources. They suggest that those resources allocated to viewing a message (the primary task) as a result of an orienting response elicited by a structural feature are not allocated generally to "processing the message," but are allocated specifically to the subprocess of encoding the message.

In a recent formulation of the limited-capacity approach, Lang (1995) suggests that television viewers are simultaneously engaged in encoding, processing, and storing a television message. She suggests that resources may be allocated independently to these three subprocesses. Various message, environmental, and individual-level variables may result in differential allocation of resources to these three concurrent ongoing processing tasks. Similar models, which also suggest that resource allocation may vary for different subprocesses, are being developed concurrently in psychology. For example, Posner (1994; Posner & Raichle, 1994) has suggested that resources are independently allocated to two subprocesses, which he calls sensory monitoring (similar to Lang's encoding) and meaning processing (similar to Lang's storage).

If we merge this model of encoding, processing, and storage with our secondary task model, then we must think about the resources being allocated to encoding and the resources being allocated to storage as separate pieces of the capacity puzzle. If we do this, one of our four pieces of capacity—*resources remaining* (not allocated to any task)—should not be affected. Each of the remaining three pieces of the puzzle, however, must be cut into two pieces. *Resources required to process the message* becomes *resources required to encode the message* and *resources required to store the message*. *Available resources* becomes *resources available for encoding* and the *resources available for storage*. *Resources allocated to processing the message* becomes *resources allocated to encoding the message* and *resources allocated to storing the message*.

Within this new framework, which of the seven pieces of the resource pie is being indexed by the STRT? The most logical candidate is *resources available at the encoding stage*. This can be inferred primarily from consideration of the nature of the secondary task itself. The secondary task requires subjects to detect and encode a probe stimulus and then to make a behavioral response. They are not required to store the secondary task probe or to process it beyond basic encoding. This means that performing the secondary task primarily requires the use of resources allocated to encoding. The encoding resources required to perform the secondary task would logically come from the pool of resources allocated to encoding the primary task, but that are not being used—that is, the available encoding resources. If there are no available encoding resources, then these resources must be borrowed from the resources being used to encode the primary task. In either case, the reaction times would logically be indexing the resources available at the encoding stage.

The resources ultimately available at encoding will be affected directly and indirectly by many aspects of the primary task. Direct influences include the structure of the message (which calls resources automatically) and the difficulty of the encoding task. These combine to determine the resources available at encoding. However, other variables will also have an indirect impact through the demands they place on overall resource allocation to all the ongoing subprocesses (retrieval, storage, rehearsal, and the like). Both message variables (e.g., difficulty, familiarity, logical or narrative structure) and subject variables (e.g., expertise in the message area, level of effort, schema development) will affect the amount of resources being allocated to ongoing processing and storage. As demands for storage and processing resources increase, overall resource demands (from all the ongoing subprocesses) may exceed the total resources in the system. When this happens, even automatic demands for resources may not be responded to fully. Thus the amount of resources available at encoding is codetermined by the resources allocated to encoding, the resources allocated to storage, the resources required for the message to be encoded, and the resources required for the message to be stored.

It makes sense to conceive of the storage subprocess as parallel to the encoding subprocess. In the same way that resources *allocated* to encoding and the resources *required* by the encoding task combine to produce the resources *available* at encoding, the resources *allocated* to storage and the resources *required* for storage should combine to produce the resources *available* for storage. It is fairly standard practice to equate memory for a message with how well a message has been processed (Craik & Lockhart, 1972; Eysenck, 1993; Lachman, Lachman, & Butterfield, 1979). It is only a small further step, which would narrow the definition slightly, to consider that memory for a message as a gross indicator of the resources available for storing a message (in much the same way that STRTs are proposed to be an indicator of resources available for encoding). If it is thought of in this way, then when the *resources required* to store a message are greater than the *resources allocated* to storing the message, the *resources available* for storing the message will be negative. In this case, memory for the message should be poor. Similarly, when the *resources allocated* to storing a message exceed the *resources required* to store a message, then *resources available* for storing the message will be positive. In this case, memory for the message should be good. If we add this to our model, we have one dependent variable (the STRT) that indexes the availability of resources at encoding and one dependent variable (memory) that indexes the availability of resources at storage. If, as the limited-capacity theory suggests, the allocation of resources to storage and the allocation of resources to encoding are separate, then resource limitations (defined as negative available resources) could appear. Depending on the viewers' situation, these limitations may be apparent at (a) both encoding and storage, (b) neither encoding nor storage, (c) encoding but not at storage, or (d) storage but not at encoding. Predicting whether (or if) resource limitations will occur will depend on the overall availability of resources within the system.

When overall resource demands (for all the subprocesses involved in a task) do not exceed a viewer's total resource capacity, then both the primary and the secondary task may be performed well. STRTs should increase or decrease as a function of the resources available at encoding. Thus STRTs will be relatively faster or slower as a function of whether the resources allocated to encoding were required to perform the encoding task fully. In addition, because the overall task does not exceed the system's total resource capacity, there should be sufficient resources to store the message, and, as a result, messages should be remembered relatively well. This, then, could result in instances where STRTs are fast (because more resources are automatically allocated to encoding than are required) and memory is good (because there are sufficient resources available to store the message). Similarly, instances might also occur where STRTs are slow, because all the resources allocated to encoding were needed to encode the message, and memory is good, because there are sufficient resources available to store the message.

On the other hand, when overall resource demands (for all the subprocesses involved) exceed the total resources available in the system, a different picture emerges. When system resources are insufficient to meet the demands of both encoding and storage, it is likely that storage will suffer. Because of the nature of the two different tasks, viewers will encode the stimulus in real time (in order to follow it), but will not have sufficient resources to store all of the information encoded (Lang, 1995). Encoding a television message must occur in real time, because the message presentation is ongoing, and many of the resources allocated to it are allocated automatically (outside of a person's control). Therefore, even when resources are scarce, the subprocess of encoding a message may get more than its share of resources. Allocation of resources to storage is less time dependent and does not, currently, appear to be driven by automatic resource allocation mechanisms. Thus it seems likely that when the system is overloaded, insufficient resources will be allocated to storage, resulting in a decline in memory for the messages. As in the previous case, where resource demands did not exceed availability, STRTs should still vary as a function of resources available at encoding. Even though the overall system is overloaded and the storage process is resource limited, there would still be resources available at encoding. Automatic calls for resources at encoding elicited by orienting responses could conceivably result in more resources being allocated to encoding than are required to encode the message. Such an overallocation of resources to encoding would only exacerbate, and in some instances could even cause, the underallocation of resources to storage. This situation would result in fast STRTs and poor memory for the messages. Similarly, instances may occur where available resources are negative at both encoding and storage, and when this occurs, the STRTs would be slow and memory would be poor.

In sum, defining secondary task reaction times as an index of the *resources available for encoding* (rather than the resources available to the entire task) and using memory to index the *resources available at storage* (rather than the resources available to the entire task) leads to a model that can predict all four combinations of data seen in the literature (slow STRTs and good memory, slow STRTs and bad memory, fast STRTs and good memory, slow STRTs and bad memory).

Using this model should also enable us to predict how any specific independent variable will affect both STRTs and memory. In particular, this model informs as to the impact of the independent variable on two pieces of the resource puzzle: (a) the resources available at encoding (in order to predict the change in STRTs) and (b) the resources available for storage (in order to predict the change in memory).

To do this, one must consider three changes: (a) the change in automatic allocation of processing resources to encoding, (b) the change in the difficulty of the encoding task, and (c) the change in the availability of resources at storage. The availability of resources at encoding, which, according to our proposal, is being indexed by secondary task reaction times, results from a combination of changes in the allocation of resources to encoding and in the difficulty of the encoding task. Thus if the allocation of processing resources to encoding increases and the encoding task difficulty does not increase, availability of resources at encoding will increase, and reaction times will get faster. On the other hand, if allocation to encoding increases, but encoding difficulty increases a greater amount, then availability will decrease and reaction times will get slower.

Memory should vary as a function of the third consideration. If an independent variable results in large amounts of resources being allocated to encoding (as a result of automatic allocation processes) and at the same time the message requires more resources for storage, then memory should decrease. In effect, encoding is hogging the resources needed for storage and the same structural features that elicit orienting (cuts, edits, and so on) also increase the amount of information available to store, and therefore increase the difficulty of the storage task. If, however, the independent variable does not alter the allocation of resources to encoding, then the availability of resources for storage should depend largely on the resources required to store the message. As the difficulty of the storage task increases, memory should decrease.

Table 11.4 shows our best predictions for the direction of change in STRT and memory as a function of each of the independent variables found in the communication literature. Entries in the second and third columns indicate whether changes in the automatic allocation of resources to encoding and the difficulty of the encoding task will go up or down in response to each of the independent variables, which are listed in the first column. The fourth column compares the second and third columns to make a prediction about the availability of resources at encoding. The fifth column predicts the change in STRT. If the prediction for available resources at encoding is "up" (corresponding to an increase in resources available at encoding), then reaction times are predicted to get faster; if the prediction is "down," then reaction times are predicted to get slower. Similarly, the sixth and seventh columns reflect our judgment as to availability of resources for storage and the resultant effect on memory performance. If the change in availability of resources at storage is predicted to decrease, then performance on memory tasks is predicted to go down. If the change in availability of resources at storage is up, then performance on memory tasks is predicted to go up. Thus Table 11.4 predicts the direction of change in STRT and memory as a function of each independent variable found in the literature. Table 11.5 compares these predictions to the actual findings in the literature.

To understand how we made these predictions and how they are reflected and tested in the tables, consider the first variable in Table 11.4, our problematic friend global visual complexity. The theoretical predictions are laid out in Table 11.4. The prediction is that as global visual complexity increases, resources automatically allocated to encoding will increase, the difficulty of the encoding task will also increase, but not as fast as the resource allocation increases (as discussed previously), and this will result in an increase in available resources. Thus we predict faster reaction times. The resources available at storage should decrease for two reasons: (a) because of the increase in resources allocated to encoding and (b) because the increase in global visual complexity also increases the difficulty of the storage task. Thus we predict that resources available at storage will go down and, therefore, memory will go down. Table 11.5 shows the study results. All five of the studies that tested global visual complexity (see Table 11.3) reported significant results in the direction predicted by the model.

This model, overall, is capable of predicting all of the combinations of memory performance and secondary task reaction times that are seen in the literature. The simple analysis reported here is not a meta-analysis. Rather, using the model derived here, we made a prediction for each independent variable as to the direction of its effect on STRT and on memory performance. Our predictions were all made based on the model presented in this chapter, not on the theoretical models used by the authors of the published works. Sometimes our predictions were the same as those made by the original authors, and sometimes they were different. We then compared our predictions for each variable to the published finding. If the published finding was significant and in the direction predicted by our model, we counted it as a finding that supported our model. If it was significant but in the wrong direction, we counted it as a finding that did not support our model. We did not include nonsignificant results ($n = 5$). As Table 11.5 shows, the model presented here accurately predicts 21 of the 25 (84%) tests found in the literature, and 12 out of 14 (85%) of the published findings related to memory performance.

Three of the four cases for which the model fails to make correct predictions involve channel presentation or audio/video redundancy questions, and the fourth involves an audio complexity manipulation. We submit that these prediction failures could result from our incomplete understanding of the

TABLE 11.4
Predictions for Resource Allocation, Reaction Times, and Memory Performance

Variable: Low to High "Levels"	Change in Resources Allocated to Encoding[a]	Change in Difficulty of Message to Encoding[b]	Available Resources Allocated to Encoding[c]	Change in Expected Reaction Times[d]	Change in Resources Available to Storage[e]	Change in Memory Performance[f]
Global visual complexity: simple to complex	up a lot	up a little	positive	faster	down	down
Local visual complexity: simple to complex	no change	up	negative	slower	down	down
Global audio complexity: simple to complex	up(?)	up less(?)	positive(?)	faster	down	down
Local audio complexity: simple to complex	no change	up	negative	slower	down	down
Visualization: no—yes	down	no change	negative	slower	up	up
Schema development: poor—good	no change	down	positive	faster	up	up
Emotion: negative—positive	down	no change	negative	slower	up	up
Analogy: present—not present	no change	down	positive	faster	up	up
Preceding teaser: no—yes	down	no change	negative	slower	down	down
Presentation channel: single—audio/video	up a little	up more(?)	negative	slower	up	up
Instructed focus: audio—video	down	no change	negative	slower	down	down
Information channel: audio—video	up	up more(?)	negative	slower	down	down
Audio/video redundancy: conflicting—high	down	down	?	?	up	up
Narrative structure: low—high	no change	down	positive	faster	up	up

NOTE: This table shows how the predictions made for each variable found in the literature were derived.

a. The likely effect of the variable on automatic calls for resources is judged. More calls for resources means an increase in resources allocated to encoding.

b. The likely increase in difficulty of encoding is assessed based primarily on how much new information the manipulation adds to the message.

c. The predicted change in difficulty of encoding (fifth column) is "subtracted" from the predicted change in resources allocated to encoding.

d. If resources available at encoding is predicted to be positive, reaction times are predicted to get faster. If resources available is predicted to be negative, slower reaction times are predicted.

e. Here, the likely effect of the variable on availability of resources to storage is judged.

f. Memory is predicted to increase when resources available at storage increase and to decrease when resources available at storage decrease.

467

TABLE 11.5
Predictions and Actual Results

				Studies Reporting			
Variable	*Levels*	*STRT Prediction*	*Memory Prediction*	*STRTs as Predicted*	*STRTs Not as Predicted*	*Memory as Predicted*	*Memory Not as Predicted*
Global visual complexity	simple	slower	better	5	0	4	0
	complex	faster	worse				
Local visual complexity	simple	faster	better	2	1	1	1
	complex	slower	worse				
Global audio complexity	simple	slower	better	1	1	1	0
	complex	faster	worse				
Local audio complexity	simple	faster	better	1	0	0	0
	complex	slower	worse				
Presentation condition	single channel	slower	better	0	1	0	0
	two channel	faster	worse				
Color/B&W	B&W	slower	better	1	0	0	1
	color	faster	worse				
Schema	poor	slower	worse	1	0	1	0
	good	faster	better				
Analogies	present	faster	better	1	0	0	0
	absent	slower	worse				

Visualization	no	faster	worse	1	1	0	0
	yes	slower	better				
Preceding teaser	no	faster	better	2	0	2	0
	yes	slower	worse				
Narrative structure	high	slower	better	1	0	1	0
	low	faster	worse				
Audio/video redundancy	high	faster	better	0	1	1	0
	medium	slower	medium				
	conflicting	slower	worse				
Channel of information	audio	faster	worse	2	0		
	video	slower	better				
Instructed focus	audio	faster	worse	1	0		
	video	slower	better				
Emotion (high arousal)	negative	faster	worse	1	0	1	0
	positive	slower	better				
Totals				21	4	12	2

NOTE: This table compares the predictions made by the model to the predictions published in the literature. A published finding is counted as supporting the prediction made by the model if it is reported as a significant effect and is in the direction predicted by the model. Effects not in the direction predicted were counted as not supporting the model. Nonsignificant effects ($n = 5$) were not included.

independent variable as well as from problems inherent in our model. The effects of single versus multiple channels of presentation, audio/video redundancy, and audio complexity on the allocation of resources to encoding and storage are still only poorly understood. In particular, very little research in this area considers the effects of audio structural features and audio manipulations on information processing. For example, we predicted there would be fewer available resources at encoding during audio/video presentations compared with single-channel presentations purely on logical grounds—no data being available to guide this prediction. It seemed likely that two channels might require more resources to encode, but this might not be the case. Predictions made in Table 11.4 may also be incorrect to the extent that the manipulations described in the literature may not have been strong enough to evoke the predicted changes. Future tests of this model should be made using independent variables that are designed and manipulated with the intent of altering the availability of resources at encoding and at storage.

CONCLUSION

In this essay we have argued that secondary task reaction times index the resources *available at encoding,* that resources *available at encoding* are dependent on the resources allocated to encoding and the resources required to encode the information in the message, and that the resources allocated to encoding are also dependent on global task demands (e.g., the resources required to process the message and the overall level of effort expended by the viewer). The model developed from these premises successfully predicts most of the published findings in this area, explains previously counterintuitive findings, and provides a framework that can explain and predict all the combinations of STRT and memory performance found in the literature (i.e., fast STRTs and good memory, fast STRTs and poor memory, slow STRTs and good memory, slow STRTs and bad memory).

To the extent that the independent variables under investigation primarily affect encoding resources, these effects can be observed as variance in STRTs. To the extent that these variables affect storage resources, these effects can be observed as variance in memory performance.

Because of the likelihood of independent allocation of resources to encoding and storage, further tests of this model should attempt to manipulate independently the resources required to encode and to store messages. Further, these studies should include both STRT and memory data as their dependent measures.

With regard to the original questions about secondary task reaction times, we hope that this framework will increase our ability to use STRTs to investigate how people process television messages. Further, we hope that the tenability of this model will continue to be examined by other researchers.

REFERENCES

Allport, A. (1989). Visual attention. In M. I. Posner (Ed.), *Foundations of cognitive science* (pp. 631-682). Cambridge: MIT Press.

Anderson, D. R., & Levin, S. R. (1976). Young children's attention to *Sesame Street. Child Development, 47,* 806-811.

Bargh, J. A. (1988). Automatic information processing: Implications for communication and affect. In L. Donohew, H. E. Sypher, & E. T. Higgins (Eds.), *Communication, social cognition, and affect* (pp. 9-32). Hillsdale, NJ: Lawrence Erlbaum.

Basil, M. D. (1994a). Multiple resource theory I: Application to television viewing. *Communication Research, 21,* 177-207.

Basil, M. D. (1994b). Multiple resource theory II: Empirical examination of specific attention to television scenes. *Communication Research, 21,* 208-231.

Basil, M. D. (1994c). Secondary reaction-time measures. In A. Lang (Ed.), *Measuring psychological responses to media messages* (pp. 85-98). Hillsdale, NJ: Lawrence Erlbaum.

Biocca, F. (1994). Continuous response measurement (CRM): A computerized tool for research on the cognitive processing of communication messages. In A. Lang (Ed.), *Measuring psychological responses to media messages* (pp. 15-64). Hillsdale, NJ: Lawrence Erlbaum.

Broadbent, D. (1958). *Perception and communication.* New York: Pergamon.

Broadbent, D. (1977). The hidden pre-attentive process. *American Psychologist, 32,* 109-118.

Cameron, G. T., Schleuder, J., & Thorson, E. (1991). The role of news teasers in the processing of news and commercials. *Communication Research, 18,* 667-684.

Chaffee, S. H., & Schleuder, J. (1986). Measurement and effects of attention to news media. *Human Communication Research, 13,* 76-107.

Cherry, C. (1953). Some experiments on the recognition of speech with one and two ears. *Journal of the Acoustical Society of America, 23,* 915-919.

Craik, F. I. M., & Lockhart, R. S. (1972). Levels of processing: A framework for memory research. *Journal of Verbal Learning and Verbal Behavior, 11,* 671-684.

Deutsch, J. A., & Deutsch, D. (1963). Attention: Some theoretical considerations. *Psychological Review, 70,* 80-90.

Eysenck, M. (1993). *Principles of cognitive psychology.* Hillsdale, NJ: Lawrence Erlbaum.

Geiger, S., & Reeves, B. (1993a). The effects of scene changes and semantic relatedness on attention to television. *Communication Research, 20,* 155-175.

Geiger, S., & Reeves, B. (1993b). We interrupt this program . . . : Attention for television sequences. *Human Communication Research, 19,* 368-387.

Gilbert, K., & Schleuder, J. (1990). Effects of color and complexity in still photographs on mental effort and memory. *Journalism Quarterly, 67,* 749-756.

Grimes, T. (1991). Mild auditory-visual dissonance in television news may exceed viewer attentional capacity. *Human Communication Research, 18,* 268-298.

Grimes, T., & Meadowcroft, J. (1995). Attention to television and some methods for its measurement. In B. R. Burleson (Ed.), *Communication yearbook 18* (pp. 133-161). Thousand Oaks, CA: Sage.

Harris, R. J. (1983). Introduction. In R. J. Harris (Ed.), *Information processing research on advertising* (pp. 241-262). Hillsdale, NJ: Lawrence Erlbaum.

Kahneman, D. (1973). *Attention and effort.* Englewood Cliffs, NJ: Prentice Hall.

Kawahara, K., Wadleigh, P. M., Hansell, R., Hazel, M., Nagami, K., & Lang, A. (1995, May). *The effects of pacing and arousal on viewers' memory for television messages.* Paper presented at the annual meeting of the International Communication Association, Albuquerque, NM.

Lachman, R., Lachman, J. L., & Butterfield, E. C. (1979). *Cognitive psychology and information processing: An introduction.* Hillsdale, NJ: Lawrence Erlbaum.

Lang, A. (1990). Involuntary attention and physiological arousal evoked by structural features and emotional content in TV commercials. *Communication Research, 17,* 275-299.

Lang, A. (Ed.). (1994). *Measuring psychological responses to media messages.* Hillsdale, NJ: Lawrence Erlbaum.

Lang, A. (1995). Defining audio/video redundancy from a limited capacity information processing perspective. *Communication Research, 22,* 86-115.

Lang, A., Chaffeur, C., Davidson, T., Funabiki, R., & Reynvaan, J. (1992, May). *Political advertising: Structure, attention, and memory.* Paper presented at the annual meeting of the International Communication Association, Miami, FL.

Lang, A., Dhillon, P., & Dong, Q. (1995). Arousal, emotion, and memory for television messages. *Journal of Broadcasting & Electronic Media, 38,* 1-15.

Lang, A., Geiger, S., Strickwerda, M., & Sumner, J. (1993). The effects of related and unrelated cuts on viewers' memory for television: A limited capacity theory of television viewing. *Communication Research, 20,* 4-29.

Lang, A., Sias, P., Chantrill, P., & Burek, J. A. (1995). Tell me a story: Narrative structure and memory for television messages. *Communication Reports, 8,* 1-9.

Lynn, R. (1966). *Attention, arousal and the orienting reaction.* Oxford: Pergamon.

McLeod, J. M., & Reeves, B. (1980). On the nature of mass media effects. In G. C. Wilhoit & H. de Bock (Eds.), *Mass communication review yearbook 2* (pp. 245-282). Beverly Hills, CA: Sage.

Meadowcroft, J. M., & Reeves, B. (1989). Influence of story schema development on children's attention to television. *Communication Research, 16,* 352-404.

Meadowcroft, J. M., & Watt, J. H. (1988, October). *Fourier analysis as a method for observing children's attention spans.* Paper submitted to the International Communication Association, Mass Communication Division.

Meadowcroft, J. M., & Watt, J. H. (1989, May). *A multi-component theory of children's attention spans.* Paper presented at the annual meeting of the International Communication Association, San Francisco.

Newhagen, J., & Reeves, B. (1992). This evening's bad news: Effects of compelling negative television news images on memory. *Journal of Communication, 42,* 25-41.

Norman, D. A. (1976). *Memory and attention.* New York: John Wiley.

Norman, D. A., & Bobrow, D. G. (1975). On data-limited and resource-limited processes. *Cognitive Psychology, 7,* 44-64.

Posner, M. I. (1978). *Chronometric explorations of mind.* Hillsdale, NJ: Lawrence Erlbaum.

Posner, M. I. (1994). Attention: The mechanisms of consciousness. *Proceedings of the National Academy of Sciences, 91,* 7398-7403.

Posner, M. I., & Raichle, M. E. (1994). *Images of mind.* New York: Scientific American Library.

Reeves, B., & Thorson, E. (1986). Watching television: Experiments on the viewing process. *Communication Research, 13,* 343-361.

Reeves, B., Thorson, E., Rothschild, M. L., McDonald, D., Hirsch, J., & Goldstein, R. (1985). Attention to television: Intrastimulus effects of movement and scene changes on alpha variation over time. *International Journal of Neuroscience, 25,* 241-255.

Reeves, B., Thorson, E., & Schleuder, J. (1986). Attention to television: Psychological theories and chronometric measures. In J. Bryant & D. Zillmann (Eds.), *Perspectives on media effects* (pp. 251-280). Hillsdale, NJ: Lawrence Erlbaum.

Schleuder, J. (1990). Effects of commercial complexity, the candidate, and issue vs. image strategies in political ads. In M. E. Goldberg, G. Gorn, & R. W. Pollay (Eds.), *Advances in consumer research* (Vol. 17, pp. 159-168). Provo, UT: Association for Consumer Research.

Schleuder, J., Cameron, G. T., & Thorson, E. (1989). Proactive interference effects of news teasers on memory for attention and emotion-eliciting commercials. In K. Rotzoll (Ed.), *Proceedings of the American Academy of Advertising* (pp. 11-16). Charleston, SC: American Academy of Advertising.

Schleuder, J., Thorson, E., & Reeves, B. (1988, May). *Effects of time compression and complexity on attention to television commercials.* Paper presented at the annual meeting of the International Communication Association, New Orleans.

Shapiro, M. A. (1986). Analogies, visualization, and mental processing of science stories. In M. L. McLaughlin (Ed.), *Communication yearbook 9* (pp. 339-355). Beverly Hills, CA: Sage.

Shiffrin, R. M., & Schneider, W. (1977). Controlled and automatic human information processing II: Perceptual learning, automatic attending, and a general theory. *Psychological Review, 84,* 127-190.

Thorson, E. (1994). Using eyes on the screen as a measure of attention to television. In A. Lang (Ed.), *Measuring psychological responses to media messages* (pp. 65-84). Hillsdale, NJ: Lawrence Erlbaum.

Thorson, E., Reeves, B., & Schleuder, J. (1985). Message complexity and attention to television. *Communication Research, 12,* 427-454.

Thorson, E., Reeves, B., & Schleuder, J. (1987). Attention to local and global complexity in television messages. In M. L. McLaughlin (Ed.), *Communication yearbook 10* (pp. 366-383). Beverly Hills, CA: Sage.

Triesman, A. M. (1960). Contextual cues in selective listening. *Quarterly Journal of Experimental Psychology, 12,* 242-248.

Triesman, A. M. (1988). Features and object: The fourteenth Bartlett Memorial Lecture. *Quarterly Journal of Experimental Psychology, 79,* 201-237.

Wickens, C. D. (1980). The structure of attentional resources. In R. Nickerson (Ed.), *Attention and performance* (Vol. 8, pp. 63-102). Hillsdale, NJ: Lawrence Erlbaum.

Wickens, C. D. (1984). Processing resources in attention. In R. Parasuraman & D. R. Davies (Eds.), *Varieties of attention* (pp. 63-102). Orlando, FL: Academic Press.

AUTHOR INDEX

SUBJECT INDEX

ABOUT THE EDITOR

MICHAEL E. ROLOFF is Professor in the Department of Communication Studies at Northwestern University. He received his Ph.D. in communication from Michigan State University in 1975. His research and teaching interests are in the general area of interpersonal influence. He has published articles and offers courses focused on persuasion, interpersonal compliance gaining, conflict management, and bargaining and negotiation. He has coedited four research volumes for Sage Publications: *Persuasion: New Directions in Theory and Research, Social Cognition and Communication, Interpersonal Processes,* and *Communication and Negotiation.* He is the author of *Interpersonal Communication: The Social Exchange Approach.* His articles have appeared in such journals as *Communication Monographs, Communication Research, Human Communication Research, International Journal of Conflict Management,* and *Personal Relationships.* In addition to editing the *Communication Yearbook,* he currently serves on the editorial boards of seven academic journals.

ABOUT THE AUTHORS

FREDERICK J. ANTCZAK received his Ph.D. from the University of Chicago, Committee on the Analysis of Ideas and the Study of Methods, in 1979. He is currently Professor and Chair of the Rhetoric Department at the University of Iowa. His research interests include 19th- and 20th-century American public address, the ethics of rhetoric, and pedagogy for the basic course in rhetoric. His recent publications include *Rhetoric and Pluralism* (1994), "Hearing Our Cassandras: Ethical Criticism and Rhetorical Receptions of Paul Erlich" (in *Social Epistemology*), "Take Me Out to the Polity," coauthored with Ira Strauber (in *American Studies*). He is also the coauthor (with Jay Satterfield) of "Pragmatism and the Prophetic Voice: William James, Cornel West, and the Openings for Invention," forthcoming in *New Perspectives on Rhetorical Invention*. He is currently working on "Teaching Public Speaking," a CD-ROM for new teachers.

MICHAEL D. BASIL (Ph.D., Stanford University, 1992) is Assistant Professor in the Department of Mass Communications and Journalism Studies at the University of Denver. His general interest is in the area of message processing, and he applies this interest to examining how people make sense of media messages by measuring the systems behind those interpretations. His research, which has looked into people's attention and memory for television messages and applied these techniques in the area of health communication, has appeared in a variety of journals, including *Journalism Quarterly, Communication Research, Journal of Broadcasting & Electronic Media, Journal of Applied Social Psychology, American Behavioral Scientist, Health Communication, Health Education Research,* and the *Journal of Health Communication.* He also serves as a reviewer for the *Journal of Broadcasting & Electronic Media* and has worked in the area of social marketing with the National Cancer Society, PBS, and Porter/Novelli.

DEBORAH A. CAI (Ph.D., Michigan State University, 1994) is Assistant Professor in the Department of Speech Communication at the University of Maryland. As an international traveler with ties to China, she has scholarly interests in intercultural communication and conflict. In particular, her current research focuses on effective communication in intercultural business negotiation. Her past works examine cultural differences in negotiation plans, enactment of face-management strategies, and the mediating effects of role on culture in business negotiation. Her research has been presented at regional and national conferences and has been published in the *Asian Journal of Communication* and *Communication Education.*

DAVID CARLONE received a master's degree from the Department of Communication Studies at the University of North Carolina at Chapel Hill in 1995. His master's thesis dealt with employee resistance to workplace control. Currently, he is a doctoral student in the Department of Communication at the University of Colorado at Boulder. Within organizational communication, his research interests include the employee experience of workplace democracy and how the workplace might be more humane. His current projects include theorizing workplace control as discursively constituted and an ethnographic project examining the creation and maintenance of political alliances. His work and interests draw heavily on cultural studies and interpretive methods.

GEORGE CHENEY (Ph.D., Purdue University, 1985) is Associate Professor in the Department of Communication Studies at the University of Montana–Missoula. His teaching and research interests include issues of identity and power in organizations, the quality of work life in contemporary society, democracy at work, and ethics in business and other institutions. He is the author of *Rhetoric in an Organizational Society: Managing Multiple Identities* (1991) as well as numerous journal articles, book chapters, and editorials. He received a Golden Anniversary Monograph Award from the Speech Communication Association in 1996 for his essay "Democracy in the Workplace: Theory and Practice From the Perspective of Communication" (*Journal of Applied Communication Research*, 1995), an earlier version of which was a "Top Three" paper in the Organizational Communication Division of ICA at the 1995 Albuquerque conference. He is currently writing a book on values, democracy, and communication in organizations. He is chair of the National Communication Association's Organizational Communication Division.

DAN DeGOOYER, JR. (M.A., University of Montana) is a graduate student at the University of Iowa. His research interests include relational perspectives of communication. He favors feminist approaches to organizing and is also interested in the talk that occurs in health care settings.

LAURA E. DRAKE (Ph.D., Michigan State University, 1995) is Visiting Professor in the Department of Communication Studies at Northwestern University. Her research interests lie in conflict management and intercultural communication. Specifically, her current research examines information exchange as an integrative conflict process versus judgment errors as distributive factors in intercultural business negotiation. Her past work investigates mediator intervention strategies in conflict, reciprocity and divergence of negotiation styles in intercultural negotiation, and information exchange processes in decision making. Her recent publications have appeared in the *International Journal of Conflict Management* and *Communication Research*.

SUSAN TYLER EASTMAN is Professor of Telecommunications at Indiana University in Bloomington. She received her B.A. from the University of California at Berkeley, her M.A. from San Francisco State University, and her Ph.D. from Bowling Green State University. She is widely known as senior editor/author of *Broadcast/Cable Programming: Strategies and Practices* (5th edition, 1997) and *Promotion and Marketing for Broadcasting and Cable* (2nd edition, 1991). She has published articles about programming theory, sports programming, and program marketing theory and practice in such journals as the *Journal of Broadcasting & Electronic Media, Journal of Communication, Critical Studies in Mass Communication, Sociology of Sport Journal,* and *Journal of Sport and Social Issues.* Her work has been published in France and Spain, and her textbooks have been translated into the languages of the former Soviet Union. Her most recent studies have focused on the role of on-air promotion within programming theory.

SHERRY DEVEREAUX FERGUSON (Ph.D., Indiana University, 1976) is Associate Professor and Chair of the Communication Department at the University of Ottawa, Canada. Her current research projects relate to issues management, crisis management, and evaluation of communication in organizations. She received the 1994 SCA PRIDE (Public Relations Innovation, Development and Educational) Award for *Mastering the Public Opinion Challenge* (1994). Other books are *Organizational Communication* (1988) and *Intercom: Readings in Organizational Communication* (1980). She has acted as consultant to the Department of Foreign Affairs, the Department of Justice, the Privy Council Office, Health Canada, Secretary of State, Communications Canada, the Department of Fisheries and Oceans, the Bureau of Management Consultants, the National Research Council, Indian and Northern Affairs, Transport Canada, and other Canadian government departments. She also trains managers and executives in issues management and strategic planning techniques. Currently she is a task force member who is contributing to rewriting the *Government Commumication Policy* for Canada.

KATHY GARVIN-DOXAS earned her B.A. in radio-television-film from the University of Texas at Austin. Currently, she is a doctoral candidate in the Department of Communication at the University of Colorado at Boulder. Her recent publications have examined the ways in which mutual knowledge is manifested in conversations, how mutual knowledge differs between conversations among friends and those among acquaintances, and the articulation of Kenneth Burke's perspective on power based on a close textual analysis of his work. Her primary area of interest is workplace democracy and participation in organizational settings. At present, she is working on a research fellowship from the National Institute of Standards and Technology for her dissertation project, which examines the implementation of work teams in a government setting and focuses on the different meanings the vocabularies of "teamwork" hold for organizational members.

SHELTON A. GUNARATNE (Ph.D., University of Minnesota, 1972) is Professor of Mass Communications at Moorhead State University in Minnesota. He has taught communication and journalism in Australia, China, and Malaysia as well during his quarter century of teaching and research. His current research interests include telecommunication in developing countries, techniques of using the Internet for communication and journalism teaching, new approaches in the practice of journalism, and UNESCO-related developments. His recent publications have appeared in *AsiaPacific MediaEducator, Javnost—The Public, Journalism & Mass Communication Educator, Jurnal Komunikasi, Media Asia,* and *Media Development.* He has been the review editor of the *Journal of International Communication* since its inception in 1994. A former journalist from Sri Lanka, he is a permanent fellow of the World Press Institute at Macalester College.

SCOTT L. HALE (M.A., University of Illinois, Urbana-Champaign, 1995) is a doctoral candidate in the Department of Speech Communication at the University of Illinois at Urbana-Champaign. His research interests center on persuasion in political communication, including the processes of public opinion formation and change, and the impact of mass media campaigns on voting behavior. He is currently engaged in a content analysis of public opinion poll questions to examine the relations between elite discourse and the content of media polls.

ANNIE LANG (Ph.D., University of Wisconsin–Madison, 1987) is Associate Professor in the Department of Telecommunications at Indiana University in Bloomington. Her research pokes and prods about the general question, how do people process media messages? In particular, she wonders how the medium in which a message is produced alters the mental processes involved in receiving a message and how the alteration in those mental processes affects the receiver's experiences of and memory for the message. In order to answer these questions, she has developed an interest in psychological measurements and their application to communication research. Her recent attempts to shed light on these issues have appeared in several journals, including *Human Communication Research, Communication Research, Journal of Broadcasting & Electronic Media,* and *Communication Reports,* and in her edited book *Measuring Psychological Responses to Media Messages.*

LAURIE K. LEWIS (Ph.D., University of California, Santa Barbara) is Assistant Professor of Speech Communication at Pennsylvania State University. She teaches and researches in the area of organizational communication, and specializes in the study of planned organizational change and organizational innovation processes. Some of her recent work in this area has been published in the *Academy of Management Review* and *Communication Monographs*; she has also presented numerous scholarly papers at academic conferences. She has consulted for a variety of both nonprofit and for-profit organizations concerning general communication issues and implementation of planned change.

W. BRADFORD MELLO is Assistant Professor of Communication at Trinity College in Washington, D.C. He has presented papers on editorial cartooning at several national conferences, including those of the Speech Communication Association and the Association for Education in Journalism and Mass Communication. He has also had the honor of speaking at the National Archives in Washington, D.C. His presentation was based on his dissertation on the films of the Memphis Belle and served as an introduction to a screening of the 1944 documentary and the 1990 docudrama about the famous B-17 bomber.

DANIEL J. O'KEEFE (Ph.D., University of Illinois, Urbana-Champaign, 1976) is Associate Professor in the Department of Speech Communication at the University of Illinois at Urbana-Champaign. His research interests concern persuasion and argument. He is the author of *Persuasion: Theory and Research*, and his work has appeared in *Communication Monographs, Human Communication Research, Communication Theory*, and other journals.

MATTHEW W. SEEGER (Ph.D., Indiana University, 1982) is Associate Professor of Communication and Assistant Dean of the Graduate School at Wayne State University in Detroit, Michigan. He teaches courses in organizational communication, communication consulting, communication theory, small group communication, communication ethics, and crisis and issue management. His research has appeared in the *Journal of Business Ethics, Central States Speech Journal, Communication Education, Southern Journal of Speech Communication,* and *International Management Journal.* His edited book *"I Gotta Tell You": Speeches of Lee Iacocca* (1994) examines rhetorical style and issue management strategies in 25 of Iacocca's best-known public addresses. His second book, *Organizational Communication Ethics,* is forthcoming. He is editor-elect of the *Free Speech Yearbook.*

DAVID R. SEIBOLD (Ph.D., Michigan State University) is Professor of Communication at the University of California, Santa Barbara. Author of nearly 100 articles on organizational change, group decision making, interpersonal influence, and health communication, he currently is editor of the *Journal of Applied Communication Research.* He serves as Chair of the Interpersonal and Small Group Interaction Division of the Speech Communication Association, and as Vice Chair of the Organizational Communication

Division of the International Communication Association. He also works closely with many business, government, and health organizations.

TIMOTHY L. SELLNOW (Ph.D., Wayne State University, 1987) is Associate Professor and Chair in the Communication Department at North Dakota State University. He teaches a variety of courses in organizational communication and graduate seminars in research methods. He also serves regularly as an organizational consultant. His research has appeared in such journals as *Argumentation and Advocacy, Communication Studies, Communication Reports, Communication Education,* and *Journal of the Association of Communication Administration.* His recent work focuses on the complexity of organizational audiences and the obstacles posed by ambiguity in organizational crisis situations.

LAURA SPEIRS-GLEBE received her B.A. in political science and communication from the University of Minnesota, Duluth, in 1995. She is currently a master's student in organizational communication at the University of Montana. Her research interests include participation, voice, and diversity in the workplace.

CYNTHIA STOHL (Ph.D., Purdue University, 1982) is Professor of Communication at Purdue University in West Lafayette, Indiana. Her research and teaching focus upon organizational and small group communication, with a primary emphasis on the dynamic relationships between and among worker participation, communication networks, and global integration. Her research on quality circles in New Zealand, semiautonomous work groups in the United States, and the social and semantic networks of managers in the European Community has appeared in several journals, including *Human Communication Research, Communication Monographs, Management Communication Quarterly, Journal of Applied Communication,* and *Discourse and Society,* and in *Communication Yearbooks 9, 10, 13,* and *16.* Her 1995 book *Organizational Communication: Connectedness in Action* won the SCA Organizational Communication Outstanding Book Award.

JOSEPH STRAUB is a master's student in organizational communication at the University of Montana. He received his B.A. in communication from the University of Colorado at Boulder in 1990. His current research is focused on the importance of communication in leadership, workplace democracy, and mediation/conflict resolution.

MARY E. STUCKEY received her Ph.D. in government and international relations from the University of Notre Dame in 1987. She is Associate Professor of Political Science at the University of Mississippi. Her interests center on the exercise of power and its consequences for members of the polity. Consequently, her research focuses on both presidential and minority politics. She is the author of several books on the presidency and presidential communication, including *The President as Interpreter-in-Chief* (1991) and *Strategic Failures in the Modern Presidency* (1997). She is also the editor of *The Theory and Practice of Political Communication Research* (1996). Her articles have appeared in such journals as *Communication Monographs, Western Journal of Communication, Communication Studies, Communication Quarterly,* and *Rhetoric Society Quarterly.* She is currently coauthoring (with Richard Morris) *Devouring Savages: The Cannibalization of Native America,* as well as other projects on First Nations peoples.

ROBERT R. ULMER (M.A., North Dakota State University, 1995) is a doctoral student and Teaching Assistant at Wayne State University in Detroit, Michigan. He teaches courses in organizational communication, public speaking, and communication theory. His research interests include communication and organizational crisis, communication ethics, and pedagogy. His research has appeared in *Argumentation and Advocacy* and the *North Dakota Journal of Speech & Theater.*

SUSAN WHALEN (Ph.D., Pennsylvania State University, 1990) is Oral Historian in Residence at the Human Rights Archives at the University of Colorado in Boulder, where she is currently directing an archival project related to human rights violations in the former Soviet Union. Her work dealing with rhetoric, social theory, and social movements has appeared in *Dissent, Critical Inquiry, Communication Theory, Quarterly Journal of Speech,* and other periodicals.